A NEW HISTORY OF IRELAND

UNDER THE AUSPICES OF THE
ROYAL IRISH ACADEMY

IX

MAPS, GENEALOGIES, LISTS

A NEW HISTORY OF IRELAND

UNDER THE AUSPICES OF THE ROYAL IRISH ACADEMY

A NEW HISTORY OF
IRELAND

EDITED BY
T. W. MOODY F. X. MARTIN
F. J. BYRNE

IX

MAPS, GENEALOGIES, LISTS

A COMPANION TO
IRISH HISTORY
PART II

OXFORD
AT THE CLARENDON PRESS
1984

Oxford University Press, Walton Street, Oxford OX2 6DP

London   New York   Toronto
Delhi   Bombay   Calcutta   Madras   Karachi
Kuala Lumpur   Singapore   Hong Kong   Tokyo
Nairobi   Dar es Salaam   Cape Town
Melbourne   Auckland

and associated companies in
Beirut   Berlin   Ibadan   Mexico City   Nicosia

Oxford is a trade mark of Oxford University Press

Published in the United States by
Oxford University Press, New York

© *Oxford University Press 1984*
on behalf of the editors and contributors

British Library Cataloguing in Publication Data

A new history of Ireland
 Vol. 9: Maps, genealogies, lists
 1. Ireland—History
 I. Moody, Theodore William
 II. Martin, Francis Xavier
 III. Byrne, Francis John
 941.5   DA910   79-41245
 ISBN 0-19-821745-5

Printed in Great Britain
at the University Press, Oxford
by David Stanford
Printer to the University

PREFACE

THIS, the second part of our 'Companion to Irish History', is a continuation of part I, with which it was originally intended to be combined. The material now presented is closely related to that in volume VIII and *vice versa*. For example, the genealogical tables and succession lists of kings and lords have their counterparts in the entries under dynastic families in the index to volume VIII. On the other hand, subjects have been omitted from, or only treated selectively in, volume VIII—such as appointments of bishops and secular officers, and meetings of parliament—because they are comprehensively treated in the present volume.

As before, we have pleasure in thanking the National Library and the libraries of Trinity College, Dublin, and the Royal Irish Academy, for their cooperation. Acknowledgements for invaluable help received from individuals are made in the introductions to the component sections of this volume. To our secretary, Richard Hawkins, and to our typist, Peggy Morgan, we are very specially indebted.

Once again we thank Dr John A. Mulcahy, of New York, and the directors of the American Irish Foundation, for their generous financial help.

We are well aware that in this volume, as in volume VIII, some errors are unavoidable, despite all our efforts to avoid them. Readers are requested to inform us of any errors they may observe in the volume, so that corrections may be included among the corrigenda to be published in volume X.

T. W. MOODY
F. X. MARTIN
F. J. BYRNE

Royal Irish Academy
December 1982

CONTENTS

PRINCIPAL CONTRIBUTORS

FRANCIS JOHN BYRNE	M.A. (N.U.I.); M.R.I.A.; professor of early and medieval Irish history, University College, Dublin
ART COSGROVE	B.A., Ph.D. (Q.U.B.); statutory lecturer in medieval history, University College, Dublin
KATHLEEN MARY DAVIES	B.A. (Manchester); cartographic adviser, 'A new history of Ireland'; coordinator, 'Atlas of Irish historic towns'
BENIGNUS MILLETT	B.A. (N.U.I), Dr Hist. Eccles. (Pontifical Gregorian University); superior of Franciscan House of Studies, Killiney, Co. Dublin
JOHN GERALD SIMMS	M.A. (Dubl., Oxon.), Ph.D. (Dubl.); M.R.I.A.; late fellow emeritus, Trinity College, Dublin (died 9 April 1979)
BRIAN MERCER WALKER	M.A. (Dubl.), Ph.D. (Dubl.); lecturer in politics, Queen's University, Belfast
CHRISTOPHER JOHN WOODS	M.A. (Cantab.), Ph.D. (Nottingham); part-time lecturer in modern history, St Patrick's College, Maynooth

ABBREVIATIONS AND CONVENTIONS

Abbreviations and conventions used in this volume are listed below. They consist of (a) the relevant items from the list in *Irish Historical Studies*, supplement 1 (Jan. 1968) and (b) abbreviations, on the same model, not included in the *Irish Historical Studies* list.

a.	*ante* (before)
A.F.M.	*Annala rioghachta Eireann: Annals of the kingdom of Ireland by the Four Masters from the earliest period to the year 1616*, ed. and trans. John O'Donovan (7 vols, Dublin, 1851; reprint New York, 1966)
A.P.F.	Archivio storico della Sancta Congregazione de Propaganda Fide, Rome
A.P.F., Atti	Atti delle congregazioni generali (MS minutes of general meetings in A.P.F.)
A.P.F., Cong. part.	Congregazioni particolari (161 MS vols in A.P.F.)
A.U.	*Annála Uladh, Annals of Ulster: otherwise Annála Senait, Annals of Senat: a chronicle of Irish affairs, 431-1131, 1155-1541*, ed. W. M. Hennessy and B. MacCarthy (4 vols, Dublin, 1887-1901)
A.V.	Archivio Segreto Vaticano
A.V., Nunz.	Nunziatura di Fiandra (MS collection in A.V.)
A.V., S. Br.	Secretaria brevium apostolicorum (MS collection in A.V.)
abd.	abdicated
abp	archbishop
admr	administrator
Anal. Hib.	*Analecta Hibernica, including the reports of the Irish Manuscripts Commission* (Dublin, 1930-)
Ann. Boyle	'The Annals in Cotton MS Titus A xxv', ed. A. M. Freeman, in *Revue celtique*, xli (1924), pp 301-30
Ann. Camb.	'Annales Cambriae', ed. E. Phillimore, in *Y Cymmrodor*, ix (1888)
Ann. Clon.	*The Annals of Clonmacnoise, being annals of Ireland from the earliest period to A.D. 1408, translated into English, A.D. 1627, by Conell Mageoghagan*, ed. Denis Murphy (Royal Society of Antiquaries of Ireland, Dublin, 1896)

Ann. Inisf.	*The Annals of Inisfallen* (*MS Rawlinson B503*), ed. and trans. Seán MacAirt (Dublin Institute for Advanced Studies, 1951)
Ann. Tig.	'The annals of Tigernach', ed. Whitley Stokes, in *Revue Celtique*, xvi–xviii (1895–7)
anon.	published anonymously
app.	appointed, formal appointment
Archiv. Hib.	*Archivium Hibernicum: or Irish historical records* (Catholic Record Society of Ireland, Maynooth, 1912–)
aux. bp	auxiliary bishop
b.	born
B.L.	British Library
B.L. Add. MS	——, Additional MS
Bk Leinster	*The Book of Leinster, formerly Lebar na Núachongbála*, ed. R. I. Best, Osborn Bergin and M. A. O'Brien (5 vols, Dublin Institute for Advanced Studies, 1954–67)
bld	blinded
bp	bishop
Brady, *Episc. succ.*	W. Maziere Brady, *The episcopal succession in England, Scotland and Ireland*, A.D. *1400 to 1875* (3 vols; Rome, 1876–7)
bt	baronet
bur.	buried
C.	*custos* (keeper)
c.	*circa* (about)
C.M.	Congregatio Missionum (Vincentians)
C.S.	chief secretary
C.S.Sp	Congregatio de Sancto Spiritu (Holy Ghost priests)
C.SS.R.	Congregatio Sanctissimi Redemptoris (Redemptorists)
Cáin Adamnáin	*Cáin Adamnáin: an Old-Irish treatise on the Law of Adamnáin*, ed. Kuno Meyer (Oxford, 1905) (Anecdota Oxoniensia)
Cal. close rolls, 1272–9 [etc.]	*Calendar of the close rolls, 1272–9* [etc.] (London, 1900–)
Cal. pat. rolls, 1232–47 [etc.]	*Calendar of the patent rolls, 1232–47* [etc.] (London, 1906–)
Cal. S.P. dom., 1547–80 [etc.]	*Calendar of state papers, domestic series, 1547–80* [etc.] (London, 1856–)

Cal. S.P. Ire., 1509-73 [etc.]	*Calendar of the state papers relating to Ireland, 1509-73* [etc.] (24 vols, London, 1860-1911)
can. reg.	canons regular of St Augustine
Census Ire., 1841 [etc.]; *Census N.I., 1926* [etc.]	[The sources denoted by these titles are the reports and other material relating to the censuses of Ireland taken by the British government and the successive Irish governments in the years indicated.]
ch.	chapter
Chron. Scot.	*Chronicum Scotorum: a chronicle of Irish affairs . . . to 1135, and supplement . . . 1141-1150*, ed. W. M. Hennessy (London, 1866)
coadj.	coadjutor
coemp.	accession as coemperor
commn	commission
commr	commissioner
con.	conservative party
conf.	confirmed in office
cons.	consecrated
cor.	coronation
cr.	created
cttee	committee
cust.	took custody of seal (chancellors); of benefice (bishops)
D.	deputy
d.	died
D.C.	deputy chancellor
D.G.	*Dublin Gazette*
D.J.	deputy justiciar
D.K.	deputy keeper
D.L.	deputy lieutenant
D.U.P.	Democratic Unionist Party
dep.	deposed
depr.	deprived
dioc.	diocese
diss.	dissolved
ed.	edited by, edition, editor or editors
el.	elected
emp.	accession as emperor
exp.	expelled

fl.	*floruit* (flourished)
Frag. ann.	*Fragmentary annals of Ireland*, ed. Joan N. Radner (Dublin Institute for Advanced Studies, 1978)
G.B.	Great Britain
G.E.C., *Peerage*	G. E. C[okayne], *The complete peerage of England, Scotland, Ireland, Great Britain and the United Kingdom* . . . (8 vols, Exeter, 1887–98; ed. Vicary Gibbs and others, 13 vols, London, 1910–59)
H.B.C.	F. M. Powicke and E. B. Fryde (ed.), *Handbook of British chronology* (Royal Historical Society, 2nd ed., London, 1961)
H.C.	house of commons
H.L.	house of lords
I.F.S.	Irish Free State
I.H.S.	*Irish Historical Studies: the joint journal of the Irish Historical Society and the Ulster Society for Irish Historical Studies* (Dublin, 1938–)
I.M.C.	Irish Manuscripts Commission
Ire.	Ireland
J.	justiciar, lord justice
K.	keeper
kg	king
kt bach.	knight bachelor
L.	lieutenant
L.C.	lord chancellor
L.C.J.	lord chief justice
l.p.	letters patent
lab.	labour (party)
lib.	liberal (party)
lib.	liberatio (delivery [of episcopal temporalities])
Lynch, *De praesulibus Hib.*	John Lynch, *De praesulibus Hiberniae potissimis catholicae religionis in Hibernia, serendae, propagandae, et conservandae authoribus*, ed. J. F. O'Doherty (Irish Manuscripts Commission, 2 vols, Dublin, 1944)
Mich.	Michaelmas
MS	manuscript

N.D.	not dated; no date of publication given, and date not ascertained
N.I.	Northern Ireland
N.I.L.P.	Northern Ireland Labour Party
N.P.	no place of publication given, and place not ascertained
nom.	nominated
O.Carm.	Order of Carmelites (friars)
O.Carth.	Order of Carthusians (monks)
O.Cist.	Order of Cistercians (monks)
O.Cruc.	Ordo Cruciferorum (Crutched friars)
O.F.M.	Order of Friars Minor (Franciscan friars)
O.F.M.Conv.	Order of Friars Minor Conventual
O.P.	Order of Preachers (Dominican friars)
O.Praem.	Order of Premonstratensians (Norbertine canons)
O.S.A.	Order of St Augustine (Augustinian friars)
O.S.B.	Order of St Benedict (Benedictine monks)
p.	*post* (after)
P.M.	prime minister
P.R.O.	Public Record Office of England
P.R.O.I.	Public Record Office of Ireland
prov.	provided
R.I.	Republic of Ireland
R.I.A. Proc.	*Proceedings of the Royal Irish Academy* (Dublin, 1836–)
R.S.A.I. Jn.	*Journal of the Royal Society of Antiquaries of Ireland* (Dublin, 1892–)
Rawl. B 502	*Rawlinson B 502; a collection of pieces in prose and verse in the Irish language . . . from the original MS in the Bodleian*, with introduction by Kuno Meyer (facsimile, Oxford, 1909)
relq.	relinquished office
remvd	formally removed from office
res.	resigned
rest.	restored
s.a.	*sub anno* (under year)
S.D.L.P.	Social Democratic and Labour Party
S.J.	Society of Jesus (Jesuits)

s.p.	*sine prole* (without issue)
sect.	section
ser.	series
succ.	succeeded
succn	succession
suffr.	suffragan
T.C.D.	Library of Trinity College, Dublin
T.D.	teachtaire dála
temp.	restitution of episcopal temporalities (royal mandate)
ter.	appointment terminated by death or removal of monarch
trs.	translated (in ecclesiastical appointments)
U.K.	United Kingdom
U.P.N.I.	Unionist Party of Northern Ireland
U.U.U.C.	United Ulster Unionist Council
U.V.F.	Ulster Volunteer Force
un.	unionist (party)
vic. ap.	vicar apostolic
vic. gen.	vicar general
V.U.P.P.	Vanguard Unionist Progressive Party
Z.C.P.	*Zeitschrift für celtische Philologie* (Halle, 1896–1943, 23 vols; Tübingen, 1953–)

The en rule (–), solidus (/), and saltire (×) are used in dates, as in the following examples.

678–80   denotes a process extending from the first to the second date.
678/80   denotes alternative dates for a specific event.
678 × 680   denotes the period within which a specific event, which cannot be more precisely dated, occurred.

Between 1582 and 1752 the solidus is also used where events are dated both in Old Style and New Style; e.g. 19/29 July 1693.

NOTE ON DATING

DURING the period 1582–1752 there was a discrepancy between the calendar used in Ireland and England and that used over a large area of continental Europe. The calendar universally used in Europe down to 1582, that introduced by Julius Caesar in 45 B.C., which provided that every fourth year should be a leap year of 366 days, was based on a calculation of the solar year at 365¼ days. This was a slight overestimate, and as a result the calendar year had by the sixteenth century come to diverge by ten days from the solar year. A new calendar was, therefore, established by Pope Gregory XIII in his bull of 24 February 1582, which corrected the over-estimate by providing that the last year of a century should not be a leap year unless the number was divisible by 400. Thus 1600 would be a leap year, but 1700 would not. The bull prescribed that the day following 4 October 1582 should be 15 October, and also that the year should begin on 1 January instead of on Lady Day, 25 March. Most catholic states adopted the Gregorian or New Style calendar in the sixteenth century, most protestant states in the eighteenth century, and Russia and the Balkan states not till the twentieth century. The Julian or Old Style calendar used in Ireland was ten days behind the New Style calendar from 5 October 1582 to 28 February 1700 (Old Style) and eleven days behind from 29 February 1700 to 2 September 1752. The Gregorian calendar was adopted in the dominions of the British crown by an act of 1751 (24 Geo. II, c. 23), which prescribed that 2 September 1752 should be followed by 14 September, and that the official beginning of the year should be 1 January in and after 1752.

In this volume, dating is according to Old Style for the day and the month, but according to New Style for the year. In the case of events in continental Europe, both styles are used. Thus, the death of Ruaidhrí Ó Domhnaill, earl of Tyrconnell, is dated 18/28 July 1608. The lists of catholic bishops present special problems of dating, which are considered in the introduction to those lists (below, p. 333).

I
MAPS

CONTENTS

INTRODUCTION

THIS section comprises over one hundred maps covering all periods of Irish history from prehistoric times. There are also maps to illustrate the physical background and to show existing provincial, county, and barony boundaries. Some maps also appear in the same or more detailed form in the appropriate volume of text, but as a rule the maps collected here are wider in scope and time scale than the text maps.

Some of the maps are based on work already published elsewhere, but the large majority are derived from primary sources, many of them being the product of new research specially undertaken for this history. The selection of topics has been partly determined by the existing state of research on the materials for Irish historical cartography.

Each map or group of maps carries the name of the contributor responsible for its contents, who has also supplied the source and any necessary comment in the appended series of notes.

We are grateful to Mr Terry Hardaker and Miss Christine Cowham, of the cartographic department of the Oxford University Press, for their cooperation and for all the expertise that they have made available to us. Mary Griffiths and Anne Weir gave valuable assistance in the assembly and plotting of data for several of the draft maps. We are specially indebted to Mary Davies for supervising this entire section and for preparing the draft maps for the press.

IRELAND IN ITS ATLANTIC AND EUROPEAN SETTING

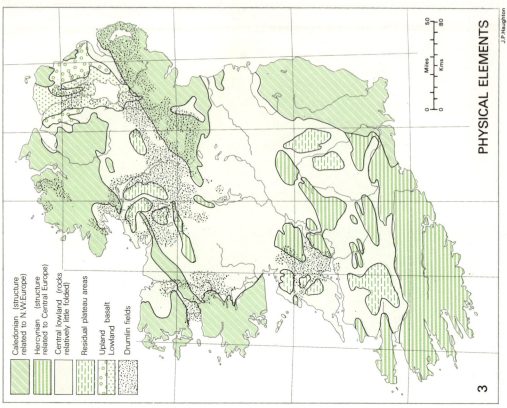

PHYSICAL ELEMENTS

Caledonian (structure related to N.W.Europe)

Hercynian (structure related to Central Europe)

Central lowland (rocks relatively little folded)

Residual plateau areas

Upland
Lowland basalt

Drumlin fields

0 — 50 Miles
0 — 80 Kms

3

J.P.Haughton

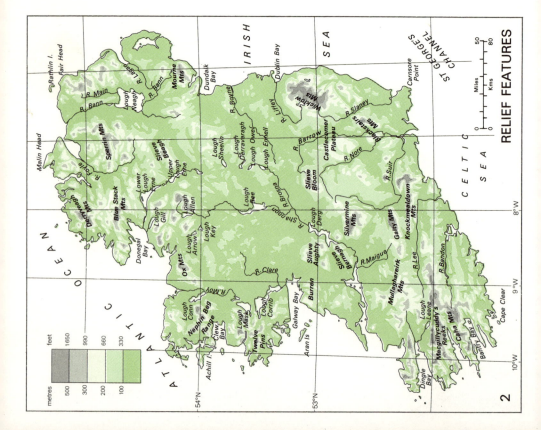

RELIEF FEATURES

feet
1650
990
660
330

metres
500
300
200
100

0 — 50 Miles
0 — 80 Kms

Rathlin I.
Fair Head
Malin Head
R. Main
R. Bann
Lough Neagh
R. Bann
R. Lagan
Mourne Mts
Dundalk Bay
Dublin Bay
R. Boyne
R. Liffey
Wicklow Mts
R. Slaney
Carnsole Point
Sperrin Mts
Slieve Beagh
Lough Sheelin
Lough Owel
Lough Derravaragh
Lough Ennell
Castlecomer Plateau
R. Barrow
R. Nore
Blackstairs Mts
Upper Lough Erne
Lower Lough Erne
Lough Erne
Slieve Bloom
R. Suir
Derryveagh Mts
Blue Stack Mts
Lough Gill
Lough Melvin
Lough Allen
Lough Key
Lough Arrow
Ox Mts
Donegal Bay
R. Shannon
R. Brosna
Lough Ree
Lough Derg
Slieve Aughty
Slieve Bernagh
Silvermine Mts
Galty Mts
Knockmealdown Mts
R. Maigue
R. Lee
R. Bandon
Mullaghareirk Mts
Lough Leane
Caha Mts
Macgillycuddy's Reeks
Dingle Bay
Bantry Bay
Cape Clear
R. Clare
R. Moy
Nephin Beg Range
Clew Bay
Achill I.
Lough Conn
Lough Cullin
Twelve Pins
Lough Mask
Lough Corrib
Galway Bay
Burren
Aran Is.
R. Suck

ATLANTIC OCEAN
IRISH SEA
CELTIC SEA
ST GEORGE'S CHANNEL

54°N
53°N
10°W
9°W
8°W

2

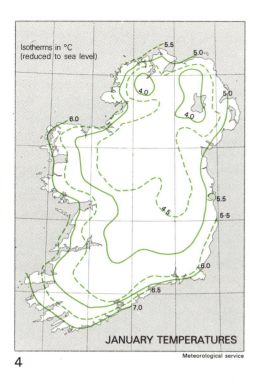

Isotherms in °C
(reduced to sea level)

5.5
5.0
4.0
5.0
6.0
4.0
4.5
5.5
5.5
6.0
6.5
7.0

JANUARY TEMPERATURES

Meteorological service

4

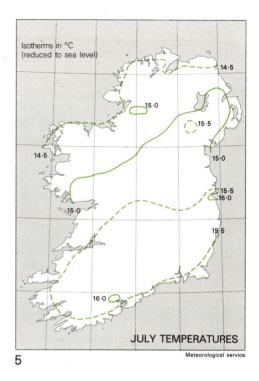

Isotherms in °C
(reduced to sea level)

14·5
15·0
15·5
14·5
15·0
15·5
16·0
15·0
15·0
15·5
16·0

JULY TEMPERATURES

Meteorological service

5

1400
1200
1400
1500
1400
1300
1400
1600
1700
1500

**MEAN ANNUAL NUMBER OF
HOURS OF BRIGHT SUNSHINE**

Meteorological service

6

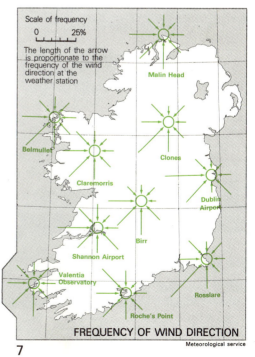

Scale of frequency

0   25%

The length of the arrow
is proportionate to the
frequency of the wind
direction at the
weather station

Malin Head

Belmullet

Clones

Claremorris

Dublin
Airport

Birr

Shannon Airport

Valentia
Observatory

Rosslare

Roche's Point

FREQUENCY OF WIND DIRECTION

Meteorological service

7

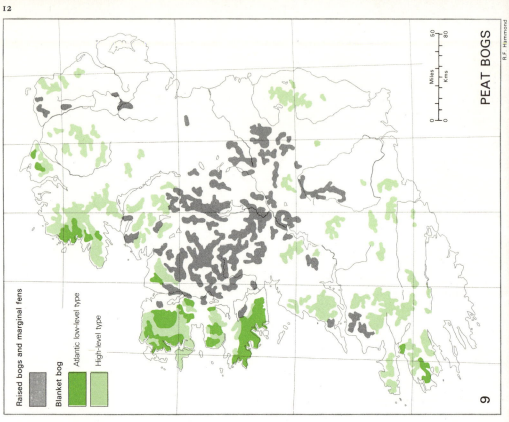

PEAT BOGS

Raised bogs and marginal fens

Blanket bog

Atlantic low-level type

High-level type

Miles

Kms

R.F. Hammond

9

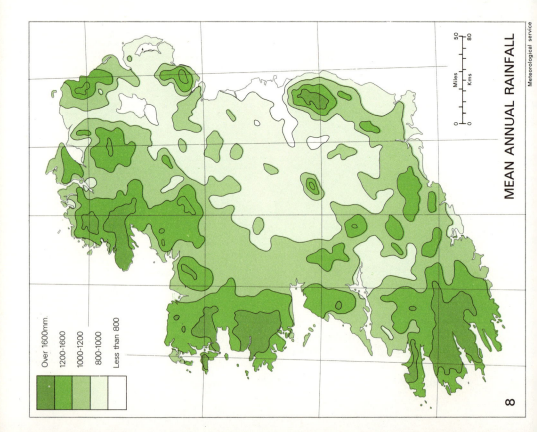

MEAN ANNUAL RAINFALL

Over 1600mm.

1200-1600

1000-1200

800-1000

Less than 800

Miles

Kms

Meteorological service

8

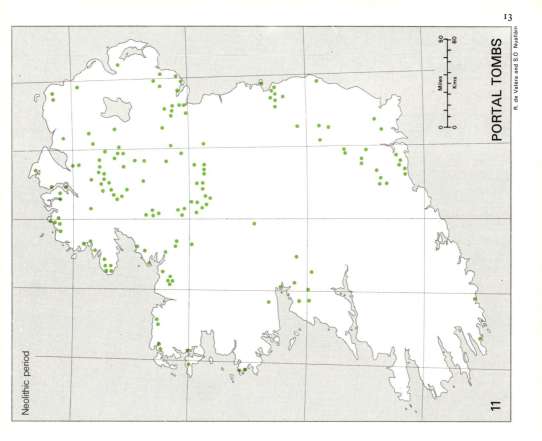

Neolithic period

PORTAL TOMBS

Miles 50
Kms 80

R. de Valéra and S.Ó Nualláin

11

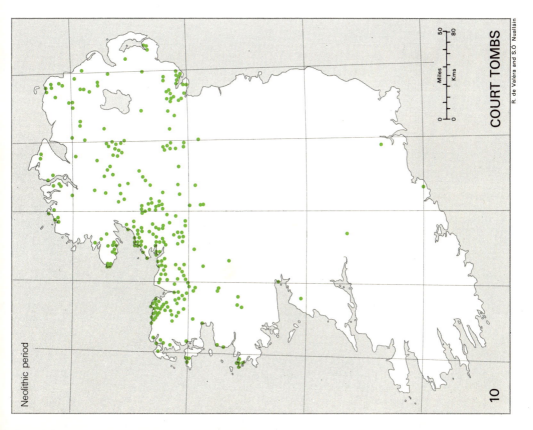

Neolithic period

COURT TOMBS

Miles 50
Kms 80

R. de Valéra and S.Ó Nualláin

10

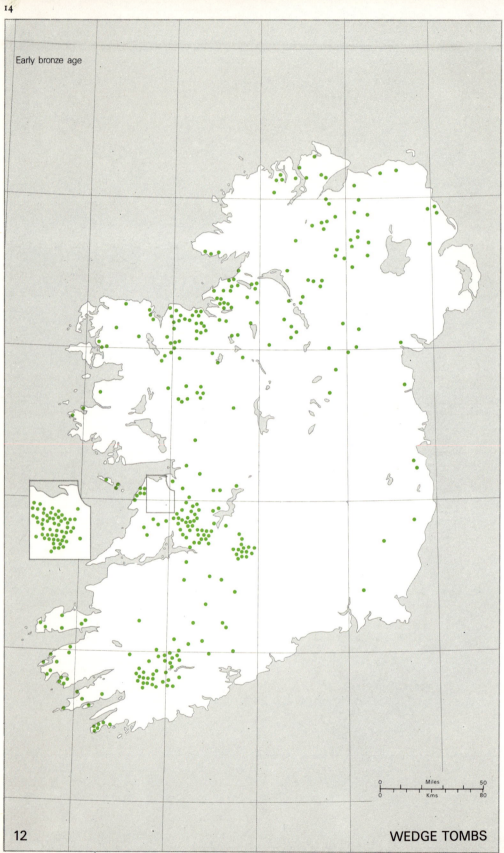

Early bronze age

Miles
0   50
0   80
Kms

WEDGE TOMBS

R. de Valéra and S.Ó. Nualláin

Tomb
Cemetery
Major cemetery

1 West Torr
2 Moneydig
3 Donegore
4 Clermont Cairn
5 Newgrange-Dowth-Knowth cemetery
6 Fourknocks
7 Seehan
8 Lugnagun Great

Ballintoy
Ballyvoy
Ballynastraid
Cross
1
Carnanmore
Tereagh
Cloghs

Craigs

Drumsurn Upper
2
Tullykittagh Upper
Templemoyle
Ballyhameen
Ballylumford
Croaghan-
Kilmonaster
cemetery
Carn
Doorat
Slieve
Gallion
3
Moyadam
Collinward
Ballybriest
Mobuy
Ballycollin
Ballynahatty
Donaghanie
Drumreagh

Magheracar
Finner
Kiltierney
Sess Kilgreen
Knocknany
Ballynolly
Waringstown
Annadorn
Reentagh
Knocknarea-Carrowmore
cemetery
Moylehid
Vicar's Cairn
Slieve
Croob
Ballynoe
Carrowhubbock South
Glen
Aughnagurgan
Carnlough Mt.
Slieve Donard
Carrowreagh
Slieve Gullion

Keshcorran-
Carrowkeel
cemetery
Scrabbagh
Feragh Beg
Laughart Lower
Carnaddy
Sheebeg
Kilin
Rockville
Sheemore

Sheean
Cornafunshin
Loughcrew cemetery
Townleyhall
Westport Demesne
5
Sheegeeragh
Drewstown Sradt
Gormanstown
Iskaroon
6
Bremore
Tara
Rush

Siregg

Croghan Hill
Caureen
7
Mountpelier
Goldenhill
Seefinnan
Broadleas-Commons
Seefin
Lugnagroagh
Church Mountain
Baltinglass Hill

Derrynahinch
Duntryleague
Shrough
Slievenaman
Boolarlisheen

Glen

Miles
0
50
Kms
0
80

13
PASSAGE-GRAVE SITES 2500-2000 B.C.

M. Herity

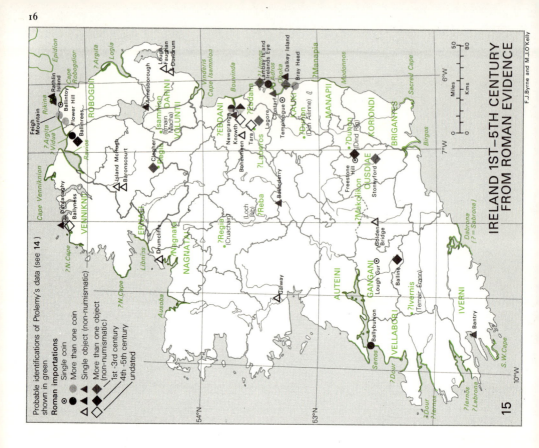

Probable identifications of Ptolemy's data (see 14) shown in green

Roman importations

	1st-3rd century	4th-5th century	undated
Single coin	⊙		
More than one coin	●	▲	◆
Single object (non-numismatic)			
More than one object (non-numismatic)	△		◇

IRELAND 1ST–5TH CENTURY FROM ROMAN EVIDENCE

15

F.J.Byrne and M.J.O'Kelly

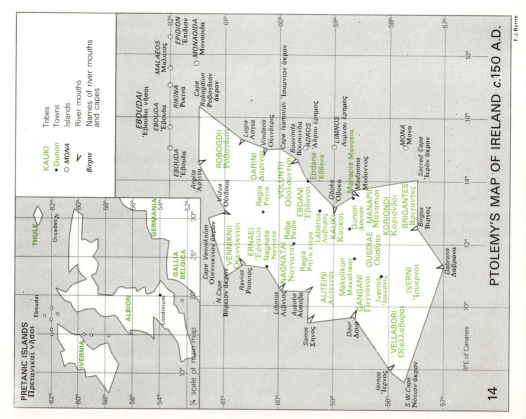

PRETANIC ISLANDS
Πρετανικαὶ νῆσοι

KAUKI	Tribes
•Dunon	Towns
○MONA	Islands
V	River mouths
Birgos	Names of river mouths and capes

PTOLEMY'S MAP OF IRELAND c.150 A.D.

14

F.J.Byrne

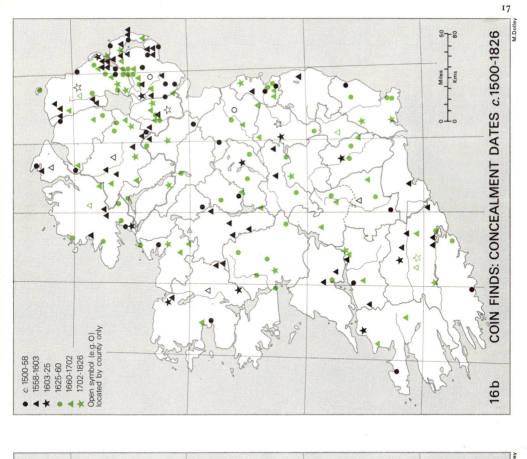

Roman period (see note 16a)
Ninth century
c. 900–97
997–1185
1185–c.1350
c.1350–c.1450
c.1450–c.1500
Open symbol (e.g.O)
located by county only

16a COIN FINDS: CONCEALMENT DATES *c.*150–*c.*1500

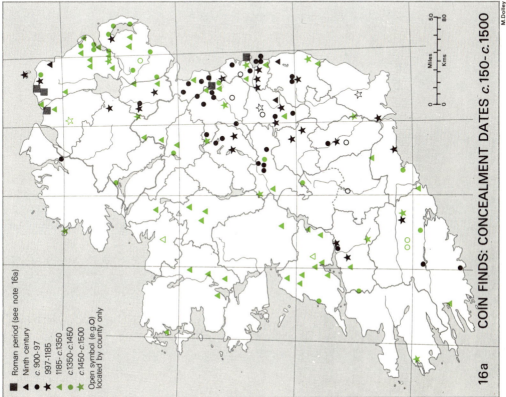

c. 1500-58
1558-1603
1603-25
1625-60
1660-1702
1702-1826
Open symbol (e.g.O)
located by county only

16b COIN FINDS: CONCEALMENT DATES *c.*1500–1826

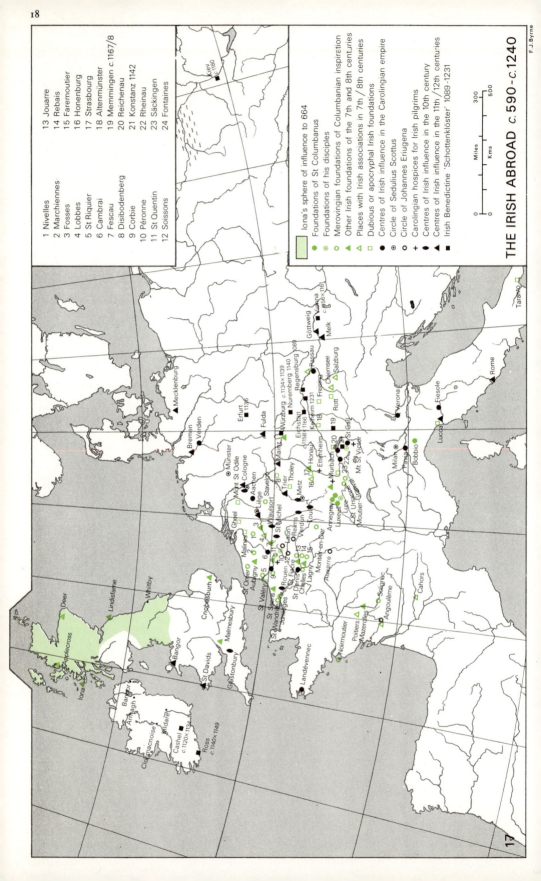

THE IRISH ABROAD c. 590–c. 1240

F. J. Byrne

1 Nivelles
2 Marchiennes
3 Fosses
4 Lobbes
5 St Riquier
6 Cambrai
7 Fescau
8 Disibodenberg
9 Corbie
10 Péronne
11 St Quentin
12 Soissons
13 Jouarre
14 Rebais
15 Faremoutier
16 Honenburg
17 Strasbourg
18 Altenmünster
19 Memmingen c.1167/8
20 Reichenau
21 Konstanz 1142
22 Rheinau
23 Säckingen
24 Fontaines

Iona's sphere of influence to 664
Foundations of St Columbanus
Foundations of his disciples
Merovingian foundations of Columbanian inspiration
Other Irish foundations of the 7th and 8th centuries
Places with Irish associations in 7th / 8th centuries
Dubious or apocryphal Irish foundations
Centres of Irish influence in the Carolingian empire
Circle of Sedulius Scottus
Circle of Johannes Eriugena
Carolingian hospices for Irish pilgrims
Centres of Irish influence in the 10th century
Centres of Irish influence in the 11th/12th centuries
Irish Benedictine 'Schottenklöster' 1089–1231

Miles
Kms
0   300
0   500

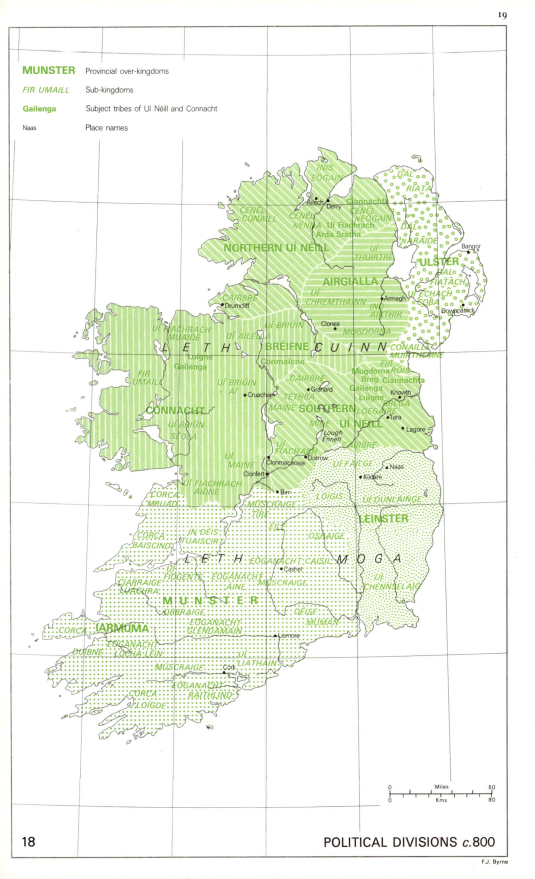

MUNSTER — Provincial over-kingdoms

FIR UMAILL — Sub-kingdoms

Gailenga — Subject tribes of Uí Néill and Connacht

Naas — Place names

INIS EÓGAIN

DÁL RIATA

Ailéch • • Derry   Ciannachta

CENÉL CONAILL   CENÉL NÉNDA   CENÉL NEÓGAIN   Uí Fiachrach   Arda Sratha   DÁL NARÁIDE

Bangor •

NORTHERN UÍ NÉILL   UÍ THUIRTRE   ULSTER   DÁL FIATÁCH

AIRGIALLA   UÍ ECHACH COBA

CAIRBRE   • Drumcliff   Uí CHREMTHAINN   • Armagh   UÍ AIRTHIR   Downpatrick •

UÍ FIACHRACH MUAIDE   UÍ AILELLA   UÍ BRIÚIN   Clones •   IND AIRTHIR   MUGDORNA

BRÉIFNE   L E T H   C U I N N   CONAILLE MUIRTHEMNE

Luigne   Conmaicne   FIR   ROIS

Gailenga   Mugdorna   Breg Ciannachta

FIR UMAILL   UÍ BRIÚIN AÍ   • Cruachain   CAIRBRE   • Granard   Gailenga   Luigne   BREGA   Knowth •

CONNACHT   TETHBA   MAINE   SOUTHERN   LOÉGAIRE   • Tara

UÍ BRIÚIN SEÓLA   MÍDE   UÍ NÉILL   • Lagore

Lough Ennell   CAIRBRE

UÍ FIACHRAID   • Durrow   UÍ FAILGE   • Naas

UÍ MAINE   Clonmacnoise •   UÍ DÚNLAINGE

Clonfert •   • Kildare

UÍ FIACHRACH AIDNE   • Birr   LÓIGIS

CORCA MRUAD   MÚSCRAIGE TÍRE   LEINSTER

CORCA BAISCIND   IN DÉIS TUAISCIRT   FILE   OSRAIGE

L E T H   M O G A

UÍ FIDGENTE   EÓGANACHT CAISIL   EÓGANACHT ÁINE   MÚSCRAIGE   UÍ CHENNSELAIG

CIARRAIGE LUACHRA   • Cashel

MUNSTER   UÍBRAIGE   DÉISE   MUMAN

CORCA IARMUMA   EÓGANACHT GLENDAMAIN   • Lismore

EÓGANACHT DUIBNE   LOCHA LÉIN   UÍ LIATHÁIN

MÚSCRAIGE   • Cork

CORCA LOÍGDE   EÓGANACHT RAITHLIND

Miles   0 ——— 50
Kms   0 ——— 80

POLITICAL DIVISIONS *c.*800

F.J. Byrne

Raid
Raid: site uncertain
Battle
Battle: site uncertain
Encampment: site uncertain
Fleet

UÍ FIDGENTE Irish kingdoms involved in war with vikings
Strangford Norse place names
Norse campaigns
812 Year of campaign

Rathlin ?
Skerries
Derry
Larne (Ulfreksfiord)
Maghera
Connor
DÁL NARAIDE
824/5
Bangor
Movilla
Inishmurray
Armagh
ULAID
Downpatrick
Strangford
UÍ MÉITH
Muckno
Carlingford
Donaghmoyne
CONAILLE
Louth 831
FIR UMAILL
CIANNACHTA
Inishbofin
CONNACHTA
(devastated 836)
Slane
Duleek
Holmpatrick
CONMAICNE
DESCERT BREG
Skerries
? Lambay
Ireland's Eye
Leixlip
Howth
Roscam
Clonmacnoise
Dalkey
Kildare
FORTUATHA LAIGEN
Glendalough
Wicklow
CORCO BAISCINN
836
TRADRAIGE DÉIS TUAISCIRT
Clonmore
Arklow
Mungret
Ferns
UÍ FIDGENTE
OSRAIGE
St Mullins
UÍ CHENNSELAIG
Begerin
Smerwick
Wexford
Waterford
Taghmon
UÍ FOTHAID TÍRE
825
Loch Léin
Lismore
Helvick
Dairinis
Cork
Cloyne
Skellig
812
824

Miles
0   50
0   80
Kms

VIKING RAIDS: THE FIRST GENERATION 795-836

F.J.Byrne and C.Doherty

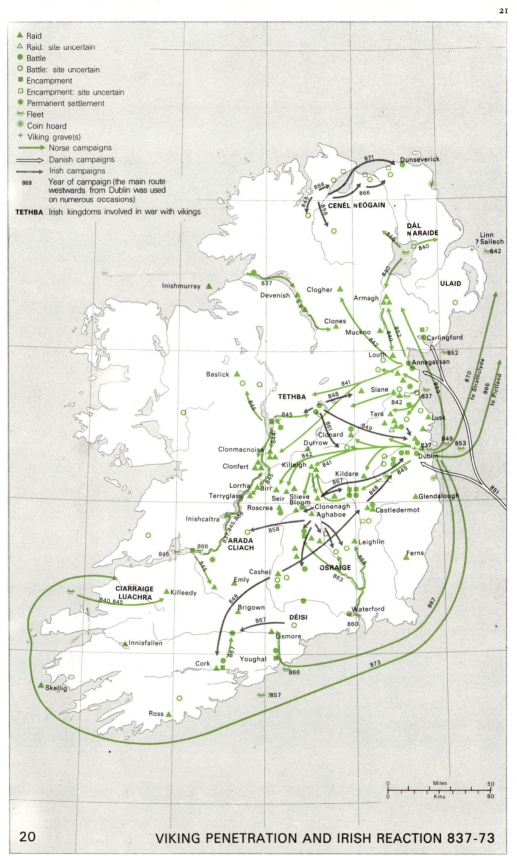

Legend

- ▲ Raid
- △ Raid: site uncertain
- ● Battle
- ○ Battle: site uncertain
- ■ Encampment
- □ Encampment: site uncertain
- ✻ Permanent settlement
- ⊢ Fleet
- ◉ Coin hoard
- ✛ Viking grave(s)
- → Norse campaigns
- ⇒ Danish campaigns
- → Irish campaigns
- 868 Year of campaign (the main route westwards from Dublin was used on numerous occasions)
- **TETHBA** Irish kingdoms involved in war with vikings

Dunseverick 871

CENÉL NEÓGAIN 866 845 856 866

DÁL NARAIDE 840

ULAID

Linn ?Sailech 842

Inishmurray 837

Devenish Clogher Armagh

Clones Muckno

Louth

Carlingford 852 852

Baslick 841 848 Slane Tara 842 Lusk 837 849 853

TETHBA 845 Clonard Durrow 849 Dublin

Clonmacnoise Killeigh 842 841 Kildare 867 845

Clonfert Seir Slieve Bloom 848 Glendalough

Lorrha Birr 845 Roscrea Clonenagh Aghaboe Castledermot

Terryglass 858 Leighlin

Inishcaltra ARADA CLIACH Ferns

845 866 Cashel OSRAIGE 863

CIARRAIGE LUACHRA Killeedy Emly Waterford 867

840.845 Brigown DÉISI 860

Innisfallen 867 Lismore

Skellig Cork Youghal 866 873

Ross 857

to Strathclyde 870 to Pictland 866 851

Miles 0 50
Kms 0 80

21

20 VIKING PENETRATION AND IRISH REACTION 837-73

F.J.Byrne and C.Doherty

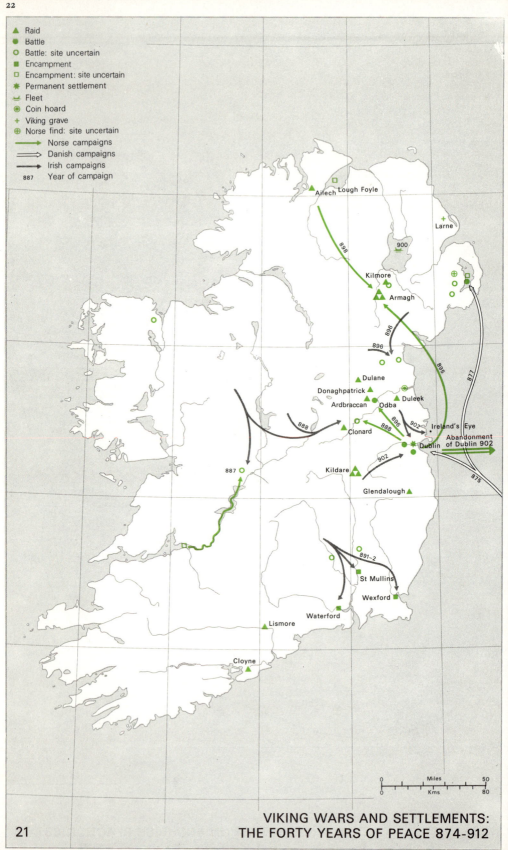

Raid
Battle
Battle: site uncertain
Encampment
Encampment: site uncertain
Permanent settlement
Fleet
Coin hoard
Viking grave
Norse find: site uncertain

Norse campaigns
Danish campaigns
Irish campaigns
887   Year of campaign

Ailech
Lough Foyle
Larne
900
Kilmore
Armagh
898
896
896
Dulane
Donaghpatrick
Duleek
Ardbraccan
Odba
888
902
Clonard
888   896   902
Ireland's Eye
Dublin
Abandonment
of Dublin 902
Kildare
887
902
Glendalough
895
877
875
891–2
St Mullins
Wexford
Waterford
Lismore
Cloyne

0   Miles   50
0   Kms   80

VIKING WARS AND SETTLEMENTS:
THE FORTY YEARS OF PEACE 874-912

F.J.Byrne and C.Doherty

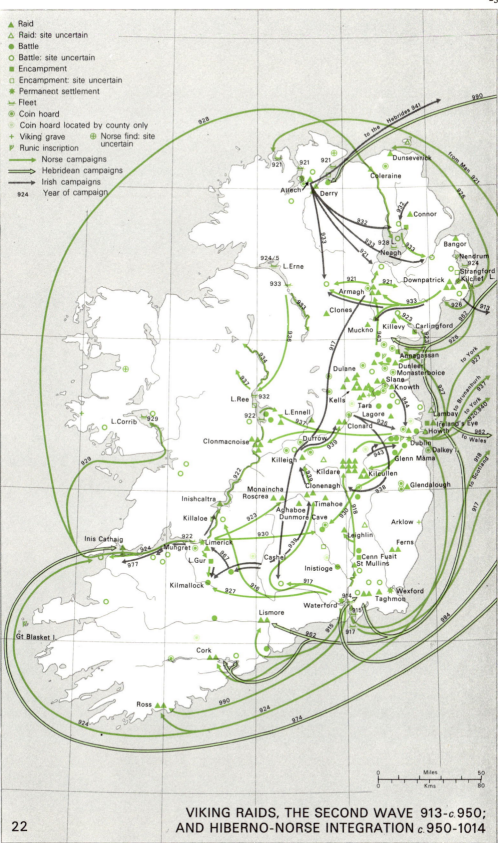

Raid
Raid: site uncertain
Battle
Battle: site uncertain
Encampment
Encampment: site uncertain
Permanent settlement
Fleet
Coin hoard
Coin hoard located by county only
Viking grave   Norse find: site uncertain
Runic inscription
Norse campaigns
Hebridean campaigns
Irish campaigns
924   Year of campaign

to the Hebrides 941
990
928
from Man 921
921 921
Dunseverick
Coleraine
Ailech Derry
921
922
Connor
932
933
933 928
Bangor
921 Neagh 933
Nendrum
924
Strangford
Kilclief L.
924/5
L.Erne
933
921 Armagh 921
Downpatrick
926 913
Clones 933
Killevy
Carlingford
962
928
Muckno 923
to York
923 928 927
Annagassan
to York
Dulane Dunleer
Monasterboice
927 937
Slane Knowth
to Brunanburh
920,340
L.Ree 932 Kells Tara
Lambay
to York
922 L.Ennell Lagore 936
Ireland's Eye
to Wales
L.Corrib 929 937 Clonard
Howth 962
Clonmacnoise Durrow 939 Dublin
to Scotland
922 Killeigh Glenn Máma 918
Kildare Kilcullen 943
Glenn Máma
Monaincha Clonenagh 938 Glendalough
Roscrea
917
Inishcaltra
Killaloe 923 Aghaboe 930 918
Dunmore Cave Leighlin
Arklow
Inis Cathaig 922 Limerick 930 939 Ferns
924 Mungret 967 Cashel Inistioge Cenn Fuait
977 L.Gur 916 St Mullins
Kilmallock 927 917 Wexford
914 Taghmon
Lismore Waterford 915 984
915 917
962
Gt Blasket I. Cork
Ross
990
924
924 974

Miles 50
0
0 Kms 80

VIKING RAIDS, THE SECOND WAVE 913-c.950;
AND HIBERNO-NORSE INTEGRATION c.950-1014

F.J.Byrne and C.Doherty

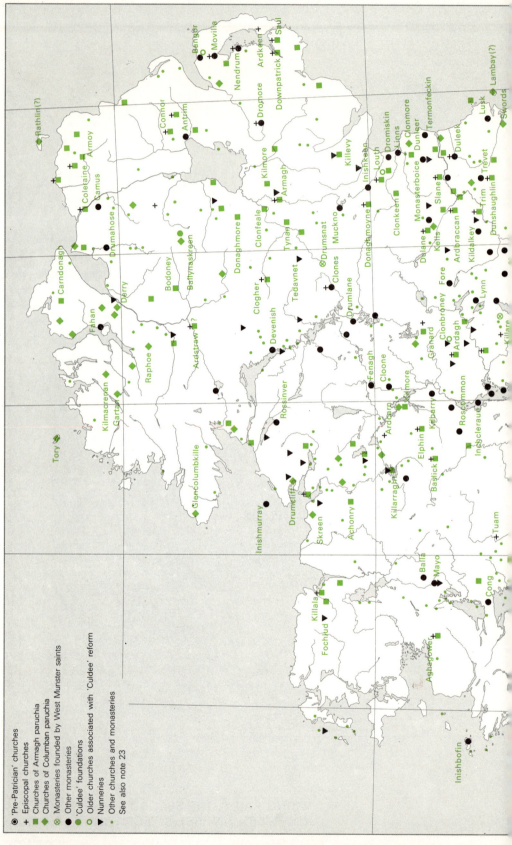

Bangor
Movilla
Nendrum
Dromore
Ardkeen
Saul
Downpatrick
Rathlin(?)
Armoy
Coletaine
Camus
Conor
Antrim
Kilmore
Killevy
Lambay(?)
Lusk
Swords
Dromiskin
Linns
Clonmore
Termonfeckin
Duleek
Trevet
Trim
Dunshaughlin
Kells
Slane
Ardbraccan
Kildalkey
Monasterboice
Dunleer
Louth
Inishkeen
Armagh
Clonfeale
Tynan
Drumsnat
Muckno
Donaghmoyne
Clonkeen
Drumahose
Donaghmore
Carndonagh
Bodoney
Ballymaskreen
Clogher
Tedavnet
Clones
Drumlane
Fore
Lynn
Killare
Derry
Devenish
Fenagh
Clonbroney
Ardagh
Fahan
Ardstraw?
Cloone
Kilmore
Granard
Raphoe
Rossinver
Kilmacrenan
Gartan
Ardcarn
Drumcliff
Achonry
Skreen
Killarragh?
Elphin
Baslick
Kilbarry
Roscommon
Iniscleraun
Tuam
Glencolumbkille
Inishmurray
Cong
Balla
Mayo
Killala
Fochjud
Aghagower
Inishbofin
Tory

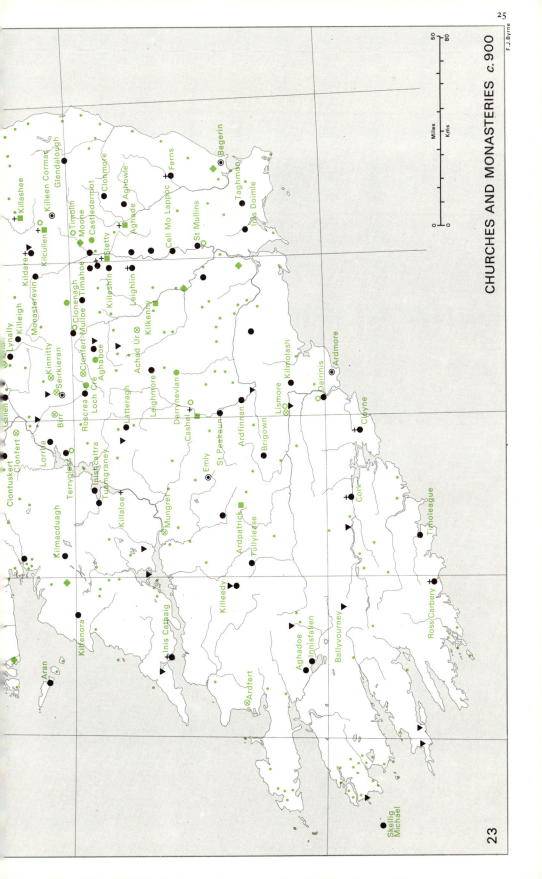

F.J.Byrne

CHURCHES AND MONASTERIES *c*.900

Miles

Kms

50

80

0

0

Killashee

Killeen Cormac

Glendalough

Kildare

Kilcullen

Timolin

Castledermot

Moone

Cloonmore

Aghowle

Ferns

Begerin

Taghmon

Inis Doimle

Killeigh

Monasterevin

Clonenagh

Timahoe

Aghade

Cell Mo Lappóc

St Mullins

Sletty

Lynally

Kildare

Clonfert-Mulloe

Killeshin

Leighlin

Kilkenny

Seirkieran

Kinnitty

Aghaboe

Achad Ur

Leighmore

Kilmolash

Birr

Roscrea

Loch Cré

Latteragh

Derrynevlan

Lismore

Dairinis

Ardmore

Clontuskert

Clonfert

Lorrha

Cashel

Ardfinnan

Cloyne

Gallen

Terryglass

Inis Cealtra

St Peakaun

Brigown

Tuamgraney

Emly

Cork

Kilmacduagh

Killaloe

Mungret

Ardpatrick

Tullylease

Timoleague

Kilfenora

Killeedy

Aghadoe

Ballyvourney

Ross Carbery

Aran

Inis Cathaig

Innisfallen

Ardfert

Skellig
Michael

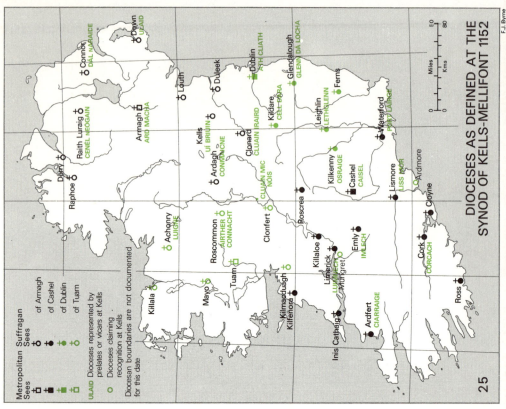

DIOCESES AS DEFINED AT THE
SYNOD OF KELLS-MELLIFONT 1152

Metropolitan Suffragan
Sees   Sees

‡   ✚   of Armagh
■□   ✚   of Cashel
■   ●   of Dublin
□   ○   of Tuam

ULAID Dioceses represented by
       prelates or vicars at Kells

○   Dioceses claiming
       recognition at Kells

Diocesan boundaries are not documented
for this date

‡ Connor
  DÁL NARAIDE

✚ Down
  ULAID

‡ Raith Luraig
  CENÉL NEOGAIN

‡ Armagh
  ARD MACHA

○ Derry

○ Raphoe

○ Achonry
  LUIGNE

○ Roscommon
  AIRTHER
  CONNACHT

Tuam

Mayo

Killala

Kilmacduagh
Kilfenora

Inis Cathaig

‡ Ardfert
  CIARRAIGE

● Killaloe

✚ Limerick
  LUIMNECH

○ Mungret

✚ Emly
  IMLECH

‡ Cork
  CORCACH

✚ Ross

Louth

✚ Duleek

Kells

✚ Ardagh

Clonard
CLUAIN IRAIRD

CLUAIN MIC
NOIS

Clonfert

● Roscrea

■ Cashel
  CAISEL

‡ Kilkenny
  OSRAIGE

✚ Lismore
  LISS MÓR

Cloyne

Cork
CORCACH

‡ Dublin
  ÁTH CLIATH

○ Glendalough
  GLENN DÁ LOCHA

● Kildare
  CELL DARA

‡ Leighlin
  LETHGLENN

✚ Ferns

Waterford
PORT LÁIRGE

Ardmore

0   80
Miles
Kms

F.J. Byrne

25

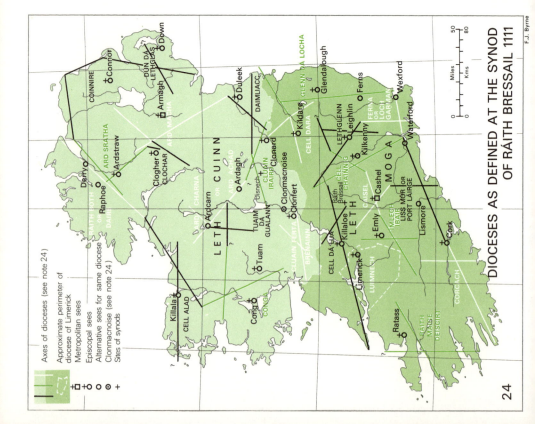

DIOCESES AS DEFINED AT THE SYNOD
OF RÁITH BRESSAIL 1111

Axes of dioceses (see note 24)

Approximate perimeter of
diocese of Limerick

Metropolitan sees

Episcopal sees

Alternative sees for same diocese

Clonmacnoise (see note 24)

Sites of synods

‡ Connor
  COINNIRE

DÚN DÁ
LETHGLAS
‡ Down

✚ Armagh
  ARD MACHA

○ Derry
○ Raphoe
  DAIRE

ARD SRATHA
✚ Ardstraw

✚ Clogher
  CLOCHAR

ARD ACHAD

TÍR CHARNA
○ Argcarn

○ Ardagh

Bisnech

TUAIM DÁ
GUALANN
✚ Tuam

Killala
CELL ALAD

Cong
CONGA

○ Clonmacnoise

LETH OR CUINN

CLUAIN
IRAIRD
Clonard

Clonfert

✚ Limerick
LUIMNECH

LUAIN
FERTA

LUAIN
BREMAINN

CELL DÁ LUA
‡ Killaloe

RÁITH
BRESSAIL

IMLEGA
IBAIR
✚ Emly

RÁITH
MAISE
DEIRGIRE
✚ Ratass

Kilkenny
CELL
CHAINNIG

Cashel
CAISEL

LETH

M O G A

LISS MÓR or
PORT LAIRGE
Lismore

Cork
CORCACH

✚ Cork

Waterford

Wexford

✚ Ferns
FERNA
OR
LOCH
GARMAN

Leighlin
LETHGLENN

✚ Kildare
CELL DARA

Glendalough
GLENN DÁ LOCHA

DAIMLIACC
✚ Duleek

0   50
Miles
Kms

F.J. Byrne

24

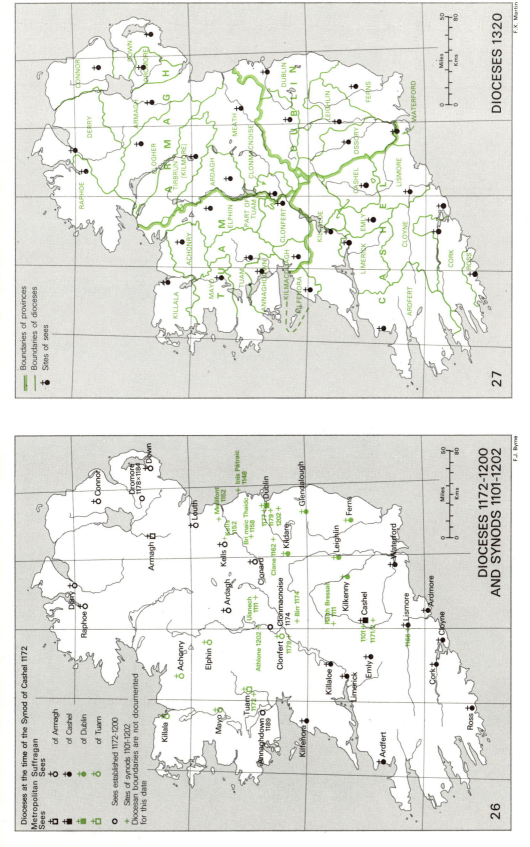

F.X. Martin

DIOCESES 1320

Boundaries of provinces
Boundaries of dioceses
Sites of sees

DOWN
ARDMORE
CONNOR
ARMAGH
DERRY
RAPHOE
CLOGHER
TIRBRUN [KILMORE]
ARDAGH
ELPHIN
PART OF TUAM
CLONMACNOISE
MEATH
DUBLIN
LEIGHLIN
FERNS
OSSORY
CASHEL
LISMORE
KILDARE
CLONFERT
ANNAGHDOWN
KILMACDUAGH
KILFENORA
TUAM
MAYO
ACHONRY
KILLALA
EMLY
LIMERICK
CLOYNE
ARDFERT
CORK
ROSS

Miles
Kms
50
80

27

F.J. Byrne

**DIOCESES 1172-1200
AND SYNODS 1101-1202**

Dioceses at the time of the Synod of Cashel 1172

Metropolitan   Suffragan
Sees   Sees
                of Armagh
                of Cashel
                of Dublin
                of Tuam

Sees established 1172-1200

Sites of synods 1101-1202

Diocesan boundaries are not documented
for this date

Down
Dromore
1178×1184
Connor
Louth
Mellifont
1152
Inis Pátraic
1148
Kells
1152
Armagh
Derry
Raphoe
Ardagh
Kells
Clonard
Brí maic Thaidc.
1158
Dublin
1177
1179
1202
Kildare
Clane 1162
Leighlin
Ferns
Glendalough
Uisnech
1111
Athlone 1202
Clonmacnoise
1174
Birr 1174
Ráith Bressail
1111
Kilkenny
Cashel
1101
1171/2
Waterford
Clonfert
1179
Elphin
Achonry
Lismore
1166
Ardmore
Killaloe
Emly
Limerick
Cloyne
Cork
Killala
Mayo
Tuam
1172
Annaghdown
1189
Kilfenora
Ardfert
Ross

Miles
Kms
50
80

26

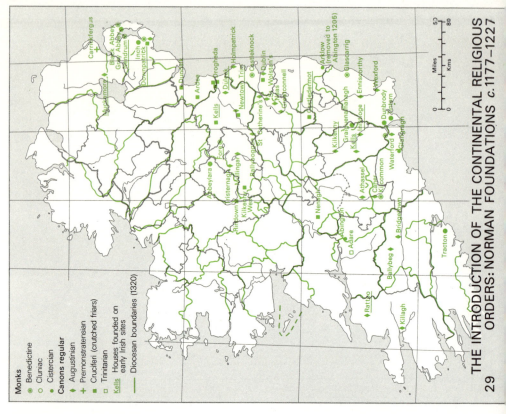

Monks
- Benedictine
- Cluniac
- Cistercian

Canons regular
- Augustinian
- Premonstratensian
- Crucifer (crutched friars)
- Trinitarian

Kells Houses founded on early Irish sites

—— Diocesan boundaries (1320)

29   THE INTRODUCTION OF THE CONTINENTAL RELIGIOUS ORDERS: NORMAN FOUNDATIONS c.1177–1227

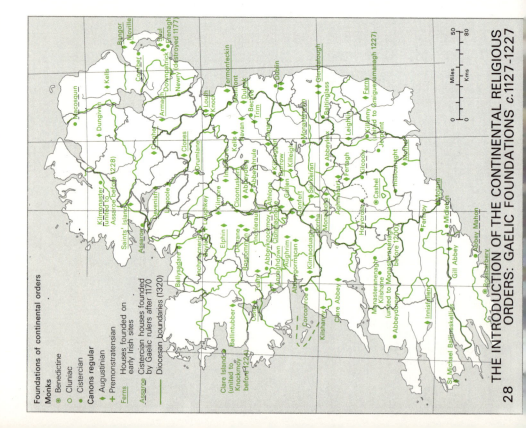

Foundations of continental orders

Monks
- Benedictine
- Cluniac
- Cistercian

Canons regular
- Augustinian
- Premonstratensian

Ferns Houses founded on early Irish sites

Assaroe Cistercian houses founded by Gaelic rulers after 1170

—— Diocesan boundaries (1320)

28   THE INTRODUCTION OF THE CONTINENTAL RELIGIOUS ORDERS: GAELIC FOUNDATIONS c.1127–1227

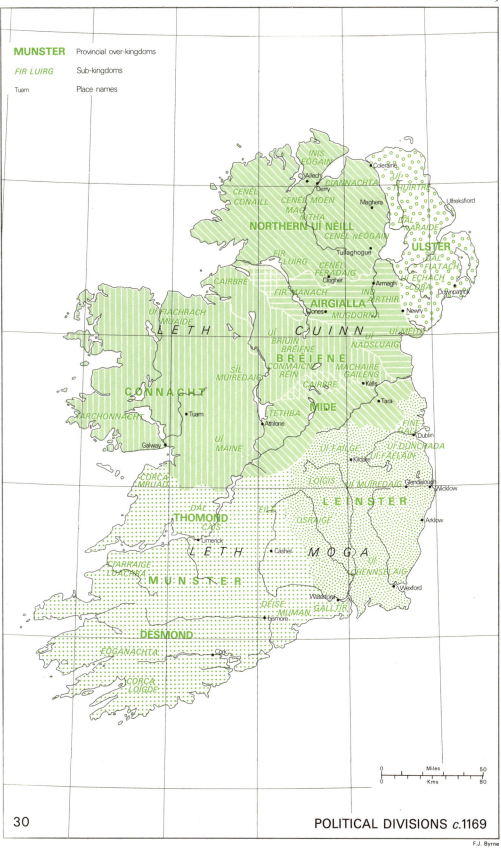

MUNSTER   Provincial over-kingdoms

FIR LUIRG   Sub-kingdoms

Tuam   Place names

INIS EÓGAIN

CIANNACHTA

Coleraine

Ailech

Derry

UÍ THUIRTRE

CENÉL CONAILL

CENÉL MOEN

MAG NITHA

Maghera

Ulfreksfiord

NORTHERN UÍ NÈILL

CENÉL NEÓGAIN

DÁL NARAIDE

ULSTER

FIR LUIRG

CENÉL FERADAIG

Tullaghogue

DÁL FIATACH

CAIRBRE

Clogher

UÍ EÇHACH COBA

FIR MANACH

IND AIRTHIR

Armagh

Downpatrick

AIRGIALLA

Clones

MUGDORNA

Newry

UÍ FIACHRACH MUAIDE

LETH   *CUINN*

UÍ MEITH

UÍ BRIÚIN BRÉIFNE

UÍ NADSLUAIG

BRÉIFNE

CONMAICNE RÉIN

MACHAIRE GAILENG

SÍL MUIREDAIG

CAIRBRE

Kells

CONNACHT

Tara

IARCHONNACHT

Tuam

TETHBA

Athlone

MIDE

FINE GALL

Dublin

UÍ MAINE

Galway

UÍ FAILGE

UÍ DÚNCHADA

UÍ FÁELÁIN

Kildare

CORCA MRUAD

LOÍGIS

UÍ MUIREDAIG

Glendalough

Wicklow

LEINSTER

DÁL CAIS

THOMOND

EILE

OSRAIGE

Arklow

Limerick

Cashel

LETH   *MOGA*

CIARRAIGE LUACHRA

UÍ CHENNSELAIG

MUNSTER

Wexford

Waterford

DÉISE MUMAN

GALLTÍR

Lismore

DESMOND

EÓGANACHTA

Cork

CORCA LOÍGDE

Miles   50

Kms   80

F.J. Byrne

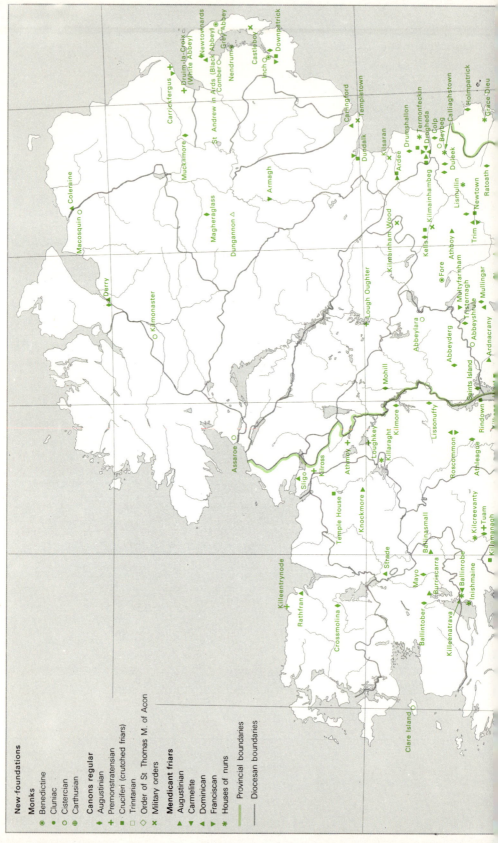

New foundations

Monks
- ◉ Benedictine
- ● Cluniac
- ○ Cistercian
- ⊕ Carthusian

Canons regular
- ◆ Augustinian
- ✛ Premonstratensian
- ■ Cruciferi (crutched friars)
- □ Trinitarian
- ◇ Order of St Thomas M. of Acon
- ✕ Military orders

Mendicant friars
- ▲ Augustinian
- ▼ Carmelite
- ◀ Dominican
- ▶ Franciscan
- ✶ Houses of nuns

— Provincial boundaries
— Diocesan boundaries

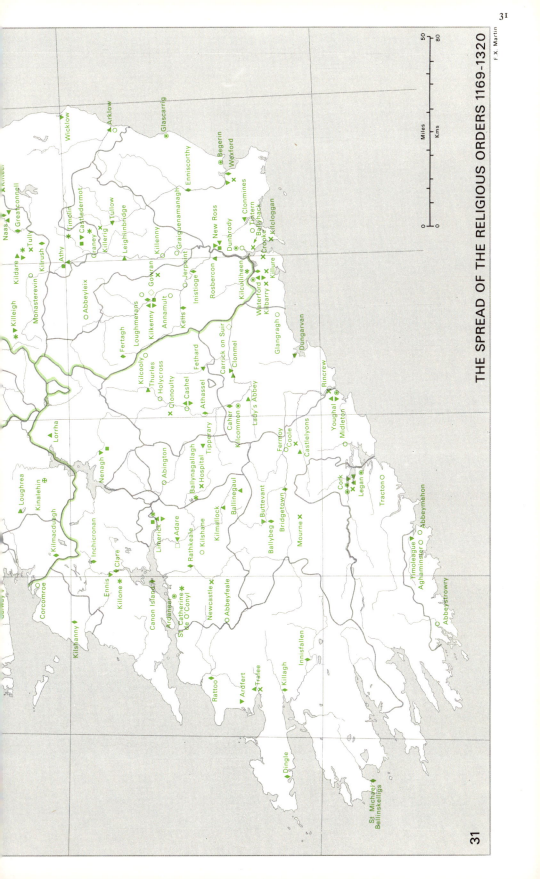

THE SPREAD OF THE RELIGIOUS ORDERS 1169-1320

F.X. Martin

Miles
Kms

Wicklow
Arklow
Glascarrig
Begerin
Wexford
Enniscorthy
Clonmines
New Ross
Tintern
Dunbrody
Ballyhack
Crooke
Kilcloggan
Hook
Rosbercon
Jerpoint
Inistioge
Kilcullen
Waterford
Killure
Kilbarry
Graiguenamanagh
Kilkenny
Gowran
Kells
Kilmurry
Castledermot
Tullow
Killerig
Leighlinbridge
Graney
Athy
Tristledermot
Timolin
Naas
Greatconnall
Kildare
Kilrush
Monasterevin
Killeigh
Abbeyleix
Fertagh
Loughmerans
Annamult
Kilkenny
Thurles
Holycross
Kilcooly
Clonoulty
Fethard
Cashel
Athassel
Carrick on Suir
Clonmel
Caher
Kilcommon
Lady's Abbey
Glangragh
Dungarvan
Rincrew
Youghal
Midleton
Fermoy
Coole
Castlelyons
Ferroy
Lorrha
Kinalehin
Loughrea
Nenagh
Abington
Ballynagallagh
Hospital
Tipperary
Ballinegaul
Kilmallock
Buttevant
Bridgetown
Mourne
Ballybeg
Cork
Legan
Tracton
Kilmacduagh
Inchicronan
Clare
Adare
Rathkeale
Kilshane
Limerick
Ennis
Killone
Corcomroe
Kilshanny
Canon Island
Iniscatty
St Catherine
de O'Conyl
Newcastle
Abbeyfeale
Rattoo
Ardfert
Tralee
Killagh
Innisfallen
Dingle
Timoleague
Aghaminster
Abbeymahon
Abbeystrowry
St Michael
Ballinskelligs

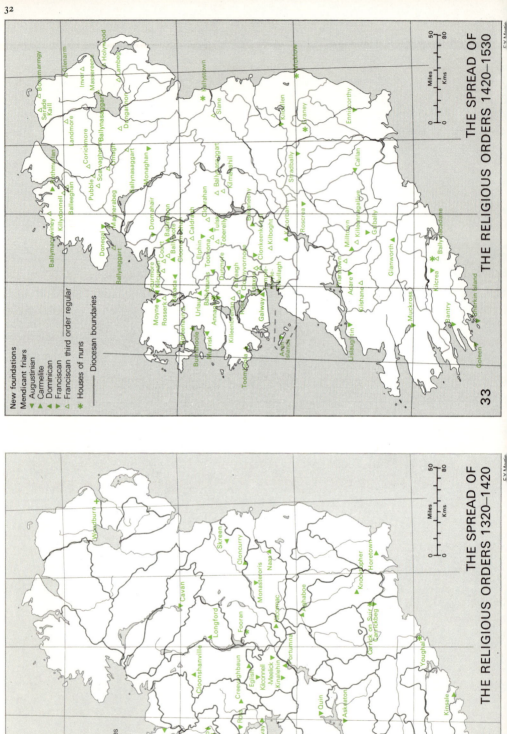
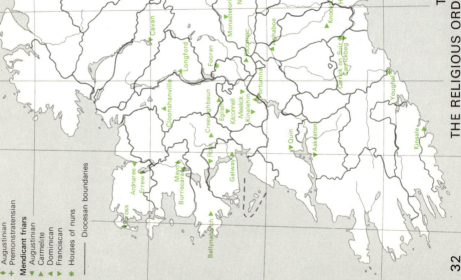

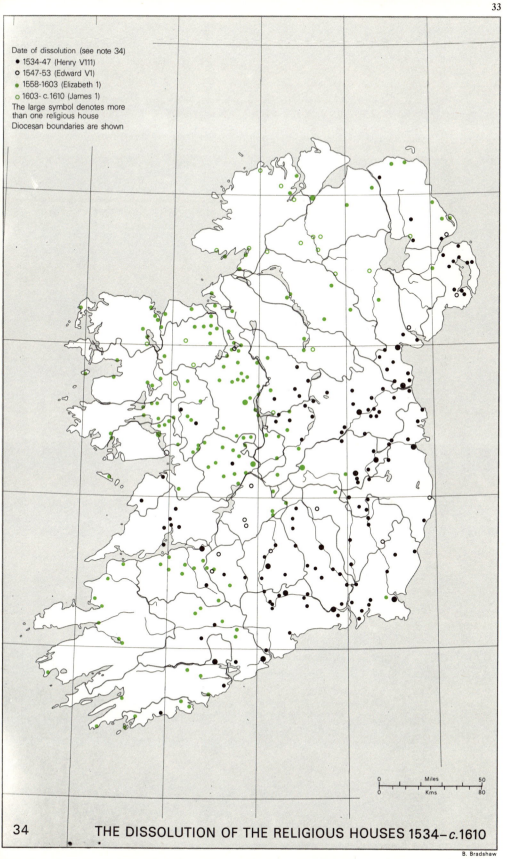

Date of dissolution (see note 34)
- ● 1534-47 (Henry V111)
- ○ 1547-53 (Edward V1)
- ● 1558-1603 (Elizabeth 1)
- ○ 1603- c.1610 (James 1)

The large symbol denotes more than one religious house
Diocesan boundaries are shown

Miles
0 ———— 50
0 ———— 80
Kms

THE DISSOLUTION OF THE RELIGIOUS HOUSES 1534–*c.*1610

B. Bradshaw

34

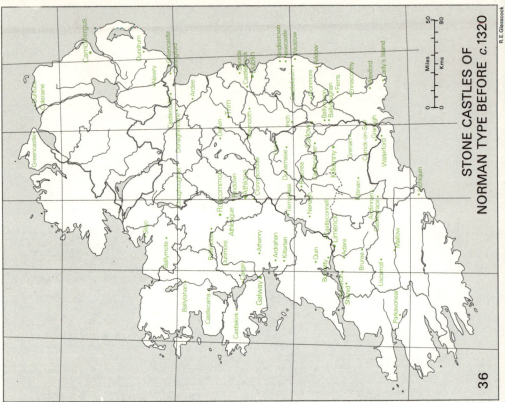

STONE CASTLES OF
NORMAN TYPE BEFORE *c.* 1320

R.E. Glasscock

36

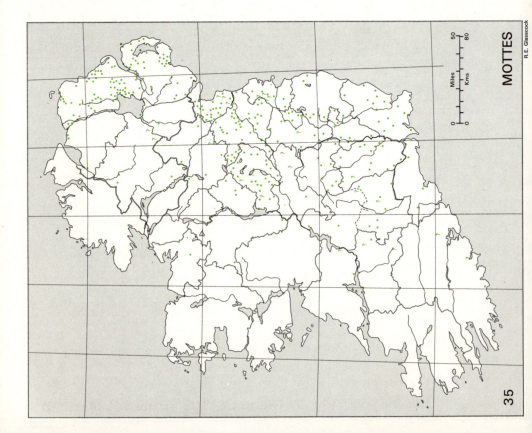

MOTTES

R.E. Glasscock

35

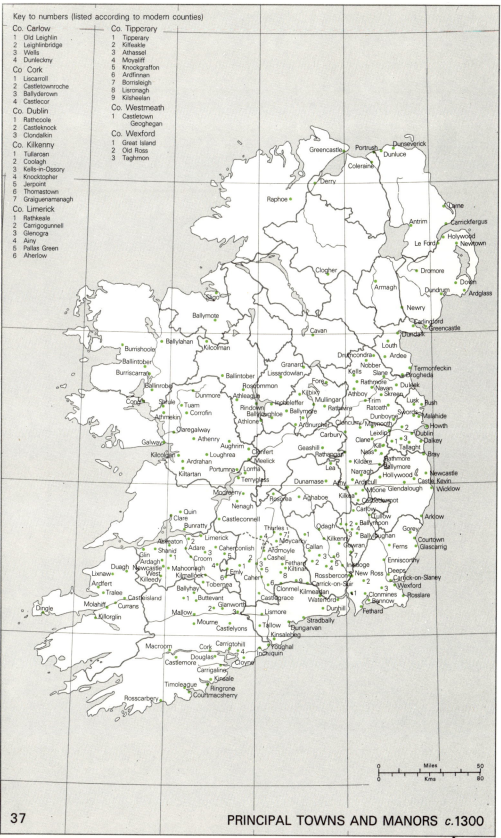

Key to numbers (listed according to modern counties)

Co. Carlow
1 Old Leighlin
2 Leighlinbridge
3 Wells
4 Dunleckny

Co Cork
1 Liscarroll
2 Castletownroche
3 Ballyderown
4 Castlecor

Co. Dublin
1 Rathcoole
2 Castleknock
3 Clondalkin

Co. Kilkenny
1 Tullaroan
2 Coolagh
3 Kells-in-Ossory
4 Knocktopher
5 Jerpoint
6 Thomastown
7 Graiguenamanagh

Co. Limerick
1 Rathkeale
2 Carrigogunnell
3 Glenogra
4 Ainy
5 Pallas Green
6 Aherlow

Co. Tipperary
1 Tipperary
2 Kilfeakle
3 Athassel
4 Moyaliff
5 Knockgraffon
6 Ardfinnan
7 Borrisleigh
8 Lisronagh
9 Kilsheelan

Co. Westmeath
1 Castletown
  Geoghegan

Co. Wexford
1 Great Island
2 Old Ross
3 Taghmon

37

PRINCIPAL TOWNS AND MANORS c.1300

R.E.Glasscock and K.W.Nicholls

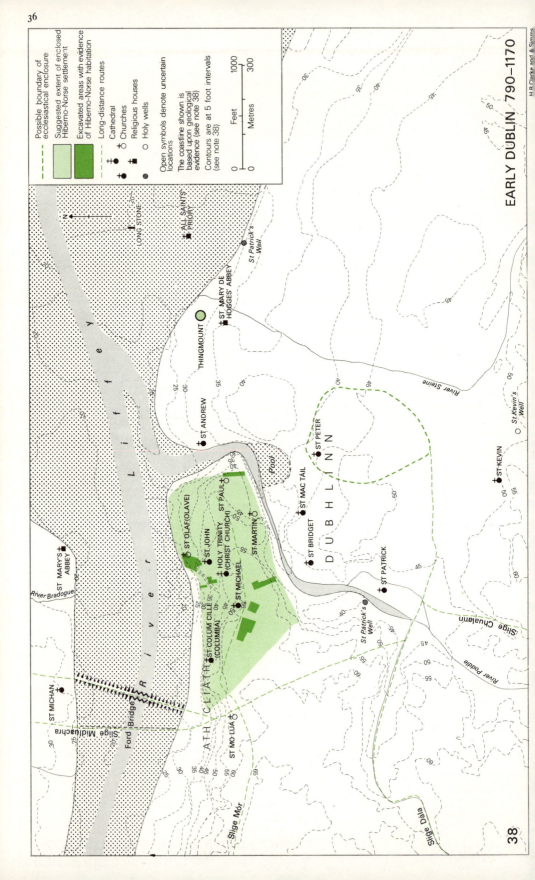

EARLY DUBLIN 790–1170

H R Clarke and A Simms

Legend:

- Possible boundary of ecclesiastical enclosure
- Suggested extent of enclosed Hiberno-Norse settlement
- Excavated areas with evidence of Hiberno-Norse habitation
- Long-distance routes

	Cathedral
	Churches
	Religious houses
	Holy wells

Open symbols denote uncertain locations

The coastline shown is based upon geological evidence (see note 38)

Contours are at 5 foot intervals (see note 38)

Feet 1000
Metres 300

0 Feet
0 Metres

N

Map labels: LONG STONE, ALL SAINTS' PRIORY, St Patrick's Well, ST MARY DE HOGGES' ABBEY, THINGMOUNT, ST ANDREW, Pool, River Steine, St Kevin's Well, ST PETER, DUBHLINN, ST MAC TAIL, ST KEVIN, ST OLAF (OLAVE), ST JOHN, ST PAUL, HOLY TRINITY (CHRIST CHURCH), ST MARTIN, ST MICHAEL, ST BRIDGET, ST PATRICK, ST COLUM CILLE (COLUMBA), St Patrick's Well, Slige Chualann, River Poddle, ATH CLIATH, ST MO LUA, ST MICHAN, River Bradogue, ST MARY'S ABBEY, Ford, Bridge, Slige Midluachra, River Liffey, Slige Mór, Slige Dála

38

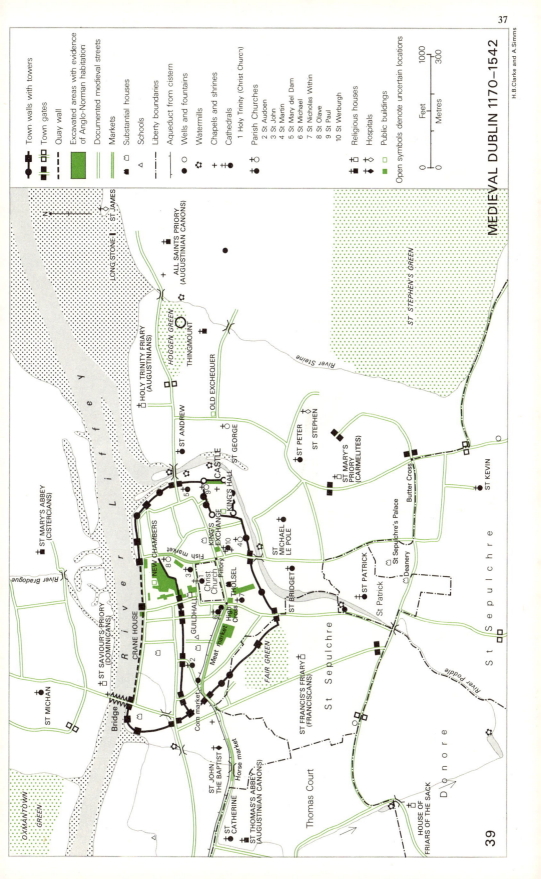

MEDIEVAL DUBLIN 1170–1542

H.B.Clarke and A.Simms

Town walls with towers
Town gates
Quay wall
Excavated areas with evidence of Anglo-Norman habitation
Documented medieval streets
Markets
Substantial houses
Schools
Liberty boundaries
Aqueduct from cistern
Wells and fountains
Watermills
Chapels and shrines
Cathedrals
1 Holy Trinity (Christ Church)
Parish Churches
2 St Audoen
3 St John
4 St Martin
5 St Mary del Dam
6 St Michael
7 St Nicholas Within
8 St Olave
9 St Paul
10 St Werburgh
Religious houses
Hospitals
Public buildings
Open symbols denote uncertain locations

Feet 1000
Metres 300

OXMANTOWN GREEN

N

LONG STONE ◇ ST JAMES

ALL SAINTS PRIORY (AUGUSTINIAN CANONS)

HOLY TRINITY FRIARY (AUGUSTINIANS)
HOGGEN GREEN
THINGMOUNT

OLD EXCHEQUER

ST ANDREW

ST GEORGE

ST PETER
ST STEPHEN

ST MARY'S PRIORY (CARMELITES)

ST STEPHEN'S GREEN

River Steine

St Sepulchre

St Sepulchre

River Poddle

Donore

St Sepulchre's Palace
Deanery
St Sepulchre
Butter Cross
ST KEVIN

ST PATRICK
St Patrick
ST PATRICK

ST BRIDGET

ST MICHAEL LE POLE

CASTLE
KING'S HALL
KING'S EXCHANGE
NEW CHAMBERS
Fish market
Christ Church
THOLSEL
High Cross
GUILDHALL
Meat market
Corn market
Horse market
CRANE HOUSE
Pillory
FAIR GREEN

Bridge

River Liffey

St Michan's ground

ST MARY'S ABBEY (CISTERCIANS)

River Bradogue

ST SAVIOUR'S PRIORY (DOMINICANS)

ST MICHAN

ST FRANCIS'S FRIARY (FRANCISCANS)

Thomas Court

ST JOHN THE BAPTIST
ST CATHERINE
ST THOMAS'S ABBEY (AUGUSTINIAN CANONS)

HOUSE OF FRIARS OF THE SACK

39

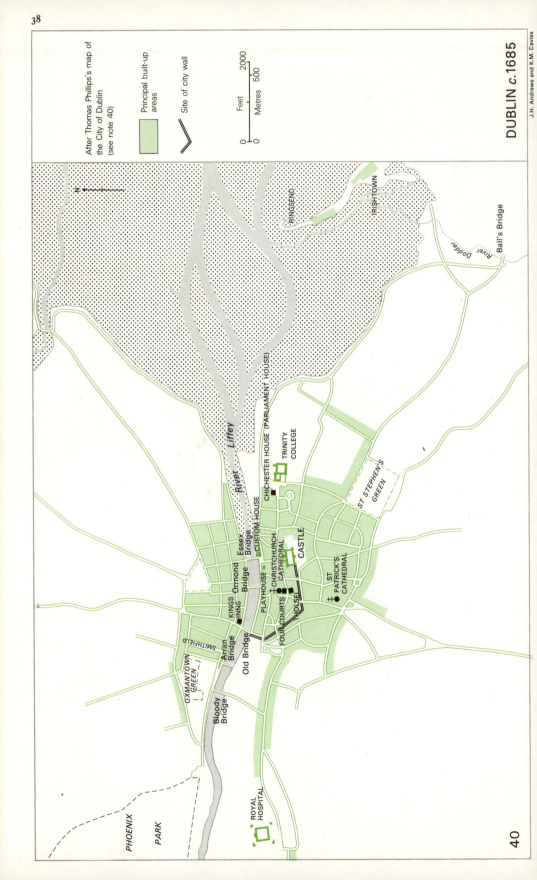

DUBLIN c.1685

After Thomas Phillips's map of
the City of Dublin
(see note 40)

Principal built-up
areas

Site of city wall

Feet   2000
         500
Metres
0   0

J.H. Andrews and K.M. Davies

N

PHOENIX

PARK

Bloody
Bridge

ROYAL
HOSPITAL

SMITHFIELD

OXMANTOWN
GREEN

Arran
Bridge

Old Bridge

KINGS
INNS

Ormond
Bridge

Essex
Bridge

River Liffey

CUSTOM HOUSE

PLAYHOUSE

FOUR COURTS

THOLSEL

CHRISTCHURCH
CATHEDRAL

CASTLE

ST
PATRICK'S
CATHEDRAL

CHICHESTER HOUSE (PARLIAMENT HOUSE)

TRINITY
COLLEGE

ST STEPHEN'S
GREEN

RINGSEND

IRISHTOWN

River Dodder

Ball's Bridge

40

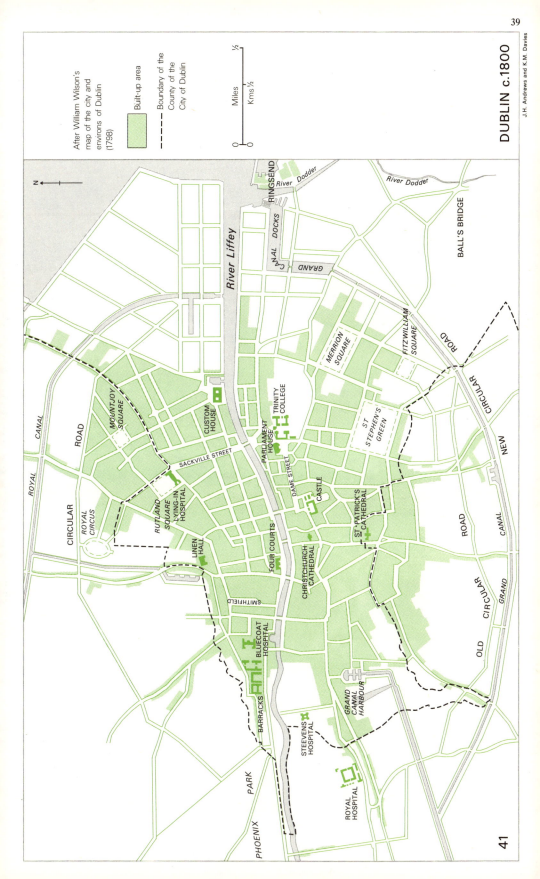

After William Wilson's map of the city and environs of Dublin (1798)

Built-up area

Boundary of the County of the City of Dublin

Miles ½

Kms ½

DUBLIN c.1800

J.H. Andrews and K.M. Davies

River Liffey

River Dodder

River Dodder

RINGSEND

CANAL DOCKS

GRAND CANAL

BALL'S BRIDGE

PHOENIX PARK

ROYAL CANAL

CIRCULAR ROAD

ROYAL CIRCUS

MOUNTJOY SQUARE

RUTLAND SQUARE

LYING-IN HOSPITAL

SACKVILLE STREET

CUSTOM HOUSE

LINEN HALL

SMITHFIELD

FOUR COURTS

BLUECOAT HOSPITAL

BARRACKS

STEVENS HOSPITAL

GRAND CANAL HARBOUR

ROYAL HOSPITAL

CHRISTCHURCH CATHEDRAL

CASTLE

DAME STREET

PARLIAMENT HOUSE

TRINITY COLLEGE

MERRION SQUARE

FITZWILLIAM SQUARE

ST STEPHEN'S GREEN

ST PATRICK'S CATHEDRAL

NEW CIRCULAR ROAD

OLD CIRCULAR ROAD

GRAND CANAL

N

41

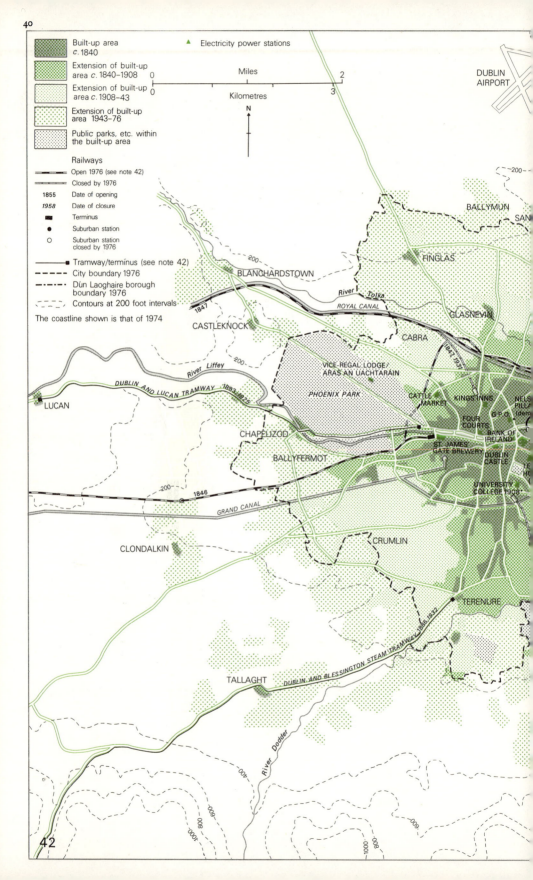

Built-up area
c. 1840

Extension of built-up
area c. 1840–1908

Extension of built-up
area c. 1908–43

Extension of built-up
area 1943–76

Public parks, etc. within
the built-up area

▲ Electricity power stations

Miles
0   2
0   3
Kilometres

N

Railways

Open 1976 (see note 42)

Closed by 1976

1855   Date of opening

1958   Date of closure

Terminus

●   Suburban station

○   Suburban station
closed by 1976

Tramway/terminus (see note 42)

City boundary 1976

Dún Laoghaire borough
boundary 1976

Contours at 200 foot intervals

The coastline shown is that of 1974

DUBLIN
AIRPORT

BALLYMUN

SAN

FINGLAS

BLANCHARDSTOWN

River   Tolka

ROYAL CANAL

GLASNEVIN

CASTLEKNOCK

CABRA

1847

1847   1931

River   Liffey

DUBLIN AND LUCAN TRAMWAY   1883   1925

200

VICE-REGAL LODGE/
ÁRAS AN UACHTARÁIN

PHOENIX PARK

CATTLE
MARKET

KINGS INNS

NELS
PILLA
(dem

LUCAN

G.P.O.

FOUR
COURTS

BANK OF
IRELAND

CHAPELIZOD

ST. JAMES'
GATE BREWERY

DUBLIN
CASTLE

BALLYFERMOT

LE
HO

200   1846

UNIVERSITY
COLLEGE 1908

GRAND CANAL

CLONDALKIN

CRUMLIN

TERENURE

DUBLIN AND BLESSINGTON STEAM TRAMWAY 1886 1932

TALLAGHT

River   Dodder

400

600

800

1000

800

600

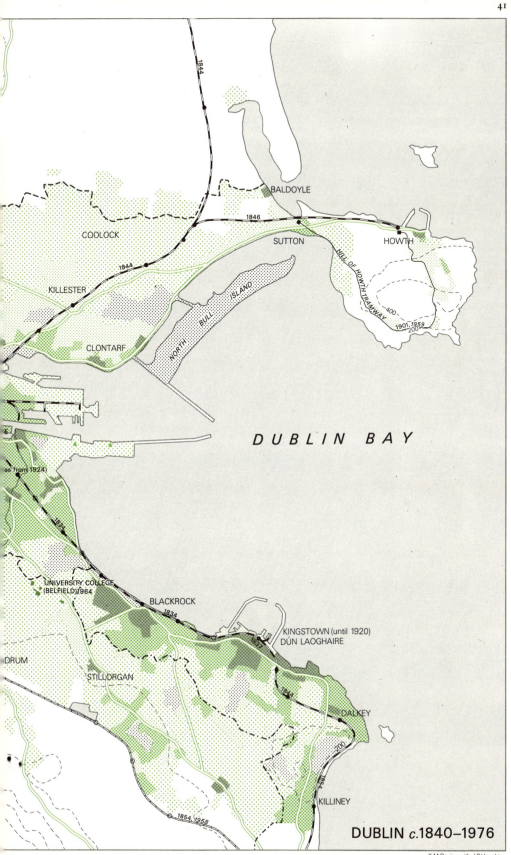

1844

BALDOYLE

1846

COOLOCK

SUTTON

HOWTH

1844

KILLESTER

HILL OF HOWTH TRAMWAY

400

CLONTARF

NORTH BULL ISLAND

1901, 1959

200

D U B L I N   B A Y

es from 1924

1834

UNIVERSITY COLLEGE
(BELFIELD) 1964

BLACKROCK

1834

KINGSTOWN (until 1920)
DÚN LAOGHAIRE

DRUM

1837

STILLORGAN

1854

DALKEY

200

1854

KILLINEY

1854, 1958

DUBLIN *c.* **1840–1976**

K.M.Davies with J.P.Haughton

42

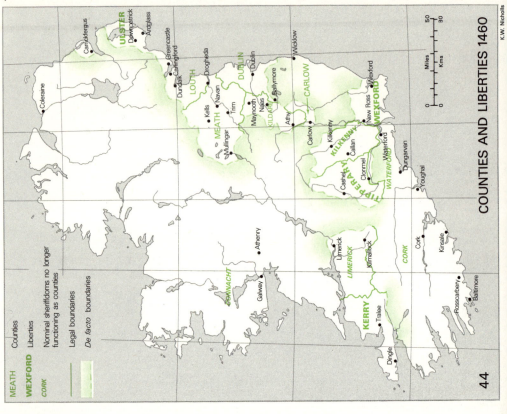

COUNTIES AND LIBERTIES 1460

44

K.W. Nicholls

MEATH   Counties
WEXFORD Liberties
CORK   Nominal sheriffdoms no longer
         functioning as counties

───── Legal boundaries
       De facto boundaries

Ulster labels: Carrickfergus, Downpatrick, Ardglass, ULSTER, Greencastle, Carlingford, Dundalk, Drogheda, Coleraine

Leinster/Meath labels: Kells, Navan, Trim, Mullingar, MEATH, Maynooth, Naas, Dublin, DUBLIN, Ballymore, KILDARE, Athy, Carlow, CARLOW, Wicklow, Kilkenny, Callan, KILKENNY, New Ross, Wexford, WEXFORD

Munster labels: Cashel, Clonmel, TIPPERARY, Waterford, WATERFORD, Dungarvan, Youghal, Cork, CORK, Kinsale, Rosscarbery, Baltimore, Limerick, LIMERICK, Kilmallock, KERRY, Tralee, Dingle

Connacht labels: Athenry, Galway, CONNACHT

Miles 0 50
Kms 0 80

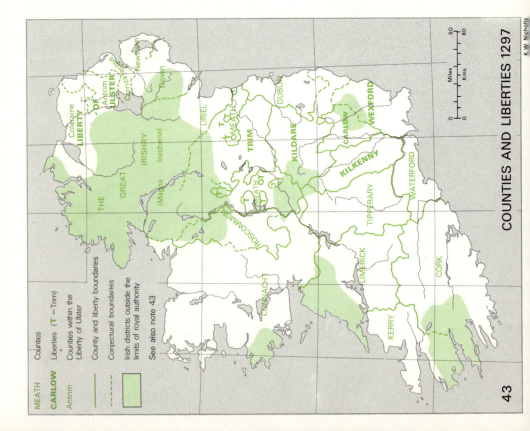

COUNTIES AND LIBERTIES 1297

43

K. W. Nicholls

MEATH   Counties
CARLOW   Liberties (T = Trim)
Antrim   Counties within the
         Liberty of Ulster

───── County and liberty boundaries
----   Conjectural boundaries
       Irish districts outside the
       limits of royal authority

See also note 43

Labels: Coleraine, LIBERTY, OF, ULSTER, Antrim, Carrickfergus, Newtown, Down, THE, GREAT, IRISHRY, (Macha Irecheria), URIEL, MEATH, TRIM, T, DUBLIN, ROSCOMMON, (Machna), MEATH OUT, KILDARE, CARLOW, WEXFORD, KILKENNY, CONNACHT, TIPPERARY, WATERFORD, LIMERICK, KERRY, CORK

Miles 0 50
Kms 0 80

1556   Date of formation of county
(for criteria of dating see note 45)

*FERNS
1578*   Impermanent counties

MEATH   Medieval counties

from Antrim
1613

DONEGAL
1585

from Donegal
1613

COLERAINE
1603

LONDONDERRY
1613

part of Tyrone
until 1613

ANTRIM
1570

Carrickfergus

TYRONE
1591

FERMANAGH
1588

ARMAGH
1571-?

DOWN
1570

SLIGO
1570

LEITRIM
1583

MONAGHAN
1587

CAVAN
1579-83

part of Armagh
until c.1630

LOUTH

MAYO
1570

ROSCOMMON
1570

LONGFORD
1570

Drogheda

MEATH

WESTMEATH
1542
formerly part
of Meath

GALWAY
1570

Galway

part of
Westmeath
until 1570

part of Galway
until 1660

KING'S COUNTY
1556

1570

KILDARE

DUBLIN

Dublin

part of Dublin
until 1606

QUEEN'S CO.
1556

WICKLOW
1577
1606

CLARE
1570

1606

nominally part
of Tipperary
until 1606

nominally part
of Kilkenny
until 1600-2

CARLOW 1606

part of Carlow
until 1606

Limerick

LIMERICK

TIPPERARY
AND
CROSS OF
TIPPERARY

Kilkenny

KILKENNY

from
Carlow
c.1550

FERNS
1578
reverted to
Wexford
c.1590

WEXFORD

KERRY

DESMOND
1571
reverted to Kerry
1606

CORK

Cork

WATERFORD

Miles
0   50
0   Kms   80

COUNTIES 1542-1613

K.W. Nicholls

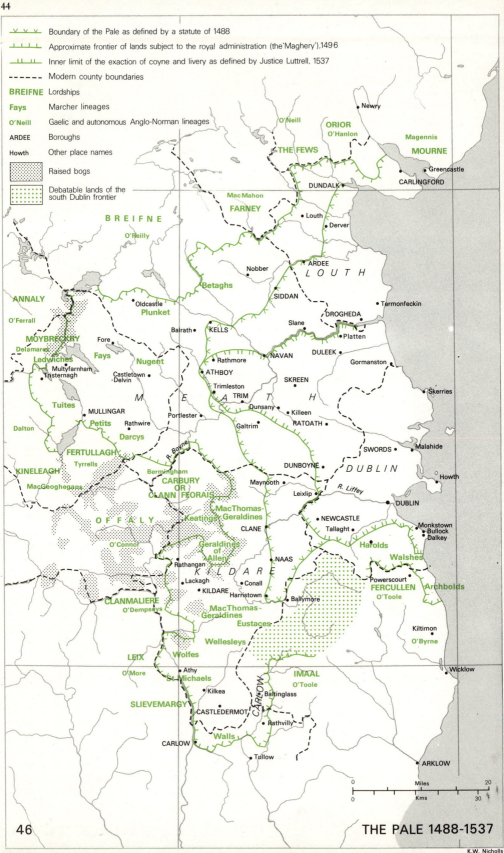

	Boundary of the Pale as defined by a statute of 1488
	Approximate frontier of lands subject to the royal administration (the 'Maghery'), 1496
	Inner limit of the exaction of coyne and livery as defined by Justice Luttrell, 1537
	Modern county boundaries
BREIFNE	Lordships
Fays	Marcher lineages
O'Neill	Gaelic and autonomous Anglo-Norman lineages
ARDEE	Boroughs
Howth	Other place names
	Raised bogs
	Debatable lands of the south Dublin frontier

Newry

O'Neill
ORIOR
O'Hanlon
Magennis
MOURNE
THE FEWS
Greencastle
DUNDALK
CARLINGFORD
MacMahon
FARNEY
Louth
Derver
BREIFNE
O'Reilly
Nobber
ARDEE
L O U T H
ANNALY
Betaghs
SIDDAN
Termonfeckin
O'Ferrall
Oldcastle
Plunket
DROGHEDA
MOYBREGGRY
Fore
Balrath
KELLS
Slane
Platten
Delamares
Ledwiches
Fays
Nugent
Rathmore
NAVAN
DULEEK
Multyfarnham
Castletown
-Delvin
ATHBOY
SKREEN
Gormanston
Tristernagh
Trimleston
M   E   A   T   H
Skerries
Tuites
MULLINGAR
Portlester
TRIM
Dunsany
Killeen
Petits
Rathwire
Galtrim
RATOATH
Dalton
Darcys
SWORDS
Malahide
R. Boyne
DUNBOYNE
D U B L I N
FERTULLAGH
Tyrrells
Bermingham
Maynooth
Howth
KINELEAGH
CARBURY
OR
CLANN FEORAIS
Leixlip
R. Liffey
MacGeoghegans
DUBLIN
O F F A L Y
Keatings
MacThomas-
Geraldines
NEWCASTLE
Monkstown
Bullock
Dalkey
O'Connor
Geraldines
of
Allen
CLANE
Tallaght
Harolds
Rathangan
NAAS
Walshes
Lackagh
Conall
FERCULLEN
Archbolds
CLANMALIERE
KILDARE
Harristown
K I L D A R E
Ballymore
O'Toole
Powerscourt
O'Dempseys
MacThomas-
Geraldines
Eustaces
Kiltimon
Wellesleys
O'Byrne
LEIX
Wolfes
O'More
Athy
IMAAL
Wicklow
St Michaels
O'Toole
Kilkea
Baltinglass
SLIEVEMARGY
CASTLEDERMOT
C A R L O W
Rathvilly
CARLOW
Walls
Tullow
ARKLOW

0		Miles		20
0		Kms		30

THE PALE 1488-1537

K.W. Nicholls

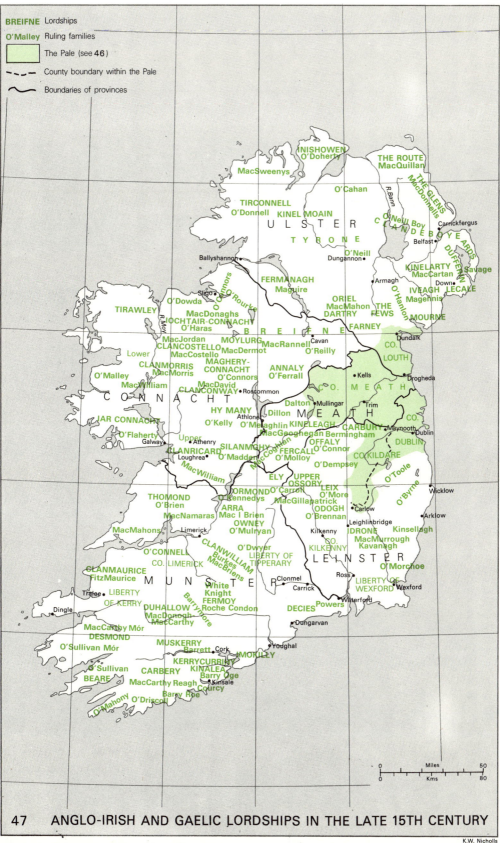

47 ANGLO-IRISH AND GAELIC LORDSHIPS IN THE LATE 15TH CENTURY

K.W. Nicholls

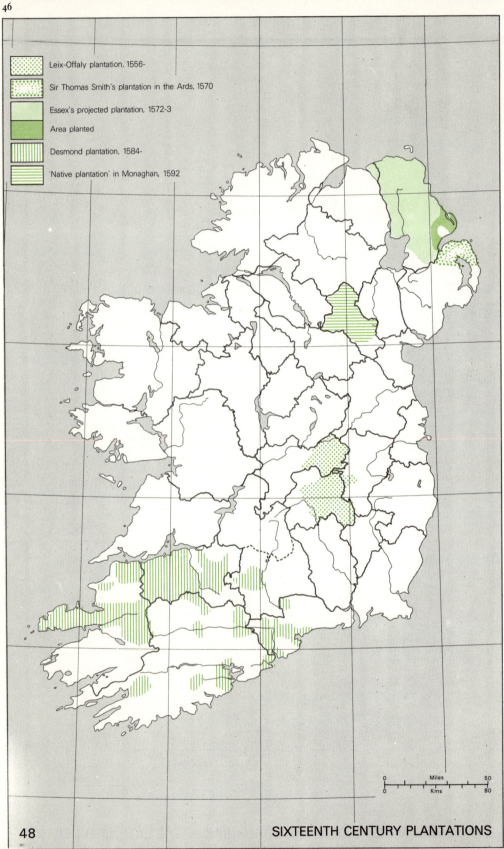

Leix-Offaly plantation, 1556-

Sir Thomas Smith's plantation in the Ards, 1570

Essex's projected plantation, 1572-3

Area planted

Desmond plantation, 1584-

'Native plantation' in Monaghan, 1592

Miles
0   50
0   80
Kms

48   **SIXTEENTH CENTURY PLANTATIONS**

K.W. Nicholls

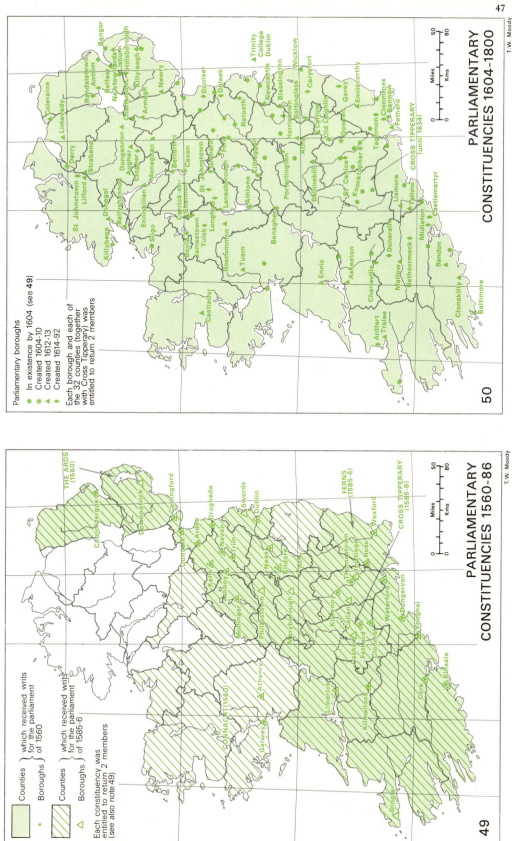

T.W. Moody

PARLIAMENTARY
CONSTITUENCIES 1604–1800

Parliamentary boroughs

● In existence by 1604 (see **49**)
◉ Created 1604-10
▲ Created 1612-13
◆ Created 1614-92

Each borough and each of
the 32 counties (together
with Cross Tipperary) was
entitled to return 2 members

Miles
Kms
50
80
0

Bangor
Randalstown
Antrim
Coleraine
Belfast
Newtownards
Lisburn
Hillsborough
Killyleagh
Newry
Dunleer
Duleek
Ratoath
▲Trinity College Dublin
Newcastle
Blessington
Wicklow
Baltinglass
▲Limavady
▲Derry
Strabane
Dungannon
Augher
Clogher
Monaghan
Cavan
Belturbet
Johnstown
Fore
Athlone
Kilbeggan
Portarlington
Harristown
Athy
Old Leighlin
Carlow
Gowran
Gorey
Enniscorthy
Fethard
CROSS TIPPERARY
(until 1634)
St Johnstown
Lifford
Ballyshannon
Donegal
Enniskillen
Carrick-on-Shannon
St Johnstown
Lanesborough
Longford
Banagher
Birr
Ballinakill
St Canice
Knocktopher
Taghmon
Clonmines
Bannow
Lismore
Tallow
Sligo
Boyle
Jamestown
Tulsk
Roscommon
Tuam
Ennis
Askeaton
Charleville
Doneraile
Midleton
Castlemartyr
Castlebar
Mallow
Rathcormack
Bandon
Clonakilty
Ardfert
Tralee
Baltimore

50

T.W. Moody

PARLIAMENTARY
CONSTITUENCIES 1560–86

Counties } which received writs
Boroughs • } for the parliament of 1560

Counties } which received writs
Boroughs △ } for the parliament of 1585-6

Each constituency was
entitled to return 2 members
(see also note 49)

THE ARDS
(1560)

Carrickfergus
Downpatrick
Carlingford
Drogheda
Ardee
Navan
Trim
Swords
▲Dublin
Kells
Athboy
Mullingar
Philipstown
Maryborough
Naas
Kildare
Thomastown
Fethard
▲Ross
Wexford
CROSS TIPPERARY
(1585-6)
FERNS
(1585-6)
Limerick
Athenry
CONNACHT (1560)
Galway
Kilmallock
Cashel
Callan
Kilkenny
Clonmel
Waterford
Dungarvan
Youghal
Cork
Kinsale
Dingle

49

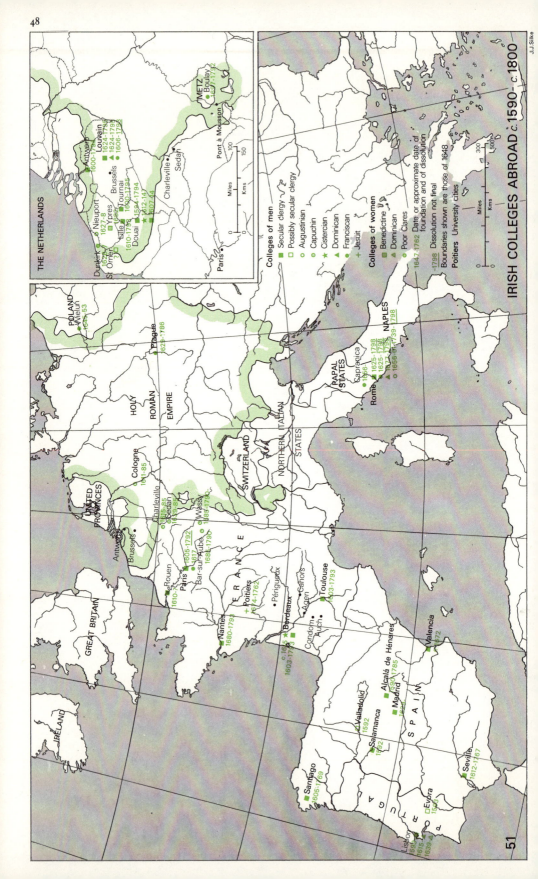

IRISH COLLEGES ABROAD c.1590– c.1800

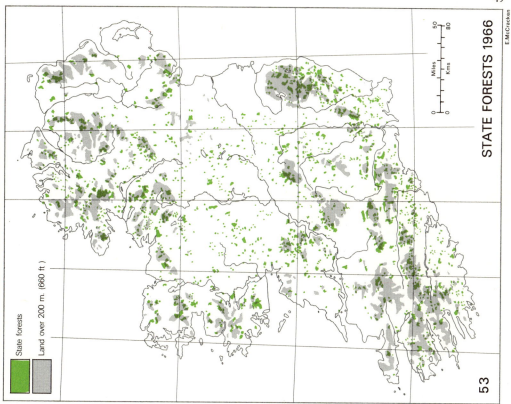

STATE FORESTS 1966

E.McCracken

State forests

Land over 200 m. (660 ft)

Miles

Kms

0   50

0   80

53

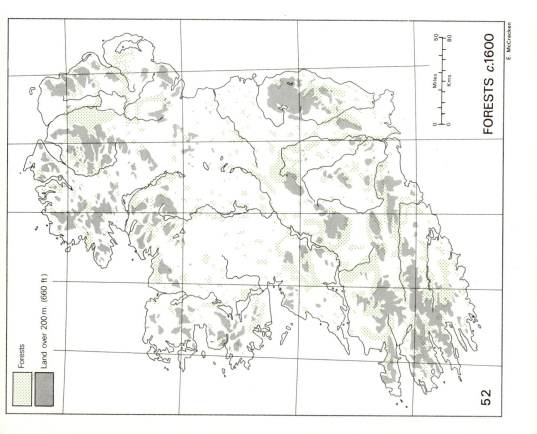

FORESTS c.1600

E. McCracken

Forests

Land over 200 m. (660 ft)

Miles

Kms

0   50

0   80

52

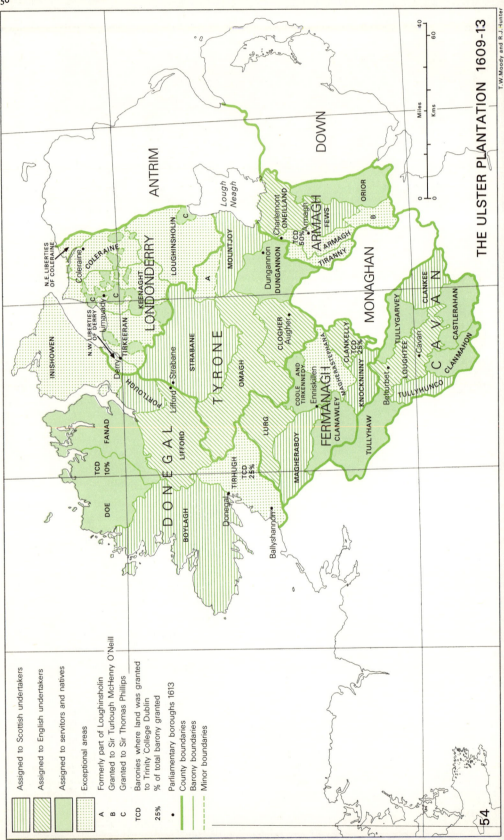

T.W.Moody and R.J.Hunter

THE ULSTER PLANTATION 1609-13

Miles

Kms

40

60

0

ANTRIM

DOWN

Lough Neagh

MONAGHAN

LONDONDERRY

COLERAINE
• Coleraine
N.E. LIBERTIES
OF COLERAINE
C
• Coleraine
C
• Limavady C
KEENAGHT
N.W. LIBERTIES
OF DERRY C
• Derry
TIRKEERAN
LOUGHINSHOLIN
A
MOUNTJOY
ONEILLAND
Charlemont
• Dungannon
DUNGANNON
Armagh
• Armagh
TCD
50%
ARMAGH
FEWS
TIRANNY
ORIOR
B

ARMAGH

INISHOWEN

PORTLOUGH

FANAD

DOE

DONEGAL

BOYLAGH

TCD
10%

TIRHUGH
• Donegal

Ballyshannon

TCD
25%

• Strabane
Lifford •
LIFFORD
STRABANE

TYRONE

OMAGH

LURG

MAGHERABOY

CLOGHER
Augher •
COOLE
AND
TIRKENNEDY
• Enniskillen
CLANAWLEY
FERMANAGH
KNOCKNINNY
TCD
25%
TULLYHAW
MAGHERASTEPHANA
CLANKELLY

TULLYGARVEY
• Cavan
LOUGHTEE
• Belturbet
TULLYHUNCO
CAVAN
CLANKEE
CASTLERAHAN
CLANMAHON

THE ULSTER PLANTATION 1609-13

Assigned to Scottish undertakers
Assigned to English undertakers
Assigned to servitors and natives
Exceptional areas
A Formerly part of Loughinsholin
B Granted to Sir Turlough McHenry O'Neill
C Granted to Sir Thomas Phillips
TCD Baronies where land was granted
to Trinity College Dublin
25% % of total barony granted
• Parliamentary boroughs 1613
County boundaries
Barony boundaries
Minor boundaries

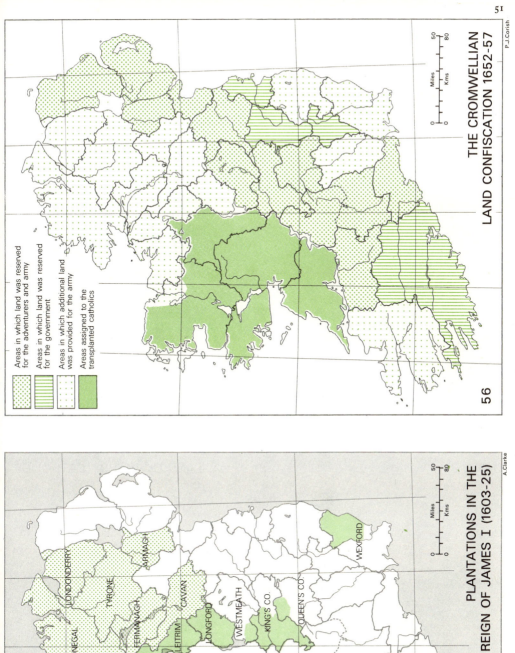

THE CROMWELLIAN
LAND CONFISCATION 1652-57

P.J.Corish

Areas in which land was reserved
for the adventurers and army

Areas in which land was reserved
for the government

Areas in which additional land
was provided for the army

Areas assigned to the
transplanted catholics

56

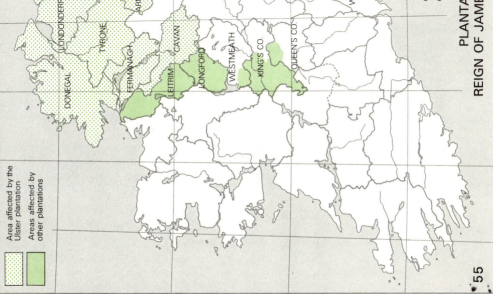

PLANTATIONS IN THE
REIGN OF JAMES I (1603-25)

A.Clarke

Area affected by the
Ulster plantation

Areas affected by
other plantations

DONEGAL

LONDONDERRY

TYRONE

ARMAGH

FERMANAGH

LEITRIM

CAVAN

LONGFORD

WESTMEATH

KING'S CO.

QUEEN'S CO.

WEXFORD

55

59%

1641

22%

1688

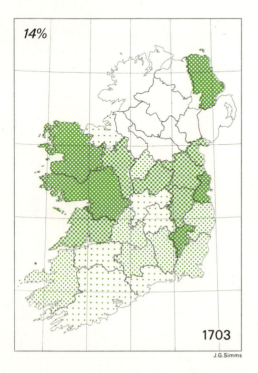

14%

1703

J.G.Simms

LAND OWNED BY CATHOLICS
1641, 1688, 1703
by counties

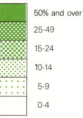

50% and over

25-49

15-24

10-14

5-9

0-4

57

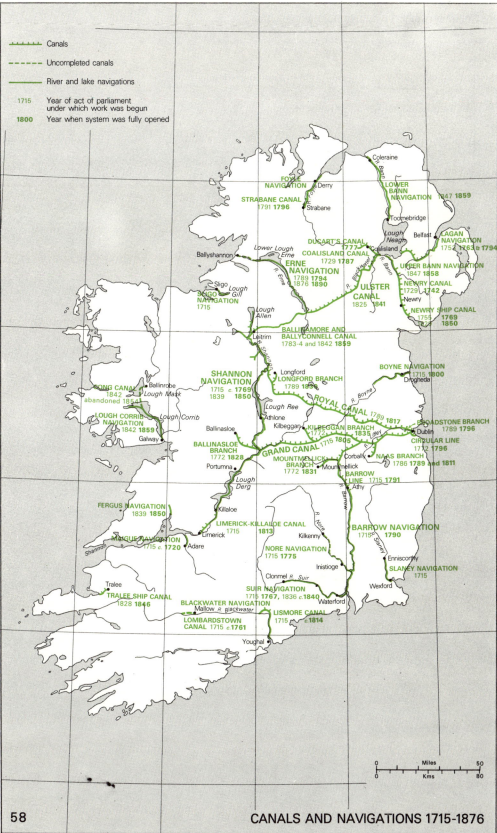

Canals

- - - - Uncompleted canals

River and lake navigations

1715   Year of act of parliament
      under which work was begun

1800   Year when system was fully opened

Coleraine

FOYLE
NAVIGATION
Derry

LOWER
BANN
NAVIGATION **1847 1859**

STRABANE CANAL
1791 1796 Strabane

Toomebridge

*Lough
Neagh* Belfast

Ballyshannon

*Lower Lough
Erne*

DUCART'S CANAL
1772
COALISLAND CANAL
1729 1787 Coalisland

LAGAN
NAVIGATION
1752 1763 & 1794

ERNE
NAVIGATION
1789 1794
1876 1890

UPPER BANN NAVIGATION
1847 1858

NEWRY CANAL
1729 1742 Newry

Sligo *Lough
Gill*

SLIGO
NAVIGATION
1715

*Lough
Allen*

ULSTER
CANAL
1825 1841

NEWRY SHIP CANAL
1755 1769
1850

BALLINAMORE AND
BALLYCONNELL CANAL
1783-4 and 1842 1859

Leitrim

CONG CANAL
1842
abandoned 1854
Ballinrobe
Lough Mask

LOUGH CORRIB
NAVIGATION
1842 1859
Galway

Lough Corrib

SHANNON
NAVIGATION
1715 c. 1769
1839 1850

Ballinasloe

BALLINASLOE
BRANCH
1772 1828

Portumna

Longford
LONGFORD BRANCH
1789 1830

Lough Ree
Athlone
Kilbeggan

KILBEGGAN BRANCH
1772 **1835**

BOYNE NAVIGATION
1715 1800
Drogheda

ROYAL CANAL
1789 1817

BROADSTONE BRANCH
1789 1796
Dublin

GRAND CANAL
1715 **1805**

MOUNTMELLICK
BRANCH
1772 1831
Mountmellick

Corbally

CIRCULAR LINE
1772 1796

NAAS BRANCH
1786 1789 and 1811

*Lough
Derg*

BARROW
LINE **1715 1791**
Athy

FERGUS NAVIGATION
1839 1850
Killaloe

LIMERICK-KILLALOE CANAL
1715 **1813**
Limerick

Kilkenny

BARROW NAVIGATION
1715 1790

MAIGUE NAVIGATION
1715 c. 1720 Adare

Shannon

NORE NAVIGATION
1715 1775

Inistioge

Enniscorthy

SLANEY NAVIGATION
1715

Tralee

TRALEE SHIP CANAL
1828 1846

BLACKWATER NAVIGATION
Mallow *R. Blackwater*

LOMBARDSTOWN
CANAL 1715 **c.1761**

Clonmel *R. Suir*

SUIR NAVIGATION
1715 1767, 1836 **c.1840**
Waterford

LISMORE CANAL
1715 **c.1814**

Wexford

Youghal

Miles
0   50
0   80
Kms

CANALS AND NAVIGATIONS 1715-1876

D. R. Delaney and W. A. McCutcheon

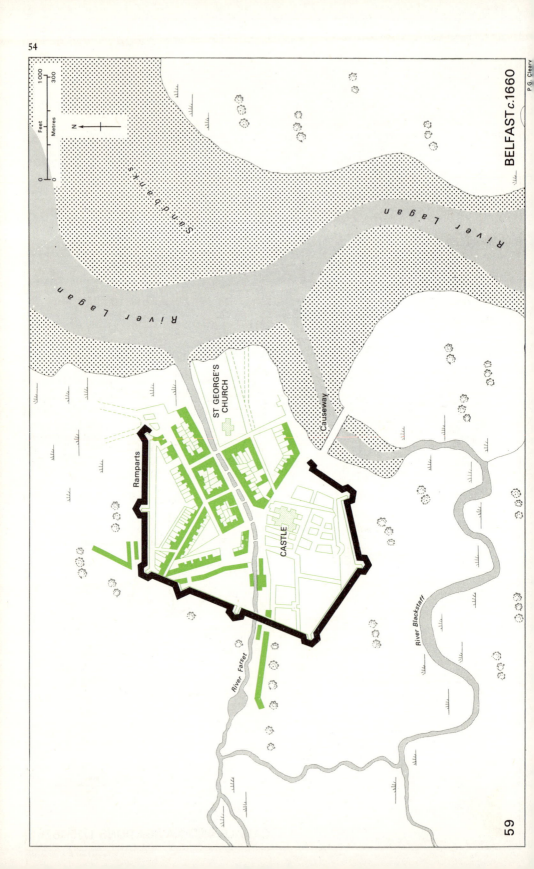

BELFAST *c.*1660

P.G. Cleary

Feet
1 000
300
Metres
0
0

N

Sand-banks

River Lagan

River Lagan

ST GEORGE'S
CHURCH

Ramparts

CASTLE

Causeway

River Farset

River Blackstaff

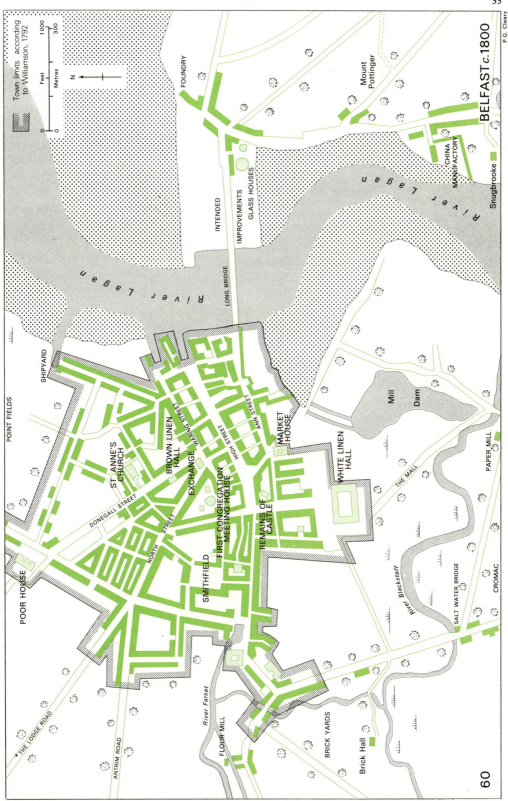

55

BELFAST c.1800

P.G. Cleary

Town limits according to Williamson, 1792

N

Feet
Metres

FOUNDRY

Mount Pottinger

CHINA MANUFACTORY

Snugbrooke

INTENDED

IMPROVEMENTS

GLASS HOUSES

River Lagan

LONG BRIDGE

River Lagan

SHIPYARD

POINT FIELDS

Mill Dam

ST ANNE'S CHURCH

BROWN LINEN HALL

WARING STREET

EXCHANGE

DONEGALL STREET

NORTH STREET

HIGH STREET

ANN STREET

MARKET HOUSE

FIRST CONGREGATION MEETING HOUSE

REMAINS OF CASTLE

WHITE LINEN HALL

THE MALL

PAPER MILL

POOR HOUSE

SMITHFIELD

River Blackstaff

SALT WATER BRIDGE

CROMAC

THE LODGE ROAD

ANTRIM ROAD

River Farset

FLOUR MILL

BRICK YARDS

Brick Hall

60

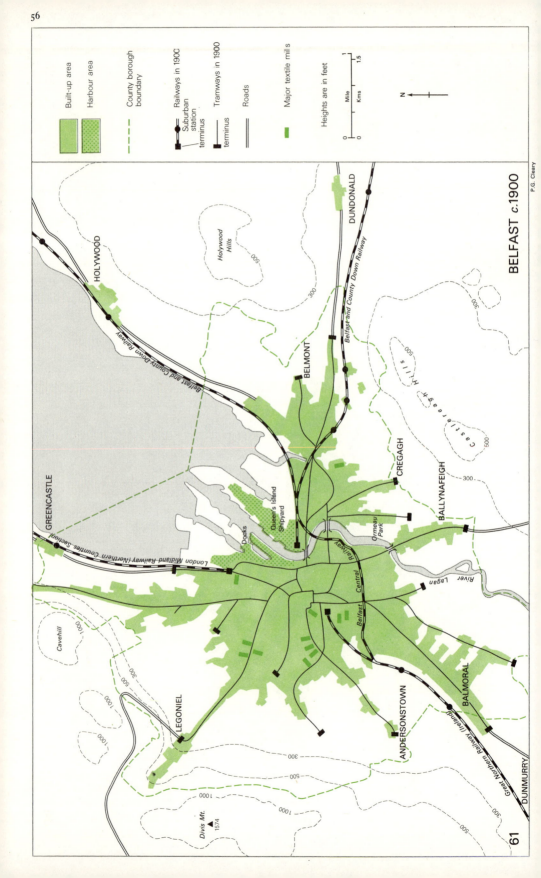

Built-up area

Harbour area

County borough boundary

Railways in 1900

Suburban station terminus

Tramways in 1900

terminus

Roads

Major textile mills

Heights are in feet

Mile

1.5

Kms

0

N

P.G. Cleary

BELFAST *c*.1900

DUNDONALD

Belfast and County Down Railway

HOLYWOOD

Holywood Hills

300

500

BELMONT

Castlereagh Hills

500

500

CREGAGH

300

BALLYNAFEIGH

Ormeau Park

GREENCASTLE

London Midland Railway (Northern Counties Section)

Belfast and County Down Railway

Docks

Queen's Island Shipyard

Belfast Central Railway

River Lagan

Cavehill

1000

300

500

1000

500

1000

LEGONIEL

1000

ANDERSONSTOWN

300

BALMORAL

Great Northern Railway (Ireland)

DUNMURRY

300

500

300

500

Divis Mt.
1574

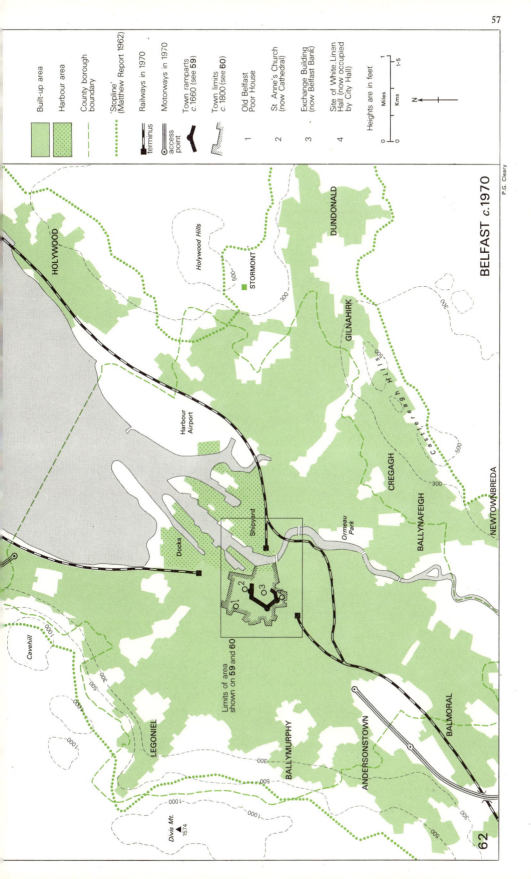

Legend:

- Built-up area
- Harbour area
- County borough boundary
- 'Stopline' (Matthew Report 1962)
- Railways in 1970
  - terminus
- Motorways in 1970
  - access point
- Town ramparts c.1660 (see **59**)
- Town limits c.1800 (see **60**)

1 Old Belfast Poor House
2 St Anne's Church (now Cathedral)
3 Exchange Building (now Belfast Bank)
4 Site of White Linen Hall (now occupied by City Hall)

Heights are in feet

Miles 0   1
Kms 0   1·5

N

BELFAST c.1970

P.G. Cleary

HOLYWOOD

Holywood Hills

500

STORMONT

DUNDONALD

300

GILNAHIRK

Castlereagh Hill

500

300

500

CREGAGH

300

BALLYNAFEIGH

NEWTOWNBREDA

Harbour Airport

Docks

Shipyard

Ormeau Park

Limits of area shown on **59** and **60**

2
3
1

Cavehill

1000

500
300

400

1000

LEGONIEL

1000

Divis Mt. ▲ 1574

1000

500

BALLYMURPHY

300

ANDERSONSTOWN

500

BALMORAL

300

62

58

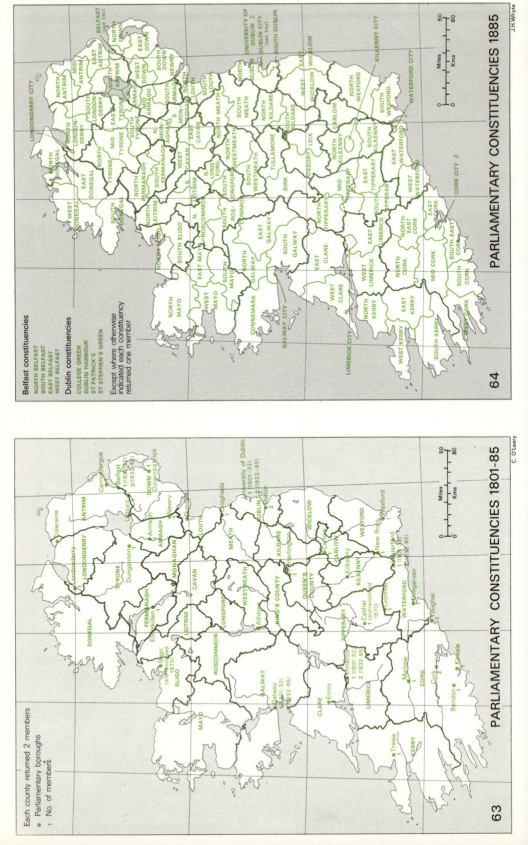

PARLIAMENTARY CONSTITUENCIES 1885

Belfast constituencies
NORTH BELFAST
SOUTH BELFAST
EAST BELFAST
WEST BELFAST

Dublin constituencies
COLLEGE GREEN
DUBLIN HARBOUR
ST PATRICK'S
ST STEPHEN'S GREEN

Except where otherwise
indicated each constituency
returned one member

64

J.H.Whyte

Each county returned 2 members
● Parliamentary boroughs
1 No. of members

PARLIAMENTARY CONSTITUENCIES 1801-85

63

C. O'Leary

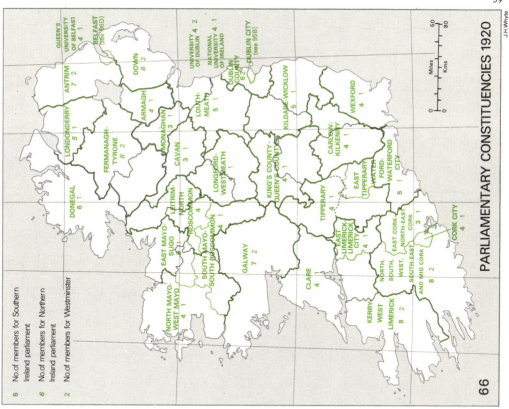

J.H.Whyte

PARLIAMENTARY CONSTITUENCIES 1920

Except where otherwise indicated each constituency returned one member

QUEEN'S
UNIVERSITY
OF BELFAST

BELFAST
(see 96D)
4   4

ANTRIM
7   2

DOWN
8   2

LONDONDERRY
5   1

ARMAGH
4   1

FERMANAGH-
TYRONE
8   2

MONAGHAN
3   1

DONEGAL
6   1

CAVAN
3

LOUTH-
MEATH
5   1

UNIVERSITY OF DUBLIN 4   2
NATIONAL
UNIVERSITY 4   1
OF IRELAND

DUBLIN CITY
(see 96B)

DUBLIN
COUNTY
6   2

KILDARE-WICKLOW
5

WEXFORD
4   1

EAST MAYO-
SLIGO

LEITRIM-
NORTH
ROSCOMMON
4

LONGFORD-
WESTMEATH
4

SOUTH MAYO-
SOUTH ROSCOMMON
4

GALWAY
7   2

CARLOW-
KILKENNY
4   1

WATER-
FORD-
WATERFORD
CITY
5   1

NORTH MAYO-
WEST MAYO
4

CLARE
4

EAST
TIPPERARY

EAST
LIMERICK
LIMERICK
CITY
4

WEST, NORTH-EAST
CORK

EAST CORK
3   1

CORK CITY
4   1

KERRY
WEST
LIMERICK
8   2

NORTH,
WEST,
SOUTH,
SOUTH-EAST
AND MID CORK
8   2

5   No. of members for Southern
    Ireland parliament

6   No. of members for Northern
    Ireland parliament

2   No. of members for Westminster

Miles 0   50
Kms 0   80

66

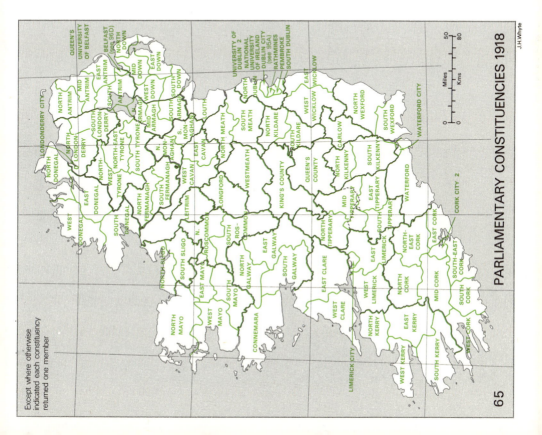

J.H.Whyte

PARLIAMENTARY CONSTITUENCIES 1918

Except where otherwise indicated each constituency returned one member

QUEEN'S
UNIVERSITY
OF BELFAST

BELFAST
(see 96D)

NORTH
DOWN

EAST
DOWN

SOUTH
DOWN

WEST
DOWN

MID
DOWN

LONDONDERRY CITY

NORTH
ANTRIM

EAST
ANTRIM

SOUTH
ANTRIM

MID
ANTRIM

NORTH
LONDON-
DERRY

SOUTH
LONDON-
DERRY

NORTH
DONEGAL

EAST
DONEGAL

NORTH
TYRONE

SOUTH
TYRONE

NORTH-EAST
TYRONE

MID
ARMAGH

NORTH
ARMAGH

S.
ARMAGH

NORTH
FERMANAGH

SOUTH
FERMANAGH

MON-
AGHAN

WEST
DONEGAL

SOUTH
DONEGAL

LEITRIM

WEST
CAVAN

EAST
CAVAN

LOUTH

NORTH-SLIGO

SOUTH SLIGO

N.
ROSCOMMON

SOUTH
ROS-
COMMON

LONGFORD

NORTH
WESTMEATH

SOUTH
WESTMEATH

NORTH
MEATH

SOUTH
MEATH

UNIVERSITY OF
DUBLIN 2
NATIONAL
UNIVERSITY
OF IRELAND
DUBLIN CITY
(see 95A)
RATHMINES
PEMBROKE
SOUTH DUBLIN

NORTH MAYO

EAST MAYO

SOUTH
MAYO

NORTH
GALWAY

EAST
GALWAY

SOUTH
GALWAY

KING'S COUNTY

QUEEN'S
COUNTY

NORTH
KILDARE

SOUTH
KILDARE

WEST
WICKLOW

EAST
WICKLOW

NORTH
CARLOW

SOUTH
KILKENNY

NORTH
KILKENNY

NORTH
WEXFORD

SOUTH
WEXFORD

WATERFORD CITY

WEST
CLARE

EAST CLARE

NORTH
TIPPERARY

MID
TIPPERARY

EAST
TIPPERARY

SOUTH
TIPPERARY

WEST
LIMERICK

EAST
LIMERICK

WATERFORD

NORTH-
EAST
CORK

EAST CORK

CONNEMARA

WEST
KERRY

NORTH
KERRY

EAST
KERRY

SOUTH
KERRY

LIMERICK CITY

NORTH
LIMERICK

NORTH
CORK

MID CORK

SOUTH
CORK

SOUTH-EAST
CORK

CORK CITY 2

WEST CORK

Miles 0   50
Kms 0   80

65

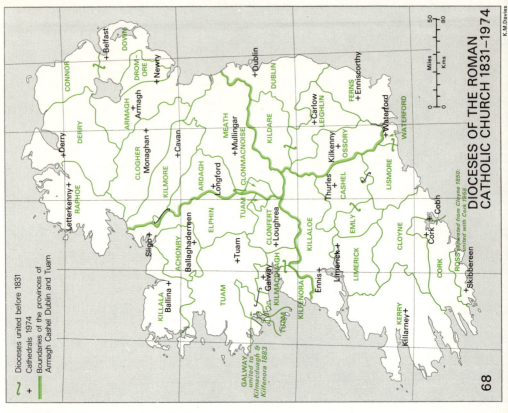

DIOCESES OF THE ROMAN
CATHOLIC CHURCH 1831–1974

K.M.Davies

Dioceses united before 1831
Cathedrals 1974
Boundaries of the provinces of
Armagh Cashel Dublin and Tuam

68

Map labels: +Belfast, DOWN, DROM-ORE, +Newry, CONNOR, ARMAGH, Armagh+, DERRY, +Derry, Letterkenny+, RAPHOE, CLOGHER, Monaghan+, +Cavan, KILMORE, ARDAGH, Longford+, MEATH, Mullingar+, +Dublin, DUBLIN, KILDARE, FERNS, +Enniscorthy, +Carlow, LEIGHLIN, Kilkenny+, OSSORY, Thurles+, CASHEL, +Waterford, WATERFORD, LISMORE, Sligo+, ACHONRY, Ballaghaderreen, ELPHIN, TUAM, +Tuam, CLONMACNOISE, CLONFERT, +Loughrea, KILMACDUAGH, Galway+, KILFENORA, KILLALOE, Ennis+, EMLY, Limerick+, LIMERICK, CLOYNE, CORK, Cork+, Cobh+, +Skibbereen, KERRY, Killarney+, KILLALA, Ballina+, TUAM, GALWAY united to Kilmacduagh & Kilfenora 1883, RQSS separated from Cloyne 1850: united with Cork 1958

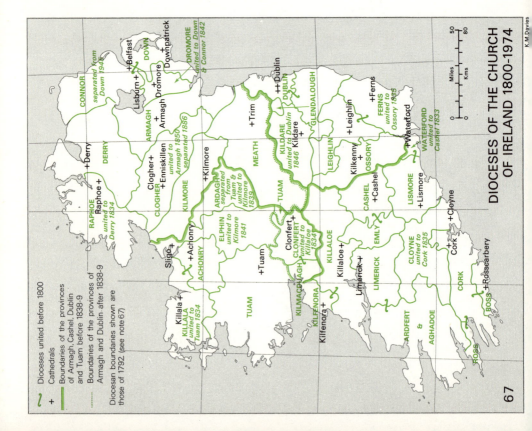

DIOCESES OF THE CHURCH
OF IRELAND 1800–1974

K.M.Davies

Dioceses united before 1800
Cathedrals
Boundaries of the provinces
of Armagh,Cashel,Dublin
and Tuam before 1838-9
Boundaries of the provinces of
Armagh and Dublin after 1838-9
Diocesan boundaries shown are
those of 1792 (see note 67)

67

Map labels: +Belfast, CONNOR separated from Down 1945, DOWN, Downpatrick+, Lisburn+, Dromore+, DROMORE united to Down & Connor 1842, +Derry, DERRY, ARMAGH, Armagh+, Raphoe+, RAPHOE united to Derry 1834, Clogher+, CLOGHER, +Enniskillen, KILMORE, +Kilmore, +Trim, MEATH, +Dublin, DUBLIN, +Ferns, FERNS united to Ossory 1835, GLENDALOUGH, KILDARE united to Dublin 1846, Kildare+, +Leighlin, LEIGHLIN, Kilkenny+, OSSORY, CASHEL, +Cashel, +Lismore, LISMORE, +Waterford, WATERFORD united to Cashel 1833, Sligo+, +Achonry, ACHONRY, ARDAGH separated from Tuam & united to Kilmore 1839, ELPHIN united to Kilmore 1841, TUAM, +Tuam, Clonfert+, CLONFERT united to Killaloe 1834, KILMACDUAGH, KILFENORA, Kilfenora+, KILLALOE, Killaloe+, Limerick+, LIMERICK, EMLY, CLOYNE united to Cork 1835, +Cloyne, CORK, Cork+, ROSS, +Rosscarbery, ARDFERT & AGHADOE, KILLALA united to Tuam 1834, Killala+

Miles 0 50
Kms 0 80

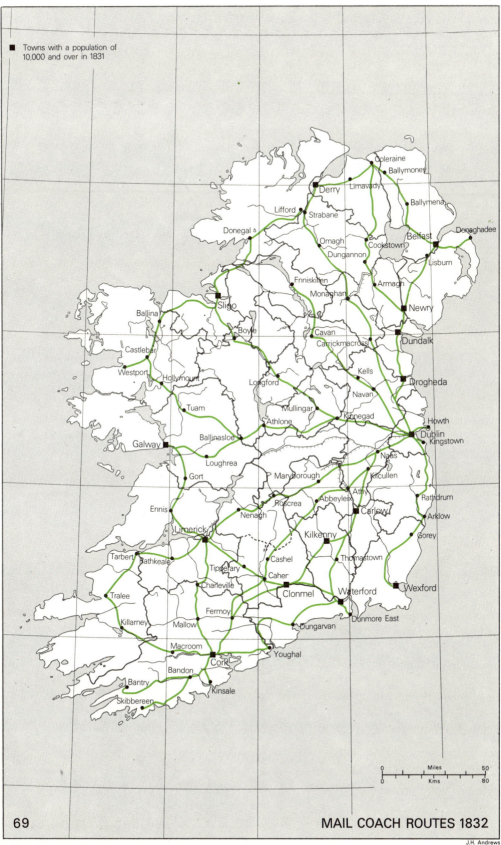

Towns with a population of
10,000 and over in 1831

Coleraine
Ballymoney
Derry
Limavady
Ballymena
Lifford
Strabane
Donegal
Belfast
Donaghadee
Omagh
Cookstown
Dungannon
Lisburn
Enniskillen
Armagh
Monaghan
Newry
Ballina
Sligo
Cavan
Dundalk
Boyle
Carrickmacross
Castlebar
Kells
Drogheda
Westport
Hollymount
Longford
Navan
Tuam
Mullingar
Howth
Ballinasloe
Athlone
Kinnegad
Dublin
Galway
Kingstown
Loughrea
Naas
Gort
Maryborough
Kilcullen
Ennis
Roscrea
Abbeyleix
Athy
Rathdrum
Nenagh
Carlow
Limerick
Kilkenny
Arklow
Tarbert
Cashel
Gorey
Rathkeale
Tipperary
Thomastown
Tralee
Charleville
Caher
Waterford
Wexford
Killarney
Fermoy
Clonmel
Dunmore East
Mallow
Dungarvan
Macroom
Youghal
Bantry
Bandon
Cork
Skibbereen
Kinsale

Miles
50
Kms
80

MAIL COACH ROUTES 1832

J.H. Andrews

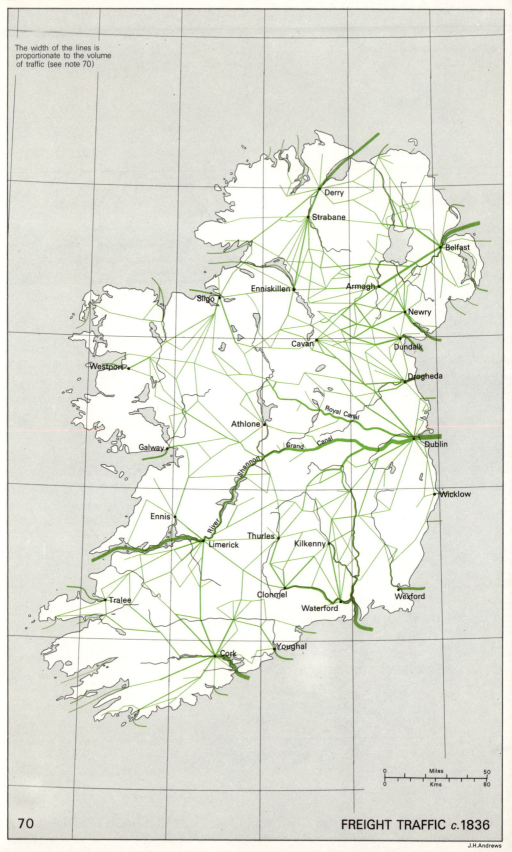

The width of the lines is proportionate to the volume of traffic (see note 70)

Derry

Strabane

Belfast

Enniskillen

Armagh

Sligo

Newry

Cavan

Dundalk

Westport

Drogheda

Royal Canal

Athlone

Grand Canal

Dublin

Galway

Shannon

Wicklow

Ennis

River

Thurles

Limerick

Kilkenny

Tralee

Clonmel

Wexford

Waterford

Cork

Youghal

Miles
0   50
0   80
Kms

FREIGHT TRAFFIC *c.*1836

J.H.Andrews

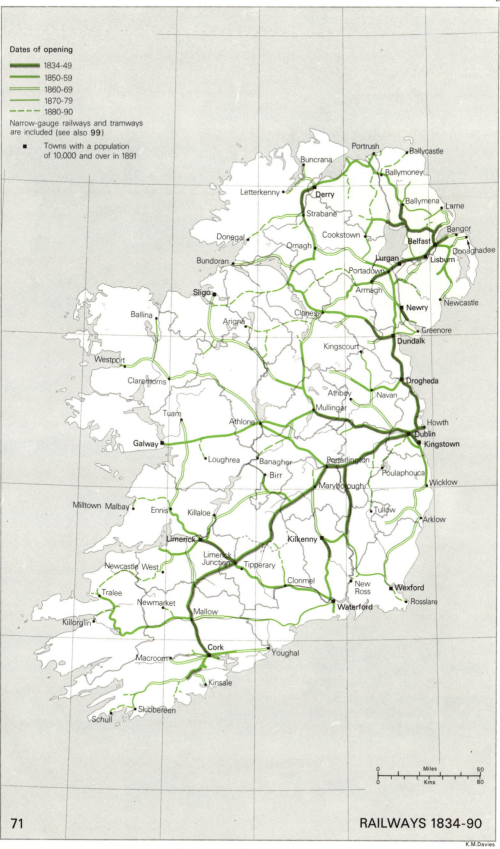

Dates of opening

1834-49
1850-59
1860-69
1870-79
1880-90

Narrow-gauge railways and tramways
are included (see also **99**)

■ Towns with a population
of 10,000 and over in 1891

Portrush
Ballycastle
Buncrana
Ballymoney
Letterkenny
Derry
Ballymena
Larne
Strabane
Bangor
Donegal
Cookstown
Belfast
Donaghadee
Omagh
Lurgan
Lisburn
Bundoran
Portadown
Sligo
Armagh
Newcastle
Ballina
Arigna
Clones
Newry
Greenore
Kingscourt
Dundalk
Westport
Drogheda
Claremorris
Athboy
Navan
Tuam
Mullingar
Howth
Athlone
Dublin
Galway
Kingstown
Loughrea
Banagher
Portarlington
Birr
Poulaphouca
Maryborough
Wicklow
Milltown Malbay
Ennis
Killaloe
Tullow
Arklow
Limerick
Kilkenny
Limerick
Junction
Tipperary
Newcastle West
Clonmel
New
Ross
Wexford
Tralee
Newmarket
Waterford
Rosslare
Killorglin
Mallow
Cork
Youghal
Macroom
Kinsale
Skibbereen
Schull

Miles
0   50
0   80
Kms

RAILWAYS 1834-90

K.M.Davies

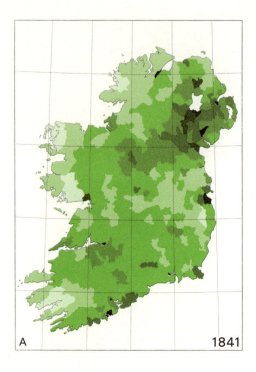

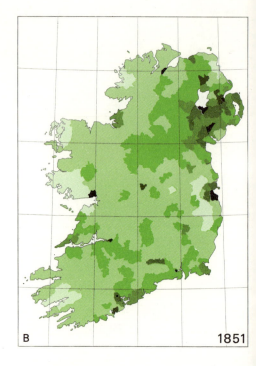

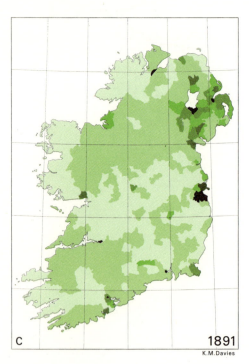

POPULATION DENSITY 1841-91
by baronies

Persons per sq. mile

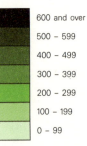

600 and over

500 – 599

400 – 499

300 – 399

200 – 299

100 – 199

0 – 99

K.M.Davies

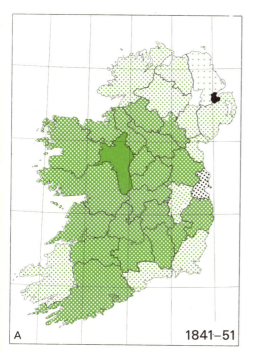

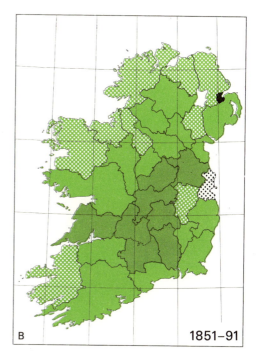

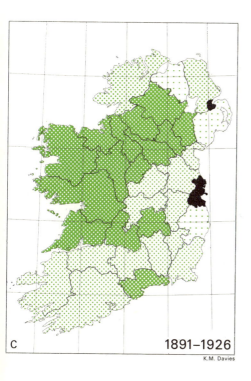

POPULATION CHANGE 1841-1926
by counties

% change in population

Increase

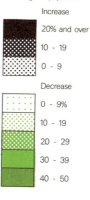

20% and over

10 - 19

0 - 9

Decrease

0 - 9%

10 - 19

20 - 29

30 - 39

40 - 50

Belfast is shown separately

K.M. Davies

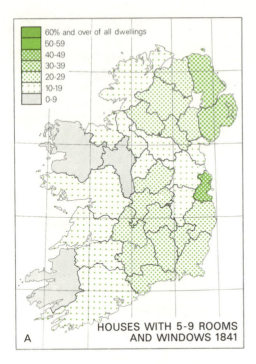

60% and over of all dwellings
50-59
40-49
30-39
20-29
10-19
0-9

A HOUSES WITH 5-9 ROOMS
AND WINDOWS 1841

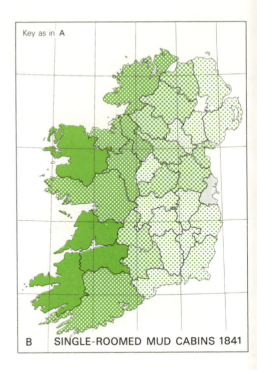

Key as in **A**

B SINGLE-ROOMED MUD CABINS 1841

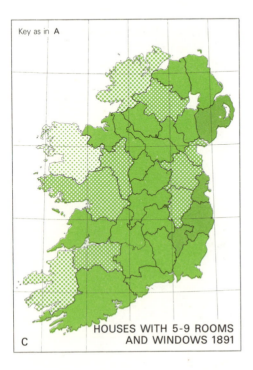

Key as in **A**

C HOUSES WITH 5-9 ROOMS
AND WINDOWS 1891

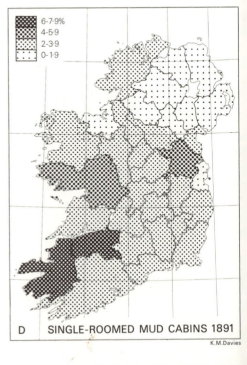

6-7·9%
4-5·9
2-3·9
0-1·9

D SINGLE-ROOMED MUD CABINS 1891

K.M.Davies

74 HOUSE STANDARDS 1841 AND 1891
by counties

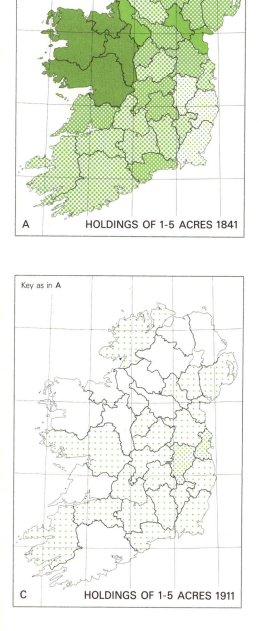

A   **HOLDINGS OF 1-5 ACRES 1841**

60% and over of all holdings (see note 75)
50-59
40-49
30-39
20-29
10-19
0-9

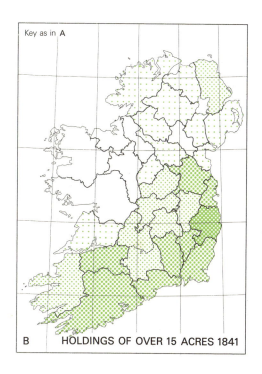

Key as in **A**

B   **HOLDINGS OF OVER 15 ACRES 1841**

Key as in **A**

C   **HOLDINGS OF 1-5 ACRES 1911**

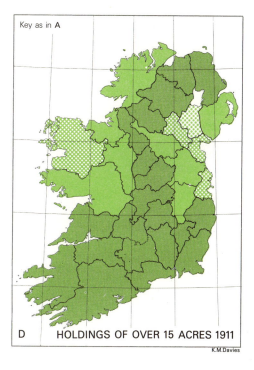

Key as in **A**

D   **HOLDINGS OF OVER 15 ACRES 1911**

K.M.Davies

FARM SIZE 1841 AND 1911
by counties

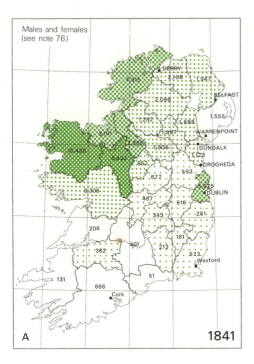

Males and females
(see note 76)

1,405 2,108 1,947

2,096

BELFAST

1,262 1,555

1,688

WARRENPOINT

3,100 1,887

DUNDALK

4,660 1,904 123

862 DROGHEDA

677 593

467 1,525 DUBLIN

3,305 516

343 261

206

362 401 161

131 213 573. Wexford

51

666

Cork

A   1841

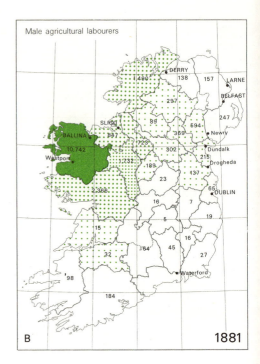

Male agricultural labourers

1,490 138 157 LARNE

BELFAST

297

247

SLIGO 89 694

BALLINA 397 369 Newry

10,742 723 302 Dundalk

Westport 1,732 189 215 Drogheda

23 137

65 DUBLIN

2,366 16 7

5 19

15

16

64 45

32 27

98 Waterford

184

B   1881

Males and females, including
non-agricultural labourers

3,386 80 22 Larne

BELFAST

79

3 62

247

Sligo 45 Newry

987 298 86 GREENORE

10,074 DUNDALK

384 26 172

Westport 7 12

2,305 2

2 0 DUBLIN

16

26 471

89

10 2

3 30

336 Wexford

31 Waterford

171 Cork

C   1901

K.M.Davies

SEASONAL MIGRATION 1841, 1881, 1901 by counties

Migrants per thousand of population

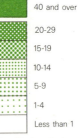

	40 and over
	20-29
	15-19
	10-14
	5-9
	1-4
	Less than 1

2,005 Number of migrants

Ports of embarkation
DUBLIN Over 1,000 migrants recorded
Newry 100-999

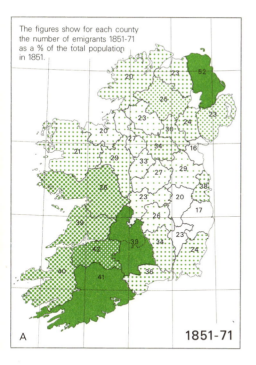

The figures show for each county the number of emigrants 1851-71 as a % of the total population in 1851.

A   1851-71

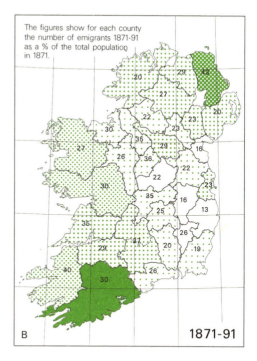

The figures show for each county the number of emigrants 1871-91 as a % of the total population in 1871.

B   1871-91

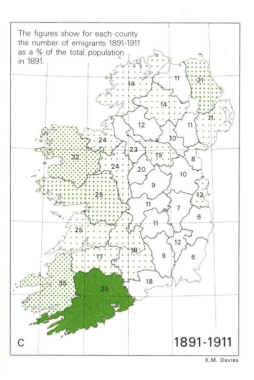

The figures show for each·county the number of emigrants 1891-1911 as a % of the total population in 1891.

C   1891-1911

K.M. Davies

EMIGRATION 1851-1911
by counties

Number of emigrants
in 1,000s

▦	120 and over
▦	100 - 119
▦	80 - 99
▦	60 - 79
▦	40 - 59
⋅	20 - 39
□	0 - 19

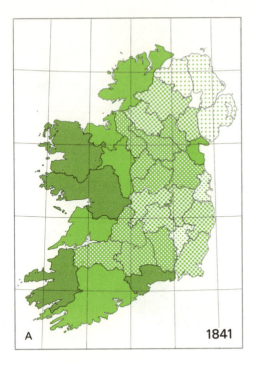

A **1841**

B **1861**

C **1891**

K.M. Davies

ILLITERACY 1841, 1861, 1891 by counties

% of persons aged 5 years old and upwards who can neither read nor write

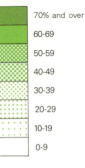

	70% and over
	60-69
	50-59
	40-49
	30-39
	20-29
	10-19
	0-9

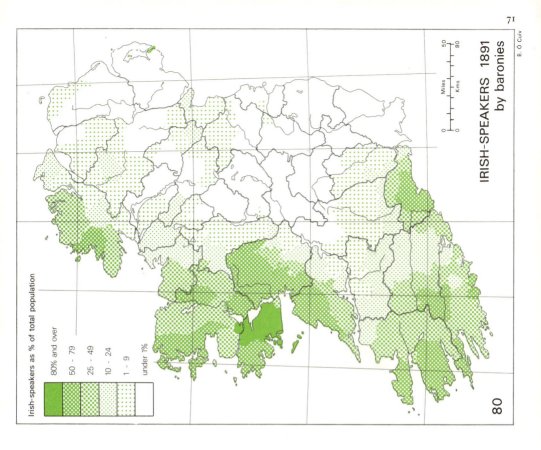

IRISH-SPEAKERS 1891
by baronies

Irish-speakers as % of total population

80% and over

50 - 79

25 - 49

10 - 24

1 - 9

under 1%

Miles

Kms

0   50
0   80

B. Ó Cuív

80

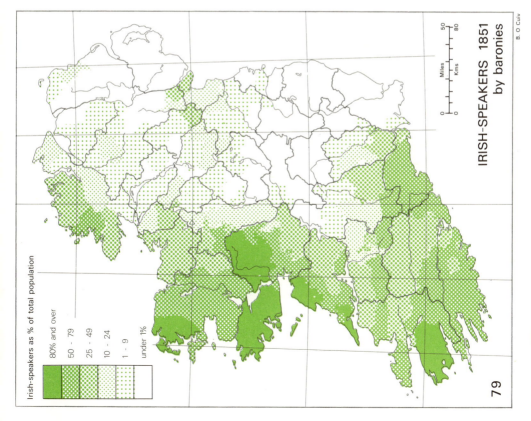

IRISH-SPEAKERS 1851
by baronies

Irish-speakers as % of total population

80% and over

50 - 79

25 - 49

10 - 24

1 - 9

under 1%

Miles

Kms

0   50
0   80

B. Ó Cuív

79

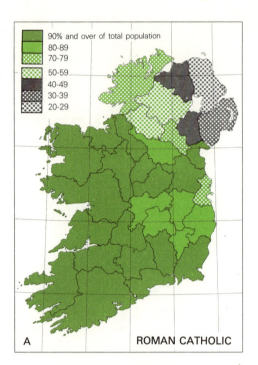

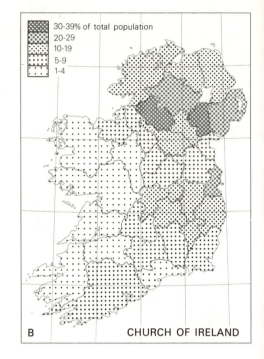

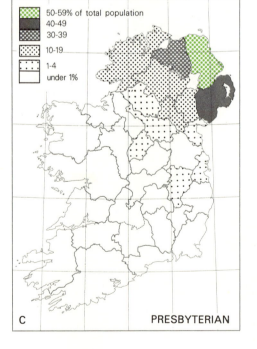

A — ROMAN CATHOLIC

- 90% and over of total population
- 80-89
- 70-79
- 50-59
- 40-49
- 30-39
- 20-29

B — CHURCH OF IRELAND

- 30-39% of total population
- 20-29
- 10-19
- 5-9
- 1-4

C — PRESBYTERIAN

- 50-59% of total population
- 40-49
- 30-39
- 10-19
- 1-4
- under 1%

D — OTHER DENOMINATIONS

- 1-4% of total population
- under 1%

K.M. Davies

RELIGIOUS DENOMINATIONS 1871
by counties

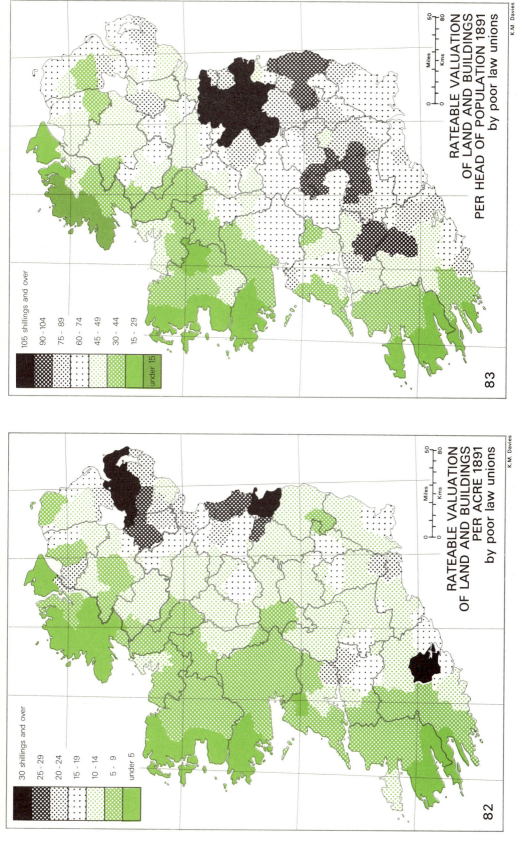

RATEABLE VALUATION
OF LAND AND BUILDINGS
PER HEAD OF POPULATION 1891
by poor law unions

K.M. Davies

105 shillings and over
90 - 104
75 - 89
60 - 74
45 - 49
30 - 44
15 - 29
under 15

83

RATEABLE VALUATION
OF LAND AND BUILDINGS
PER ACRE 1891
by poor law unions

K.M. Davies

30 shillings and over
25 - 29
20 - 24
15 - 19
10 - 14
5 - 9
under 5

82

Miles 0   50
Kms 0   80

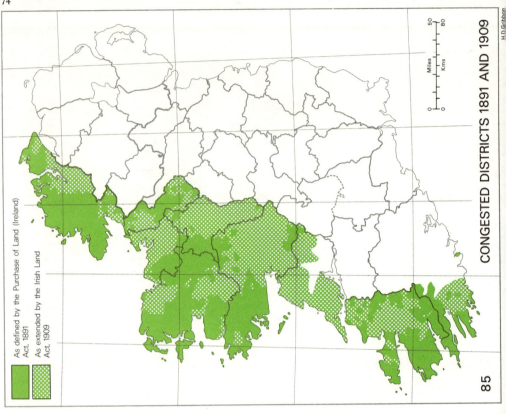

CONGESTED DISTRICTS 1891 AND 1909

As defined by the Purchase of Land (Ireland) Act, 1891

As extended by the Irish Land Act, 1909

H.D.Gribbon

85

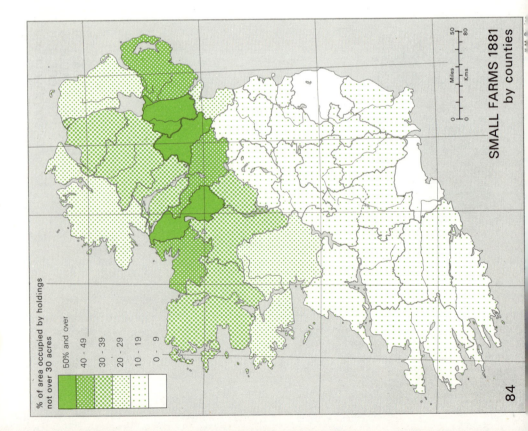

SMALL FARMS 1881
by counties

% of area occupied by holdings not over 30 acres

50% and over

40 - 49

30 - 39

20 - 29

10 - 19

0 - 9

84

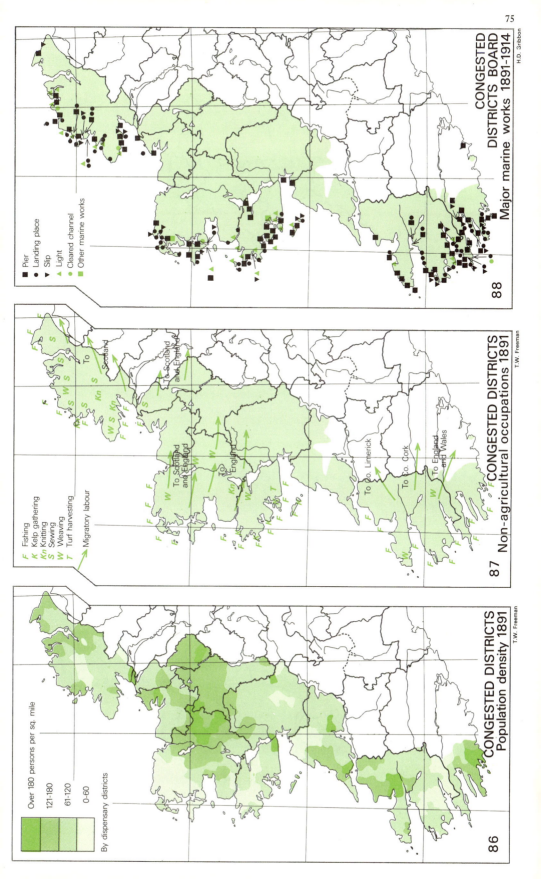

CONGESTED DISTRICTS BOARD
Major marine works 1891-1914

H.D. Gribbon

Pier ■
Landing place ●
Slip ▼
Light ◀
Cleared channel ●
Other marine works ■

88

CONGESTED DISTRICTS
Non-agricultural occupations 1891

T.W. Freeman

F Fishing
K Kelp gathering
Kn Knitting
S Sewing
W Weaving
T Turf harvesting

→ Migratory labour

To Scotland
To Scotland and England
To England
To Co. Limerick
To Co. Cork
To England and Wales

87

CONGESTED DISTRICTS
Population density 1891

T.W. Freeman

Over 180 persons per sq. mile
121-180
61-120
0-60

By dispensary districts

86

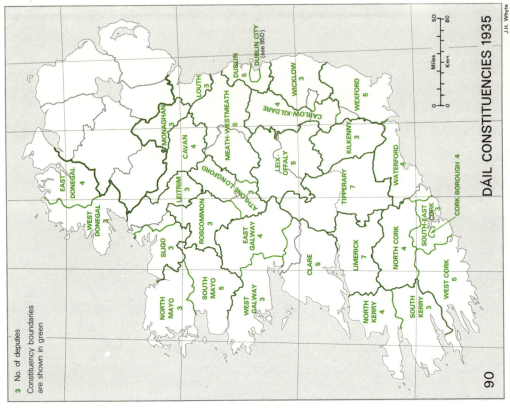

3 No. of deputies

Constituency boundaries are shown in green

DÁIL CONSTITUENCIES 1935

90

J.H. Whyte

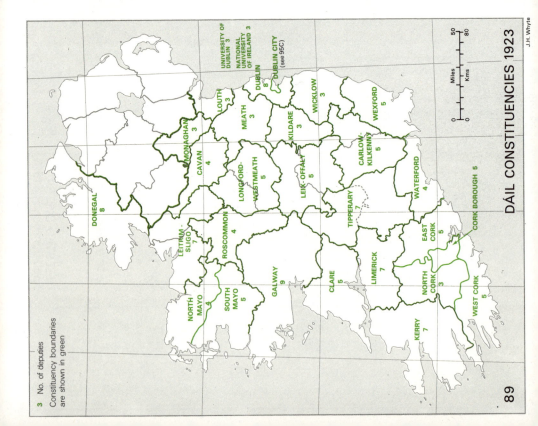

3 No. of deputies

Constituency boundaries are shown in green

DÁIL CONSTITUENCIES 1923

89

J.H. Whyte

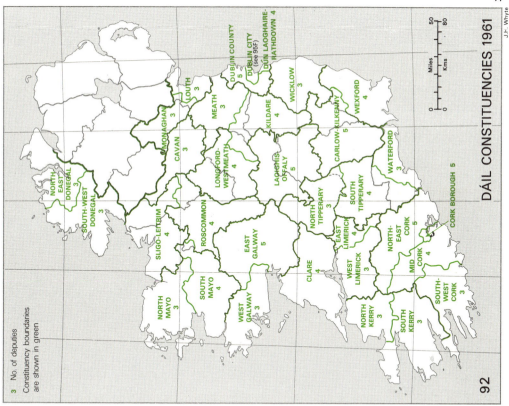

DÁIL CONSTITUENCIES 1961

3 No. of deputies
Constituency boundaries
are shown in green

NORTH EAST DONEGAL 3
SOUTH-WEST DONEGAL 3
MONAGHAN 3
CAVAN 3
LOUTH 3
MEATH 3
DUBLIN COUNTY 5
DUBLIN CITY (see 95F)
DÚN LAOGHAIRE-RATHDOWN 4
WICKLOW 3
KILDARE 4
LONGFORD-WESTMEATH 4
LAOGHIS-OFFALY 5
CARLOW-KILKENNY 5
WEXFORD 4
WATERFORD 3
SLIGO-LEITRIM 4
ROSCOMMON 3
EAST GALWAY 5
NORTH TIPPERARY 3
SOUTH TIPPERARY 4
NORTH MAYO 3
SOUTH MAYO 3
WEST GALWAY 3
CLARE 4
EAST LIMERICK 3
WEST LIMERICK 3
NORTH-EAST CORK 5
MID CORK 4
SOUTH-WEST CORK 3
CORK BOROUGH 5
NORTH KERRY 3
SOUTH KERRY 3

92

J.H. Whyte

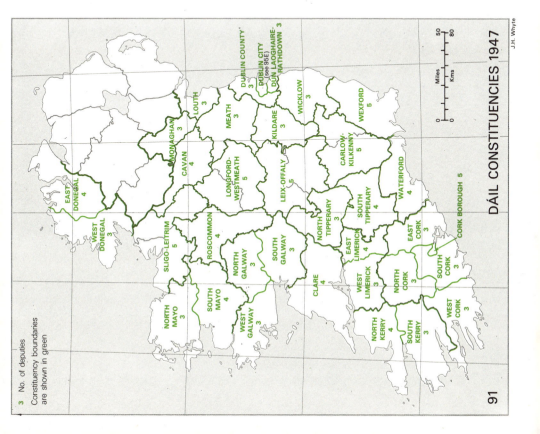

DÁIL CONSTITUENCIES 1947

3 No. of deputies
Constituency boundaries
are shown in green

EAST DONEGAL 4
WEST DONEGAL 3
MONAGHAN 3
CAVAN 4
LOUTH 3
MEATH 3
DUBLIN COUNTY 3
DUBLIN CITY (see 95E)
DÚN LAOGHAIRE-RATHDOWN 3
WICKLOW 3
KILDARE 3
LONGFORD-WESTMEATH 5
LEIX-OFFALY 5
CARLOW-KILKENNY 5
WEXFORD 5
WATERFORD 4
SLIGO-LEITRIM 5
ROSCOMMON 4
NORTH GALWAY 3
SOUTH GALWAY 3
NORTH TIPPERARY 3
SOUTH TIPPERARY 4
NORTH MAYO 3
SOUTH MAYO 4
WEST GALWAY 3
CLARE 4
EAST LIMERICK 4
WEST LIMERICK 3
NORTH CORK 3
EAST CORK 3
SOUTH CORK 3
WEST CORK 3
CORK BOROUGH 5
NORTH KERRY 4
SOUTH KERRY 3

91

J.H. Whyte

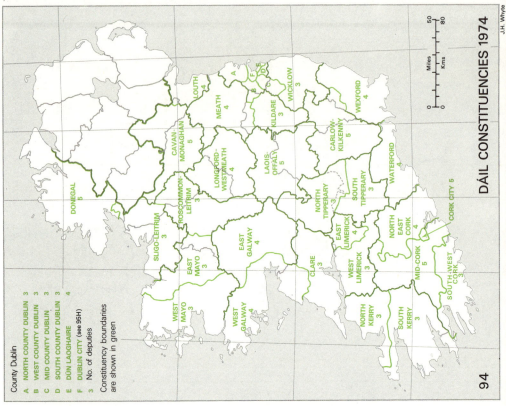

J.H. Whyte

County Dublin

A NORTH COUNTY DUBLIN 3
B WEST COUNTY DUBLIN 3
C MID COUNTY DUBLIN 3
D SOUTH COUNTY DUBLIN 3
E DÚN LAOGHAIRE 4
F DUBLIN CITY (see 95H)
3 No. of deputies

Constituency boundaries
are shown in green

94

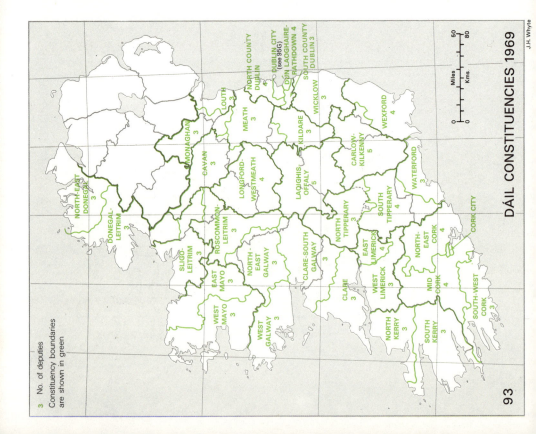

DÁIL CONSTITUENCIES 1969

J.H. Whyte

3 No. of deputies
Constituency boundaries
are shown in green

93

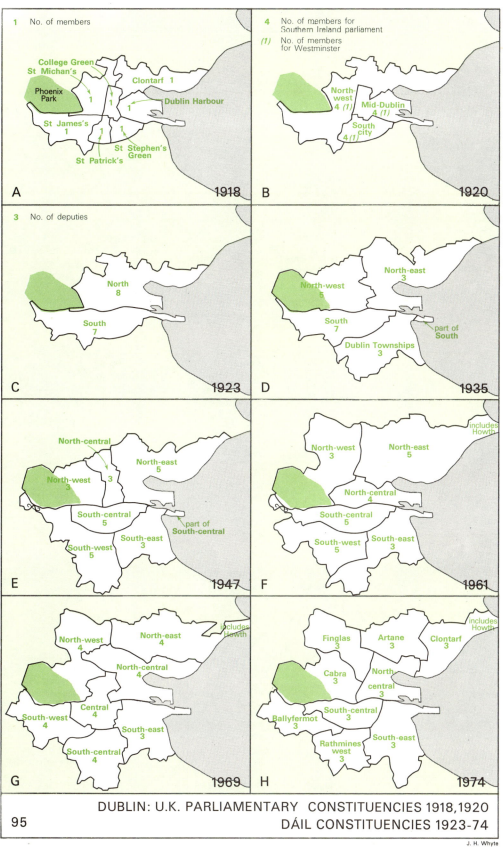

A   **1918**
B   **1920**
C   **1923**
D   **1935**
E   **1947**
F   **1961**
G   **1969**
H   **1974**

1   No. of members

4   No. of members for
Southern Ireland parliament
(1) No. of members
for Westminster

3   No. of deputies

A (1918)

College Green
St Michan's
Phoenix Park
St James's
St Patrick's
St Stephen's Green
Clontarf 1
Dublin Harbour
1 · 1 · 1 · 1 · 1

B (1920)

North-west 4 (1)
Mid-Dublin 4 (1)
South city 4 (1)

C (1923)

North 8
South 7

D (1935)

North-west 5
North-east 3
South 7
Dublin Townships 3
part of South

E (1947)

North-central
North-west 3
3
North-east 5
South-central 5
South-west 5
South-east 3
part of South-central

F (1961)

North-west 3
North-east 5
North-central 4
South-central 5
South-west 5
South-east 3
includes Howth

G (1969)

North-west 4
North-east 4
North-central 4
Central 4
South-west 4
South-central 4
South-east 3
includes Howth

H (1974)

Finglas 3
Artane 3
Clontarf 3
Cabra 3
North-central 3
Ballyfermot
South-central 3
Rathmines west 3
South-east 3
includes Howth

DUBLIN: U.K. PARLIAMENTARY CONSTITUENCIES 1918, 1920
DÁIL CONSTITUENCIES 1923-74

J. H. Whyte

80

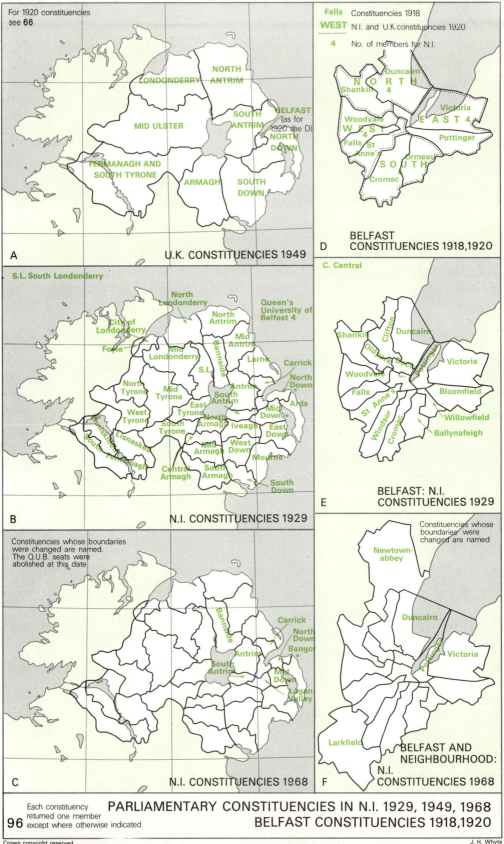

For 1920 constituencies see **66**

A   U.K. CONSTITUENCIES 1949

NORTH ANTRIM
LONDONDERRY
MID ULSTER
SOUTH ANTRIM
BELFAST (as for 1920: see D)
NORTH DOWN
FERMANAGH AND SOUTH TYRONE
ARMAGH
SOUTH DOWN

Falls   Constituencies 1918
WEST   N.I. and U.K. constituencies 1920
4   No. of members for N.I.

NORTH 4
Duncairn
Shankill
Woodvale
WEST 4
Falls
St Anne's
EAST 4
Victoria
Pottinger
SOUTH
Ormeau
Cromac

D   BELFAST CONSTITUENCIES 1918,1920

S.L. South Londonderry

North Londonderry
City of Londonderry
Foyle
Mid Londonderry
North Antrim
Mid Antrim
Queen's University of Belfast 4
Bannside
Larne
Carrick
North Down
North Tyrone
Mid Tyrone
S.L.
Antrim
South Antrim
Ards
West Tyrone
East Tyrone
North Armagh
Iveagh
Mid Down
East Down
Enniskillen
South Fermanagh
Lisnaskea
South Tyrone
Mid Armagh
West Down
Mourne
Central Armagh
South Armagh
South Down

B   N.I. CONSTITUENCIES 1929

C. Central

Shankill
Clifton
Duncairn
Oldpark
Dock
Pottinger
Victoria
Woodvale
C.
Falls
St Anne's
Bloomfield
Windsor
Cromac
Willowfield
Ballynafeigh

E   BELFAST: N.I. CONSTITUENCIES 1929

Constituencies whose boundaries were changed are named. The Q.U.B. seats were abolished at this date

Bannside
Carrick
North Down
Bangor
Antrim
South Antrim
Mid Down
Lagan Valley

C   N.I. CONSTITUENCIES 1968

Constituencies whose boundaries were changed are named

Newtown-abbey
Duncairn
Pottinger
Victoria
Larkfield

F   BELFAST AND NEIGHBOURHOOD: N.I. CONSTITUENCIES 1968

96   Each constituency returned one member except where otherwise indicated

PARLIAMENTARY CONSTITUENCIES IN N.I. 1929, 1949, 1968
BELFAST CONSTITUENCIES 1918,1920

Crown copyright reserved   J. H. Whyte

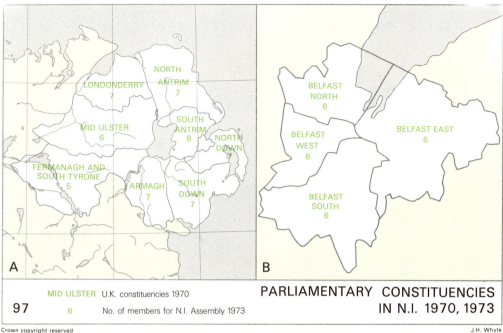

MID ULSTER U.K. constituencies 1970

97

6 No. of members for N.I. Assembly 1973

PARLIAMENTARY CONSTITUENCIES
IN N.I. 1970, 1973

J.H. Whyte

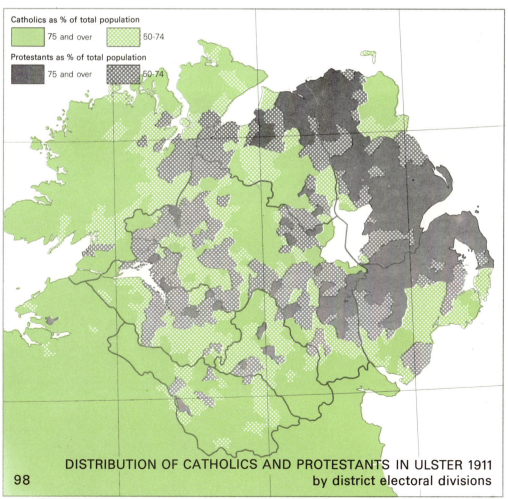

Catholics as % of total population

75 and over 50-74

Protestants as % of total population

75 and over 50-74

DISTRIBUTION OF CATHOLICS AND PROTESTANTS IN ULSTER 1911
by district electoral divisions

98

K.M.Davies

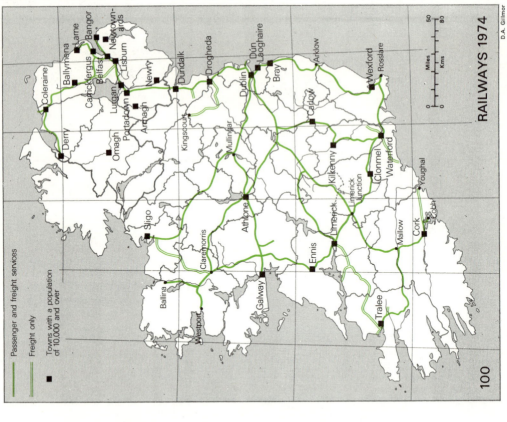

RAILWAYS 1974

Passenger and freight services

Freight only

Towns with a population of 10,000 and over

Coleraine · Derry · Larne · Bangor · Ballymena · Carrickfergus · Belfast · Lisburn · Newtown-ards · Lurgan · Portadown · Armagh · Newry · Omagh · Dundalk · Drogheda · Kingscourt · Mullingar · Dublin · Dún Laoghaire · Bray · Carlow · Arklow · Wexford · Rosslare · Sligo · Ballina · Claremorris · Athlone · Westport · Galway · Ennis · Kilkenny · Limerick · Limerick Junction · Clonmel · Waterford · Youghal · Tralee · Mallow · Cork · Cobh

Miles 0 50
Kms 0 80

D.A. Gillmor

100

RAILWAYS 1926

Railways

Narrow-gauge railways

Tramways

Towns with a population of 10,000 and over

Carndonagh · Ballycastle · Bangor · Coleraine · Larne · Ballymena · Belfast · Newtown-ards · Lisburn · Lurgan · Portadown · Armagh · Newry · Derry · Strabane · Clones · Kingscourt · Dundalk · Drogheda · Omagh · Glenties · Bundoran · Sligo · Mullingar · Dublin · Dún Laoghaire · Burton Port · Killybegs · Claremorris · Athlone · Birr · Carlow · Arklow · Wexford · Rosslare · Killala · Ennis · Kilkenny · Limerick · Limerick Junction · Clonmel · Waterford · Youghal · Achill · Westport · Galway · Foynes · Kilkee · Mallow · Cork · Cobh · Clifden · Tralee · Caherciveen · Kenmare · Bantry · Dingle

Miles 0 50
Kms 0 80

K.M.Davies

99

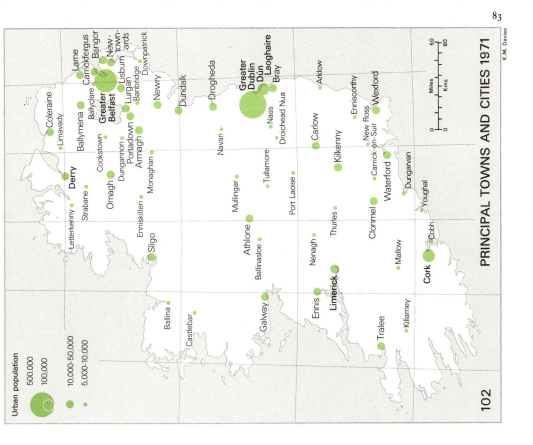

PRINCIPAL TOWNS AND CITIES 1971

Urban population

- 500,000
- 100,000
- 10,000–50,000
- 5,000–10,000

Larne
Coleraine
Limavady
Ballymena
Ballyclare
Carrickfergus
Bangor
New-town-ards
Greater Belfast
Lisburn
Lurgan
Banbridge
Downpatrick
Newry
Derry
Strabane
Cookstown
Portadown
Dungannon
Armagh
Omagh
Monaghan
Letterkenny
Enniskillen
Sligo
Ballina
Castlebar
Dundalk
Drogheda
Navan
Greater Dublin
Dún Laoghaire
Bray
Naas
Droichead Nua
Arklow
Enniscorthy
New Ross
Wexford
Mullingar
Tullamore
Port Laoise
Carlow
Kilkenny
Carrick-on-Suir
Clonmel
Waterford
Dungarvan
Youghal
Cobh
Cork
Mallow
Killarney
Tralee
Limerick
Ennis
Nenagh
Thurles
Athlone
Ballinasloe
Galway

Miles
Kms
0   50
0   80

102

K.M. Davies

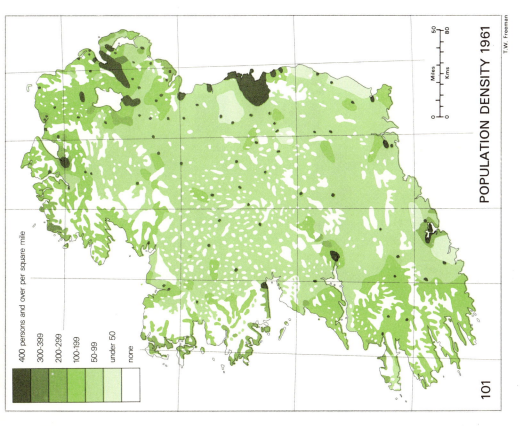

POPULATION DENSITY 1961

400 persons and over per square mile
300–399
200–299
100–199
50–99
under 50
none

Miles
Kms
0   50
0   80

101

T.W. Freeman

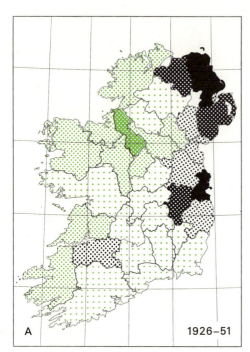

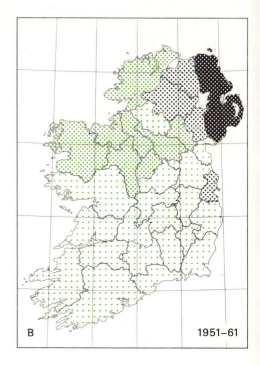

A   1926–51

B   1951–61

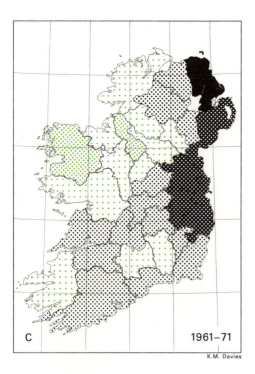

C   1961–71

K.M. Davies

POPULATION CHANGE 1926-71
by counties

% change in population

Increase

20% and over

10–19

0– 9

Decrease

0– 9%

10–19

20–29

Belfast county borough is
shown separately

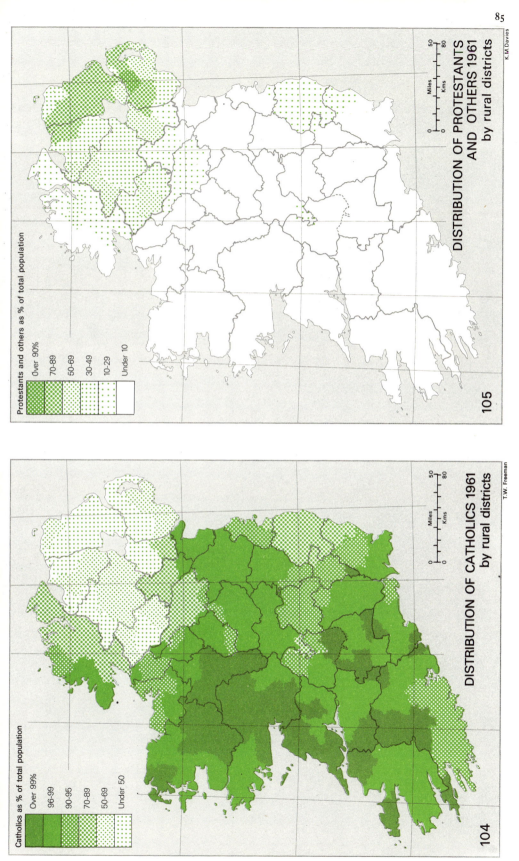

85

Protestants and others as % of total population

| Over 90% |
| 70-89 |
| 50-69 |
| 30-49 |
| 10-29 |
| Under 10 |

DISTRIBUTION OF PROTESTANTS
AND OTHERS 1961
by rural districts

Miles
Kms
0   50
0   80

K.M.Davies

105

Catholics as % of total population

| Over 99% |
| 96-99 |
| 90-95 |
| 70-89 |
| 50-69 |
| Under 50 |

DISTRIBUTION OF CATHOLICS 1961
by rural districts

Miles
Kms
0   50
0   80

T.W. Freeman

104

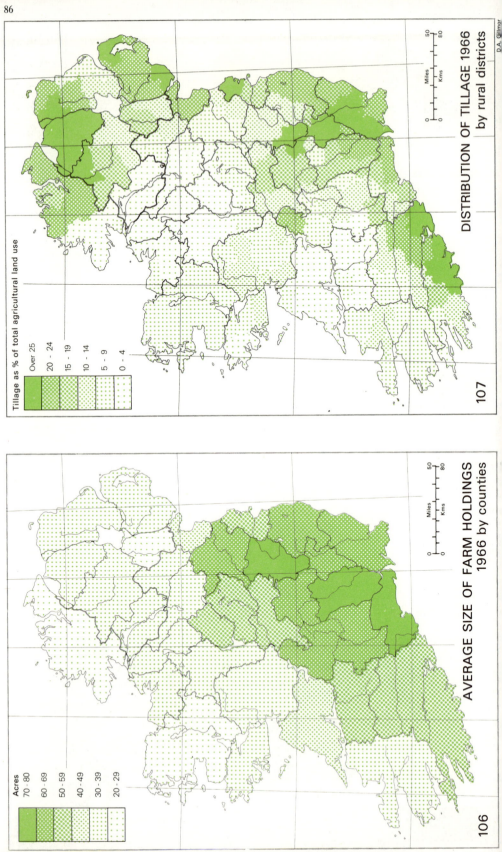

Tillage as % of total agricultural land use

Over 25
20 - 24
15 - 19
10 - 14
5 - 9
0 - 4

DISTRIBUTION OF TILLAGE 1966
by rural districts

107

D.A. Gillmor

Acres
70 - 80
60 - 69
50 - 59
40 - 49
30 - 39
20 - 29

AVERAGE SIZE OF FARM HOLDINGS
1966 by counties

106

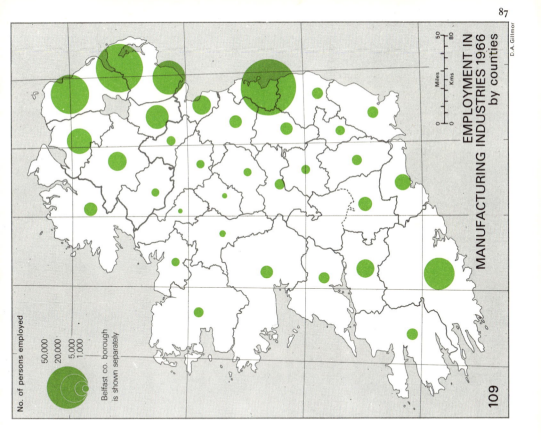

No. of persons employed

50,000
20,000
5,000
1,000

Belfast co. borough
is shown separately

EMPLOYMENT IN
MANUFACTURING INDUSTRIES 1966
by counties

Miles
0   50
Kms
0   80

D.A. Gillmor

109

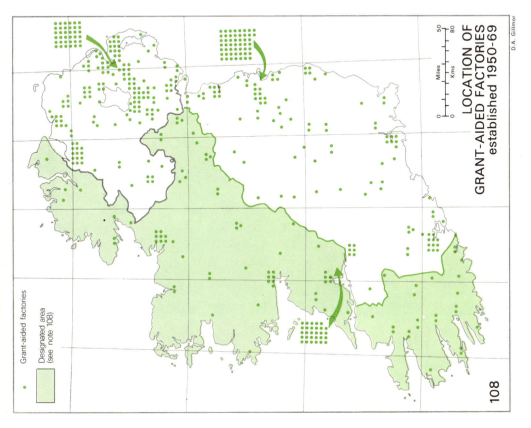

Grant-aided factories

Designated area
(see note 108)

LOCATION OF
GRANT-AIDED FACTORIES
established 1950-69

Miles
0   50
Kms
0   80

D.A. Gillmor

108

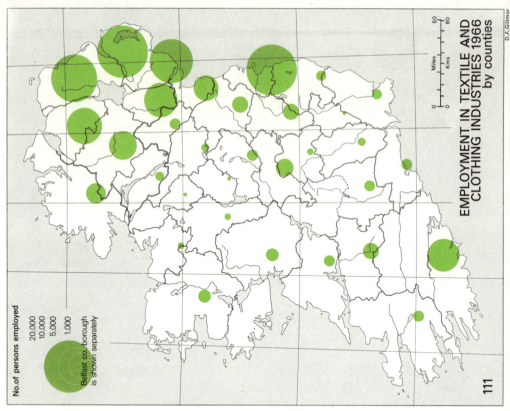

No. of persons employed

20,000
10,000
5,000
1,000

Belfast co. borough
is shown separately

0   Miles   50
0   Kms   80

D.A.Gillmor

EMPLOYMENT IN TEXTILE AND
CLOTHING INDUSTRIES 1966
by counties

111

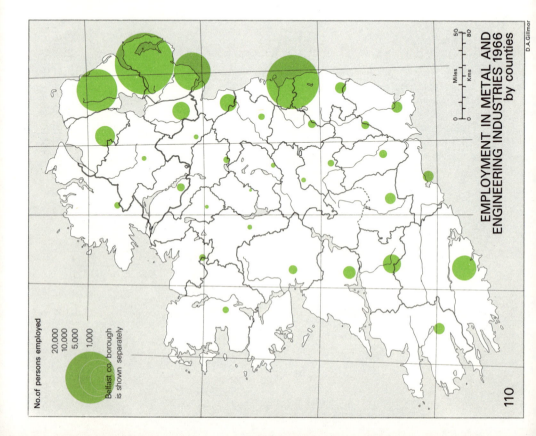

No. of persons employed

20,000
10,000
5,000
1,000

Belfast co. borough
is shown separately

0   Miles   50
0   Kms   80

D.A.Gillmor

EMPLOYMENT IN METAL AND
ENGINEERING INDUSTRIES 1966
by counties

110

89

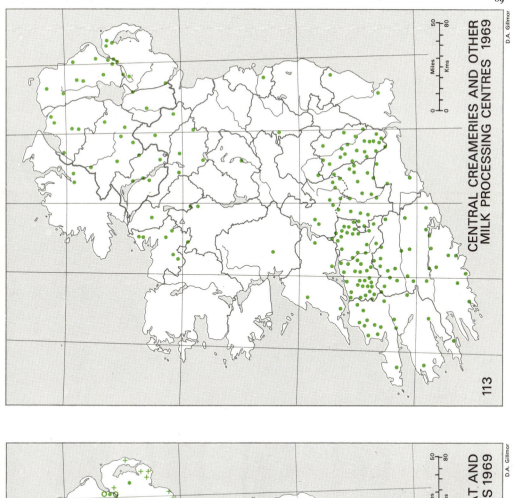

CENTRAL CREAMERIES AND OTHER
MILK PROCESSING CENTRES 1969

113

D.A. Gillmor

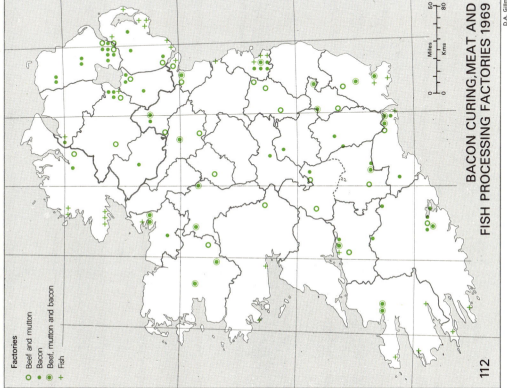

Factories
○ Beef and mutton
• Bacon
◉ Beef, mutton and bacon
+ Fish

BACON CURING, MEAT AND
FISH PROCESSING FACTORIES 1969

112

D.A. Gillmor

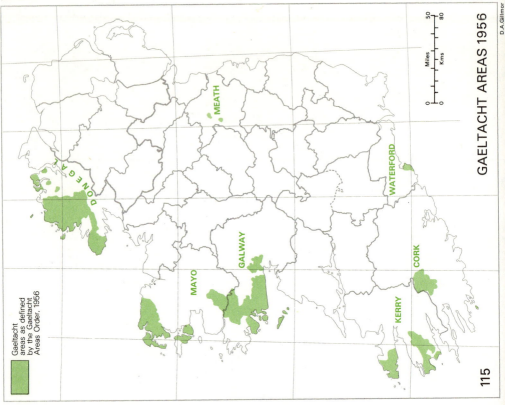

GAELTACHT AREAS 1956

Gaeltacht
areas as defined
by the Gaeltacht
Areas Order, 1956

DONEGAL

MAYO

GALWAY

MEATH

WATERFORD

KERRY

CORK

Miles
0   50
Kms
0   80

115

D.A.Gillmor

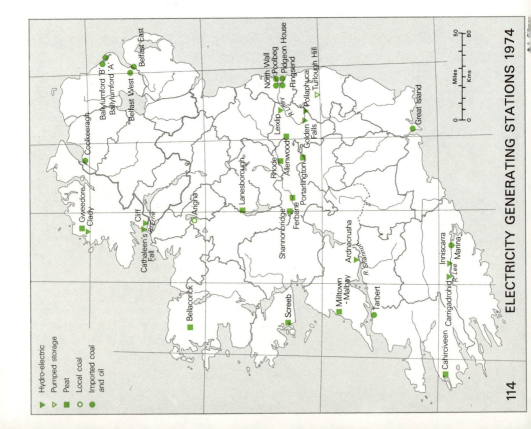

ELECTRICITY GENERATING STATIONS 1974

Hydro-electric
Pumped storage
Peat
Local coal
Imported coal
and oil

Belfast East
Ballylumford 'B'
Ballylumford 'A'
Belfast West
Coolkeeragh
Gweedore
Clady
Cliff
Cathaleen's
Fall
R. Erne
Annagh
Bellacorick
Screeb
Milltown
-Malbay
Tarbert
Ardnacrusha
R. Shannon
Cahirciveen
Carrigadrohid
Inniscarra
R. Lee
Marina
Shannonbridge
Ferbane
Portarlington
Lanesborough
Rhode
Allenwood
Leixlip
R. Liffey
North Wall
Poolbeg
Pigeon House
Ringsend
Pollaphuca
Golden
Falls
Turlough Hill
Great Island

Miles
0   50
Kms
0   80

114

A PLANNING AND INDUSTRIAL DEVELOPMENT AUTHORITY REGIONS

Donegal

Northern Ireland

North-west

North-east

West

Midlands

East

Mid-west

South-east

South-west

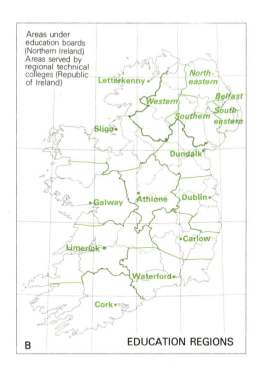

B EDUCATION REGIONS

Areas under education boards (Northern Ireland) Areas served by regional technical colleges (Republic of Ireland)

Letterkenny •

North-eastern

Western

Belfast

Southern

South-eastern

Sligo •

Dundalk •

• Galway

Athlone

Dublin •

Limerick •

• Carlow

Waterford •

Cork •

C HEALTH BOARD AREAS

Northern

North western

Western

Eastern

Southern

North eastern

Western

Midland

Eastern

Mid-western

South-eastern

Southern

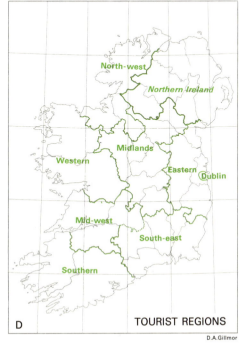

D TOURIST REGIONS

North-west

Northern Ireland

Midlands

Western

Eastern

Dublin

Mid-west

South-east

Southern

D.A.Gillmor

116   ADMINISTRATIVE REGIONS 1974

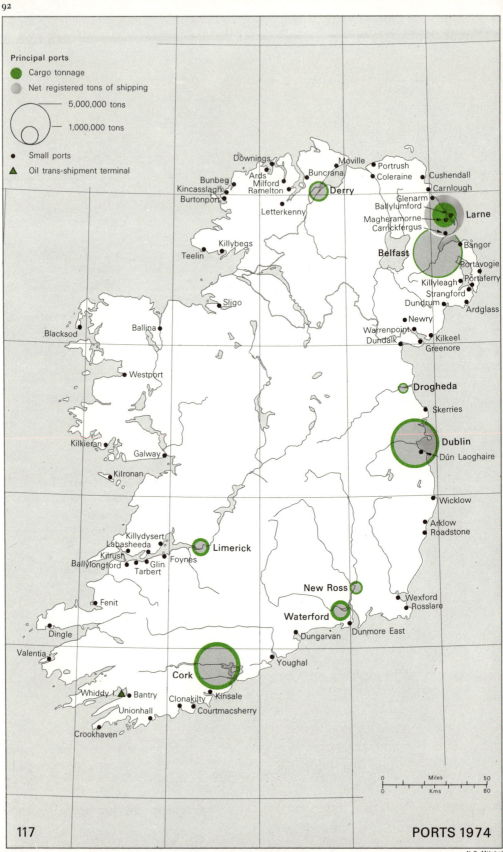

Principal ports
- Cargo tonnage
- Net registered tons of shipping

5,000,000 tons

1,000,000 tons

• Small ports
▲ Oil trans-shipment terminal

Downings
Moville
Portrush
Cushendall
Bunbeg
Ards
Buncrana
Coleraine
Carnlough
Kincasslagh
Milford
Derry
Burtonport
Ramelton
Glenarm
Ballylumford
Letterkenny
Magheramorne
Larne
Carrickfergus
Killybegs
Belfast
Teelin
Bangor
Portavogie
Killyleagh
Portaferry
Strangford
Sligo
Dundrum
Ardglass
Blacksod
Ballina
Newry
Warrenpoint
Westport
Dundalk
Kilkeel
Greenore

Drogheda
Skerries

Dublin
Kilkieran
Dún Laoghaire
Galway
Kilronan

Wicklow

Arklow
Roadstone
Killydysert
Labasheeda
Limerick
Kilrush
Glin
Foynes
Ballylongford
Tarbert
Fenit
New Ross
Wexford
Rosslare
Waterford
Dingle
Dungarvan
Dunmore East
Valentia
Youghal
Cork
Whiddy I. ▲ Bantry
Clonakilty
Kinsale
Unionhall
Courtmacsherry
Crookhaven

Miles 50
Kms 80

PORTS 1974

N.C. Mitchel

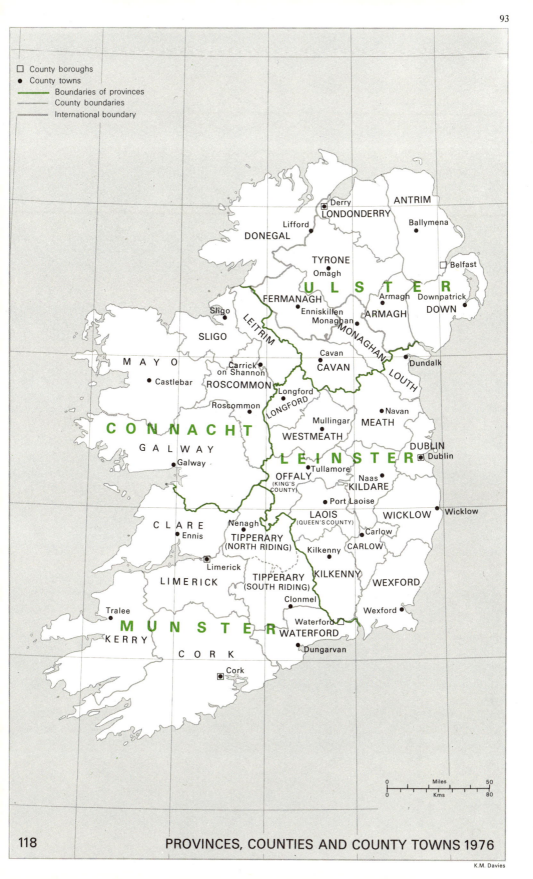

PROVINCES, COUNTIES AND COUNTY TOWNS 1976

K.M. Davies

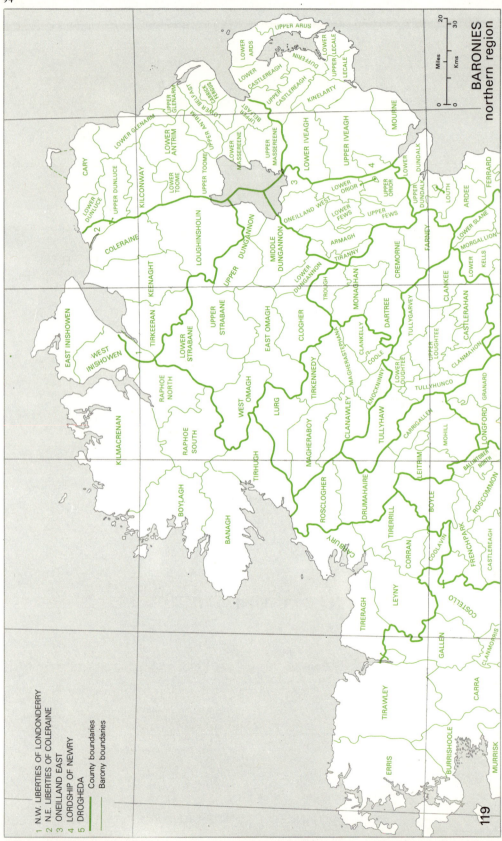

BARONIES
northern region

1 N.W. LIBERTIES OF LONDONDERRY
2 N.E. LIBERTIES OF COLERAINE
3 ONEILLAND EAST
4 LORDSHIP OF NEWRY
5 DROGHEDA

County boundaries
Barony boundaries

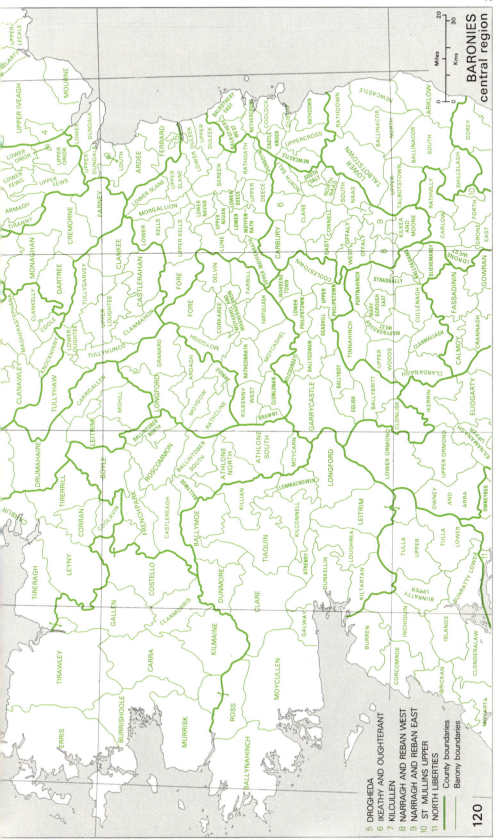

BARONIES
central region

Miles
Kms

5 DROGHEDA
6 IKEATHY AND OUGHTERANT
7 KILCULLEN
8 NARRAGH AND REBAN WEST
9 NARRAGH AND REBAN EAST
10 ST MULLINS UPPER
11 NORTH LIBERTIES

—— County boundaries
—— Barony boundaries

120

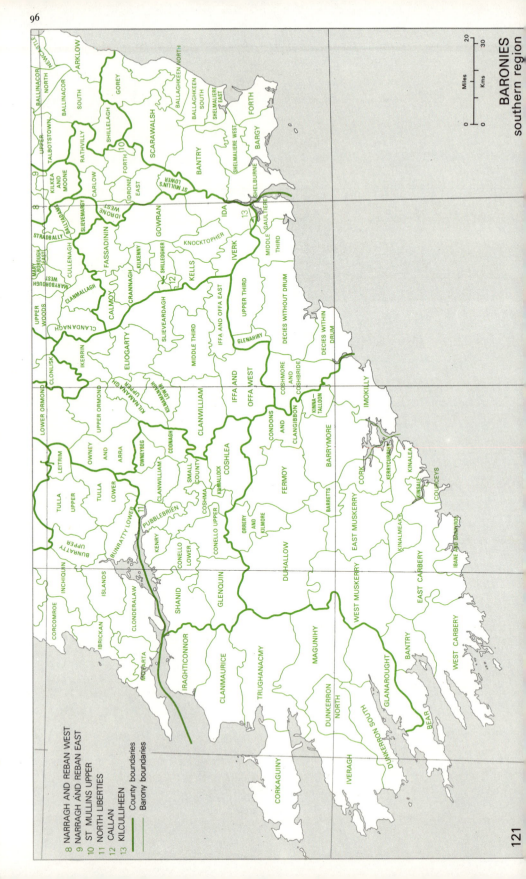

BARONIES
southern region

Miles
Kms

County boundaries
Barony boundaries

121

NOTES TO THE MAPS

1 THE ATLANTIC AND EUROPEAN SETTING
Base adapted from Rand McNally Geo-Physical Globe, copyright Rand-McNally & Company, R.L. 75-GP1-1.

2 RELIEF FEATURES

3 PHYSICAL ELEMENTS, by J. P. Haughton
See J. P. Haughton, 'The physical environment', above, i; Geological Survey of Ireland, *Geological map of Ireland, scale 1:750,000* (3rd ed., Dublin, 1961). Drumlin fields based on F. M. Synge and Nicholas Stephens, 'The quaternary period in Ireland—an assessment, 1960' in *Ir. Geography*, iv (1959–63), fig. 1, p. 123.

4 JANUARY TEMPERATURES, by the Meteorological Service
Based on map supplied by P. K. Rohan, Meteorological Service, Department of Transport and Power, Dublin.

The averages are for the years 1939–60.

5 JULY TEMPERATURES, by the Meteorological Service
Source and note as for 4.

6 MEAN ANNUAL NUMBER OF HOURS OF BRIGHT SUNSHINE, by the Meteorological Service
Source and note as for 4.

7 FREQUENCY OF WIND DIRECTION, by the Meteorological Service
Source and note as for 4.

8 MEAN ANNUAL RAINFALL, by the Meteorological Service
Source and note as for 4.

9 PEAT BOGS, by R. F. Hammond
See Royal Irish Academy, *Atlas of Ireland* (Dublin, 1979), map 'Peat', pp 26–7.

Raised bogs consist of dome-shaped cushions of sphagnum mosses that have developed over fen peats in low-lying areas under the control of atmospheric precipitation. Fen peats without a sphagnum cover are found occupying wet hollows where the conditions are unsuitable for sphagnum. Blanket bogs, as the name suggests, have surfaces that conform to the underlying topography, both upland and lowland, and their extensive occurrence in western areas is related to conditions of high rainfall, high humidity, and low evaporation.

10 COURT TOMBS, by Ruaidhrí de Valera and Seán Ó Nualláin
Redrawn from Ruaidhrí de Valera and Seán Ó Nualláin, *Survey of the megalithic tombs of Ireland* (3 vols., Dublin, 1961–72), ii, map 3.

11 PORTAL TOMBS, by Ruaidhrí de Valera and Seán Ó Nualláin
Redrawn from de Valera and Ó Nualláin, *Survey*, iii, fig. 85.

12 WEDGE TOMBS, by Ruaidhrí de Valera and Seán Ó Nualláin
Redrawn from de Valera and Ó Nualláin, *Survey*, iii, fig. 86.

13 PASSAGE-GRAVE SITES, 2500-2000 B.C., by Michael Herity
Redrawn from Michael Herity, *Irish passage graves: neolithic tomb-builders in Ireland and Britain, 2500 B.C.* (Dublin: Irish University Press, 1974), pp 206-7.

14 PTOLEMY'S MAP OF IRELAND, *c.* 150 A.D., by F. J. Byrne
Based on the reconstruction in Ordnance Survey, *Map of Roman Britain*, scale 16 miles to one inch (3rd ed., 1956), p. 20, from the data in Carl Müller, *Claudii Ptolomaei Geographia* (Paris, 1883), lib. II, cap. ii. See J. G. Rylands, *The geography of Ptolemy elucidated* (Dublin, 1893); G. H. Orpen, 'Ptolemy's map of Ireland' in *R.S.A.I. Jn.*, xxiv (1894), pp 115-28; T. F. O'Rahilly, *Early Irish history and mythology* (Dublin, 1946), pp 1-42; Julius Pokorny, 'Die Geographie Irlands bei Ptolemaios' in *Z.C.P.*, xxix (1954), pp 94-120; J. J. Tierney, 'The Greek geographic tradition and Ptolemy's evidence for Irish geography' in *R.I.A. Proc.*, lxxvi (1976), sect. C, no. 14, pp 257-65. The choice among the variant readings of the proper names has been guided chiefly by O'Rahilly, except for the *Ernaei* (alias *Erdini*, *Erpeditani*), for whom see Alfred Holder, *Alt-keltischer Sprachschatz*, i (Leipzig, 1896; reprint, Graz, 1961), col. 1464.

Ptolemy derived his information about Ireland largely through Marinus of Tyre (*c.* 100 A.D.) from Philemon (*c.* 40 A.D.), though his knowledge of the northern coasts may owe something to surveys made in preparation for Agricola's proposed invasion (*c.* 83 A.D.). The central meridian through Ireland (12° east of the Canaries) is correct relative to London (20° east), which is, however, itself 2° too far east and 2° 30′ too far north. The southern coast of Ireland is placed between 5° and 6° too far north and the northern coast 6° 30′ too far north. The north-east point of Ireland is 2° too far east (probably because it was surveyed from Scotland, which is notoriously distorted by Ptolemy), and the south-west point is similarly 2° too far west, which suggests that it was calculated from Spain, which Ptolemy places too far west.

For more recent discussion of Roman finds, see the papers read at the colloquium on Hiberno-Roman relations and material remains published in *R.I.A. Proc.*, lxxvi (1976), sect. C, nos 6-15, pp 169-292.

15 IRELAND 1ST-5TH CENTURY FROM ROMAN EVIDENCE,
by F. J. Byrne and M. J. O'Kelly
The identifications of sites mentioned by Ptolemy incorporate two emendations: (*a*) the assumption made by Müller on the evidence of Marcian that *Isamnion* was a town and not a cape, and its consequent identification with Emain Machae, as proposed by Pokorny and O'Rahilly; (*b*) the hypothesis that the river-name *Dabrona* is a double error conflating two separate names—that of the *Sabrona* or Lee (O.Ir. *Sabrann*) and that of the *Labrona* or Roughty (O.Ir. *Labrann*). All river-names from the *Iernos* clockwise to the *Argita* should therefore be moved one point north or east. The latter emendation places the *Senos* or Shannon in a recognisably deep estuary and enables the *Libnios* to be identified with the Erne (O.Ir. *Lemain*) and the *Ravios* with the Roe (O.Ir. *Raue, Roa*); the *Argita* may then be identified with either the Bush or the Sixmile Water at Larne. Note that Ptolemy has grossly underestimated the extent of the western coastline between the Shannon and Moy estuaries, which accords with the suggestion made in the previous note that his information on the northern coast derived from a different source than that on the south-west.

16a COIN FINDS: CONCEALMENT DATES, *c.* 150–*c.* 1500, by Michael Dolley

A coin find here defined as two or more coins lost or concealed apparently on the same occasion. Map 15 shows additional sites where single Roman coins have been found.

16b COIN FINDS: CONCEALMENT DATES, *c.* 1500–1826, by Michael Dolley

See 16a. On 5 Jan. 1826 the Anglo-Irish and English currencies were assimilated in accordance with 6 Geo. IV, *c.* 79.

17 THE IRISH ABROAD, *c.* 590–1231, by F. J. Byrne

J. F. Kenney, *The sources for the early history of Ireland*, i (New York, 1929), pp 486–621. For the dates of foundation of the Schottenklöster see Ludwig Hammermayer, 'Die irischen Benediktiner—"Schottenklöster" in Deutschland und ihr institutioneller Zusammenschluss vom 12. bis 16. Jahrhundert' in *Studien und Mitteilungen zur Geschichte des Benediktiner-Ordens und seiner Zweige*, Band 87, Heft iii–iv (Ottobeuren, 1976), pp 249–337.

The term 'Carolingian empire' here refers to the period after the coronation of Charlemagne in 800.

18 POLITICAL DIVISIONS, *c.* 800, by F. J. Byrne

The indispensable source-book for any student of early Irish place-names and political geography is Edmund Hogan, *Onomasticon Goedelicum* (Dublin, 1910). This pioneering work omits very few place-names mentioned in early and medieval Irish literary and historical documents, but needs careful revision. There is no indication to the non-specialist of the date of the sources used, which vary from the seventh to the seventeenth century.

Precise boundaries for all Irish kingdoms at any given date are difficult and sometimes impossible to ascertain. Here, as in map 30 below, only those of the major provincial divisions are tentatively indicated. Reasons of scale do not permit inclusion of all the tribal kingdoms.

By the eighth century, documentary evidence, chiefly that of the annals, genealogies, and hagiography, is full enough to allow a reasonable amount of certainty as to the main political divisions, which had now assumed the 'classical' character that was to remain largely unchanged until the eleventh century. A theoretical division of Ireland into Leth Cuinn ('Conn's half') and Leth Moga ('Mug Nuadat's half') along a line between Dublin and Galway Bay had won general acceptance. The former denoted the hegemony of the descendants of Conn, the Connachta and Uí Néill (to whom the Airgialla and Uí Maini were attached by genealogical fiction), i.e., the supremacy of the high-kings of Tara. It did not, however, include the rump of the ancient province of Ulster, where the Ulaid (Dál Fiatach) and Cruthin (Dál nAraidi and Uí Echach Cobo) maintained their independence east of the river Bann. Mug's half never resulted in a real supremacy of Cashel over the province of Leinster.

19 VIKING RAIDS: THE FIRST GENERATION, 795–836, by F. J. Byrne and Charles Doherty

This and the following three maps are based on an exhaustive collection of all references to viking and Hiberno-Norse activity recorded in *A.F.M.*, *A.U.*, *Ann. Boyle*, *Ann. Clon.*, *Ann. Inisf.*, *Ann. Tig.*, *Chron. Scot.*, as well as 'The Annals of Roscrea', ed. Dermot Gleeson and Seán Mac Airt in *R.I.A. Proc.*, lix (1958), sect. C, no. 3, pp 138–80, all of which can with some confidence be regarded as based on contemporary records. Later literary and saga material has been ignored. However, the opening section (chs. i–xxv) of the twelfth-century text *Cogadh Gaedhel re Gallaibh; The war of the Gaedhil with the Gaill*, ed. J. H. Todd (Rolls series, London, 1867), has been used with caution in the compilation of maps 19 and 20, as it draws on early annalistic material, some of which is no longer extant. For information as to the dates of coins and coin-hoards we are grateful to Professor Michael Dolley. Reasons of space render it impossible to add the date of every battle and raid to maps on this scale.

Note that indisputable examples of Norse place-names are confined to coastal areas, with the exception of Leixlip, Co. Kildare. The queries at Rathlin and Lambay refer to the uncertainty over which of these sites represents the Old Irish *Rechru* or *Rechrainn*.

20 VIKING PENETRATION AND IRISH REACTION, 837–73, by F. J. Byrne and Charles Doherty

Sources as for 19.

Note that the direction of the arrow indicating the attempt by Danes from England in 851 to take over the Norse bases at Dublin, Annagassan, and Carlingford is dictated by artistic convenience; it does not imply that this expedition actually came from southern rather than northern Britain.

21 VIKING WARS AND SETTLEMENTS: THE FORTY YEARS OF PEACE, 874–912, by F. J. Byrne and Charles Doherty

Sources as for 19.

The directions of the arrows for the Danish raids of 875 and 877 do not imply that the expeditions came from southern Britain; see A. P. Smyth, *Scandinavian Dublin and York*, i (Dublin, 1975), pp 18–26. The inland viking encampments on the upper Barrow and Nore were destroyed during this period and never reestablished.

22 VIKING RAIDS, THE SECOND WAVE, 913–*c*. 950; AND HIBERNO-NORSE INTEGRATION, *c*. 950–1014, by F. J. Byrne and Charles Doherty

Sources as for 19.

After *c*. 950 the campaigns mounted by the Hiberno-Norse (such as those of Dublin in north Leinster and Meath) may be viewed rather as incidents in internal Irish politics than as viking raids. Viking raids in the strict sense were carried out in the second half of the tenth century by Danes based in the Hebrides, and were more often than not directed against the Hiberno-Norse towns. The site of the battle of Clontarf, N.E. of Dublin, is marked on this map, but without an arrow to indicate the expedition of Jarl Sigurd of Orkney to aid Dublin and Leinster against Brian Bóruma in the war which is conventionally regarded as the last major incident in Ireland's viking age.

23 CHURCHES AND MONASTERIES, *c*. 900, by F. J. Byrne

Sites based on Aubrey Gwynn and R. N. Hadcock, *Medieval religious houses, Ireland* (London, 1970); Ordnance Survey of Ireland, *Monastic Ireland*, scale 1:625,000 [by R. N. Hadcock] (Dublin, 1959; revised ed., 1965), with revisions. These sources do not always reflect the relative importance of the various churches as shown in the annals and hagiography.

Not all early Irish churches were monasteries: many were mere cells, while others were *Eigenkirchen* attached to the estates of noble families. Some, but not all, early episcopal churches had adopted a monastic constitution by the eighth century, and most of these were absorbed into the Patrician *paruchia* of Armagh. The Columban churches dependent on Iona are listed on the evidence supplied by William Reeves, *The life of St Columba . . . by Adamnan* (Dublin, 1857), pp 276–85. The west Munster saints whose foundations are signalled by the symbol x are Ciarán of Saigir (allegedly pre-Patrician), Brendan of Birr, Brendan of Clonfert, Fínán Camm of Kinnitty, Nessán of Mungret, and Mo Lua of Clonfertmulloe.

It is not certain that all the sites here marked were flourishing at the date given (*c.* 900). The nunnery at Derry, for instance, does not seem to be explicitly mentioned before the twelfth century, while the monastery at Linns on the Co. Louth coast had been destroyed to make way for a viking encampment at Annagassan in the ninth century, a fate which was shared for a time by St Mullins in Co. Wexford where the community seems to have moved to the daughter-house of Timolin, Co. Kildare; see maps 20-22. Many nunneries were ephemeral, and that at Killeady, Co. Limerick, had been replaced by a male monastery at some date before the twelfth century. The query at Ardstraw, Co. Tyrone, refers to the fact that, although claimed as a Patrician church as early as the seventh century, the community seem to have been hostile to Armagh and claimed Bishop Eógan to have been the founder of an independent episcopal church, a status which it enjoyed in the ninth century. The queries at Rathlin and Lambay refer (as in map 19) to the uncertainty as to which of these sites represents the Columban church of *Rechru* or *Rechrainn*.

The Patrician (Armagh) church marked at Kilkenny is not Cell Chainnig itself, which was a church in the *paruchia* of Aghaboe, but Martorthech in Mag Roigni.

24 DIOCESES AS DEFINED AT THE SYNOD OF RÁITH BRESSAIL, 1111, by F. J. Byrne

Our information as to the dioceses set up at this synod and their extent is based upon the lost Book of Clonenagh, as cited by Geoffrey Keating, *Foras feasa ar Éirinn; The history of Ireland*, ed. D. Comyn and P. S. Dinneen (Irish Texts Society, 4 vols, London, 1902-14), iii, 298-307. Gilbert (Gilla-Espuic), bishop of Limerick, who presided as papal legate, had well-defined boundaries for his proposed diocese; the others were only vaguely defined, usually by four named points; the lines between these are marked as axes on the map. Six points are given for Connor and none for Down, but it is apparent that the original four points for each have been conflated by scribal error (the dioceses were briefly united during St Malachy's first episcopate, 1124-32). Four dioceses are given a choice of two sees: Derry-Raphoe; Ardcarne-Ardagh; Lismore-Waterford; Ferns-Wexford. Clonmacnoise was deliberately excluded, but at the synod of Uisnech later in the year it obtained western Mide from Clonard, which then became the see for eastern Mide, Duleek being suppressed (*Chron. Scot.*, 1107 [= 1111]).

25 DIOCESES AS DEFINED AT THE SYNOD OF KELLS-MELLIFONT, 1152, by F. J. Byrne

The book of Clonenagh is one of the main sources, as cited by Keating, *Foras feasa*, iii, 312-17, and by Sir James Ware, *De Hibernia et antiquitatibus ejus* (London, 1654; 2nd ed., 1658), ch. xvi (see B.L., Add. MS 4783, f. 34). Lists of the provincial organisation as defined at the synod are to be found in papal records: the 'Provinciale' of Albinus (Vat. Ottoboni Latinus 3057, written 1188-9 [A]; Montpellier, École de Médecine, MS 92, 12th century [B]) and the 'Liber Censuum' of Cencius Camerarius, dating from 1192 (Vat. Latinus, 8486 [C]); also B.L. Add. MS 4783, f. 60 [D]; Ware, op. cit.). None of these texts, however, gives any indication of the boundaries of the dioceses there established. The tendency in the native sources (as in the Irish annals for long after) is to name the dioceses by their territories rather than by their episcopal sees: thus *Airther Connacht* for Roscommon, *Cenél nEógain* for Ráith Luraig, *Luigne* for Achonry.

For vicissitudes in the history of individual dioceses see the notes to maps 26 and 27 below and also the notes to the succession lists of bishops, 1111-1534 (below, section III).

26 DIOCESES, 1170-1200, SYNODS, 1101-1202, by F. J. Byrne

The *Gesta Regis Henrici Secundi*, ed. William Stubbs (2 vols, London, 1867) gives a complete list of the hierarchy arranged according to the four ecclesiastical provinces, from the submissions of the bishops to Henry II at the second synod of Cashel in 1172. This list, and the Vatican, Montpellier, and Ware texts for the Kells-Mellifont settlement have been conveniently assembled by Breandán Ó Cíobháin in *Dinnseanchas*, v, no. 2 (1972), pp 52-6; the same scholar has collected further documentation on the Irish diocesan system for the twelfth and thirteenth centuries in ibid., v, no. 3 (1973), pp 71-85. The *Gesta* names the four metropolitans and also the suffragans of the Armagh province. Clonmacnoise is again absent, but the synod of Birr (1174) assigned it to the diocese of western Mide (and probably transferred it from the province of Tuam to that of Armagh). Between 1172 and 1200 two new dioceses gained recognition: Annaghdown and Dromore. Note the change of the east Connacht see from Roscommon to Elpin.

It is difficult to ascertain which of the many assemblies mentioned in the sources qualify for recognition as legitimate synods. St Bernard speaks of several synods convened by St Malachy as papal legate (1141-8), but only that of Inis Pátraic is known for certain: the assembly at Terryglass in 1144 (at which he is not recorded as having been present) was a peace conference between Toirrdelbach Ua Conchobair and Toirrdelbach Ua Briain; and the assembly of the Connacht clergy in 1143 was concerned with the reconciliation of Ua Conchobair to his son Ruaidrí. Probably also the assembly of clergy for the consecration of Cormac's chapel at Cashel in 1134 does not rank as a synod, any more than that for the consecration of Mellifont in 1157. The meetings presided over by the high-kings Muirchertach Mac Lochlainn and Ruaidrí Ua Conchobair at Áth na Dairbrige (Derver, north Co. Meath) and Athboy (Co. Meath) in 1161 and 1167 respectively, although they dealt with some matters pertaining to the church, seem to partake of the nature of royal assemblies rather than of synods properly so called. All these have accordingly been ignored on this map.

27 DIOCESES, 1320, by F. X. Martin

Based on Ordnance Survey of Ireland, *Monastic Ireland*.

For the Irish dioceses in 1302-22, see the ecclesiastical taxation of Ireland, edited by H. S. Sweetman and G. F. Handcock in *Calendar of documents relating to Ireland, 1302-1307* (London, 1886), pp ix-xxi, and the qualifications added by G. J. Hand, 'The dating of the early fourteenth-century ecclesiastical valuations of Ireland' in *Ir. Theological Quarterly*, xxiv (1957), pp 271-4. Since the parishes composing the dioceses are listed in the valuations, we can determine precisely the boundaries of these sees. Ossory and Ferns are not included in the valuations but the relevant information about them can be established from W. H. Grattan-Flood, *History of the diocese of Ferns* (Waterford, 1916) and William Carrigan, *History and antiquities of the diocese of Ossory* (4 vols, Dublin, 1905).

For the evolution, amalgamation, and disappearance of Irish dioceses in the medieval period, see the notes to the succession lists of bishops, 1111-1534 (below, section III). For the tangled problems of the western dioceses, see H. T. Knox, *Notes on the early history of the dioceses of Tuam, Killala, and Achonry* (Dublin, 1904), which also includes information on the dioceses of Mayo and Annaghdown and the wardenship of Galway. For the proposals and negotiations during 1325-7 for amalgamation of various dioceses, see the documents published by John Hagan in *Archiv. Hib.*, vi (1917), pp 132-42, and the commentary by J. A. Watt, 'Negotiations between Edward II and John XXII concerning Ireland' in *I.H.S.*, x, no. 37 (Mar. 1956), pp 1-20; J. A. Watt, *The church and the two nations in medieval Ireland* (Cambridge, 1970), pp 192-6.

1320 is the earliest date at which ecclesiastical boundaries can be shown.

28 THE INTRODUCTION OF THE CONTINENTAL RELIGIOUS
ORDERS: GAELIC FOUNDATIONS, *c.* 1127–1227, by Marie-Thérèse
Flanagan

Sites based on Aubrey Gwynn and R. N. Hadcock, *Medieval religious houses, Ireland;*
Ordnance Survey of Ireland, *Monastic Ireland;* Peter Harbison, *Guide to the national
monuments of Ireland* (2nd ed., London, 1975); Lord Killanin and M. V. Duignan, *Shell
guide to Ireland* (revised ed., London, 1967).

The Irish annals provide some information on foundation dates of Irish houses. Charters
of foundation and/or confirmation are extant for many of the Norman houses. These
provide precise details of the site and dates of foundation. A few original documents have
survived. The majority of texts, however, are later copies, to be found principally in
cartularies and enrolments of the Irish and English chanceries. They are scattered through
a wide series of publications, but a number have been collected in W. Dugdale, *Monasticon
Anglicanum*, vi, pt 2 (London, 1830), pp 1123–49. Papal confirmations to Irish monastic
houses may be conveniently consulted in M. P. Sheehy, *Pontificia Hibernica* (2 vols,
Dublin, 1962–5). The Cistercian order kept tables of the dates of foundation of its houses,
and the Irish evidence has been examined and collated by Gearóid Mac Niocaill, *Na
manaigh liatha in Éirinn, 1142–c. 1600* (Baile Atha Cliath, 1959). Information including
maps for the Augustinian houses that followed the Arroasian observance is to be found in
L. Mills, *L'ordre des chanoines réguliers d'Arrouaise* (2 vols, Brugge, 1969). Useful evidence
for the adoption of the Arroasian observance by a number of Irish houses in the twelfth
century is afforded by the breviary of St Mary's Abbey, Trim, which reflects twelfth-century
custom; see Aubrey Gwynn, 'A breviary from St Mary's abbey, Trim' in *Ríocht na
Midhe*, ii (1963–6), pp 290–98. Romanesque architectural remains are also a useful indication
of twelfth-century foundation. Romanesque sites have been listed by Liam de Paor,
'Cormac's chapel: the beginnings of Irish romanesque' in Etienne Rynne (ed.), *North
Munster Studies: essays in commemoration of Monsignor Michael Moloney* (Limerick 1967),
pp 133–45.

Help is acknowledged with thanks from Professor F. J. Byrne.

29 THE INTRODUCTION OF THE CONTINENTAL RELIGIOUS
ORDERS: NORMAN FOUNDATIONS, *c.* 1177–1277, by Marie-
Thérèse Flanagan

Sources and notes as for 28.

30 POLITICAL DIVISIONS, *c.* 1169, by F. J. Byrne

Sources as for 18.

In the twelfth century the boundaries of the medieval dioceses are a useful guide to the
extent of many of the over-kingdoms, while the barony divisions in the midlands, Leinster,
and Munster usually reflect the lesser political units of pre-Norman Ireland, but all
attempts to draw precise borders for this period must remain approximations. The
twelfth century saw great changes in Irish political geography and many boundaries were
in a state of flux at the time of the Norman invasion.

31 THE SPREAD OF THE RELIGIOUS ORDERS, 1169–1320, by F. X.
Martin

Gwynn and Hadcock, *Medieval religious houses: Ireland.*

32 THE SPREAD OF THE RELIGIOUS ORDERS, 1320–1420, by F. X.
Martin

Source as for 31.

33 THE SPREAD OF THE RELIGIOUS ORDERS, 1420–1534, by F. X. Martin

Source as for 31.

34 THE DISSOLUTION OF THE RELIGIOUS HOUSES, 1534–*c*. 1610, by Brendan Bradshaw

Based on Ordnance Survey of Ireland, *Monastic Ireland*. The chronology of the dissolution is based on Gwynn and Hadcock, *Medieval religious houses: Ireland*, except where a different conclusion is reached in Brendan Bradshaw, *The dissolution of the religious orders in Ireland under Henry VIII* (Cambridge, 1973).

The date of dissolution shown is that on which the property was appropriated by the crown, even though the religious community itself may have survived, as at Multyfarnham, Kilcullen, Kilmallock, and Ennis (Bradshaw, op. cit., pp 140–45, 166–7, 170–71). Patents that never took effect are disregarded. Some religious communities were transformed into colleges of secular priests before their final dissolution as here shown.

35 MOTTES, by R. E. Glasscock

G. H. Orpen, *Ireland under the Normans, 1169–1333* (4 vols, Oxford, 1911–20); R. E. Glasscock, 'Mottes in Ireland' in *Château Gaillard*, vii (1974), pp 95–110; T. E. McNeill, 'Ulster mottes: a checklist' in *Ulster Journal of Archaeology*, xxxviii (1975), pp 49–59.

The first castles built by the Anglo-Normans were of wood surrounded by a palisade, on top of an artificial mound known as a motte; sometimes an already existing mound was used, as, for instance, in the case of the neolithic burial mound at Knowth.

Help is acknowledged with thanks from B. J. Graham, the late N. W. English, and other local correspondents.

36 STONE CASTLES OF NORMAN TYPE BEFORE *c*. 1320, by R. E. Glasscock

Based mainly on H. G. Leask, *Irish castles and castellated houses* (revised ed., Dundalk, 1951).

Some of the castles named have been removed completely, and there are only fragmentary remains of others.

37 PRINCIPAL TOWNS AND MANORS, *c*. 1300, by R. E. Glasscock and K. W. Nicholls

Calendar of documents relating to Ireland, 1293–1301, 1302–7 (London, 1881, 1886); J. T. Gilbert (ed.), *Historical and municipal documents of Ireland, A.D. 1172–1320* (London, 1870); Orpen, *Normans*; A. J. Otway-Ruthven, 'The character of Norman settlement in Ireland' in *Hist. Studies*, v (1965), pp 75–84; A. J. Otway-Ruthven, 'The medieval county of Kildare' in *I.H.S.*, xi (1958–9), pp 181–99; Gearóid Mac Niocaill, *Na buirgéisí, XII–XV aois* (Baile Atha Cliath, 1964).

For recent work in this field see B. J. Graham, 'The towns of medieval Ireland' in R. A. Butlin (ed.), *The development of the Irish town* (London, 1977), pp 28–60; B. J. Graham, 'The evolution of urbanization in medieval Ireland' in *Journal of Historical Geography*, v (1979), pp 111–25.

38 EARLY DUBLIN, 790–1170, by H. B. Clarke and Anngret Simms

Based on many sources. See Breandán Ó Riordáin, 'Excavations at High Street and Winetavern Street, Dublin' in *Medieval Archaeology*, xv (1971), pp 73–85; National Museum of Ireland, *Viking and medieval Dublin* (Dublin, 1973); H. B. Clarke, 'The topographical development of early medieval Dublin' in *R.S.A.I. Jn.*, cvii (1977), pp 29–51.

The early medieval coastline is shown as the boundary between alluvium and boulder clay taken from the drift map of the six-inch Geological Survey of Ireland (1915). This does not rule out the possibility of early medieval settlement on the alluvium, for the Viking Long Stone and the later priory of All Saints were erected on slob land that was presumably dry and firm for most of the time. (According to Professor John de Courcy, some correlation may exist between the modern 16.5 foot O.D. contour and the coastline in the middle ages.) The River Liffey was certainly much broader than it is now and therefore shallower, but the way in which tidal movements influenced the configuration of the estuary is difficult to estimate. The contours, at five-foot intervals, were surveyed only recently and may have been modified locally by building activities, particularly in Georgian areas of the modern city. The western end of a narrow ridge of boulder clay was probably the site of the primary settlement in this district, perhaps a small fishing village, called *Áth Cliath*. The exact location of the nearby ford is unknown: the alignment on the map is suggested on purely topographical grounds.

The topography of early medieval Dublin was also influenced by the presence of the River Poddle. Its lower reaches were tidal and a pool on the site of the present castle gardens may have been scoured out by tidal movements. South of the pool, the modern street pattern is strongly reminiscent of ecclesiastical enclosures as they are known from air photographs of monastic sites in Ireland. This street outline corresponds to the boundary of the Anglo-Norman parish of St Peter, which is presumptive evidence that St Peter's was the principal church within the enclosure. Nearby, to the west and south, lay a number of other churches with Irish dedications, together with three holy wells. The suggestion is, therefore, that monastic *Dubhlinn*, taking its name from the adjacent pool, was situated between the Poddle and the Steine. This would explain why the sources refer to two Irish place-names in this district. There were two distinct settlements: the purely secular *Áth Cliath* and the ecclesiastical or quasi-ecclesiastical *Dubhlinn*. The death of Abbot Siadal in 790 is the earliest datable reference to Dublin and is therefore taken as the starting date for this map.

Dubhlinn was the name adopted by the vikings for their stronghold constructed across the pool from the Irish churches. The viking settlement has been depicted at its greatest extent: the initial stronghold was almost certainly smaller and is likely to have been located on the eastern part of the ridge. The most recent archaeological excavations (1978) on the western side of Fishamble Street have revealed a series of earthen banks and a large number of superimposed wooden houses. The earliest features on this site date back to the first half of the tenth century. Access to the bridge north-west of the later town must have been by means of causeways built over the sloblands.

Help is acknowledged with thanks from Patrick Healy, Breandán Ó Riordáin, A. J. Otway-Ruthven, Thomas Reilly, Patrick Wallace, and Peter Walsh.

39 MEDIEVAL DUBLIN, 1170-1542, by H. B. Clarke and Anngret Simms

Based on many sources. For a more detailed map see Ordnance Survey of Ireland, *Dublin c. 840 to c. 1540: the medieval town in the modern city* (Dublin, 1978), scale 1 : 2,500. See also John Speed, *The theatre of the empire of Great Britaine . . .* (London, 1611), inset to map following p. 141; Allen and Sons, *Map of Dublin with the parishes and the other divisions accurately laid down* (3rd ed., Dublin, 1826); C. T. McCready, *Dublin street names, dated and explained* (Dublin, 1892); M. V. Ronan, 'The Poddle river and its branches' in *R.S.A.I. Jn.*, lvii (1927), pp 39-46; J. B. Maguire, 'Seventeenth-century plans of Dublin Castle' in *R.S.A.I. Jn.*, civ (1974), pp 5-14; P. F. Wallace, 'Wood Quay, the growth of thirteenth-century Dublin' in *Dublin Arts Festival 1976* (Dublin, 1976), pp 22-4; Anngret Simms, 'Medieval Dublin: a topographical analysis' in *Ir. Geography*, xii (1979), pp 25-41.

Hiberno-Norse Dublin came under Anglo-Norman control on 21 September 1170. The late medieval coastline has been conjectured on the basis of John Speed's map of Dublin in the early seventeenth century. Archaeological evidence demonstrates how, from *c.* 1200 onwards, the river-bed was filled in progressively by the construction of post-and-wattle walls on the river parallel to the original town wall. Whether the final quay-wall was effectively fortified under the threat of attack by Robert Bruce in 1317 is uncertain: Prickett's Tower is the only known wall-tower between Bridge Gate and Fyan's Castle. Most of the streets that are documented for the medieval period have been plotted and the principal streets named (several had more than one name). Other streets are recorded, but their location is unknown. The outline of the castle is based on a detailed plan of 1673. As Dublin had no central market-place, streets with special market functions are distinguished on the map. The boundaries of the five liberties (areas of private jurisdiction) are shown as they existed in the early nineteenth century. These boundaries probably differed very little from those of the middle ages. Most of the liberty of Christ Church was situated north of the Liffey, beyond the limits of this map. The map terminates in 1542, when an act of parliament (33 Hen. VIII, sess. 2, c. 5) provided for the suppression of religious houses.

Help is acknowledged with thanks as for 38.

40 DUBLIN, *c.* 1685, by J. H. Andrews and K. M. Davies

Based largely upon Thomas Phillips, 'An exact survey of the City of Dublin and part of the harbour anno 1685' (B.L., K. op 53, 8 and 9; National Library of Ireland, MS 2557). See also Bernard de Gomme, 'The city and suburbs of Dublin, 1673' (National Maritime Museum, Greenwich, Dartmouth collection, 11); Thomas Dineley's drawing of Trinity College, Dublin, 1680 (N.L.I., MS 392), reproduced above, iii, facing p. 450.

The street pattern shown by Phillips has been somewhat simplified. On some copies of Phillips, Arran Bridge (built 1681; see J. T. Gilbert, *History of the city of Dublin*, (3 vols, Dublin, 1859), i, 388) is omitted, and two other non-existent bridges are shown. Phillips also shows Ormond Bridge too far to the east, and this has been rectified.

Help is acknowledged with thanks from E. J. McParland and the late J. G. Simms.

41 DUBLIN, *c.* 1800, by J. H. Andrews and K. M. Davies

Based on William Wilson, *Modern plan of the city and environs of Dublin* (London and Dublin, 1798).

The Royal Circus was not in fact built.

42 DUBLIN, *c.* 1840–1976, by K. M. Davies with J. P. Haughton

Based on the Ordnance Survey by permission of the government (permit no. 2865).

Ordnance Survey, *County Dublin*, sheets nos 13–26, scale 1 : 10,560 (Dublin, 1843); Ordnance Survey, *County Dublin*, sheets nos 13–26, scale 1 : 10,560 (Dublin, 1910–12); Ordnance Survey of Ireland, *Dublin*, scale 1 : 25,000 (Dublin, 1948); Ordnance Survey of Ireland, *Dublin district*, scale 1 : 63,360 (Dublin, 1974); built-up areas in 1976 based on material supplied by the assistant director, Ordnance Survey of Ireland; S. Maxwell Hajducki, *A railway atlas of Ireland* (Newton Abbot, 1974), pp 21–2, 38; information from Coras Iompair Eireann. See also R. C. Flewitt, 'The Hill of Howth tramway, G.N.R.' in *Journal of the Irish Railway Record Society*, vii (1965), pp 90–105; A. T. Newham, 'The Dublin and Lucan tramway' (locomotion paper no. 29), Oakwood Press ([1964]), pp 1–40; A. T. Newham, 'The Dublin & Blessington steam tramway' in *Journal of the Irish Railway Record Society*, iii (1954), pp 181–200.

The built-up areas are simplified. This is particularly true of Dun Laoghaire county borough where the pattern of development was complex, but where the map is designed to show the early development along the coast and the recent rapid growth of suburbs in adjoining areas of south County Dublin. A significant part of the growth of the city shown as occurring between 1908 and 1943 consisted of corporation housing schemes under way in the 1940s, which extended the city into Crumlin and neighbouring districts to the south-west and Cabra to the north-west, together with a number of areas (e.g. Marino, to the south-west of Killester) on the north-east side.

The south city site in Earlsfort Terrace occupied by University College, Dublin, was that of the 'Great Exhibition' of 1865. The exhibition buildings were taken over and extended to serve as the headquarters of the Royal University (1880-1909). University College, as provided for by the Irish Universities Act, 1908, was housed in the Royal University buildings and in new buildings erected close by.

The map shows both passenger and freight railway lines operating in 1976 (those in the harbour area are simplified). The branch line to Howth is open to passenger traffic only, while the inner of the two lines circling north-eastern Dublin and all lines in the harbour area are open to freight traffic only.

In addition to the three tramways shown, a network of tram routes served the city and the south-eastern suburbs as far as Dalkey: the first routes were opened in 1872 and the last tram ran in 1949.

43 COUNTIES AND LIBERTIES, 1297, by K. W. Nicholls

The only general survey (though outdated) of the formation of the counties is that by C. Litton Falkiner: 'The counties of Ireland: their origin, constitution and gradual delimitation' in *Illustrations of Irish history and topography* (London, 1904), pp 103-42. For the medieval Irish counties, see A. J. Otway-Ruthven, 'Anglo-Irish shire government in the thirteenth century' in *I.H.S.*, v, no. 17 (Mar. 1946), pp 1-28; A. J. Otway-Ruthven, 'The medieval county of Kildare' in *I.H.S.*, xi, no. 43 (Mar. 1959), pp 181-99, and map; A. J. Otway-Ruthven, *A history of medieval Ireland* (London, 1968), pp 173-87.

Contemporary records, especially the justiciary and plea rolls, provide evidence for the location of a particular place within a particular county. For the actual boundary lines, those of the ecclesiastical divisions—dioceses and rural deaneries—have been followed in the absence of other information. The boundaries of the rural deaneries normally coincided with those of the cantreds, the sub-units of the co-administration.

The liberty of Trim and the county of Meath, representing respectively the Geneville and Verdon shares of the lordship of Meath, were inextricably intermingled. For their limits the map by A. J. Otway-Ruthven ('The partition of the de Verdon lands in Ireland in 1332' in *R.I.A. Proc.*, lxvi (1968), sect. C, no. 5, pp 401-55), has been followed with some slight modifications, but there must have been a number of enclaves within the liberty of Trim belonging to the county. The county of Meath was created in 1297; previously its territory was reckoned as part of Co. Dublin.

Within all the liberties the cross or church lands were exempt from the liberty jurisdiction. Those in the Leinster liberties were reckoned as part of Co. Dublin; those in Trim belonged until 1297 to Dublin and after that date to Meath. The cross lands included some areas of considerable extent, but were for the most part scattered in fragments too small to be plotted on a map of this scale.

Although the five sub-counties of the liberty of Ulster are shown on this map, it is possible that their emergence as counties rather than bailiwicks belongs to the opening years of the fourteenth century. They were in existence by 1333.

The boundaries between the liberties of Kildare and Wexford and the county of Dublin are only tentative; the liberty of Wexford is taken as coterminous with the diocese of Ferns and the eastern extension of the liberty (later county) of Kildare as comprising those portions of the rural deaneries of Arklow and Wicklow which were not within the cross of Dublin.

44 COUNTIES AND LIBERTIES, 1460, by K. W. Nicholls

See above, iii, pp 1-25. C. A. Empey and Katharine Simms, 'The ordinances of the White Earl and the problem of coign in the later middle ages' in *R.I.A. Proc.*, lxxv (1975), sect. C, no. 8, pp 161-87.

The outer boundaries of the counties and liberties have been delimited by the known existence of Gaelic or gaelicised lordships where the shire or liberty administration did not function. Although nominal sheriffs of Connacht and Cork continued to be appointed throughout the fifteenth century, there is no evidence that they exercised any effective authority. In Limerick the sheriff's authority was confined to the central and eastern portion of the county. Kerry was a liberty of the earls of Desmond, while Waterford had a line of hereditary sheriffs whose authority, limited to the eastern portion of the county, was often exercised in defiance of crown and parliament. Tipperary was a recognised liberty of the earls of Ormond, but although Kilkenny and the crosslands of Co. Tipperary were in theory subject to royal jurisdiction, they had from before 1430 been annexed to the Ormond liberty. Wexford was a liberty of the earl of Shrewsbury. The liberty of Ulster was formally united to the crown by the accession of Edward IV but retained its theoretical status under a nominal seneschal. Only the counties of Dublin, Louth (or Uriel), Meath, Kildare, and (perhaps) Carlow can be said to have functioned fully as units of the royal administration, although the authority of the sheriff of Dublin in the foothills south of Dublin must have been at best exiguous.

45 COUNTIES, 1542-1613, by K. W. Nicholls

See Litton Falkiner, 'The counties of Ireland', note 43 above.

The dates given for the formation of counties are those of their official creation, where known; where no formal instrument survives, the date given is that indicated by contemporary evidence of their existence. The formal creation of a county, however, did not necessarily involve its functioning as such; it is doubtful whether the counties of Armagh and Tyrone, for example, functioned to any extent before 1603. Of the ephemeral counties, Desmond presents little difficulty: documentary evidence survives for its formation in 1571 and for its annexation to Kerry in 1606. No formal instrument of creation survives for the county of Ferns, but it was in existence by 1579 and returned members to the parliament of 1586; it seems to have disappeared soon after, the area being reannexed to Co. Wexford (although certain places in the extreme north of the merged counties are sometimes referred to as being in Co. Carlow, to which Arklow then belonged). The county of Wicklow created in 1577 seems not to have functioned and ceased to exist some time after 1586, a somewhat larger county of that name being recreated in 1606.

A number of minor changes took place in the boundaries of medieval counties, as in those of Cork with Limerick and Waterford. The medieval boundary between Limerick and Tipperary would seem to have been completely forgotten, owing no doubt to the emergence of autonomous Gaelic lordships which straddled it. The present boundary seems to have emerged in the early Elizabethan period, leaving the district of Arra, in the north-west of Co. Tipperary, unshired until it was annexed to the county of the cross of Tipperary in 1606. The latter otherwise consisted of a number of detached portions whose exact limits are difficult to discover, but which included the towns of Cashel and Fethard. The cross of Tipperary was merged with Co. Tipperary for practical purposes in 1621, when the liberty was taken into the hands of the crown; it was formally annexed in 1662.

The date 1570 for the formal erection of Co. Clare is rather misleading, as a sheriff of Thomond had already existed for some years; but at this date Clare was annexed to the province of Connacht, where it remained until the restoration. Co. Cavan is referred to as newly erected in 1579, but does not seem to have been fully operational until 1584.

County Tyrone, as constituted in 1591, included also the area subsequently formed in 1603 into the county of Coleraine.

County boundaries were largely stabilised by 1613, although minor changes have been made since, notably by the local government act of 1898.

46 THE PALE, 1488-1537, by K. W. Nicholls

The boundaries of the Pale were defined by an act of parliament in 1488 (4 Hen. VII, c. 1); see Charles McNeill (ed.), *Calendar of Archbishop Alen's register, c. 1172-1534* (Dublin, 1950), pp 250-51; John D'Alton, *History of the county of Dublin* (Dublin, 1838), p. 34. By an act of Poynings' parliament, 1494 (10 Hen. VII, c. 34, printed in Agnes Conway, *Henry VII's relations with Scotland and Ireland, 1485-1498* (Cambridge, 1932), pp 215-16), a ditch and rampart were ordered to be constructed along what appears to have been the line defined in 1488; part of this line, however (that stretching south-westward from Tallaght in Co. Dublin), had already been provided with a defensive earthwork before 1475 (see *Statute rolls of the parliament of Ireland, 12th and 13th to the 21st and 22nd years of the reign of King Edward IV*, ed. James F. Morrissey (Dublin, 1939), pp 442-5), and it is possible that other portions had also been fortified. Justice Luttrell, writing in 1537, defined a narrower area (marked on the map), outside which the gentry were accustomed to exact coyne and livery from their tenants (*State papers, Henry VIII* (11 vols, London, 1830-52) ii, 500).

The boundary of the 'maghery' (*machaire*), the area in which the common law and the authority of the Dublin administration effectively functioned, has been defined by the existence of autonomous Gaelic or gaelicised lordships.

47 ANGLO-IRISH AND GAELIC LORDSHIPS IN THE LATE 15TH CENTURY, by K. W. Nicholls

For a general explanation see above, iii, 4-19. See also the more detailed map of lordships, ibid., pp 2-3.

48 SIXTEENTH-CENTURY PLANTATIONS, by K. W. Nicholls

See above, iii, 77-9, 95-7, 113-15.

The area shown for the Leix-Offaly plantation includes, in its east-central part, the district of Clanmaliere, which in fact was regranted *in toto* to its native possessors, the O'Dempseys.

Sir Thomas Smith's plantation in the Ards left no permanent traces, even in the legal title to the area. While the Essex plantation in Antrim was in general a failure, it was responsible for a small degree of new settlement in the Carrickfergus area (perhaps exaggerated on the map).

The Desmond plantation differed from the others shown in that it only extended to forfeited lands intermingled with others which remained unforfeited and in the possession of the original owners; only in some few parts of the area indicated, therefore, was the totality of the land included in the plantation. For the same reasons, the areas marked are only approximate.

The Monaghan settlement of 1592 consisted of a redistribution of the land on an entirely new basis among the existing native chiefs and landowners; only a few minimal holdings were reserved for new settlers. The portion of Co. Monaghan not included in the settlement, the barony of Farney (left unshaded), had been granted in 1575 to the earl of Essex (but not under plantation conditions); it does not seem to have been effectively occupied by his heirs until after 1603.

49 PARLIAMENTARY CONSTITUENCIES, 1560–86, by T. W. Moody

T. W. Moody, 'The Irish parliament under Elizabeth and James I' in *R.I.A. Proc.*, xlv (1939), sect. C, no. 6, pp 41–81, and sources there cited.

In 1560 election writs were issued to 20 counties and 29 towns. The counties comprised the modern counties of Leinster, except Wicklow and Longford; the modern counties of Munster; Connacht, treated as a single county; and in Ulster the counties of Antrim, Down, and the Ards. Ten counties (King's, Queen's, Cork, Kerry, Limerick, Clare, Connacht, Antrim, Down, and the Ards) and one town (Kilmallock) appear not to have returned members.

In 1585 Connacht and the Ards disappear from the county constituencies and nine new counties appear: Wicklow, Ferns, and Longford; Cross Tipperary; Galway, Mayo, Sligo, and Roscommon; Cavan. Ferns and Cross Tipperary were respectively the portions of Wexford and Tipperary outside the palatine jurisdiction in those counties and directly administered by the crown. The towns receiving writs included all those on the 1560 list (except Athy) and eight additional towns.

50 PARLIAMENTARY CONSTITUENCIES, 1604–1800, by T. W. Moody

Moody, 'Irish parliament'; J. C. Beckett, *The making of modern Ireland* (London, 1966), map of parliamentary cities and boroughs; J. H. Andrews, above, iii, 454–77.

By 1613, when the first Irish parliament of the century met, the county constituencies (except Cross Tipperary, which continued until 1634) had all assumed their modern form. Trinity College, Dublin, had been given the right to return two members. Between 1604 and 1613 the number of towns entitled to send members was more than doubled (from 37 to 77). By 1692 the total stood at 117, and there it remained till the extinction of the Irish parliament in 1800. From 1692 to 1800 the constituencies as a whole thus numbered 150.

In this map the names of towns that appear on map 49 are not repeated, though their locations are shown.

51 IRISH COLLEGES ABROAD, *c.* 1590–*c.* 1800, by J. J. Silke

See above, iii, 587–633.

Bordeaux secular college had offshoots at Perigueux, Cahors, Agen, Condom, and Auch. Cologne was founded as an Irish college, but became the centre of a Capuchin mission. Sedan was also the centre of a Capuchin mission to France, where Irish Capuchins gained practical experience.

Irish students attended the English colleges at Douai (founded 1568), Valladolid (1589), Seville (1589), and St Omer (1592–3), and the Scots college, founded at Paris (1580), transferred to Pont-à-Mousson (1581–90), and reopened at Douai in 1593. Irish regular clergy were trained at the houses of their brethren all over Europe.

52 FORESTS, *c.* 1600, by Eileen McCracken

Redrawn from Eileen McCracken, 'The woodlands of Ireland *circa* 1600' in *I.H.S.*, xi, no. 44 (Sept. 1959), p. 272; see also her *The Irish woods since Tudor times* (Newton Abbot, 1971).

These forests are deciduous hardwoods, principally oak and ash, with hazel, holly, alder, and willow.

53 STATE FORESTS, 1966, by Eileen McCracken

Redrawn from McCracken, *Ir. woods*, map 9, pp 144–5, by permission of David and Charles. The state forests are almost all coniferous, with sitka spruce, lodgepole pine, and

Norway spruce as the main species. The amount of natural deciduous woodland that has survived is negligible. Woods in private hands are mostly deciduous plantations on old estates; they cover about 90,000 acres and are scattered and individually of too small extent to be shown on a map of this scale.

54 THE ULSTER PLANTATION, 1609-13, by T. W. Moody and R. J. Hunter
Irish patent rolls of James I: facsimile of the Irish record commissioners' calendar prepared prior to 1830, with foreword by M. C. Griffith (I.M.C., Dublin, 1966); 'Ulster plantation papers, 1608-13', ed. T. W. Moody, in *Anal. Hib.*, no. 8 (1938); T. W. Moody, *The Londonderry plantation, 1609-41* (Belfast, 1939); R. J. Hunter, 'The Ulster plantation in the counties of Armagh and Cavan' (M.Litt. thesis, T.C.D., 1969); J. G. Simms, 'Donegal in the Ulster plantation' in *Ir. Geography*, vi, no. 4 (1972), pp 386-93; J. H. Andrews, 'The maps of the escheated counties of Ulster, 1609-10' in *R.I.A. Proc.*, lxxiv (1974), sect. C, no. 4, pp 133-70; P. S. Robinson, 'The plantation of County Tyrone in the seventeenth century' (Ph.D. thesis, Q.U.B., 1974).

The map shows the broad pattern of the plantation arrangements in the six escheated counties in terms of plantation 'precincts'. These correspond with modern baronies, or represent subdivisions of baronies (e.g. Doe + Fanad = Kilmacrenan), or combinations of baronies (e.g. Knockninny = Knockninny + Coole). Mountjoy and Dungannon represent subdivisions of the then barony of Dungannon, now represented by the three baronies, Upper, Middle, and Lower Dungannon. In general each precinct was assigned to one of the three classes of grantees specified in the key to the map. But there were important exceptions to this principle of appropriation.

(1) In each of the six counties the former 'termon and erenagh' land, which was interspersed among the lands granted to the planters, was assigned almost entirely to the bishops of the established church. In Londonderry, church land amounted to 23% of the whole area, in Armagh to 20%, and in Cavan to 10%.

(2) Certain grants made shortly before the plantation were not interfered with. These included lands granted in 1603 to Sir Turlough McHenry O'Neill in the Fews, and in 1605 to Sir Henry Óg O'Neill in Tiranny and Dungannon; and lands of dissolved monasteries, granted for the most part to servitors, which in County Armagh amounted to almost 10% of the whole county, mainly in the baronies of Armagh, the Fews and Orior.

(3) Under the plantation scheme lands were assigned to corporate towns and a free-school in each county; and Trinity College, Dublin, received 95,000 acres in Counties Armagh, Donegal and Fermanagh.

(4) An area marked out for exceptional treatment was the county of Londonderry, formed in 1613 as a combination of (*a*) the former county of Coleraine, (*b*) the barony of Loughinsholin, detached from Tyrone (except the south-west corner), (*c*) Derry and its north-western liberties, and (*d*) Coleraine and its north-eastern liberties. All the temporal land in this county, except an area of 4% granted to a servitor, Sir Thomas Phillips, and 10% to native Irish, went to the city of London under a special agreement of 28 January 1610.

(5) Five exceptional baronies were: (*a*) Inishowen, granted (except the church land) to Sir Arthur Chichester, the lord deputy, in February 1610; (*b*) Tirhugh, where Trinity College had 25% of the area and the rest was divided between the church, servitors, native Irish, a school, and Ballyshannon fort; (*c*) Armagh, half of which went to Trinity College and the rest to the church and to servitors; (*d*) Tiranny, mainly granted to the church and to native Irish; (*e*) Magheraystephana, where the greater part of the temporal land was granted to Conor Roe Maguire and the rest to a Scottish undertaker, Lord Burley.

(6) Two other exceptional areas were (a) the south-west corner of Loughinsholin, which, detached from the rest of the barony in 1613, when the county of Londonderry was formed, and added to Dungannon barony, was granted principally to the archbishop of Armagh and a native grantee, Brian Crossagh O'Neill; (b) the southern half of Fews barony, which went to Sir Turlough McHenry O'Neill (see (2) above).

(7) In Co. Cavan native Irish grantees received 10% of the land in Loughtee (assigned to English undertakers), and Old English owners held 14% of the county, mainly in Clanmahon, Castlerahan, and Clankee.

Help is acknowledged with thanks from P. S. Robinson.

55 PLANTATIONS IN THE REIGN OF JAMES I (1603-25), by Aidan Clarke
See above, iii, 187-232.

56 THE CROMWELLIAN LAND CONFISCATION, 1652-7, by P. J. Corish
See above, iii, 360-75.

57 LAND OWNED BY CATHOLICS, 1641, 1688, 1703, by J. G. Simms
See above, iii, 422-9. See also T. W. Moody and F. X. Martin (ed.), *The course of Irish history* (Cork and New York, 1967), p. 201.

58 CANALS AND NAVIGATIONS, 1715-1876, by D. R. Delany and W. A. McCutcheon
V. T. H. Delany and D. R. Delany, *The canals of the south of Ireland* (Newton Abbot, 1966), pp 228-35. W. A. McCutcheon, *The canals of the north of Ireland* (Dawlish and London, 1965), pp 168-73. See also W. A. McCutcheon, 'Inland navigations in the north of Ireland' in *Technology and Culture*, vi, no. 4 (1965), pp 596-620; K. B. Nowlan (ed.), *Travel and transport in Ireland* (Dublin, 1973); individual canal histories.

59 BELFAST, 1660, by P. G. Cleary
Street patterns, principal buildings, gardens, and ramparts based on two sources. (1) An anonymous map of Belfast, reputed to be the earliest surviving map of the town, and ascribed to 1660 in the early nineteenth century: see John Dubourdieu, *A statistical survey of the county of Antrim* (Dublin, 1812); it may be a reproduction of a plan contained in Thomas Phillips, 'Survey of the fortifications of towns and harbours of Ireland', c. 1685, P.R.O.N.I., T1720. (2) Thomas Phillips, 'The ground plan of Belfast and the design for erecting a citadel upon the strand, anno 1685', P.R.O.N.I., T 8 22.

Area around Belfast based on 'Map of Belfast Lough, c. 1570', P.R.O., M.P.F. 77; P.R.O.N.I., T1493/41; G. Collins, 'Hydrographic survey of Carrickfergus Lough [Belfast Lough], 1693', P.R.O.N.I., D754/2; 'Plan of the town of Belfast, anno 1757', P.R.O.N.I., T1541/7; Francis Dobbs, 'A plan of the attack and defence of the town of Belfast, by the volunteers, on the 20th July 1781', reproduced in George Benn, *A history of the town of Belfast from the earliest times to the close of the eighteenth century* (London, 1877), facing p. 630; James Lawson, 'Map of Belfast Lough with a plan of the town of Belfast, 1789', P.R.O.N.I., D671/P10/2.

For the dating of these maps, see Lavens M. Ewart, 'Belfast maps' in *Ulster Journal of Archaeology*, series II, i (1895), pp 62-9; J. H. Andrews, 'Christopher Saxton and Belfast Lough' in *Ir. Geography*, v, pt 3 (1965), pp 1-5.

60 BELFAST, 1800, by P. G. Cleary

James Williamson, *A map of the town and environs of Belfast, taken to a distance of one Irish mile from the Exchange, surveyed in 1791* (Belfast and Dublin: Marcus Ward & Co., 1863).

61 BELFAST, 1900, by P. G. Cleary

Ordnance Survey, *County Antrim*, sheets 56-65, *County Down*, sheets 4, 5, 9, scale 1:10,560, 2nd ed. (1904); *Map of city boundary extensions* (Belfast and Dublin: Marcus Ward & Co., 1896); Baird's *Irish railway and steamboat guide* (Belfast, 1908).

62 BELFAST, 1970, by P. G. Cleary

Based upon the Ordnance Survey map with the sanction of the controller of H.M. Stationery Office, crown copyright reserved.

Ordnance Survey, *County Antrim*, sheets 60-64, *County Down*, sheets 4, 5, 9, scale 1:10,560 (1966-7); Building Design Partnership, *Belfast urban area, interim planning policy* (Belfast, 1967); R. H. Mathew, *Belfast regional survey and plan* (Belfast: H.M.S.O., 1964).

The rapid growth of Belfast since 1900 has meant that the built-up area has reached, and in many areas spilled over, the 1896 county boundary. The Mathew report 'stopline' represents an attempt to curb this growth, but by 1970 continued expansion was already putting the 'line' under heavy pressure.

63 PARLIAMENTARY CONSTITUENCIES, 1801-85, by Con O'Leary

Act for the union of Great Britain and Ireland, 1800 (39 & 40 Geo. III, c. 67); G. C. Bolton, *The passing of the Irish act of union: a study in parliamentary politics* (Oxford, 1966) pp 196-7; Representation of the People (Ireland) Act, 1832 (2 & 3 Will. IV, c. 88); Act to disfranchise the boroughs of Sligo and Cashel, 1870 (33 & 34 Vict., c. 38); *Report of the commissioners appointed under the act 15 & 16 Vict., c. 57, for the purpose of making inquiry into the existence of corrupt practices at the last election for Cashel, together with the minutes of evidence*, pp 1-394 [C. 9], H.C. 1870, xxxii, 1-410; corresponding report for Sligo, pp 1-418 [C. 48], H.C. 1870, xxxii, 621-1054.·

The 33 parliamentary boroughs were selected on a population basis, estimated from the returns of taxation, particularly hearth money. Sligo and Cashel were disfranchised following revelations of gross bribery and corruption, in election petitions tried in 1869 and investigations by election commissioners in 1870.

64 PARLIAMENTARY CONSTITUENCIES, 1885, by J. H. Whyte

Phillips' handy atlas of the counties of Ireland: special edition, showing the new parliamentary divisions (London, [c. 1885]).

65 PARLIAMENTARY CONSTITUENCIES, 1918, by J. H. Whyte

Redistribution of Seats (Ireland) Act, 1918 (7 & 8 Geo. V, c. 65).

66 PARLIAMENTARY CONSTITUENCIES, 1920, by J. H. Whyte

Government of Ireland Act, 1920 (10 & 11 Geo. V, c. 67), schedule 5.

67 DIOCESES OF THE CHURCH OF IRELAND, 1800-1974, by K. M. Davies

H.B.C., pp 351-79; *Church of Ireland Directory, 1974* (Dublin, 1974). See also D. H. Akenson, *The church of Ireland: ecclesiastical reform and revolution, 1800-1885* (New Haven and London, 1971).

The diocesan boundaries are based upon Richard Mant, *History of the Church of Ireland* (London, 1840), map facing p. 1, taken from Daniel Beaufort, *Memoir of a map of Ireland* (London, 1792). Minor boundary changes have occurred during the period covered by the map, but these are too small to be shown on this scale; a manuscript map showing the boundaries of the modern dioceses on a scale of 1 : 575,000 is available from the General Synod of the Church of Ireland, Dublin.

Not all the cathedrals were in existence by 1800. Trim dates only from 1955 and Sligo from 1962; both were formerly parish churches.

Help is acknowledged with thanks from R. H. Sherwood.

68 DIOCESES OF THE ROMAN CATHOLIC CHURCH, 1831-1974, by K. M. Davies

Irish Catholic Directory (Dublin, 1975); Ordnance Survey of Ireland, *Ireland, scale 1:575,000, showing catholic diocesan boundaries and names* (Dublin, 1963).

The diocese of Galway covered a slightly larger area prior to 1893. Help is acknowledged with thanks from the Rev. Martin Coen.

69 MAIL COACH ROUTES, 1832, by J. H. Andrews

Based on 'A new map of Ireland, shewing the post towns and mail conveyances throughout . . .' in *Report from the select committee on turnpike roads in Ireland*, H.C. 1831-2 (645), xvii, appendix, map 2.

In the original map different kinds of postal service are distinguished by hand colouring. Where the colours contradict the tables of mail coach routes printed in the same appendix, the latter have been presumed correct.

70 FREIGHT TRAFFIC, *c.* 1836, by J. H. Andrews

Based on *Atlas to accompany the second report of the railway commissioners, Ireland* (Dublin, 1838), plate III.

The original map uses bands of varying thickness to show traffic volume. An attempt has been made here to reproduce this effect, but precise numerical values cannot be assigned to the different widths. The report does not give the exact date of the statistics for road and inland water traffic on which the map is based.

71 RAILWAYS, 1834-90, by K. M. Davies

S. Maxwell Hajducki, *A railway atlas of Ireland* (Newton Abbot, 1974), pp 2-37; Ordnance Survey, *Map of Ireland*, scale 1:1,000,000 (1919); *Census Ire., 1891*, general report, tables 71-3.

72 POPULATION DENSITY, 1841, 1851, 1891, BY BARONIES, by K. M. Davies

Census Ire., 1841; ——, *1851;* ——, *1891*, county tables.

73 POPULATION CHANGES, 1841-1926, BY COUNTIES, by K. M. Davies

Census Ire., 1926, i, table 2; *Census N.I., 1926*, general report, table 3.

74 HOUSE STANDARDS, 1841 and 1891, BY COUNTIES, by K. M. Davies

Census Ire., 1841; report, p. xiv; appendix to report, centesimal tables, pp lvi-lviii; *Census Ire., 1891*, county tables.

The census returns divided houses into four classes of which the lowest or fourth class—'all mud cabins having only one room'—and the second class—'a good farm house, or in towns, a house in a small street having from 5 to 9 rooms and windows'—are illustrated here. For a more detailed map for 1841, see T. W. Freeman, *Pre-famine Ireland* (Manchester, 1951), p. 150; Professor Freeman's help is acknowledged with thanks.

75 FARM SIZE, 1841 and 1911, BY COUNTIES, by K. M. Davies

Census Ire., 1841, miscellaneous tables, III, 3; *Census Ire., 1911*, general report, table 151.
   Holdings of less than one acre are not included.

76 SEASONAL MIGRATION, 1841, 1881, 1901, BY COUNTIES, by K. M. Davies

Census Ire., 1841, report, pp xxvi–xxvii; miscellaneous tables, II, 3; *Agricultural statistics, Ireland, 1881. Report and tables relating to migratory agricultural labourers*, p. 3, table I [C 3150], H.C. 1882, lxxiv, 191; *Agricultural statistics, Ireland, 1901. Report and tables relating to Irish migratory agricultural and other labourers*, p. 10, table I [C 850], H.C. 1902, cxvi, pt 2, 96, 107.

The 1841 census returns covered both males and females embarking for Great Britain from Irish ports from 13 May to 31 August 1841, the majority of whom were expected to return to Ireland at the close of the harvest season. The enumerators of agricultural statistics collected figures for Irish male migratory agricultural labourers annually from 1880, including those who migrated within Ireland. From 1901 the tables included non-agricultural labourers as well as females (the figure for Co. Wicklow is made up entirely of Arklow fishermen who went to the fishing grounds of south-west Ireland and then on to join the Scottish herring fleets).

77 EMIGRATION, 1851–1911, BY COUNTIES, by K. M. Davies

Census Ire., 1911, county tables.

78 ILLITERACY, 1841, 1861, 1891, BY COUNTIES, by K. M. Davies

Census Ire., 1841, appendix to the report, centesimal tables, pp lvi–lix; *Census Ire., 1861*, pt II, i, pl. II; *Census Ire., 1891*, general report, plate II.

79 IRISH-SPEAKERS, 1851, BY BARONIES, by Brian Ó Cuív

Census Ire., 1851, county tables; see also Brian Ó Cuiv, *Irish dialects and Irish-speaking districts* (Dublin, 1951).

80 IRISH-SPEAKERS, 1891, BY BARONIES, by Brian Ó Cuív

Census Ire., 1891, county tables; Ó Cuiv, *Irish dialects*.

81 RELIGIOUS DENOMINATIONS, 1871, BY COUNTIES, by K. M. Davies

Census Ire., 1871, county tables.

82 RATEABLE VALUATION OF LAND AND BUILDINGS PER ACRE, 1891, BY POOR LAW UNIONS, by K. M. Davies

Census Ire., 1891, general report, plate IV and accompanying table.

83 RATEABLE VALUATION OF LAND AND BUILDINGS PER
   HEAD OF POPULATION, 1891, BY POOR LAW UNIONS, by
   K. M. Davies

Source as for 82.

84 SMALL FARMS, 1881, BY COUNTIES, by K. M. Davies

Census Ire., 1881, general report, table 49.

85 CONGESTED DISTRICTS, 1891 and 1909, by H. D. Gribbon

Purchase of Land (Ireland) Act, 1891 (54 & 55 Vict., c. 48); Irish Land Act, 1909
(9 Edw. VII, c. 42).

   The congested districts board was established in 1891 under the Purchase of Land
(Ireland) Act, 1891, to investigate and alleviate poverty in the poorest areas of Co. Donegal,
the five counties of Connacht, Co. Kerry, and the western part of Co. Cork. Poor law
electoral divisions where the total rateable value divided by the number of inhabitants was
less than £1.50 were defined as 'congested'. The board used government funds to improve
roads, build piers and harbours, improve stock, establish factories, and encourage fisheries,
and worked with other government agencies to reallocate land and construct light railways.

86 CONGESTED DISTRICTS: POPULATION DENSITY, 1891 [BY
   DISPENSARY DISTRICTS], by T. W. Freeman

Based on T. W. Freeman, 'The congested districts of western Ireland' in *Geographical
Review*, xxxiii (1943), fig. 2, p. 4.

87 CONGESTED DISTRICTS: NON-AGRICULTURAL OCCUPA-
   TIONS, 1891, by T. W. Freeman

Base line reports of the congested districts board.

   Every poor law electoral division was surveyed and for each a comprehensive report
was prepared on a standard pattern: an example, the report for Glenties, Co. Donegal,
is given in W. L. Micks, *An account of the constitution, administration and dissolution of
the congested districts board for Ireland from 1891 to 1923* (Dublin, 1925), pp 241–58. In
many areas the income from the small farms was supplemented by seasonal migration,
emigrants' remittances, fishing, local labouring, and domestic crafts.

88 CONGESTED DISTRICTS BOARD: MAJOR MARINE WORKS,
   1891–1914, by H. D. Gribbon

Eighteenth report of the congested districts board for Ireland, 1909, pp 1–148 [Cd 4927],
H.C. 1909, xvi, and subsequent reports up to 1914.

89 DÁIL CONSTITUENCIES, 1923, by J. H. Whyte

Based on maps in franchise section, Department of Local Government, Dublin. Help
from the secretary of the department is acknowledged with thanks.

90 DÁIL CONSTITUENCIES, 1935, by J. H. Whyte

Source as for 89.

91 DAIL CONSTITUENCIES, 1947, by J. H. Whyte

Source as for 89.

92 DÁIL CONSTITUENCIES, 1961, by J. H. Whyte
Source as for 89.

93 DÁIL CONSTITUENCIES, 1969, by J. H. Whyte
Source as for 89.

94 DÁIL CONSTITUENCIES, 1974, by J. H. Whyte
Source as for 89.

95 DUBLIN: U.K. PARLIAMENTARY CONSTITUENCIES, 1918-20,
   and DÁIL CONSTITUENCIES, 1923-74, by J. H. Whyte
Source for A as for 65. Source for B as for 66. Source for C-H as for 89.

96 PARLIAMENTARY CONSTITUENCIES IN N.I., 1929, 1949, 1968, and
   BELFAST CONSTITUENCIES, 1918, 1920, by J. H. Whyte
A, B, and E are based on Ordnance Survey of Northern Ireland, *Map showing parliamentary constituencies of Northern Ireland*, scale 1:253,400 (Belfast, 1959). C and F are based on Ordnance Survey of Northern Ireland, *Map showing parliamentary constituencies of Northern Ireland*, scale 1:253,440 (Belfast, 1969). These maps are reproduced under the sanction of the controller of H.M. Stationery Office, crown copyright reserved.

   Source for D as for 65 and 66.

97 PARLIAMENTARY CONSTITUENCIES IN N.I., 1970, 1973, by J. H.
   Whyte
Based on maps supplied by Ordnance Survey of Northern Ireland, and reproduced under the sanction of the controller of H.M. Stationery Office, crown copyright reserved.

98 DISTRIBUTION OF CATHOLICS AND PROTESTANTS IN
   ULSTER, 1911, BY DISTRICT ELECTORAL DIVISIONS, by K. M.
   Davies
Census Ire., 1911, county tables.

   No figures are available for Northern Ireland district electoral divisions in 1926, but the Irish Free State figures for border areas at that date do not differ to any great extent from those for 1911. It seems reasonable to suppose, therefore, that this map gives a close approximation to the distribution pattern at the time of partition. See also Geoffrey J. Hand, introduction to *Report of the Irish boundary commission, 1925* (Shannon, 1969), and the map of distribution of majorities (ibid., appendix 7).

99 RAILWAYS, 1926, by K. M. Davies
Hajducki, *Railway atlas of Ireland*, pp 38-9; Ordnance Survey, *Map of Ireland*, scale 1:1,000,000 (1919); *Census Ire., 1926*, i, table 7; *Census N.I., 1926*, general report, table 3. See also Michael H. C. Baker, *Irish railways since 1916* (London, 1972).

   The standard gauge in Ireland is 5 feet 3 inches and the narrow gauge is 3 feet. The distinction between railways (particularly narrow-gauge lines) and tramways is not always clear; some lines served as both at different dates. The Dublin and Blessington steam tramway was standard gauge.

   Help is acknowledged with thanks from J. E. Killen.

100 RAILWAYS, 1974, by D. A. Gillmor
Based on information from Coras Iompair Éireann, Dublin.

101 POPULATION DENSITY, 1961, by T. W. Freeman

Redrawn from T. W. Freeman, *Ireland* (4th ed., London, 1969), p. 133, by permission of Methuen & Co. Ltd.

102 PRINCIPAL TOWNS AND CITIES, 1971, by K. M. Davies

Census Ire., *1971*, i, table 8; *Census N.I.*, *1971*, preliminary report, table 3.

   'Greater Belfast' includes Holywood and Newtownabbey. 'Greater Dublin' includes Clondalkin, Lucan, and Tallaght.

103 POPULATION CHANGE, 1926–71, BY COUNTIES, by K. M. Davies

Census Ire., *1971*, i, table 5; *Census N.I.*, *1971*, preliminary report, table 2.

104 DISTRIBUTION OF CATHOLICS, 1961, BY RURAL DISTRICTS,
      by T. W. Freeman

Census Ire., *1961*, vii, pt 1, table 8; *Census N.I.*, *1961*, county tables.

105 DISTRIBUTION OF PROTESTANTS AND OTHERS, 1961, BY
      RURAL DISTRICTS, by K. M. Davies

Sources as for 104.

106 AVERAGE SIZE OF FARM HOLDINGS, 1966, BY COUNTIES, by
      D. A. Gillmor

Information supplied by Central Statistics Office, Dublin, and by Ministry of Agriculture, Belfast.

   The map shows the average area of crops and pasture per holding; holdings of less than one acre have been omitted from the calculations. The metric equivalents (in brackets) are: 20 acres (8.09 hectares), 30 (12.14), 40 (16.19), 50 (20.23), 60 (24.28), 70 (28.33), 80 (32.37).

107 DISTRIBUTION OF TILLAGE, 1966, BY RURAL DISTRICTS, by
      D. A. Gillmor

Irish Statistical Bulletin, 46 (4), (1971); information for N.I. supplied by Ministry of Agriculture, Belfast.

108 LOCATION OF GRANT-AIDED FACTORIES, ESTABLISHED
      1950–69, by D. A. Gillmor

Information supplied by Industrial Development Authority, Dublin, and by Ministry of Commerce, Belfast.

   The map shows the distribution of new manufacturing establishments to which government grants were paid during the period 1950–69 under schemes for the promotion of new industry. The 'designated areas' are those parts of the Republic of Ireland, mainly in western districts, that qualified for incentives higher than those available in the remainder of the state during the 1960s.

109 EMPLOYMENT IN MANUFACTURING INDUSTRIES, 1966, BY
      COUNTIES, by D. A. Gillmor

Census Ire., *1966*, iii, table 4; *Census N.I.*, *1966*, general report, table 16.

110 EMPLOYMENT IN METAL AND ENGINEERING INDUSTRIES,
      1966, BY COUNTIES, by D. A. Gillmor

Source as for 109.

111 EMPLOYMENT IN TEXTILE AND CLOTHING INDUSTRIES, 1966, BY COUNTIES, by D. A. Gillmor

Source as for 109.

112 LOCATION OF BACON CURING, MEAT AND FISH PROCESS-ING FACTORIES, 1969, by D. A. Gillmor

Information supplied by Department of Agriculture, Dublin, and by Ministry of Agriculture, Belfast.

113 CENTRAL CREAMERIES AND OTHER MILK PROCESSING CENTRES, 1969, by D. A. Gillmor

Information supplied by Department of Agriculture, Dublin, and by Ministry of Agriculture, Belfast.

The majority of creameries are run by cooperative societies owned largely by farmer members.

114 ELECTRICITY GENERATING STATIONS, 1974, by D. A. Gillmor

Information supplied by Electricity Supply Board, Dublin, and by Electricity Board for Northern Ireland, Belfast.

115 GAELTACHT AREAS, 1956, by D. A. Gillmor

Information supplied by Roinn na Gaeltachta, Dublin.

116 ADMINISTRATIVE REGIONS, 1974, by D. A. Gillmor

Information supplied by Departments of Education, Health, and Local Government, Dublin; Bórd Failte Éireann, Dublin; Industrial Development Authority, Dublin; Department of Education, Bangor, Co. Down; Department of Health and Social Services, Belfast.

117 PORTS, 1974, by N. C. Mitchel

Information supplied by harbour commissioners of Belfast, Cork, Drogheda, Limerick, Londonderry, New Ross, and Waterford; Dublin Port and Docks Board; Larne Harbour Ltd; Warrenpoint Harbour Authority; Department of Transport and Power, Dublin; Department of Commerce, Belfast; Gulf Oil Terminals (Ireland) Ltd. See also J. H. Andrews, 'The pattern of trade in Ireland's smaller seaports' in *Ir. Geography*, iv, no. 2 (1960), pp 93-8; R. A. Butlin, 'The Bantry Bay crude oil terminal' in *Ir. Geography*, v, no. 5 (1968), pp 481-4.

Net registered tonnage refers to the tonnage of ships below decks and is a measure of the actual cargo capacity. The recent practice of carrying containers on deck is detracting from its value as a measure of port usage, but in 1974 it remained of sufficient significance to justify its use on this map.

The Whiddy Island oil terminal transhipped middle-eastern and other crude oil, destined for British and continental refineries, from 1969 until operations were suspended after the *Betelgeuse* disaster in 1979. In 1974 the cargo tonnage handled was considerably greater than that for any other Irish port.

Help is acknowledged with thanks from John de Courcy Ireland.

118 PROVINCES, COUNTIES, AND TOWNS, 1976, by K. M. Davies

119 BARONIES: NORTHERN REGION

Based on Ordnance Survey of Ireland, *County boundaries; barony boundaries*, scale 1 : 633,600 (Dublin 1938).

The barony was a division of the county used in the raising of local revenue and the maintenance of public roads and bridges and other services. These functions were taken over by the system of representative local government established by the local government act of 1898 (61 & 62 Vict., c. 37). Barony boundaries were inherited from territories of medieval or earlier origin, with some modifications in the eighteenth and nineteenth centuries.

120 BARONIES: CENTRAL REGION

Source and note as for 119.

121 BARONIES: SOUTHERN REGION

Source and note as for 119.

II

GENEALOGICAL TABLES

CONTENTS

INTRODUCTION

THE following forty-two tables present the succession to kingship within the major dynasties of early and medieval Ireland, together with the succession to the major Anglo-Norman lordships. The first thirteen deal with the period prior to the Norman invasion, although for practical reasons—the eclipse of the Mac Lochlainn and Mac Duinn Sléibe families in 1241 and 1201 (tables 3 and 6) and the continuity of political power in Connacht and Munster (tables 11 and 12)—a cut-off point at 1169 would have been artificial. Tables 14–33 detail the major lordships of Gaelic Ireland in the later middle ages; tables 14, 21, 23, 24, and 28 are continuations of tables 2, 8, 11, 10, and 12; some overlapping has been allowed in order to render each table self-explanatory. Similarly, tables 32 and 33 begin earlier than 1169.

Within these two sections the order is roughly geographical, beginning with the north and moving clockwise to finish in the west; but the largely Scandinavian character of the Dublin kingship warrants placing table 13 on its own: lack of genealogical data precluded extending the table beyond the year 1094 to the extinction of the kingship in 1171. Thus the O'Rourkes and O'Reillys find their place as tables 32 and 33 at the end of the Gaelic section because of their historical and genealogical connection with Connacht, even though the O'Reillys were regarded by the O'Neills in the sixteenth century as within their hegemony of Ulster. The far-flung interests of the FitzGeralds and de Burghs forbid any neat geographical arrangement of the Anglo-Norman tables (34-40), and the smaller lordships of Meath and Leinster have been relegated to the end (41-2).

Succession of individuals is marked by numerals to correspond with the succession lists in the next section, which are designed to be complementary to the genealogical tables. Disputed successions or periods of shared rule are indicated by the addition of (a), (b), (c), etc. after the ruler's numeral, and the period of rule is shown under the name, the final year being that of death unless otherwise indicated by abd = abdicated, bld = blinded, dep. = deposed; in such instances d. indicates the year of death. Gaelic rulers who by formal agreement shared sovereignty, either as delegates or as equal partners, or who ruled half of a partitioned territory, are designated *leth-ríg* 'joint [literally 'half'] kings' to distinguish them from more hostile rival aspirants. The term *tánaiste* is explained above (viii, 75). Uncertainty or illegitimacy of descent or relationship is shown by broken lines. In some cases (e.g. the foot of table 2), for reasons of space, undistinguished individuals in a pedigree are omitted and the number of generations indicated by a figure.

The complications of the Gaelic system of succession to lordship are amply illustrated in the tables, but the feudal custom of partition among coheiresses and the gaelicisation of the de Burghs render tables 39–42 scarcely less complex. The vexed question of the enumeration of the earls of Desmond has been dealt with in a manner which is somewhat at variance with that employed in volume III of the New History (see below, table 36, and note on pp 232–3 to succession list of earls of Desmond).

As in volume VIII (see pp 4–5) Irish proper names in this and the following section are written according to an Old Irish standard up to A.D. 900, no attempt being made to restore older archaic or proto-Irish forms. A Middle Irish standard has been adopted for the period 901–1333. In both cases we have been somewhat conservative, for certain changes (i.e. final -a for original final -o) had occurred well before 900, and Classical Modern Irish had evolved already by 1200, although the new orthography is not commonly found in manuscripts until the end of the fourteenth century. However, a few Middle Irish forms have remained uncorrected in the portions of the genealogical tables referring to the period before 900; where discrepancies occur, the forms appearing in the succession lists are to be preferred.

The lower-case 'mac' and 'ua' mean 'son' and 'grandson'; as elements in the formation of surnames, which came into general use in the eleventh century, they are written Mac and Ua (Ó after 1216).

Anglo-Norman surnames such as FitzGerald are written with the second element in capitals throughout the medieval period; they are to be distinguished from forms such as 'fitz Gerald', which are patronymics.

Tables 1–13 are by F. J. Byrne. Tables 14–42 are based on material prepared by K. W. Nicholls, but the editors bear responsibility for their present format.

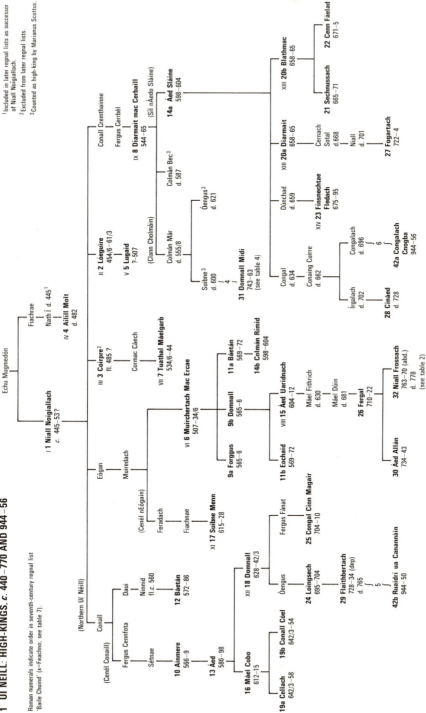

1 Uí Néill: HIGH-KINGS, c. 440–770 AND 944–56

Roman numerals indicate order in seventh-century regnal list
'Baile Chuind' (x=Feachno; see table 7).

[1] Included in later regnal lists as successor of Niall Noigiallach.
[2] Excluded from later regnal lists.
[3] Counted as high-king by Marianus Scottus.

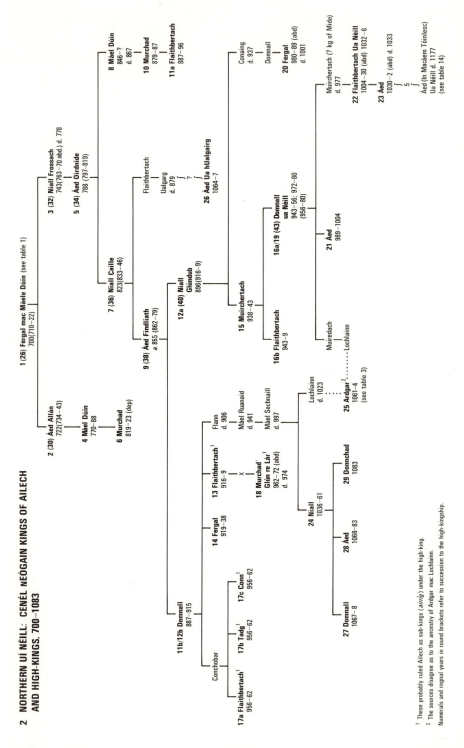

2 NORTHERN UÍ NÉILL: CENÉL NEÓGAIN KINGS OF AILECH
AND HIGH-KINGS, 700–1083

1 (26) Fergal mac Máele Dúin (see table 1)
700/710–22)

2 (30) Áed Allán
722(734–43)

3 (32) Niall Frossach
743(763–70 abd.) d. 778

4 Máel Dúin
770–88

5 (34) Áed Oirdnide
788 (797–819)

6 Murchad
819–23 (dep)

7 (36) Niall Caille
823(833–46)

8 Máel Dúin
846–?
d. 867

Flaithbertach

Ualgarg
d. 879

9 (38) Áed Findliath
a. 855 (862–79)

10 Murchad
879–87

11a Flaithbertach
887–96

11b/12b Domnall
887–915

12a (40) Niall
Glúndub
896(916–9)

26 Áed Ua hUalgairg
1064–7

Conchobar

17a Flaithbertach[1]
956–62

17b Tadg[1]
956–62

17c Conn[1]
956–62

14 Fergal
919–38

13 Flaithbertach[1]
916–9

x

18 Murchad[1]
Glún re Lár[1]
962–72 (abd)
d. 974

Flann
d. 906

Máel Ruanaid
d. 941

Máel Sechnaill
d. 997

15 Muirchertach
938–43

16b Flaithbertach
943–9

16a/19 (43) Domnall
ua Néill
943–56: 972–80
(956–80)

Conaing
d. 937

Domnall

20 Fergal
980–89 (abd)
d. 1001

Muircheartach (? kg of Mide)
d. 977

21 Áed
989–1004

22 Flaithbertach Ua Néill
1004–30 (abd) 1032–6

23 Áed
1030–2 (abd) d. 1033

5

Áed (In Macáem Tóinlesc)
Ua Néill d. 1177
(see table 14)

Muiredach

Lochlainn

Lochlainn
d. 1023

25 Ardgar[2]........Lochlainn
1061–4
(see table 3)

24 Niall
1036–61

27 Domnall
1067–8

28 Áed
1068–83

29 Donnchad
1083

[1] These probably ruled Ailech as sub-kings (airríg) under the high-king.

[2] The sources disagree as to the ancestry of Ardgar mac Lochlainn.

Numerals and regnal years in round brackets refer to succession to the high-kingship.

3 NORTHERN UÍ NÉILL: MAC LOCHLAINN KINGS OF CENÉL NEÓGAIN, 1083–1241

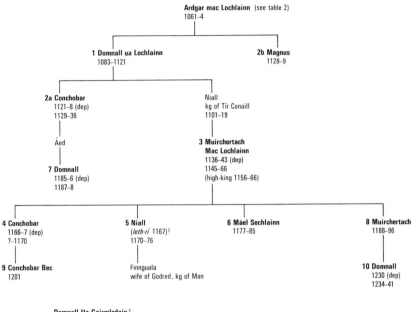

Ardgar mac Lochlainn (see table 2)
1061–4

1 Domnall ua Lochlainn
1083–1121

2b Magnus
1128–9

2a Conchobar
1121–8 (dep)
1129–36

Niall
kg of Tír Conaill
1101–19

Áed

3 Muirchertach
Mac Lochlainn
1136–43 (dep)
1145–66
(high-king 1156–66)

7 Domnall
1185–6 (dep)
1187–8

4 Conchobar
1166–7 (dep)
?–1170

5 Niall
(leth-rí 1167)[1]
1170–76

6 Máel Sechlainn
1177–85

8 Muirchertach
1188–96

9 Conchobar Bec
1201

Finnguala
wife of Godred, kg of Man

10 Domnall
1230 (dep)
1234–41

Domnall Ua Gairmledaig[2]
1143–5 (dep)
d.1160

Ruaidrí Ua Flaithbertaig[2]
1186–7

[1] Shared kingdom with Áed Ua Néill.
[2] These two kings came from distant branches of the Cenél nEógain.

For the succession of the rival Ua Néill kings of Cenél nEógain from 1167 to 1234 see table 14.

4 SOUTHERN UÍ NÉILL: CLANN CHOLMÁIN KINGS OF MIDE AND HIGH-KINGS, 766–1030

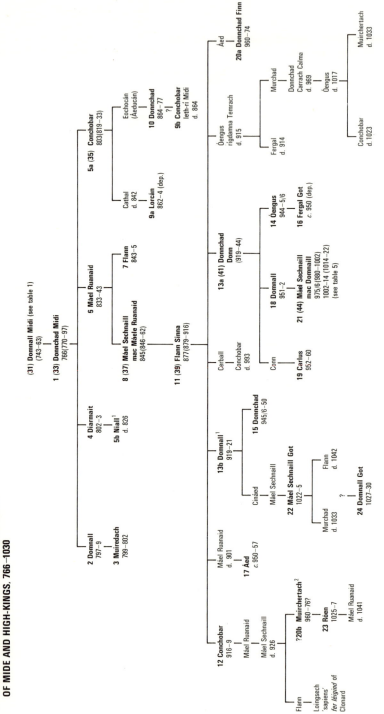

[1] May have acted as provincial sub-kings under the high-kings.

[2] 20b is more probably to be identified with Muirchertach (d.977) son of Domnall ua Néill (see table 2).

Numerals and regnal years in round brackets refer to succession to the high-kingship.

5 SOUTHERN UÍ NÉILL: UA MÁEL SECHLAINN
KINGS OF MIDE, 1030–1184

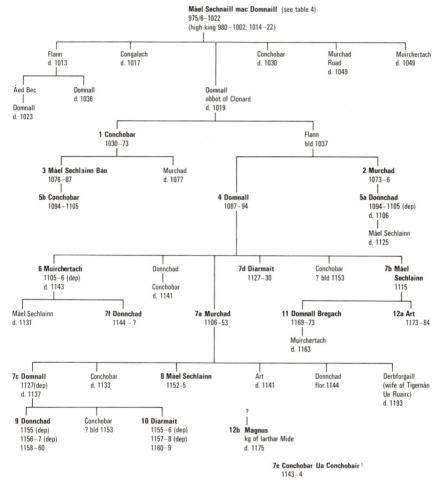

Máel Sechnaill mac Domnaill (see table 4)
975/6–1022
(high-king 980–1002; 1014–22)

Flann
d. 1013

Congalach
d. 1017

Conchobar
d. 1030

Murchad
Ruad
d. 1049

Muirchertach
d. 1049

Áed Bec
|
Domnall
d. 1023

Domnall
d. 1036

Domnall
abbot of Clonard
d. 1019

1 Conchobar
1030–73

Flann
bld 1037

3 Máel Sechlainn Bán
1076–87

Murchad
d. 1077

2 Murchad
1073–6

5b Conchobar
1094–1105

4 Domnall
1087–94

5a Donnchad
1094–1105 (dep)
d. 1106
|
Máel Sechlainn
d. 1125

6 Muirchertach
1105–6 (dep)
d. 1143

Donnchad
|
Conchobar
d. 1141

7d Diarmait
1127–30

Conchobar
? bld 1153

7b Máel
Sechlainn
1115

Máel Sechlainn
d. 1131

7f Donnchad
1144 – ?

7a Murchad
1106–53

11 Domnall Bregach
1169–73
|
Muirchertach
d. 1163

12a Art
1173–84

7c Domnall
1127(dep)
d. 1137

Conchobar
d. 1133

8 Máel Sechlainn
1152–5

Art
d. 1141

Donnchad
flor.1144

Derbforgaill
(wife of Tigernán
Ua Ruairc)
d. 1193

9 Donnchad
1155 (dep)
1156–7 (dep)
1158–60

Conchobar
? bld 1153

10 Diarmait
1155–6 (dep)
1157–8 (dep)
1160–9

?
|
12b Magnus
kg of Iarthar Mide
d. 1175

7e Conchobar Ua Conchobair [1]
1143–4

[1] Son of high-king Toirrdelbach Ua Conchobair of Connacht.

6   KINGS OF ULSTER (DÁL FIATACH) TO 1201

For numbers 4. 8. 9. 11. 16. 18. 20.
23. 26. 29a 35. 38. 43. see table 7.

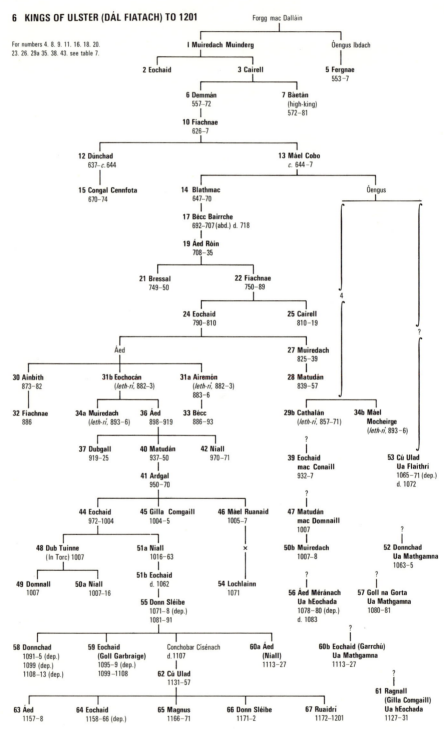

Forgg mac Dalláin

I Muiredach Muinderg

Óengus Ibdach

2 Eochaid   3 Cairell

5 Fergnae
553–7

6 Demmán
557–72

7 Báetán
(high-king)
572–81

10 Fiachnae
626–7

12 Dúnchad
637–c. 644

13 Máel Cobo
c. 644–7

Óengus

15 Congal Cennfota
670–74

14 Blathmac
647–70

17 Bécc Bairrche
692–707 (abd.) d. 718

19 Áed Róin
708–35

21 Bressal
749–50

22 Fiachnae
750–89

4

24 Eochaid
790–810

25 Cairell
810–19

Áed

27 Muiredach
825–39

?

30 Ainbíth
873–82

31b Eochocán
(leth-rí, 882–3)

31a Airemón
(leth-rí, 882–3)
883–6

28 Matudán
839–57

32 Fiachnae
886

34a Muiredach
(leth-rí, 893–6)

36 Áed
898–919

33 Bécc
886–93

29b Cathalán
(leth-rí, 857–71)

34b Máel
Mocheirge
(leth-rí, 893–6)

37 Dubgall
919–25

40 Matudán
937–50

42 Niall
970–71

?

39 Eochaid
mac Conaill
932–7

53 Cú Ulad
Ua Flaithrí
1065–71 (dep.)
d. 1072

41 Ardgal
950–70

?

44 Eochaid
972–1004

45 Gilla Comgaill
1004–5

46 Máel Ruanaid
1005–7

47 Matudán
mac Domnaill
1007

?

48 Dub Tuinne
(In Torc) 1007

51a Niall
1016–63

×

50b Muiredach
1007–8

52 Donnchad
Ua Mathgamna
1063–5

49 Domnall
1007

50a Niall
1007–16

51b Eochaid
d. 1062

54 Lochlainn
1071

?

56 Áed Méránach
Ua hEochada
1078–80 (dep.)
d. 1083

57 Goll na Gorta
Ua Mathgamna
1080–81

55 Donn Sléibe
1071–8 (dep.)
1081–91

?

58 Donnchad
1091–5 (dep.)
1099 (dep.)
1108–13 (dep.)

59 Eochaid
(Goll Garbraige)
1095–9 (dep.)
1099–1108

Conchobar Císénach
d. 1107

60a Áed
(Niall)
1113–27

60b Eochaid (Garrchú)
Ua Mathgamna
1113–27

62 Cú Ulad
1131–57

?

63 Áed
1157–8

64 Eochaid
1158–66 (dep.)

65 Magnus
1166–71

66 Donn Sléibe
1171–2

67 Ruaidrí
1172–1201

61 Ragnall
(Gilla Comgaill)
Ua hEochada
1127–31

7 KINGS OF ULSTER (CRUTHIN) TO 972

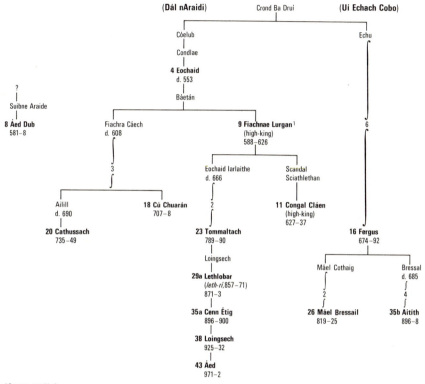

(Dál nAraidi)   Crond Ba Druí   (Uí Echach Cobo)

Cóelub   Echu

Condlae

4 Eochaid
d. 553

Báetán

?
Suibne Araide

8 Áed Dub
581–8

Fiachra Cáech
d. 608

9 Fiachnae Lurgan[1]
(high-king)
588–626

6

3

Eochaid Iarlaithe
d. 666

Scandal
Sciathlethan

Ailill
d. 690

18 Cú Chuarán
707–8

2

11 Congal Cláen
(high-king)
627–37

20 Cathussach
735–49

23 Tommaltach
789–90

16 Fergus
674–92

Loingsech

Máel Cothaig

Bressal
d. 685

29a Lethlobar
(*leth-rí*, 857–71)
871–3

2

4

35a Cenn Étig
896–900

26 Máel Bressail
819–25

35b Aitith
896–8

38 Loingsech
925–32

43 Áed
971–2

[1] See note to table 1.

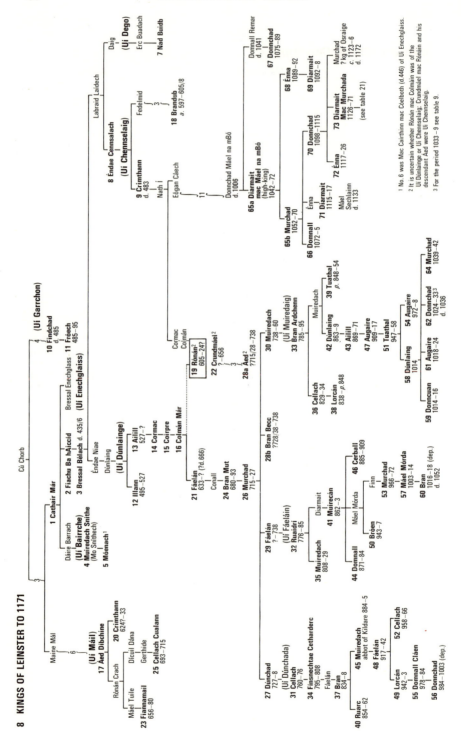

8 KINGS OF LEINSTER TO 1171

[1] No. 6 was Mac Caírthinn mac Coelbóth (d.446) of Uí Enechglaiss.

[2] It is uncertain whether Rónán mac Colmáin was of the Uí Dúnlainge or Uí Chennselaig; Crundmáel mac Rónáin and his descendant Áed were Uí Chennselaig.

[3] For the period 1033–9 see table 9.

9 KINGS OF OSRAIGE, 842–1176

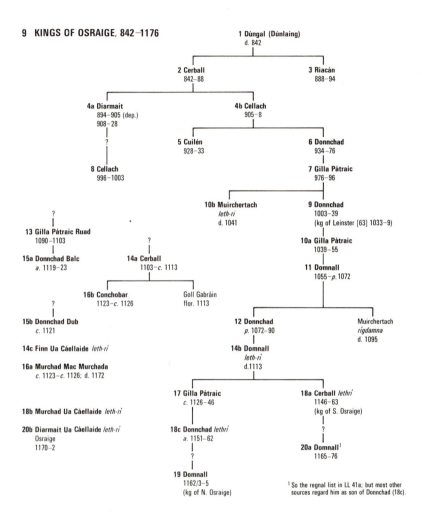

1 Dúngal (Dúnlaing)
d. 842

2 Cerball
842–88

3 Riacán
888–94

4a Diarmait
894–905 (dep.)
908–28

4b Cellach
905–8

5 Cuilén
928–33

6 Donnchad
934–76

8 Cellach
996–1003

7 Gilla Pátraic
976–96

10b Muirchertach
leth-ri
d. 1041

9 Donnchad
1003–39
(kg of Leinster [63] 1033–9)

13 Gilla Pátraic Ruad
1090–1103

14a Cerball
1103–*c.* 1113

10a Gilla Pátraic
1039–55

15a Donnchad Balc
a. 1119–23

11 Domnall
1055–*p.* 1072

16b Conchobar
1123–*c.* 1126

Goll Gabráin
flor. 1113

15b Donnchad Dub
c. 1121

12 Donnchad
p. 1072–90

Muirchertach
rigdamna
d. 1095

14c Finn Ua Cáellaide *leth-ri*

14b Domnall
leth-ri
d.1113

16a Murchad Mac Murchada
c. 1123–*c.* 1126; d. 1172

18b Murchad Ua Cáellaide *leth-ri*

17 Gilla Pátraic
c. 1126–46

18a Cerball *lethri*
1146–63
(kg of S. Osraige)

20b Diarmait Ua Cáellaide *leth-ri*
Osraige
1170–2

18c Donnchad *lethri*
a. 1151–62

20a Domnall[1]
1165–76

19 Domnall
1162/3–5
(kg of N. Osraige)

[1] So the regnal list in LL 41a; but most other
sources regard him as son of Donnchad (18c).

10 KINGS OF MUNSTER (EÓGANACHT) TO 1024

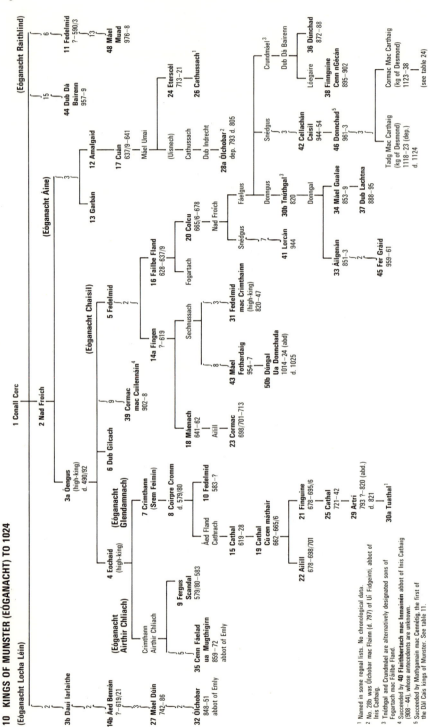

(Eóganacht Locha Léin)

(Eóganacht Raithlind)

(Eóganacht Áine)

(Eóganacht Chaisil)

(Eóganacht Glendamnach)

(Eóganacht Airthir Chliach)

1 Named in some regnal lists. No chronological data.

2 No. 28b was Ólchobar mac Flainn (d. 797) of Uí Fidgeinti, abbot of Inis Cathaig.

3 Truithgal and Cruindmáel are alternatively designated sons of Fogartach mac Failbe Fland.

4 Succeeded by 40 Flaithbertach mac Inmainén abbot of Inis Cathaig (908–44), whose antecedents are unknown.

5 Succeeded by Mathgamain mac Cennétig, the first of the Dál Cais kings of Munster. See table 11.

11 DÁL CAIS KINGS OF MUNSTER AND THOMOND, 951–1194

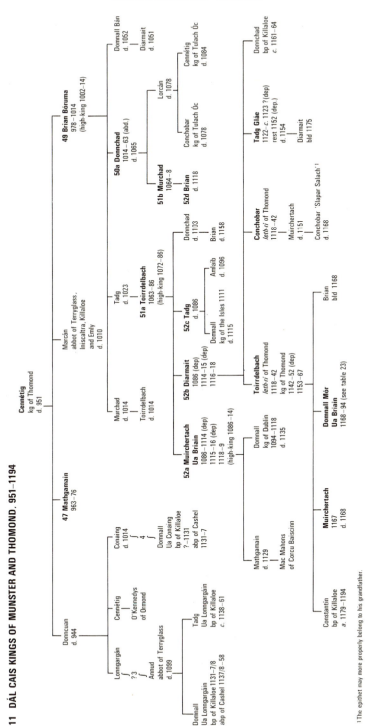

[1] The epithet may more properly belong to his grandfather.

12 KINGS OF CONNACHT TO 1224

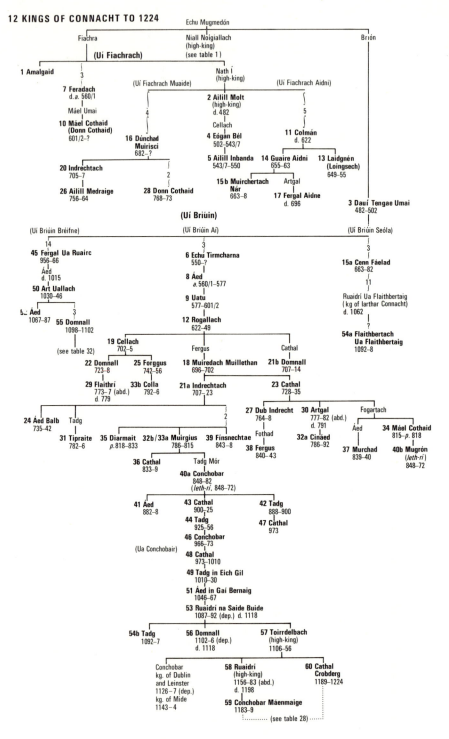

13 KINGS OF DUBLIN, 853–1094

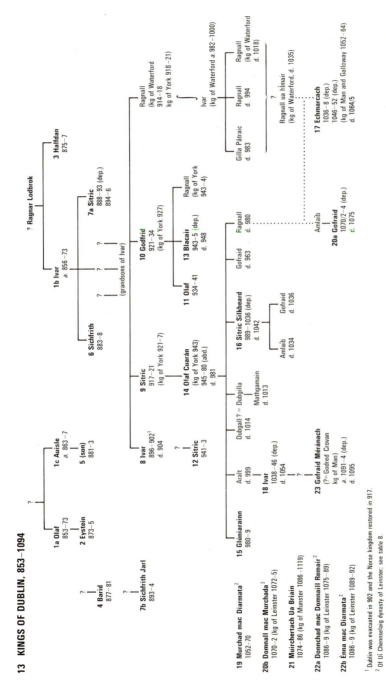

[1] Dublin was evacuated in 902 and the Norse kingdom restored in 917.

[2] Of Uí Chennselaig dynasty of Leinster; see table 8.

14 O'NEILLS OF TYRONE: Ó NÉILL, KINGS OF TÍR EÓGAIN AND EARLS OF TYRONE, 1166–1616

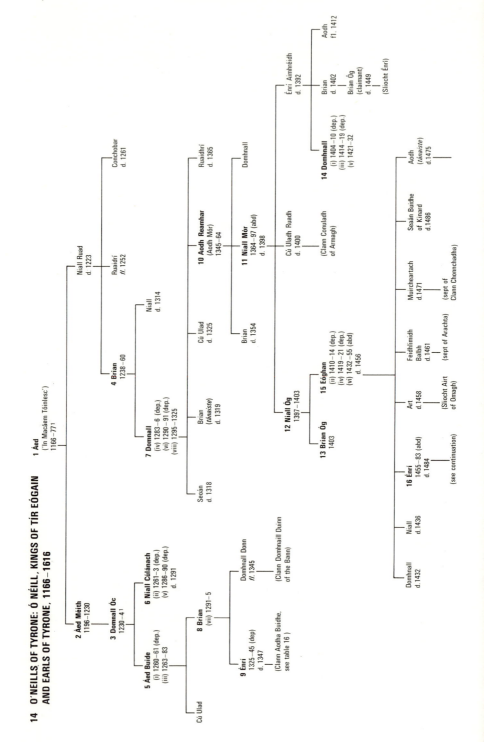

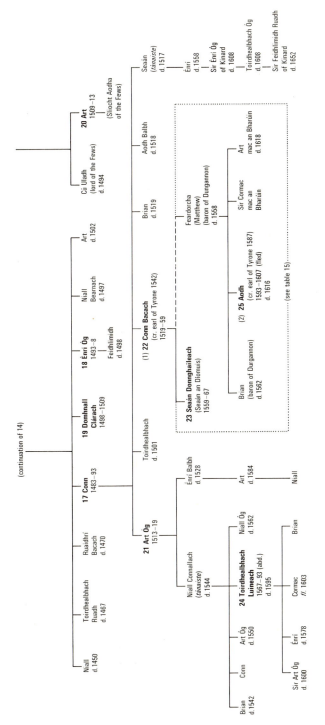

(continuation of 14)

20 Art
1509–13
(Sliocht Aodha
of the Fews)

Cú Uladh
(lord of the Fews)
d. 1494

Seaán
(tánaiste)
d. 1517

Énri
d. 1558

Sir Énri Óg
of Kinard
d. 1608

Toirdhealbhach Óg
d. 1608

Sir Feidhlimidh Ruadh
of Kinard
d. 1652

Aodh Balbh
d. 1518

Brian
d. 1519

Feardorcha
(Matthew)
(baron of Dungannon)
d. 1558

Sir Cormac
mac an
Bharúin

Art
mac an Bharúin
d. 1618

Art
d. 1502

Niall
Bearnach
d. 1497

Feidhlimidh
d. 1498

18 Énri Óg
1483–8

**19 Domhnall
Clárach**
1498–1509

17 Conn
1483–93

Ruaidhri
Bacach
d. 1470

Toirdhealbhach
Ruadh
d. 1467

Niall
d. 1450

Toirdhealbhach
d. 1501

(1) **22 Conn Bacach**
(cr. earl of Tyrone 1542)
1519–59

Brian
(baron of Dungannon)
d. 1562

(2) **25 Aodh**
(cr. earl of Tyrone 1587) (fled)
1593–1607
d. 1616

23 Seaán Donnghaileach
(Seaán an Díomuis)
1559–67

(see table 15)

21 Art Óg
1513–19

Énri Balbh
d. 1528

Art
d. 1584

Niall

Niall Connallach
(tánaiste)
d. 1544

**24 Toirdhealbhach
Luineach**
1567–93 (abd.)
d. 1595

Art Óg
d. 1550

Niall Óg
d. 1562

Cormac
fl. 1603

Brian

Conn

Énri Óg
d. 1578

Brian
d. 1542

Sir Art Óg
d. 1600

[1] For details of the period 1166–1241, see table 3

Numerals in parentheses indicate succession to the earldom of Tyrone.

15 O'NEILLS OF TYRONE: DESCENDANTS OF CONN BACACH Ó NÉILL

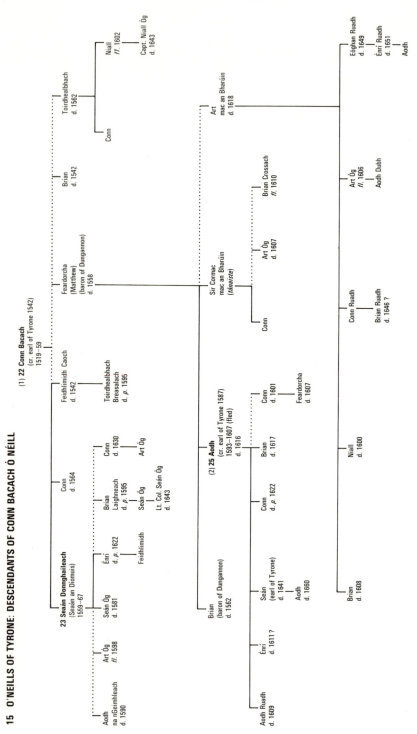

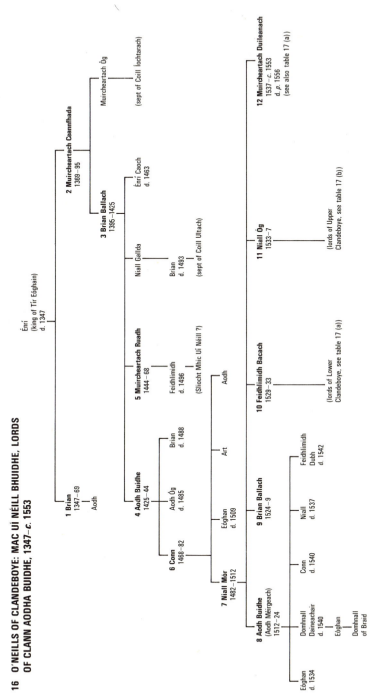

16 O'NEILLS OF CLANDEBOYE: MAC UÍ NÉILL BHUIDHE, LORDS OF CLANN AODHA BUIDHE, 1347–c. 1553

17(A) O'NEILLS OF LOWER[1] CLANDEBOYE: MAC UÍ NÉILL BHUIDHE ÍOCHTAR, *c.* 1553–1617

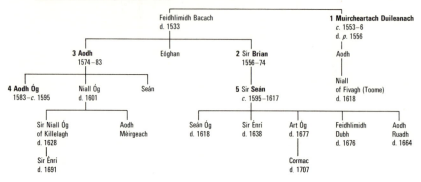

17(B) O'NEILLS OF UPPER[2] CLANDEBOYE: MAC UÍ NÉILL BHUIDHE UACHTAR, *c.* 1553–1619

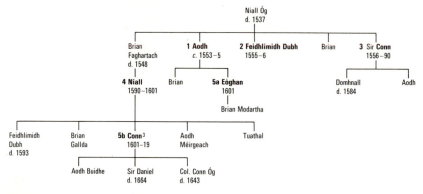

[1] i.e. northern.

[2] i.e. southern.

[3] Sold two-thirds of his land in 1605 and subsequently lost most of the remainder.

18 O'DONNELLS OF TYRCONNELL: Ó DOMHNAILL, KINGS OF TÍR CONAILL AND EARL OF TYRCONNELL, c. 1201–1608

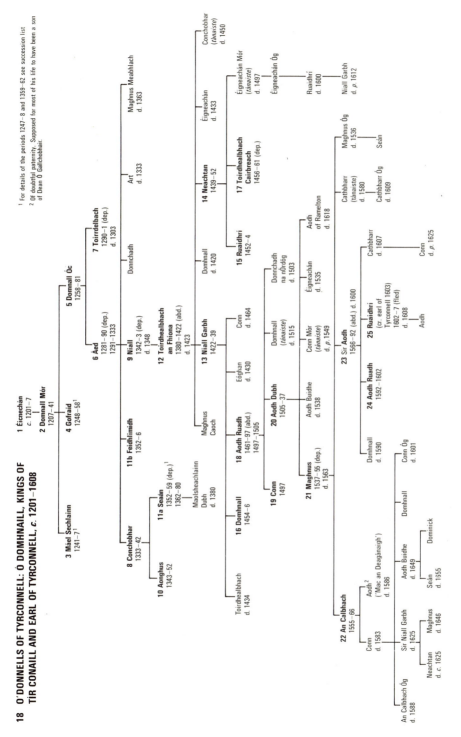

[1] For details of the periods 1247–8 and 1359–62 see succession list

[2] Of doubtful paternity. Supposed for most of his life to have been a son of Dean Ó Gallchobhair.

19 MACMAHONS OF ORIEL: MAC MATHGHAMHNA, KINGS OF OIRGHIALLA, c.1200–1590

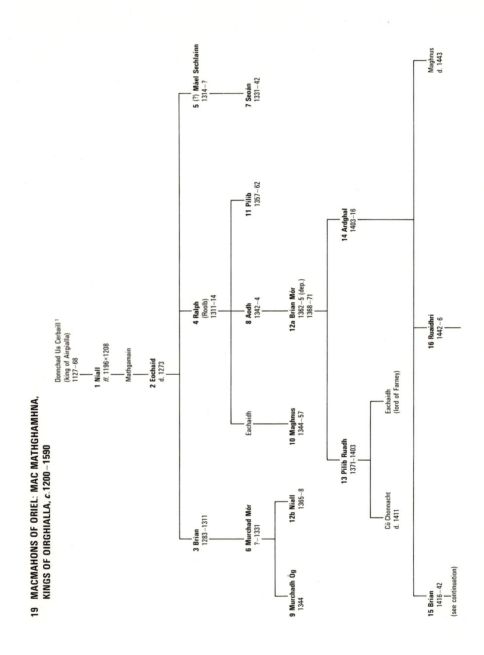

Donnchad Ua Cerbaill [1]
(king of Airgialla)
1127–68

1 Niall
fl. 1196×1208

Mathgamain

2 Eochaid
d. 1273

3 Brian
1283–1311

4 Ralph
(Roolb)
1311–14

5 (?) Mael Sechlainn
1314–?

6 Murchadh Mór
?–1331

Eachaidh

7 Seoán
1331–42

8 Aodh
1342–4

11 Pilib
1357–62

9 Murchadh Óg
1344

10 Maghnus
1344–57

12a Brian Mór
1362–5 (dep.)
1368–71

12b Niall
1365–8

13 Pilib Ruadh
1371–1403

Cú Chonnacht
d. 1411

Eachaidh
(lord of Farney)

14 Ardghal
1403–16

Maghnus
d. 1443

15 Brian
1416–42
(see continuation)

16 Ruaidhri
1442–6

(continuation of 19)

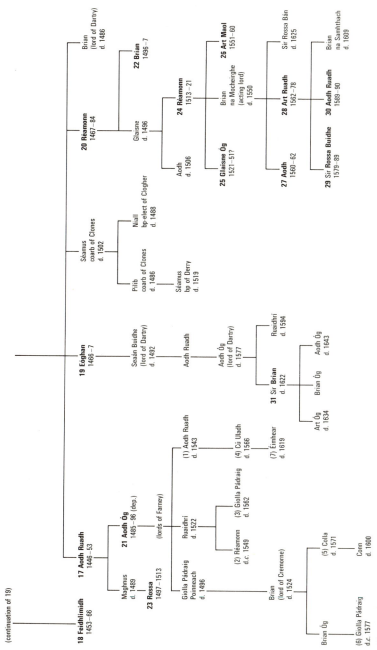

18 Feidhlimidh 1453–66

17 Aodh Ruadh 1446–53

Maghnus d. 1489

21 Aodh Óg 1485–96 (dep.)

(lords of Farney)

23 Rossa 1497–1513

Giolla Pádraig Ponneach d. 1496

Ruaidhri d. 1522

(1) Aodh Ruadh d. 1543

(2) Réamonn d.c. 1549

(3) Giolla Pádraig d. 1562

(4) Cú Uladh d. 1566

(7) Éimhear d. 1619

Brian (lord of Cremorne) d. 1524

(5) Colla d. 1571

Conn d. 1600

Brian Óg

(6) Giolla Pádraig d.c. 1577

19 Eóghan 1466–7

Seaán Buidhe (lord of Dartry) d. 1492

Aodh Ruadh

Aodh Óg (lord of Dartry) d. 1577

31 Sir Brian d. 1622

Ruaidhri d. 1594

Art Óg d. 1634

Brian Óg

Aodh Óg d. 1643

Séamus coarb of Clones d. 1502

Pilib coarb of Clones d. 1486

Niall bp-elect of Clogher d. 1488

Séamus bp of Derry d. 1519

Brian (lord of Dartry) d. 1486

20 Réamonn 1467–84

Glaisne d. 1492

Aodh d. 1506

22 Brian 1496–7

Glaisne d. 1496

Brian na Mocheirghe (acting lord) d. 1550

24 Réamonn 1513–21

25 Glaisne Óg 1521–51?

26 Art Maol 1551–60

27 Aodh 1560–62

28 Art Ruadh 1562–78

Sir Rossa Bán d. 1625

29 Sir Rossa Buidhe 1579–89

30 Aodh Ruadh 1589–90

Brian na Samhthach d. 1609

[1] The alleged descent of the MacMahons from Donnchad is highly suspect.

20 MAGUIRES OF FERMANAGH: MÁG UIDHIR, KINGS OF FIR MANACH AND BARONS OF ENNISKILLEN, *c.* 1282-1645

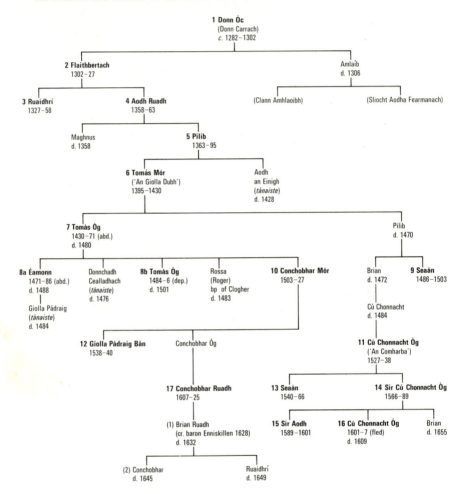

Numerals in parentheses indicate the succession of the barons of Enniskillen.

21 MACMURROUGHS (KAVANAGH): MAC MURCHADHA (CAOMHÁNACH), KINGS OF UÍ CHEINNSEALAIGH AND LEINSTER, 1171–1603

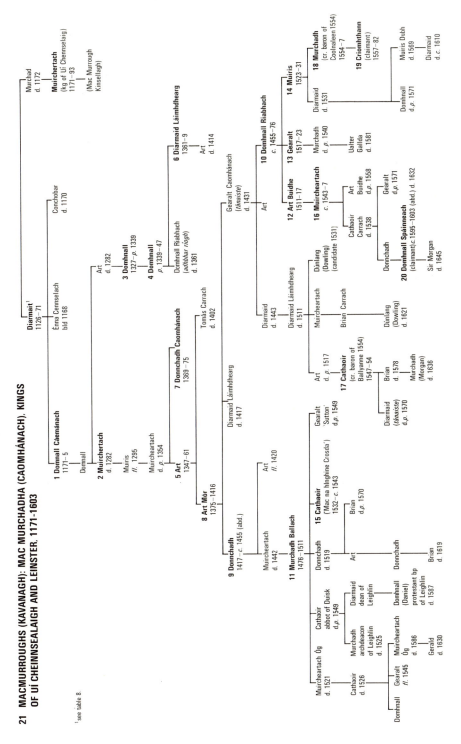

¹ see table 8.

22 O'CONNOR FALY: Ó CONCHOBHAIR FAILGHE.
KINGS OF UÍ FAILGHE, c. 1051 – c. 1556

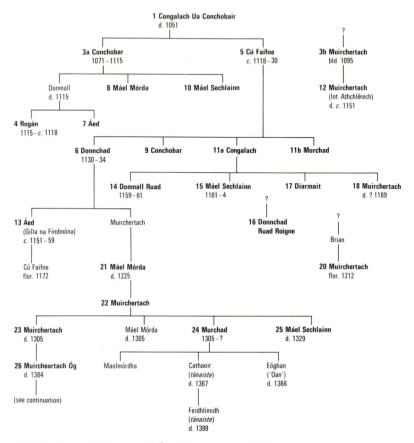

NOTE: The following kings of Uí Failghe were not of the Ó Conchobhair family but of Clann Máel Ugra:

2 Gilla Pátraic mac Conchobair Ua Sibleáin, 1051 – 71

19 Diarmait mac Con Broga Ua Dimmasaig, a. 1172 – 93

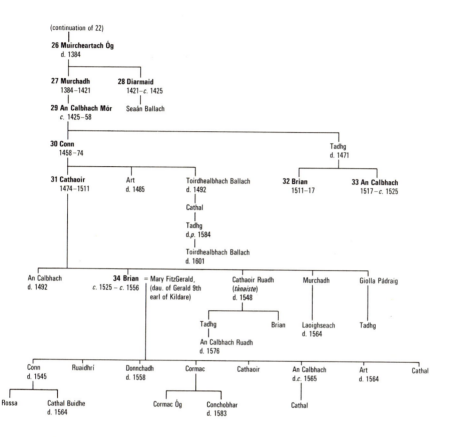

(continuation of 22)

26 **Muircheartach Óg**
d. 1384

27 **Murchadh**   28 **Diarmaid**
1384–1421   1421–c. 1425

29 **An Calbhach Mór**   Seaán Ballach
c. 1425–58

30 **Conn**   Tadhg
1458–74   d. 1471

31 **Cathaoir**   Art   Toirdhealbhach Ballach   32 **Brian**   33 **An Calbhach**
1474–1511   d. 1485   d. 1492   1511–17   1517–c. 1525

                                 Cathal

                                 Tadhg
                                 d.p. 1584

                                 Toirdhealbhach Ballach
                                 d. 1601

An Calbhach   34 **Brian** = Mary FitzGerald,   Cathaoir Ruadh   Murchadh   Giolla Pádraig
d. 1492   c. 1525 – c. 1556 (dau. of Gerald 9th   (*tánaiste*)
                 earl of Kildare) d. 1548

                                 Tadhg   Brian   Laoighseach   Tadhg
                                                                 d. 1564

                                 An Calbhach Ruadh
                                 d. 1576

Conn   Ruaidhrí   Donnchadh   Cormac   Cathaoir   An Calbhach   Art   Cathal
d. 1545   d. 1558   d.c. 1565   d. 1564

Rossa   Cathal Buidhe   Cormac Óg   Conchobhar   Cathal
            d. 1564   d. 1583

23 O'BRIENS: Ó BRIAIN, KINGS AND EARLS OF THOMOND, 1168-1657

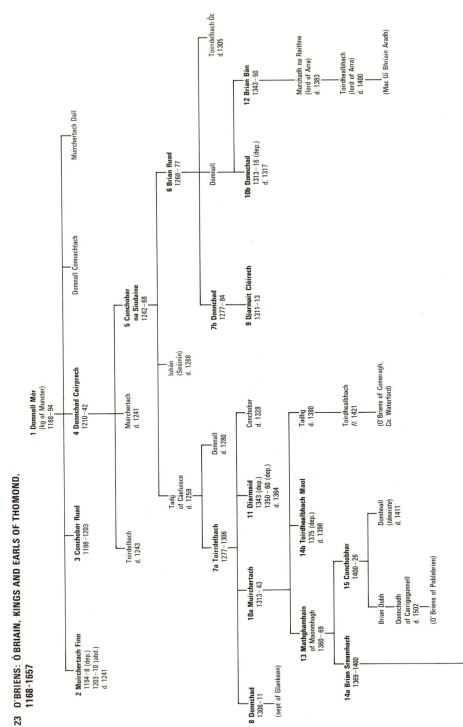

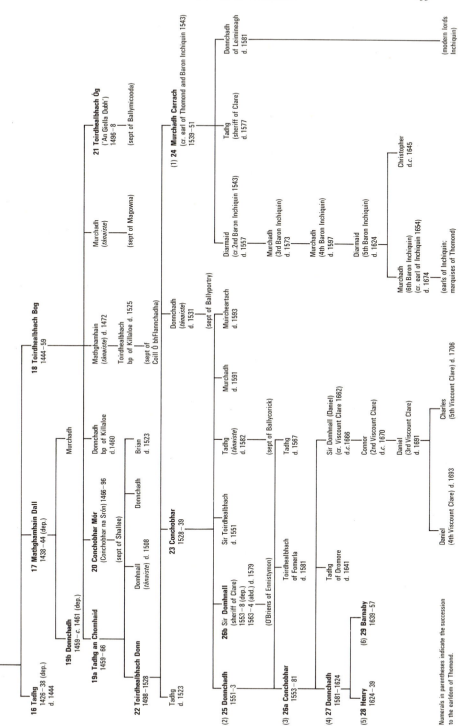

Numerals in parentheses indicate the succession
to the earldom of Thomond.

24 MACCARTHYS OF DESMOND: MAC CARTHAIG, KINGS OF DESMOND, 1118–1262

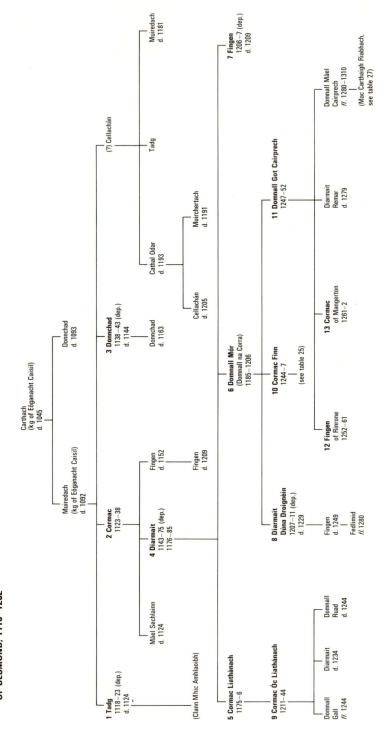

25 MACCARTHYS OF DESMOND: MAC CARTHAIGH MÓR, KINGS OF DESMOND AND EARLS OF CLANCARE, 1262 – c. 1640

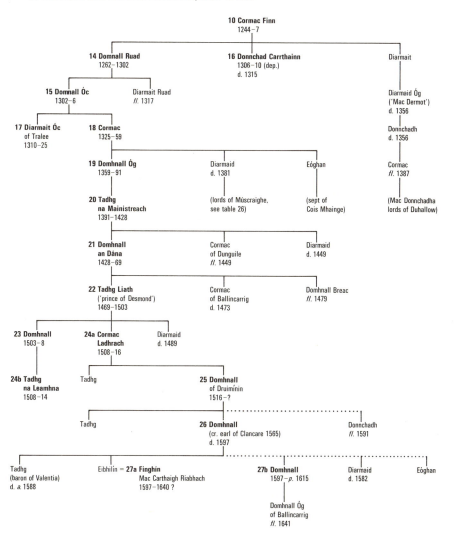

**26 MACCARTHYS OF MUSKERRY: MAC CARTHAIGH MÚSCRAIGHE,
LORDS OF MUSKERRY AND EARLS OF CLANCARTY, 1359–1734**

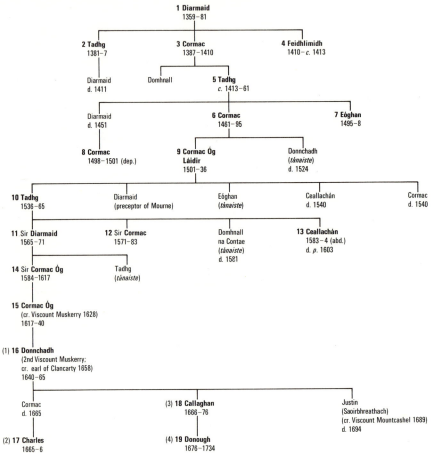

Numerals in parentheses indicate the succession to the earldom of Clancarty.

27 MACCARTHY REAGH : MAC CARTHAIGH RIABHACH, LORDS OF CAIRBRE [CARBERY, CO. CORK], 1366–*c.* 1600

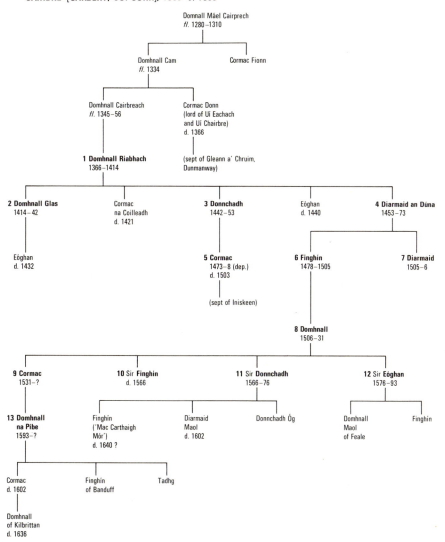

28 O'CONNORS: Ó CONCHOBHAIR, KINGS OF CONNACHT, 1106–1345

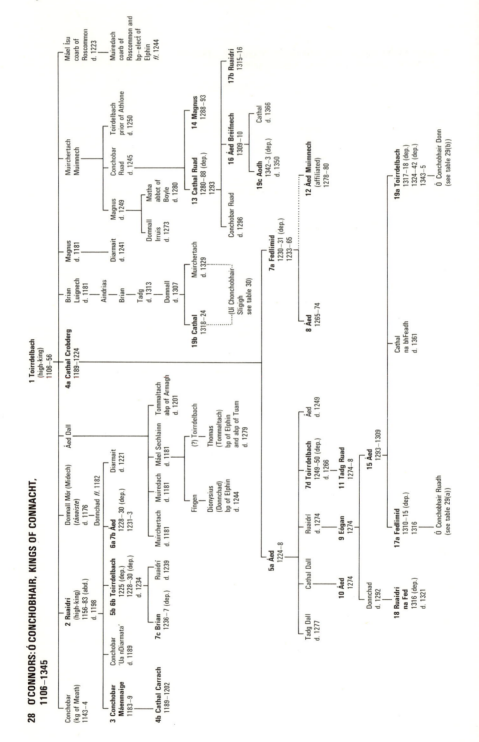

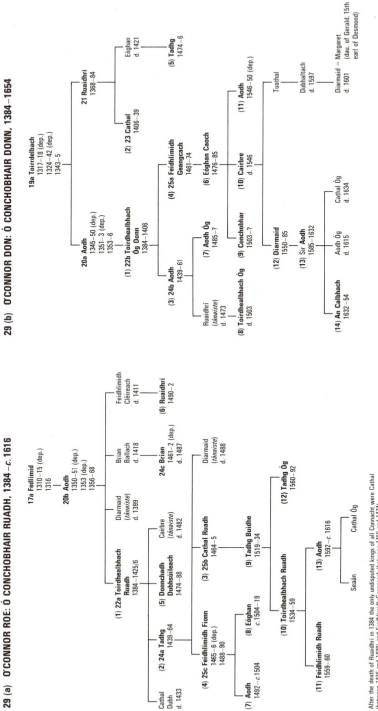

29 (a) O'CONNOR ROE: Ó CONCHOBHAIR RUADH, 1384–c. 1616

29 (b) O'CONNOR DON: Ó CONCHOBHAIR DONN, 1384–1654

After the death of Ruaidhri in 1384 the only undisputed kings of all Connacht were Cathal (between 1426 and 1439) and Feidhlimidh Geangcach (between 1466 and 1474).

Numerals 17a to 25 and all dates before 1474 indicate succession to the kingship of Connacht: see table 28.

Numerals in parentheses and all dates after 1474 indicate Ó Conchobhair Ruadh and Ó Conchobhair Donn successions.

**30   O'CONNOR SLIGO: Ó CONCHOBHAIR SLIGIGH,
LORDS OF CAIRBRE [CARBURY, CO. SLIGO], 1318–1634**

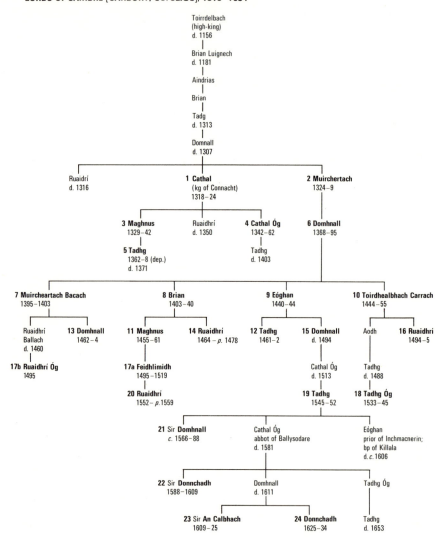

31 O' KELLYS OF HY MANY: Ó CEALLAIGH, KINGS OF UÍ MHAINE, c. 1200 – c. 1611

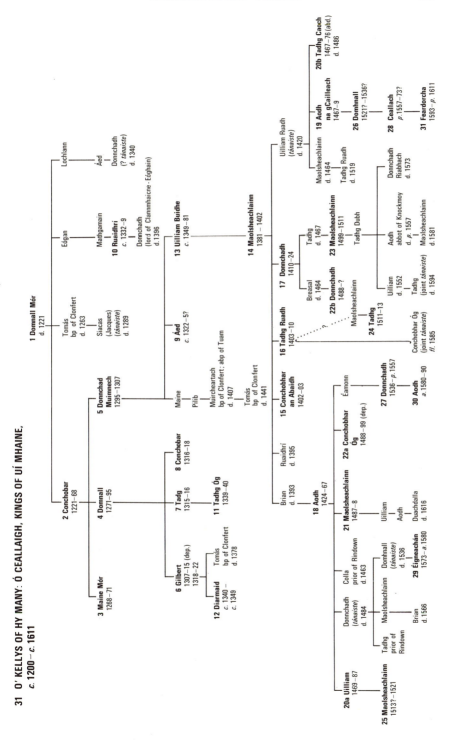

32 O'ROURKES OF BREIFNE: Ó RUAIRC, KINGS OF BRÉIFNE, c.1128–1605

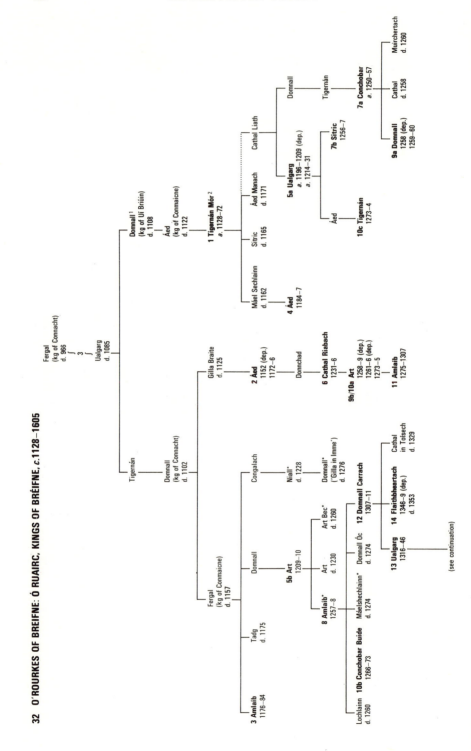

(see continuation)

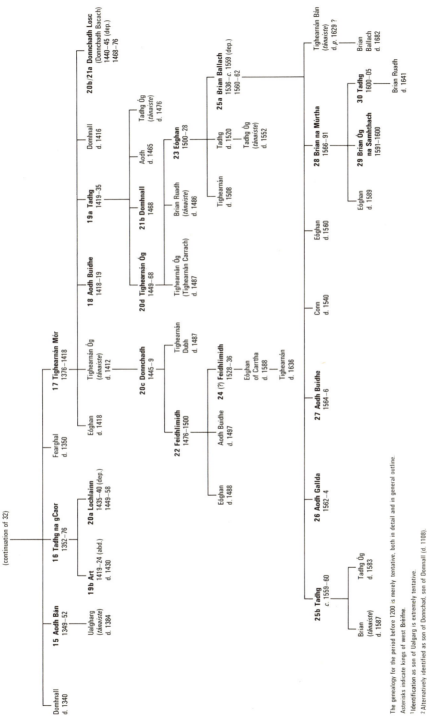

(continuation of 32)

Domhnall
d. 1340

15 **Aodh Bán**
1349–52

Ualgharg
(*tánaiste*)
d. 1384

16 **Tadhg na gCaor**
1352–76

19b **Art**
1419–24 (abd.)
d. 1430

20a **Lochlainn**
1435–40 (dep.)
1449–58

Eóghan
d. 1488

Fearghal
d. 1350

17 **Tighearnán Mór**
1376–1418

Eóghan
d. 1418

Tighearnán Óg
(*tánaiste*)
d. 1412

Domhnall
d. 1416

Aodh
d. 1465

Tadhg Óg
(*tánaiste*)
d. 1476

19a **Tadhg**
1419–35

18 **Aodh Buidhe**
1418–19

21b **Domhnall**
1468

Brian Ruadh
(*tánaiste*)
d. 1486

23 **Eóghan**
1500–28

20b/21a **Donnchadh Losc**
(Donnchadh Bacach)
1440–45 (dep.)
1468–76

22 **Feidhlimidh**
1476–1500

Aodh Buidhe
d. 1497

20c **Donnchadh**
1445–9

Tighearnán
Dubh
d. 1487

20d **Tighearnán Óg**
1449–68

Tighearnán Óg
(Tighearnán Carrach)
d. 1487

24 (?) **Feidhlimidh**
1528–36

Eóghan
of Carrtha
d. 1588

Tighearnán
d. 1636

Tighearnán
d. 1508

Tadhg
d. 1520

Tadhg Óg
(*tánaiste*)
d. 1552

25a **Brian Ballach**
1536–c. 1559 (dep.)
1560–62

Tighearnán Bán
(*tánaiste*)
d.p. 1629 ?

Brian
Ballach
d. 1682

26 **Aodh Gallda**
1562–4

27 **Aodh Buidhe**
1564–6

Conn
d. 1540

Eóghan
d. 1560

28 **Brian na Múrtha**
1566–91

Eóghan
d. 1589

29 **Brian Óg
na Samhthach**
1591–1600

30 **Tadhg**
1600–05

Brian Ruadh
d. 1641

25b **Tadhg**
c. 1559–60

Brian
(*tánaiste*)
d. 1587

Tadhg Óg
d. 1583

The genealogy for the period before 1200 is merely tentative, both in detail and in general outline.

Asterisks indicate kings of west Bréifne.

[1] Identification as son of Ualgarg is extremely tentative.

[2] Alternatively identified as son of Donnchad, son of Domnall (d. 1108).

33   O'REILLYS OF EAST BREIFNE : Ó RAGHALLAIGH, KINGS OF MUINTIR MAOILMHORDHA, *c*. 1161–1607

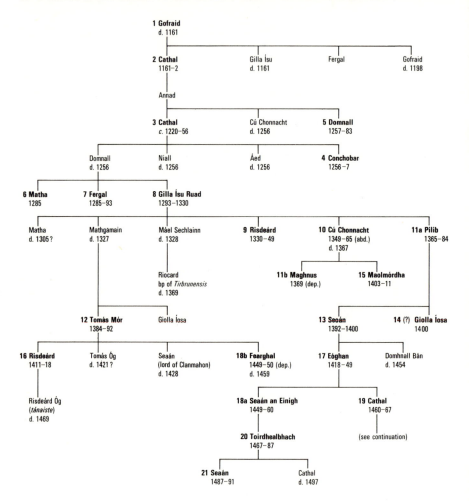

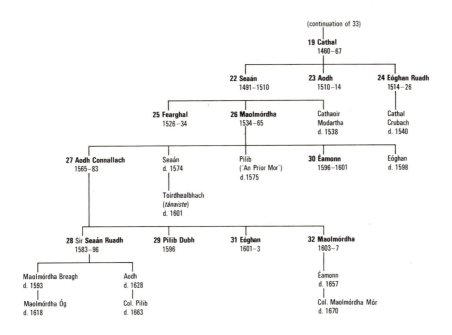

(continuation of 33)

19 Cathal
1460–67

22 Seaán
1491–1510

23 Aodh
1510–14

24 Eóghan Ruadh
1514–26

25 Fearghal
1526–34

26 Maolmórdha
1534–65

Cathaoir
Modartha
d. 1538

Cathal
Crubach
d. 1540

27 Aodh Connallach
1565–83

Seaán
d. 1574

Pilib
('An Prior Mor')
d.1575

30 Éamonn
1596–1601

Eóghan
d. 1598

Toirdhealbhach
(*tánaiste*)
d. 1601

28 Sir **Seaán Ruadh**
1583–96

29 Pilib Dubh
1596

31 Eóghan
1601–3

32 Maolmórdha
1603–7

Maolmórdha Breagh
d. 1593

Aodh
d. 1628

Éamonn
d. 1657

Maolmórdha Óg
d. 1618

Col. Pilib
d. 1663

Col. Maolmórdha Mór
d. 1670

34 (a) FITZGERALDS, CAREWS, BARRYS, DESCENDANTS OF NESTA

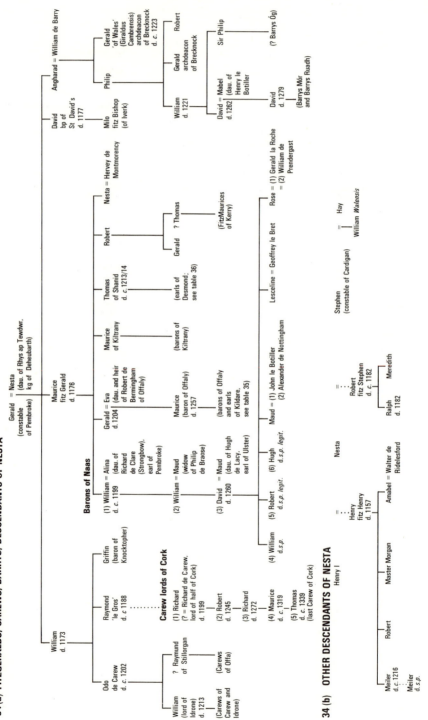

34 (b) OTHER DESCENDANTS OF NESTA

35 FITZGERALDS, EARLS OF KILDARE, 1316–1773, AND THEIR ANTECEDENTS

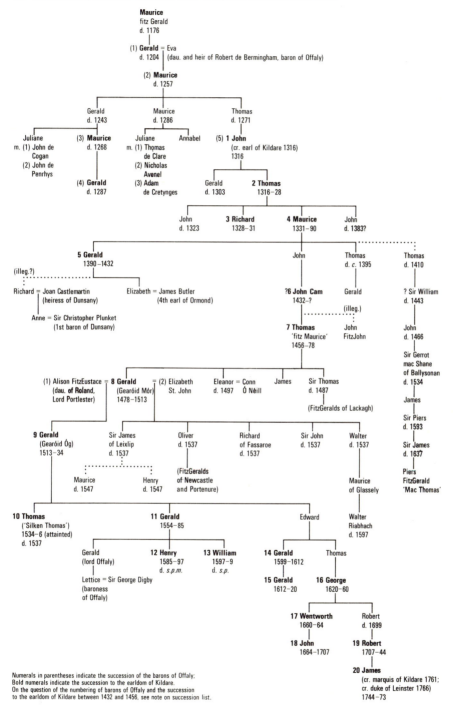

Numerals in parentheses indicate the succession of the barons of Offaly;
Bold numerals indicate the succession to the earldom of Kildare.
On the question of the numbering of barons of Offaly and the succession
to the earldom of Kildare between 1432 and 1456, see note on succession list.

36 FITZGERALDS, EARLS OF DESMOND, 1329–1632, AND THEIR ANTECEDENTS

Thomas fitz Maurice. fitz Gerald of Shanid d. c. 1213/14 = Sadhbh

Margery (dau. and co-heir of Thomas fitz Anthony, lord of Decies and Desmond) = **John** of Shanid d. 1261 — Maurice

Maurice d. 1261
Thomas* d. 1298

(1) Katherine (dau. of Richard de Burgh, 3rd earl of Ulster) = **1 Maurice*** (cr. earl of Desmond 1329) 1298–1356 = (2) Aneline (dau. of Nicholas fitz Maurice of Kerry)

Sir John of Glincarbry d.p. 1299
Sir Thomas of Glincarbry d.p. 1348 (Knights of Glin)

(?) Philip
Gilbert of Meane
Sir Thomas d.p. 1346
Sir Maurice d.p. 1372
Sir Maurice (the 'White Knight') d. 1414 (White Knights)

(?) Maurice
Sir Richard d. 1356
Sir Maurice (sheriff of Desmond) d.a. 1401

Sir Maurice d. 1346

Richard d. 1442 (seneschals of Imokilly)

Nicholas (bp of Ardfert) d.a. 1450 (Knights of Kerry)

Thomas d.a. 1309
Sir John d. 1324
Sir Thomas ('le nève') d.p. 1390 (Mac Thomases of Munster)

2 Maurice* 1356–7
Nicholas (an idiot)
3 Gerald* (Gearóid Iarla) 1357–98

4 John* 1398–9
6 Thomas* 1401–11 (dep.) d. 1420
Maurice d. 1452 (FitzGeralds of Brohill)

5 Maurice* (de facto earl) 1399–1401
8 Thomas* 1463–8

7 James* 1411–63

Joan Cam = Thomas FitzGerald (7th earl of Kildare)

Sir Gerrot* d. 1486
John* d. 1583

13b John (de facto earl) 1534–6
Sir Gerrot Óg d.p. 1520

Maurice abp of Cashel d. 1524
Gerald* mac Shane d. 1553

9 James 1468–87
10 Maurice Bacach 1487–1520
Thomas

11 James 1520–29
Maurice

12 Thomas 1529–34
[13a] James 1534–41

Joan = (1) James Butler (9th earl of Ormond and Ossory) (2) Sir Francis Bryan (3) Gerald FitzGerald (15th earl of Desmond)

Sir Maurice* (cr. Viscount Decies 1569) d. 1572
Sir James* d. 1581
Gerald* d. 1600
Gerrot d. 1569
Sir John* d. 1620

(3) Evelyn (dau. of Mac Carthaigh Mór) =
Sir Maurice an Torteáin d. 1564
John Óg d.p. 1580

14 James 1536–58 = (1) Joan Roche
(2) Mór (dau. of Maolruanaidh Ó Cearbhaill) =
Sir James d. 1580
Sir John d. 1582

15 Gerald 1558–83 (attainted)
[16b] James 1600–01

Thomas d. 1567
James fitz Maurice d. 1578
Thomas Óg d. 1581
Gerald d. 1588
Maurice d. 1588

Sir Thomas Ruadh of Conna d. 1595 = **[17] John** 1607–p. 1615
[18] Gerald p. 1615–32

[16a] James (the 'Súgán Earl') 1598–1601 (dep.) d. 1607

Thomas d. 1520

For enumeration of succession to the earldom of Desmond see note on succession list.
Bracketed numerals indicate earls who were not in de facto possession.
Asterisks indicate lords of Decies.

37 BUTLERS, EARLS AND DUKES OF ORMOND, 1328 – 1745, AND THEIR ANTECEDENTS

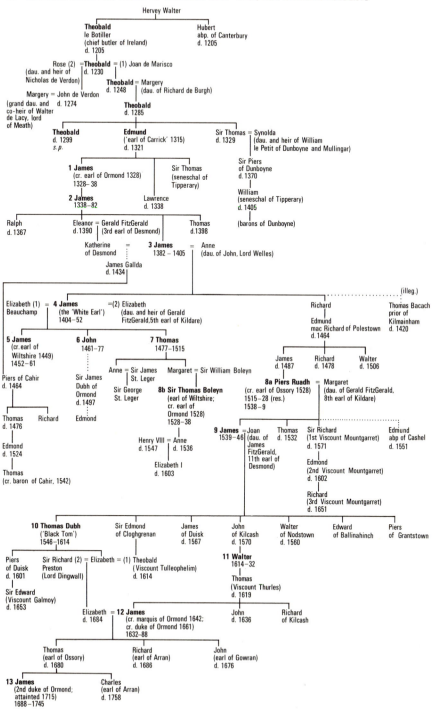

38 EARLS OF ULSTER AND LORDS OF CONNACHT, 1205–1460 (De BURGH, De LACY, AND MORTIMER)

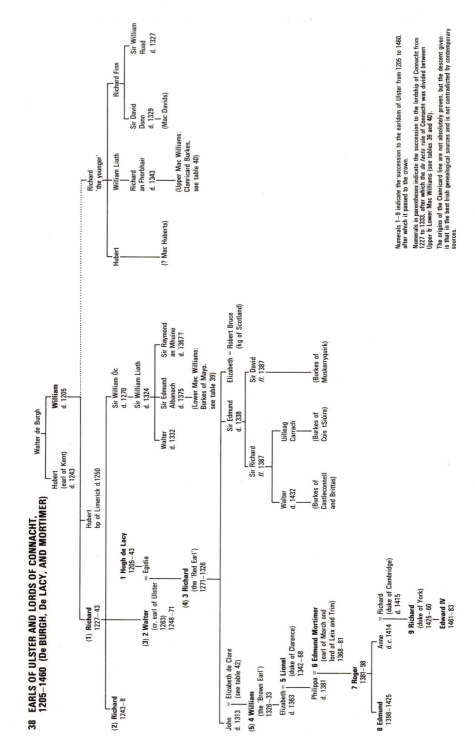

Numerals 1–9 indicate the succession to the earldom of Ulster from 1205 to 1460, after which it passed to the crown.

Numerals in parentheses indicate the succession to the lordship of Connacht from 1227 to 1333, after which the *de facto* rule of Connacht was divided between Upper & Lower Mac Williams (see tables 39 and 40).

The origins of the Clanricard line are not absolutely proven, but the descent given is that in the best Irish genealogical sources and is not contradicted by contemporary sources.

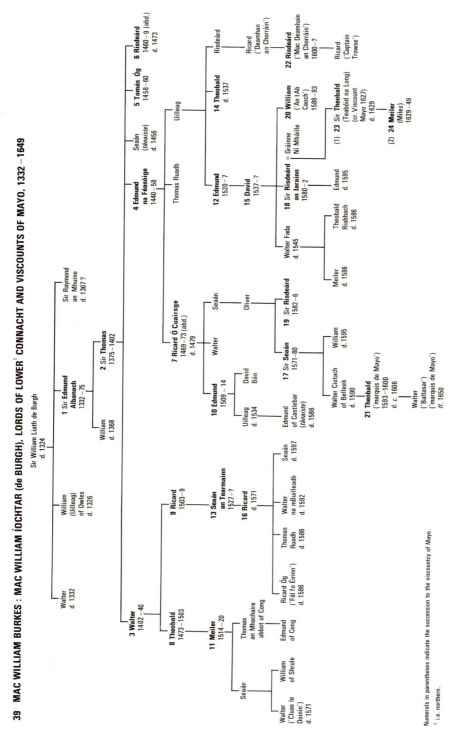

39 MAC WILLIAM BURKES : MAC WILLIAM ÍOCHTAR (de BURGH), LORDS OF LOWER¹ CONNACHT AND VISCOUNTS OF MAYO, 1332–1649

Numerals in parentheses indicate the succession to the viscountcy of Mayo.

¹ i.e. northern.

40 BURKES OF CLANRICARD: MAC WILLIAM UACHTAR (DE BURGH), LORDS OF UPPER¹ CONNACHT AND EARLS OF CLANRICARD, 1332–1722

Numerals in parentheses indicate the succession to the earldom of Clanricard.

¹ i.e. southern.

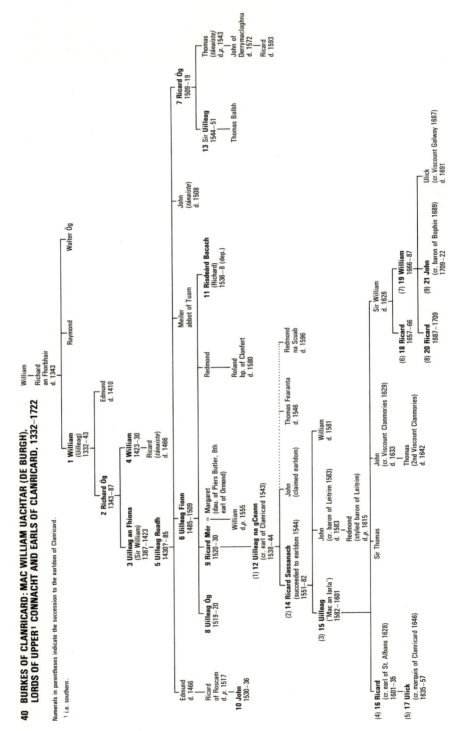

41 MEATH LORDSHIPS

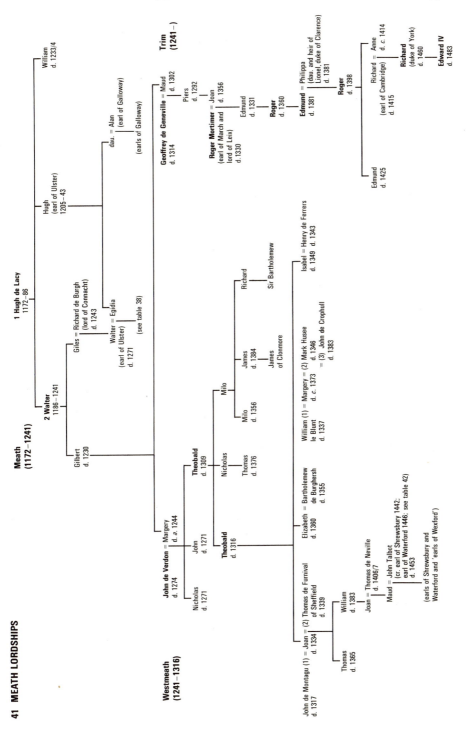

Meath
(1172–1241)

1 Hugh de Lacy
1172–86

Westmeath
(1241–1316)

Trim
(1241–)

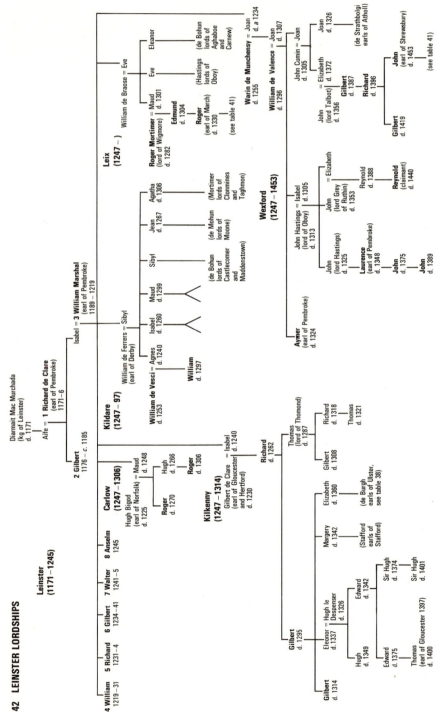

42　LEINSTER LORDSHIPS

**Leinster
(1171–1245)**

CORRIGENDA

Small discrepancies in orthography, style, and dating between the genealogical tables and the corresponding succession lists have arisen, primarily because further research was being carried out on the succession lists after the tables had reached final proof stage. Where such discrepancies occur the information in the succession lists may therefore be taken as based on more recent research; and the following should be substituted for the corresponding statements in the tables.

TABLE 1

ix 8	Diarmait mac Cerbaill 544–64/5
19a	Cellach 642/3–56/8
xiii 20a	Diarmait 656/8–65/6
xiii 20b	Blathmac 656/œ–œŒ/6
21	Sechnussach 66/6–71

TABLE 2

9(38)	Áed Findliath *a.* 855 (862/3–79)

TABLE 4

17	Áed *c.* 950–51

TABLE 5

2	Murchad 1073 (dep.); d. 1076 abbot of Clonard
3	Máel Sechlainn Ban 1073–87

TABLE 6

12	Dúnchad 637/9–*c.* 644
15	Congal Cennfoto 670–74

TABLE 7

11	Congal Clóen (high king) 627–37/9

TABLE 8

19	Rónán 605/8–24?

TABLE 10

15	Cathal 619/21–28
22	Ailill 695/701
32	Ólchobar 847–59, abbot of Emly
35	Fenn Fáelaid ua Mughthigirn 859–72, abbot of Emly

TABLE 10 (*cont.*)

40   Flaithbertach mac Inmainén, abbot of Inis Cathaig (914–22 abd; d. 944)

41   Lorcán 922–?

42   Cellachán *a.* 941–54

TABLE 13

14   Olaf Cuarán (kg of York ?–943)

TABLE 32

24   Feidhlimidh [deleting ?]

'E 33

In title read 'Maoilmhordha'

TABLE 37

11   Walter 1614–33

12   James . . . 1633–88

For the uncertainty of absolute dating before the eighth century see the introduction to 'Prehistoric and early Ireland', above, viii, 9.

In table 10, both Olchobar and Cenn Fáelaid may have belonged to the dynasty of Eóghanacht Áine (see Donnchadh Ó Corráin in *Celtica*, xiii (1980), pp 150–68).

III

SUCCESSION LISTS

CONTENTS

ROMAN CATHOLIC BISHOPS FROM 1534
by Benignus Millett and C. J. Woods

BISHOPS OF THE CHURCH OF IRELAND FROM 1534
by Brendan Bradshaw, J. G. Simms, and C. J. Woods

MODERATORS OF PRESBYTERIAN CHURCHES FROM 1690
by John M. Barkley

VICE-PRESIDENTS OF THE CONFERENCE AND PRESIDENTS OF THE METHODIST CHURCH IN IRELAND FROM 1868   by Ernest W. Gallagher   449

RULERS OF ENGLAND, SCOTLAND, WALES, AND MAN FROM *a.* 500

PRINCIPAL OFFICERS OF THE CENTRAL GOVERNMENT IN IRELAND, 1172–1922

GENERAL INTRODUCTION

THESE lists of officeholders, lay and ecclesiastical, are intended to provide chronological structures for all periods and many aspects of Irish history and its context in the history of the British Isles, Europe, and the world. Selection has, of course, been difficult: for example, we have excluded judges in Ireland (other than chancellors) because of the bulk and complexity of the subject, but have included Roman emperors because of their intrinsic importance in the European context. We should have been glad to include local officers such as mayors and sheriffs, but, partly from lack of material and of scholarly research for some areas, partly from the very wealth of materials on others, and partly from compelling reasons of space, we have limited our choice to the mayors and lord mayors of Dublin and the lords president of Munster and Connacht.

In the spelling of personal names in the early and medieval period our practice is as set out on page 126 above.

We have pleasure in acknowledging our indebtedness to the many standard reference-publications which we have used and to which tribute is paid in the headnotes to the various lists. We are especially grateful to the Royal Historical Society for cordially permitting us to use the invaluable material in its *Handbook of British chronology* and its *Handbook of dates*. Generally we have organised this material in a different form, and often, especially in the list of early and medieval bishops, we have made corrections in the light of new research. We are also grateful to the many scholars, contributors to this history and others, who have helped us by checking and presenting lists, based on, or drawn from, standard publications. All these are mentioned in the appropriate headnotes.

HIGH-KINGS AND
PROVINCIAL KINGS

F. J. BYRNE

INTRODUCTION

THESE lists of the succession to the major Irish kingdoms complement the material presented in genealogical tables 1-13 (above, pp 1-139). The annals are the most reliable historical source, but use has also been made of the Middle Irish regnal lists in prose and verse. For discussion of the latter, see T. F. O'Rahilly, *Early Irish history and mythology* (Dublin, 1946), pp 409-18; F. J. Byrne, 'Clann Ollaman uaisle Emna' in *Studia Hibernica*, iv (1964), pp 54-94; and M. O. Anderson, *Kings and kingship in early Scotland* (Edinburgh and London, 1973), pp 103-18, 223-4. The Leinster and Connacht regnal lists for the sixth and seventh centuries were distorted by dynastic propaganda: the later dominance of the Uí Dúnlainge and Uí Briúin respectively was projected backwards. A more reliable version for Connacht has been attempted by critical use of the annals (though the possibility remains that a separate provincial kingship of all Connacht, as distinct from the Uí Néill high-kingship, did not emerge until the eighth century), but for Leinster the absence of early annalistic material renders such emendation impossible. The later annals—such as *Ann. Tig.*, interpolated entries in *A.U.*, and *A.F.M.*—have themselves been contaminated by the regnal lists, and the pseudo-historical dates they assign to various early kings have accordingly been ignored; on the other hand, fifth- and sixth-century dates from *A.U.* and *Ann. Inisf.* have been utilised (as in the chronology in volume VIII), although their absolute accuracy cannot be guaranteed; those referring to the kings of Ulster (pp 197-9) are probably the most reliable. In spite of the shortcomings of regnal lists and genealogies, their value is appreciated when, as in the case of Dublin (pp 208-10), a succession must be constructed from the annalistic evidence alone.

The succession of rulers is not numbered in these lists as in the genealogical tables, but the names appear in the order denoted by numerals in these tables. In cases of shared or disputed kingship the name of the claimant with the longest period of tenure (denoted by (a) after the numeral in the genealogical table) is given first, followed by those of his rivals or partners (denoted by (b), etc., in the table).

The list of high-kings is based on the official reckonings which became standardised in the Middle Irish schools of the eleventh and twelfth centuries, and attempts to illustrate the development of the theory of the high-kingship as found in the ten earliest regnal lists, exemplified by sigla in the notes (below, pp 192–4). All dates have been supplied from the annals, with the exception of the conjectural date for the obit of Niall Noígiallach, for which see F. J. Byrne, *Irish kings and high-kings* (London, 1973), pp 80–81. The earliest list is that in the 'Baile Chuind', composed *c.* 675 and preserved in two sixteenth-century manuscripts (ed. G. Murphy, *Ériu*, xvi (1952), pp 145–51); it shows considerable divergences from the Middle Irish doctrine and clearly does not envisage an unbroken succession of Uí Néill high-kings. The earliest manuscript list is that in MS Palatino-Vaticanus 830, f. 15b, the autograph of the Chronicle of Marianus Scottus (Máel Brigte), who died at Mainz in 1082 (ed. B. MacCarthy, in *Todd lecture series*, iii (1892), pp 93–6). It seems to be based on a list first drawn up in the reign of Áed Oirdnide mac Néill (797–819) and continued in the reign of Flann Sinna (879–916); it exhibits some interesting differences from the official eleventh-century version standardised by Flann Mainistrech, *fer léigind* of Monasterboice (d. 1056), in his poem 'Ríg Themra tóebaige iar tain' (*Bk Leinster*, iii, 509–15), written between 1014 and 1022, and elaborated by Gilla Cáemáin mac Gilla Samthainne (*fl.* 1072) in his poem 'Atá sund forba fessa' (ibid., pp 491–5). With these the prose list in *Ann. Inisf.*, written before 1092, is in broad, though not absolute, agreement. The same doctrine is reiterated in three twelfth-century sources: the prose list in *Rawl. B 502*, pp 135b–137a (see M. A. O'Brien, *Corpus genealogiarum Hiberniae*, i (Dublin, 1962), pp 124–5), written *c.* 1130; Gilla Mo Dutu Ua Casaide's poem 'Ériu óg inis na náem' (see MacCarthy, op cit., pp 408–37, and *Lebor Gabála Érenn: the book of the taking of Ireland*, ed. R. A. S. Macalister, v (Dublin, 1956), pp 540–65), written in 1143, which extends the list down to his own day; and the prose list in *Bk Leinster*, i, 94–9, which ends with the reign of Ruaidrí Ua Conchobair (the notice of his death in 1198 is probably an addition by a later hand). An earlier list is provided by 'Baile in Scáil' (ed. from fifteenth- and sixteenth-century MSS by Kuno Meyer in *Z.C.P.*, iii (1901), pp 457–66; xiii (1921), pp 371–82; and by Rudolf Thurneysen, ibid., xx (1935), pp 213–27), which was probably written *c.* 862, but which has reached us in a redaction made between 1022 and 1036. It is just possible that the synchronisms in the fifteenth-century MS Laud Misc. 610 (ed. Kuno Meyer in *Z.C.P.*, ix (1913), pp 471–81) derive from a list originally drawn up in the reign of Domnall Midi (743–63), but they too have suffered the attentions of an eleventh-century editor and reflect the official doctrine too closely to have any independent value (see O'Rahilly, pp 412–18; Anderson, pp 223–4).

HIGH-KINGS, *c.* 453-1183

[B] = Síl nÁedo Sláine of Brega (Southern Uí Néill)
[C] = Cenél Conaill (Northern Uí Néill)
[D] = Dál Cais of Thomond
[E] = Cenél nEógain of Ailech (Northern Uí Néill)
[F] = Uí Fiachrach of Connacht
[M] = Clann Cholmáin of Mide (Southern Uí Néill)
[SM] = Síl Muiredaig of Uí Briúin Aí (Connacht)

	accession	death unless otherwise stated
Niall Noígiallach[1]	?	?453
Lóeguire mac Néill	454/6	461/3
Coirpre mac Néill[2]	*fl.* 485	
Ailill Molt mac Nath Í[3] [F]	?	482
Lugaid mac Lóeguiri	?	507
Muirchertach Mac Ercae[4] [E]	507	534/6
Tuathal Máelgarb mac Coirpri[5]	534/6	544
Diarmait mac Cerbaill	544	564/5
Forggus mac Muirchertaig[6] [E]	564/5	566
Domnall Ilchelgach mac Muirchertaig[6] [E]		
Ainmere mac Sétnai[6,7] [C]	566	569
Báetán mac Muirchertaig[6,7] [E]	569	572
Eochaid mac Domnaill[6,7] [E]		
Báetán mac Ninnedo[6,8] [C]	572	586
Áed mac Ainmerech[6,9] [C]	586	598
Áed Sláine mac Diarmato[6] [B]	598	604
Colmán Rímid mac Báetáin[6,10] [E]		
Áed Allán (alias Uaridnach) mac Domnaill[11] [E]	604	612
Máel Cobo mac Áedo[6,12] [C]	612	615
Suibne Menn mac Fiachnai[13] [E]	615	628
Domnall mac Áedo[14] [C]	628	Jan. 642/3
Cellach mac Máele Cobo[6,15] [C]	642/3	656/8
Conall Cóel mac Máele Cobo[6,15] [C]		654
Diarmait mac Áedo Sláine [B]	656/8	665/6
Blathmac mac Áedo Sláine [B]		
Sechnussach mac Blathmaic[6] [B]	665/6	*c.* 1 Nov. 671
Cenn Fáelad mac Blathmaic[6,16] [B]	671	675
Fínsnechtae Fledach mac Dúnchado[17] [B]	675	695
Loingsech mac Óengusso[14,18] [C]	695	12 July 704
Congal Cinn Magair mac Fergusso[19] [C]	704	710
Fergal mac Máele Dúin[20] [E]	710	11 Dec. 722
Fogartach mac Néill[19] [B]	722	724

	accession	death unless otherwise stated
Cínáed mac Írgalaig[21] [B]	724	728
Flaithbertach mac Loingsig[22] [C]	728	dep. 734
		d. 765
Áed Allán mac Fergaile[23] [E]	734	743
Domnall Midi mac Murchado [M]	743	20 Nov. 763
Niall Frossach mac Fergaile[24] [E]	763	abd. 770
		d. 778
Donnchad Midi mac Domnaill[25] [M]	770	797
Áed Oirdnide mac Néill[22] [E]	797	819
Conchobar mac Donnchado[25,26] [M]	819	833
Niall Caille mac Áedo[22,26] [E]	833	846
Máel Sechnaill I mac Máele Ruanaid[14,23] [M]	846	27 Nov. 862
Áed Findliath mac Néill[22,27] [E]	862/3	20 Nov. 879
Flann Sinna mac Máele Sechnaill[23,28] [M]	879	25 May 916
Niall Glúndub mac Áeda[14,29] [E]	916	15 Sept. 919
Donnchad Donn mac Flainn [M]	919	944
Congalach Cnogba mac Máel Mithig[14,30] [B]	944	956
Domnall ua Néill[14,22,31] [E]	956	980
Máel Sechnaill II mac Domnaill[14,31] [M]	980	abd. 1002
		rest. 1014
		d. 2 Sept. 1022
Brian Bóruma mac Cennétig[14,22] [D]	1002	23 Apr. 1014
[Interregnum 1022-72][32]		

Ríg Érenn co fressabra 'high-kings with opposition'

	accession[33]	
Toirrdelbach ua Briain, kg of Munster[14,34] [D]	1063(1072)	14 July 1086
Domnall Mac Lochlainn, kg of Ailech[35] [E]	1083(1090)	9 Feb. 1121
Muirchertach Ua Briain, kg of Munster[14,36] [D]	1086(1093)	13 Mar. 1119
Toirrdelbach Ua Conchobair, kg of Connacht[23,37] [SM]	1106(1120/21)	20 May 1156
Muirchertach Mac Lochlainn, kg of Ailech[14,22] [E]	1136(1149/50)	1166
Ruaidrí Ua Conchobair, kg of Connacht[14,23] [SM]	1156(1166)	abd. 1183
		d. 2 Dec. 1198

SIGLA

B	= 'Baile Chuind'	L	= *Bk Leinster*, i, 94-9
C	= Gilla Cáemáin mac Gilla Samthainne	La	= Synchronisms in Laud Misc. 610
D	= Gilla Mo Dutu Ua Casaide	M	= Marianus Scottus
F	= Flann Mainistrech	R	= *Rawl. B 502*, pp 135b-137a
I	= *Ann. Inisf.*, pp 40-44	S	= 'Baile in Scáil'

Footnotes on next page

¹ *S* inserts Colla Óss (i.e. Colla Uais, one of the legendary 3 Collas, ancestors of the Airgialla) as Niall's successor; *M* gives him as his immediate predecessor and agrees with *C, F, I, L, La, R* in including Nath Í mac Fiachrach [F] (d. 445) as high-king after Niall.

² Only in *B*.

³ Ailill precedes Lóeguire in *S*.

⁴ 'Mac Ercéni', *B*; the identification in all later sources with Muirchertach mac Muiredaig of Cenél nEógain may be false.

⁵ 'Óengarb', *B*; Tuathal is after Lóeguire (see note 3) and before Lugaid in *S*.

⁶ Not in *B*.

⁷ Ainmere and the joint reign of Báetán and Eochaid are placed after Muirchertach Mac Ercae and before Diarmait in *S*; Ainmere succeeds Báetán and Eochaid in *C, D, F, L, La, R*; *M* inserts Muiredach Muinderg, kg of Ulster, before Ainmere.

⁸ Not in *I, M,* or *S*; *M* replaces him by an unknown Báetán mac Murchada who is succ. after 16 years by another Ainmere; all other sources assign Báetán mac Ninnedo a reign of only 1 year (*A.U.* records his death as 'kg of Tara' in 586). The Ulster genealogies claim that Muiredach Muinderg (see note 7), his son Cairell, and his grandson Báetán mac Cairill, kg of Ulster 572–c. 581, were high-kings of Ireland, and Báetán's claim is referred to by *D* and *R*.

⁹ *M* gives Colmán Bec mac Diarmato, kg of Mide 555/8–587, a joint reign of 13 years with Áed mac Ainmerech, and further inserts Suibne mac Colmáin Máir [M], kg of Mide 587–600, with a reign of 6 years after Áed mac Ainmerech and before Áed Sláine.

¹⁰ Not in *M* or *S*, which give Áed Sláine a sole reign of 4 and 8 years respectively.

¹¹ 'Aíd Olláin', *B*, which places him between Tuathal Máelgarb and Diarmait mac Cerbaill; *S* distinguishes between 'Áed Uáredach mac Domnaill', who is placed before Áed Sláine, and 'Áedh Olldain', who succeeds the latter.

¹² Not in *M* or *S*; *M* substitutes a 9-year reign of Óengus mac Colmáin Máir [M], kg of Mide from *a*. 612 to 621, who is in fact styled *rex nepotum Néill* in *A.U.* 621.

¹³ *B* gives Suibne a predecessor 'Feachno', who may be his father, but who more probably is Fiachnae mac Báetáin maic Echach (Fiachnae Find or Fiachnae Lurgan), Cruthin kg of Ulster 588–626, whose grandson Congal Clóen, kg of Ulster 627–37/9, is stated in the law-tract 'Bech-bretha' to have been kg of Tara; *D* tacitly recognises the latter's claim by dividing the regnal years of Domnall mac Áedo into 9 or 10 years before and 7 after the battle of Mag Roth (637/9); *D* further states that the Ulaid regarded Báetán mac Cairill (see note 8), Fiachnae Find and Eochaid Iarlaithe, kg of Dál nAraidi 645–66, as high-kings.

¹⁴ Expressly styled 'kg of Ireland' in *A.U.*

¹⁵ Not in *S*; *A.U.* 643 admits that some claimed a quadripartite reign of Cellach and Conall jointly with Diarmait and Blathmac.

¹⁶ Given as 'mac Crundmaíl' in *D, L, La*.

¹⁷ 'Snechta Fína', the last identifiable name in *B*, which proceeds to prophesy 5 further kgs by vague kennings; *S* places Fínsnechtae before Sechnussach.

¹⁸ *I* inserts a single year of Fogartach after Loingsech.

¹⁹ *S* assigns Congal and Fogartach a joint reign of 14 years and asserts that both are buried at Clonard.

²⁰ Buried at Durrow.

²¹ Not in *S*.

²² Buried at Armagh.

²³ Buried at Clonmacnoise.

²⁴ Buried at Iona.

²⁵ Buried at Clonard.

²⁶ With opposition from Fedelmid mac Crimthainn, kg of Munster 820–47; *Ann. Inisf.*, 721, also claims the high-kingship for earlier Munster kgs, viz Óengus mac Nad Froích (d. 490/92), his son Eochaid, and Cathal mac Finguine 721–42; *D* mentions but does not accept Fedelmid's claim, but *L* omits Niall Caille and admits Fedelmid as *rí Érenn co fressabra*, 'kg of Ireland with opposition'.

²⁷ 'In Cóel Cresen Óed Ólach', *S*, the first of 15 kgs there prophesied under vague kennings; the first 8 were glossed by the names of historical kgs by the eleventh-century redactor.

²⁸ The last name in *M*, where no regnal years are given.

²⁹ Buried at Kells.

³⁰ With opposition from Ruaidrí ua Canannáin [C], 944–50; *I* assigns Congalach and Ruaidrí a joint reign of 12 years; Congalach is buried at Monasterboice.

³¹ Domnall ua Néill and the first half of Máel Sechnaill's reign are ignored in *I*; *F* ends 1014 × 1022; *C, I, La, R* end 1022.

³² This is the doctrine of the medieval schools, but Donnchad mac Briain [D], kg of Munster 1014–63 (d. 1065), claimed to be kg of Ireland, while the redactor of *S* makes the same claim for his comtemporary

Flaithbertach Ua Néill [E], kg of Ailech 1004–36; *L* reckons an interregnum of 42 or 52 years from 1022 but claims that Diarmait mac Máel na mBó, kg of Leinster 1042–72, was high-king 'with opposition'; *D* reckons an interregnum of 72 years 1022–94.

[33] To provincial kingship; the year in which pretension to high-kingship was first made is in brackets.

[34] *L* agrees with *A.U.* in recognising Toirrdelbach ua Briain, Muirchertach Ua Briain, Muirchertach Mac Lochlainn, and Ruaidrí Ua Conchobair as high-kings of Ireland.

[35] Not in *L*; buried at Derry; *D* assigns 23 or 25 years of joint rule to Domnall Mac Lochlainn and Muirchertach Ua Briain.

[36] Buried at Killaloe.

[37] *L* reckons an interregnum of 36 years after the death of Muirchertach Ua Briain, but admits Toirrdelbach Ua Conchobair as high-king 'with opposition'; *D*, writing in 1143, acknowledges Toirrdelbach as high-king of Ireland.

CENÉL NEÓGAIN KINGS OF AILECH, 700–1185

Many of these kings were also high-kings and are listed above as such.

	accession	death unless otherwise stated
Fergal mac Máele Dúin	700	11 Dec. 722
Áed Allán mac Fergaile	722	743
Niall Frossach mac Fergaile	743	abd. 770
		d. 778
Máel Dúin mac Áedo	770	788
Áed Oirdnide mac Néill	788	819
Murchad mac Máele Dúin	819	dep. 823
Niall Caille mac Áedo	823	846
Máel Dúin mac Áedo	846	dep. or abd. ?
		d. 867
Áed Findliath mac Néill	a. 855	20 Nov. 879
Murchad mac Máele Dúin	879	887
Flaithbertach mac Murchado	887	896
Domnall mac Áedo	887	915
Niall Glúndub mac Áedo	896	15 Sept. 919
Flaithbertach mac Domnaill[1]	916	919
Fergal mac Domnaill	919	938
Muirchertach mac Néill	938	26 Feb. 943
Domnall ua Néill (mac Muirchertaig meic Néill)	943	980
Flaithbertach mac Muirchertaig meic Néill	943	949
Flaithbertach mac Conchobair[1]	956	962
Tadg mac Conchobair[1]	956	962
Conn mac Conchobair[1]	956	962
Murchad Glún re Lár mac Flaithbertaig[1]	962	abd. 972
		d. 974
Fergal mac Domnaill meic Conaing	980	abd. 989
		d. 1001
Áed mac Domnaill Ua Néill	989	1004

	accession	death unless otherwise stated
Flaithbertach Ua Néill	1004	abd. 1030 rest. 1032 d. 1036
Áed mac Flaithbertaig Ua Néill	1030	abd. 1032 d. 1033
Niall mac Máel Sechnaill	1036	1061
Ardgar mac Lochlainn	1061	1064
Áed Ua hUalgairg	1064	1067
Domnall mac Néill	1067	1068
Áed mac Néill	1068	1083
Donnchad mac Néill	1083	1083
Domnall ua (Mac) Lochlainn	1083	9 Feb 1121
Conchobar mac Domnaill	1121	dep. 1128 rest. 1129 d. 1136
Magnus ua (Mac) Lochlainn	1128	1129
Muirchertach Mac Lochlainn	1136	dep. 1143 rest. 1145 d. 1166
Domnall Ua Gairmledaig	1143	dep. 1145 d. 1160
Conchobar mac Muirchertaig Mac Lochlainn	1166	dep. 1167 rest. (?) d. 1170
Niall mac Muirchertaig Mac Lochlainn[2]	1167	dep.(?) rest. 1170 d. 1176
Aed ('In Macáem Tóinlesc') Ua Néill[2]	1167	1177
Máel Sechlainn mac Muirchertaig Mac Lochlainn	1177	1185

[1] Probably ruled Ailech as sub-king (*airrí*) when the kg of Ailech was high-king.
[2] *Leth-rí*.

CLANN CHOLMÁIN KINGS OF MIDE, 766–1184

Many of these kings were also high-kings and are listed above as such.

	accession	death unless otherwise stated
Donnchad Midi mac Domnaill	766	797
Domnall mac Donnchado	797	799
Muiredach mac Domnaill	799	802
Diarmait mac Donnchado	802	803

	accession	death unless otherwise stated
Conchobar mac Donnchado	803	833
Niall mac Diarmato[1]	?	826
Máel Ruanaid mac Donnchado	833	843
Fland mac Máele Ruanaid	843	845
Máel Sechnaill mac Máele Ruanaid	845	22 Nov. 862
Lorcán mac Cathail	862	dep. 864
Conchobar mac Donnchado[2]	?	864
Donnchad mac Eochocáin (Áeducáin)	864	877
Fland Sinna mac Máele Sechnaill	877	25 May 916
Conchobar mac Flainn	916	919
Donnchad Donn mac Flainn	919	944
Domnall mac Flainn[1]	919	921
Óengus mac Donnchada	944	945/6
Donnchad mac Domnaill	945/6	950
Fergal Got mac Óengussa	c. 950	dep. c. 950
Áed mac Máel Ruanaid	c. 950	951
Domnall mac Donnchada	951	952
Carlus mac Cuinn	952	960
Donnchad Finn mac Áeda	960	974
Muirchertach mac Máel Sechnaill[3]	960	?976
Máel Sechnaill mac Domnaill	975/6	2 Sept. 1022
Máel Sechnaill Got mac Máel Sechnaill	1022	1025
Róen mac Muirchertaig	1025	1027
Domnall Got[4]	1027	1030
Conchobar ua Máel Sechlainn	1030	1073
Murchad mac Flainn Ua Máel Sechlainn	1073	dep. 1073 d. 1076
Máel Sechlainn Bán mac Conchobair Ua Máel Sechlainn	1073	1087
Domnall mac Flainn Ua Máel Sechlainn	1087	1094
Donnchad mac Murchada Ua Máel Sechlainn[5]	1094	dep. 1105 d. 1106
Conchobar mac Máel Sechlainn Ua Máel Sechlainn[5]	1094	1105
Muirchertach mac Domnaill Ua Máel Sechlainn	1105	dep. 1106 d. 1143
Murchad mac Domnaill Ua Máel Sechlainn[6]	1106	1153
Máel Sechlainn mac Domnaill Ua Máel Sechlainn	1115	1115
Domnall mac Murchada Ua Máel Sechlainn	1127	dep. 1127 d. 1137
Diarmait mac Domnaill Ua Máel Sechlainn	1127	1130
Conchobar Ua Conchobair[7]	1143	1144
Donnchad mac Muirchertaig Ua Máel Sechlainn	1144	?
Máel Sechlainn mac Murchada Ua Máel Sechlainn	1152	1155

	accession	death unless otherwise stated
Donnchad mac Domnaill Ua Máel Sechlainn	1155	dep. 1155 rest. 1156 dep. 1157 rest. 1158 d. 1160
Diarmait mac Domnaill Ua Máel Sechlainn	1155	dep. 1156 rest. 1157 dep. 1158 rest. 1160 d. 1169
Domnall Bregach mac Máel Sechlainn meic Domnaill Ua Máel Sechlainn	1169	1173
Art mac Máel Sechlainn meic Domnaill Ua Máel Sechlainn	1173	1184
Magnus Ua Máel Sechlainn[8]	?	1175

[1] May have acted as provincial sub-king (*airrí*) when the kg of Mide was high-king.
[2] *Leth-rí.*
[3] Probably should be identified with Muirchertach (d. 977), son of Domnall ua Néill; see tables 2 and 4, pp 128-9.
[4] Antecedents unknown.
[5] Mide was partitioned between Donnchad and Conchobar in 1094 by Muirchertach Ua Briain.
[6] Deposed and restored on several occasions.
[7] Son of High-king Toirrdelbach Ua Conchobair of Connacht.
[8] Antecedents unknown; kg of Iarthar Mide.

KINGS OF ULSTER TO 1201

[DA] = Dál nAraidi (Cruthin)
[UE] = Uí Echach Cobo (Cruthin)
*   = antecedents unknown

All other kings are of the Ulaid dynasty of Dál Fiatach.

	accession	death unless otherwise stated
Muiredach Muinderg mac Forggo (high-king)		
Eochaid mac Muiredaig Muindeirg		
Cairell mac Muiredaig Muindeirg (high-king)		
Eochaid mac Condlai [DA]	?	553
Fergnae mac Óengusso Ibdaig	553	557
Demmán mac Cairill	557	572
Báetán mac Cairill (high-king)	572	c. 581
Áed Dub mac Suibni Araidi [DA] *	c. 581	588
Fiachnae Lurgan mac Báetáin maic Echach [DA] (high-king)	588	626

	accession	death unless otherwise stated
Fiachnae mac Demmáin	626	627
Congal Clóen mac Scandail Sciathlethain [DA] (high-king)	627	637/9
Dúnchad mac Fiachnai	637/9	c. 644
Máel Cobo mac Fiachnai	c. 644	647
Blathmac mac Máele Cobo	647	670
Congal Cennfoto mac Dúnchado	670	674
Fergus mac Áedáin [UE]	674	692
Bécc Bairrche mac Blathmaic	692	abd. 707 d. 718
Cú Chuaráin mac Dúngaile Eilni [DA]	707	708
Áed Róin mac Bécce Bairrche	708	735
Cathussach mac Ailello [DA]	735	749
Bressal mac Áedo Róin	749	750
Fiachnae mac Áedo Róin	750	789
Tommaltach mac Indrechtaig [DA]	789	790
Eochaid mac Fiachnai	790	810
Cairell mac Fiachnai	810	819
Máel Bressail mac Ailello [UE]	819	825
Muiredach mac Eochado	825	839
Matudán mac Muiredaig	839	857
Lethlobar mac Loingsig [DA][1]	857	873
Cathalán mac Indrechtaig[1]	857	871
Ainbíth mac Áedo	873	882
Airemón mac Áedo[2]	882	886
Eochocán mac Áedo[2]	882	883
Fiachnae mac Ainbíth	886	886
Bécc mac Airemóin	886	893
Muiredach mac Eochocáin[3]	893	896
Máel Mocheirge mac Indrechtaig[3]	893	896
Cenn Étig mac Lethlobair [DA]	896	900
Aitíth mac Laigni [UE]	896	898
Áed mac Eochocáin	898	919
Dubgall mac Áeda	919	925
Loingsech mac Cinn Étig [DA]	925	932
Eochaid mac Conaill *	932	937
Matudán mac Áeda	937	950
Ardgal mac Matudáin	950	970
Niall mac Áeda	970	971
Áed mac Loingsig [DA]	971	972
Eochaid mac Ardgail	972	1004
Gilla Comgaill mac Ardgail	1004	1005
Máel Ruanaid mac Ardgail	1005	1007
Matudán mac Domnaill *	1007	1007
Dub Tuinne ('In Torc') mac Eochada	1007	1007
Domnall mac Duib Thuinne	1007	1007
Niall mac Duib Thuinne	1007	1016

	accession	death unless otherwise stated
Muiredach mac Matudáin *	1007	1008
Niall mac Eochada	1016	1063
Eochaid mac Néill meic Eochada	?	1062
Donnchad Ua Mathgamna *	1063	1065
Cú Ulad Ua Flaithrí *4	1065	dep. 1071 d. 1072
Lochlainn Ua Máel Ruanaid	1071	1071
Donn Sléibe mac Eochada	1071	dep. 1078 rest. 1081 d. 1091
Áed Méránach Ua hEochada *	1078	dep. 1080 d. 1083
Goll na Gorta Ua Mathgamna *	1080	1081
Donnchad mac Duinn Sléibe	1091	dep. 1095 rest. and dep. 1099 rest. 1108 dep. 1113
Eochaid (Goll Garbraige) mac Duinn Sléibe	1095	1108 dep. and rest. 1099
Áed (Niall) mac Duinn Sléibe	1113	1127
Eochaid (Garrchú) Ua Mathgamna *	1113	1127
Ragnall (Gilla Comgaill) Ua hEochada *	1127	1131
Cú Ulad mac Conchobair Chísénaig Mac Duinn Sléibe	1131	1157
Áed mac Con Ulad Mac Duinn Sléibe	1157	1158
Eochaid mac Con Ulad Mac Duinn Sléibe	1158	dep. 1166
Magnus Mac Con Ulad Mac Duinn Sléibe	1166	1171
Donn Sléibe mac Con Ulad Mac Duinn Sléibe	1171	1172
Ruaidrí mac Con Ulad Mac Duinn Sléibe	1172	1201

[1] *Leth-rí* 857-71; Lethlobar subsequently reigned to 873.
[2] *Leth-rí* 882-3; Airemón subsequently reigned to 886.
[3] *Leth-rí.*
[4] Probably of Leth Cathail branch of Dál Fiatach.

KINGS OF LEINSTER TO 1171

[UB]   = Uí Bairrche
[UC]   = Uí Chennselaig
[UD]   = Uí Dúnlainge
[UD:D] = Uí Dúnlainge : Uí Dúnchada
[UD:F] = Uí Dúnlainge : Uí Fáeláin
[UD:M] = Uí Dúnlainge : Uí Muiredaig
[UE]   = Uí Enechglaiss
[UG]   = Uí Garrchon
[UM]   = Uí Máil

	accession	death unless otherwise stated
Cathaír Már		
Fiachu ba hAiccíd mac Cathaír		
Bressal Bélach mac Fiachach		435/6
Muiredach Sníthe mac Dáiri Barraich (Mo Sníthech) [UB]		
Móenach mac Muiredaig [UB]		
Mac Caírthinn mac Cóelboth [UE]		446
Nad Buidb mac Eirc Buadaig maic Dego		
Éndae Cennselach mac Labrado Laídig		
Crimthann mac Éndai Chennselaig [UC]		483
Findchad mac Garrchon [UG]		485
Fróech mac Findchado [UG]		495
Illann mac Dúnlainge [UD]		527
Ailill mac Dúnlainge [UD]		
Cormac mac Ailello [UD][1]		
Coirpre mac Cormaic [UD][1]		
Colmán Már mac Coirpri [UD][1]		
Áed Díbchíne mac Senaig Díbig [UM]		
Brandub mac Echach [UC]	a. 597	605/8
Rónán mac Colmáin [UC or UD?]	?	624
Crimthann mac Áedo Díbchíni [UM]	624	633
Fáelán mac Colmáin [UD]	633	abd. or dep.? d. 666
Crundmáel mac Rónáin [UC]	?	656
Fiannamail mac Máele Tuile [UM]	?	680
Bran Mut mac Conaill [UD]	680	693
Cellach Cualann mac Gerthidi [UM]	693	715
Murchad mac Brain [UD]	715	727
Dúnchad mac Murchado [UD]	727	728
Áed mac Colggen [UC]	?715/28	19 Aug. 738
Bran Bec mac Murchado [UD]	?728/38	738
Fáelán mac Murchado [UD]	?738	738
Muiredach mac Murchado [UD]	738	760
Cellach mac Dúnchado [UD:D]	760	776

	accession	death unless otherwise stated
Ruaidrí mac Fáeláin [UD:F]	776	785
Bran Ardchenn mac Muiredaig [UD:M]	785	795
Fínsnechtae Cetharderc mac Cellaig [UD:D]	795	808 dep. 805[2] rest. 806
Muiredach mac Ruadrach [UD:F]	808	829
Cellach mac Brain [UD:M]	829	834
Bran mac Fáeláin [UD:D]	834	838
Lorcán mac Cellaig [UD:M]	838	*p.* 848
Tuathal mac Muiredaig alias mac Máele Brigte [UD:M]	?	854
Ruarc mac Brain [UD:D]	854	862
Muirecán mac Diarmato [UD:F]	862	863
Dúnlaing mac Muiredaig [UD:M]	863	869
Ailill mac Dúnlainge [UD:M]	869	871
Domnall mac Muirecáin [UD:F]	871	884
Muiredach mac Brain [UD:D], abbot of Kildare	884	885
Cerball mac Muirecáin [UD:F]	885	909
Augaire mac Ailella [UD:M]	909	917
Fáelán mac Muiredaig [UD:D]	917	942
Lorcán mac Fáeláin [UD:D]	942	943
Bróen mac Máel Mórda [UD:F]	943	947
Tuathal mac Augaire [UD:M]	947	958
Cellach mac Fáeláin [UD:D]	958	966
Murchad mac Finn [UD:F]	966	972
Augaire mac Tuathail [UD:M]	972	978
Domnall Cláen mac Lorcáin [UD:D]	978	984
Donnchad mac Domnaill Cláin [UD:D]	984	dep. 1003
Máel Mórda mac Murchada [UD:F]	1003	1014
Dúnlaing mac Tuathail [UD:M]	1014	1014
Donncuan mac Dúnlainge [UD:M]	1014	1016
Bran mac Máel Mórda [UD:F]	1016	dep. 1018 d. 1052
Augaire mac Dúnlainge [UD:M]	1018	1024
Donnchad mac Dúnlainge [UD:M]	1024	dep. 1033 d. 1036
Donnchad mac Gilla Pátraic[3]	1033	1039
Murchad mac Dúnlainge [UD:M]	1039	1042
Diarmait mac (Donnchada) Máel na mBó [UC]	1042	7 Feb. 1072
Murchad mac Diarmata [UC][4]	1052	21 Nov. 1070
Domnall mac Murchada [UC]	1072	1075
Donnchad mac Domnaill Remair [UC][5]	1075	1089
Énna mac Diarmata [UC]	1089	1092
Diarmait mac Énna [UC]	1092	1098
Donnchad mac Murchada [UC]	1098	1115

	accession	death unless otherwise stated
Diarmait mac Énna Mac Murchada [UC]	1115	1117
Énna mac Donnchada Mac Murchada [UC]	1117	1126
Diarmait mac Donnchada Mac Murchada [UC][6]	1126/a. 1132	a. 1 May 1171

[1] These names are taken from the Uí Dúnlainge pedigree; their actual rule is very doubtful.

[2] The high-king Áed Oirdnide divided Leinster between Muiredach mac Ruadrach [UD:F] and Muiredach mac Brain [UD:M].

[3] Kg of Osraige 1003–39; see below.

[4] Ruled as sub-king and kg of Dublin under his father; see below, p. 209.

[5] Conchobar Ua Conchobair, kg of Uí Failge 1071–1115, made an attempt to claim the kingship of Leinster in 1079.

[6] The high-king Toirrdelbach Ua Conchobair intruded his son Conchobar as kg of Dublin and Leinster on Énna's death in 1126, and after his expulsion by the Leinstermen in 1127 nominated Domnall mac Cerbaill Mac Fáeláin [UD:F], kg of Uí Fáeláin (d. 1141), as kg of Leinster, but apparently without effect.

KINGS OF OSRAIGE, a. 842–1176

* = antecedents unknown

	accession	death unless otherwise stated
Dúngal (Dúnlaing)	?	842
Cerball mac Dúnlainge	842	888
Riacán mac Dúnlainge	888	894
Diarmait mac Cerbaill	894	dep. 905 rest. 908 d. 928
Cellach mac Cerbaill	905	908
Cuilén mac Cellaig	928	933
Donnchad mac Cellaig	934	976
Gilla Pátraic mac Donnchada	976	996
Cellach mac Diarmata	996	1003
Donnchad mac Gilla Pátraic[1]	1003	1039
Gilla Pátraic mac Donnchada	1039	1055
Muirchertach mac Gilla Pátraic[2]	?	1041
Domnall mac Gilla Pátraic	1055	p. 1072
Donnchad mac Domnaill	p. 1072	1090
Gilla Pátraic Ruad *	1090	1103
Cerball *	1103	c. 1113
Domnall mac Donnchada Mac Gilla Pátraic[2]	?	1113
Finn Ua Cáellaide *[2]	?	?
Donnchad Balc mac Gilla Pátraic Ruaid	a. 1119	1123
Donnchad Dub *	c. 1121	c. 1121
Murchad Mac Murchada[3]	c. 1123	dep. c. 1126 d. 1172
Conchobar mac Cerbaill	1123	c. 1126

	accession	death unless otherwise stated
Gilla Pátraic mac Domnaill Mac Gilla Pátraic	c. 1126	1146
Cerball mac Domnaill Mac Gilla Pátraic[4]	1146	1163
Murchad Ua Cáellaide *[2]	?	?
Donnchad mac Gilla Pátraic Mac Gilla Pátraic[2]	a. 1151	1162
Domnall (?mac Donnchada) Mac Gilla Pátraic[5]	1162/3	1165
Domnall (?mac Cerbaill) Mac Gilla Pátraic[6]	1165	1176
Diarmait Ua Cáellaide *[2]	1170	1172

[1] Kg of Leinster 1033-9.
[2] *Leth-rí.*
[3] Of Uí Chennselaig: apparently brother of Énna and Diarmait Mac Murchada, kgs of Leinster 1117-26 and 1126-71.
[4] Kg of south Osraige: the regnal list in *Bk Leinster*, i, 190, states that Cerball was expelled by Diarmait Mac Murchada and replaced by Murchad Ua Cáellaide and Donnchad mac Gilla Pátraic; subsequently Diarmait imprisoned Donnchad and restored Cerball as *leth-rí* with Murchad; finally Cerball ruled jointly with Donnchad.
[5] Kg of north Osraige.
[6] See note on table 9.

KINGS OF MUNSTER TO 1119, OF DESMOND TO 1176, AND OF THOMOND TO 1194

[Á]	= Eóganacht Áine
[AC]	= Eóganacht Airthir Chliach
[C]	= Eóganacht Chaisil
[D]	= Dál Cais
[F]	= Uí Fidgeinti
[G]	= Eóganacht Glendamnach
[L]	= Eóganacht Locha Léin
[R]	= Eóganacht Raithlind
*	= antecedents unknown

	accession	death unless otherwise stated
Conall Corc mac Luigthig		
Nio Froích mac Cuirc		
Óengus mac Nad Froích (high-king)		490/92
Dauí Iarlaithe mac Maithni [L]		
Eochaid mac Óengusso (high-king)		
Fedelmid mac Óengusso [C]		
Dub Gilcach mac Óengusso		
Crimthann (Srem Feimin) mac Echado [G]		

	accession	death unless otherwise stated
Coirpre Cromm mac Crimthainn [G]	?	579/80
Fergus Scandal mac Crimthainn Airthir Chliach [AC]	579/80	583
Fedelmid mac Coirpri Chruimm [G]	583	?
Fedelmid mac Tigernaig [R]		590/93
Amalgaid mac Éndai [Á]	?	?
Garbán (Gabrán) mac Éndai [Á]	?	?
Fíngen mac Áedo Duib [C]	?	619
Áed Bennán mac Crimthainn [L]	?	619/21
Cathal mac Áedo Flaind Chathrach [G]	619/21	628
Faílbe Fland mac Áedo Duib [C]	628	637/9
Cuán mac Amalgado [Á]	637/9	641
Máenach mac Fíngin [C]	641	662
Cathal Cú cen Máthair mac Cathail [G]	662	665/6
Colcu mac Faílbi Flaind [C]	665/6	678
Finguine mac Cathail Con cen Máthair [G]	678	695/6
Ailill mac Cathail Con cen Máthair [G]	695/6	698/701
Cormac mac Ailello maic Máenaig [C]	698/701	713
Eterscél mac Máele Umai [Á]	713	721
Cathal mac Finguine [G] (high-king)	721	742
Cathussach mac Eterscélai [Á]	?	?
Máel Dúin mac Áedo [L]	742	786
Ólchobar mac Duif Indrecht [Á]	?	dep. or abd. 793 d. 805
[Ólchobar mac Flaind [F], abbot of Inis Cathaig		797][1]
Artrí mac Cathail [G]	793	abd. c. 820 d. 821
Tuathal mac Artroig [G][2]	?	?
Tnúthgal mac Donngusso (Donngaile) [C][2]	820	820
Fedelmid mac Crimthainn [C] (high-king)	820	28 Aug. 847
Ólchobar mac Cináedo [L or Á?], abbot of Emly	847	851
Áilgenán mac Donngaile [C]	851	853
Máel Gualae mac Donngaile [C]	853	859
Cenn Fáelad ua Mugthigirn [AC or Á ?], abbot of Emly	859	872
Dúnchad mac Duib dá Bairenn [C]	872	888
Dub Lachtna mac Máele Gualae [C]	888	895
Finguine Cenn nGécán mac Lóegairi [C]	895	902
Cormac mac Cuilennáin [C], bp of Cashel	902	908
Flaithbertach mac Inmainén *, abbot of Inis Cathaig	914	abd. 922 d. 944
Lorcán mac Coinlígáin [C]	922	?
Cellachán Caisil mac Buadacháin [C]	a. 940	954
Máel Fothardaig mac Flainn [C]	954	957

	accession	death unless otherwise stated
Dub dá Bairenn mac Domnaill [R]	957	959
Fer Gráid mac Cléirig [C]	959	961
Donnchad mac Cellacháin [C]	961	963
Mathgamain mac Cennétig [D]	963	976
Máel Muad mac Brain [R]	976	978
Brian Bóruma mac Cennétig [D] (high-king)	978	23 Apr. 1014
Donnchad mac Briain [D]	1014	abd. 1063 d. 1065
Dúngal mac Máel Fothardaig Ua Donnchada [C]	1014	abd. 1024 d. 1025
Toirrdelbach ua Briain [D] (high-king)	1063	14 July 1086
Murchad mac Donnchada [D]	1064	1068
Muirchertach mac Toirrdelbaig Ua Briain [D] (high-king)	1086	dep. 1114 rest. 1115 dep. 1116 rest. 1118 d. 13 Mar. 1119
Diarmait mac Toirrdelbaig Ua Briain [D]	1086	dep. 1086 rest. 1114 dep. 1115 rest. 1116 d. 1118
Tadg mac Toirrdelbaig Ua Briain [D]	1086	1086
Brian mac Murchada Ua Briain [D]	1118	1118
Toirrdelbach mac Diarmata Ua Briain [D][3]	1118	dep. 1152 rest. 1153 d. 1167
Conchobar mac Diarmata Ua Briain [D][4]	1118	1142
Tadg Gláe mac Diarmata Ua Briain [D][5]	1122	dep. c. 1123? rest. and dep. 1152 d. 1154
Tadg Mac Carthaig [C][6]	1118	dep. 1123 d. 1124
Cormac Mac Carthaig [C][6]	1123	1138
Donnchad Mac Carthaig [C][6]	1138	dep. 1143 d. 1144
Diarmait mac Cormaic Mac Carthaig [C][6]	1143	dep. 1175 rest. 1176 d. p. 25 Apr 1185
Muirchertach mac Toirrdelbaig Ua Briain [D][5]	1167	1168
Cormac Liathánach mac Diarmata Mac Carthaig [C][6]	1175	1176
Domnall Mór mac Toirrdelbaig Ua Briain [D][5]	1168	1194

Footnotes on next page

¹ Ólchobar mac Flaind's inclusion as kg in some sources may be due to confusion with Ólchobar mac Duib Indrecht.
² May be variant identifications of the same kg.
³ *Leth-rí* of Thomond 1118–42; kg of Thomond 1142–52, 1153–67.
⁴ *Leth-rí* of Thomond 1118–42; kg of Dublin 1141–2.
⁵ Kg of Thomond; see table 11.
⁶ Kg of Desmond; see table 24.

KINGS OF CONNACHT TO 1183

[B]	= Uí Briúin
[BA]	= Uí Briúin Aí
[BA:C]	= Uí Briúin Aí: Síl Cathail
[BA:M]	= Uí Briúin Aí: Síl Muiredaig
[BB]	= Uí Briúin Bréifne
[BS]	= Uí Briúin Seóla
[F]	= Uí Fiachrach
[FA]	= Uí Fiachrach Aidni
[FM]	= Uí Fiachrach Muaide

	accession	death unless otherwise stated
Amalgaid mac Fiachrach [F]		
Ailill Molt mac Nath Í [B] (high-king)	?	482
Dauí Tengae Umai mac Briúin [F]	482	502
Eógan Bél mac Cellaig [F]	502	543/7
Ailill Inbandae mac Eógain Beóil [F]	543/7	550
Echu Tirmcharnae mac Fergusso [BA]	550	?
Feradach mac Rossa [F]	?	a. 560/61
Áed mac Echach Tirmcharnai [BA]	a. 560/61	577
Uatu mac Áedo [BA]	577	601/2
Máel Cothaid (Donn Cothaid) mac Máele Umai [F]	601/2	?
Colmán mac Cobthaig [FA]	?	622
Rogallach mac Uatach [BA]	622	649
Laidgnén (Loingsech) mac Colmáin [FA]	649	655
Guaire Aidni mac Colmáin [FA]	655	663
Cenn Fáelad mac Colggen [BS]	663	682
Muirchertach Nár mac Guairi Aidni [FA]	663	668
Dúnchad Muirisci mac Tipraiti [FM]	682	?
Fergal Aidni mac Artgaile [FA]	?	696
Muiredach Muillethan mac Fergusso [BA]	696	702
Cellach mac Rogallaig [BA]	702	705
Indrechtach mac Dúnchado Muirisci [FM]	705	707
Indrechtach mac Muiredaig Muillethain [BA:M]	707	723
Domnall mac Cathail [BA]	707	714
Domnall mac Cellaig [BA]	723	728

	accession	*death unless otherwise stated*
Cathal mac Muiredaig Muillethain [BA]	728	735
Áed Balb mac Indrechtaig maic Muiredaig Muillethain [BA: M]	735	742
Forggus mac Cellaig [BA]	742	756
Ailill Medraige mac Indrechtaig maic Dúnchado Muirisci [FM]	756	764
Dub Indrecht mac Cathail maic Muiredaig Muillethain [BA: C]	764	768
Donn Cothaid mac Cathail maic Ailello [FM]	768	773
Flaithrí mac Domnaill [BA]	773	abd. 777 d. 779
Artgal mac Cathail maic Muiredaig Muillethain [BA: C]	777	abd. 782 d. 791
Tipraite mac Taidg [BA: M]	782	786
Cináed mac Artgaile [BA: C]	786	792
Muirgius mac Tommaltaig [BA: M]	786	815
Colla mac Fergusso [BA]	792	796
Máel Cothaid mac Fogartaig [BA: C]	815	p. 818
Diarmait mac Tommaltaig [BA: M]	p. 818	833
Cathal mac Muirgiusso [BA: M]	833	839
Murchad mac Áedo [BA: C]	839	840
Fergus mac Fothaid [BA: C]	840	843
Fínsnechtae mac Tommaltaig [BA: M]	843	848
Conchobar mac Taidg Móir [BA: M][1]	848	882
Mugrón mac Máele Cothaid [BA: C][1]	848	872
Áed mac Conchobair [BA: M]	882	888
Tadg mac Conchobair [BA: M]	888	900
Cathal mac Conchobair [BA: M]	900	925
Tadg mac Cathail [BA: M]	925	956
Fergal (mac Airt) ua Ruairc [BB]	956	966
Conchobar mac Taidg [BA: M]	966	973
Cathal mac Taidg meic Conchobair [BA: M]	973	973
Cathal mac Conchobair [BA: M]	973	1010
Tadg in Eich Gil mac Cathail meic Conchobair [BA: M]	1010	1030
Art Uallach mac Áeda Ua Ruairc [BB]	1030	1046
Áed in Gaí Bernaig mac Taidg in Eich Gil Ua Conchobair [BA: M]	1046	1067
Áed mac Airt Uallaig Ua Ruairc [BB]	1067	1087
Ruaidrí na Saide Buide mac Áeda in Gaí Bernaig Ua Conchobair [BA: M]	1087	dep. 1092 d. 1118
Flaithbertach Ua Flaithbertaig [BS]	1092	1098
Taidg mac Ruaidrí na Saide Buide Ua Conchobair [BA: M]	1092	1097
Domnall mac Tigernáin Ua Ruairc [BB]	1098	1102

	accession	death unless otherwise stated
Domnall mac Ruaidrí na Saide Buide Ua Conchobair [BA:M]	1102	dep. 1106 d. 1118
Toirrdelbach mac Ruaidrí na Saide Buide Ua Conchobair [BA:M] (high-king)	1106	20 May 1156
Ruaidrí mac Toirrdelbaig Ua Conchobair [BA:M] (high-king)	1156	abd. 1183 d. 2 Dec. 1198

¹ *Leth-rí* 848-72; Conchobar subsequently reigned to 882.

KINGS OF DUBLIN, 853-1171

	accession	end of reign
Olaf (Amlaíb)¹	853	873
Ivar (Ímar)¹	856²	873
Auisle (O.N. Hásli)¹	863²	867
Eystein, son of Olaf (Oistin mac Amlaíb)	873	875
[?Halfdan (Alband), brother of Ivar	?873/5	877]
Barid or Barith (Bard)	875/7	881
Son of Auisle	881	883
[?Eoloir, son of Járnkné (mac Iercne)³	?	?]
Sichfrith, son of Ivar	?883	888
Sitric (O.N. Sigtryggr), son of Ivar	888	dep. 893 rest. 894 d. 896
Sichfrith Járl	893	894
Ivar, grandson of Ivar	896	dep. 902 d. 904
[Interregnum 902-17: Dublin abandoned by Norse]		
Sitric, grandson of Ivar (Sigtryggr Gale)	917	921⁴
Godfrid (Guthfrith), grandson of Ivar	921	934⁵
Olaf (Anlaf), son of Godfrid (Olaf Godfridsson)	934	941⁶
[?Sitric⁷	941	943]
Blacair mac Gofraid (?O.N. Blákkr Godfridsson)	943	dep. 945 d. 948
Olaf Cuarán (Anlaf; O.N. Óláfr Sigtryggsson Kváran)	945	abd 980 d. 981
Glúniarainn, son of Olaf Cuarán (O.N. Járnkné Óláfsson)	980	989
Sitric, son of Olaf (Sitric mac Amlaíb; O.N. Sigtryggr Óláfsson Silkiskeggi; Sihtric Silkbeard)	989	dep. 1036 d. 1042

	accession	end of reign
Echmarcach mac Ragnaill	1036	dep. 1038
		rest. 1046
		dep. 1052[8]
		d. 1064/5
Ivar Haraldsson (Ímar mac Arailt)	1038	dep. 1046
		d. 1054
Murchad mac Diarmata meic Máel na mB[9]	1052	21 Nov. 1070
Diarmait mac Máel na mBó[10] *or* Domnall mac Murchada meic Diarmata[11]	1070	7 Feb. 1072
Gofraid mac Amlaíb meic Ragnaill	?1070/72	dep. 1074
		d. 1075
(Toirrdelbach ua Briain, king of Munster 1063–86, given kingship of Dublin 1072)		
Muirchertach mac Toirrdelbaig Ua Briain[12]	1074	1086
[?Énna mac Diarmata meic Máel na mBó[13] *or* [?Donnchad mac Domnaill Remair meic Máel na mBó[14]	1086	1089]
Gofraid Méránach (Godred Crovan, kg of Man)	a. 1091	dep. 1094
		d. 1095
Domnall mac Muirchertaig Ua Briain	?1094	dep. 1118
		d. 1135
[?Donnchad mac Murchada meic Diarmata[15]	?	1115]
[?Diarmait mac Énna[16]	1115	1117]
Énna mac Donnchada Mac Murchada[17]	1118	1126
Conchobar mac Toirrdelbaig Ua Conchobair[18]	1126	dep. 1127
		d. 1144
Thorkell	*fl.* 1133	?
Conchobar Ua Briain, kg of Thomond	1141	1142
Ottar, grandson of Ottar	1142	1148
Ragnall mac Torcaill (Thorkellsson)[19]	?	d. 1146
Brótar mac Torcaill	1146	1160
Asculf (Ascall mac [Ragnaill meic] Torcaill)	1160	?dep. 1162
		rest. 1166
		dep. 1170
		d. *c.* 16 May 1171
Diarmait mac Donnchada Mac Murchada[20]	1162	dep. 1166
		rest. 1170
		d. *c.* 1 May 1171

[1] Joint kgs.
[2] Reign may have begun earlier.
[3] *Fl.* 886; doubtful kg.
[4] Kg of York 921–7.
[5] Kg of York 927.

⁶ Kg of York ?937.

⁷ Kg of York ?-943.

⁸ Kg of Man and Galloway 1052-64; see below, p. 466.

⁹ Representing Diarmait mac Máel na mBó, kg of Leinster 1042-72; Murchad possibly ruled jointly with his son Domnall.

¹⁰ ? ruling directly.

¹¹ Kg of Leinster 1072-5; briefly rest. as kg of Dublin and Leinster 1074-5.

¹² Kg of Munster 1086-1119.

¹³ Kg of Leinster 1089-92.

¹⁴ Kg of Leinster 1075-89.

¹⁵ Kg of Leinster 1098-1115.

¹⁶ Kg of Leinster 1115-17.

¹⁷ Kg of Leinster 1117-26.

¹⁸ Kg of Mide 1143-4.

¹⁹ Called *mormáer Átha Cliath* (*A.U.*), *rí Átha Cliath* (*Ann. Tig.*).

²⁰ Kg of Leinster 1126-71.

LATER GAELIC KINGS AND LORDS

F. J. BYRNE

INTRODUCTION

THESE lists are in effect a re-presentation of part of the data given in genea-logical tables 14–33 (above, pp 140–65); while the tables show the structure of relationships in a ruling lineage, the lists show only those individuals who successively held the lordship. Some indication of relationships has been given by the use of patronymics and, where necessary, by explanatory foot-notes. The list of kings of Tír Conaill (p. 214) includes Ruaidrí Ó Canannáin (1247–8) and Cathal Óg Ó Conchobhair Sligigh (1359–62). Not being O'Donnells, they are shown in square brackets; their interruption of O'Donnell possession of the kingship is insufficient to warrant a change in the heading of the list. So too in the list of Uí Failghe (pp 217–18), Gilla Pátraic Ua Sibleáin (1051–71) and Diarmait Ua Dímmusaig (c. 1172–93) do not belong to the O'Connor Faly family.

Successions are not numbered in these lists (except in the case of peerages, where the succession is indicated in brackets after the name), but names appear in the order denoted by numerals in the genealogical tables. The order in which names appear in cases of shared or disputed kingship is explained in the introduction to the lists of high-kings and provincial kings, above, p. 189.

KINGS OF TÍR EÓGAIN AND EARLS OF TYRONE, 1185–1616

After the death of Domnall mac Muirchertaig Mac Lochlainn in 1241 the kingship of Tír Eógain remained in O'Neill hands. In the following list all the successors of Brian mac Néill Ruaid are O'Neills.

Numerals in round brackets indicate the succession of earls of Tyrone.

	accession	death unless otherwise stated
Domnall mac Áeda Mac Lochlainn	1185	dep. 1186 rest. 1187 d. 1188
Ruaidrí Ua Flaithbertaig	1186	1187
Muirchertach mac Muirchertaig Mac Lochlainn	1188	1196

	accession	death unless otherwise stated
Áed Méith mac Áeda Ua Néill	1196	1230
Conchobar Bec mac Conchobair Mac Lochlainn	1201	1201
Domnall Óc mac Áeda Méith Ó Néill	1230	1234
Domnall mac Muirchertaig Mac Lochlainn	1230	dep. 1230 rest. 1234 d. 1241
Brian mac Néill Ruaid Ó Neill	1238	16 May 1260
Áed Buide mac Domnaill Óic	1260	dep. 1261 rest. 1263 d. 1283
Niall Cúlánach mac Domnaill Óic	1261	dep. 1263 rest. 1286 dep. 1290 d. 1291
Domnall mac Briain	1283	dep. 1286 rest. 1290 dep. 1291 rest. 1295 d. 1325
Brian mac Áeda Buide	1291	1295
Énrí mac Briain meic Áeda Buide	1325	dep. 1345 d. 1347
Aodh Reamhar (Aodh Mór) mac Domhnaill	1345	1364
Niall Mór mac Aodha Reamhair	1364	abd. 1397 d. 1398
Niall Óg mac Néill	1397	1403
Brian Óg mac Néill Óig	1403	1403
Domhnall mac Énrí Aimhréidh	1404	dep. 1410 rest. 1414 dep. 1419 rest. 1421 d. 1 Jan. 1432
Eóghan mac Néill Óig	1410	dep. 1414 rest. 1419 dep. 1421 rest. 1432 abd. 1455 d. 1456
Énrí mac Eóghain	1455	abd. 1483 d. 1484
Conn mac Énrí	1483	8 Jan. 1493
Énrí Óg mac Énrí	1493	21 July 1498
Domhnall Clárach mac Énrí	1498	6 Aug. 1509
Art mac Aodha	1509	1513
Art Óg mac Cuinn	1513	1519
Conn Bacach mac Cuinn (1)[1]	1519	a. 17 July 1559

	accession	death unless otherwise stated
Seaán Donnghaileach (Seaán an Díomuis) mac Cuinn Bhacaigh	1559	21 June 1567
Toirdhealbhach (Turlough) Luineach mac Néill Chonnalaigh	1567	abd. 1593 d. c. 10 Sept. 1595
Aodh (Hugh) mac Firdorcha (2)[2]	1593	fled 1607 d. 10/20 July 1616

[1] Created earl of Tyrone 1 Oct. 1542.
[2] Became earl of Tyrone de jure on the death of his brother Brian 12 Apr. 1562.

O'NEILLS OF CLANDEBOYE: MAC UÍ NÉILL BHUIDHE, LORDS OF CLANN AODHA BUIDHE, 1347-c.1553

	accession	death unless otherwise stated
Brian mac Énrí	1347	1369
Muircheartach Ceannfhada mac Énrí	1369	1395
Brian Ballach mac Muircheartaigh	1395	1425
Aodh Buidhe mac Briain	1425	May 1444
Muircheartach Ruadh mac Briain	1444	1468
Conn mac Aodha Buidhe	1468	1482
Niall Mór mac Cuinn	1482	11 Apr. 1512
Aodh Buidhe (Aodh Méirgeach) mac Néill	1512	c. Sept. 1524
Brian Ballach mac Néill	1524	1529
Feidhlimidh Bacach mac Néill	1529	1533
Niall Óg mac Néill	1533	1537
Muircheartach Duileanach mac Néill	1537	p. 1556[1]

[1] See next list.

O'NEILLS OF LOWER CLANDEBOYE: MAC UÍ NÉILL BHUIDHE ÍOCHTAR, c.1553-1617

	accession	death unless otherwise stated
Muircheartach Duileanach mac Néill	c. 1553	p. 1556
(Sir) Brian mac Feidhlimidh	1556	1574
Aodh mac Feidhlimidh	1574	1583
Aodh Óg mac Aodha	1583	c. 1595
(Sir) Seán mac Briain	c. 1595	1617

O'NEILLS OF UPPER CLANDEBOYE: MAC UÍ NÉILL BHUIDHE UACHTAR, *c.*1553-1619

	accession	death unless otherwise stated
Aodh mac Néill Óig	*c.* 1553	1555
Feidhlimidh Dubh mac Néill Óig	1555	1556
(Sir) Conn mac Néill Óig	1556	1590
Niall mac Briain	1590	1601
Eóghan mac Aodha	1601	1601
Conn mac Néill	1601	1619

O'DONNELLS OF TYRCONNELL: Ó DOMHNAILL, KINGS OF TÍR CONAILL AND EARL OF TYRCONNELL, *c.*1201-1608

	accession	death unless otherwise stated
Éicnechán	*c.* 1201	1207
Domnall Mór mac Éicnecháin	1207	autumn 1241
Máel Sechlainn mac Domnaill	1241	1247
[Ruaidrí Ó Canannáin	1247	1248]
Gofraid mac Domnaill	1248	1258
Domnall Óc mac Domnaill	1258	1281
Áed mac Domnaill Óic	1281	dep. 1290 rest. 1291 d. 1333
Toirrdelbach mac Domnaill Óic	1290	dep. 1291 d. 1303
Conchobhar mac Aodha	1333	1342
Niall mac Aodha	1342	dep. 1343 d. 1348
Aonghus mac Conchobhair	1343	1352
Seoán mac Conchobhair	1352[1]	dep. 1359 rest. 1362 d. 1380
Feidhlimidh mac Aodha	1352[1]	1356
[Cathal Óg Ó Conchobhair Sligigh	1359	3 Nov. 1362]
Toirdhealbhach an Fhíona mac Néill	1380	abd. 1422 d. 1423
Niall Garbh mac Toirdhealbhaigh	1422	1439
Neachtan mac Toirdhealbhaigh	1439	1452
Ruaidhrí mac Neachtain	1452	7 Apr. 1454
Domhnall mac Néill Ghairbh	1454	28 May 1456
Toirdhealbhach mac Neachtain Cairbreach	1456	dep. 1461

	accession	death unless otherwise stated
Aodh Ruadh mac Néill Ghairbh	1461	abd. 26 May 1497 rest. 1497 d. 11 July 1505
Conn mac Aodha Ruaidh	1497	19 Oct. 1497
Aodh Dubh mac Aodha Ruaidh	1505	5 July 1537
Maghnus mac Aodha Duibh	1537	dep. 1555 d. 9 Feb. 1563
An Calbhach mac Maghnusa	1555	26 Oct. 1566
(Sir) Aodh mac Maghnusa	1566	abd. 1592 d. 1600
Aodh Ruadh mac Aodha	1592	31 Aug./10 Sept. 1602
Ruaidhrí mac Aodha[2]	1602	fled 1607 d. 18/28 July 1608

[1] Kingship disputed.
[2] Created earl of Tyrconnell 27 Sept. 1603.

MACMAHONS OF ORIEL: MAC MATHGHAMHNA, KINGS OF OIRGHIALLA, TO 1590

	accession	death unless otherwise stated
Niall (?mac Donnchada)	*fl.* 1196 × 1208	?
Eochaid mac Mathghamna meic Néill	?	1273
Brian mac Eochada	1283	1311
Ralph (Roolb) mac Eochada	1311	1314
?Máel Sechlainn mac Eochada	1314	?
Murchad Mór mac Briain	?	1331
Seoán mac Maoilsheachlainn	1331	1342
Aodh mac Rooilbh	1342	1344
Murchadh Óg mac Murchadha	1344	1344
Maghnus mac Eochadha	1344	1357
Pilib mac Rooilbh	1357	1362
Brian Mór mac Aodha	1362	dep. 1365 rest. 1368 d. 1371
Niall mac Murchadha	1365	1368
Pilib Ruadh mac Briain	1371	1403
Ardghal mac Briain	1403	Feb. 1416
Brian mac Ardghail	1416	1442
Ruaidhrí mac Ardghail	1442	1446
Aodh Ruadh mac Ruaidhrí	1446	31 Mar. 1453
Feidhlimidh mac Briain	1453	1466
Eóghan mac Ruaidhrí	1466	1467

	accession	death unless otherwise stated
Réamonn mac Ruaidhrí	1467	Nov. 1484
Aodh Óg mac Aodha Ruaidh	1485	dep. 16 Sept. 1496
Brian mac Réamoinn	1496	1497
Rossa mac Maghnusa	1497	1513
Réamonn mac Glaisne	1513	c. 1 Apr. 1521
Glaisne Óg mac Réamoinn	1521	?1551
Art Maol mac Réamoinn	1551	1560
Aodh mac Briain	1560	1562
Art Ruadh mac Briain	1562	1578
(Sir) Rossa Buidhe mac Airt	1579	Aug. 1589
Aodh Ruadh mac Airt	1589	Sept./Oct. 1590

MAGUIRES OF FERMANAGH: MÁG UIDHIR, KINGS OF FIR MANACH, c.1282–1625

	accession	death unless otherwise stated
Donn Óc (Donn Carrach)	c. 1282	1302
Flaithbertach mac Duinn	1302	1327
Ruaidhrí mac Flaithbheartaigh	1327	1358
Aodh Ruadh mac Flaithbheartaigh	1358	1363
Pilib mac Aodha Ruaidh	1363	16 Mar. 1395
Tomás Mór ('An Giolla Dubh') mac Pilib	1395	13 Nov. 1430
Tomás Óg mac Tomáis	1430	abd. 1471 d. 1480
Éamonn mac Tomáis Óig	1471	abd. 6 Nov. 1486 d. 1488
Tomás Óg mac Tomáis Óig	1484	dep. 1486 d. 1501
Seaán mac Pilib meic Tomáis Mhóir	1486	1503
Conchobhar Mór mac Tomáis Óig	1503	1527
Cú Connacht Óg ('An Comharba') mac Con Connacht	1527	1538
Giolla Pádraig Bán mac Conchobhair Mhóir	1538	1540
Seaán mac Con Connacht Óig	1540	1566
(Sir) Cú Chonnacht Óg mac Con Connacht Óig	1566	17 June 1589
(Sir) Aodh mac Con Connacht Óig[1]	1589	1601
Cú Chonnacht Óg mac Con Connacht Óig[1]	1601	fled 1607 d. 1609
Conchobhar Ruadh mac Conchobhair Óig meic Conchobhair Mhóir	1607	1625

[1] Son of Cú Chonnacht Óg (1566–89).

MACMURROUGHS (KAVANAGH): MAC MURCHADHA (CAOMHÁNACH), KINGS OF LEINSTER, 1171–1603

	accession	death unless otherwise stated
Domnall Cáemanach mac Diarmata	1171	1175
Muirchertach mac Domnaill[1]	?	21 July 1282
Domhnall mac Airt	1327	*p.* 1339
Domhnall mac Domhnaill	*p.* 1339	5 June 1347
Art mac Muircheartaigh	1347	1361
Diarmaid Láimhdhearg mac Domhnaill	1361	1369
Donnchadh Caomhánach mac Muircheartaigh	1369	26 July 1375
Art Mór mac Airt	1375	31 Dec. 1416
Donnchadh mac Airt Mhóir	1417	abd. *c.* 1455
Domhnall Riabhach mac Gearailt	*c.* 1455	1476
Murchadh Ballach mac Muircheartaigh	1476	1511
Art Buidhe mac Domhnaill Riabhaigh	1511	25 Nov. 1517
Gearalt mac Domhnaill Riabhaigh	1517	1523
Muiris mac Domhnaill Riabhaigh	1523	1531
Cathaoir ('Mac na hInghine Crosda') mac Murchadha Ballaigh	1532	*c.* 1543
Muircheartach mac Airt Bhuidhe	*c.* 1543	1547
Cathaoir mac Airt[2]	1547	1554
Murchadh mac Muiris[3]	1554	1557
Criomthann mac Murchadha[4]	1557	1582
Domhnall Spáinneach mac Donnchadha[4]	*c.* 1595	abd. 1603 d. 1632

[1] Attempted to revive extinct kingship, which was successfully restored in 1327.
[2] Created baron of Ballyanne 8 Feb. 1554.
[3] Created baron of Coolnaleen 1554.
[4] Claimant.

O'CONNOR FALY: Ó CONCHOBHAIR FAILGHE, KINGS OF UÍ FAILGHE, *a.* 1051–*c.* 1556

	accession	death unless otherwise stated
Congalach Ua Conchobair	?	1051
[Gilla Pátraic mac Conchobair Ua Sibleáin[1]	1051	1071]
Conchobar mac Congalaig[2]	1071	1115
Muirchertach[3]	?	bld 1095
Rogán mac Domnaill meic Conchobair	1115	*c.* 1118
Cú Faifne mac Congalaig	*c.* 1118	1130
Donnchad mac Con Faifne	1130	1134

	accession	death unless otherwise stated
Áed mac Domnaill	1134	?
Máel Mórda mac Conchobair	?	?
Conchobar mac Con Faifne[4]	?	?
Máel Sechlainn mac Conchobair	?	?
Congalach mac Con Faifne	?	?
Murchad mac Con Faifne[5]	?	?
Muirchertach mac Muirchertaig (Int Athchlérech)[3]	?	c. 1151
Áed mac Donnchada (Gilla na Findmóna)	c. 1151	1159
Domnall Ruad mac Congalaig	1159	1161
Máel Sechlainn mac Congalaig	1161	1164
Donnchad Ruad Roigne[3]	1164	?
Diarmait mac Congalaig	?	?
Muirchertach mac Congalaig	?	?1169
[Diarmait mac Con Broga Ua Dímmusaig[1]	a. 1172	1193]
Muirchertach mac Briain[3]	fl. 1212	?
Máel Mórda mac Muirchertaig meic Donnchada	?	1225
Muirchertach mac Máel Mórda	1225	?
Muirchertach mac Muirchertaig	?	c. 13 June 1305
Murchad mac Muirchertaig	1305	?
Máel Sechlainn mac Muirchertaig	?	1329
Muircheartach Óg mac Muircheartaigh[6]	?	1384
Murchadh mac Muircheartaigh Óig	1384	1421
Diarmaid mac Muircheartaigh Óig	1421	c. 1425
An Calbhach Mór mac Murchadha	c. 1425	1458
Conn mac an Chalbhaigh	1458	autumn 1474
Cathaoir mac Cuinn	1474	1511
Brian mac Taidhg meic an Chalbhaigh	1511	1517
An Calbhach mac Taidhg	1517	c. 1525
Brian mac Cathaoir	c. 1525	c. 1556

[1] Of Clann Máel Ugra.
[2] Claimed kingship of Leinster 1079.
[3] Ancestry unknown.
[4] Reigned for 3 months.
[5] His reign of 2 years interrupted that of his brother Congalach.
[6] Son of the Muirchertach who d. 1305. His cousin Cathaoir mac Murchadha, who d. 1367, was *tánaiste* and may have been kg in succn to Máel Sechlainn; see K. W. Nicholls, *Gaelic and gaelicised Ireland* (Dublin, 1972), p. 174.

O'BRIENS: Ó BRIAIN, KINGS AND EARLS OF THOMOND, 1168–1657

Numerals in round brackets indicate the succession of earls of Thomond.

	accession	death unless otherwise stated
Domnall Mór mac Toirrdelbaig	1168	1194
Muirchertach Finn mac Domnaill Móir	1194	dep. 1198
		rest. 1203
		abd. 1210
		d. 1241
Conchobar Ruad mac Domnaill Móir	1198	1203
Donnchad Cairprech mac Domnaill Móir	1210	1242
Conchobar na Siudaine mac Donnchada	1242	22 May 1268
Brian Ruad mac Conchobair	1268	p. 11 May 1277
Toirrdelbach mac Taidg	1277[1]	Aug. 1306
Donnchad mac Briain Ruaid	1277[1]	1284
Donnchad mac Toirrdelbaig	1306	1311
Diarmait Cléirech mac Donnchada[2]	1311	c. 1 June 1313
Muirchertach mac Toirrdelbaig	1313[1]	1343
Donnchad mac Domnaill	1313[1]	dep. 1316
		d. 17 Aug. 1317
Diarmaid mac Toirdhealbhaigh	1343	dep. 1343
		rest. 1350
		dep. 1360
		d. 1364
Brian Bán mac Domhnaill	1343	1350
Mathghamhain mac Muircheartaigh	1360	1369
Brian Sreamhach mac Mathghamhna	1369	1400
Toirdhealbach Maol mac Muircheartaigh	1375	dep. 1375
		d. 1398
Conchobhar mac Mathghamhna	1400	13 Apr. 1426
Tadhg mac Briain	1426	dep. 1438
		d. 1444
Mathghamhain Dall mac Briain	1438	dep. 1444
Toirdhealbhach Bog mac Briain	1444	1459
Tadhg an Chomhaid mac Toirdhealbhaigh	1459[1]	1466
Donnchadh mac Mathghamhna Daill	1459[1]	dep. c. 1461
Conchobhar Mór (Conchobhar na Srón) mac Toirdhealbhaigh	1466	1496
Toirdhealbach Óg ('An Giolla Dubh') mac Toirdhealbhaigh	1496	1498
Toirdhealbhach Donn mac Taidhg	1498	1528
Conchobhar mac Toirdhealbhaigh Duinn	1528	1539
Murchadh Carrach mac Toirdhealbhaigh Duinn (1)[3]	1539	7 Nov. 1551

	accession	death unless otherwise stated
Donnchadh mac Conchobhair (2)	1551	1 Apr. 1553
Conchobhar mac Donnchadha (3)	1553[4]	Jan. 1581
(Sir) Domhnall mac Conchobhair[5]	1553[4]	dep. 1558 rest. 1563 abd. 1564 d. 1579
Donnchadh mac Conchobhair (4)[6]	1581	5 Sept. 1624
Henry mac Donnchadha (5)	1624	a. 22 Apr. 1639
Barnaby mac Donnchadha (6)	1639	a. 15 Nov. 1657

[1] Kingship disputed.
[2] Son of Donnchad mac Briain Ruaid.
[3] Created earl of Thomond and Baron Inchiquin 1 July 1543.
[4] Kingship disputed.
[5] Son of Conchobhar who d. 1539.
[6] Son of Conchobhar who d. 1581.

MACCARTHYS OF DESMOND: MAC CARTHAIGH MÓR, KINGS OF DESMOND AND EARL OF CLANCARE, 1118–?1640

	accession	death unless otherwise stated
Tadg mac Muiredaig	1118	dep. 1123 d. 1124
Cormac mac Muiredaig	1123	1138
Donnchad mac Muiredaig	1138	dep. 1143 d. 1144
Diarmait mac Cormaic	1143	dep. 1175 rest. 1176 d. p. 25 Apr. 1185
Cormac Liathánach mac Diarmata	1175	1176
Domnall Mór (Domnall na Corra) mac Diarmata	1185	1 Dec. 1206
Fíngen mac Diarmata	1206	dep. c. 1 Feb. 1207 d. 1209
Diarmait Dúna Droignéin mac Domnaill[1]	1207	dep. 1211 d. 1229
Cormac Óc Liathánach mac Cormaic	1211	1244
Cormac Finn mac Domnaill	1244	1247
Domnall Got Cairprech mac Domnaill	1247	29 Aug. 1252
Fíngen mac Domnaill Guit	1252	29 Sept. 1261
Cormac mac Domnaill Guit	1261	1262
Domnall Ruad mac Cormaic Finn	1262	1302

	accession	death unless otherwise stated
Domnall Óc mac Domnaill Ruaid	1302	24 Sept. 1306
Donnchad Carrthainn mac Cormaic Finn	1306	dep. 1310
		d. 1315
Diarmait Óc mac Domnaill Óic	1310	1325
Cormac mac Domnaill Óic	1325	1359
Domhnall Óg mac Cormaic	1359	1391
Tadhg na Mainistreach mac Domhnaill Óig	1391	1428
Domhnall an Dána mac Taidhg	1428	1469
Tadhg Liath mac Domhnaill	1469	1503
Domhnall mac Taidhg Léith	1503	1508
Cormac Ladhrach mac Taidhg Léith	1508[2]	1516
Tadhg na Leamhna mac Domhnaill	1508[2]	1514
Domhnall mac Cormaic	1516	?
Domhnall mac Domhnaill[3]	?	a. 12 Feb. 1597
Finghín (Mac Carthaigh Riabhach) mac Donnchadha	1597[2]	?1640
Domhnall mac Domhnaill	1597[2]	p. 1615

[1] Diarmait continued to dispute the kingship with Cormac until his death in 1229.
[2] Kingship disputed.
[3] Created earl of Clancare 24 June 1565.

MACCARTHYS OF MUSKERRY: MAC CARTHAIGH MÚSCRAIGHE, LORDS OF MUSKERRY AND EARLS OF CLANCARTY, 1359–1734

Numerals in round brackets indicate the succession of earls of Clancarty.

	accession	death unless otherwise stated
Diarmaid mac Cormaic	1359	1381
Tadhg mac Diarmada	1381	1387
Cormac mac Diarmada	1387	1410
Feidhlimidh mac Diarmada	1410	c. 1413
Tadhg mac Cormaic	c. 1413	1461
Cormac mac Taidhg	1461	1495
Eóghan mac Taidhg	1495	1498
Cormac mac Diarmada meic Taidhg	1498	dep. 1501
Cormac Óg Láidir mac Cormaic[1]	1501	1536
Tadhg mac Cormaic Óig	1536	1565
(Sir) Diarmaid mac Taidhg	1565	1571
(Sir) Cormac mac Taidhg	1571	1583
Ceallachán mac Taidhg	1583	abd. 1584
		d. p. 1603

	accession	death unless otherwise stated
(Sir) Cormac Óg mac Diarmada	1584	1617
Cormac Óg mac Cormaic Óig[2]	1617	1640
Donnchadh mac Cormaic Óig (1)[3]	1640	4 Aug. 1665
Charles mac Cormaic (2)	1665	22 Sept. 1666
Callaghan mac Donnchadha (3)	1666	21 Nov. 1676
Donough mac Callaghan (4)[4]	1676	1 Oct. 1734

[1] Son of Cormac mac Taidhg, d. 1495.
[2] Created Viscount Muskerry 15 Nov. 1628.
[3] Son of Lord Muskerry; created earl of Clancarty 27 Nov. 1658.
[4] Title forfeited 11 May 1691.

MACCARTHY REAGH: MAC CARTHAIGH RIABHACH, LORDS OF CAIRBRE (CARBERY, CO. CORK), 1366–c. 1600

	accession	death unless otherwise stated
Domhnall Riabhach mac Domhnaill Chairbrigh	1366	1414
Domhnall Glas mac Domhnaill Riabhaigh	1414	1442
Donnchadh mac Domhnaill Riabhaigh	1442	1453
Diarmaid an Dúna mac Domhnaill Riabhaigh	1453	1473
Cormac mac Donnchadha	1473	dep. 1478 d. 1503
Finghín mac Diarmada an Dúna	1478	1505
Diarmaid mac Diarmada an Dúna	1505	1506
Domhnall mac Finghín	1506	1531
Cormac mac Domhnaill	1531	?
(Sir) Finghín mac Domhnaill	?	1566
(Sir) Donnchadh mac Domhnaill	1566	1576
(Sir) Eóghan mac Domhnaill	1576	1593
Domhnall na Píbe mac Cormaic	1593	?

O'CONNORS: Ó CONCHOBHAIR, KINGS OF CONNACHT, 1183-1474

The kingship of Connacht was in frequent dispute, and the form of this list does not permit all changes of tenure to be accurately recorded.

[D] = Ó Conchobhair Donn
[R] = Ó Conchobhair Ruadh

	accession	death unless otherwise stated
Conchobar Máenmaige mac Ruaidrí	1183	1189
Cathal Crobderg mac Toirrdelbaig	1189	1224
Cathal Carrach mac Conchobair Máenmaige	1189	d. 1202
Áed mac Cathail Chrobdeirg	1224	1228
Toirrdelbach mac Ruaidrí	1225	dep. 1225 rest. 1228 dep. 1230 d. 1234
Áed mac Ruaidri	1228	dep. 1230 rest. 1231 d. 1233
Fedlimid mac Cathail Chrobdeirg	1230	dep. 1231 rest. 1233 d. 1265
Brian mac Toirrdelbaig	1236	dep. 1237
Toirrdelbach mac Áeda meic Cathail Chrobdeirg	1249	dep. 1250 d. 1266
Áed mac Fedlimid	1265	3 May 1274
Eógan mac Ruaidrí	1274	c. 3 Aug. 1274
Áed mac Cathail Daill	1274	c. 17 Aug. 1274
Tadg Ruad mac Toirrdelbaig	c. Aug. 1274	1278
Áed Muimnech (? mac Fedlimid)	1278	1280
Cathal Ruad mac Conchobair Ruaid	1280	dep. 1288 d. 1293
Magnus mac Conchobair Ruaid	1288	1293
Áed mac Eógain	1293	1309
Áed Bréifnech mac Cathail Ruaid	1309	1310
Fedlimid mac Áeda[1]	1310	dep. 1315 rest. 23 Feb. 1316 d. 10 Aug. 1316
Ruaidrí mac Cathail Ruaid	1315	23 Feb. 1316
Ruaidrí na Fed mac Donnchada	1316	dep. 1316 d. 1321
Toirrdelbach mac Áeda	1317	dep. 1318 rest. 1324 dep. 1342 rest. 1343 d. 15 Oct. 1345

	accession	death unless otherwise stated
Cathal mac Domnaill	1318	25 Aug. 1324
Aodh mac Aodha Bréifnigh	1342	dep. 1343
		d. 1350
Aodh mac Toirdhealbhaigh	1345	dep. 1350
		rest. 1351
		dep. and rest.
		1353
		d. 1356
Aodh mac Feidhlimidh	1350	dep. 1351
		rest. and dep.
		1353
		rest. 1356
		d. autumn
		1368
Ruaidhrí mac Toirdhealbhaigh	1368	25 Nov. 1384
Toirdhealbhach Ruadh mac Aodha meic		
Feidhlimidh [R]	1384	1425/6
Toirdhealbhach Óg Donn mac Aodha		
meic Toirdhealbhaigh [D]	1384	9 Dec. 1406
Cathal mac Ruaidhrí [D]	1406	19 Mar. 1439
Tadhg mac Toirdhealbhaigh Ruaidh [R]	1439	18 Aug. 1464
Aodh mac Toirdhealbhaigh Óig [D]	1439	15 May 1461
Brian mac Briain Bhallaigh [R]	1461	dep. 1462
		d. 1487
Feidhlimidh Geangcach mac	1461	1474
Toirdhealbhaigh Óig [D]		
Cathal Ruadh mac Taidhg [R]	1464	30 Mar. 1465
Feidhlimidh Fionn mac Taidhg [R]	1465	dep. 1466
		rest. 1488
		d. 12 Apr. 1490
Feidhlimidh Geangcach mac Toirdhealbhaig		
Óig [D]		

[1] Grandson of Eógan, d. 1274.

O'CONNOR ROE: Ó CONCHOBHAIR RUADH, 1384–c. 1616

	accession	death unless otherwise stated
Toirdhealbhach Ruadh mac Aodha meic		
Feidhlimidh	1384	1425/6
Tadhg mac Toirdhealbhaigh Ruaidh	1439	18 Aug. 1464
Cathal Ruadh mac Taidhg	1464	30 Mar. 1465
Feidhlimidh Fionn mac Taidhg	1465	dep. 1466
		rest. 1488
		d. 12 Apr. 1490

	accession	death unless otherwise stated
Donnchadh Dubhshúileach mac Toirdhealbhaigh Ruaidh	1474	1488
Ruaidhrí mac Feidhlimidh Chléirigh	1490	1492
Aodh mac Feidhlimidh Fhinn	1492	c. 1504
Eóghan mac Feidhlimidh Fhinn	c. 1504	1519
Tadhg Buidhe mac Cathail Ruaidh	1519	1534
Toirdhealbhach Ruadh mac Taidhg Bhuidhe	1534	1559
Feidhlimidh Ruadh mac Toirdhealbhaigh Ruaidh	1559	1560
Tadhg Óg mac Taidhg Bhuidhe	1560	1592
Aodh mac Toirdhealbhaigh Ruaidh	1592	c. 1616

O'CONNOR DON: Ó CONCHOBHAIR DONN, 1384–1654

	accession	death unless otherwise stated
Toirdhealbhach Óg Donn mac Aodha meic Toirdhealbhaigh	1384	9 Dec. 1406
Cathal mac Ruaidhrí	1406	19 Mar. 1439
Aodh mac Toirdhealbhaigh Óig	1439	15 May 1461
Feidhlimidh Geangcach mac Toirdhealbhaigh Óig[1]	1461	1474
Tadhg mac Eóghain	1474	1476
Eóghan Caoch mac Feidhlimidh Gheangcaigh	1476	1485
Aodh Óg mac Aodha	1485	?
Toirdhealbhach Óg mac Ruaidhrí	?	1503
Conchobhar mac Eóghain Chaoich	1503	?
Cairbre mac Eóghain Chaoich	?	1546
Aodh mac Eóghain Chaoich	1546	dep. 1550
Diarmaid mac Cairbre	1550	1585
(Sir) Aodh mac Diarmada	1585	1632
An Calbhach mac Aodha	1632	1654

[1] Accepted by both lines as O'Connor 1466–74.

O'CONNOR SLIGO:[1] Ó CONCHOBHAIR SLIGIGH, LORDS OF CAIRBRE (CARBURY, CO. SLIGO), 1318-1634

	accession	death unless otherwise stated
Cathal mac Domnaill	1318	1324
Muirchertach mac Domnaill	1324	1329
Maghnus mac Cathail	1329	1342
Cathal Óg mac Cathail[2]	1342	3 Nov. 1362
Tadhg mac Maghnusa	1362	dep. 1368
		d. 1371
Domhnall mac Muircheartaigh	1368	18 Dec. 1395
Muircheartach Bacach mac Domhnaill	1395	1403
Brian mac Domhnaill	1403	1440
Eóghan mac Domhnaill	1440	1444
Toirdhealbhach Carrach mac Domhnaill	1444	1455
Maghnus mac Briain	1455	1461
Tadhg mac Eóghain	1461	1462
Domhnall mac Muircheartaigh Bhacaigh	1462	1464
Ruaidhrí mac Briain	1464	p. 1478
Domhnall mac Eóghain	?	14 Mar. 1494
Ruaidhrí mac Toirdhealbhaigh Carraigh	1494	1495
Feidhlimidh mac Maghnusa	1495[3]	1519
Ruaidhrí Óg mac Ruaidhrí Bhallaigh	1495[3]	1495
Tadhg Óg mac Taidhg	1533	1545
Tadhg mac Cathail Óig	1545	1552
Ruaidhrí mac Feidhlimidh	1552	p. 1559
(Sir) Domhnall mac Taidhg	c. 1556	5 Jan. 1588
(Sir) Donnchadh mac Cathail Óig	1588	1609
(Sir) An Calbhach mac Domhnaill	1609	1625
Donnchadh mac Domhnaill	1625	1634

[1] The style 'O'Connor Sligo' seems to have been formally adopted first by Tadhg Óg in 1536.
[2] Also kg of Tír Conaill, 1359-62.
[3] Kingship disputed.

O'KELLYS OF HY MANY: Ó CEALLAIGH, KINGS OF UÍ MHAINE, a. 1221-c. 1611

	accession	death unless otherwise stated
Domnall Mór	?	1221
Conchobar mac Domnaill Móir	1221	1268
Maine Mór mac Conchobair	1268	1271
Domnall mac Conchobair	1271	1295

	accession	death unless otherwise stated
Donnchad Muimnech mac Conchobair	1295	1307
Gilbert mac Domnaill	1307	dep. 1315 rest. 1318 d. 1322
Tadg mac Domnaill	1315	1316
Conchobar mac Domnaill	1316	1318
Áed mac Donnchada Muimnig	c. 1322	?1325
Ruaidhrí mac Mathghamhna	c. 1332	29 Oct. 1339
Tadhg Óg mac Taidhg	1339	1340
Diarmaid mac Gilbert	c. 1340	c. 1349
Uilliam Buidhe mac Donnchadha Muimhnigh	c. 1349	1381
Maolsheachlainn mac Uilliam Buidhe	1381	1402
Conchobhar an Abaidh mac Maolsheachlainn	1402	1403
Tadhg Ruadh mac Maolsheachlainn	1403	13 Oct. 1410
Donnchadh mac Maolsheachlainn	1410	10 Oct. 1424
Aodh mac Briain	1424	1467
Aodh na gCailleach mac Uilliam Ruaidh	1467	13 Feb. 1469
Uilliam mac Aodha[1]	1469[2]	1487
Tadhg Caoch mac Uilliam Ruaidh	1467[2]	abd. 1476 d. 1486
Maolsheachlainn mac Aodha[1]	1487	1488
Conchobhar Óg mac Aodha[1]	1488[2]	dep. 1499
Donnchadh mac Breasail	1488[2]	?
Maolsheachlainn mac Taidhg	1499	1511
Tadhg mac Maolsheachlainn	1511	1513
Maolsheachlainn mac Uilliam	?1513	1521
Domhnall mac Aodha na gCailleach	?1521	?1536
Donnchadh mac Éamoinn	1536	p. 1557
Ceallach mac Domhnaill[3]	p. 1557	?1573
Éigneachán mac Domhnaill[4]	1573	a. 1580
Aodh mac Donnchadha	a. 1580	1590
Feardorcha mac Ceallaigh	1593	p. 1611

[1] Son of Aodh mac Briain.
[2] Kingship disputed.
[3] Son of Domhnall mac Aodha na gCailleach.
[4] Son of Domhnall mac Donnchadha, *tánaiste*, d. 1536.

O'ROURKES OF BREIFNE: Ó RUAIRC, KINGS OF BRÉIFNE, a. 1128–1605

	accession	death unless otherwise stated
Tigernán Mór mac Áeda	a. 1128	1172
Áed mac Gilla Braite	1152	dep. 1152
		rest. 1172
		d. 1176
Amlaíb mac Fergaile	1176	1184
Áed mac Máel Sechlainn	1184	1187
Ualgarg mac Cathail Léith	a. 1196	dep. 1209
		rest. a. 1214
		d. 1231
Art mac Domnaill	1209	1210
Cathal Riabach mac Donnchada	1231	1236
Conchobar mac Tigernáin	a. 1250[1]	1257
Sitric mac Ualgairg	1256[1]	1257
Amlaíb mac Airt	1257	1258
Domnall mac Conchobair	1258	dep. 1258
		rest. 1259
		d. 1260
Art mac Cathail Riabaig	1258	dep. 1259
		rest. 1261
		dep. 1266
		rest. 1273
		d. 1275
Conchobar Buide mac Amlaíb	1266	1273
Tigernán mac Áeda	1273	1274
Amlaíb mac Airt	1275	1307
Domnall Carrach mac Amlaíb[2]	1307	1311
Ualgarg mac Domnaill Charraig	1316	1346
Flaithbheartach mac Domhnaill Charraigh	1346	dep. 1349
		d. 1353
Aodh Bán mac Ualghairg	1349	1352
Tadhg na gCaor mac Ualghairg	1352	1376
Tighearnán Mór mac Ualghairg	1376	c. 1 Feb. 1418
Aodh Buidhe mac Tighearnáin Mhóir	1418	1419
Tadhg mac Tighearnáin Mhóir	1419[1]	1435
Art mac Taidhg na gCaor	1419[1]	abd. 1424
		d. 1430
Lochlainn mac Taidhg na gCaor	1435	dep. 1440
		rest. 1449
		d. 1458
Donnchadh Losc (Donnchadh Bacach) mac Tighearnáin Mhóir	1440	dep. 1445
		rest. 1468
		d. 1476
Donnchadh mac Tighearnáin Óig[3]	1445	1449

	accession	death unless otherwise stated
Tighearnán Óg mac Taidhg	1449	1468
Domhnall mac Taidhg	1468	1468
Feidhlimidh mac Donnchadha	1476	1500
Eóghan mac Tighearnáin Óig[4]	1500	1528
Feidhlimidh mac Feidhlimidh	1528	1536
Brian Ballach mac Eóghain	1536	dep. *c.* 1559 rest. 1560 d. 1562
Tadhg mac Briain Bhallaigh	*c.* 1559	1560
Aodh Gallda mac Briain Bhallaigh	1562	1564
Aodh Buidhe mac Briain Bhallaigh	1564	1566
Brian na Múrtha mac Briain Bhallaigh	1566	3 Nov. 1591
Brian Óg na Samhthach mac Briain na Múrtha	1591	1600
Tadhg mac Briain na Múrtha	1600	1605

[1] Kingship disputed.
[2] Son of Amlaíb mac Airt, d. 1258.
[3] Son of Tighearnán Óg mac Tighearnáin Mhóir, *tánaiste*, d. 1412.
[4] Son of Tighearnán Óg mac Taidhg, d. 1468.

O'REILLYS OF EAST BREIFNE: Ó RAGHALLAIGH, KINGS OF MUINTIR MAOILMHÓRDHA, *a.*1161–1607

	accession	death unless otherwise stated
Gofraid	?	1161
Cathal mac Gofraid	1161	1162
Cathal mac Annaid	*c.* 1220	*c.* 3 May 1256
Conchobar mac Cathail	1256	1257
Domnall mac Annaid	1257	1283
Matha mac Domnaill[1]	1285	1285
Fergal mac Domnaill[1]	1285	1293
Gilla Ísu Ruad mac Domnaill[1]	1293	1330
Risdeárd mac Giolla Íosa Ruaidh	1330	1349
Cú Chonnacht mac Giolla Íosa Ruaidh	1349	abd. 1365 d. 1367
Pilib mac Giolla Íosa Ruaidh	1365	1384
Maghnus mac Con Connacht	1369	dep. 1369
Tomás Mór mac Mathghamhna	1384	1392
Seoán mac Pilib	1392	1400
?Giolla Íosa mac Pilib	1400	1400
Maolmhórdha mac Con Connacht	1403	1411
Risdeárd mac Tomáis Mhóir	1411	1418

	accession	*death unless otherwise stated*
Eóghan mac Seoáin	1418	1449
Seaán an Einigh mac Eóghain	1449²	3 Sept. 1460
Fearghal mac Tomáis Mhóir	1449²	dep. 1450
		d. 1459
Cathal mac Eóghain	1460	1467
Toirdhealbhach mac Seaáin an Einigh	1467	1 Sept. 1487
Seaán mac Toirdhealbhaigh	1487	*a.* 25 Nov. 1491
Seaán mac Cathail	1491	1510
Aodh mac Cathail	1510	1514
Eóghan Ruadh mac Cathail	1514	1526
Fearghal mac Seaáin	1526	1534
Maolmhórdha mac Seaáin	1534	1565
Aodh Connallach mac Maolmhórdha	1565	1583
(Sir) Seaán Ruadh mac Aodha Connallaigh	1583	1596
Pilib Dubh mac Aodha Connallaigh	1596	1596
Éamonn mac Maolmhórdha	1596	1601
Eóghan mac Aodha Connallaigh	1601	1603
Maolmhórdha mac Aodha Connallaigh	1603	1607

¹ Son of Domnall mac Cathail, d. 1256.
² Kingship disputed.

ANGLO-NORMAN LORDS

F. J. BYRNE

INTRODUCTION

In the same manner as in the preceding section, these lists are based on genealogical tables 34-40 (above, pp 166-74) and show those individuals who held the major Anglo-Norman lordships. Problems of enumerating successions are discussed in headnotes to individual lists.

EARLS OF KILDARE AND THEIR ANTECEDENTS, 1169-1773

Numerals in round brackets indicate the succession of earls of Kildare. Between the death of Gerald fitz Maurice in 1432 and the official recognition of Thomas 'fitz Maurice' in 1456, the evidence for the succession is not clear; John fitz John is shown below as sixth earl, but in G.E.C., *Peerage*, vii, 226-8, the title is assigned to his father, who may on the other hand have died before 1432.

The numbering of barons of Offaly also presents difficulties. In G.E.C., *Peerage*, x, 10-20, Gerald fitz Maurice (d. 1204) is considered the first FitzGerald baron of Offaly, and his successors are numbered accordingly. However, his entitlement rests on his being the first husband of Eve, daughter of Robert de Bermingham, lord of Offaly. All of Eve's three husbands might be considered barons of Offaly in consequence, and the third, Geoffrey de Marisco, was actually known by the title. The date of her father Robert's death is unknown, and he may have survived Gerald. The strongest evidence in favour of Gerald's having obtained possession is the fact that his brother Thomas was enfeoffed in part of Offaly. See G. H. Orpen, *Ireland under the Normans, 1169-1333* (4 vols, Oxford, 1911-20; reprint, Oxford, 1968), iii, 113.

	succession	death unless otherwise stated
Maurice fitz Gerald[1]		1 Sept. 1176
Gerald fitz Maurice	1176	*a.* 15 Jan. 1204
Maurice fitz Gerald	1204	*c.* 27 May 1257
Maurice fitz Gerald	1257	*c.* 25 July 1268
Gerald fitz Maurice	1268	1287
John fitz Thomas (1)[2]	1287	12 Sept. 1316
Thomas fitz John (2)	1316	5 Apr. 1328
Richard fitz Thomas (3)	1328	7 July 1331
Maurice fitz Thomas (4)	1331	May/Aug. 1390[3]

	succession	death unless otherwise stated
Gerald fitz Maurice (5)	1390	13 Oct. 1432[4]
John fitz John (?6)	1432	?
Thomas 'fitz Maurice' (7)	1456[5]	25 Mar. 1478
Gerald (Gearóid Mór) 'fitz Maurice' (8)	1478	3 Sept. 1513
Gerald (Gearóid Óg) fitz Gerald (9)	1513	2 Sept. 1534
Thomas ('Silken Thomas') fitz Gerald (10)	1534	3 Feb. 1537
Gerald fitz Gerald (11)	1553[6]	16 Nov. 1585
Henry (12)	1585	1 Aug. 1597
William (13)	1597	early Apr. 1599
Gerald (14)	1599	11 Feb. 1612
Gerald (15)	1612	11 Nov. 1620
George (16)	1620	a. 29 May 1660[7]
Wentworth (17)	1660	5 Mar. 1664
John (18)	1664	9 Nov. 1707
Robert (19)	1707	20 Nov. 1744
James (20)[8]	1744	19 Nov. 1773

[1] Arrived in Ire. 1169.
[2] Created earl of Kildare 14 May 1316.
[3] G.E.C., *Peerage*, gives *p*. May; *H.B.C.*, p. 461 gives 15 Aug.
[4] *Calendar of Ormond deeds, 1413–1509* (Dublin, 1935), no. 101.
[5] Recognised as earl.
[6] The earldom was under attainder since May 1536; Gerald was created earl of Kildare and baron of Offaly by letters patent 13 May 1553.
[7] *H.B.C.*, p. 461.
[8] Created earl of Offaly and marquis of Kildare 3 Mar. 1761; created duke of Leinster 26 Nov. 1766.

EARLS OF DESMOND AND THEIR ANTECEDENTS, 1176–1632

Numerals in round brackets indicate the succession of earls of Desmond. The lordship of Decies passed into Geraldine hands following the marriage of John fitz Thomas of Shanid to Margery, daughter of Thomas fitz Anthony, lord of Decies and Desmond; it descended with the earldom until the time of the eighth earl. For the succession down to 1620, see genealogical table 36, above.

In this list the numbering of earls of Desmond after the fourth earl differs from the numbering in other sources; in particular from that in volume III of this history (*Early modern Ireland, 1534–1691*), e.g. index, p. 707, where the earls numbered below as 8, 10, 11, 12, 13a, 13b, 14, 15, 16a, and 16b appear respectively as 7, 9, 10, 11, 12, 11a, 13, 14, 16, and 15. The sequence given in volume III was a refinement on those given in other sources, but remained based on the same principles; use of a suffixed 'a', as in the numbering of John fitz Thomas (d. 1536), was an expedient adopted to meet immediate needs without reference to the general requirements of succession lists of lordships. In the present list the sequence is based on the principles used in the lists of Irish kingships and lordships (see above, p. 189).

Thus Maurice fitz Gerald appears as fifth earl; John fitz Thomas is numbered 13b (considered as a rival to James fitz Maurice, rather than a brief successor to Thomas fitz Thomas); and James fitz Gerald, for similar reasons, is numbered 16b.

	succession	death unless otherwise stated
Thomas fitz Maurice fitz Gerald of Shanid	1176[1]	c. 1213/14
John fitz Thomas of Shanid	c. 1213/14	?23 July 1261
Thomas fitz Maurice	1261	4 June 1298
Maurice fitz Thomas (1)[2]	1298	25 Jan. 1356
Maurice fitz Maurice (2)	1356	1357
Gerald fitz Maurice (Gearóid Iarla) (3)	1357	?12 Oct. 1398
John fitz Gerald (4)	1398	11 Oct. 1399
Maurice fitz Gerald (5)[3]	1399	1401
Thomas fitz John (6)	?1401[4]	dep. 1411 d. a. 10 Aug. 1420
James fitz Gerald (7)	1411	1463
Thomas fitz James (8)	1463	15 Feb. 1468
James fitz Thomas (9)	1468	7 Dec. 1487
Maurice Bacach fitz Thomas (10)	1487	1520
James fitz Maurice (11)	1520	18 June 1529
Thomas fitz Thomas (12)	1529	1534
James fitz Maurice (13a)	1534	1541
John fitz Thomas (13b)[3]	1534	1536
James fitz John (14)	1536[5]	14 Oct. 1558
Gerald fitz James (15)	1558	11 Nov. 1583[6]
James fitz Thomas 'the Súgán Earl' (16a)	10 Oct. 1598	dep. 1601[7] d. a. 28 Apr. 1607
James fitz Gerald (16b)	1 Oct. 1600[8]	c. 7 Nov. 1601
John fitz Thomas (17)	1607	?p. 1615
Gerald fitz John (18)	?p. 1615	1632

[1] Succ. his father Maurice fitz Gerald, who arrived in Ire. in 1169.
[2] Created earl of Desmond 27 Aug. 1329.
[3] De facto earl.
[4] Styled earl of Desmond 8 Sept. 1407.
[5] Son of John fitz Thomas; proclaimed himself earl on the death of James fitz Maurice, but not officially recognised until later.
[6] Attainted and deprived of all honours and estates 15 Nov. 1582; the earldom was subsequently under attainder until 1600.
[7] Attainted 10 Mar. 1601; captured 29 May 1601 and imprisoned in Tower of London until death.
[8] Created earl of Desmond to neutralise the claim of his cousin James, the 'Súgán Earl'; on his death his honours were extinguished.

EARLS AND DUKES OF ORMOND AND THEIR ANTECEDENTS, 1185–1745

Numerals in round brackets indicate the succession of earls of Ormond; except for 8b (Thomas Boleyn), all belong to the Butler family.

	succession	death unless otherwise stated
Theobald Walter[1]		1205
Theobald	1205	1230
Theobald	1230	1248
Theobald	1248	1285
Theobald	1285	1299
Edmund[2]	1299	13 Sept. 1321
James (1)[3]	1321	a. 18 Feb. 1338
James (2)	1338	c. 1 Nov. 1382
James (3)	1382	7 Sept. 1405
James 'the White Earl' (4)	1405	23 Aug. 1452
James (5)[4]	1452	c. 1 May 1461
John (6)	1461	a. 15 June 1477
Thomas (7)	1477	3 Aug. 1515
Piers Ruadh (8a)[5]	1515	26 Aug. 1539
Thomas Boleyn (8b)	cr. 8 Dec. 1529	12 Mar. 1539
James (9)	1539	28 Oct. 1546
Thomas Dubh 'Black Tom' (10)	1546	22 Nov. 1614
Walter (11)	1614	24 Feb. 1633
James (12)[6]	1633	21 July 1688
James (13)[7]	1688	5/16 Nov. 1745

[1] Arrived in Ire. 1185.   [2] Granted earldom of Carrick 1 Sept. 1315, but never created earl.
[3] Created earl of Ormond 16 × 31 Oct. 1328.   [4] Created second earl of Wiltshire 8 July 1449.
[5] Resigned earldom 18 Feb. 1528; created earl of Ossory 23 Feb. 1528; rest. as earl of Ormond after Boleyn's death.
[6] Created marquis of Ormond 30 Aug. 1642; created duke of Ormond in the Irish peerage 30 Mar. 1661, and in the English peerage 9 Nov. 1682.   [7] Second duke, attainted 20 Aug. 1715.

EARLS OF ULSTER AND LORDS OF CONNACHT, 1205–1483

Numerals in round brackets indicate the succession of earls of Ulster.

	succession	death unless otherwise stated
William de Burgh, lord of Connacht		1205
Hugh de Lacy (1)	1205[1]	1243
Richard de Burgh, lord of Connacht	1227	summer 1243
Richard de Burgh, lord of Connacht	1243	1248

	succession	death unless otherwise stated
Walter de Burgh, lord of Connacht (2)[2]	1248	28 July 1271
Richard de Burgh 'the Red Earl' (3)	1271	a. 24 June 1326
William de Burgh 'the Brown Earl' (4)	1326	6 June 1333
Lionel Plantagenet (5)[3]	1342	17 Oct. 1368
Edmund Mortimer, 3rd earl of March (6)[4]	1368	26/7 Dec. 1381
Roger Mortimer, 4th earl of March (7)	1381	20 July 1398
Edmund Mortimer, 5th earl of March (8)	1398	18 Jan. 1425
Richard Plantagenet, 3rd duke of York, 5th earl of Cambridge, and 6th earl of March (9)[5]	1425	30 Dec. 1460
Edward Plantagenet, 7th earl of March (10)[6]	1460	9 Apr. 1483

[1] Created earl of Ulster 29 May 1205; forfeited 1210; rest. 20 Apr. 1227.

[2] Created earl of Ulster 15 July 1263.

[3] Third son of Edward III; became earl of Ulster by marriage to Elizabeth, daughter and heir of the fourth earl; created duke of Clarence 13 Nov. 1362.

[4] Married Philippa, daughter and heir of the fifth earl, c. May 1368.

[5] Became earl of Ulster in right of his mother Anne, sister of the eighth earl.

[6] Became kg as Edward IV, 4 Mar. 1461, after which the earldom of Ulster and lordship of Connacht passed to the crown.

LOWER MAC WILLIAM AND VISCOUNTS OF MAYO, 1332-1649

Numerals in round brackets indicate the succession of viscounts of Mayo.

	succession	death unless otherwise stated
(Sir) Edmund Albanach mac William	1332	4 Nov. 1375
(Sir) Thomas	1375	1402
Walter	1402	7 Sept. 1440
Edmund na Féasóige	1440	1458
Tomás Óg	1458	1460
Risdeárd	1460	abd 1469 d. 1473
Ricard Ó Cuairsge	1469	abd 1473 d. 1479
Theobald	1473	5 Mar. 1503
Ricard	1503	7 July 1509
Edmund	1509	23 Feb. 1514
Meiler	1514	28 Apr. 1520
Edmund	1520	29 Sept. 1527
Seaán an Tearmainn	1527	?
Theobald	?	1537
David	1537	?
Ricard	?	1571
(Sir) Seaán	1571	1580

	succession	death unless otherwise stated
(Sir) Risdeárd an Iarainn	1580	1582
(Sir) Risdeárd	1582	1586
William 'An tAb Caoch'	1586	1593
Theobald[1]	1593	c. 1606
Risdeárd 'Mac Deamhain an Chorráin'	1600	?
(Sir) Theobald 'Teabóid na Long' (1)[2]	?	18 June 1629
Meiler (Miles) (2)	1629	1649

[1] Fled to Spain, where he died, having been granted the title 'marquis de Mayo'.
[2] Created Viscount Mayo 21 June 1627.

UPPER MAC WILLIAM AND EARLS OF CLANRICARD, 1332–1722

Numerals in round brackets indicate the succession of earls of Clanricard.

	succession	death unless otherwise stated
William (Uilleag) Mac William	1332	1343
Richard Óg	1343	1387
(Sir William) Uilleag an Fhíona	1387	1423
William	1423	1430
Uilleag Ruadh	?1430	1485
Uilleag Fionn	1485	1509
Ricard Óg	1509	31 Aug. 1519
Uilleag Óg	1519	24 Apr. 1520
Ricard Mór	1520	Apr. 1530
John	1530	1536
Risdeárd Bacach	1536	dep. 1538
Uilleag na gCeann (1)[1]	1538	19 Oct. 1544
(Sir) Uilleag	1544	1551
Ricard Sassanach (2)[2]	1551	24 July 1582
Uilleag 'Mac an Iarla' (3)	1582	20 May 1601
Ricard (4)[3]	1601	12 Nov. 1635
Ulick (5)[4]	1635	July 1657
Ricard (6)	1657	Aug. 1666
William (7)	1666	Oct. 1687
Ricard (8)	1687	1709
John (9)[5]	1709	17 Oct. 1722

[1] Created earl of Clanricard 1 July 1543.
[2] Succeeded to the earldom 1544.
[3] Created earl of St Albans 23 Aug. 1628.
[4] Created marquis of Clanricard 21 Feb. 1646; as he died without male issue, this title and the earldom of St Albans were not transmitted to his successors.
[5] Created baron of Bophin 2 Apr. 1689.

HEADS OF CHURCHES TO *c.*1200

F. J. BYRNE

INTRODUCTION

IN this section twelve representative churches have been selected for which a fairly full list of heads can be culled from the annals. Where annalistic obits are the only source, it is impossible to be certain that there are no gaps in the record. Only in the case of Armagh is there an official list (of 'coarbs of Patrick') which, by and large, agrees with the annalistic evidence. In the case of Bangor, there is a list dating from the seventh century in the *Antiphonary of Bangor* (ed. F. E. Warren, 2 vols, London, 1893–5) which also agrees with the annalistic evidence. The martyrologies[1] are a valuable source of information, and provide the day of the month for the death of many early ecclesiastics, particularly for the period before 800. Only for Iona do the annals provide such circumstantial detail for the early period.

These lists give the heads of the old Irish foundations. In the twelfth century most of these houses gave way to the newer diocesan chapters or were refounded as houses of Augustinian canons as happened at Bangor, refounded by St Malachy *c.*1124. The old order continued longest at Derry, where it lasted well into the thirteenth century. The last abbot of Ferns (d. 1172) was probably abbot of the new house of Augustinian canons founded by Diarmait Mac Murchada *c.*1160.

[1] *Félire Oengusso Céli Dé: the martyrology of Oengus the Culdee*, ed. Whitley Stokes (London, 1905), compiled *c.* 800; *Martyrology of Tallaght*, ed. R. I. Best and H. J. Lawlor (London, 1931), also compiled *c.*800; and *Félire Huí Gormáin: the martyrology of Gorman*, ed. Whitley Stokes (London, 1895), compiled in the twelfth century but incorporating much earlier material.

ARMAGH

(ARD MACHAE)

Comarbai Pátraic 'heirs of St Patrick'

The church of Armagh, traditionally founded in 444, was episcopal in origin, but after the middle of the eighth century the 'heir of Patrick' was always an abbot and the office of bishop of Armagh was subordinate to that of the abbot until Cellach (Celsus) and St Malachy restored episcopal government in the twelfth century. Bishops are therefore listed separately from 750 onwards. The early coarbs are given the titles accorded them in the annals and lists, but all were bishops, while the term 'abbot' may in some cases be an anachronism. Members of the Clann Sínaig are denoted by an asterisk: see Tomás Ó Fiaich, 'The church of Armagh under lay control' in *Seanchas Ard Mhacha* (1969), v, no. 1, pp 75-127.

	death unless otherwise stated
bishops	
Pátraic (Patricius; St Patrick)	17 Mar. 457/61 or 493
Sechnall mac Restituit (St Secundinus)[1]	27 Nov. 447/8
Sen-Phátraic[1]	24 Aug. —
Benén mac Sescnén (St Benignus)	9 Nov. 467/8
Iarlaithe mac Treno	3 Feb. 481
Cormac, bp and abbot[2]	17 Feb. 497
Dubthach, bp	513
Ailill I, bp	13 Jan. 526
Ailill II, bp	1 July 536
Dubthach (Duach), abbot[3]	548
Fedelmid Find, abbot	578
Carláen (Cáerlan, Ciarláech, Cairellán), bp	24 Mar. 588
Eochu (Eochaid), abbot	598
Senach, abbot	610
Mac Laisre, abbot	12 Sept. 623
Tómméne, bp	10 Jan. 661
Ségéne, bp[4]	24 May 688
Fland Feblae mac Scandláin, abbot and bp	715
Suibne *nepos* Mruichessaich (mac Crundmaíl), bp	21 June 730
Congus, bp (also scribe)	750
abbots	
Céle Petair	758
Fer dá Chrích mac Suibni	768
Cú Dínaisc mac Conasaig	?res. *c.* 772
	d. 791
*Dub dá Leithe I mac Sínaig	793
Airechtach ua Fáeláin	794
Fóendelach mac Móenaig	795
Gormgal mac Dindataig (Dindanaig, Dindagaid, Indnotaig)[5]	806
*Condmach mac Duib dá Leithe[6]	807
Torbach mac Gormáin	16 July 808
Toicthech ua Tigernaig[7]	809
Nuadu (also bp and anchorite)	812
Flandgus (Fergus) mac Loingsig	826
Artrí mac Conchobair, bp[8]	dep. 827/8
	d. 833
[?Suibne mac Forandáin (Fairnig)[9]	830]
Eógan Mainistrech mac Ainbthig[10]	834
Forindán mac Murgile (also bp and scribe)[11]	852
Diarmait ua Tigernáin[11]	852

abbots	*death unless otherwise stated*
[?Cathassach[12]	856]
Féthgno mac Nechtain, bp	6 Oct. 874
Máel Cobo mac Crundmaíl[13]	dep. 877
	rest. 877/8
	d. 888
Ainmere ua Fáeláin	dep. 877/8
	d. 879
Cathassach mac Robartaig, bp	883
Máel Brigte mac Tornáin[14]	22 Feb. 927
Ioseph mac Fathaig (also bp and anchorite)	936
Máel Pátraic mac Máel Tuile, bp	936
Cathassach mac Doiligén, bp	957
Muiredach mac Fergussa	dep. 965
	d. 966
*Dub dá Leithe II mac Cellaig[15]	**June 998**
Muirecén mac Ciaracáin[16]	res. 1001
	d. 1005
*Máel Muire mac Eochada (Eochocáin)[17]	3 June 1020
*Amalgaid mac Máel Muire	1049
*Dub dá Leithe III mac Máel Muire[18]	1 Sept. 1064
Cummascach Ua hErodáin (abbot 1060–63/4)[19]	1074
*Máel Ísu mac Amalgada	18 Dec. 1091
*Domnall mac Amalgada	Aug. 1105
*Cellach mac Áeda meic Máel Ísu (Celsus), bp (abp 1106)	1 Apr. 1129
*Muirchertach mac Domnaill	17 Sept. 1134
*Niall mac Áeda meic Máel Ísu	res. 1137
	d. 1139

archbishops	
Máel Máedóc Ua Morgair (Malachias; St Malachy), abp 1132[20]	res. 1136
	d. 2 Nov. 1148
Gilla Meic Liac mac Diarmata meic Ruaidrí (Gelasius)[21]	27 Mar. 1174
Conchobar mac Meic Con Caille (St Concors), can. reg.[22]	1175
Gilla in Choimded Ua Caráin (Gillebertus)	*c.* Jan. 1180
Tommaltach mac Áeda Ua Conchobair (Thomas)[23]	1201

bishops	
Affiath	794
Nuadu[24]	812
Artrí mac Conchobair[24]	833
Forindán mac Murgile[24]	852
Máel Pátraic mac Findchon (also scribe and anchorite)	863

bishops	*death unless otherwise stated*
Féthgno mac Nechtain[24]	6 Oct. 874
Cathassach mac Robartaig[24]	883
Mochtae daltae Féthgno (also scribe and anchorite)[25]	893
Máel Aithgin	895
Cellach mac Sóergussa (also anchorite)	903
Máel Ciaráin mac Eochocáin[26]	915
Ioseph mac Fathaig[24]	936
Máel Pátraic mac Máel Tuile[24]	936
Cathassach mac Doiligén[24]	957
Cathassach mac Murchadáin	967
Máel Muire mac Scandláinn	994
Airmedach mac Coscraig (also scribe)	1006
[?Cenn Fáelad Sabaill (anchorite)[27]	1012]
Máel Tuile	1032
Áed Ua Forréid[28]	1056
Máel Pátraic mac Airmedaig	1096
Cáenchomrac Ua Baígill (cons. 29 May 1099)	1106
Máel Coluim Ua Brolcháin (cons. 13 Sept. 1107)[29]	1122
Máel Brigte Ua Brolcháin[30]	29 Jan. 1139
Amlaím Ua Muirethaig[31]	1185

[1] The names of Secundinus (of Dunshaughlin) and of the chimerical 'Old Patrick' occur here in the Book of Leinster list: see H. J. Lawlor and R. I. Best, 'The ancient list of the coarbs of Patrick' in *R.I.A. Proc.*, xxxv, sect. C, no. 9 (1919), pp 316–62; but *A.U.* call Iarlaithe 'third bp of Armagh'.

[2] Styled *heres Patricii* in *A.U.*, 'first abbot' in the official list.

[3] Perhaps identical with Bp 'Dauid Farannaini' (Dauid mac Guairi uí Farannáin), whose obit is interpolated in a late hand, *A.U.* 551.

[4] After Ségéne the Book of Leinster inserts a Forannán (unknown to the other MSS of the list and to the annals) with a reign of 1 year.

[5] Also abbot of Clones; omitted from the list together with Fland Rói mac Cummascaig, who took the abbacy by force (his grandfather, Conchobar, was killed in 698), rival to Fóendelach.

[6] In opposition to Fóendelach and Gormgal; recognised as coarb, *A.U.* 804.

[7] Not in the official list.

[8] Bp of Armagh since 794; acting as coarb (or on behalf of Flandgus?) in 818, 823, 825.

[9] *Abbas duorum mensium*, *A.U.*; abbot of Devenish, *Chron. Scot.*; not in list.

[10] Also *fer léigind* of Monasterboice and (since 830) abbot of Clonard.

[11] Rival abbots.

[12] Only in *Ann. Inisf.* and *Frag. ann.*; but *A.F.M.* call him *fer tigis* 'oeconomus'.

[13] The 4 years assigned to his successor Cathassach, who died in retirement in 883, suggest that Máel Cobo's capture by the Norse in 879 put an end to his tenure of office.

[14] Also coarb of Colum Cille 891.

[15] Also coarb of Colum Cille 989; *A.U.* give his obit as 5th Nones of June, which is meaningless.

[16] Of Both Domnaig (Bodoney, Co. Tyrone); acting as coarb 993.

[17] Son of *fer léigind* Eochaid ua Flainn (d. 1004) and nephew of Dub dá Leithe II.

[18] *Fer léigind* since 1046.

[19] In opposition to Dub dá Leithe III.

[20] Son of *fer léigind* Mugrón Ua Morgair (d. 5 Oct. 1102); bp of Down and Connor 1124–37, bp of Down 1137–48.

[21] Abbot of Derry since 1121.

[22] Abbot of SS Paul and Peter, Armagh (can. reg.); d. at Lémenc near Chambéry in Savoy on visit to Rome. Omitted in the Book of Leinster list, which substitutes 'int epscop hua Muredaig', presumably Amlaím Ua Muirethaig (see bishops).

[23] Bp of Elphin since *c.*1174; grandson of High-king Toirrdelbach Ua Conchobair (d. 1156).
[24] Also abbot: see preceding list.
[25] i.e. pupil or fosterson of Féthgno.
[26] Also abbot of Clones and Mucknoe.
[27] Said to be a 'pilgrim', therefore probably not bp of Armagh; from Saul.
[28] May have resigned bishopric when he became *fer léigind* in 1049.
[29] Died in Derry; see below, pp 278, 280.
[30] Máel Coluim and Máel Brigte may have combined duties as bps under the old regime with diocesan care over Cenél nEógain (Ardstraw/Derry).
[31] Succeeded Muiredach Ua Cobthaig (d. 10 Feb. 1173) as bp of Ráith Lúraig/Derry; d. at Dún Cruthnai (County Londonderry); buried at Derry. But he is styled 'bp of Armagh and Cenél Feradaig' (*A.U.* 1185) and appears to be reckoned as coarb of Patrick in the Book of Leinster list.

BANGOR

(BENNCHOR)

Comarbai Comgaill

abbots	*death unless otherwise stated*
Comgall moccu Araidi	10 May 601 or 602/5
Béugnae mac Daigri	22 Aug. 606/9
Sinlán moccu Min	28 Feb. 610/12
[Áedán, anchorite of Bangor[1]	610/12]
Finntan Óentreib	613/15
Mac Laisre	16 May 646/7
Ségán moccu Chuind	10 Sept. 663
Berach	21 Apr. 665
Cumméne	17 Sept. 665
Colum	1 Oct. 665
Áedán moccu Chuind	9 Oct. 665
Baíthéne	666
Crítán	16 Sept. 669
[Máel Rubai mac Elgonaig, abbot of Applecross[2]	res. 671
	d. 21 Apr. 722]
Cammán (Colmán)	679/80
Crónán moccu Chualni	6 Nov. 691
Cenn Fáelad *nepos* Áedo Bricc	8 Apr. 705
Flann Óentreib	15 Dec. 728
Sárán	1 Aug. 747
Suairlech	13 Dec. 761
Fidbadach	767
Snédcheist mac Tuamchon	778[3]
Conall mac int Saír	778[3]
Augustín	27 Oct. 780
Sírne	4 Dec. 791
Tómás (Tómmae)	22 Apr. 794
Airmedach mac Conaill	800

abbots	death unless otherwise stated
Mac Óige	802
Robartach	805[4]
Máel Tuili mac Dondgaile	res. 817
	d. 820
Máel Gaimrid	839
Airindán	849
Móengal	871
Ferchar mac Congusso	881
Rogaillnech	884
Indrechtach mac Dobailén	906
Móenach mac Siadail	921
Céle Dabaill mac Scannail	res. 928
	d. 14 Sept. 929[5]
Muiredach	940
Máel Cothaid mac Lachtnáin	953
(Dub Innse, bp[6]	953)
Tanaide mac Uidir	958[7]
Cellach ua Bánáin	968
Ardgal mac Cosracháin	*c.* 975[8]
Sínach mac Muirthilén	981
Diarmait ua Máel Telcha, bp	1016
Máel Brigte ua Críchidén	1025
Óengus ua Cruimthir	1030
Máel Martain mac Assída	1055
Colmán ua hAirechtaig	1058
Augéne mac in Bécánaig	1068
Lergus Ua Cruimthir	1097
Óengus Ua Gormáin, bp	1123[9]
Muirchertach Ua hIndrechtaig	3 Oct. 1131[10]

[1] Reckoned as abbot in the Antiphonary of Bangor.
[2] Reckoned as abbot of Bangor in the Martyrology of Tallaght and *A.F.M.* (671, 721), but not in the Antiphonary or early annals.
[3] *A.F.M.* 773.
[4] *A.F.M.* 800.
[5] At Rome.
[6] Apparently did not hold office of abbot.
[7] Killed by Norse.
[8] *A.F.M.*; *Chron. Scot.*, 973.
[9] At Lismore.
[10] At Armagh.

CLONARD

(CLUAIN IRAIRD)

Comarbai Finnéin[1]

abbots	*death unless otherwise stated*
Finnio moccu Thelduib (St Finnian)	12 Dec. 549/552
Senach, bp	21 Aug. *c.* 590
Diarmait[2]	615
Colmán moccu Thelduib (Mo Cholmóc), bp	8 Feb. 654
Oisséne Foto	1 May 654
Ultán moccu Chungai	665
[?Da Beóóc (Mo Bécóc)[3]	689/90]
Colmán ua hEirc[4]	5 Dec. 701
Dub Dúin ua Fáeláin, bp	718
Áelchú	732
Fiannamail mac Geirtidi	736
(Tólae mac Dúnchado, bp	738)
Forindán	12 Feb. 745
Do Dímmóc[5]	3 Mar. 748
Bécc Laitne	763
Loarn	765
Airlid	772
Góedel	776
(Fulartach, bp	29 Mar./21 Dec. 779)
Dub dá Bairenn	787
Crundmáel Dromma Inesclainn[6]	793
(Clothchú, bp and anchorite)	796)
Dub dá Bairenn ua Dubáin	805
Crundmáel mac Odráin	820
Clemens, bp	826
Cormac mac Suibni, bp (also scribe)	830
Eógan Mainistrech[7]	834
Comsud, bp (also anchorite)	858
Suairlech ind Eidnén mac Ciaráin, bp[8]	4 Dec. 870
Dálach mac Máele Raitte	862
Áedán	19 July 882
Ailbrén mac Maichtig	884
Cormac[9]	885
Cú Chongelt	888
(Rumann mac Cathassaig, bp	921)
Colmán mac Ailella[10]	926
Ferdomnach mac Flannacáin	932
Máel Mochta (also scribe)	942
Máel Feichíne	944
Célechair mac Robartaig[11]	954
[?Máenach[12]	956]

abbots	*death unless otherwise stated*
Béccán mac Lachtnáin, bp	973
Tuathal mac Máel Ruba (ua Dubánaig)	993
Ferdomnach	1008
Fachtna	1011
Flaithbertach mac Domnaill[13]	1014
Domnall mac Máel Sechnaill[14]	1019
Tuathal ua Dubánaig, bp[15]	1028/30
Cellach ua Cléirchén	1043
Ferdomnach ua hInnascaig	1048
Tuathal Ua Follamain	1055
Murchad mac Flainn Ua Máel Sechlainn[16]	1076
Muirchertach mac Loingsig Ua Máel Sechlainn	1092
(Máel Muire Ua Dúnáin, bp	24 Dec. 1117)
Conchobar Ua Follamain	1117
[?**Gilla Críst Ua hEcháin**[17]	1136]
Ua Follamain[18]	1150
[?Conchobar Dall mac Domnaill Ua Máel Sechlainn	bld 1153]

[1] The title 'coarb of Finnian' is ambiguous, as it may also refer to abbots of Moville, County Down, founded by Finnian *nepos* Fiatach (d. 10 Sept. 579/80); abbots of Clonard are sometimes called 'coarbs of Finnian and Mo Cholmóc'. Bps who did not hold the office of abbot are here placed between round brackets. For later diocesan bishops of Clonard see below, pp 285-6.

[2] Styled 'third abbot' in *A.U.*; the martyrologies commemorate a Fiachrai, abbot of Glenn Suilige (Glenswilly) and Clonard, at 8 Feb., but he is not recorded in the annals.

[3] Probably the saint commemorated at 26 May: of Cluain Aird Mo Bécóc (Kilpeacon, County Limerick) rather than of Clonard.

[4] 'Colman hoa hOircc' (*Cáin Adamnáin*).

[5] Also anchorite and abbot of Kildare (since 698).

[6] From Dromiskin, County Louth.

[7] *Fer léigind* of Monasterboice; also abbot of Armagh (since 827/8).

[8] Of Int Eidnén (Inan, in parish of Killyon, County Meath).

[9] Also bp of Duleek.

[10] Also bp and scribe, and abbot of Clonmacnoise (since 904).

[11] Also abbot of Clonmacnoise (since 952).

[12] Also *fer léigind* of Armagh; possibly abbot of Moville.

[13] Son of Domnall, kg of Mide (951-2), and brother of the high-king Máel Sechnaill mac Domnaill (980-1022); also abbot of Clonmacnoise (since 1003).

[14] Son of Máel Sechnaill mac Domnaill.

[15] His obit at 1030 in *A.F.M.* is presumably a duplicate of that at 1028.

[16] Grandson of Abbot Domnall, and kg of Mide ('for three nights' according to the annals) in 1073; also abbot of Kells in 1055, where he was killed by the kg of Gailenga in 1076.

[17] Probably abbot of Moville or possibly of Clooncraff, Co. Roscommon.

[18] Died at Kells.

CLONFERT

(CLUAIN FERTAE BRÉNAIND)

Comarbai Brénaind

abbots	death unless otherwise stated
Brénaind moccu Altai	16 May 577/8
Fintan Corach (Corad)	21 Feb. 592
Senach	604
Senach Garb mac Buidi	10 Sept. 621
Ségán Carrthach	636
Cumméne Foto mac Fiachnai, bp	12 Nov. 661/2
Fáelán[1]	*fl.* 696/7
Fachtnae mac Folachtáin	729
Fiachnae ua Maic Niad	752
Cellán	753
Suibne	762
Crimthann mac Rechtgaile	766
Ceithernach ua hErmono (?Rumono)	773
Flaithnio mac Congaile	781
Mac Flaithniad	783
Tipraite mac Ferchair[2]	786
Muiredach	792
Muiredach mac Ólchobair	802
Tipraite mac Ceithernaig	817
Ólchobar mac Cummascaig	820
Ruithnél, bp	826
Coinnecán	?dep. 838
	d. 849
Fedelmid mac Crimthainn[3]	28 Aug. 847
Rechtabrae	850
Mugrón ua Cinn Fáelad	885
Máel Tuili mac Cilléni	888
Máel Petair ua Cuáin[4]	895
Áed mac Ailella	916
Áed mac Cellaig	958
Eógan ua Catháin	981
Máel Petair ua Tolaig	992
Óengus ua Flainn	1036
Coscrach mac Aingeda (also abbot of Killaloe)	1040
Diarmait mac Máel Brénainn[5]	1074
Coinnecán Ua Flainn	1081
Cenn Fáelad Ua hÓcáin[6]	1091
Ua Corcráin, bp	1094
Gilla Muire Ua Fogartaig (Máel Muire Ua Fócarta)	1112
Máel Brénainn Ua hÁnradáin[7]	1132/4
Gilla Meic Aiblén Ua hAnmchada	1166

The following bishops are recorded who did not hold the office of coarb or abbot.[8]

bishops	death unless otherwise stated
Móenu	1 Mar. 572
Eitchén	578
Cenn Fáelad	807
Laithbertach mac Óengusso	822
Cormac mac Áedáin	922
Ciarán ua Gabla	953
Cathal mac Cormaic	963
Eochu mac Scolaige	1031

[1] 'Faelan ho Cluain Ferta Brenaind' (*Cáin Adamnáin*).

[2] *A.U.* records his obit in 786, and that of Tipraite mac Ferchair *ó Chluain Ferta Brénaind*, i.e. 'from Clonfert' (not explicitly styled abbot) in 795; it is possible that the same person is intended and that the earlier obit is an error for his resignation of office.

[3] Kg of Munster since 820; according to *Ann. Inisf.* he took the abbacy of Cork in 836 and in 838 'sat in the abbatial chair of Clonfert' and became high-king.

[4] Also bp and abbot of Terryglass; took the abbacy of Clonfert in 891.

[5] Died at Ardfert.

[6] Of Dál Cais: took the abbacy in 1082.

[7] The obit of Gilla Brénainn Ua hÁnradáin in *A.F.M.* 1134 is probably a duplicate of that of Máel Brénainn in 1132.

[8] For bishops of the diocese of Clonfert after 1111 see below, pp 324-6.

CLONMACNOISE

(CLUAIN MOCCU NÓIS)

Comarbai Ciaráin[1]

See John Ryan, 'The abbatial succession at Clonmacnois' in *Féil-sgríbhinn Eóin Mhic Néill* (Dublin, 1940), pp 490-507, and his *Clonmacnois: a historical summary* (Dublin, 1973).

abbots	death unless otherwise stated
Ciarán mac int Saír[2]	9 Sept. 544 or 548/9
Óenu moccu Loígse[3]	20 Jan. 570
Mac Nisse[4]	13 June 585
Ailithir[5]	599
To Lua Foto (Lucaill)[6]	614
Columbán moccu Bairddéni (Columbanus filius Bairddaeni)[7]	628
Crónán moccu Loígde[8]	18 July 638
Áedlug mac Cammáin[9]	26 Feb. 652
Báetán moccu Chormaic[10]	1 Mar. 664
Colmán Cass mac Fualascaig[11]	665
Cumméne[12]	665
Colmán[13]	683

abbots	*death unless otherwise stated*
Forcrón	686
Crónán Becc (Crón)[14]	6 Apr. 694
Osséne Frémainne mac Galluist[15]	?dep. *a.* 696/7
	d. 706
Faílbe Becc[16]	713
Cuindles[17]	724
Fland Fine ua Colla (Fland Cualann)[18]	733
Conmáel ua Lóchéni[19]	737
Cellach mac Ségdai[20]	740
[Commán mac Fáelchon[21]	26 Dec. 747]
Luccreth (Lucraid)[22]	29 Apr. 753
Cormac[23]	762
Rónán[24]	764
[Ua Miannaig[25]	768]
Folachtach[26]	770
Forbassach ua Cernaig[27]	771
Collbran	776
Rechtnio (Rechtabrae)[28]	784
Snéidriagail[29]	786
Murgal[30]	789
Sóerbergg	791
Ioseph ua Cernaig[31]	794
Anaile[32]	799
[Tuathgal[33]	811]
Foirchellach Fobair[34]	814
Suibne mac Cuanach[35]	816
Rónán[36]	res. 823
	d. 844
Cétadach[37]	850
Condmach[38]	868
Martan[39]	869
Ferdomnach[40]	872
Eógan Topair[41]	876
Máel Tuili ua Cuanach[42]	877
Máel Pátraic[43]	885
Máel Brigte na Gamnaide[44]	892
Blathmac mac Tairchedaig[45]	896
Dedimus ua Foirbthen[46]	dep. 901
	d. 923
Ioseph[47]	904
Colmán mac Ailella[48]	926
[Máel Giric[49]	929]
Tipraite mac Ainnséine[50]	931
Ainmere ua Cathla (ua Cathaláin)[51]	948
Ferdomnach ua Máenaig[52]	952
Célechair mac Robartaig[53]	954
Cormac ua Cillín[54]	966

Tuathal, bp	971
Dúnchad ua Bráeín[55]	res. 976
	d. 16 Jan. 988/9
Máel Finnia mac Speláin (ua Máenaig)[56]	992
Ua Beculáin	dep. 1002
Flannchad ua Ruaidíne (ua Ruadáin)[57]	1003
Flaithbertach mac Domnaill[58]	1014
Muiredach mac Mugróin[59]	1025
Bressal Conaillech[60]	1030
Loingsech ua Flaithnén[61]	1042
Echtigern Ua hEgráin[62]	1052
[Máel Finnéin mac Cuinn na mBocht[63]	1056]
Ailill Ua hAirechtaig[64]	1070
[Máel Ciaráin mac Cuinn na mBocht[65]	1079]
Tigernach Ua Bráeín[66]	1088
Ailill Ua Nialláin[67]	1093
Mac Raith Ua Flaithnén[68]	res. 1096
	d. 1100
[Cormac Mac Cuinn na mBocht[69]	1103]
Flaithbertach Ua Loingsig	1109
Gilla Críst Ua Máel Eóin	1127
Domnall Ua Dubthaig[70]	17 Mar. 1136
Máel Mochta Ua Fidabra (Ua Máel Sechlainn)[71]	1173
Áed Ua Máel Eóin[71]	1153
Tigernach Ua Máel Eóin[71]	1172
Máel Ciaráin Ua Fidabra	1187

bishops

Tuathchar	889
Máel Odar	890
Cairpre Cromm	904
Loingsech	919
Fer Dálach	922
Dúnchad mac Suthainén	942
Óenucán mac Écertaig[72]	949
Dúnadach mac Écertaig[73]	955
Tuathal[74]	971
Máenach mac Máel Míchil	971
Flann mac Máel Míchil[75]	979
Conaing ua Coscraig	998
Máel Póil[76]	1001
Conaing mac Áedacáin[77]	1010
Flaithbertach mac Loingsig[78]	1037
Célechair Mugdornach mac Cuinn na mBocht[79]	1067
Gilla Críst Ua hEchtigirn[80]	1104
Muiredach Ua Máel Dúin	1105

¹ Bps who were not abbots are listed separately below; for diocesan bps of Clonmacnoise after 1111 see below, pp 275-7.

² Of Latharnai Molt; Ryan adduces reasons for believing 545 to be the correct year of his death.

³ Of Loíges Réto.

⁴ Of Ulaid.

⁵ Of Múscraige.

⁶ Of Corcu Moga.

⁷ Of Dál mBairdd Ulad.

⁸ Of Corcu Loígde.

⁹ Of Gailenga in Choraind.

¹⁰ Of Conmaicne Mara.

¹¹ Of Corcu Moga.

¹² Of Grecraige Locha Teichet.

¹³ From Airtech; probably of Ciarraige Airtig.

¹⁴ From Cuailgne; probably of Conailli Muirtheimne.

¹⁵ Of Calraige Tethbae; possibly identical with 'Oisine mac Glais abp Cluana Ferta Molua' (abbot of Clonfertmulloe) in *Cáin Adamnáin*, where Faílbe Becc appears as abbot of Clonmacnoise; although Osséne's epithet refers to Frewin, County Westmeath, his father's name suggests Pictish origin, and the tract on the monastery of Tallaght (ed. E. J. Gwynn and W. J. Purton, in *R.I.A. Proc.*, xxix, sect. C, no. 5 (1911), p. 162, § 85) refers to the expulsion of a foreigner (*deórad*) whom Adomnán of Iona had appointed to the abbacy of Clonmacnoise.

¹⁶ Of Gailenga in Choraind.

¹⁷ Of Sogain Connacht.

¹⁸ Of Uí Chremthainn.

¹⁹ Of Ciannachta Breg.

²⁰ From Buidemnach; of Conmaicne.

²¹ St Commán, founder of Roscommon; styled abbot of Clonmacnoise in *A.F.M.* only, probably in error.

²² Of Corcu Loígde.

²³ Of Uí Maini.

²⁴ Of Luigni.

²⁵ *Abb sruithe Cluana moccu Nóis*, i.e. abbot of the seniors or house of seniors, apparently a subordinate office to that of the coarb of Ciarán.

²⁶ From Tech Tuae (Taghadoe, Co. Kildare).

²⁷ Of Uí Briúin.

²⁸ Of Uí Maini.

²⁹ Of Calraige Áelmaige.

³⁰ Of Uí Fiachrach.

³¹ Of Ciannachta Breg.

³² Of Uí Briúin.

³³ *Abb sruithe* (see n. 25).

³⁴ From Fore; of Gailenga Móra.

³⁵ Of Uí Briúin Seóla.

³⁶ Of Luigni Rossa Temrach.

³⁷ Of Uí Chormaic Máenmaige.

³⁸ Of Cenél nEchach Gall.

³⁹ Of Dartraige Coininnse; also abbot of Devenish.

⁴⁰ Of Mugdornai.

⁴¹ Of Uí Chremthainn.

⁴² Of Grecraige Arda in Luigni Connacht.

⁴³ From Tech Ingine Lingaig; of Uí Maini.

⁴⁴ Of Fir Umaill.

⁴⁵ Of Bregmaine.

⁴⁶ Held office of *tánaise abbad* at his death.

⁴⁷ From Loch Con; of Uí Fiachrach.

⁴⁸ Of Conailli Muirtheimne; also bp, scribe, and abbot of Clonard (since 888).

⁴⁹ *Abb tige sruithe* (see n. 25).

⁵⁰ Of Uí Briúin.

⁵¹ Of Uí Maic Uais Midi; also abbot of Lecan (Lackan, Co. Westmeath).

⁵² Of Corcu Moga; also abbot of Glendalough (since 950), where he died.

⁵³ Of Uí Maic Uais Midi; also abbot of Clonard (since 944).

⁵⁴ Of Uí Fiachrach Aidni; also abbot of Roscommon and Tomgraney.

⁵⁵ Of Síl Muiredaig; died at Armagh.

⁵⁶ Of Uí Beccon.

⁵⁷ Of Corcu Moga.

⁵⁸ Of Clann Cholmáin; brother of High-king Máel Sechnaill (980-1022); also abbot of Clonard (since 1011).

⁵⁹ From Imlech Fordeórad; also abbot of Roscommon.

⁶⁰ Of Conailli Muirtheimne.

⁶¹ Of Cuircni; also abbot of Tomgraney.

⁶² Of Sogain Ua Maine; also abbot of Roscommon; d. in retirement at Clonard.

⁶³ Of Mugdornai, son of Conn na mBocht, head of the Céli Dé (d. 1059/60). Probably not abbot; only so styled in *A.F.M.*, which may however refer to his son Cormac (d. 1103).

⁶⁴ Of Corcu Roíde.

⁶⁵ Styled abbot only in *A.F.M.*; 'head of the poor', *A.U.*

⁶⁶ Of Síl Muiredaig; also abbot of Roscommon.

⁶⁷ Also abbot of Roscrea and Kilmacduagh.

⁶⁸ Of Uí Fiachrach Fella; also abbot of Tomgraney; d. at Aghaboe.

⁶⁹ Styled abbot only in *Chron. Scot.*; *tánaise abbad* or 'prior', *Ann. Tig.*, *A.F.M.*; son of Máel Finnéin and grandson of Conn na mBocht according to *A.F.M.*

⁷⁰ Apparently first diocesan bp as well as abbot of Clonmacnoise; also bp of Elphin; d. at Clonfert.

⁷¹ Máel Mochta was abbot in 1141, and in 1158 *Ann. Tig.* and *Ann. Clon.* refer to 'two coarbs of Ciarán'.

⁷² Of Mugdornai Maigen; son of Luchairén, scribe (d. 863), son of Eógan, anchorite (d. 847), son of Áeducán, abbot of Louth (since 822), who d. at Clonmacnoise in 835, son of Torbach, abbot of Armagh (807-8), son of Gormán, abbot of Louth (d. at Clonmacnoise 758); also abbot of the 'Little Church'.

⁷³ Brother of Óenucán; great-grandfather of Conn na mBocht; the claim that he was of the Uí Chellaig Breg seems spurious (see John V. Kelleher, 'The Táin and the annals' in *Ériu*, xxii (1971), p. 126).

⁷⁴ Became abbot in 966; see above.

⁷⁵ Also *fer léigind* and coarb of Cluain Deochra.

⁷⁶ Also abbot of Fore.

⁷⁷ Of Mugdornai Maigen.

⁷⁸ Also *fer léigind*.

⁷⁹ Son of Conn na mBocht and father of Máel Muire (killed 1106), one of the scribes of *Lebor na hUidre*.

⁸⁰ Also abbot of Ardagh.

CORK

(CORCACH MÁR MUMAN)

Comarbai Báirri[1]

abbots[2]	death unless otherwise stated
Suibne mac Máele Umai	682
Roisséne	686/7
Mend Maiche mac Duib dá Bárcc	*fl.* 69
. . . .	
Dónait mac To Ence	8 May 764
Selbach mac Con Alltai	772/4
T'Éróc	792
Condmach mac Dónait	800

abbots	*death unless otherwise stated*
Conaing mac Dónait	816/17
Forbassach	823
Fland mac Fairchellaig[3]	21 Dec. 825
Dúnlaing mac Cathassaig[4]	dep. 834
	d. 836
Fedelmid mac Crimthainn[5]	28 Aug. 847
Colum mac Airechtaig	851
Daniél ua Liathaidi[6]	863
Rechtabrae mac Murchado	868
(Domnall, bp and scribe	877)
Arggatán mac Forindáin	?res. 897
	d. 899
(Sóerbrethach mac Connaid, bp	896)
Ailill mac Eógain[7]	908
Flann mac Loíge	913
Fínnechta	928
Ailill mac Cuirc	951
(Cathmug, bp[8]	961)
(Fínnechta, bp	978)
Colum mac Ciarucáin	989
Flaithem	1001
Cellach ua Menngoráin	1007
Cormac mac Dúnlaing	1016
Cellach ua Selbaig, bp	res. 1025
	d. 1036
Niall ua Meic Duib	1026
Art ua hAirt	1027
Cathal Martír	1034
Óengus mac Catháin, bp	1036
Dub dá Leithe Ua Cináeda[9]	1057
Mugrón Ua Mutáin, bp and *fer léigind*[9]	1057
Cléirech Ua Selbaig	1085
(Ua Cochláin, bp[10]	1096)
Mac Bethad Ua hÁilgenáin[10]	1106
Gilla Pátraic Ua Selbaig	1109
Gilla Pátraic Ua hÉnna[11]	—
Domnall Ua Selbaig	1140
Finn mac meic Céilechair Ua Cennéitig[12]	1152
Gilla Pátraic mac Donnchada Mac Carthaig[13]	1157

[1] Báirre (St Findbarr) is commemorated on 25 Sept., and may have lived in the sixth century.

[2] Bps who were not also abbots are given between round brackets; for diocesan bps of Cork after 1111 see below, pp 295-6.

[3] Also abbot of Lismore (since 814) and Emly (since 819).

[4] The first of the 2 obits in *A.F.M.* 833, 835, is probably an error for his deposition; *A.U.* record his death at Cashel *sine communione* in 836.

[5] Kg of Munster (since 820); also abbot of Clonfert (since 838), scribe and anchorite.

[6] Also abbot of Lismore (since 825).

[7] Styled *princeps Triúin Corcaige* 'abbot of Trian Corcaige' i.e. of the Third of Cork, in *A.U.*

⁸ Also abbot of Lismore (since 959).
⁹ It is not clear whether Dub dá Leithe preceded or succeeded Mugrón, who was killed at Ros Ailithir (Roscarbery) by Ua Flainn Arda (*Ann. Inisf.*), or by his own community (*Ann. Tig.*, *Chron. Scot.*), or by 'robbers' of the Corcu Loígde (*A.F.M.*).
¹⁰ According to *Ann. Inisf.* Ua hÁilgenáin was of the Dál Cais and succeeded Ua Selbaig in 1085; *A.F.M.* are therefore probably mistaken in styling Ua Cochláin 'coarb of Báirre'.
¹¹ Not in the annals, but he is recorded in the genealogies of Dál Cais as first cousin of Domnall Ua hÉnna, bp of Killaloe (d. 1098), and as himself being abbot of Cork and bp of Killaloe; see list of bps of Killaloe (pp 300–1). He must have died well before 1131, when Domnall Ua Conaing was translated from Killaloe to Cashel.
¹² Of Dál Cais; also abbot of Terryglass (since 1108).
¹³ Son of Donnchad Mac Carthaig, kg of Desmond (1138–43; d. 1144).

EMLY

(IMBLECH IBAIR)

Comarbai Ailbi¹

abbots²	death unless otherwise stated
Conaing ua Daint	661
Cuán	686
Díbléne Elnai³	*fl.* 696/7
Conamail mac Carthaig	708
Cellach	720
Fer dá Chrích⁴	742
Abnér	760
Cennselach mac Con Bairnne	768
Senchán⁵	774
Senchán⁵	781
Senchán, bp⁵	11 Dec. 785
Cuán	787
Rechtabrae mac Mugthigirn⁶	819
Fland mac Fairchellaig⁷	21 Dec. 825
Ólchobar mac Cináedo⁸	851
Fínán	852
Máel Tuili	858
Maine mac Uargusso	858
Cenn Fáelad ua Mugthigirn⁹	872
Rudgal (Ruidgel) mac Fingaile, bp	882
Cú cen Máthair	887
Eógan mac Cinn Fáelad¹⁰	890
Mescell mac Cummascaig	899
Flann mac Conaill	904
Tipraite mac Máel Finn, bp	913
Mac Lenna¹¹	935
Eochu mac Scannláin	942
(Uarach, bp	954)
Máel Cellaig mac Áeda	957
Fáelán mac Cáellaide, bp	980

abbots	*death unless otherwise stated*
Tipraite	dep. 986
Cétfaid dalta Riata[12]	989
Marcán mac Cennéitig[13]	res. 995
	d. 1010
Colum ua Laigenáin[14]	1002
Dub Sláine ua Lorcáin[15]	1004
Sáerbrethach[16]	1025
(Máel Finnia, bp	1039)
Máel Ísu Ua Flainn Chua	res. 1046
	d. 1058
Clothna Muimnech	1048
Cairpre Ua Lígda[17]	dep. 1052
	d. 1058
Muiredach mac Carthaig[18]	*fl.* 1052
	?dep. —
	d. 1092
Máel Mórda	1074
Máel Ísu Ua hÁrrachtáin	1092
Diarmait Ua Flainn Chua, bp and *fer léigind*	1114
Conchobar Ua Lígda	1122
Máel Mórda Ua Clothna	1164

[1] The death of Bp Ailbe of Emly is variously recorded in the annals and martyrologies on 10 and 12 Sept. and 30 Dec. in 527/8, 534, and 542; by the twelfth century his feast was celebrated on 12 Sept.

[2] Bps who were not also abbots are given between round brackets; for diocesan bps of Emly after 1111 see below, pp 297-8.

[3] 'Diblaine Elnai abb Imlechai Ibair', *Cáin Adamnáin*; but the late and unreliable introduction to this tract mentions a certain Fóelán as abbot of Emly.

[4] Also abbot of Leighlin.

[5] It is not certain that there were 3 successive abbots of this name: only the second is recorded in *Ann. Inisf.*, while only the first and third appear in *A.F.M.* 769, 780.

[6] Of Eóganacht Airthir Chliach.

[7] Also abbot of Lismore (since 814) and Cork (since 823).

[8] Of Eóganacht Locha Léin or Áine; kg of Munster 847-51.

[9] Of Eóganacht Airthir Chliach or Áine; nephew of Abbot Rechtabrae and kg of Munster 859-72.

[10] Son of Kg-abbot Cenn Fáelad ua Mugthigirn.

[11] Also abbot of Liath Mór Mo Cháemóc (Leighmore, County Tipperary).

[12] 'Fosterson of Riata'; probably to be identified with Cétfaid mac Con Duib of Dál Cais: see Donnchadh Ó Corráin, 'Dál Cais—church and dynasty' in *Ériu*, xxiv (1973), p. 53, n. 4.

[13] Brother of Brian Bóruma, kg of Munster (978-1014); also abbot of Iniscaltra (since 969), Killaloe (since 991), and Terryglass (since 1008).

[14] Of Eóganacht Áine; took abbacy in 995 (*Ann. Inisf.*).

[15] Probably first cousin of Brian Bóruma; ignored by *Ann. Inisf.*

[16] Probably Sáerbrethach mac Donnchada, father of Carthach, kg of Eóganacht Chaisil (d. 1045) and ancestor of the MacCarthys.

[17] Also *fer léigind*; killed in battle in 1058, by which time he seems to have regained the abbacy.

[18] Seized the abbacy in 1052; son of Carthach mac Sáerbrethaig (d. 1045) and kg of Eóganacht Caisil 1057-92.

FERNS

(FERNAE MÁR MÁEDÓC)

Comarbai Máedóc

abbots	death unless otherwise stated
Áed mac Sétnai (St Aidan, Máedóc), bp[1]	31 Jan. *c.* 624/5
Da Chua Luachrae (Crónán)	22 June 654
[?To Ernóc mac Finntain[2]	8 Feb. 663]
Commán, bp[3]	18 Mar. 678
Máel Dogair, bp[3]	678
Díraith, bp[3]	27 July 693
Mo Ling Luachair[4]	17 June 696/7
Cilléne, bp[3]	31 Aug. 715
Airechtach mac Cuanach	742
Bressal mac Colgan	749
Reóthaide	763
Dub Indrecht mac Fergusso	781
[Crónán Liae Fernae[5]	791]
Fiannachtach	799
Cilléne[6]	817
Findchellach	862
Diarmait	870
Lachtnán mac Mochthigirn[7]	875
Fergil	883
Lachtnán	905
Laidcnén[8]	939
Flathgus	946
Fínnechta mac Lachtnáin[9]	958
Cairpre mac Laidcnén[10]	967
Conaing mac Catháin	977
Conn ua Laidcnén	997
Conchobar (Cairpre) Ua Laidcnén[11]	1043
Diarmait Ua Rodacháin, bp	1050
Conaing Ua Fairchellaig[12]	1059
Murchad Ua Laidcnén	1062
Úgaire Ua Laidcnén	1085
Cairpre Ua Ceithernaig, bp	1095
Cellach Ua Colmáin, bp[13]	1117
Brigtén Ua Catháin	1172

---

[1] Also founder of Drumlane, County Cavan, and Rossinver, County Leitrim. His obit occurs only in the later annals at 624/5 and also at *c.*656; the latter obit may be that of St Máedóc of Clonmore (Cluain Már Máedóc), i.e. Bp Áed ua Dúnlainge (11 Apr.); in the eleventh century the *acta* and *paruchiae* of the 2 saints were merged.

[2] Also anchorite; the notes to the *Félire Óengusso* identify 'Ternóc' with Onchú ua ind Éicis, also commemorated on 8 Feb., who is associated with Clonmore, not Ferns.

[3] These names are also found among those of the *familia* Mundu, or members of the community of

Taghmon (founded by St Munnu or Fintan mac Tulchain, d. 21 Oct. 635/7), commemorated in the *Martyrology of Tallaght* at 21 Oct.

⁴ Founder of St Mullins, Co. Carlow.

⁵ Probably not abbot.

⁶ In 817 the *familia* of Ferns were defeated with the loss of 400 men by the *familia* of Taghmon led by Cathal mac Dúnlainge, *secnap* or *oeconomus* of Ferns (since *a.* 783?) and Sil Máele Uidir kg of Ui Chennselaig (809-19); an interregnum in the abbacy may have followed.

⁷ Also bp of Kildare.

⁸ Also abbot of Tallaght.

⁹ Of Síl Máel Uidir.

¹⁰ Also abbot of St Mullins.

¹¹ Also abbot of St Mullins.

¹² Also abbot of Drumlane; 'coarb of Máedóc in Connacht and Leinster', *A.F.M.*

¹³ For diocesan bishops of Ferns see below, pp 311-12.

GLENDALOUGH

(GLENN DÁ LOCHA)

Comarbai Cóemgein[1]

abbots	death unless otherwise stated
Cóemgen mac Cóemloga (St Kevin)	3 June 622
Colmán Cerbb, bp	12 Dec. 657/60
Dairchell moccu Rétai, bp[2]	3 May 678
Do Chumae Conóc[3]	687
Dub Gualae[4]	712
Énchorach ua Dodáin	769
Máel Combair	790
Ceithernach	799
Mimthenach[4]	800
Áed[5]	809
Échtbrann[5]	809
Guaire	810
Eterscél mac Cellaig, bp	814
Suibne mac Ioseph	836
Suibne ua Teimnén	842
Daniél[6]	868
Fechtnach	875
Dúngal mac Baíthíne, bp	904
Cormac mac Fidbrain, bp	927
(Nuadu, bp	930)
Flann ua hAnaile[7]	950
Ferdomnach ua Máenaig[8]	952
Flann ua hÁeducáin	957
Martan[9]	959
Crunnmáel	972
Ailill mac Laignig	973
Cairpre ua Corra	974

abbots	*death unless* *otherwise stated*
Dúnchad ua Mancháin	1003
Conn ua Diugraid	1014
Flann ua Cellaig	1030
Conaing ua Cerbaill[10]	1031
Cathassach ua Cathail[10]	dep. 1031
	d. 1045
Murchad ua Nióc	1032
(Máel Brigte ua Máel Finn, bp	1041)
Cináed mac Muiredaig	1068
In Breithem Ua Mancháin	1095
(Cormac Ua Máíl, bp	1101)
Tuathal Ua Cathail	13 May 1106
Gilla Comgaill Ua Tuathail[11]	1127
Gilla Pátraic mac Tuathail Ua Cathail[11]	1128
Dúnlaing Ua Cathail	1153
Lorcán Ua Tuathail (Laurentius;	cons. abp of Dublin
St Laurence O'Toole)	1162
	d. 14 Nov. 1180

[1] Bps who did not hold the office of abbot are placed between round brackets; for diocesan bps of Glendalough after 1111 see below, p. 313.

[2] Of the Dál Riatai; he may also be commemorated among the *familia* Mundu of Taghmon at 21 Oct. in the Martyrology of Tallaght.

[3] So (with variants) in all the annals; but possibly two names have been conflated; cf. Mo Chonnóc (19 Dec.).

[4] The verb *periit* used in the obits of Dub Gualae and Mimthenach suggests a violent death.

[5] It is uncertain whether Áed (*A.F.M.*) preceded or succ. Échtbrann (*Ann. Inisf.*).

[6] Also abbot of Tallaght.

[7] Probably grandson of *secnap* Anaile (d. 886).

[8] Also abbot of Clonmacnoise (since 948).

[9] Also anchorite and abbot of Tallaght.

[10] It is uncertain whether Conaing preceded or succeeded Cathassach, who was blinded in 1031 by Domnall ua Dúnlaing, grandson of Dúnlaing mac Tuathail, Uí Muiredaig kg of Leinster (1014).

[11] Gilla Comgaill, father of Muirchertach Ua Tuathail, kg of Uí Muiredaig (1141-64), and grandfather of St Laurence O'Toole, was killed by the Fortuatha Laigen in 1127; and Gilla Pátraic, son of the previous abbot Tuathal Ua Cathail, was killed by the Uí Muiredaig in 1128.

IONA

(Í COLUIM CILLE)

Comarbai Coluim Cille

William Reeves, *The life of St Columba, founder of Hy; written by Adamnan* . . . (Dublin, 1857); A. O. Anderson, *Early sources of Scottish history, A.D. 500 to 1286* (2 vols, Edinburgh, 1922); *Adomnán's life of Columba*, ed. A. O. Anderson and M. O. Anderson (London, 1961), pp 78-102.

The Columban *paruchia* or confederation of churches, comprising many houses in Ireland and Scotland (see Reeves, pp 276-98), was centred upon Iona until the beginning of the ninth century, when its headquarters were moved to Kells (County Meath), after which a separate Scottish *paruchia*, centred on Dunkeld, appears to have been organised. The link between the Scottish and Irish *paruchiae* finally dissolved *c.* 986; the headship of the Irish *paruchia* was subsequently ambulatory between Kells, Raphoe, and Derry.

abbots	*death unless otherwise stated*
Colum Cille mac Fedelmtheo (St Columba)	9 June 597
Báethíne mac Brénaind	9 June 598/601
Laisrén mac Feradaig	**16 Sept. 605/8**
Fergno Britt mac Faílbi (Virgno)	2 Mar. 623/4
Ségéne mac Fiachnaí	12 Aug. 652
Suibne moccu Fir Thrí (? moccu Thuirtri)[1]	11 Jan. 657
Cumméne Find (Cummeneus Albus)	24 Feb. 669
Faílbe mac Pípáin	22 Mar. 679
Adomnán mac Rónáin (Adamnanus; St Eunan)	23 Sept. 704/5
Conamail mac Faílbi (of Uí Maic Uais)	?dep. 707
	d. 11 Sept. 710
Dúnchad mac Cinn Fáelad[2]	?dep. *c.* June 713
	rest.—
	res. 716
	d. 25 May 717
Dorbbéne Foto[3]	28 Oct. 713
Fáelchú mac Dorbbéni	?dep. 722
	?rest.
	d. 724
Fedelmid	?dep. *a.* 724
	d. 759
Cilléne Foto	726
Cilléne Droichtech	752
Sléibéne	res. *a.* 766
	d. 767
Suibne	res. 771
	d. 772
Bressal mac Ségéni	801
Connachtach	802
Cellach mac Congaile	res. 814
	d. 815
Diarmait daltae Daigri[4]	?res. 831
Indrechtach ua Fínsnechtai	res. *a.* 854
	d. 854[5]
Cellach mac Ailello (also abbot of Kildare since 852)	865
Feradach mac Cormaic	880
Fland mac Máele Dúin	20 Apr. 891
Máel Brigte mac Tornáin (also abbot of Armagh since 883)	22 Feb. 927
Dubthach mac Dubáin, abbot of Raphoe	938

abbots	death unless otherwise stated
[?Cáenchomrac, abbot of Iona[6]	947]
Robartach, abbot of Raphoe	954
Dub Dúin ua Stepháin	959
Dub Scoile mac Cináeda	964
Mugrón, abbot and bp of Iona, 'coarb of Colum Cille in Ire. and Scotland'	980/81
Máel Ciaráin ua Maigne, abbot of Iona	24 Dec. 986[7]
Dúnchad ua Robacháin, abbot of Raphoe	989
Dub dá Leithe mac Cellaig (also abbot of Armagh since 965)	June 998
[?Máel Brigte mac Rímeda, abbot of Iona[8]	1005]
Muiredach Mac Críchain, abbot of Raphoe (also *fer léigind* of Armagh)	res. 1007 d. 1011
Ferdomnach, abbot of Kells	1008
Máel Muire ua hUchtáin, abbot of Kells	1009
Flandabra, 'coarb of Iona'	1025
Máel Eóin ua Toráin, 'coarb of Derry'	1025
Máel Muire Ua hUchtáin, abbot of Kells and Raphoe	1040
Murchad mac Flainn Ua Máel Sechlainn, abbot of Kells (?)[9]	*fl.* 1055 ?dep. *a.* 1057 d. 1076
Robartach mac Ferdomnaig, abbot of Kells	1057
Gilla Críst Ua Máel Doraid, 'coarb of Colum Cille in Ire. and Scotland'	1062
Mac Meic Báethéne, abbot of Iona	1070 (killed)
Domnall mac Robartaig, abbot of Kells	res. *a.* 1098 d. 1098
Donnchad mac meic Máenaig, abbot of Iona	1099
Ferdomnach Ua Clucáin, abbot of Kells	1114
Máel Brigte mac Rónáin, abbot of Kells	1117[10]
Conaing Ua Becléigind, abbot of Kells	1128
Gilla Adamnáin Ua Coirthén, abbot of Kells	—
Gilla Meic Liac mac Diarmata meic Ruaidrí (Gelasius), abbot of Derry (since 1121)	cons. abp of Armagh 1137 d. 27 Mar. 1174
Muiredach Ua Clucáin, abbot of Kells	1154
Flaithbertach Ua Brolcháin, abbot of Derry[11]	1175
Gilla Meic Liac Ua Branáin, abbot of Derry	res. 1198
Gilla Críst Ua Cernaig, abbot of Derry	1210
Fonachtan Ua Branáin, abbot of Derry (Ua Brónáin)	1220
Flann Ua Brolcháin, abbot of Derry	dep. 1220
Muirchertach Ua Milliucáin, abbot of Derry (also *fer léigind*)	*fl.* 1226
[Máel Isu Ua Daigre, *airchinnech* of Derry[12]	8 Dec. 1219]

abbots	death unless otherwise stated
[Gofraid Ua Daigre, *airchinnech* of Derry[13]	*fl.* 1220 d. 1233]
[Amalgaid Ua Fergail (Ua Firgil), abbot of *Recles* of Derry[14]	*fl.* 1204]

[1] 'Mac Cuirtri', *A.U.*
[2] Took office in 707.
[3] Took office in 713; ruled 5 months.
[4] Pupil or fosterson of Daigre; no notice of his resignation or death in the annals.
[5] Killed in England on pilgrimage to Rome.
[6] In *A.F.M.* only; not styled coarb of Colum Cille.
[7] Killed by Danes.
[8] Not styled coarb of Colum Cille.
[9] Also abbot of Clonard since 1055; kg of Mide briefly in 1073; killed in round tower of Kells by kg of Gailenga in 1076.
[10] Killed by Áed Ua Ruairc, kg of Bréifne (d. 1122).
[11] Acting as coarb of Colum Cille, 1150.
[12] Since the death of Mac Raith Ua Daigre in 1180.
[13] *A.U.*'s account of his dispute with Abbot Muirchertach over the office of *fer léigind*, *s.a.* 1226, makes it clear that the *airchinnech* was subordinate to the *comarbae*.
[14] Intruded as abbot of Iona by northern Irish clergy in 1204, in opposition to Cellach (Celsus; Celestinus), O.S.B., first abbot of new Benedictine monastery (cf. letter to him of Innocent III, 9 Dec. 1203) founded by Reginald (Ragnall) son of Sumarlaide (*fl.* 1192).

KILDARE

(CELL DARO)

Comarbai Brigte

The church of Kildare was a double monastery of nuns and monks and an episcopal see ruled by an abbess (*abbatissa, dominatrix*), who was the 'heir of Brigit' (*comarbae Brigte*), and by a bishop. The abbess of Kildare was deprived of her privilege of precedence over bishops at the synod of Kells-Mellifont in 1152. It is not clear whether the office of abbot was identical with that of bishop before *c.* 700, but thereafter it was separate and appears to have lapsed after 967. For diocesan bishops of Kildare after 1111 see below, pp 313-15.

abbesses	death unless otherwise stated
Brigit ingen Dubthaig (St Brigit)[1]	1 Feb. 521 or 524/6
Der Lugdach[2]	1 Feb. —
. . . .	
Gnáthnat (Gnáthat)[3]	690
Sébdann ingen Cuirc	732
Aiffrica (Affraic)	743
Martha ingen maic Dubáin	758
Lerthan	773
Condál ingen Murchado	797

abbesses	*death unless otherwise stated*
Fine	805
Muirenn ingen Cellaig[4]	831
Affraic	834
Cathán	855
Tuilelaith ingen Uargalaig	10 Jan. 885
Cobflaith ingen Duib Dúin	916
Muirenn ingen Suairt[5]	26 May 918
Muirenn ingen Flannacáin meic Colmáin[5]	964
Muirenn ingen Congalaig	979
Eithne ingen Suairt	1016
Lann ingen meic Selbacháin	1047
Dub Dil	1072
Gormlaith ingen Murchada[6]	1112
Ingen Cerbaill Meic Fáeláin[7]	dep. 1127
Mór ingen Domnaill Uí Chonchobair Failge[8]	dep. 1132 d. 1167
Sadb ingen Glúniarainn Meic Murchada[9]	1171

bishops	
Conláed ua hEimri (St Conleth)	3 May 520
Áed Dub mac Colmáin[10]	639
Máel Dobarchon	19 Feb. 709
Eóthigern	762[11]
Lomthuile	787
Snéidbran	787
Tuathchar, scribe	834
Orthanach ua Cóellámae Cuirrig	840
Áedgen Britt, scribe and anchorite	864
Móengal	870
Robartach mac na Cerddae[12]	875
Lachtnán mac Mochthigirn[13]	875
Suibne ua Fínsnechtai	881
Scandal	884
Lergus mac Cruinnén	888
Crunnmáel	931
Anmchad	981
Máel Martain	1030
Máel Brigte	1042
Máel Brigte mac int Saír Ua Brolcháin	1097
Áed Ua hEremóin	1100
Ferdomnach[14]	1101
[?Máel Finnéin Mac Donngaile[15]	1108]

abbots	
Áed Dub mac Colmáin[16]	639
Óengus mac Áedo Find[17]	—
Brandub mac Fiachrach[18]	—

abbots	*death unless otherwise stated*
Lóchéne Mend Sapiens	696[19]
Forindán	698
Do Dímmóc[20]	3 Mar. 748
Cathal mac Forindáin	752
Muiredach mac Cathail	787
Eódus ua Dícolla	798
Fáelán mac Cellaig[21]	804
Muiredach mac Cellaig[21]	823
Áed mac Cellaig[21]	828
Siadal mac Feradaig	830
Artrí mac Fáeláin[22]	852
Cellach mac Ailello[23]	865
Cobthach mac Muiredaig[24]	870
Muiredach mac Brain[25]	885
Tuathal mac Ailbi	886
Dubán	905
Flannacán ua Riacáin[26]	922
Cuilén mac Cellaig	955[27]
Muiredach mac Fáeláin[28]	967

[1] Of Fothairt; *ingen* = daughter.

[2] Not in the annals; the martyrologies also record the abbesses Comnat at 1 Jan. and Tuilelath (Talulla) at 6 Jan.

[3] Also ninth abbess of Killeevy, County Armagh (since *c*. 665). Killeevy (Cell Sléibe) was founded by St Mo Ninne (or Dar Ercae, d. 6 July *c*. 516/7).

[4] Of Uí Dúnchado; daughter of Cellach mac Dúnchado (kg of Leinster 760-76) and sister of Finsnechtae Cetharderc (kg of Leinster 795-808).

[5] Of Fothairt.

[6] Daughter of Murchad (kg of Dublin 1052-70), son of Diarmait mac Máel na mBó (Uí Chennselaig kg of Leinster 1042-72).

[7] Cerball Mac Fáeláin, kg of Uí Fáeláin, was killed by Donnchad Ua Conchobair (kg of Uí Failge 1130-4) while defending the abbacy for his daughter.

[8] Daughter (?) of Domnall Ruad (kg of Uí Failge 1159-61) and thus great-niece of Donnchad (see previous note); or more probably daughter of Domnall (d. 1115), son of Conchobar Ua Conchobair (kg of Uí Failge 1071-1115).

[9] Niece (?) of Diarmait Mac Murchada, kg of Leinster (1126-71).

[10] Also abbot; brother of the Uí Dúnlainge kg of Leinster, Fáelán mac Colmáin (*fl.* 633).

[11] Killed by priest in church of Kildare.

[12] Also scribe and abbot of Killeigh.

[13] Also abbot of Ferns (since 870).

[14] Styled 'bp of Leinster' already in 1096.

[15] Abbot of Terryglass and 'chief bp of Leinster'; not specifically styled bp of Kildare.

[16] Also bp; see above.

[17] Nephew of Áed Dub; only recorded in the genealogies.

[18] Of Uí Dúnlainge, fifth in descent from Illann mac Dúnlainge, kg of Leinster (495-527); only recorded in the genealogies.

[19] Assassinated, according to *A.U.*

[20] Also anchorite and abbot of Clonard (since 745).

[21] These 3 abbots were sons of Cellach mac Dúnchado (kg of Leinster 760-76) and brothers of Finsnechtae Cetharderc (kg of Leinster, 795-808) and of the abbess Muirenn (805-31).

[22] Of Uí Dúnchado; possibly son of Abbot Fáelán or grandson of Finsnechtae Cetharderc and brother of Bran mac Fáelán, kg of Leinster (834-8).

[23] Also abbot of Iona (since *c*. 854); d. in Pictland.

²⁴ Possibly of Uí Dúnchado and son of Abbot Muiredach mac Cellaig; or of Uí Fáeláin, son of Muiredach mac Ruadrach, kg of Leinster (808-29).
²⁵ Of Uí Dúnchado; great-grandson of Finsnechtae Cetharderc and kg of Leinster (884-5).
²⁶ Also *rígdamna* of Leinster (*A.F.M.*); possibly of Síl nÉladaig, grandson of Riacán mac Echthigirn, kg of Uí Chennselaig (876-93).
²⁷ Killed, according to *A.F.M.*
²⁸ Of Uí Dúnchado; grandson of Kg-abbot Muiredach mac Brain, son of Fáelán, kg of Leinster (917-42), and brother of Lorcán and Cellach, kings of Leinster (942-3) and (958-66); killed by Olaf Cuarán, kg of Dublin (945-80) and by his own nephew Cellach mac Lorcáin (d. 967).

LISMORE

(LES MÁR MO CHUTU)

Comarbai Mo Chutu

abbots	death unless otherwise stated
Carrthach (Mo Chutu)	14 May 637/9
[?Conodur¹	*fl.* 696/7]
Iarnlach (Iarlug, Iarlaga), bp	16 Jan. 700
Cuandae (Cuanu)	4 Feb. 701
Colmán mac Findbairr (Mo Cholmóc)²	22 Jan. 703
Crónán ua hÉcáin	1 June 718
Colmán ua Lítáin	25 July 730
Mac Óige	3 Dec. 752/3
Tríchmech (Trígmech), bp	7 July 760
Áedán	19 July 768
Suairlech mac Ciaráin	4 Dec. 774
Órach, also abbot of Inis Doimle³	781
Áedán moccu Raichlich (mac uí Raichlich), bp	16 Mar. 814
Fland mac Fairchellaig, also abbot of Cork and Emly	21 Dec. 825
Daniél ua Liathaidi, also abbot of Cork	863
Fland mac Forbassaig	894
Máel Brigte mac Máel Domnaig	912
[Cormac mac Mothla⁴	920]
Ciarán mac Ciarmacáin	938
Diarmait	953
Diarmait mac Torpthai	954
Máenach mac Cormaic	959
Cathmug, also bp of Cork	961
Cináed mac Máel Chiaráin	965
Cormac mac Máol Chiaráin	983
Ua Máel Sluaig	1024
Muiredach Ua Rebacháin	1041
Cináed mac Aichir	1063
Máel Dúin Ua Rebacháin	1090

bishops[5]	*death unless otherwise stated*
Gilla Mo Chutu Ua Rebacháin	1129
Rónan	9 Feb. 763
Cináed ua Con Minn, also bp of Inis Cathaig	958

[1] Only in *Ann. Inisf.* (707) and *Cáin Adamnáin*, where it seems an error for Conodor of Fore (d. 3 Nov. 707).

[2] Without title in *Cáin Adamnáin*.

[3] Inch, Co. Wexford.

[4] Bp and *secnap* of Lismore, abbot of Kilmolash, kg of Déise.

[5] For later diocesan bishops of Lismore see below, pp 303-4.

BISHOPS, 1111–1534

F. J. BYRNE

INTRODUCTION

THIS is a revised version of the list in *H.B.C.*, pp 307–51, compared with Conrad Eubel, *Hierarchia catholica medii aevi* (vol. i, 2nd ed., Munich, 1913; vols ii and iii, Munich, 1901–10), with the Irish annals for the period 1098–1534, and with the material up to 1261 provided in M. P. Sheehy (ed.), *Pontificia Hibernica* (2 vols, Dublin, 1962–5), and for 1254–72 in A. F. O'Brien, 'Episcopal elections in Ireland, *c.* 1254–72' in *R.I.A. Proc.*, lxxiii, sect. C, no. 5 (1973), pp 129–76. Valuable corrections and additions are due to the researches of Mr K. W. Nicholls (from material in B.L., Add. MSS 4789 and 4799, the calendars of papal letters,[1] and other sources) and of Fr Benignus Millett, O.F.M. The editors are particularly grateful to the bishops of the Roman Catholic church for the many notes and queries which they transmitted either personally or through their diocesan historians in the process of compilation.

For the origin and development of the diocesan system in Ireland between 1111 and 1327, see maps 24–7 and the accompanying notes (above, pp 101–2).

The twelfth-century annals record the obits of the following bishops, whose sees it has not been possible to determine:

Ua Ruadgussa[2]	d. 1126
Mac Raith Ua Faíllecháin[2]	d. 1143
Ua Menngoráin[3]	d. 1147
Ua Noídenáin[4]	d. 1148
Ua Gormgaile[5]	d. 1149
Ua Muirgiussa[6]	d. 1161

[1] *Calendar of entries in the papal registers relating to Great Britain and Ireland: papal letters, 1198–1304* [etc.] (London, 1893–   ).
[2] These may possibly have been bps of Emly.
[3] Possibly bp of Cork.
[4] Possibly bp of Glendalough.
[5] Possibly bp of Ráith Lúraig (Derry).
[6] Possibly to be identified with Gilla na Náem Laignech (d. 1160/61), bp of Glendalough.

CONCORDANCE OF VARIANT ENGLISH, IRISH, AND LATIN NAMES OF DIOCESES

variant names of diocese	names entered under	province
Achad Conaire	Achonry	Tuam
Achadensis	Achonry	Tuam
Ail Finn	Elphin	Tuam
Airgialla	Clogher	Armagh
Airther Connacht	Elphin	Tuam
Aladensis	Killala	Tuam
Ardachad	Ardagh	Armagh
Ardachadensis	Ardagh	Armagh
Ard Ferta Brénainn	Ardfert	Cashel
Ard Macha	Armagh	Armagh
Ar(d)machanus	Armagh	Armagh
Ard Mór	Ardmore	Cashel
Ardmorensis	Ardmore	Cashel
Ard Sratha	Derry	Armagh
Ardstraw	Derry	Armagh
Artfertensis	Ardfert	Cashel
Áth Cliath	Dublin	Dublin
Bistagnensis	Glendalough	Dublin
Bréifne	Tirbrunensis	Armagh
Caisel Muman	Cashel	Cashel
Casselensis	Cashel	Cashel
Cathagensis	Scattery Island	Cashel
Cell Da Lua	Killaloe	Cashel
Cell Dara	Kildare	Dublin
Cell Finnabrach	Kilfenora	Cashel
Cell Meic Duach	Kilmacduagh	Tuam
Cell Mór	Tirbrunensis	Armagh
Cenannas Mór	Tirbrunensis	Armagh
Cenannensis	Tirbrunensis	Armagh
Cenél nEógain	Derry	Armagh
Ciarraige	Ardfert	Cashel
Clochar mac nDaimíne	Clogher	Armagh
Clochorensis	Clogher	Armagh
Clonard	Meath	Armagh
Clonensis	Clonmacnoise	Armagh
	Cloyne	Cashel
Cluain Ferta Brénainn	Clonfert	Tuam
Cluain Iraird	Meath	Armagh
Cluain moccu Nóis	Clonmacnoise	Armagh
Cluain Uama	Cloyne	Cashel
Cluanfertensis	Clonfert	Tuam
Clunardensis	Meath	Armagh

variant names of diocese	names entered under	province
Conderensis	Connor	Armagh
Conmaicne	Ardagh	Armagh
Connachta	Tuam	Tuam
Connere	Connor	Armagh
Corcach Mór Muman	Cork	Cashel
Corcagiensis	Cork	Cashel
Corco Loígde	Ross	Cashel
Corco Mruad	Kilfenora	Cashel
Daire Coluim Chille	Derry	Armagh
Dál nAraide	Connor	Armagh
Damliacc Cianáin	Duleek	Armagh
Darensis	{ Kildare	Dublin
	{ Derry	Armagh
Derensis	Derry	Armagh
Dromorensis	Dromore	Armagh
Druim Mór	Dromore	Armagh
Duacensis	Kilmacduagh	Tuam
Dublinensis	Dublin	Dublin
Dún Lethglaisse	Down	Armagh
Dunensis	Down	Armagh
Earipolensis	Ossory	Dublin
Éile	Roscrea	Cashel
Elfinensis	Elphin	Tuam
Enach Dúin	Annaghdown	Tuam
Enachdunensis	Annaghdown	Tuam
Ergalensis	Clogher	Armagh
Ferna Mór Máedóc	Ferns	Dublin
Fernensis	Ferns	Dublin
Finnabarensis	Kilfenora	Cashel
Glendalachensis	Glendalough	Dublin
Glenn dá Locha	Glendalough	Dublin
Iarmuma	Ardfert	Cashel
Imlech Ibair	Emly	Cashel
Imilicensis	Emly	Cashel
Inis Cathaig	Scattery Island	Cashel
Insulensis	Scattery Island	Cashel
Kells	Tirbrunensis	Armagh
Kenanensis	Tirbrunensis	Armagh
Kerry	Ardfert	Cashel
Kilmore	Tirbrunensis	Armagh

variant names of diocese	names entered under	province
Laonensis	Killaloe	Cashel
Lethglenn	Leighlin	Dublin
Lethglennensis	Leighlin	Dublin
Limiricensis	Limerick	Cashel
Lismorensis	Lismore	Cashel
Liss Mór Mo Chutu	Lismore	Cashel
Louth	Clogher	Armagh
Lugdunensis	Clogher	Armagh
Lugmad	Clogher	Armagh
Luigne	Achonry	Tuam
Luimnech	Limerick	Cashel
Lumnicensis	Limerick	Cashel
Maghera	Derry	Armagh
Mag nAí	Elphin	Tuam
Mag nEó na Saxan	Mayo	Tuam
Maionensis	Mayo	Tuam
Mide	Meath	Armagh
Midensis	Meath	Armagh
Na Tuatha	Elphin	Tuam
Osraige	Ossory	Dublin
Ossoriensis	Ossory	Dublin
Port Láirge	Waterford	Cashel
Ráith Both	Raphoe	Armagh
Ráith Lúraig	Derry	Armagh
Rathlurensis	Derry	Armagh
Rathpotensis	Raphoe	Armagh
Roscommon	Elphin	Tuam
Ross Ailithir	Ross	Cashel
Ross Commáin	Elphin	Tuam
Ross Cré	Roscrea	Cashel
Rossensis	Ross	Cashel
Síl Muiredaig	Elphin	Tuam
Tír Conaill	Raphoe	Armagh
Tír mBriúin	Tirbrunensis	Armagh
Triburnensis	Tirbrunensis	Armagh
Tuadmuma	Killaloe	Cashel
Tuaim dá Gualann	Tuam	Tuam
Tuamensis	Tuam	Tuam

variant names of diocese	names entered under	province
Uí Amalgada	Killala	Tuam
Uí Briúin	Tirbrunensis	Armagh
Uí Chennselaig	Ferns	Dublin
Uí Echach	Dromore	Armagh
Uí Fiachrach Aidne	Kilmacduagh	Tuam
Uí Fiachrach Muaide	Killala	Tuam
Uí Maine	Clonfert	Tuam
Ulaid	Down	Armagh
Waterfordensis	Waterford	Cashel
Ymlicensis	Emly	Cashel

PROVINCE OF ARMAGH

DIOCESE OF ARMAGH (Ard Macha; Ar(d)machanus)

archbishops	accession	death unless otherwise stated
Cellach mac Áeda meic Máel Ísu, abbot of Armagh (Celsus)	el. abbot p. 12 Aug. 1105 cons. bp 23 Sept. 1105 abp 1106	1 Apr. 1129
Máel Máedóc Ua Morgair,[1] abbot of Bangor and bp of Down and Connor (Malachias; St Malachy)	el. and cons. 1132 installed 1134	res. 1136 d. 2 Nov. 1148
Gilla Meic Liac mac Diarmata meic Ruaidrí, abbot of Derry (Gelasius)	el. and cons. 1137	27 Mar. 1174
Conchobar mac Meic Con Caille, can. reg., abbot of SS Paul and Peter, Armagh (St Concors)	el. and cons. c. 1174	1175
Gilla in Choimded Ua Caráin, bp of Raphoe (Gillebertus)	el. and cons. c. 1175	c. Jan. 1180
Tommaltach mac Áeda Ua Conchobair, bp of Elphin (Thomas)	el. and cons. a. Feb. 1180 res. 1184 rest. c. 1186/7	1201
Máel Ísu Ua Cerbaill, bp of Clogher (Malachias)	el. 1184	1186/7
Echdonn Mac Gilla Uidir, can. reg., abbot of Bangor (Eugenius)	el. and cons. 1202 temp. 30 Aug. 1206 (suffr. in Exeter and Worcester 1207)	p. 11 Aug. 1216

archbishops	accession	death unless otherwise stated
Luke Netterville, archdeacon of Armagh	el. *a.* Aug. 1217 temp. 16 Sept. 1219	17 Apr. 1227
Donatus Ó Fidabra, bp of Clogher	trs. *c.* Aug. 1227 temp. 20 Sept. 1227	*a.* 17 Oct. 1237
Robert Archer, O.P.	el. *a.* 4 Apr. 1238 (never cons.)	
Albrecht Suerbeer of Cologne (Albertus)	prov. *a.* 4 Mar. 1239 temp. *c.* 30 Sept. 1240 cons. 30 Sept. 1240	trs. to Prussia-Livonia 10 Jan. 1246 d. *c.* 1273
Rainaldo, O.P. (Raigned; Reginaldus)	prov. *a.* 28 Oct. 1247 cons. *a.* 28 Oct. 1247 temp. 28 Oct. 1247	*p.* July 1256
Abraham Ó Conalláin, archpriest of Armagh and chaplain to Hugo, cardinal-priest of St Sabina	el. *p.* 20 Feb. 1257 conf. by Alexander IV 18 Dec. 1257 cons. *a.* 16 Mar. 1258 temp. 16 Mar. 1258	21 Dec. 1260
Máel Pátraic Ó Scannail, O.P., bp of Raphoe (Patricius)	el. *c.* Mar. 1261 conf. *a.* 13 Aug. 1261 trs. 5 Nov. 1261 temp. 20 Apr. 1262	16 Mar. 1270
Nicol Mac Máel Ísu, canon of Armagh (Nicolaus; 'Nicholas of Ardagh')	el. *p.* 9 May 1270 conf. 14 July 1272 temp. 23 Sept. 1272 lib. 27 Oct. 1272	10 May 1303
Michael Mac Lochlainn, O.F.M. (Mauricius), lector of Armagh convent	el. *a.* 31 Aug. 1303 (never cons.)	el. bp Derry 1319
Dionysius, dean of Armagh	prov. by Benedict XI 1303/4 (never cons.)	res. *c.* 1304
John Taaffe	prov. 27 Aug. 1306 cons. *p.* 27 Aug. 1306	*a.* 6 Aug. 1307
Walter Jorz, O.P., royal chaplain	prov. 6 Aug. 1307 cons. 6 Aug. 1307 temp. 30 Sept. 1307	res. *a.* 13 Nov. 1311
Roland Jorz, O.P.	prov. 13 Nov. 1311 cons. 13 Nov. 1311 temp. 15 Sept. 1312 lib. 20 Dec. 1312	suspended 1316? res. *a.* 22 Aug. 1322; suffr. in Canterbury 1323; in York 1332
Stephen Segrave, dean of Lichfield	prov. 16 Mar. 1321 temp. 31 July 1323 cons. Apr. 1324	27 Oct. 1333

archbishops	accession	death unless otherwise stated
David Mág Oireachtaigh, dean of Armagh	el. *a.* July 1334 prov. 4 July 1334 cons. *a.* 26 July 1334 temp. 16 Mar. 1335	16 May 1346
Richard FitzRalph, dean of Lichfield ('Richard of Dundalk')	el. *a.* July 1346 prov. 31 July 1346 fealty 15 Feb. 1347 temp. 15 Apr. 1347 cons. 8 July 1347	16 Nov. 1360
Milo Sweetman, treasurer of Ossory	prov. 29 Oct. 1361 cons. 17/21 Nov. 1361 temp. 5 Feb. 1362	11 Aug. 1380
Thomas Ó Calmáin, O.F.M.	prov. by Clement VII 14 Jan. 1381 (without effect)	—
John Colton, dean of St Patrick's, Dublin	prov. *p.* Jan. 1381 cons. 1381 temp. 9 Mar. 1383	res. *a.* Apr. 1404 d. 27 Apr. 1404
Nicholas Fleming, canon of St Patrick's, Dublin	prov. 18 Apr. 1404 cons. 1 May 1404 prov. (again) 11 Nov. 1404	*p.* 22 June 1416
Richard Talbot	el. 1416 (never cons.)	el. abp of Dublin *p.* May 1417
Robert FitzHugh, chancellor of St Patrick's, Dublin	el. *p.* May 1417 (annulled by Martin V 10 Jan. 1418)	—
John Swayne	prov. 10 Jan. 1418 cons. *c.* 2 Feb. 1418	res. 27 Mar. 1439 d. *a.* Oct. 1442
John Prene, archdeacon of Armagh	prov. 27 Mar. 1439 cons. Nov. 1439	June 1443
John Mey	prov. 26 Aug. 1443	1456
John Bole (Bull), can. reg., abbot of St Mary's, Navan, and bp-elect of Kildare	prov. 2 May 1457 cons. *a.* 13 June 1457	18 Feb. 1471
John Foxhalls (Foxholes), O.F.M.	prov. 16 Dec. 1471 cons. *p.* Dec. 1471	*a.* 23 Nov. 1474
Edmund Connesburgh	prov. 5 June 1475 cons. *c.* 1475 conf. by Edward IV 20 May 1478 (did not get possession; suffr. in Ely 1477; in Norwich 1502)	res. Nov. 1477 trs. to Chalcedon 1478 d. *p.* 1502

archbishops	accession	death unless otherwise stated
Ottaviano Spinelli, nuncio apostolic (Octavianus de Palatio)	app. apostolic admr by Sixtus IV 19 Apr. 1477 prov. *c.* 3 July 1478 cons. *a.* 29 Oct. 1479	June 1513
John Kite, canon of Salisbury and Exeter, sub-dean of Windsor	prov. 24 Oct. 1513 cons. *p.* Oct. 1513	trs. to Carlisle 12 July 1521 d. 11 June 1537
George Cromer, priest of Chichester dioc.	prov. 2 Oct. 1521 cons. *c.* Dec. 1521	suspended by Paul III 23 July 1539 depr. 16 Mar. 1542 d. 16 Mar. 1543

¹ St Malachy apparently held the united bishoprics of Down and Connor until his resignation from the primacy, whereupon he remained bishop of the diocese of Down only. In some early sources his surname is given as Ua Mongair.

DIOCESE OF ARDAGH (*Ardachad; Conmaicne; Ardachadensis*)²

bishops	accession	death unless otherwise stated
Mac Raith Ua Móráin	*a.* Mar. 1152	res. 1166 d. 1168
Gilla Críst Ua hEóthaig	*a.* 1172	1178
Ua hÉislinnén	—	1188
Annud Ua Muiredaig (Adam)	—	1216
Robert, O.Cist., abbot of St Mary's, Dublin	1217	27 May 1224
M., can. reg., prior of Inis Mór³	*c.* 1224	*c.* 1229
Joseph Mac Teichthecháin alias Mac Eódaig ('Magoday'), archdeacon of Ardagh⁴	el. 1227 cons. *c.* 1228	1230
Mac Raith Mac Serraig, archdeacon of Ardagh³	el. and cons. *c.* 1229	1230
Thomas³	*fl. c.* 1230	—
Gilla Ísu mac in Scélaige Ó Tormaid, priest of Ardagh dioc. (Gelasius)⁴	el. and cons. *c.* 1232	1237
Jocelinus, O.Cist., monk of St Mary's, Dublin³	el. and cons. *c.* 1232 temp. 1 Mar. 1233	res. *a.* 1237
Brendán Mac Teichthecháin alias Mac Eódaig ('Magoday')	el. *c.* 1238	res. 15 Oct. 1252 d. 1255
Milo of Dunstaple	el. *a.* 20 May 1256 temp. 13 Jan. 1257	23 Oct. 1288

bishops	accession	death unless otherwise stated
Matha Ó hEóthaig (Matthaeus), canon of Ardagh	el. Nov. 1289 fealty 28 Jan. 1290 temp. 8 Apr. 1290	1322
Robert Wirsop, O.S.A.	prov. 5 Apr. 1323 (did not get possession)	trs. to Connor 20 June 1323
Seoán Mág Eóaigh, archdeacon of Ardagh	el. *a.* Mar. 1324 prov. 19 Mar. 1324 cons. *a.* 12 May 1324 temp. 20 Oct. 1324	1343
Eóghan alias Maolsheachlainn Ó Fearghail (Audovenus)	prov. 1343 cons. 1347	1367
Uilliam Mac Carmaic, canon of Ardagh	prov. 1367 cons. *a.* 26 Aug. 1369	*a.* Aug. 1373
Cairbre Ó Fearghail, archdeacon of Ardagh (Carolus)[5]	el. *a.* Sept. 1373 conf. *p.* Sept. 1373	1378
John Aubrey, O.P., friar of Trim[5]	el. *a.* Sept. 1373 prov. 29 Apr. 1374	—
Seoán Ó Fraoich[5]	—	1396
Henry Nony, O.P.	prov. 29 Apr. 1392 (did not get possession; suffr. in Exeter 1396–9; in Bath 1400)	*p.* 1400
Comedinus Mac Brádaigh (Gillebertus)	prov. 20 Oct. 1395 cons. *p.* 19 Aug. 1396	*a.* Feb. 1400
Adam Leyns (Lexid), O.P.	prov. 15 Feb. 1400	June 1416
Conchobhar Ó Fearghail, dean of Ardagh (Cornelius)	el. *p.* June 1416 prov. 17 Feb. 1418 cons. 3 Feb. 1419	1423
Risdeárd Ó Fearghail, O.Cist., abbot of Granard	el. *a.* Jan. 1425 prov. 11 Jan. 1425 cons. *p.* 25 May 1425	*c.* June 1444
Mac Muircheartaigh, official of Ardagh ('an t-oifiséal óg')	el. 1444 (never cons.)	res. 1445
Cormac Mág Shamhradháin, can. reg., prior of Drumlane	prov. 6 Nov. 1444 cons. *p.* 19 Feb. 1445	res. *c.* 1462
Seaán Ó Fearghail	prov. 30 July 1462 (bulls expedited 26 Nov. 1462) prov. (again) 28 July 1469	*a.* Aug. 1479
?Jacobus (?Johannes)	—	(suffr. in Salisbury 1466; in Exeter 1478–9)
Donatus Ó Fearghail, canon of Ardagh	prov. 12 Oct. 1467	*a.* 28 July 1469

bishops	accession	death unless otherwise stated
Uilliam mac Donnchadha Ó Fearghail, lord of Anghaile and abbot *in commendam* of Granard (O.Cist.)	prov. 4 Aug. 1480 cons. 11 June 1482	1516
Ruaidhrí Ó Maoileóin, canon of Tuam and Clonmacnoise and admr of Clonmacnoise dioc., *c.* 1520–40 (Rogerius)	prov. 14 Dec. 1517	1540

[2] Ardagh and Ardcarn (Co. Roscommon) were named as alternative sees for an east Connacht diocese (presumably for the Uí Briúin Bréifne and their vassal state of Conmaicne) at the synod of Ráith Bressail in 1111, but at the synod of Kells–Mellifont in 1152 a greatly expanded kingdom of Bréifne was incorporated into the new diocese of Kells (see below under Tirbrunensis), while Conmaicne was formed into an independent diocese with its see at Ardagh. Ardcarn was now included in the diocese of Roscommon–Elphin, and never achieved true status as an episcopal see. The Connacht origins of both Uí Briúin Bréifne and Conmaicne led to claims by the abps of Tuam that Tirbrunensis and Ardagh rightfully belonged to that province; the dispute between Tuam and Armagh lasted from 1177 until 1326 and resulted in a schism within the diocese of Ardagh in 1224.

[3] Of the Tuam obedience.

[4] Of the Armagh obedience.

[5] It is uncertain whether either of the rival candidates in the disputed election of 1373 obtained possession of the see: Cairbre Ó Fearghail died at Avignon, and it is doubtful whether John Aubrey is to be identified with Seoán Ó Fraoich.

DIOCESE OF ARDSTRAW (*Ard Sratha; Cenél nEógain*)[6]:
see DERRY

[6] The synod of Ráith Bressail proposed Ardstraw as the see for a diocese comprising the western part of Cenél nEógain, excluding the Inis Eógain peninsula (Inishowen), which was assigned to Derry–Raphoe, as well as the east of Co. Londonderry, which was assigned to Connor. It is unlikely that this scheme was accepted in the north. Ardstraw, as chief church of the Airgiallan kingdom of Uí Fiachrach Arda Sratha (though within the over-kingdom of Cenél nEógain), was claimed by the diocese of Clogher, but had finally been incorporated into the diocese of Derry by *c.* 1240. Letters procured by Bp David Ó Brácáin of Clogher from Pope Alexander IV (14 Mar. 1258) for the recovery of the deanery of Ardstraw were of no effect.

DIOCESE OF CLOGHER (*Airgialla; Clochar mac nDaimíne; Clochorensis; Ergalensis*)[7]

bishops	accession	death unless otherwise stated
Cináeth Ua Baígill	—	1135
Gilla Críst Ua Morgair (Christianus)	1135	1138
Áed Ua Cáellaide, can. reg., prior of Louth (Edanus)	1138	res. *a.* May 1178 d. 29 Mar. 1182
Mael Ísu Ua Cerbaill (Malachias)[8]	el. *a.* 18 May 1178	1186/7

bishops	accession	death unless otherwise stated
Gilla Críst Ua Mucaráin, can. reg., abbot of Clones (Christinus)	c. 1187	1193
Máel Ísu Ua Máel Chiaráin, O.Cist., abbot of Mellifont	a. Sept. 1194	1197
Gilla Tigernaig Mac Gilla Rónáin, can. reg., prior of Louth (Thomas)	c. 1197	1218
Donatus Ó Fidabra, can. reg., prior of Louth	c. 1218	trs. to Armagh c. Aug. 1227
Nehemias Ó Brácáin, O.Cist., prior of Mellifont[9]	el. Sept. 1227	a. 15 Nov. 1240
David Ó Brácáin, O.Cist., monk of Mellifont	el. c. 1245	1267
Michael Mac in tSaír, official of Armagh	el. a. Sept. 1268 cons. 9 Sept. 1268	?res. a. 1287 d. 1288
Matthaeus Mac Cathasaig I	el. a. 29 June 1287 cons. 29 June 1287	a. 1310
Henricus	fl. 1310	c. 1316
Gelasius alias Cornelius Ó Bánáin, can. reg., abbot of Clones	el. c. 1316 cons. c. 1316	1319
Nicolaus Mac Cathasaigh	el. 23 Feb. 1320 cons. 1320	1356
Brian Mac Cathmhaoil (Bernardus)	el. p. Sept. 1356 prov. c. 1357	1358
Matthaeus Mac Cathasaigh II	el. c. 1361 cons. p. Feb. 1362	—
Aodh Ó hEóthaigh (alias Ó Néill) (Odo)	—	27 July 1369
Johannes Ó Corcráin, O.S.B., monk of Würzburg	prov. 6 Apr. 1373	?c. 1389
Art Mac Cathmhaoil	prov. 15 Feb. 1390 cons. a. 28 Apr. 1390	10 Aug. 1432
Piaras Mág Uidhir (Petrus)	prov. 31 Aug. 1433	res. a. July 1447 d. 5 Dec. 1450
Rossa mac Tomáis Óig Mág Uidhir (Rogerius)	prov. 21 July 1447 cons. a. 6 Jan. 1450	1483
Florence Woolley, O.S.B.	prov. 20 Nov. 1475 (did not get possession; suffr. in Norwich 1478–1500)	1500
Niall mac Séamuis Mac Mathghamhna	prov. a. 14 June 1484 (bulls not expedited)	1488
John Edmund de Courcy, O.F.M.	prov. 14 June 1484 (bulls expedited 14 Sept. 1484)	trs. to Ross 26 Sept. 1494

bishops	accession	death unless otherwise stated
Séamus mac Pilib Mac Mathghamhna	prov. 5 Nov. 1494 (did not take effect)	trs. to Derry 26 Nov. 1503
Andreas	prov. 10 June 1500	—
Nehemias Ó Cluainín, O.S.A.	prov. 24 Jan. 1502	res. 1503
Giolla Pádraig Ó Condálaigh, can. reg., abbot of Clones (Patricius)	prov. 6 Mar. 1504	a. Dec. 1504
Eoghan Mac Cathmhaoil (Eugenius)	prov. 4 Apr. 1505	1515
Pádraig Ó Cuilín, O.S.A.	prov. 11 Feb. 1517	a. 26 Mar. 1534

⁷ The diocese of Clogher envisaged at the synod of Ráith Bressail was very small, corresponding to the ancient core of the Airgiallan kingdom of Uí Chremthainn. At the synod of Kells–Mellifont the diocese was assigned the whole of the western Airgialla over-kingdom ruled by Donnchad Ua Cerbaill (d. 1168). It was in recognition of Ua Cerbaill's support that St Malachy as primate had c. 1135/6 allowed his brother, Bp Gilla Críst Ua Morgair, to remove the see from Clogher to the Ua Cerbaill capital at Louth, thus granting away from Armagh the territory of Co. Louth. Clogher itself had fallen under control of the Cenél nEógain sept of Cenél Feradaig and was thus unsuitable as an Airgiallan see. But the Anglo-Norman settlement of Co. Louth ('English Oriel') resulted in the transfer of this area back to the diocese of Armagh c. 1192, although as late as c. 1233 Bp Nehemias styled himself *episcopus Lugdunensis*. On his translation to Armagh, Bp Donatus had earlier (10 Oct. 1227) tried to resolve the dispute by petitioning for the union of Armagh and Clogher, and on 15 Nov. 1240, some time after the death of Bp Nehemias, Pope Gregory IX issued a new commission to examine this proposal, but without effect. Bp David Ó Brácáin was still pursuing his claims to Louth in 1252 and 1257.

⁸ Assumed the archbishopric of Armagh briefly on the resignation of Abp Tommaltach Ua Conchobair in 1184.

⁹ His election was opposed by the dean, precentor, and chancellor, probably in view of the proposed union of the diocese with that of Armagh, a circumstance which also accounts for the prolonged vacancy after his death (which occurred well before 15 Nov. 1240).

DIOCESE OF CLONARD (*Cluain Iraird; Clunardensis*): see MEATH

DIOCESE OF CLONMACNOISE (*Cluain moccu Nóis; Clonensis*)

bishops	accession	death unless otherwise stated
?Domnall mac Flannacáin Ua Dubthaig, abbot of Roscommon and bp of Elphin¹⁰	?1111	17 Mar. 1136
Muirchertach Ua Máel Uidir¹¹	a. Mar. 1152	1187
Cathal Ua Máel Eóin	—	6 Feb. 1207
Muiredach Ua Muirecén	el. c. 1207	1214
Áed Ó Máel Eóin I	el. 1214	1220
Máel Ruanaid Ó Modáin	el. 1220	?res. a. 1227 d. 1230

bishops	*accession*	*death unless otherwise stated*
Áed Ó Máel Eóin II, O.Cist. (Elias)	el. *a.* 1227	res. 27 Apr. 1235 d. 1237
Thomas FitzPatrick, dean of Clonmacnoise	el. *a.* Apr. 1236 temp. *p.* 18 Apr. 1236	*c.* 1252
Tomás Ó Cuinn, O.F.M., custos of Drogheda	el. *a.* Nov. 1252 conf. 26 Nov. 1252 temp. *p.* 20 Feb. 1253	18 Nov. 1278
Anonymous, O.F.M.	el. *a.* 20 July 1280	—
Gillebertus, dean of Clonmacnoise	el. *a.* 18 Feb. 1282 temp. 18 Feb. 1282 (bld; never cons.)	res. 13 Sept. 1289
Uilliam Ó Dubthaig, O.F.M.	el. *a.* 18 July 1290 temp. 6 Oct. 1290	*a.* Aug. 1297
Uilliam Ó Finnéin, O.Cist., abbot of Kilbeggan	el. 1298	*a.* 28 Aug. 1302
Domnall Ó Bráein, O.F.M., guardian of Killeigh	el. *a.* 26 Oct. 1302 temp. *p.* 14 Apr. 1303	—
Lughaidh Ó Dálaigh	—	1337
Henricus, O.P.	el. *c.* 1337	*a.* 1368
Simon, O.P. prior of Roscommon	prov. 11 May 1349 (did not take effect)	trs. to Derry 18 Dec. 1349
Richard Braybroke	cons. *a.* 28 Aug. 1369	*a.* Sept. 1371
Hugo	cons. *a.* 25 Sept. 1371	*p.* 1380
Philippus Ó Maoil[12]	—	res. *a.* 30 Jan. 1388 d. 1420
Milo Corr, O.F.M.	prov. 30 Jan. 1388 (again) 9 Nov. 1389	*a.* Sept. 1397
Philip Nangle, O.Cist., abbot of Granard[12]	prov. *a.* 24 Nov. 1397 cons. *a.* 26 Nov. 1397	*a.* Sept. 1423
David Prendergast, O.Cist.	prov. 24 Sept. 1423 (did not take effect)	—
Cormac Mac Cochláin, dean of Clonmacnoise (Cornelius)	prov. 10 Jan. 1425 (again) 8 July 1426 cons. *p.* 2 Aug. 1426	22 June 1444
Seaán Ó Dálaigh, O.F.M.	prov. 18 Sept. 1444	*a.* 26 Mar. 1487
Thomas	*a.* 27 Oct. 1449	—
Robertus	—	—
William, can. reg., prior of Brinkburn	prov. 14 July 1458 (suffr. in Durham)	*p.* 1484
Jacobus	1480	1486
Johannes[13]	?prov. 1486	1486/7
Walter Blake, canon of Tuam and Annaghdown	prov. 26 Mar. 1487	1508
Tomás Ó Maolalaidh, O.F.M.	*c.* 1509	trs. to Tuam 19 June 1514

bishops	accession	death unless otherwise stated
Quintinus Ó hUiginn, O.F.M.	prov. 10 Nov. 1516 (admr of Down and Connor p. 1520)	a. 16 June 1539

[10] May have been abbot as well as bishop (see above, p. 248). At this time Clonmacnoise was a centre of Connacht influence east of the Shannon and its claims to episcopal status were ignored by the synod of Ráith Bressail, which assigned western Mide to the see of Clonard and eastern Mide (Brega) to Duleek. But later in the same year (1111) Abbot Gilla Críst Ua Máel Eóin (d. 1127) convened a local synod at Uisnech, which decreed the suppression of Duleek, assigning its diocese to Clonard and creating Clonmacnoise an episcopal see for western Mide.

[11] Was present at the synod of Kells–Mellifont in 1152, but the status of his see does not seem to have been recognised; however, the textual error in the decrees of the synod which represents Achonry as two dioceses ('Achad' and 'Conaire') may be accompanied by a corresponding omission of Clonmacnoise due to haplography with Clonfert, in which case Clonmacnoise would have been a suffragan see of the province of Tuam. But neither Bp Muirchertach nor his see figure among the episcopal submissions to Henry II in 1171/2, and it seems that the synod of Brí mac Taidg in 1158 saw another attempt to suppress the see. At the synod of Birr in 1174 Clonmacnoise was awarded the whole diocese of western Mide and probably then transferred from the province of Tuam to that of Armagh, but the Anglo-Norman settlement of Meath ensured that most of this territory passed once more under the control of Clonard-Meath, and the diocese of Clonmacnoise remained diminutive in extent.

[12] It is possible that it was Ó Maoil rather than Nangle who had been abbot of Granard.

[13] It seems probable that Johannes is identical with Bp Seaán Ó Dálaigh.

DIOCESE OF CONNOR (Connere; Dál nAraide; Conderensis)

bishops	accession	death unless otherwise stated
Flann Ua Sculu	—	1117
Máel Máedóc Ua Morgair (Malachias; St Malachy)[14]	1124	res. 1136 d. 2 Nov. 1148
Máel Pátraic Ua Bánáin	a. Mar. 1152	res. a. 1172 d. 1174
Nehemias	a. 1172	a. 1178
Reginaldus	c. 1178	p. 19 Apr. 1225
Eustachius, archdeacon of Connor	el. a. 5 May 1226 temp. 5 May 1226	a. Oct. 1241
Adam, O.Cist., abbot of Warden, Bedfordshire	el. a. 27 Jan. 1242 temp. 27 Jan. 1242 cons. Sept. 1242	7 Nov. 1244
Isaac of Newcastle	el. a. 4 Apr. 1245 temp. 8 May 1245	c. 6 Oct. 1256
William of Portroyal, O.S.B., monk of Winchester	prov. 27 Oct. 1257 temp. 7 Jan. 1258	a. 16 July 1260
William de la Hay	el. 10 Oct. 1260 cons. p. 21 Mar. 1261 temp. p. 21 Mar. 1261 (suffr. in Lincoln 1262)	a. 25 Dec. 1262
Robert Fleming	el. 3 Feb. 1263 temp. p. Feb. 1263	25 Nov. 1274
Petrus 'de Dunach-' ('Dunath')	el. a. 2 Mar. 1275	a. Jan. 1292

bishops	accession	death unless otherwise stated
Johannes, rector of St Mary's, 'Corryton'	el. *a.* 23 Jan. 1292 temp. 27 Apr. 1293	*c.* 1319
Richard	el. *c.* 1320	—
James of Couplith	el. *a.* 26 July 1321 (did not get possession)	—
John of Eglecliff, O.P., bp of Glasgow	trs. *a.* 5 Mar. 1323 (did not get possession)	trs. to Llandaff 20 June 1323 d. 2 Jan. 1346
Robert Wirsop, O.S.A., bp of Ardagh	trs. 20 June 1323	*a.* May 1324
Jacobus Ó Cethernaig, bp of Annaghdown	trs. 7/15 May 1324 temp. 22 Dec. 1324	1351
William Mercier, archdeacon of Down	prov. 8 July 1353 cons. *p.* 12 Aug. 1353 temp. 2 Nov. 1353	1374
Paulus, rector of Aghohill	prov. 11 Dec. 1374 temp. 10 May 1376 lib. 4 July 1377	1389
Johannes, archdeacon of Connor	el. *a.* 29 Mar. 1389 temp. 23 July 1389 prov. 9 Nov. 1389	*c.* 1416
Seaán Ó Luachráin	prov. 22 May 1420	*a.* Feb. 1421
Eóghan Ó Domhnaill ('Machivenan'), canon of Raphoe dioc. (Eugenius)	prov. 5 May 1421 cons. *p.* June 1422	trs. to Derry 9 Dec. 1429
Domhnall Ó Mearaich, bp of Derry	trs. 9 Dec. 1429	*a.* 28 Jan. 1431
John Fossade (Festade), archdeacon of Connor	prov. 28 Jan. 1431 cons. *p.* 2 June 1431 **bp of Down and Connor 1442-50**	1450
Patricius	prov. *a.* 1459	*a.* 1459
Simon Elvington, O.P.	prov. 12 Feb. 1459 (suffr. in Salisbury and Exeter 1459-81; vicar of Gillingham 1463-75)	1481

[14] St Malachy ruled both Down and Connor from his monastery at Bangor, but resigned jurisdiction over Connor after 1137. For the subsequent union of the two dioceses see below under Down.

DIOCESE OF DERRY (*Daire Coluim Chille; Cenél nEógain; Darensis; Derensis*)

bishops	accession	death unless otherwise stated
?Máel Coluim Ua Brolcháin[15]	cons. 13 Sept. 1107	1122
?Máel Brigte Ua Brolcháin[15]	—	29 Jan. 1139
?Ua Gormgaile	—	1149

bishops	accession	death unless otherwise stated
Muiredach Ua Cobthaig (Mauricius)	*a.* Mar. 1152	10 Feb. 1173
Amlaím Ua Muirethaig	—	1185
Fogartach Ua Cerballáin I (Florentius)	1185	1230
Gilla in Choimded Ó Cerballáin, O.P. (Germanus)	el. *c.* 1230	1279
Fogartach Ó Cerballáin II (Florentius)	el. *c.* 1280	*c.* 24 July 1293
Michael, treasurer of Derry	el. *a.* 10 Oct. 1293 temp. 8 Feb. 1294 (never cons.)	—
Énrí Mac Airechtaig ('O'Reghly'), O.Cist. (Henry of Ardagh)	el. by abp of Armagh *a.* 12 Aug. 1294 (again) *a.* Mar. 1295 temp. 16 June 1295	1297
Gofraid Mac Lochlainn	el. *a.* 26 June 1297 temp. *p.* 26 June 1297	*c.* 1315
Áed Ó Néill (Odo)	el. 1316	June 1319
Michael Mac Lochlainn, O.F.M. (Mauricius), lector of Armagh convent	el. *p.* 19 Aug. 1319	*a.* 18 Dec. 1349
Simon, O.P., bp of Clonmacnoise	trs. 18 Dec. 1349	*p.* 1380
Johannes	—	*a.* July 1391
John Dongan, O.S.B.	prov. *a.* 11 July 1391 (suffr. in London 1392)	trs. to Down 16 Sept. 1394
Seoán Ó Mocháin, priest of Achonry dioc. (?and bp of Elphin)	prov. 16 Sept. 1394 (did not take effect)	1395
Aodh (Hugo)	prov. *a.* 25 Feb. 1398	?res. *a.* Aug. 1401
Seoán Ó Flannabhra, O.Cist., abbot of Macosquin	prov. 19 Aug. 1401	*a.* Feb. 1415
Domhnall Mac Cathmhaoil, canon of Leighlin dioc.	prov. 20 Feb. 1415 (never cons.)	*a.* Oct. 1419
Domhnall Ó Mearaich	prov. 16 Oct. 1419	trs. to Connor 9 Dec. 1429
Eoghan Ó Domhnaill, bp of Connor (Eugenius)	trs. 9 Dec. 1429	*a.* Sept. 1433
Johannes 'Oguguin' alias 'Ogubun', canon of Derry	prov. 18 Sept. 1433 cons. *p.* 17 Oct. 1433	d. or res. *a.* 1456
Bartholomaeus Ó Flannagáin, O.Cist., monk of Assaroe	prov. 27 May 1458	res. 1463
Johannes	*c.* 1464	*a.* Apr. 1466
Nicholas Weston	prov. 21 Feb. 1466	Dec. 1484
Domhnall Ó Fallamhain, O.F.M.	prov. 16 May 1485 cons. *p.* July 1487	5 July 1501

bishops	accession	death unless otherwise stated
Séamus mac Pilib Mac Mathghamhna, bp of Clogher	trs. 26 Nov. 1503	1519
Ruaidhrí Ó Domhnaill, dean of Raphoe	prov. 11 Jan. 1520	8 Oct. 1550/51

[15] These two members of the Cenél Feradaig family closely associated with Derry are styled bps of Armagh (see above, p. 240); they probably ruled the embryonic diocese of Cenél nEógain from that city in the transitional period before the grasp of the Clann Sínaig on the office of coarb of Patrick was finally loosened. Muiredach Ua Cobthaig established the see at Ráith Lúraig (Co. Londonderry), but is styled *episcopus Tarensis* in his submission to Henry II in 1171/2, and was buried at Derry: see below under Maghera. The see was finally transferred to Derry by Bp Gilla in Choimded Ó Cerballáin in 1247, and the removal was confirmed by Pope Innocent IV on 4 Nov. 1254.

DIOCESE OF DOWN (*Dún Lethglaisse; Ulaid; Dunensis*)

bishops	accession	death unless otherwise stated
Máel Muire	—	1117
Óengus Ua Gormáin, abbot of Bangor	—	1123
Máel Máedóc Ua Morgair, [16] abbot of Bangor (Malachias I; St Malachy)	1124	2 Nov. 1148
Máel Ísu mac in Chléirig Chuirr (Malachias II)	a. Mar. 1152	1175
Gilla Domangairt Mac Cormaic (Gilla Domnaig Mac Carmaic), can. reg., abbot of Bangor	1175	1175
Amlaím (?Ua hEcháin), abbot of Saul and ex-abbot of Mellifont[17]	1175	1175
Echmílid (?mac Máel Martain) (Malachias III)[18]	c. 1176	res. a. 1202 d. 1204
Radulphus, O.Cist., abbot of Melrose	c. 1202	—
Thomas	a. 1224	1242
Randulphus	a. May 1251	a. Nov. 1257
Reginaldus, archdeacon of Down	el. a. Apr. 1258 temp. p. 21 Oct. 1258 cons. p. Oct. 1258	trs. to Cloyne 13 Apr. 1265
Thomas Lydel, archdeacon of Down	el. a. Apr. 1258 (again) 1265 cons. p. 5 July 1265 temp. 5 Nov. 1266 (suffr. in Lincoln 1270)	a. Feb. 1277
Nicholas le Blund, O.S.B., prior of Down	el. a. 19 Mar. 1277 temp. p. 29 Mar. 1277	a. 28 Mar. 1305

bishops	accession	death unless otherwise stated
Thomas Ketel, parson of 'Lesmoghan'	el. *a.* 18 Aug. 1305 temp. *p.* 18 Aug. 1305	*c.* 20 Mar. 1314
Thomas Bright, O.S.B., prior of Down	el. *p.* 20 Mar. 1314	1327
John of Balyconingham	el. *a.* Aug. 1328 temp. 4 Aug. 1328	trs. to Cork *a.* Jan. 1329 trs. to Down 5 Jan. 1330 (without effect)
Ralph of Kilmessan, O.F.M.	prov. *a.* Jan. 1329 temp. 1 Apr. 1329 trs. to Cork 5 Jan. 1330 (without effect)	Aug. 1353
Richard Calf I, O.S.B., prior of Down	prov. 4 Dec. 1353 cons. *a.* 23 Dec. 1353 temp. 6 Mar. 1354	16 Oct. 1365
Robert of Aketon (Acton), O.S.A.	el. 18 Nov. 1365 (did not get possession)	res. *a.* Feb. 1366 prov. to Kildare 2 May 1366
William White, can. reg., prior of Greatconnell	prov. *a.* Dec. 1367 temp. 30 June 1367	*c.* 10 Aug. 1368
Richard Calf II, O.S.B., prior of Down	prov. 19 Feb. 1369 temp. 28 Apr. 1369	16 May 1386
John Ross, O.S.B., prior of Down	prov. *a.* 8 Nov. 1386	*a.* Sept. 1394
John Dongan, O.S.B., bp of Derry	trs. 16 Sept. 1394 temp. 26 July 1395	res. *a.* 28 July 1413
John Sely, O.S.B., prior of Down[19]	prov. 28 July 1413	depr. *a.* Nov. 1442 d. *a.* 26 Apr. 1445
Ralph Alderle, can. reg., prior of Newark	prov. 26 Apr. 1445 (did not get possession)	—
Thomas Pollard, O.Carth.	prov. 21 June 1447 cons. 27 Aug. 1447	*a.* June 1451
Richard Wolsey, O.P.	prov. 21 June 1451 (suffr. in Lichfield 1452-65; in Worcester 1465-79; in Hereford 1479)	res. *a.* Aug. 1453 d. *p.* 1479

[16] See above under Armagh and Connor.

[17] Having been expelled from the abbacy of Mellifont, Amlaím, son of the abbot of Moville, was intruded into the abbacy of Saul in 1170, with the support of Magnus Mac Duinn Sléibe, king of Ulster, expelling the canons regular there established by St Malachy. The wording of his obit in *A.U.* suggests that his tenure of the episcopacy was equally uncanonical.

[18] Also the son of an abbot of Moville, presumably of Máel Martain, who, together with Bp Máel Ísu, had tried to prevent the expulsion of the canons from Saul in 1170.

[19] Pope Eugenius IV issued a bull on 29 July 1439 providing for the union of Down and Connor on the death or resignation of either bp. This should have taken effect on the deprivation of John Sely, but Primate Prene was opposed to the union, which does not seem to have become fully effective until the episcopate of Thomas Knight.

DIOCESE OF DOWN AND CONNOR

bishops	accession	death unless otherwise stated
Thomas Knight, O.S.B., prior of Daventry	prov. 24 Aug. 1453 cons. 31 May 1456 (suffr. in London 1459-63)	1463
Tadhg Ó Muirgheasa, can. reg., prior of St Catherine's, Waterford (Thaddaeus)	prov. 10 July 1469 cons. 10 Sept. 1469	p. July 1480
Tiberio Ugolino	prov. 14 Feb. 1483 (again) 12 Sept. 1484 (again) 1 Sept. 1485 cons. 12 Mar. 1489	a. Apr. 1519
Robert Blyth, O.S.B., abbot of Thorney	prov. 16 Apr. 1520	depr. by Paul III 1539 suffr. in Ely 1539-41 d. p. 19 Oct. 1547

DIOCESE OF DROMORE (Druim Mór; Uí Echach; Dromorensis)[20]

bishops	accession	death unless otherwise stated
Ua Ruanada	a. 1197	—
Geraldus, O.Cist., monk of Mellifont	a. 15 Apr. 1227 fl. 1237	—
Andreas, archdeacon of Dromore	el. a. Oct. 1245	—
Tigernach I	el. c. 1284	—
Gervasius	1290	—
Tigernach II	—	1309
Florentius Mac Donnocáin, canon of Dromore	el. c. 1309 temp. c. 1309	—
Milo	fl. 20 Oct. 1366	—
Christophorus	fl. 28 Aug. 1369	—
Cornelius	—	a. Nov. 1382
Johannes ('O'Lannio'; 'O Lannub'), O.F.M.	temp. 10 Nov. 1382	—
Thomas Orwell, O.F.M., bp of Killala	trs. a. Nov. 1398 (suffr. in Ely and Norwich 1389-1406)	p. 1406

bishops	accession	death unless otherwise stated
John Waltham, can. reg., bp of Ossory	trs. 14 May 1400	trs. (again) to Ossory 9/11 Oct. 1402
Roger Appleby, can. reg., prior of Nuneaton and bp of Ossory	trs. 9/11 Oct. 1402	trs. to Waterford a. Oct. 1407
Richard Payl, O.P.	prov. 30 Dec. 1407 cons. a. 11 Nov. 1408	trs. to Sodor 30 May 1410 d. a. 20 Apr. 1422
John Chourles, O.S.B., monk of Bury St Edmunds	prov. 16 July 1410 cons. a. 4 Jan. 1411 (suffr. in Canterbury 1420–33; in London 1419–26; in Rochester 1423)	12 June 1433
Marcus[21]	fl. 1410	—
Seaán Ó Ruanadha	fl. 1414	—
Nicholas Wartre, O.F.M.	prov. 17 Mar. 1419 (suffr. in Rochester 1419–26; in York 1420–45)	p. 1445
Thomas Rackelf, O.S.A.	prov. 31 Jan. 1429 cons. 21 Dec. 1433 (suffr. in Durham 1441–6)	1453
William	—	a. June 1431
David Chirbury, O.Carm.	prov. 22 June 1431 (suffr. in St David's 1437)	p. 1451
Thomas Scrope alias Bradley, O.Carm.	prov. 1434? (suffr. in Norwich 1450–77; in Canterbury 1469)	res. a. 1440 d. 15 Jan. 1492
Thomas Radcliff	cons. 1 Feb. 1450 (suffr. in Durham until 1487)	res. 1454/5
Donatus 'O hEndua' or 'O hEndna' (?Ó hAnluain; ?Ó hÉanna)	prov. c. 1454/5 cons. p. 17 Apr. 1456	—
Richard Messing, O.Carm.	prov. 29 July 1457 (suffr. in York 1458–62)	a. June 1463
William Egremond, O.S.A.	prov. 15 June 1463 (suffr. in York 1463–1501)	p. 1501
Aonghus (Aeneas)	—	a. Aug. 1476
Robert Kirke, O.Cist.	prov. 28 Aug. 1476	a. Apr. 1480
Yvo Guillen, canon of St Malo	prov. 14 Apr. 1480	a. Apr. 1483
Georgius de Brana ('an t-easbog Gréagach')	prov. 18 Apr. 1483 cons. 4 May 1483 (suffr. in St Andrew's 1484–5; in London and Worcester 1497)	trs. to Elphin 15 Apr. 1499

bishops	accession	death unless otherwise stated
Tadhg Ó Raghallaigh, O.S.A. (Thaddaeus)	prov. 30 Apr. 1511 (suffr. in London 1511) prov. to Ross 24 Dec. 1519	a. June 1526

[20] This diocese, corresponding to the Irish kingdom of Uí Echach Coba, may have been first established at the synod held in Dublin in 1192 by the papal legate, Muirges Ua hÉnna, abp of Cashel.

[21] Primate Fleming's register refers to Marcus as 'a bp sojourning in the diocese of Dromore'; he does not therefore seem to have been actual bp of that see, which remained without a resident pastor for much of the fifteenth century.

DIOCESE OF DULEEK (Damliacc Cianáin)

bishops	accession	death unless otherwise stated
Gilla Mo Chua mac Camchuarta	—	1117
[Congalach[22]	—	1127]
[Áed[23]	—	1160]

[22] Congalach was 'coarb of Cianán' and possibly therefore abbot rather than bp.

[23] Áed is not specifically styled bp in his obit. It seems probable that the diocese was never properly established in spite of the decrees of Ráith Bressail (see above under Clonmacnoise) and of Kells-Mellifont. By 1171/2 it seems already to have been absorbed into that of Clonard (see below under Meath).

DIOCESE OF KELLS (Cenannas Mór; Kenanensis):
see TIRBRUNENSIS

DIOCESE OF KILMORE (Cell Mór): see TIRBRUNENSIS

DIOCESE OF LOUTH (Lugmad; Lugdunensis): see CLOGHER

DIOCESE OF MAGHERA (Ráith Lúraig; Rathlurensis):
see DERRY[24]

[24] The choice of the obscure church of Ráith Lúraig as the see for the diocese of Cenél nEógain at the synod of Kells–Mellifont (which also nominated the church of Derry, apparently as an alternative see), was motivated by two factors: an affirmation of Cenél nEógain control over the east of Co. Londonderry, which had been assigned to the diocese of Connor at the synod of Ráith Bressail (see above under Ardstraw), and a desire for an episcopal see which would not be overshadowed by the great Columban church of Derry, whose abbot, Flaithbertach Ua Brolcháin (see above, p. 258), was awarded the status of mitred abbot at the synod of Brí mac Taidg in 1158.

On 3 Apr. 1471 Thomas Ingleby obtained a provision to this extinct see from Pope Paul II and appears as a suffragan in Lincoln on 1 Feb. 1475 and apparently again in London on 25 Apr. 1491.

DIOCESE OF MEATH (Mide; Midensis)[25]

bishops	accession	death unless otherwise stated
Máel Muire Ua Dúnáin[26]	a. 1096	24 Dec. 1117
Eochaid Ua Cellaig	a. 11 Nov. 1133	1140
Étrú Ua Miadacháin (Eleuzerius)	a. Mar. 1152	1173
Echthigern Mac Máel Chiaráin (Eugenius)	a. Mar. 1177	1191
Simon Rochfort	el. 1192	a. Aug. 1224
Dónán Dé (Deodatus)	el. Aug. 1224 (never cons.)	p. 21 Oct. 1226
Ralph Petit, archdeacon of Meath	el. a. 30 Mar. 1227 temp. 30 Mar. 1227	c. 28 Sept. 1230
Richard de la Corner	el. and cons. 1231	a. 29 June 1252
Hugh of Taghmon, rector of Killulagh	el. a. 23 Dec. 1252 temp. 20 Feb. 1253 conf. by Innocent IV 31 Oct. 1254 cons. p. June. 1255	c. 30 Jan. 1282
Geoffrey Cusack, O.F.M.	el., conf. (by abp of Armagh), and cons. a. July 1253	res. July 1253 d. a. Oct. 1254
Walter de Fulbourn, dean of Waterford	el. and cons. (by abp of Armagh) a. Jan. 1283 (did not get possession)	trs. to Waterford 12 July 1286
Thomas St Leger, archdeacon of Kells	el. a. 5 Nov. 1282 prov. 12 July 1286 cons. 3 Nov. 1287	Dec. 1320
Seoán Mac Cerbaill, bp of Cork (John MacCarwill)	trs. 20 Feb. 1321 temp. 23 June 1322	trs. to Cashel 19 Jan. 1327
William of St Paul, O.Carm.	prov. 16 Feb. 1327 cons. c. Feb. 1327 temp. 24 July 1327	July 1349
William St Leger	prov. 5 Oct. 1349 temp. 24 Feb. 1350 cons. 2 May 1350	24 Aug. 1352
Nicholas Allen, can. reg., abbot of St Thomas's, Dublin	el. a. Jan. 1353 prov. 9 Jan. 1353 cons. 31 Jan. 1353 temp. 15 Mar. 1353	15 Jan. 1367
Stephen de Valle (Wall), bp of Limerick	trs. 19 Feb. 1369 temp. 13 Feb. 1370 (again) 6 Sept. 1373	10 Nov. 1379
William Andrew, O.P., bp of Achonry	trs. 1380 (suffr. in Canterbury 1380) temp. 12 Nov. 1380	28 Sept. 1385

bishops	accession	death unless otherwise stated
Alexander Petit (de Balscot), bp of Ossory	trs. 10 Mar. 1386	10 Sept. 1400
Robert Montayne, rector of Kildalkey	prov. 7 Feb. 1401 cons. *a.* 13 Sept. 1401	24 May 1412
Edward Dantsey, archdeacon of Exeter	prov. 31 Aug. 1412 temp. 11 Apr. 1413	4 Jan. 1430
William Hadsor	prov. 29 May 1430	28 May 1433
William Silk, canon of Cashel and Ossory and vicar of Delvin	el. *a.* 30 Aug. 1433 prov. 22 Sept. 1434 cons. *p.* 14 Oct. 1434	9 May 1450
Edmund Ouldhall, O. Carm.	prov. 7 Aug. 1450	9 (?29) Aug. 1459
William Sherwood, priest of dioc. of York	prov. 26 Mar. 1460	3 Dec. 1482
John Payne, O.P., prior of English province	prov. 17 Mar. 1483 temp. 16 July 1483 cons. *a.* 4 Aug. 1483	6 May 1507
William Rokeby, vicar of Halifax	prov. 28 May 1507	trs. to Dublin 28 Jan. 1512
Hugh Inge, O.P.	prov. 28 Jan. 1512	trs. to Dublin 27 Feb. 1523
Richard Wilson, can. reg., prior of Drax and bp of Negropont	prov. 27 Feb. 1523 (suffr. in York 1523-9)	res. *a.* Sept. 1529
Edward Staples, master of St Bartholomew's Hospital, London	prov. 3 Sept. 1529	depr. 29 June 1554 d. *c.* 1560

[25] For the vicissitudes of the territory of Mide in the diocesan arrangements of the twelfth century, see above under Clonmacnoise. The see remained at Clonard until 1202 when Bp Simon Rochfort transferred it to the Anglo-Norman centre of Newtown by Trim. The Augustinian priory which he founded there provided the cathedral church, but the diocese remained without a chapter. By 1216 it had absorbed the Co. Meath portion of the diocese of Kells, including the see itself (see below under Tirbrunensis), and apparently most of western Mide which had been assigned to Clonmacnoise in 1174.

[26] Máel Muire styled himself bp of Mide in 1096 and died at Clonard. He presided at Ireland's first papal legate at the first synod of Cashel in 1101, and spent most of his career as chief ecclesiastical adviser to the high-king Muirchertach Ua Briain. Hence *Ann. Tig.* and *Ann. Boyle* style him 'chief bp of Munster'. But there seems to be little evidence to support the seventeenth-century tradition that he was ever bp of Killaloe.

DIOCESE OF RAPHOE (*Ráith Both; Tír Conaill; Rathpotensis*)

bishops	accession	death unless otherwise stated
?Eóin Ua Gairedáin[27]	—	—
?Domnall Ua Garbáin[27]	—	—
?Feidlimid Ua Sída[27]	—	—

bishops	*accession*	*death unless otherwise stated*
Gilla in Choimded Ua Caráin (Gillebertus)	a. 1156	trs. to Armagh c. 1175
Anonymous	—	res. a. 18 May 1198
Máel Ísu Ua Doirig	a. 1204	res. a. 7 Mar. 1252
Máel Pátraic Ó Scannail, O.P.[28] (Patricius)	el. c. Nov. 1253 cons. 30 Nov. 1253	trs. to Armagh 5 Nov. 1261
Giovanni de Alneto, O.F.M. (Johannes)	prov. 3 Dec. 1264	res. 28 Apr. 1265
Cairpre Ó Scuapa, O.P.	prov. p. 28 Apr. 1265 (suffr. in Canterbury 1273)	9 May 1274
Fergal Ó Firgil (Florentius)	c. 1275	1299
Tomás Ó Naán, archdeacon of Raphoe	el. a. 1306 (never cons.)	1306
Énrí Mac in Chrossáin (Henricus)	c. 1306	1319
Tomás Mac Carmaic Uí Domnaill, O.Cist., abbot of Assaroe	el. 1319	1337
Pádraig Mac Maonghail	—	a. Oct. 1367
Conchobhar Mac Carmaic Uí Dhomhnaill, O.Cist., abbot of Assaroe and canon of Raphoe (Cornelius)	prov. 23 Dec. 1367	res. 21 Feb. 1397 d. 1399
Seoán Mac Meanmain, O.Cist., monk of Assaroe	prov. 21 Feb. 1397	—
Eóin Mac Carmaic (Johannes)	prov. a. 8 Dec. 1400	1419
Lochlainn Ó Gallchobhair I, dean of Raphoe (Laurentius)	el. a. 27 Feb. 1420 prov. 28 Feb. 1420	1438
Cornelius Mac Giolla Bhrighde, dean of Raphoe	prov. 20 July 1440 cons. p. 30 July 1440	a. June 1442
Lochlainn Ó Gallchobhair II, canon and official of Raphoe (Laurentius)	prov. 18 June 1442 cons. p. 23 July 1443	a. Nov. 1479
Johannes de Rogeriis, priest of Roman church (?Seaán Mac Ruaidhrí)	prov. 12 Nov. 1479	a. Nov. 1483
Meanma Mac Carmaic, dean of Raphoe (Menelaus Mac Carmacáin)	prov. 4 Nov. 1483	res. 6 Feb. 1514 d. 9 May 1515
Conn Ó Catháin, cleric of Derry dioc. (Cornelius)	prov. 6 Feb. 1514	depr. (?)1534 d. p. 1550

bishops	accession	death unless otherwise stated
Éamonn Ó Gallchobhair, dean of Raphoe	prov. 11 May 1534	26 Feb. 1543

[27] These bps, 'Sean O Gairedain, Donell O Garvan, Felemy O Syda', are known only from a seventeenth-century catalogue of the bps of Raphoe. The dominance of the Columban church in this diocese helps to explain the obscurity of the early bps.

[28] Upon his consecration he was appointed vic. gen. of the diocese of Armagh during the absence of Abp Rainaldo at the papal court 1253-6.

DIOCESE OF TIRBRUNENSIS (Bréifne; Tír mBriúin; Uí Briúin; Triburnensis)[29]

bishops	accession	death unless otherwise stated
Áed Ua Finn	—	1136
Muirchertach Ua Máel Mochéirge	—	1149
Tuathal Ua Connachtaig (Thaddaeus)	a. Mar. 1152	1179
Anonymous, O.Cist.	el. and cons. a. 1185	—
M. Ua Dobailén	a. Aug. 1202	1211
Flann Ó Connachtaig (Florentius)	—	1231
Congalach Mac Idneóil	a. c. 1233	res. a. May 1250 d. 1250
Simon Ó Ruairc	el. a. 20 June 1251	1285
Mauricius, can. reg., abbot of Kells	el. a. Oct. 1286	1307
Matha Mac Duibne	—	1314
Pátraic Ó Cridecáin	el. a. 1320	1328
Conchobhar Mac Conshnámha (Ford)	—	1355
Riocard Ó Raghallaigh	el. c. 1356	1369
Johannes	el. a. 1373	c. 1389
Thomas Rushook, O.P., bp of Chichester	trs. c. 1388	?res. 1390 d. c. 1393
Seoán Ó Raghallaigh I	p. 2 Nov. 1389	1393
Nicol (alias Ruaidhrí) Mac Brádaigh	prov. a. 27 Aug. 1395 cons. a. July 1398	1421
John Stokes	— (suffr. in Lichfield 1407; in Worcester 1416)	—
David Ó Faircheallaigh	prov. by Gregory XII c. 1408/9 cons. c. 1408/9	—

bishops	accession	death unless otherwise stated
Domhnall Ó Gabhann, vicar of Ballintemple (Donatus)	prov. 13 Aug. 1421 cons. p. 30 June 1422	res. c. 1445
Aindrias Mac Brádaigh, archdeacon of Tirbrunensis	prov. 9 Mar. 1445	1455
Fear Síthe Mág Dhuibhne, can. reg., prior of Drumlane (Tycheus)	prov. 11 July 1455	27 Nov. 1464
Seaán Ó Raghallaigh II, can. reg., abbot of Kells	prov. 17 May 1465	a. Nov. 1476
Cormac Mág Shamhradháin, can. reg., prior of Drumlane[30]	prov. 4 Nov. 1476	Dec. 1512
Tomás mac Aindriais Mac Brádaigh[30]	prov. 20 Oct. 1480	29 July 1511
Diarmaid Ó Raghallaigh	prov. 28 Jan. 1512	a. June 1530
Edmund Nugent, can. reg., prior of Tristernagh	prov. 22 June 1530	depr. 5 Nov. 1540 d. c. 1550

[29] For the origins of this diocese see above under Ardagh. The synod of Kells–Mellifont designated Kells as the see for Tigernán Ua Ruairc's kingdom of Bréifne. After the Anglo-Norman settlement of north Co. Meath this part of the diocese was absorbed into that of Meath: the expulsion of a Cistercian bp of Kells (who may perhaps be identical with Bp M. Ua Dobailén) by the bp of Meath is recorded c. 1185, and by 1216 the episcopal status of Kells had been abolished by Bp Simon Rochfort of Meath. Bréifne or Tír mBriúin was thus left without a diocesan see, and the division of the territory in the thirteenth century between the rival lordships of Ua Ruairc and Ua Ragallaig compounded the difficulties. In 1453 or 1454 Bp Aindrias Mac Brádaigh obtained the consent of Pope Nicholas V to erect the obscure parish church of Kilmore, on the border between the two lordships, into a cathedral, thus overriding the claims of the more important church of Drumlane, which was closely linked with the O'Rourkes.

[30] These two rival bps were both present and recognised as bps of Kilmore at provincial councils held by Primate Octavian in 1492 and 1495; Cormac represented the Ó Ruairc interest and Tomás that of Ó Raghallaigh.

PROVINCE OF CASHEL

DIOCESE OF CASHEL (Caisel Muman; Casselensis)

archbishops	accession	death unless otherwise stated
Máel Ísu Ua hAinmere, O.S.B., bp of Waterford (Malchus)[1]	c. 1111	res. — d. 1135
Máel Ísu Ua Fogluda	—	1131
Domnall Ua Conaing, bp of Killaloe	trs. 1131	1137
Domnall Ua Lonngargáin, bp of Killaloe	trs. 1137/8	1158

archbishops	accession	death unless otherwise stated
Domnall Ua hUalacháin (Donatus)	a. 1172	1182
Muirges Ua hÉnna, O.Cist. (Matthaeus; Mauricius)	a. 1185	1206
Donnchad Ua Lonngargáin I (Donatus; Dionysius)	c. 1208	a. July 1216
Donnchad Ó Lonngargáin II, O.Cist. (Donatus)	el. 1216	res. a. Aug. 1223 d. 1232
Michael Scottus	prov. 1223 (never cons.)	res. 1223 d. a. 1235
Mairín Ó Briain, can. reg., bp of Cork (Marianus)	el. p. 19 Aug. 1223 trs. 20 June 1224 temp. 25 Aug. 1224 (again) 20 Jan. 1225	res. a. 6 June 1237 d. 1238
David mac Cellaig Ó Gilla Pátraic, O.P., bp of Cloyne	trs. a. Dec. 1238 conf. 1239	4 Apr. 1253
David Mac Cerbaill (O.Cist. 1269), dean of Cashel (MacCarwill)	el. a. 17 Aug. 1254 prov. 17 Aug. 1254 temp. 19 Feb. 1255	a. 4 Sept. 1289
Stiamna Ó Brácáin, archdeacon of Glendalough and canon of Cashel (Stephanus)	el. a. 31 Jan. 1290 prov. 21 Aug. 1290 temp. 27 Mar. 1291	25 July 1302
Mauricius Mac Cerbaill, archdeacon of Cashel	el. a. 17 May 1303 fealty 24 May 1303 prov. 17 Nov. 1303 temp. 28 July 1304	c. 25 Mar. 1316
William FitzJohn, bp of Ossory	trs. 26 Mar. 1317 temp. p. 3 Mar. 1318	15 Sept. 1326
Seoán Mac Cerbaill, bp of Meath (John MacCarwill)	trs. 19 Jan. 1327 temp. 18 May 1327 fealty 26 Sept. 1327	c. 27 July 1329
Walter le Rede, bp of Cork	trs. 20 Oct. 1329 temp. 20 July 1330 lib. 19 Aug. 1330	17 June 1331
Eóin Ó Gráda, treasurer of Cashel	prov. 27 Mar. 1332 temp. 12 June 1332 lib. 9 July 1332	8 July 1345
Radulphus Ó Ceallaigh (? Ó Caollaidhe), O.Carm., bp of Leighlin	trs. 9 Jan. 1346 temp. 9 Mar. 1346 lib. 4 Apr. 1346 (suffr. in Winchester 1346)	20 Nov. 1361
George Roche (de Rupe), canon of Cashel	a. 12 Sept. 1362	c. 1362
Tomás Mac Cearbhaill, abp of Tuam	trs. a. 8 Mar. 1365	8 Feb. 1372

archbishops	accession	death unless otherwise stated
Philip of Torrington, O.F.M.	prov. 5 Sept. 1373 temp. 19 Dec. 1373 lib. 19 Sept. 1374	1380
Michael, O.F.M., minister of Irish province	prov. by Clement VII 22 Oct. 1382	trs. to Sodor 15 July 1387 d. p. 1398
Peter Hackett	prov. by Urban VI (no date) temp. 28 Oct. 1385	c. 1405
Risdeárd Ó hÉidigheáin (Richard O'Hedian)	prov. a. 6 Apr. 1406 cons. a. 17 June 1406 temp. 14 Sept. 1408	21 July 1440
John Cantwell I, archdeacon of Ossory	el. a. Nov. 1440 prov. 21 Nov. 1440 cons. a. 28 Mar. 1442	14 Feb. 1451/2
John Cantwell II, dean of Cashel	prov. 2 May 1452 cons. p. 2 May 1452	1482
David Creagh, canon of Limerick	prov. 10 May 1484 cons. 14 June 1484	5 Sept. 1503
Maurice FitzGerald	c. 1504	a. Oct. 1524
Edmund Butler, O.S. Trin.	prov. 21 Oct. 1524 cons. p. 3 Jan. 1525	5 Mar. 1551

¹ Máel Ísu Ua hAinmere was appointed first abp of Cashel at the synod of Ráith Bressail in 1111, but appears to have resigned that dignity shortly afterwards to retire to his original see of Waterford.

DIOCESE OF ARDFERT (Ard Ferta Brénainn; Ciarraige; Iarmuma; Artfertensis)²

bishops	accession	death unless otherwise stated
Anmchad Ua hAnmchada	—	1117
Máel Brénainn Ua (Mac) Rónáin	a. Mar. 1152	21/2 Sept. 1161
Domnall Ua Connairche	—	1193
David Ua Duib Díthrib	el. a. 1197 conf. by Innocent III 1200/01	1207
Anonymous	—	c. 1217
John, O.S.B., of St Alban's, priest of Limerick dioc.	el. c. 1217 cons. a. 28 Feb. 1218 (suffr. in Canterbury c. 1222)	depr. 18 June 1224 d. 14 Oct. 1245
Gillebertus, dean of Ardfert	el. a. 28 Feb. 1218 conf. p. 16 July 1219 temp. p. 7 May 1225	res. p. 24 Apr. 1235

bishops	accession	death unless otherwise stated
Brendán, provost of Ardfert	el. *p.* 6 Dec. 1236 conf. 17 Nov. 1237	res. *p.* 1 Aug. 1251 d. *a.* 20 Apr. 1252
Christianus, O.P., friar of Tralee	el. *a.* 23 Feb. 1253 cons. *p.* 17 Aug. 1253	*a.* 20 Aug. 1256
Philippus, canon of Ardfert	el. *a.* 23 Mar. 1257 cons. *p.* 23 Mar. 1257 temp. 16 June 1257	*a.* 4 July 1264
Johannes, archdeacon of Ardfert	el. *a.* 3 Mar. 1265 temp. *p.* 3 Mar. 1265	*a.* 6 June 1286
Nicolaus	el. *p.* 28 June 1286	14 Mar. 1288
Nicol Ó Samradáin, O.Cist., abbot of Odorney	el. *p.* 26 Apr. 1288 temp. *p.* 10 Aug. 1288 lib. 25 Apr. 1289	1335
Edmund of Caermarthen, O.P.	prov. 24 Sept. 1331 cons. 24 Sept. 1331 temp. 27 Jan. 1332 (did not get possession)	—
Ailín Ó hEichthighirn, canon of Ardfert	el. *c.* 1335 prov. 18 Nov. 1336 cons. 18 Nov. 1336	2 Dec. 1347
John de Valle (Wall), canon of Ardfert	el. *a.* Oct. 1348 prov. 22 Oct. 1348 temp. 10 Mar. 1349	*a.* Oct. 1372
Cornelius Ó Tighearnaigh, O.F.M.	prov. 22 Oct. 1372 temp. 10 Feb. 1373	*c.* 1379
William Bull	temp. 14 Feb. 1380	*c.* 1404
Nicholas Ball	prov. *a.* Oct. 1404	trs. to Emly 2 Dec. 1405
Tomás mac Muircheartaigh Ó Ceallaigh, O.P.	prov. *a.* 10 Mar. 1405	trs. to Clonfert 11 Mar. 1405
John Attilburgh alias Artilburch, O.S.B., monk of Bermondsey and penitentiary apostolic	prov. 10 Mar. 1405 conf. by Alexander V 25 Oct. 1409	*a.* Jan. 1411
Nicholas fitz Maurice FitzGerald	prov. *a.* 17 Sept. 1408 conf. by John XXIII 27 Jan. 1411	*a.* Apr. 1450
Maurice Stack, dean of Ardfert	prov. 30 Jan. 1450 cons. *p.* 29 Apr. 1450	*a.* Jan. 1452
Mauricius Ó Conchobhair	prov. 26 Jan. 1452 cons. *p.* 11 Feb. 1452	*a.* Sept. 1458
John Stack	prov. 18 Sept. 1458 cons. *c.* 1461 conf. by Sixtus IV 15 Mar. 1488	*a.* Oct. 1488

bishops	accession	death unless otherwise stated
John Pigge, O.P.	prov. 27 Mar. 1461 (rector in London 1462–83)	res. *a.* 22 June 1473 trs. to Beirut *a.* Jan. 1475
Philip Stack, archdeacon of Ardfert	prov. 22 June 1473 (again) 27 Oct. 1488	*a.* Nov. 1495
John FitzGerald	prov. 20 Nov. 1495	*a.* May 1536

[2] The obscure site of Ratass (Ráith Maige Deiscirt) was designated as the see for Ciarraige at the synod of Ráith Bressail, but Anmchad Ua hAnmchada is styled bp of Ardfert at his death, and this was the site confirmed at the synod of Kells–Mellifont: it lay in the kingdom of Ciarraige, but the diocese also included Corco Duibne and Eóganacht Locha Lein, and the king of the last-named territory, Amlaíb Ua Donnchada, seems to have tried to move the see to Aghadoe (Achad dá Eó) in 1158, when he was defeated and killed by the forces of Thomond.

DIOCESE OF ARDMORE (*Ard Mór; Ardmorensis*)[3]

bishops	accession	death unless otherwise stated
Eugenius	*a.* 1153 (suffr. in Lichfield 1184/5)	—
?Ua Selbaig[4]	—	1205

[3] The synod of Kells–Mellifont deferred judgement on the alleged episcopal status of the churches of Mungret (Mungairet), Co. Limerick, and Ardmore, Co. Waterford. Limerick was powerful enough to quash the claims of Mungret, but Ardmore, as chief church of St Declan, patron of the Déise, maintained its existence as a see for some fifty years. The cathedral was built by the archpriest, Máel Étain Ua Duib Rátha (d. 1203), and the last reference to the diocese occurs in a papal letter of 1210.

[4] Died at Cork; his see is not mentioned, and he may have been bp of Ross.

DIOCESE OF CLOYNE (*Cluain Uama; Clonensis*)[5]

bishops	accession	death unless otherwise stated
Gilla na Náem Ua Muirchertaig (Nehemias)	*a.* 1148	1149
Ua Dubchróin, abbot of Cloyne	—	1159
Ua Flannacáin	—	1167
Matthaeus Ua Mongaig	*fl.* 1173 × 1177	1192
Laurentius Ua Súillebáin	*a.* 1201	1205
C.	*c.* 1205	—
Lucas	*a.* 1218	1223
Florentius, archdeacon of 'Belaghathe' (Ballyhay)	el. *a.* 24 Aug. 1224 (never cons.)	—
William, O.Cist., prior of Fermoy	el. *a.* 20 July 1226 (never cons.)	—

bishops	accession	death unless otherwise stated
Daniel	el. *p.* 31 Aug. 1226	*p.* Oct. 1234
David mac Cellaig Ó Gilla Pátraic, O.P.	el. *a.* Sept. 1237	trs. to Cashel *a.* Dec. 1238
Ailinn Ó Súillebáin, O.P.	*c.* 1240 conf. 1240	trs. to Lismore *p.* 26 Oct. 1246
Daniel, O.F.M.	el. *a.* 12 Oct. 1247 cons. *p.* 12 Oct. 1247 temp. 2 July 1248	*a.* 2 June 1264
Reginaldus, bp of Down	trs. 13 Apr. 1265	7 Feb. 1274
Alanus Ó Longáin alias Ó Lonngargáin, O.F.M.	el. *a.* 18 Feb. 1275 temp. 21 Feb. 1275 lib. 21 Apr. 1275	*c.* 5 Jan. 1284
Nicholas of Effingham	el. *p.* 18 Mar. 1284 temp. 2 Sept. 1284	June 1321
Mauricius Ó Solcháin, archdeacon of Cloyne	prov. 2 Oct. 1321 temp. 1 Aug. 1322 cons. *p.* 25 Aug. 1323	31 Mar. 1333
John Brid, O.Cist., abbot of Combe	prov. 10 Aug. 1333 cons. *a.* 9 Oct. 1333 temp. 16 Sept. 1335	*c.* 1351
John Whitekot	el. *a.* June 1351 prov. 8 June 1351 cons. *a.* 27 June 1351 temp. 18 Sept. 1351	7 Feb. 1362
John Swaffham, O.Carm.	prov. 1 Mar. 1363 temp. 14 July 1363	trs. to Bangor 2 July 1376 d. 24 June 1398
Richard Wye, O.Carm.	prov. 2 July 1376 temp. 9 Nov. 1376	depr. *a.* 16 Mar. 1394
Gerald Caneton, O.S.A.	prov. 16 Mar. 1394 temp. 9 Nov. 1394	trs. to Elphin *c.* 1405
Adam Payne, O.S.A.	prov. 26 July 1413	res. *a.* 15 June 1429 d. *a.* Jan. 1432

[5] This diocese was created after the synod of Ráith Bressail out of the ancient territories of Eóganacht Glennamnach, Fir Maige Féine, and Úí Liatháin, at the expense of the dioceses of Emly, Cork, and Lismore, and was recognised at the synod of Kells-Mellifont. After the union with Cork in 1429 (see below) a titular bp of 'Cloyne', Thomas Hartepyry, is found as a suffragan in Hereford in 1490.

DIOCESE OF CORK (*Corcach Mór Muman; Corcagiensis*)

bishops	accession	death unless otherwise stated
?Ua Menngoráin	—	1147
Gilla Áeda Ua Maigín, can. reg., canon of Cong and abbot of Gill Abbey (Gregorius)	*a.* 1148	1172
Gregorius Ua hÁeda	*fl.* 1173×1177	1182
Reginaldus I, archdeacon of Cork	*c.* 1182	1187
Aicher (Aggirus)	*c.* 1187	1188
Murchad Ua hÁeda	*a.* 1192	1206
Mairín Ua Briain, can. reg., canon of Christchurch, Dublin (Marianus)	*a.* 1208	trs. to Cashel 20 June 1224
Gillebertus, archdeacon of Cork	el. *a.* 5 June 1225	*p.* 1237
Laurentius, dean of Cashel	el. *a.* 5 May 1248	*a.* 27 Mar. 1265
William of Jerpoint, O.Cist.	el. *p.* 27 Mar. 1265 temp. 28 Nov. 1266	*a.* 8 July 1267
Reginaldus II, treasurer of Cashel	el. *a.* 5 Aug. 1267	16 Dec. 1276
Robertus Mac Donnchada, O.Cist.	el. *a.* 8 May 1277 temp. 11 June 1277 lib. 13 Oct. 1277	6 Mar. 1302
Seoán Mac Cerbaill, dean of Cork (John MacCarwill)	el. 30 Apr. 1302 temp. 12 June 1302 lib. 20 July 1302	trs. to Meath 20 Feb. 1321
Philip of Slane, O.P., friar of St Mary of the Island	prov. 20 Feb. 1321 temp. 16 July 1321	*a.* Mar. 1327
Walter le Rede, canon of Cork	prov. 20 Mar. 1327 cons. *a.* 12 July 1327 temp. 18 Oct. 1327	trs. to Cashel 20 Oct. 1329
John of Ballyconingham, bp of Down	trs. *a.* Jan. 1329 temp. 30 May 1330	29 May 1347
John Roche	el. *a.* Dec. 1347 cons. Dec. 1347	4 July 1358
Gerald Barry, dean of Cork	prov. *a.* 14 Feb. 1359 temp. 2 Feb. 1360 prov. (again) by Urban V 8 Nov. 1362	4 Jan. 1393
Roger Ellesmere	prov. 3 Dec. 1395 temp. 31 Mar. 1396	*a.* 14 Feb. 1406
Richard Kynmoure, priest of Dublin dioc.	prov. *a.* 6 Oct. 1406	*a.* June 1409

bishops	accession	death unless otherwise stated
Milo FitzJohn, dean of Cork	prov. by Gregory XII July 1409 (again) by Martin V 11 Jan. 1418	mid-June 1431
Patrick Foxe, dean of Ossory	prov. by Alexander V 14 Oct. 1409 conf. by John XXIII 25 May 1410	trs. to Ossory 15 Dec. 1417
John Paston alias Wortes, O.S.B., prior of Brownholm	prov. 23 May 1425 (did not get possession)	p. 1459

DIOCESE OF CORK AND CLOYNE[6]

bishops	accession	death unless otherwise stated
Jordan Purcell, chancellor of Limerick	prov. 15 June 1429 conf. 6 Jan. 1432 temp. 25 Sept. 1432	res. p. 18 Apr. 1469 d. c. 1477
Gerald FitzGerald, canon of Cloyne[7]	prov. a. 3 Feb. 1462	res. a. June 1499
William Roche, archdeacon of Cloyne[7]	prov. 26 Oct. 1472 cons. a. 1475	res. a. Apr. 1490
Tadhg Mac Carthaigh (Thaddaeus)[7]	prov. 21 Apr. 1490	24 Oct. 1492
Patrick Cant (Condon), O.Cist., abbot of Fermoy	prov. 15 Feb. 1499 (annulled 26 June 1499)	—
John fitz Edmund FitzGerald	prov. 26 June 1499	a. 27 Aug. 1520
John Bennett alias Ferret, priest of Cloyne dioc.	prov. 28 Jan. 1523	1536

[6] On the petition of Edward II, Pope John XXII issued a bull on 31 July 1327 providing for the union of Cork with Cloyne on the death of either incumbent, but this plan was not put into effect (it was part of a more ambitious scheme for the reduction in the number of Irish dioceses in favour of sees within easier control of the royal administration in Ireland). An attempt by Bp Richard Wye of Cloyne (10 Sept. 1376) was also unsuccessful. Bp Adam Payne of Cloyne obtained confirmation of the union from Pope Martin V on 21 Sept. 1418, but it was opposed by Bp Milo FitzJohn of Cork, and did not take place until the provision of Jordan Purcell to both sees in 1429.

[7] The provision of Gerald FitzGerald ignored the claims of William Roche, who had been granted right of succession to Bp Jordan Purcell in 1461; the rivalry was further protracted by the provision of Tadhg Mac Carthaigh (who had been provided in error to Ross in 1482) on the resignation of Roche, and was only ended by the provision of John FitzGerald in 1499.

DIOCESE OF EMLY (*Imlech Ibair; Imilicensis; Ymlicensis*)

bishops	accession	death unless otherwise stated
Diarmait Ua Flainn Chua	—	1114
Gilla in Choimded Ua hArdmaíl (Deicola)[8]	a. Mar. 1152	—
Máel Ísu Ua Laigenáin, O.Cist., abbot of Baltinglass	—	1163
Ua Meic Stia	a. 1172	1173
Ragnall Ua Flainn Chua	—	1197
?Isaac Ua hAnmchada[9]	—	—
M.[9] William, canon of Emly	a. 1205 / el. c. 1209 (never cons.)	a. 1209 / depr. 5 Jan. 1211
Henry, O.Cist., abbot of Bindon	el. 1212	a. 13 July 1227
John Collingham, chancellor of Emly	el. a. 13 July 1227 / conf. by Gregory IX 1228 / cons. a. 25 June 1228 / temp. p. 25 June 1230	a. 14 June 1236
Daniel, prior of the Hospital of St John's, Dublin	el. a. Apr. 1238 / temp. p. 8 Apr. 1238 (did not get possession)	—
Christianus	el. a. 18 Oct. 1238	a. 12 Dec. 1249
Gillebertus Ó Dubartaig, dean of Emly	el. a. Oct. 1251 / temp. 12 Oct. 1251	9 Oct. 1265
Laurentius 'of Dunlak', precentor of Emly	el. a. 30 Mar. 1266 (never cons.)	—
Florentius Ó hAirt	el. and conf. a. 17 Apr. 1266 / temp. p. 17 Apr. 1266	18 Jan. 1272
Matthaeus Mac Gormáin, archdeacon of Emly	el. p. 3 Apr. 1272 / temp. 18 June 1272 / lib. 2 Aug. 1272	24 Mar. 1275
David Ó Cossaig, O.Cist., abbot of Holycross	el. a. 24 June 1275 / temp. 2 Aug. 1275 / lib. 14 Sept. 1275	11 June 1281
William de Clifford, papal chaplain	prov. 1 Oct. 1286	a. 10 Aug. 1306
Thomas Quantok (Cantok), chancellor of Ire. and canon of Emly	el. a. 3 Sept. 1306 / temp. 3 Sept. 1306	4 Feb. 1309
William Roughead	el. a. May 1309 / temp. 14 May 1309	15 June 1335
Richard le Walleys (Walsh)	el. a. 16 Aug. 1335 / temp. 16 Aug. 1335	a. 11 Jan. 1353

bishops	*accession*	*death unless otherwise stated*
John Esmond, bp-elect of Ferns	prov. 11 Jan. 1353 (again) 28 Feb. 1356 temp. 27 Apr. 1356	4 Apr. 1362
David Penlyn (Foynlyn), canon of Emly	prov. 4 July 1362 cons. *a.* June 1363	—
William, archdeacon of Emly	prov. 7 June 1363 temp. 11 Oct. 1363	*a.* Dec. 1405
Nicholas Ball, bp of Ardfert	trs. 2 Dec. 1405	*a.* Apr. 1421
John Rishberry, O.S.A.	prov. 21 Apr. 1421 (bulls not expedited)	—
Robert Windell, O.F.M.	prov. 14 Jan. 1423 (suffr. in Norwich 1424; in Worcester 1433; in Salisbury 1435–41)	depr. 1425 d. 1441
Thomas de Burgh, can. reg., canon of Clare Abbey	prov. 19 Dec. 1425 cons. *p.* 23 Feb. 1428	*a.* Sept. 1444
Robert Portland, O.F.M.	prov. 5 Mar. 1429 (did not take effect)	trs. to Tiberias 1444 suffr. in Winchester 1456
Cornelius Ó Cuinnlis, O.F.M.	prov. 11 Sept. 1444 cons. *a.* 16 Jan. 1445	trs. to Clonfert 30 Aug. 1448
Conchobhar Ó Maolalaidh, O.F.M., bp of Clonfert (Cornelius)	trs. 30 Aug. 1448	trs. to Elphin 20 Oct. 1449
Uilliam Ó hÉidigheáin, bp of Elphin	trs. 20 Oct. 1449	*p.* Feb. 1475
Pilib Ó Cathail, canon of Emly	prov. 1 Dec. 1475 cons. *p.* 9 Jan. 1476	*a.* Nov. 1494
Donatus Mac Briain[10]	prov. 10 Nov. 1494	res. *a.* Apr. 1498 suffr. in Worcester 1500
Cinnéidigh Mac Briain, canon of Emly (Carolus)	prov. 30 Apr. 1498	*a.* Oct. 1505
Tomás Ó hUrthaile	prov. 6 Oct. 1505 cons. *c.* 1507	1542

[8] Diarmait Ua Flainn Chua had been abbot of Emly since 1092 (see above, p. 253); Gilla in Choimded attended the synod of Kells–Mellifont as vicar-general for an unnamed bp of Emly; it is possible, but by no means certain, that the bps Ua Ruadgussa (d. 1126) and Mac Raith Ua Faíllecháin (d. 1143), whose sees are not recorded, may have been bps of Emly.

[9] 'Isaac O Hanmy' is mentioned by Bishop William de Clifford in 1302 as an early thirteenth-century predecessor; he may be identical with M. if that initial stands for Máel Ísu.

[10] Lynch, *De praesulibus Hib.*, ii, 64, inserts at this point three bps who are otherwise unknown, but cites no authentic record for any of them: Cathaldus Ó Murchu, from Leinster; Dermicius Ó Cahill; and Edmund Pillin.

DIOCESE OF KILFENORA (Cell Finnabrach; Corco Mruad; Finnabarensis)[11]

bishops	accession	death unless otherwise stated
Anonymous	*fl.* 1171	—
?A.[12]	*fl. c.* 1189?	—
F.	*a.* 1205	—
Johannes	*a.* 1224	—
Christianus	*fl.* 1251 × 1254	*a.* Dec. 1255
Anonymous	—	*a.* 28 Feb. 1264
Mauricius	el. *p.* 3 Mar. 1265	*a.* 14 July 1273
	cons. *a.* 12 Feb. 1266	
	temp. 12 Feb. 1266	
Florentius Ó Tigernaig,	el. *a.* 18 Sept. 1273	*a.* 12 July 1281
can. reg., abbot of Kilshanny	temp. 30 Nov. 1273	
Congalach Ó Lochlainn,	el. *a.* Sept. 1281	*a.* 21 Dec. 1298
dean of Kilfenora	temp. 6 Sept. 1281	
(Carolus)		
Simon Ó Cuirrín, O.P.	el. 16 May 1300	*a.* 26 Dec. 1302
	conf. 22 July 1300	
Mauricius Ó Briain (?O.S.B.)[13]	el. *a.* 10 June 1303	1319
	temp. 8 Oct. 1303	
	lib. 6 May 1304	
Risdeárd Ó Lochlainn	cons. 17 Apr. 1323	3 Feb. 1359
Dionysius	—	*a.* Oct. 1372
Henricus, dean of Killaloe	prov. 6 Oct. 1372	—
Cornelius	—	*c.* 1389
Patricius,	el. *a.* Feb. 1390	*a.* Jan. 1421
archdeacon of Kilfenora	prov. 28 Feb. 1390	
	cons. *p.* 19 Mar. 1390	
Feidhlimidh mac	prov. 15 Jan. 1421	*a.* Aug. 1433
Mathghamhna	cons. *p.* 6 Feb. 1421	
Ó Lochlainn, canon of		
Kilfenora (Florentius)		
Fearghal, dean of Kilfenora	prov. 7 Aug. 1433	*a.* Nov. 1434
Dionysius Ó Connmhaigh,	prov. 17 Nov. 1434	res. 12 Dec.
archdeacon of Kilfenora	cons. 26 Dec. 1434	1491
Muircheartach mac	prov. 12 Dec. 1491	1510
Murchadha Ó Briain,	(bulls expedited 26 Aug.	
canon of Killaloe	1492)	
(Mauricius 'Othesi')		
Mauricius Ó Ceallaigh, O.F.M.	prov. 6 Nov. 1514	*a.* 21 Nov. 1541

[11] This diocese, corresponding to the sub-kingdom of Corco Mruad, was the only one to survive of three set up at the synod of Kells–Mellifont at the expense of Killaloe (see below under Roscrea and Scattery Island).

[12] The existence of this bp is attested only in a forged charter of the fifteenth century.

[13] The suggestion that he may have been a Benedictine monk is based on the occurrence of his name in a seventeenth-century copy of a necrology from the Irish Benedictine Schottenkloster of Würzburg.

DIOCESE OF KILLALOE (*Cell Da Lua; Tuadmuma; Laonensis*)

bishops	accession	death unless otherwise stated
Domnall Ua hÉnna I	—	1 Dec. 1098
Gilla Pátraic Ua hÉnna, abbot of Cork[14]	—	—
Domnall Ua Conaing	—	trs. to Cashel 1131
Domnall Ua Lonngargáin	*c.* 1131	trs. to Cashel 1137/8
Tadg Ua Lonngargáin	*c.* 1138	1161
Donnchad mac Diarmata Ua Briain	*c.* 1161	1164
Constantín mac Toirrdelbaig Ua Briain	*a.* 1179	1194
Diarmait Ua Conaing	1194	1195
Conchobar Ua hÉnna (Cornelius)	*a.* 1201	1216
Domnall Ó hÉnna II, archdeacon of Killaloe (Donatus)	el. 1216 conf. by Honorius III 1219 cons. 1221	*c.* 1225
Robert Travers	el. *a.* 14 Jan. 1217 cons. *p.* 14 Jan. 1217	depr. 1221 (again) May 1226
Domnall Ó Cennéitig, archdeacon of Killaloe (Donatus)	el. *a.* 1231 temp. *p.* 20 Aug. 1231	*a.* 22 Nov. 1252
Ísóc Ó Cormacáin, dean of Killaloe (Isaac)	el. *a.* 5 Apr. 1253 prov. 23 June 1253 cons. 23 June 1253 temp. 1 Oct. 1253	res. *a.* 10 Nov. 1267
Mathgamain Ó hÓcáin, dean of Killaloe (Matthaeus)	el. *a.* 20 Mar. 1268 temp. 26 Mar. 1268	12 Aug. 1281
Mauricius Ó hÓcáin, precentor of Killaloe	el. 23 Nov. 1281 temp. 15 Feb. 1282 lib. 6 July 1282	*a.* Oct. 1298
David Mac Mathgamna, dean of Killaloe	el. 7 Jan. 1299 temp. 22 Apr. 1299 cons. May 1299	9 Feb. 1317
Tomás Ó Cormacáin I, archdeacon of Killaloe	el. *a.* 2 July 1317 temp. 2 July 1317	31 July 1322
Brian Ó Coscraig, dean of Killaloe (Benedictus)	el. *a.* 1 Aug. 1323	*c.* 1325
David Mac Briain, canon of Killaloe ('David of Emly')	el. *a.* May 1326 prov. 25 May 1326 temp. 26 Sept. 1326	12 Dec. 1342

bishops	*accession*	*death unless otherwise stated*
'Unatus O Heime' (?Uaithne Ó hÉnna)	?el. 1326	1334
Tomás Ó hÓgáin, canon of Killaloe	temp. 22 Apr. 1343	30 Oct. 1354
Tomás Ó Cormacáin II, archdeacon of Killaloe	el. *a.* May 1355 prov. 27 May 1355 temp. 12 Aug. 1355	1382
Mathghamhain Mág Raith (Matthaeus)	prov. *a.* Aug. 1389 temp. 1 Sept. 1391	*a.* Feb. 1400
Donatus Mág Raith, can. reg., abbot of Clare Abbey	prov. *a.* 8 Feb. 1400 cons. *a.* 9 Apr. 1400	*p.* Aug. 1421
Robert Mulfield, O.Cist., monk of Meaux (Yorkshire)[15]	prov. 9 Sept. 1409 (did not get possession)	suffr. in Lichfield *c.* 1418-40
Eugenius Ó Faoláin, bp of Kilmacduagh[15]	trs. 6 July 1418	*a.* 24 July 1431
Thaddaeus Mág Raith I, can. reg., abbot of Clare Abbey[16]	prov. 25 Oct. 1423 cons. *p.* 5 Nov. 1423 temp. 1 Sept. 1431	*a.* July 1443
Séamus Ó Lonnghargáin, bp of Annaghdown[16]	trs. 9 Dec. 1429 cons. *c.* Dec. 1429 prov. (again) 24 July 1431	res. *c.* July 1443
Donnchadh mac Toirdhealbhaigh Ó Briain (Donatus)	prov. 26 July 1443 cons. *p.* 12 Aug. 1443	*a.* Aug. 1460
Thaddaeus Mág Raith II, rector of Dromcliffe and Kilmayley	prov. 18 Aug. 1460 cons. 2 Sept. 1460	*a.* May 1463
Matthaeus Ó Gríobhtha, archdeacon of Limerick	prov. 23 May 1463 cons. *p.* 7 July 1463	*c.* Sept. 1483
Toirdhealbhach mac Mathghamhna Ó Briain (Theodoricus; Thaddaeus)	prov. 19 Sept. 1483	1525
Séamus Ó Cuirrín, priest of Meath dioc.	prov. 24 Aug. 1526	res. 5 May 1542 d. *a.* June 1554

[14] Attested only in the genealogies.

[15] Both appointed in the lifetime of Bp Donatus Mág Raith; Eugenius was resident for some years in a portion of the diocese.

[16] Rival bps from 1429 to 1443.

DIOCESE OF LIMERICK (*Luimnech; Limericensis; Lumnicensis*)

bishops	accession	death unless otherwise stated
Gilli alias Gilla Espaic (Gillebertus)	el. *c.* 1106	res. 1140 d. 1145
Patricius	cons. by Abp Theobald of Canterbury 1140 (may not have got possession)	*p.* Dec. 1148
Erolb	—	1151
Torgestius (Torgesli)	*a.* Mar. 1152	1167
Brictius	*fl.* 1167 × 78	*c.* 1186 × 1189
Donnchad Ua Briain (Donatus)	*a.* 1190	*a.* 5 Dec. 1207
Edmund	*a.* July 1215	1222
Hubert de Burgh, can. reg., prior of Athassel	cust. 11 Mar. 1223 el. *a.* 7 May 1224 temp. *c.* 21 Apr. 1225	14 Sept. 1250
Robert of Emly, archdeacon of Limerick	el. *a.* 11 Apr. 1251 temp. 6 Jan. 1252	8 Sept. 1272
Gerald Marshal, archdeacon of Limerick	el. *a.* 11 Jan. 1273 temp. 17 Jan. 1273	10 Feb. 1302
Robert of Dundonald, canon of Limerick	el. *a.* 2 May 1302 temp. 30 July 1302 lib. 23 Sept. 1302	3 May 1311
Eustace de l'Eau (de Aqua)	el. *c.* 20 Nov. 1312 temp. *p.* 1 Dec. 1312	3 May 1336
Maurice Rochfort (de Rupe)	el. *a.* Nov. 1336 temp. 7 Nov. 1336 cons. 6 Apr. 1337	9 June 1353
Stephen Lawless, chancellor of Limerick	prov. 19 Feb. 1354 cons. *a.* 7 Apr. 1354 temp. 29 Apr. 1354 lib. 13 May 1354	28 Dec. 1359
Stephen de Valle (Wall), dean of Limerick	el. *a.* Nov. 1360 prov. 6 Nov. 1360 temp. 2 Mar. 1361	trs. to Meath 19 Feb. 1369
Peter Curragh, canon of Ferns	prov. 19 Feb. 1369 fealty 4 Aug. 1369 temp. 10 Feb. 1370	trs. to Ross *c.* 1399
Bernardus Ó Conchobhair, bp of Ross	trs. *c.* 1399 (did not take effect)	—
Conchobhar Ó Deadhaidh, O.F.M., archdeacon of Killaloe and coarb of Dysert O'Dea (Cornelius O'Dea)	prov. 23 May 1400	res. *a.* Oct. 1426 d. 27 July 1434
John of Mothel, can. reg.	prov. 7 Oct. 1426 temp. 23 Jan. 1427	res. *a.* Apr. 1458 d. 1468

bishops	accession	death unless otherwise stated
Thomas Leger, can. reg., canon of Dunstable	prov. 10 May 1456	depr. 23 Nov. 1456
William Creagh alias Russell, canon of Limerick	prov. 19 Apr. 1458	a. July 1469
Thomas Arthur, treasurer of Limerick	prov. 14 July 1469 cons. 10 Sept. 1469	19 July 1486
Richard Stackpoll	prov. 18 Sept. 1486	a. 20 Nov. 1486
John Dunowe, canon of Exeter	prov. 20 Nov. 1486 (suffr. in Exeter 1489)	a. Apr. 1489
John Folan, rector of Clonmore, Armagh dioc.	prov. 24 Apr. 1489	30 Jan. 1522
Seaán Ó Cuinn, O.P.	prov. 21 Oct. 1524 cons. a. 3 Jan. 1525	res. 9 Apr. 1551 d. 1554/5

DIOCESE OF LISMORE (Liss Mór Mo Chutu; Lismorensis)[17]

bishops	accession	death unless otherwise stated
Niall mac Meic Áedacáin	—	1113
Ua Daigthig	—	1119
Máel Ísu Ua hAinmere, O.S.B. (Malchus)[18]	—	1135
Máel Muire Ua Loingsig	—	?res. c. 1151 d. 1159
Gilla Críst Ua Connairche, O.Cist., abbot of Mellifont (Christianus)	cons. 1151	res. c. 1179 d. 1186
Felix	el. c. 1179	res. 1202
Malachias, O.Cist.	el. c. 1202 cons. a. 5 Nov. 1203	a. 1216
Thomas	el. a. June 1216 cons. a. June 1216	a. Dec. 1218
Robert of Bedford, royal clerk and bp-elect of Glendalough	el. a. 13 Dec. 1218 temp. 13 Dec. 1218 cons. a. 17 Apr. 1219	a. Nov. 1223
Griffin Christopher, chancellor of Lismore	el. a. 6 Nov. 1223 temp. 6 Nov. 1223 (again) 8 July 1225 (again) 11 July 1227 cons. a. 25 Apr. 1228	res. 17 July × 8 Aug. 1246 d. p. 22 Aug. 1252
Ailinn Ó Súillebáin, O.P., bp of Cloyne	trs. p. 26 Oct. 1246 temp. 25 May 1248	a. 27 Apr. 1253
Thomas, treasurer of Lismore	el. a. 25 July 1253 temp. p. 27 July 1253 cons. p. 15 Oct. 1253	a. 2 July 1270

bishops	accession	death unless otherwise stated
John Roche, precentor of Lismore	el. *a.* 20 Aug. 1270 temp. *p.* 20 Aug. 1270	11 June 1279
Richard Corre, chancellor of Lismore	el. 19 July 1279 cons. *p.* 24 Oct. 1279 temp. 18 Nov. 1279	Oct. 1308
William Fleming	el. *p.* 24 Nov. 1308	Nov. 1321
John Leynagh	el. *p.* 13 Dec. 1321 cons. 17 Apr. 1323	Dec. 1354
Thomas le Reve, canon of Lismore[19]	prov. 14 May 1358 temp. 24 Aug. 1358 bp of Lismore and Waterford 16 June 1363	*a.* Sept. 1394

[17] The Hiberno-Norse city of Waterford had already been established as a suffragan see of Canterbury as early as 1096, but the synod of Ráith Bressail in 1111 set up a diocese for the neighbouring kingdom of the Déise, leaving a choice between Waterford and Lismore as the episcopal see. In 1152 the synod of Kells–Mellifont divided this into two separate dioceses; for the claims of Ardmore to represent the Déise, see n. 3 above (p. 293).

[18] Consecrated bp of Waterford in 1096 and elevated to the metropolitan see of Cashel *c.* 1111, Máel Ísu, a leading figure in the church reform, died at Lismore; see n. 1 above (p. 291) and n. 27 below (p. 309).

[19] On 18 Nov. 1356, Edward ordered the temporalities of Lismore, then vacant, to be delivered to Roger Cradock, bp of Waterford, in accordance with the terms of the bull of John XXII (31 July 1327; see above, n. 6 (p. 296)). This was not done, and although Innocent VI confirmed the letter of union in 1355, he provided le Reve to the see of Lismore in 1358. After Cradock's translation from Waterford to Llandaff, Urban V effected the delayed union in 1363.

DIOCESE OF LISMORE AND WATERFORD

bishops	accession	death unless otherwise stated
Thomas le Reve, bp of Lismore	prov. 16 June 1363 temp. 7 Oct. 1363	*a.* Sept. 1394
Robert Read, O.P.	prov. 9 Sept. 1394	trs. to Carlisle 26 Jan. 1396 trs. to Chichester 5 Oct. 1396 d. June 1415
Thomas Sparkford, priest of Exeter dioc.	prov. 27 Jan. 1396	*a.* 11 July 1397
John Deping, O.P.	prov. 11 July 1397 temp. 14 Oct. 1397	4 Feb. 1400
Thomas Snell, archdeacon of Glendalough	prov. 26 May 1400 temp. 16 Nov. 1400	trs. to Ossory 11 Mar. 1407
Roger Appleby, can. reg., bp of Dromore	trs. *a.* Oct. 1407	*a.* Aug. 1409

bishops	accession	death unless otherwise stated
John Geese, O.Carm.	prov. 23 Aug. 1409 depr. by John XXIII Feb. 1414 prov. (again) 4 Dec. 1422 (suffr. in London 1424)	22 Dec. 1425

Thomas Colby, O.Carm., bp
    of Elphin
	trs. by John XXIII
	    Feb. 1414
		a. Dec. 1422

Richard Cantwell, archdeacon of Lismore	prov. 27 Feb. 1426	7 May 1446
Robert Poer, dean and archdeacon of Lismore	prov. 2 Sept. 1446 cons. a. 23 Aug. 1447	c. 1472
Richard Martin, O.F.M.	prov. 9 Mar. 1472	—
John Bulcomb (de Cutwart)	prov. 17 Mar. 1475	res. a. 17 Oct. 1483
Nicol Ó hAonghusa, O.Cist., abbot of Fermoy	prov. 20 May 1480	—
Thomas Purcell	prov. 17 Oct. 1483 cons. p. 6 Nov. 1483	res. 13 Apr. 1519
Nicholas Comyn, bp of Ferns	trs. 13 Apr. 1519	depr. 21 July 1550

DIOCESE OF ROSCREA (Ross Cré; Éile)[20]

bishops	accession	death unless otherwise stated
Ísác Ua Cuanáin	—	1161
?Ua Cerbaill[21]	—	1168

[20] This diocese was established at the synod of Kells-Mellifont at the expense of Killaloe, but did not survive the revival of Dál Cais power under Domnall Mór Ua Briain (kg of Thomond 1168-94).

[21] As this bp bore the name of the ruling family of Éile it seems likely that he was of Roscrea rather than of Ross, as he is styled by A.F.M.

DIOCESE OF ROSS (Ross Ailithir; Corco Loígde; Rossensis)

bishops	accession	death unless otherwise stated
Nechtan Mac Nechtain[22]	—	1160
?Ua Cerbaill*	—	1168
Benedictus	fl. 1173×1177	—
Mauricius	fl. 1192×1195	c. 1195
Daniel	el. c. 1196 cons. a. Jan. 1198	1223
Florentius (?Ua Selbaig)[23]	el. c. 1196 conf. by Innocent III 17 Sept. 1198	?1205

bishops	*accession*	*death unless otherwise stated*
Fíngen Ó Clothna (Florentius)	el. *p.* 7 May 1224	res. *a.* 22 Jan. 1253
Mauricius, precentor of Cloyne	el. *a.* 16 July 1253 cons. *p.* 2 Mar. 1254 temp. *p.* 18 July 1254 lib. 11 Sept. 1254	res. *c.* 25 Apr. 1265
Ualter Ó Mithigéin, O.F.M.	el. *a.* 23 Sept. 1269 temp. *p.* 23 Sept. 1269	*a.* 13 Dec. 1274
Matthaeus	el. *c.* 1269 conf. by Gregory X 28 Dec. 1272 (did not get possession)	—
Petrus Ó hUallacháin, O.Cist. (?Patricius)	el. *a.* 25 Mar. 1275 temp. 25 Mar. 1275 lib. 14 Apr. 1275	21 Sept. 1290
Laurentius, canon of Ross	el. *a.* 12 Jan. 1291 temp. 12 Jan. 1291 lib. 10 Apr. 1291	*a.* 8 Mar. 1310
Matthaeus Ó Finn	el. *p.* 8 Mar. 1310 temp. *p.* 8 Mar. 1310	16 Oct. 1330
Laurentius Ó hUallacháin	el. 30 Apr. 1331 temp. 14 Aug. 1331	1335
Dionysius	el. 1336	1377
Bernardus Ó Conchobhair, O.F.M.	temp. 3 Feb. 1379	trs. to Limerick *c.* 1399
Peter Curragh, bp of Limerick	trs. *c.* 1399 (did not take effect)	—
Thaddaeus Ó Ceallaigh, O.Cist., abbot of Maure (Abbeymahon)	prov. *c.* 1399 (did not take effect)	—
Mac Raith Ó hEidirsgeóil, archdeacon of Ross (Macrobius; Matthaeus)	prov. *a.* 4 Aug. 1401 (annulled 25 June 1403)	1418
Stephen Brown, O.Carm.	prov. 24 Apr. 1399 temp. 6 May 1402 prov. (again) 25 June 1403 (suffr. in St David's 1408; in Wells 1410; in Hereford 1418; in Worcester 1420)	*p.* 1420
Walter Formay, O.F.M.	prov. 14 Nov. 1418	*a.* Sept. 1423
John Bloxworth, O.Carm.	prov. 24 Sept. 1423 (did not take effect)	—
Conchobhar Mac Fhaolchadha, O.F.M. (Cornelius)	prov. 19 Aug. 1426	*a.* Dec. 1448
Maurice Brown	—	*a.* July 1431
Walter of Leicester, O.P.	prov. 13 July 1431	—

bishops	accession	death unless otherwise stated
Richard Clerk, cleric of Meath dioc.	prov. 10 Mar. 1434 (suffr. in London 1434–41; in Canterbury 1439–65; in Salisbury 1454)	p. 1465
Domhnall Ó Donnabháin, cleric of Ross dioc.	prov. 4 Nov. 1448	res. a. 1474 d. a. 1474
Johannes	(suffr. in Bath 1450–60)	a. Mar. 1460
Robert Colynson, priest of York dioc.	prov. 19 Mar. 1460	—
John Hornse	(suffr. in Norwich 1466–9; in Bath 1479–81)	p. 1481
Aodh Ó hEidirsgeóil, canon of Ross (Odo)	prov. 24 Mar. 1474 cons. 11 Apr. 1474	a. Sept. 1494
Tadhg Mac Carthaigh, cleric of Cork dioc. (Thaddaeus)	prov. 29 Mar. 1482 cons. 3 May 1482	depr. 3 Aug. 1483 prov. to Cork and Cloyne 21 Apr. 1490
John Edmund de Courcy, O.F.M., bp of Clogher	trs. 26 Sept. 1494	res. 4 Nov. 1517
Seaán Ó Muirthile, O.Cist., abbot of Maure (Abbeymahon)	prov. 4 Nov. 1517	9 Jan. 1519
Tadhg Ó Raghallaigh, O.S.A., bp of Dromore (Thaddaeus)[24]	prov. 24 Dec. 1519	a. June 1526
Bonaventura	fl. 27 Mar. 1523	—
Diarmaid Mac Carthaigh, O.S.A.	prov. 6 June 1526	1552

* See note 21 on p. 305.

[22] A.F.M. falsely duplicate his obit, along with that of several other ecclesiastics (see below, nn 7, 8 to the province of Dublin (pp 313, 315), and n. 2 to the province of Tuam (p. 320)) s.a. 1085.

[23] For the possible identification of the unsuccessful claimant Florentius with Ua Selbaig see above, n. 4 (p. 293).

[24] Held the two sees of Dromore and Ross 1519–26.

DIOCESE OF SCATTERY ISLAND (Inis Cathaig; Cathagensis; Insulensis)[25]

bishops	accession	death unless otherwise stated
Áed Ua Bécháin (?O.S.B.) (Edanus)[26]	—	1188
Cerball Ua hÉnna	—	c. 1193
Tomás Mac Mathghamhna, O.F.M.	prov. 11 May 1360 cons. p. 11 May 1360	depr. 20 Dec. 1366

bishops	accession	death unless otherwise stated
Richard Belmer, O.P.	prov. 1414 (suffr. in Bath 1414–18; in Exeter 1418–33)	trs. to Achonry 12 Apr. 1424
?Dionysius	—	a. 1447
John Grene, can. reg., prior of Leighs	prov. 30 Mar. 1447 (vicar in Lincoln dioc. 1458; suffr. in York 1452–62; in Canterbury 1465–7)	p. 1467

[25] Established at Kells–Mellifont at the expense of Killaloe, Ardfert, and Limerick, to represent the interests of the Corco Baiscinn in west Clare and the Uí Fidgente of west Limerick, it did not survive the twelfth century (see above, nn 11, 20 (pp 299, 305)). Afterwards its church became collegiate, with traditional rights over certain churches on both banks of the Shannon.

[26] The suggestion that he was a Benedictine is based upon the Würzburg necrology (see above, n. 13 (p. 299)).

DIOCESE OF WATERFORD (Port Láirge; Waterfordensis)

bishops	accession	death unless otherwise stated
Máel Ísu Ua hAinmere, O.S.B., monk of Winchester (Malchus)[27]	cons. 27 Dec. 1096	1135
Toistius	a. Mar. 1152	—
Augustinus Ua Selbaig	el. 6 Oct. 1175	1182
Robert I	fl. 1195 × 1198	a. Oct. 1204
David the Welshman[28]	el. a. 19 Oct. 1204	1209
Robert II	el. p. June 1210	a. Apr. 1223
William Wace, royal clerk	el. a. 5 Apr. 1223 temp. 6 Apr. 1223	a. 19 Apr. 1225
Walter, O.S.B., prior of St John's, Waterford	el. c. 20 Aug. 1227 temp. p. 20 Aug. 1227	1 Aug. 1232
Stephen, O.S.B., prior of St John's, Waterford	el. a. 19 Dec. 1232 temp. p. 19 Dec. 1232	a. Mar. 1250
Henry, archdeacon of Waterford	el. a. 11 Mar. 1250 temp. p. 11 Mar. 1250	a. 20 July 1251
Philip, dean of Waterford	el. a. 26 Mar. 1252 temp. 14 June 1252	a. 15 Apr. 1254
Walter de Southwell, prior of the Hospital of St John's, Dublin	el. a. 2 Apr. 1255 conf. by Alexander IV 2 Apr. 1255	c. 24 Mar. 1271
Stephen de Fulbourn	el. a. 10 June 1274 temp. 28 Oct. 1274 lib. p. 6 Jan. 1275	trs. to Tuam 12 July 1286
Walter de Fulbourn, bp of Meath	trs. 12 July 1286	a. 14 Dec. 1307

bishops	accession	death unless otherwise stated
Matthew	el. 7 Feb. 1308	18 Dec. 1322
Nicholas Welifed	cons. 17 Apr. 1323 temp. 28 July 1323	27 June 1337
Richard Francis	el. *a.* Apr. 1338 temp. 6 Apr. 1338 (suffr. in Exeter 1338)	*c.* 1349
Robert Elyot	el. *c.* 1349 cons. *c.* June 1349	depr. *a.* Mar. 1350 prov. to Killala 8 June 1351
Roger Cradock, O.F.M.	prov. 2 Mar. 1350 temp. 17 Aug. 1350 (again) 10 May 1352	trs. to Llandaff Dec. 1361 d. *a.* 22 June 1382

[27] Abp of Cashel from *c.* 1111 until his resignation at a date unknown, he seems to have resided at Lismore for the most part: see above, nn 1, 18 (pp 291, 304).

[28] Murdered by Ua Fáeláin, kg of the Déise.

PROVINCE OF DUBLIN

DIOCESE OF DUBLIN (*Áth Cliath; Dublinensis*)[1]

bishops	accession	death unless otherwise stated
Dúnán (Donatus)	*c.* 1028	6 May 1074
Gilla Pátraic, O.S.B., monk of Worcester (Patricius)	cons. 1074	10 Oct. 1084
Donngus, O.S.B. (Donatus)	cons. *p.* Aug. 1085	22 Nov. 1095
Samuel Ua hAingliu (?O.S.B.)	cons. 27 Apr. 1096	*a.* Sept. 1121

archbishops

Gréne (Gregorius)[2]	cons. 2 Oct. 1121 abp Mar. 1152	8 Oct. 1161
Lorcán Ua Tuathail, abbot of Glendalough (Laurentius; St Laurence O'Toole)	cons. 1162	14 Nov. 1180
John Cumin, archdeacon of Bath and royal clerk	el. 6 Sept. 1181 temp. 6 Sept. 1181 cons. 21 Mar. 1182	*c.* Nov. 1212
Henry of London, archdeacon of Stafford	el. *a.* Mar. 1213 temp. *a.* Mar. 1213 cons. *c.* Aug. 1213	*a.* Nov. 1228
Luke, royal chaplain and dean of St Martin's, London	el. *a.* 13 Dec. 1228 temp. 22 Jan. 1229 prov. *a.* 11 Oct. 1229 cons. *p.* May 1230	12 Dec. 1255

archbishops	accession	death unless otherwise stated
Fulk de Sandford, treasurer of London	prov. 27 July 1256 temp. *c.* Oct. 1256 cons. *a.* 25 Mar. 1257	4 May 1271
John de Derlington, O.P.	prov. 8 Feb. 1279 temp. 27 Apr. 1279 cons. 27 Aug. 1279	29 Mar. 1284
John de Sandford, dean of St Patrick's	el. *a.* 20 July 1284 conf. 30 May 1285 temp. 6 Aug. 1285 cons. 7 Apr. 1286	2 Oct. 1294
Thomas de Chadworth, dean of St Patrick's	el. *a.* 28 Apr. 1295 (never cons.) el. (again) 14 Feb. 1299	—
William of Hotham, O.P., prior of English province	prov. 24 Apr. 1296 temp. 23 Nov. 1296 lib. 2 Feb. 1297 cons. *c.* Nov. 1297	27 Aug. 1298
Richard de Ferings, canon of Canterbury	prov. *c.* June 1299 cons. *a.* 1 July 1299 temp. 1 June 1300	17 Oct. 1306
Richard de Haverings, precentor of Dublin	el. *a.* 30 Mar. 1307 prov. 10 July 1307 temp. 13 Sept. 1307 (never cons.)	res. 21 Nov. 1310
John Lech, canon of Dunkeld	prov. 16 May 1311 cons. *a.* 18 May 1311 temp. 20 July 1311	10 Aug. 1313
Alexander Bicknor, canon of St Patrick's and treasurer of Ire.	prov. 20 Aug. 1317 cons. 25 Aug. 1317 temp. 9 Sept. 1317	14 July 1349
John of St Paul, canon of St Patrick's	prov. 4 Sept. 1349 temp. 16 Dec. 1349 cons. 14 Feb. 1350	9 Sept. 1362
Thomas Minot, canon of St Patrick's	prov. 20 Mar. 1363 cons. 16 Apr. 1363 temp. 21 Sept. 1363	10 July 1375
Robert Wikeford, archdeacon of Winchester	prov. 12 Oct. 1375 temp. 30 Jan. 1376	29 Aug. 1390
Robert Waldeby, O.S.A., bp of Aire (Gascony)	trs. 14 Nov. 1390 temp. 27 July 1391	trs. to Chichester 25 Oct. 1395 trs. to York 5 Oct. 1396 d. 6 Jan. 1398
Richard Northalis, O.Carm., bp of Ossory	trs. 25 Oct. 1395 temp. 4 Feb. 1396	20 July 1397

archbishops	accession	death unless otherwise stated
Thomas Cranley	prov. a. 26 Sept. 1397 cons. p. 26 Sept. 1397 temp. 21 Dec. 1397	25 May 1417
Richard Talbot, abp-elect of Armagh	el. p. May 1417 prov. 20 Dec. 1417 cons. a. Aug. 1418	15 Aug. 1449
Michael Tregury	prov. a. 24 Oct. 1449 temp. 10 Feb. 1450	21 Dec. 1471
John Walton, can. reg., abbot of Oseney	prov. 4 May 1472 cons. a. 27 Aug. 1472 temp. 15 Aug. 1474 (again) 20 May 1477	res. 14 June 1484
Walter FitzSimons, precentor of St Patrick's	prov. 14 June 1484 cons. 26 Sept. 1484	14 May 1511
William Rokeby, bp of Meath	trs. 28 Jan. 1512 temp. 22 June 1512	29 Nov. 1521
Hugh Inge, O.P., bp of Meath	trs. 27 Feb. 1523	3 Aug. 1528
John Alen	prov. 3 Sept. 1529 cons. 13 Mar. 1530	28 July 1534[3]

[1] The Hiberno-Norse city-state of Dublin became the first of the new regular episcopal sees in Ireland and was subject to Canterbury, although c. 1098 × 1102 Bp Samuel displayed metropolitan pretensions. The diocese of Glendalough, established at the synod of Ráith Bressail in 1111, evidently envisaged the eventual incorporation of Dublin (see above, map 24 and note) under the primacy of Armagh.

[2] Elected by the citizens of Dublin in defiance of Abp Cellach of Armagh, and cons. at Canterbury. The elevation of the see of Dublin to metropolitan rank by the papal legate Cardinal Paparo in 1152 broke the connection with Canterbury.

[3] Murdered during the revolt of Silken Thomas.

DIOCESE OF FERNS (Ferna Mór Máedóc; Uí Chennselaig; Fernensis)

bishops	accession	death unless otherwise stated
Cellach Ua Colmáin	—	1117
?Máel Eóin Ua Dúnacáin[4]	—	1125
Ua Cattáin	—	1135
Joseph Ua hÁeda	fl. 1160 × 1161	1183
Ailbe Ua Máel Muaid, O.Cist., abbot of Baltinglass (Albinus)	c. 1186 (suffr. in Winchester 1201, 1214)	1223
John of St John, treasurer of Ire.	el. a. 6 July 1223 cons. a. 2 Apr. 1224	a. Oct. 1253
Geoffrey of St John, treasurer of Limerick	el. a. 5 Mar. 1254 temp. p. 16 Mar. 1254	c. 21 Apr. 1258

bishops	accession	death unless otherwise stated
Hugh of Lamport, treasurer of Ferns	el. *a*. 11 July 1258 temp. 27 Sept. 1258	15 May 1282
Richard of Northampton, dean of Ferns	el. 28 July 1282 temp. 13 Oct. 1282 cons. 1283	13 Jan. 1304
Simon of Evesham	el. *p*. 12 Mar. 1304 cons. 22 June 1304	1 Sept. 1304
Robert Walrand	el. *p*. 14 Feb. 1305 cons. *p*. 13 Apr. 1305	17 Nov. 1311
Adam of Northampton	el. *a*. 14 Mar. 1312 temp. 14 Mar. 1312 cons. 18 June 1312	29 Oct. 1346
Hugh de Saltu (of Leixlip)	el. *a*. 10 Mar. 1347 cons. 8 Apr. 1347	depr. 1347
Geoffrey Grandfeld, O.S.A., suffr. in Lincoln *c*. 1342	prov. 5 Mar. 1347 cons. June 1347 temp. 15 Nov. 1347	22 Oct. 1348
John Esmond, archdeacon of Ferns	el. 1349 cons. 1349 (did not get possession)	depr. 1349 trs. to Emly 11 Jan. 1353
William Charnells, O.P., apostolic penitentiary	prov. 19 Apr. 1350 cons. 19 Apr. 1350 temp. 15 Oct. 1350	July 1362
Thomas Dene, archdeacon of Ferns	prov. *a*. 15 Apr. 1363 cons. 18 June 1363 temp. 26 May 1363	27 Aug. 1400
Patrick Barrett, can. reg., canon of Kells in Ossory	prov. 10 Dec. 1400 cons. Dec. 1400 temp. 11 Apr. 1401	10 Nov. 1415
Robert Whittey, precentor of Ferns	prov. 16 Feb. 1418	res. 5 Oct. 1457 d. 1458
Tadhg Ó Beirn, O.S.B., prior of Glascarrig (Thaddaeus)	prov. 8 Oct. 1451 (did not take effect)	—
John Purcell I, canon of Ferns and archdeacon of Lismore	prov. 4 Oct. 1457	*a*. Oct. 1479
Laurence Nevill	prov. 26 Oct. 1479 temp. 20 May 1480	1503
Edmund Comerford	cons. 1505	15 Apr. 1509
Nicholas Comyn	prov. 3 Aug. 1509 cons. 20 Jan. 1510	trs. to Lismore and Waterford 13 Apr. 1519
John Purcell II, can. reg., canon of St Catherine's, Waterford	prov. 13 Apr. 1519 cons. 6 May 1519	20 July 1539

[4] Styled *ardepscup Lagen* 'chief bp of Leinster' by *Ann. Inisf.*, and 'bp of Uí Chennselaig' by *A.F.M.*; he died at Leighlin and may have been bp of that see.

DIOCESE OF GLENDALOUGH (*Glenn dá Locha; Bistagnensis; Glendalachensis*)[5]

bishops	accession	death unless otherwise stated
Áed Ua Modáin	—	1126
Anonymous[6]	*a.* 1140	—
Gilla na Náem Laignech[7]	*a.* Mar. 1152	res. *c.* 1157 d. 7 Apr. 1160/61
Cináed Ua Rónáin (Celestinus; Clemens)	*c.* 1157	1173
Máel Callann Ua Cléirchén (Malchus)	*a.* 1176	1186
Macrobius, archdeacon of Dublin	—	*c.* 1192
William Piro	1192	*a.* 30 July 1212
Robert of Bedford, royal clerk	el. *c.* 1213/14 (did not get possession)	el. bp of Lismore *a.* 13 Dec. 1218
Michael	—	*a.* 22 Oct. 1481
Denis White, O.P.	prov. 22 Oct. 1481 (did not get possession)	res. 30 May 1497
Johannes	—	*a.* 10 Nov. 1494
Ivo Ruffi, O.F.M.	prov. 10 Nov. 1494	*a.* 21 Aug. 1500
Francis FitzJohn, O.F.M., of Cordoba	prov. 21 Aug. 1500	—

[5] For the diocese of this name established at Ráith Bressail, see above, n. 1. The diocese established at Kells–Mellifont surrounded Dublin on the south and west and included the Uí Muiredaig territories in south Kildare soon to be settled by Anglo-Normans. As the see remained in Irish territory there was strong pressure to have it absorbed into the diocese of Dublin, which was effectively under royal control, and the union of the two dioceses was confirmed by Innocent III, 25 Feb. 1216, and again by Honorius III, 6 Oct. 1216.

[6] Attested only in the *Vita S. Laurentii*, he died some time before St Laurence O'Toole succeeded to the abbacy of Glendalough in 1153; possibly to be identified with Bp Ua Noídenáin, d. 1148.

[7] His obit is wrongly given in *A.F.M., s.a.* 1085; he died in Würzburg as head of the Schottenkloster there.

DIOCESE OF KILDARE (*Cell Dara; Darensis*)

bishops	accession	death unless otherwise stated
Cormac Ua Cathassaig	—	1146
Ua Duibín	—	1148
Finn mac Máel Muire Mac Cianáin	*a.* Mar. 1152	—
Finn mac Gussáin Ua Gormáin, O.Cist., abbot of Newry[8]	—	1160

bishops	*accession*	*death unless otherwise stated*
Malachias Ua Brain	*c.* 1161	1 Jan. 1175
Nehemias	*a.* Mar. 1177	—
	fl. 1180 × 1190	
Cornelius Mac Fáeláin, archdeacon of Kildare ('Mag Gelain')	1206	*a.* Mar. 1223
Ralph of Bristol, treasurer of St Patrick's, Dublin	el. *a.* 12 Mar. 1223 temp. *p.* 12 Mar. 1223	24 Aug. 1232
John of Taunton, canon of Kildare	el. *a.* 6 Aug. 1233 temp. 11 Nov. 1233	*c.* 22 June 1258
Simon of Kilkenny, canon of Kildare	el. *a.* 21 Oct. 1258 temp. *p.* 21 Oct. 1258 lib. 5 Feb. 1259	20 Apr. 1272
Nicholas Cusack, O.F.M.	prov. 27 Nov. 1279 cons. 15 May × 7 Sept. 1280 temp. 24 Dec. 1280 lib. 18 Feb. 1281	5 Sept. 1299
Walter Calf (le Veel), chancellor of Kildare	el. *a.* Jan. 1300 temp. 5 Jan. 1300	*c.* 29 Nov. 1332
Richard Houlot	el. *a.* May 1333 prov. 24 May 1333 cons. 18 Oct. 1333 temp. 5 Feb. 1334 lib. 26 Apr. 1334	24 June 1352
Thomas Giffard, chancellor of Kildare	el. *p.* June 1352 prov. 21 Nov. 1352 cons. *a.* 31 Dec. 1352	25 Sept. 1365
Robert of Aketon (Acton), O.S.A., bp-elect of Down	el. 18 Nov. 1365 prov. 2 May 1366 temp. 23 Mar. 1367	res. *a.* Apr. 1404
John Maddock, canon of Kildare	prov. 9 Apr. 1404	*a.* July 1431
William fitz Edward, archdeacon of Kildare	prov. 20 July 1431 (again) 14 Aug. 1431	Apr. 1446
Geoffrey Hereford, O.P.	prov. 23 Aug. 1447 cons. 20 Apr. 1449 (suffr. in Hereford 1449)	res. 1454 d. *a.* 1464
John Bole (Bull), can. reg., abbot of St Mary's, Navan	el. *c.* 1456/7 (never cons.)	prov. to Armagh 2 May 1457
Richard Lang	prov. *a.* Aug. 1464 (bulls never expedited) cons. *c.* 1464	depr. 28 July 1474 (suffr. in Chichester 1480; in Winchester 1488)

bishops	accession	death unless otherwise stated
David Conel, archdeacon of Kildare	prov. 28 July 1474 cons. *p.* 6 Sept. 1474	*a.* Apr. 1475
James Wall, O.F.M. (?Edmund)	prov. 5 Apr. 1475 (suffr. in London 1485–91)	28 Apr. 1494
William Barrett (Barnett)	(suffr. in Winchester 1502–25; in York 1530)	res. *a.* 1492
Edward Lane	—	*c.* 1513
Thomas Dillon, can. reg., prior of St Peter's, Drogheda	prov. 24 Aug. 1526	*a.* July 1529
Walter Wellesley, can. reg., prior of Greatconnell	prov. 1 July 1529 temp. 23 Sept. 1531	*a.* 18 Oct. 1539

[8] Died at Killeigh, Co. Offaly; his obit is duplicated in *A.F.M.* at 1085.

DIOCESE OF LEIGHLIN (Lethglenn; Lethglennensis)

bishops	accession	death unless otherwise stated
?Máel Eóin Ua Dúnacáin[9]	—	1125
Sluaigedach Ua Catháin	—	1145
Dúngal Ua Cáellaide	*a.* Mar. 1152	1181
Johannes I	*fl.* 1192	—
Johannes II, O.Cist., abbot of Monasterevin	cons. 18 Sept. 1198	*c.* 1201
Herlewin, O.Cist.	*a.* 1202	*a.* Apr. 1217
Richard Fleming, archdeacon of Leighlin	*c.* 1217	*a.* Nov. 1228
William, archdeacon of Leighlin	el. *a.* Nov. 1228	*a.* 21 Apr. 1252
Thomas, can. reg., prior of Greatconnell	el. *a.* 4 Sept. 1252 prov. 7 Jan. 1253 temp. *p.* 9 Mar. 1253	25 Apr. 1275
Nicholas Chever, archdeacon of Leighlin	el. *a.* Nov. 1275 temp. 7 Mar. 1276 conf. 28 Sept. 1276	20 July 1309
Maurice de Blancheville	el. *a.* 11 Nov. 1309 temp. *p.* 13 Nov. 1309	*a.* Nov. 1320
Meiler le Poer	el. 5 Nov. 1320 cons. 12 Apr. 1321	*a.* Apr. 1349
Radulphus Ó Ceallaigh (?Ó Caollaidhe), O.Carm.	prov. 6 Feb. 1344 cons. Feb. 1344 (did not take effect; suffr. in York 1344)	trs. to Cashel 9 Jan. 1346
William St Leger	el. *a.* 3 Nov. 1348 (did not take effect)	—

bishops	*accession*	*death unless otherwise stated*
Thomas of Brakenberg, O.F.M.	prov. 20 Mar. 1349 cons. 30 Mar. 1349 temp. 15 Aug. 1349	July 1360
Johannes III	prov. 1360	1361
William, archdeacon of Leighlin	prov. 14 Jan. 1362 (never cons.)	1362
John Young, treasurer of Leighlin	prov. 20 Feb. 1363 temp. 21 Sept. 1363	*c.* 12 Feb. 1385
John Griffin	temp. 2 Aug. 1385	trs. to Ossory 2 July 1399
Richard Bocomb, O.P.	prov. 1 Oct. 1400 (suffr. in Exeter and Salisbury)	res. *a.* July 1419
Seaán Ó Maolagáin, rector of Lynn, Meath dioc.	prov. 5 July 1419 temp. 1 Sept. 1422	1431
Thomas Fleming, O.F.M.	prov. 29 Apr. 1432	—
Diarmaid	—	*a.* Feb. 1464
Milo Roche, O.Cist., abbot of Tracton	prov. 3 Feb. 1464	*a.* Apr. 1490
John Caroys, can. reg., canon of All Hallows, Dublin	prov. 10 Oct. 1483	—
Galebrandus de Andree,O.F.M.	prov. 15 Nov. 1484	—
Nicolaus 'Magwyr' (?Mág Uidhir; ?Mág Dhuibhidhir)	prov. 21 Apr. 1490	*c.* 1512
Thomas Halsey, notary apostolic and cleric of Lincoln dioc.[10]	prov. 20 May 1513 (suffr. in York 1519)	*p.* Aug. 1521
Mauricius Ó Deóradháin, O.P.[11]	prov. 19 Jan. 1524	1525
Matthew Sanders, cleric of Leighlin dioc.	prov. 10 Apr. 1527	23/4 Dec. 1549

[9] May have been bp of Ferns: see n. 4 above (p. 312).

[10] An absentee bp, he was also custos of the English hospice in Rome and was described as bp of Elphin by Erasmus in letters written 8 Feb. 1512 and 23 Aug. 1521. The diocese was administered in his absence by the chancellor, Cathaoir Mac Murchadha Caomhánach.

[11] Murdered by the archdeacon, Murchadh Mac Murchadha Caomhánach, son of Cathaoir the chancellor (see above, genealogical table 21).

DIOCESE OF OSSORY (*Osraige; Earipolensis; Ossoriensis*)[12]

bishops	*accession*	*death unless otherwise stated*
Domnall Ua Fócarta alias Ua Fogartaig[13]	*a.* Mar. 1152	1178
Felix Ua Duib Sláine, O.Cist., abbot of Ossory[14]	*a.* 1180	24 Jan. 1202
Hugo de Rous (Rufus), can. reg., canon of Kells in Ossory	*c.* 1202	*a.* Dec. 1218

bishops	accession	death unless otherwise stated
Peter Mauveisin, can. reg., canon of St Patrick's, Dublin	el. *a.* 8 Dec. 1218 cons. *p.* 31 Aug. 1220 temp. *p.* 8 Mar. 1221	*a.* Mar. 1231
William of Kilkenny, chancellor of Kilkenny	el. *p.* 16 Mar. 1231 temp. *p.* 25 June 1231	res. *a.* 8 May 1232
Walter de Brackley, canon of Ossory	el. *a.* 13 June 1232 temp. *p.* 25 Mar. 1233 cons. *a.* 15 July 1233	*a.* 12 Oct. 1243
Geoffrey de Tourville, archdeacon of Dublin, treasurer and chancellor of Ire.	el. *p.* 5 Feb. 1244 temp. *p.* 13 June 1244 lib. 17 Oct. 1244 cons. *a.* 17 Jan. 1245	*a.* 18 Oct. 1250
Hugh de Mapilton, archdeacon of Dublin ('Hugh of Glendalough')	el. *a.* 17 Apr. 1251 temp. 18 May 1251 cons. $\bar{p}$. 20 Aug. 1251	*a.* 4 June 1260
Geoffrey St Leger, treasurer of Ossory	el. *a.* 29 June 1260 temp. 4 July 1260	10 Jan. 1287
Roger of Wexford, dean of Ossory	el. *a.* 22 June 1287 temp. 24 July 1287 cons. 3 Nov. 1287	28 June 1289
Michael d'Exeter, dean of Ossory	el. 28 Sept. 1289 temp. 2 Nov. 1289 lib. 6 Feb. 1290	12 July 1302
William FitzJohn, canon of Ossory	el. 10 Sept. 1302 temp. 24 Oct. 1302 lib. 9 May 1303 cons. *p.* 6 Jan. 1303	trs. to Cashel 26 Mar. 1317
Richard Ledred (Leatherhead), O.F.M.	prov. 24 Apr. 1317 cons. *c.* May 1317 temp. 14 July 1317 lib. 3 Mar. 1318	*c.* 1361
John de Tatenhale, O.P., apostolic penitentiary	prov. 8 Nov. 1361 cons. *a.* 14 Dec. 1361 temp. 12 Feb. 1362	*p.* Mar. 1364
William	*a.* Feb. 1366	—
John of Oxford, O.S.A.	—	*c.* 1370
Alexander Petit (de Balscot), canon of Ossory	el. 19 Dec. 1370 prov. 10 Feb. 1371 temp. 12 May 1371	trs. to Meath 10 Mar. 1386
Richard Northalis, O.Carm.	el. 1386 prov. *a.* 17 Feb. 1387 cons. *a.* 4 Dec. 1387	trs. to Dublin 25 Oct. 1395
Thomas Peverall, O.Carm.	prov. *a.* 3 Nov. 1395 temp. 4 Feb. 1396	trs. to Llandaff 2 July 1398 trs. to Worcester 4 July 1407 d. 1/2 Mar. 1419

bishops	accession	death unless otherwise stated
John Waltham, can. reg.	prov. *a.* 1 Feb. 1398 temp. 20 Mar. 1399	trs. to Dromore 14 May 1400
John Griffin, bp of Leighlin	trs. 2 July 1399 temp. 7 Feb. 1400	*p.* June 1400
Roger Appleby, can. reg., prior of Nuneaton	prov. 26 Sept. 1400 temp. 3 Jan. 1401 lib. 6 Apr. 1401	trs. to Dromore 9/11 Oct. 1402
John Waltham, can. reg., (again) bp of Dromore	trs. 9/11 Oct. 1402	5 Nov. 1405
Thomas Snell, bp of Lismore and Waterford	trs. 11 Mar. 1407	16 Oct. 1417
Patrick Foxe, bp of Cork	trs. 15 Dec. 1417	20 Apr. 1421
Dionysius Ó Deadhaidh, precentor of Limerick	prov. 4 July 1421	*a.* 12 Dec. 1426
Thomas Barry, rector of Theversham, Ely dioc.	prov. 19 Feb. 1427	3 Mar. 1460
David Hacket	prov. 4 July 1460	24 Oct. 1478
Seaán Ó hÉidigheáin	prov. 15 Jan. 1479 cons. 21 Feb. 1479	6 Jan. 1487
Oliver Cantwell, O.P.	prov. 26 Mar. 1487 temp. 28 Feb. 1496	9 Jan. 1527
Milo Baron (FitzGerald), can. reg., prior of Inistiogue	prov. 8 June 1528	1 July × 27 Sept. 1550

[12] Explicitly styled the diocese of Kilkenny (Cell Cainnig) at the synod of Ráith Bressail, its boundaries remained virtually unchanged at Kells–Mellifont. Later claims that the original see was St Cainnech's chief foundation of Aghaboe are baseless.

[13] The first recorded bp, he is said by Keating to have attended the synod of Kells–Mellifont as vic. gen. of an unnamed absent bp; Keating similarly describes Gilla in Choimded Ua hArdmaíl of Emly (see above, n. 8 (p. 298) to province of Cashel), but in both cases the parallel text in B.L., Add. MS 4783 styles them bps in 1152.

[14] Probably abbot of Jerpoint, where he was buried, or of a monastery at Kilkenny which was later refounded at Jerpoint.

PROVINCE OF TUAM

DIOCESE OF TUAM (*Tuaim dá Gualann; Connachta; Tuamensis*)

bishops	accession	death unless otherwise stated
Cathussach Ua Conaill	—	1117
Muiredach Ua Dubthaig (Mauricius)[1]	*a.* 1134	15/16 May 1150

archbishops

Áed Ua hOissín, abbot of Tuam[2]	*a.* Mar. 1152 abp Mar. 1152	1161
Cadla Ua Dubthaig (Catholicus)	*a.* 1167	1201

archbishops	accession	death unless otherwise stated
Felix Ua Ruanada, can. reg., prior of Saul	1202	res. 23 Mar. 1235 d. 1238
?F. (?Ó Conchobair)[3]	cons. 1218/19	p. 23 June 1223
Máel Muire Ó Lachtáin (Marianus), dean of Tuam	el. a. 6 Apr. 1236 temp. p. 6 Apr. 1236 cons. 1236	a. 25 Dec. 1249
Flann Mac Flainn (Florentius), chancellor of Tuam	el. a. 27 May 1250 temp. 25 July 1250 cons. 25 Dec. 1250	a. 29 June 1256
Walter de Salerno, dean of St Paul's, London	prov. 29 May 1257 cons. 2 Sept. 1257 temp. 6 Nov. 1257	a. 22 Apr. 1258
Tommaltach Ó Conchobair (Thomas), bp of Elphin	el. p. 17 July 1258 trs. 23 Mar. 1259 temp. 20 July 1259	16 June 1279
Nicol Mac Flainn	el. a. 20 Oct. 1283 (never cons.)	—
Stephen de Fulbourn, bp of Waterford	trs. 12 July 1286 temp. 15 Sept. 1286	3 July 1288
William de Bermingham, rector of Athenry	el. c. autumn 1288 prov. 2 May 1289 temp. 29 Sept. 1289	Jan. 1312
Máel Sechlainn Mac Áeda (Malachias), bp of Elphin	el. c. Mar. 1312 trs. 19 Dec. 1312 temp. 1 Apr. 1313	10 Aug. 1348
Tomás Mac Cearbhaill, archdeacon of Cashel	prov. 26 Nov. 1348 temp. 6 Oct. 1349	trs. to Cashel a. 8 Mar. 1365
Eóin Ó Gráda, archdeacon of Cashel	prov. p. 20 Nov. 1364 temp. 19 July 1365	19 Sept. 1371
Gregorius Ó Mocháin I, bp of Elphin	trs. 7 May 1372 temp. 24 Nov. 1372	1383
Gregorius Ó Mocháin II	prov. by Clement VII c. 1384	depr. by Urban VI 5 May 1386 d. 1392
Uilliam Ó Cormacáin	prov. by Urban VI 5 May 1386 temp. 15 Mar. 1387	trs. to Clonfert 27 Jan. 1393
Muircheartach mac Pilib Ó Ceallaigh, bp of Clonfert (Mauricius)	el. summer 1392 trs. 26 Jan. 1393	29 Sept. 1407
John Babingle alias Baterley, O.P.	prov. by Gregory XII a. 25 Oct. 1408 prov. by Alexander V 2 Sept. 1409 conf. by John XXIII 25 May 1410	prov. to Achonry 1410

archbishops	accession	death unless otherwise stated
Cornelius, O.F.M.	prov. 7 Oct. 1411 (did not take effect)	—
John de Bermingham (Winfield)	prov. 7 June 1430 cons. *p.* 5 Dec. 1430	1437
Tomás mac Muircheartaigh Ó Ceallaigh, O.P., bp of Clonfert	trs. 15 July 1438 (did not get possession)	1441
John de Burgh, can. reg., abbot of Cong	prov. 9 Oct. 1441 cons. *c.* Nov./Dec. 1441	*a.* Dec. 1450
Donatus Ó Muireadhaigh, can. reg., dean of Tuam	prov. 2 Dec. 1450 cons. *p.* Dec. 1450	17 Jan. 1485
Walter Blake, canon of Tuam and Annaghdown	prov. 8 Aug. 1483 (did not take effect)	prov. to Clonmac- noise 26 Mar. 1487
Uilliam Seóighe (Joyce), priest of Tuam dioc.	prov. 16 May 1485	28 Dec. 1501
Philip Pinson, O.F.M., suffr. in Hereford	prov. 2 Dec. 1503 (did not take effect)	5 Dec. 1503
Muiris Ó Fithcheallaigh, O.F.M. (Maurice O'Fihely, Mauricius de Portu; 'Flos Mundi')	prov. 26 June 1506	25 Mar. 1513
Tomás Ó Maolalaidh, O.F.M., bp of Clonmacnoise	trs. 19 June 1514	28 Apr. 1536

[1] Styled *senóir Érend* 'senior of Ire.' already in 1123 on the inscription on the Cross of Cong, Ua Dubthaig seems to have been claiming metropolitan status as early as 1134, although Tuam's claims were not formally recognised until after his death.

[2] His obit is falsely duplicated by *A.F.M. s.a.* 1085. He had been 'coarb of Iarlaithe', i.e., abbot of Tuam, since at least 1123. The death of a previous coarb, Muirges Ua Nióc, in religious retirement, is recorded in 1128, and he too was probably abbot rather than bp of Tuam.

[3] This abp's consecration is attested in an agreement between him and the convent of Kilcreevanty of 23 June 1223. That he was an Ó Conchobair is suggested by a reference to him in *Chartularies of St Mary's abbey, Dublin, . . . and annals of Ireland, 1162–1370*, ed. J. T. Gilbert (2 vols, 1884–6), *c.* 1230 as uncle of Ruaidrí Ó Conchobair, kinsman of Fedlimid (kg of Connacht, 1230–1, 1233–65). Abp Felix Ua Ruanada had sought refuge in Dublin as early as 1213, and in 1216 had been captured and imprisoned by Máel Ísu Ó Conchobair, coarb of Roscommon.

DIOCESE OF ACHONRY (*Achad Conaire; Luigne; Achadensis*)

bishops	accession	death unless otherwise stated
Máel Ruanaid Ua Ruadáin	*a.* Mar. 1152	1170
Gilla na Náem Ua Ruadáin (Gelasius)	*a.* 1179	?res. *a.* 1208 d. 1214
Clemens Ua Sniadaig	*a.* 1208	1219

bishops	accession	death unless otherwise stated
Connmach Ó Torpaig, O.Cist., abbot of Mellifont (Carus)	el. *a.* 10 Mar. 1220	16 Jan. 1227
Gilla Ísu Ó Cléirig (Gelasius)	—	1230
Tomás Ó Ruadáin	—	1237
Áengus Ó Clúmáin	—	res. *a.* 14 Nov. 1248 d. 1264
Tomás Ó Maicín ('Thomas Enliser')	el. *p.* 14 Feb. 1251 cons. *a.* 20 June 1251 temp. *p.* 20 June 1251	*a.* 1 June 1265
Tomás Ó Miadacháin, archdeacon of Achonry (Dionysius)	el. *a.* 27 Apr. 1266 cons. 19 Dec. 1266	*c.* 27 Nov. 1285
Benedictus Ó Brácáin (Ó Brócáin)	el. *p.* 29 Apr. 1286 temp. 17 Sept. 1286	19 Mar. 1312
David of Kilheny[4]	el. *p.* 1 May 1312 temp. 1 Aug. 1312	1344
Nicol alias Muircheartach Ó hEadhra, O.Cist., monk of Assaroe	prov. 22 Oct. 1348 cons. 22 Oct. 1348 temp. 19 Mar. 1349	1373
William Andrew, O.P.	prov. 17 Oct. 1373 temp. 1 Aug. 1374 (suffr. in Canterbury 1380)	trs. to Meath 1380
Simon, O.Cist.	prov. *a.* 9 July 1385 (suffr. in London 1385; in Winchester 1385-95; in Canterbury 1386; in Lichfield 1387)	*p.* 1395
Donatus Ó hEadhra	—	1396
Johannes	prov. *a.* 13 Sept. 1396	—
Tomás mac Muirgheasa Mac Donnchadha	—	1398
Brian mac Seaáin Ó hEadhra (Bernardus)	prov. *a.* Sept. 1400 cons. *a.* 26 Jan. 1401	1409
Maghnus Ó hEadhra, canon of Achonry (Magonius; 'an t-eapscob ruadh')	prov. 14 Apr. 1410 cons. *a.* 30 June 1410	1435
John Babingle alias Baterley, O.P., abp of Tuam	prov. 1410	res. 1420 (suffr. in Salisbury 1425) d. *a.* June 1430
Richard Belmer, O.P., titular bp of Scattery Island	prov. 12 Apr. 1424 cons. 14 June 1424 (suffr. in Exeter 1418-33; in Worcester and Hereford 1426-33)	*a.* Sept. 1436

bishops	accession	death unless otherwise stated
Tadhg Ó Dálaigh, O.P. (Thaddaeus)	prov. 3 Sept. 1436	a. 15 Oct. 1442
James Blakedon, O.P.	prov. 15 Oct. 1442 (suffr. in Salisbury, Wells, Exeter and Worcester 1442–53)	trs. to Bangor 7 Feb. 1453 d. 24 Oct. 1464
Cornelius Ó Mocháin, O.Cist.	prov. 15 Oct. 1449 conf. 5 Apr. 1452	a. July 1473
Brian Ó hEadhra (Benedictus; Bernardus)	prov. 2 Sept. 1463	a. May 1484
Nicholas Forden	prov. 22 Apr. 1470	—
Robert Wellys, O.F.M.	prov. 14 July 1473 cons. 4 June 1475 (did not get possession)	—
Thomas FitzRichard	—	a. Oct. 1492
Tomás Ó Conghaláin	prov. 10 May 1484	1508
John Bustamente	prov. 23 Sept. 1489 (did not take effect)	—
Thomas Ford (de Rivis), can. reg., canon of St Petroc's, Bodmin	prov. 8 Oct. 1492 (suffr. in Lichfield 1495; in Lincoln 1496–1504)	p. 1504
?Rogerius	—	a. 6 Nov. 1508
?An Cosnamhach	prov. 6 Nov. 1508	a. 22 Aug. 1516
Eugenius Ó Flannagáin, O.P.	prov. 22 Dec. 1508	a. June 1522
?Milorius	prov. 22 Aug. 1516	a. 14 Sept. 1517
?William	prov. 14 Sept. 1517	—
Cormac Ó Snighe (?Ó Sniadhaigh)	prov. 15 June 1522	a. June 1547

[4] Pope John XXII's bull of 31 July 1327 sanctioned the union of the three dioceses of Annaghdown, Kilmacduagh, and Achonry with that of Tuam. The union of Achonry with Tuam should have taken place on the death of Bp David in 1344, but in 1346 the chapter of Achonry, with agreement from the abp and chapter of Tuam, petitioned Clement VI for the dissolution of the union, of which no more is heard.

DIOCESE OF ANNAGHDOWN (Enach Dúin; Enachdunensis)[5]

bishops	accession	death unless otherwise stated
Conn Ua Mellaig (Concors)	a. 17 Sept. 1189	1202
Murchad Ua Flaithbertaig	c. 1202	1241
Tomás Ó Mellaig I, O.Praem., abbot of Cella Parva (Annaghdown)[6]	cons. c. 1242 (suffr. in Lincoln 1246)	?depr. 28 May 1247 d. a. 27 May 1250
Conchobar, canon of Annaghdown (Concors)	el. a. 12 Jan. 1251 temp. p. 8 May 1251	—

bishops	accession	death unless otherwise stated
Thomas[7]	—	a. 12 Sept. 1263
John d'Ufford, archdeacon of Annaghdown	el. a. 14 Mar. 1283 (never cons.)	res. c. 1289 app. archdeacon of Tuam
Gillebertus Ó Tigernaig, O.F.M.	el. c. 1306 conf. by Richard Taaffe, vicar-general of Armagh 1306/7 cons. a. 15 July 1308 temp. 15 July 1308 (suffr. in Winchester 1313; in Worcester 1313–14; in Hereford 1315)	a. 16 Dec. 1323
Jacobus Ó Cethernaig	prov. 16 Dec. 1323	trs. to Connor 7/15 May 1324
Robert Petit, O.F.M., ex-bp of Clonfert	prov. 27 Oct. 1325 temp. p. 22 June 1326 (suffr. in Salisbury 1326)	28 Apr. 1328
Albertus	prov. a. Sept. 1328 temp. 23 Sept. 1328	—
Tomás Ó Mellaig II[8]	el. c. 1328/9 (never cons.)	c. 24 June 1330
Dionysius	el. a. Mar. 1359 (probably never cons.)	—
Johannes	a. 6 July 1393	a. Oct. 1394
Henry Trillow, O.F.M.	prov. 26 Oct. 1394 (suffr. in Exeter, Salisbury, and Winchester 1395–1401)	a. 25 Jan. 1402
John Bryt, O.F.M.	prov. 25 Jan. 1402 (suffr. in Winchester 1402; in Lincoln 1403–4; in York 1417–20)	p. 1420
John Wynn	prov. a. 17 Dec. 1408	—
Henricus (?Matthaeus)	—	a. June 1421
John Boner alias Camere, can. reg., of Winchester dioc.	prov. 9 June 1421 (suffr. in Salisbury and Hereford 1421; in Exeter 1438)	a. 1446
Seaán Mac Brádaigh, O.Carm.	prov. 15 Oct. 1425	—
Séamus Ó Lonnghargáin	prov. 10 Dec. 1428	trs. to Killaloe 9 Dec. 1429
Donatus Ó Madagáin, archdeacon of Annaghdown	prov. 19 Nov. 1431	—
Thomas Salscot	prov. 8 July 1446 (suffr. in Lincoln 1449; in Exeter 1458)	p. 1458

bishops	accession	death unless otherwise stated
Redmund de Bermingham, dean of Tuam (Réamonn mac Uilliaim Mac Feórais)[9]	prov. 18 May 1450 cons. May 1450	1451
Thomas Barrett (Tomás Bairéad)	prov. 17 Apr. 1458 (suffr. in Exeter 1458 and 1468–75; in Wells 1482–5)	p. 1485
François Brunand, O.Carm.	prov. a. 4 Dec. 1494 (suffr. in Geneva)	p. 1504

[5] This diocese was probably created at the provincial synod of Clonfert convened by St Laurence O'Toole as papal legate in 1179 to represent the Ua Flaithbertaig territory of Iarchonnacht.

[6] On 28 May 1247 Pope Innocent IV instructed the abp of Tuam to examine charges that Tomás, alleged to be the son of a bp and a nun, had simoniacally intruded himself into the see.

[7] In the summer of 1253 the see of Annaghdown was united to that of Tuam, and its temporalities assigned to Tuam. Nevertheless, royal licence to elect on the death of a bp 'Thomas' was granted on 12 Sept. 1263, though there is no record of any consequent action.

[8] In spite of his bull of 31 July 1327 (see above, n. 4 (p. 322)), Pope John XXII provided Albertus to the see of Annaghdown in 1328, while the chapter had elected Tomás Ó Mellaig. Abp Máel Sechlainn Mac Áeda of Tuam opposed the election, and Bp Tomás, with the support of Edward III, appealed his case at Avignon, apparently without success. Although the chapter of Annaghdown petitioned for the dissolution of the union to Clement VI in 1350 and to Innocent VI in 1359/60, the abps of Tuam maintained the union. Nevertheless, a full chapter, with dean and archdeacon, remained at Annaghdown, and some schismatic elections (not to mention papal provisions of English absentees) occurred in the 15th century.

[9] In answer to the challenge of this provision Abp Donatus Ó Muireadhaigh described himself on 16 Dec. 1450 as 'elect of Tuam and Annaghdown'.

DIOCESE OF CLONFERT (Cluain Ferta Brénainn; Uí Maine; Cluanfertensis)

bishops	accession	death unless otherwise stated
Muiredach Ua hÉnlainge	—	1117
Gilla Pátraic Ua hAilchinned	—	1149
Petrus Ua Mórda, O.Cist., abbot of Grellach dá Iach[10]	c. 1150	27 Dec. 1171
Máel Ísu Mac in Baird	1172	1173
Celechair Ua hAirmedaig	a. 1179	1186
Muirchertach Ua Máel Uidir, bp of Clonmacnoise[11]	1186	1187
Domnall Ua Finn[12]	—	1195
Muirchertach Ua Carmacáin	—	1203
Máel Brigte Ua hEruráin, Columban monk of Derry	el. 1205	—
Cormac Ó Luimlín (Carus)	a. 1224	c. 19 June 1259
Tomás mac Domnaill Móir Ó Cellaig, dean of Clonfert	el. a. 7 Nov. 1259 temp. 11 Nov. 1259	6 Jan. 1263

bishops	accession	death unless otherwise stated
Giovanni de Alatre, nuncio apostolic (Johannes)	prov. *a.* Sept. 1266 temp. 29 Sept. 1266 cons. 19 Dec. 1266	trs. to Benevento 2 Oct. 1295 trs. to Capua 2 Jan. 1301 d. *a.* June 1304
Robertus, O.S.B., monk of Christchurch, Canterbury	prov. 2 Jan. 1296 cons. *a.* 21 Apr. 1296 temp. 24 Sept. 1296 (suffr. in Canterbury 1296-1307)	*a.* Dec. 1307
Gregorius Ó Brócaig	el. *a.* 22 Mar. 1308 temp. *p.* 22 Mar. 1308	1319
Robert Petit, O.F.M.	el. 10 Feb. 1320 cons. *c.* 1320 (suffr. in Worcester 1322; in Exeter 1324)	depr. *c.* 1323 prov. to Annaghdown 27 Oct. 1325
Seoán Ó Leaáin, canon of Clonfert and archdeacon of Kilmacduagh	el. 10 Nov. 1319 prov. 6 Aug. 1322 cons. 20 Sept. 1322 temp. 29 Dec. 1322	7 Apr. 1336
Tomás mac Gilbert Ó Ceallaigh	*a.* 14 Oct. 1347	1378
Muircheartach mac Pilib Ó Ceallaigh (Mauricius)	prov. *a.* 6 Mar. 1378 cons. 1378	trs. to Tuam 26 Jan. 1393
Uilliam Ó Cormacáin, abp of Tuam	trs. 27 Jan. 1393	depr. 1398
David Corre, O.F.M.	prov. 20 Mar. 1398 (did not take effect)	—
Énrí Ó Connmhaigh	prov. *c.* July 1398	trs. to Kilmac-duagh 11 Mar. 1405
Tomás mac Muircheartaigh Ó Ceallaigh, O.P., bp of Ardfert	trs. 11 Mar. 1405	trs. to Tuam 15 July 1438
Cobhthach Ó Madagáin	el. 1410 (never cons.)	1410
Seaán Ó hEidhin, O.F.M., minister of Irish province	prov. 18 July 1438 (again) 25 Oct. 1441 (suffr. in London, Exeter, and Worcester 1443-59)	1459
John White, O.F.M.	prov. 25 Oct. 1441 (did not get possession)	res. July 1448
Conchobhar Ó Maolalaidh, O.F.M. (Cornelius)	prov. 22 May 1447 (again) 18 July 1448	trs. to Emly 30 Aug. 1448
Cornelius Ó Cuinnlis, O.F.M., bp of Emly	trs. 30 Aug. 1448	res. 1463 d. *p.* 1469

bishops	accession	death unless otherwise stated
Matthaeus Mág Raith, can. reg., abbot of Clare Abbey	prov. 22 June 1463	1507
David de Burgh	prov. 5 July 1508	1509
Dionysius Ó Mórdha, O.P.	prov. 7 Nov. 1509	1534

[10] Grellach dá Iach (location unknown) was the first of three sites inhabited by the Cistercian community which finally settled at Boyle.

[11] Held the two sees of Clonfert and Clonmacnoise 1186-7.

[12] Styled 'coarb of Brénainn' in the *Annals of Loch Cé* and *A.U.* and 'abbot of Clonfert' in *Ann. Inisf.*, he may not have been bp.

DIOCESE OF ELPHIN (*Ail Finn; Airther Connacht; Mag nAí; Na Tuatha; Síl Muiredaig; Elfinensis*)

bishops	accession	death unless otherwise stated
Domnall mac Flannacáin Ua Dubthaig, abbot of Roscommon and bp of Clonmacnoise	?1111	17 Mar. 1136
Flannacán Ua Dubthaig	—	res. *a.* 1152 d. 1168
Máel Ísu Ua Connachtáin	*a.* Mar. 1152	1174
Tommaltach mac Áeda Ua Conchobair (Thomas)	—	trs. to Armagh *a.* Feb. 1180
Floirint Ua Riacáin Uí Máelruanaid, O.Cist., abbot of Boyle	*c.* 1180	1195
Ardgar Ua Conchobair	*a.* 14 Feb. 1206	1215
Dionysius Ó Mórda	*fl.* 1217 × 1221	res. 1229 d. 15 Dec. 1231
Alanus	*c.* 1230 (probably did not get possession)	—
Donnchad mac Fíngein Ó Conchobair (Dionysius; Donatus)	cons. 1231	24 Apr. 1244
Eóin Ó Mugróin, archdeacon of Elphin[13]	el. *p.* 12 June 1244 prov. 18 Aug. 1245 temp. *p.* 4 Sept. 1245 cons. 1245	1246
Tommaltach mac Toirrdelbaig Ó Conchobair (Thomas), dean of Annaghdown	el. *a.* 21 Aug. 1246 cons. 21 Jan. 1247	trs. to Tuam 23 Mar. 1259
Máel Sechlainn mac Taidg Ó Conchobair, archdeacon of Clonmacnoise (Milo)	el. *a.* 30 Jan. 1260 conf. by abp of Armagh *a.* 8 Nov. 1260 temp. 8 Nov. 1260 cons. *c.* Nov. 1260	9 Jan. 1262

bishops	accession	death unless otherwise stated
Tomás mac Fergail Mac Diarmata, O.Cist., abbot of Boyle	el. *a*. 26 Jan. 1260 temp. 10 May 1262	1265
Muiris mac Néill Ó Conchobair, O.P. (Mauricius)	el. *p*. 27 Feb. 1266 temp. *p*. 23 Apr. 1266	*c*. 5 Dec. 1284
Amlaím Ó Tommaltaig	el. and conf. 1285 (never cons.)	1285
Gilla Ísu mac in Liathánaig Ó Conchobair, O.Praem., abbot of Loch Cé (Gelasius)	el. 10 Aug. 1285 temp. 5 Mar. 1286	*a*. Sept. 1296
Máel Sechlainn Mac Briain, O.Cist., abbot of Boyle (Malachias)	el. *a*. 2 Nov. 1296 temp. 7 Sept. 1297	*a*. Mar. 1303
Marianus Ó Donnabair, O.P.	el. Sept./Oct. 1296	1297
Donnchad Ó Flannacáin, O.Cist., abbot of Boyle (Donatus)	el. *a*. 28 June 1303 temp. *p*. 28 June 1303	22 June 1307
Cathal Ó Conchobair, O.Praem., abbot of Loch Cé (Carolus)	el. *p*. 2 Sept. 1307 cons. *c*. Oct. 1307 temp. 12 Mar. 1309	res. 1310 d. 1343
Máel Sechlainn Mac Áeda, canon of Elphin (Malachias)	el. *p*. 2 Sept. 1307 prov. 22 June 1310 cons. 22 June 1310 temp. 7 Dec. 1310	trs. to Tuam 19 Dec. 1312
Lúirint Ó Lachtnáin, canon of Elphin (Laurentius)	prov. 21 Jan. 1313 cons. *p*. 19 Feb. 1313 temp. 22 Sept. 1314	1326
Seoán Ó Fínnachta	el. and cons. 1326 temp. *p*. 31 Dec. 1326	1354
Carolus	el. *c*. 1355	depr. 1357
Gregorius Ó Mocháin, provost of Killala	prov. 27 Feb. 1357	trs. to Tuam 7 May 1372
Thomas Barrett, archdeacon of Annaghdown (Tomás Bairéad)	prov. 16 June 1372 temp. 24 Nov. 1372 depr. by Clement VII 17 Jan. 1383 (without effect)	1404
Seoán Ó Mocháin, ?priest of Achonry dioc.	prov. by Clement VII *p*. 17 Jan. 1383	?trs. to Derry 16 Sept. 1394
Seaán Ó Gráda	prov. *a*. 12 Oct. 1407	1417
Gerald Caneton, O.S.A., bp of Cloyne	trs. *c*. 1405 (did not take effect)	1412
Thomas Colby, O.Carm.	prov. by John XXIII 18 Mar. 1412 (did not take effect)	trs. to Lismore and Waterford Feb. 1414

bishops	accession	death unless otherwise stated
Robert Fosten alias Forster, O.F.M.	prov. 16 Feb. 1418 (suffr. in Durham 1426)	p. 1430
Edmund Barrett (Éamonn 'mac an easbuig' Bairéad)	prov. 1421	1421
Johannes	—	depr. 26 Jan. 1429 d. a. Mar. 1434
Laurentius Ó Beólláin, canon of Elphin	prov. 26 Jan. 1429	a. Dec. 1429
Uilliam Ó hÉidigheáin	prov. 2 Dec. 1429	trs. to Emly 20 Oct. 1449
Conchobhar Ó Maolalaidh, O.F.M., bp of Emly (Cornelius)	trs. 20 Oct. 1449	1468
Nicol Ó Flannagáin, O.P.	prov. 7 June 1458 (again) 10 July 1469	res. Sept. 1494
'Hugo Arward' (?Aodh Mac an Bhaird)	prov. 24 Jan. 1487	?1495
Riocard Mac Briain Ó gCuanach, O.P.	prov. 22 June 1492	p. 1501
Cornelius Ó Flannagáin	a. 1501	—
Georgius de Brana, bp of Dromore	trs. 15 Apr. 1499	18 Aug.× 27 Dec. 1529
Christopher Fisher, custos of the English hospice in Rome	prov. 12 Dec. 1508	—
John Maxey, O.Praem., abbot of Welbeck	prov. 7 Apr. 1525 (suffr. in York 1525)	15 Aug. 1536

[13] There was a disputed election, most of the diocesan clergy electing Tomás Ó Cuinn, O.F.M. (later to be bp of Clonmacnoise; see above, p. 276), and the junior members of the chapter Muiredach Ó Conchobair, coarb of Roscommon.

DIOCESE OF KILLALA (Cell Alaid; Uí Amalgada; Uí Fiachrach Muaide; Aladensis)

bishops	accession	death unless otherwise stated
Ua Máel Fogmair I	—	1137
Ua Máel Fogmair II	—	1151
Ua Máel Fogmair III	a. 1179	—
Domnall Ua Bécda (Donatus)	a. 29 Mar. 1199	1206
?Muiredach Ua Dubthaig[14]	fl. 1208	—
Áengus Ó Máel Fogmair (Elias)	a. 1224	1234

bishops	accession	death unless otherwise stated
Donatus	1235 *fl.* 7 Sept. 1244	—
Seoán Ó Laidig, O.P.	el. *p.* 22 June 1253 cons. 7 Dec. 1253	res. *p.* 21 Feb. 1264 d. 1275
Seoán Ó Máel Fogmair	—	25 Oct. 1280
Donnchad Ó Flaithbertaig, dean of Killala (Donatus)	el. *a.* 16 Apr. 1281 temp. 29 Sept. 1281	*c.* Feb. 1306
John Tankard alias Seoán Ó Laithim, archdeacon of Killala	el. 13 June 1306 temp. *p.* 13 June 1306 cons. *c.* 1307	1343
James de Bermingham, canon of Killala	el. and cons. 1344	*c.* 1346
Uilliam Ó Dubhda, canon of Killala	el. 1344 prov. 26 June 1346 temp. 25 Mar. 1348	1350
Robert Elyot, ex-bp of Waterford	prov. 8 June 1351	depr. by Clement VII *a.* 17 Jan. 1383 d. *a.* Jan. 1390
Brian mac Donnchadha Ó Dubhda	el. 1381	1381
Thomas Lodowys, O.P.	prov. 9 Aug. 1381 (did not take effect)	—
Conchobhar Ó Coineóil, canon of Tuam (Cornelius)	prov. by Clement VII *a.* 19 Feb. 1383	1422/3
Thomas Orwell, O.F.M.	prov. 31 Jan. 1390 (suffr. in Ely and Norwich 1389–1406)	trs. to Dromore *a.* Nov. 1398
Tomás mac Uilliaim Duibh Bairéad (Thomas Barrett; 'an t-easbog Tóimíneach')	prov. *a.* 14 Apr. 1400 temp. 12 Mar. 1401	25 Jan. 1425
Muircheartach Cléireach mac Donnchadha Ó Dubhda	el. *c.* 1403 (never cons.)	1403
Fearghal Ó Martain, O.S.A., papal penitentiary	prov. 26 Sept. 1425 cons. 11 Nov. 1427	30 Jan. 1431/2
Thaddaeus 'Mac Creagh'	prov. *a.* Sept. 1431	—
Brian Ó Coineóil (Bernardus)	prov. 30 Jan. 1432 dep. 1436 rest. 1439	31 May 1461[15]
Maghnus Ó Dubhda, archdeacon of Killala	el. 1436	22 Feb. 1436
Robert Barrett, provost of Killala	prov. 3 July 1447 (did not take effect)	1447
Ruaidhrí Bairéad (Barrett), O.S.A.	prov. 3 Mar. 1452 (did not take effect)	*p.* May 1458

bishops	accession	death unless otherwise stated
Thomas	prov. *a.* 7 Jan. 1453 (did not take effect)	—
Richard Viel, O.Carth., prior of Wittam, Bath dioc.	prov. 17 Oct. 1459 (did not take affect)	—
Richard de Burgh	prov. *a.* 24 May 1460 (did not take effect)	*a.* 24 May 1460
Meiler d'Exeter	prov. *p.* 31 May 1461	*a.* 2 Dec. 1461
Donatus Ó Conchobhair, O.P., friar of Rathfran	prov. 2 Dec. 1461	*p.* Oct. 1467
Tomás Bairéad, can. reg., canon of Crossmolina (Thomas Barrett)	prov. 9 Feb. 1470 (suffr. in Ely 1497)	*p.* 1497
Seaán Ó Caissín, O.F.M. (Johannes de Tuderto)	prov. 18 Jan. 1487	res. 1490
Thomas Clerke, archdeacon of Sodor	prov. 4 May 1500	res. 1505 d. 1508 as vicar of Chedsey in Somerset
Malachias Ó Clúmháin, priest of Clonfert dioc.	prov. 12 Feb. 1506 cons. 3 Sept. 1508	*a.* 1513
Risdeárd Bairéad, canon of Killala (Richard Barrett)	prov. 7 Jan. 1513	*a.* Nov. 1545

[14] He is mentioned in the *Annals of Loch Cé*, 1208, where the context suggests that his see may have been Killala.

[15] Murdered by the son of Maghnus Ó Dubhda.

DIOCESE OF KILMACDUAGH (*Cell Meic Duach; Uí Fiachrach Aidne; Duacensis*)

bishops	accession	death unless otherwise stated
?Ua Cléirig[16]	—	1137
Ímar Ua Ruaidín	—	1176
Mac Gilla Cellaig Ua Ruaidín	*a.* 1179	1204
I. Ua Cellaig	*a.* Feb. 1206	1215
Máel Muire Ó Connmaig	—	1224
Áed, precentor of Kilmacduagh (Odo)	el. *a.* 12 May 1227 temp. *p.* 12 May 1227	—
Conchobar Ó Muiredaig	—	1247
Gilla Cellaig Ó Ruaidín, archdeacon of Kilmacduagh (Gillebertus)	el. *a.* 5 May 1248 temp. *p.* 5 May 1248	*a.* 9 Nov. 1253
Mauricius Ó Leaáin, canon of Kilmacduagh	el. *a.* 15 May 1254 temp. *p.* 15 May 1254	*c.* 10 Nov. 1283

bishops	*accession*	*death unless otherwise stated*
David Ó Sétacháin	el. *p.* 27 Mar. 1284 temp. 18 July 1284	*a.* 13 June 1290
Lúirint Ó Lachtnáin, O.Cist., abbot of Knockmoy (Laurentius)	el. *a.* 10 Aug. 1290 temp. *p.* 10 Aug. 1290	*a.* 1 Mar. 1307
Lucas	el. *c.* 1307	1325
Johannes	el. *a.* May 1326 temp. 14 May 1326	*c.* 1357
Nicol Ó Leaáin, dean of Kilmacduagh[17]	prov. 16 Nov. 1358 cons. 1360 temp. 13 Sept. 1365	*a.* Oct. 1393
Gregorius Ó Leaáin	prov. 13 Oct. 1393 cons. *c.* 1394 conf. 30 Aug. 1396	1397
Énrí Ó Connmhaigh, bp of Clonfert	trs. 11 Mar. 1405	—
Dionysius	—	*a.* May 1410
Eugenius Ó Faoláin, dean of Cloyne	prov. 21 Sept. 1409 (bulls expedited 25 May 1410)	trs. to Killaloe 6 July 1418
Diarmaid Ó Donnchadha	prov. *c.* July 1418 cons. *c.* July 1418	*a.* Oct. 1419
Nicol Ó Duibhghiolla	el. *a.* Oct. 1419 (did not take effect)	—
Seaán Ó Connmhaigh, O.Cist., abbot of Corcomroe	prov. 23 Oct. 1419	*a.* May 1441
Dionysius Ó Donnchadha, dean of Kilmacduagh	prov. 10 May 1441	*a.* Dec. 1478
Cornelius 'O'Mullony' (?Ó Maoldomhnaigh)	prov. 8 Jan. 1479	res. 8 Mar. 1503
Matthaeus Ó Briain, archdeacon of Killaloe	prov. 8 Mar. 1503	*a.* Aug. 1533
Malachias 'O'Mullony' (?Ó Maoldomhnaigh)	prov. 4 Aug. 1533 (did not take effect)	—
Christopher Bodkin	prov. 3 Sept. 1533 cons. 4 Nov. 1533	opp. to Tuam 15 Feb. 1537 d. 1572

[16] His see is not mentioned at his obit in *A.F.M.*, but is suggested by his surname, which is that of one of the ruling families of Uí Fiachrach Aidne.

[17] The union of Kilmacduagh with Tuam in accordance with the bull of John XXII (see above, n. 4 (p. 322)) should have taken effect on the death of Bp Johannes, but the chapter, with the agreement of the abp and chapter of Tuam, petitioned Innocent VI for the dissolution of the union, of which no more is heard.

DIOCESE OF MAYO (*Mag nEó na Saxan; Maionensis*)[18]

bishops	accession	death unless otherwise stated
Gilla Ísu Ua Mailín	*a.* 1172	1184
Céle Ua Dubthaig	—	1210
?Patricius, archdeacon of Mayo[19]	el. *c.* 1210 (never cons.)	res. 1216 d. 1216?
William Prendergast, O.F.M.	prov. 16 July 1428 (did not take effect)	—
Nicolaus 'Wogmay', O.F.M.	prov. 17 July 1430	*p.* Oct. 1436
Martinus Campania, O.Cist., monk of Clarus Campus, in Utrecht dioc.	prov. 29 Apr. 1432 (suffr. in Münster and Utrecht)	res. *a.* 31 Aug. 1439
Aodh Ó hUiginn, can. reg., abbot of Mayo (Odo)	prov. 31 Aug. 1439	depr. *a.* Jan. 1448 d. 1478
Simon de Düren, O.S.A.	prov. 12 Aug. 1457 (suffr. in Münster and Worms 1461)	28 Aug. 1470
John Bell, O.F.M.	prov. 4 Nov. 1493 (suffr. in London 1499; in Salisbury and Exeter 1501; in Canterbury and Lichfield 1503; in Bath and Wells 1519-26; in Lincoln 1507-*c.* 1530)	*c.* 1541

[18] This see was established at the synod of Kells–Mellifont in 1152, but was united to Tuam by the papal legate John of Salerno when he installed Felix Ua Ruanada as abp in 1202. It is probable that Bp Céle Ua Dubthaig was the rival candidate for the archbishopric who was expelled from Tuam by the legate, and that the see of Mayo was being used as a backdoor to ensure succession to the archbishopric by members of the Ua Dubthaig family. The case for the revival of the diocese was raised before Pope Innocent III in 1216 and rejected. In 1217 it was alleged to Honorius III that John of Salerno had been deceived and that the abp of Armagh had since (possibly at the synod of Tuam in 1211) reversed his decision, but the papal legate, James of St Victor, upheld the sentence in 1221, and the union was finally confirmed by Gregory IX on 3 July 1240.

[19] He is called *espuc Cnuic Muaidhe* 'bp of Knockmoy' (a Cistercian monastery in Co. Galway, diocese of Tuam) at his obit in the *Annals of Loch Cé*.

DIOCESE OF ROSCOMMON (*Ross Commáin*): see ELPHIN

ROMAN CATHOLIC BISHOPS
FROM 1534

BENIGNUS MILLETT AND C. J. WOODS

INTRODUCTION

THE following tables are based on those contributed by the late Maureen Wall to *H.B.C.*, pp 383–412. The footnotes in *H.B.C.* formed an integral part of the lists and have consequently been reproduced, with amendments where necessary. Except where otherwise indicated, corrections to the dates given in *H.B.C.* have been made in accordance with the dates and sources cited in the *Hierarchia catholica medii et recentioris aevi* (iv, ed. Patritius Gauchat, Münster, 1935; v–viii, ed. Remigius Ritzler and Pirminus Sefrin, Padua, 1952–79). From 1958 the lists have been compiled from *Acta Apostolicae Sedis*, the official publication of the holy see, and from *Annuario Pontificio*, published annually by the Tipografia Poliglotta, Vatican City. Maureen Wall's introduction, in *H.B.C.*, pp 379–83, to the lists of catholic bishops from 1534, contains much valuable information not reproduced here.

Accurate dating for the period from 4 October 1582 to 14 September 1752, when both the Old and the New Style calendars were in use (see above, viii, 2–3), raises problems because, in many cases, it is difficult to establish which calendar is being used in the source from which a date is drawn. Provisions were made at Rome, and were therefore consistently dated in New Style. Consecrations, however, occasionally took place in Ireland; several bishops, on the other hand, died on the Continent. Our knowledge of them derives from documents which may or may not use the same calendar as that in use where the event took place. Every effort has been made to overcome these fruitful sources of uncertainty. Following the general practice of this history, Old Style dates are shown unaltered (except that the year is taken as beginning on 1 January), while dates of provision, and other dates which in documentary origin are clearly New Style, have been shown in both styles, e.g.

Mateo de Oviedo, O.F.M.	prov. 25 Apr./5 May 1600 cons. *a.* 5 July 1600	[d.] 31 Dec. 1609/ 10 Jan. 1610

Dates of uncertain style are indicated by daggers (†). In a few cases it has been possible to ascertain that New Style was being used by the source, although the exact day cannot be established; in these cases '(N.S.)' has been added after the date. The names of vicars apostolic, temporary adminis-

trators, coadjutors who did not succeed, and bishops whose provision did
not take effect are shown in brackets. Bishops of the reformation period who
were recognised by the crown and consequently appear also in the list of
bishops of the established church (below, pp. 337-91) are marked with an
asterisk. Auxiliary bishops are not included unless they became full bishops.

In curial usage a bishop was provided to a see by the pope in consistory,
and a papal bull of provision was issued to him. From the pontificate of
Gregory XIV (1590-91) there were special norms, somewhat modified by
Urban VIII (1623-44), governing the preliminary investigations. These
norms prescribed a detailed process of inquiry, made through the sacred
congregation of the consistory or through the datary by an examination of
witnesses under oath, concerning the state of a see and the suitability of the
candidate proposed as bishop. In accordance with the norms for nominating
bishops to dioceses outside Italy, the appointments should have been
entrusted to the congregation of the consistory. However, the unsettled
conditions in Ireland during the seventeenth century compelled the holy
see to hold the processes of inquiry, almost without exception, in Rome and
to entrust them to the datary.[1] After these preliminary investigations had
been brought to a successful conclusion, the stages in the provision of a
candidate were as follows: the preconisation of the candidate was made in
secret consistory, usually but not always by a cardinal; the pope, at the
same meeting, provided him to the see; and a papal bull of provision was
issued to the candidate. But the extant registers of the processes of the
consistory and the datary show clearly that they contain inquiries for only
slightly more than half the number of episcopal provisions in Ireland during
the seventeenth century. Circumstances had led the pope or his advisers to
change the procedures; and while the appropriate inquiries were indeed
made, the role played by the datary or the consistory was handed over to the
Sacra Congregatio de Propaganda Fide (Sacred Congregation for the Propa-
gation of the Faith; referred to below as Propaganda), which for more
than 250 years—up to 3 November 1908—had a decisive say in the appointment of bishops to Irish dioceses.

From its establishment in 1622 the new congregation was keenly interested
in the nomination of bishops to sees in Ireland, but for many years it did
not have the appropriate faculties or legal competence to deal directly with
this problem. On 24 January 1623, when one of the cardinals proposed that
new bishops be appointed to vacant sees in Ireland, the congregation decided
that this business and another be dealt with by the holy office.[2] Though the

[1] See the informative introduction by Cathaldus Giblin to his 'The *processus datariae* and the
appointment of Irish bishops in the seventeenth century' in Franciscan Fathers (ed.), *Father Luke
Wadding* (Dublin, 1957), pp 508-19.
[2] Brendan Jennings (ed.), 'Acta Sacrae Congregationis de Propaganda Fide, 1622-1650' in *Archivium
Hibernicum*, xxii (1959), p. 30.

provision of bishops to Irish dioceses came up for discussion at Propaganda during this and the next decade, it is clear from the minutes of the general meetings that during those years the ultimate curial decision, subject to the pope's approval, rested with the holy office.[3] The same minutes reveal that Propaganda was consulted, and expected to be consulted, on this question, and that towards the end of the 1630s Propaganda had begun to assume curial competence for episcopal appointments in Ireland. This had clearly emerged in 1641.[4] The assessor of the holy office reported an order of Innocent X to a general meeting of Propaganda on 22 January 1647 to the effect that ten bishops and one coadjutor bishop were to be provided to Irish dioceses, and that the cardinals of Propaganda were to prepare the processes of inquiry and make the preconisations in secret consistory. The members of the congregation, obviously satisfied that this was a positive attempt by the pope to tidy up the somewhat confused curial practice regarding Irish provisions, gratefully accepted this papal assignment.[5]

The next change in curial practice came during the puritan persecution. In an effort to keep provisions to Irish sees secret, it was decided to issue a papal brief to a bishop-elect, not a papal bull. This was done for the first time in 1657, when Edmund O'Reilly was provided to Armagh and Anthony MacGeoghegan was translated from Clonmacnoise to Meath. From 1657 until well into the nineteenth century, with the exception of the short reign of James II when there was a return to former practice, each candidate provided to an Irish diocese was issued with a papal brief of provision. This more simplified form of papal document could be easily folded and smuggled past the watchful eyes of government officials and spies at the English and Irish ports. Vicars apostolic were always appointed by papal brief.

While Propaganda controlled the appointments of Irish bishops, the stages in a provision, after the preliminary inquiry had been made through papal nuncios, internuncios and others, were as follows: the nomination of the candidate to the appropriate see by Propaganda; the approval given by the pope, i.e. the papal provision; and the issuing of a papal brief of provision. The second stage—the actual papal provision—was the important one. The pope's approval was sometimes given on the same day as the congregation's nomination, but more frequently it was given some days later. The papal brief of provision was usually issued within a few weeks of the provision. It should be noted that when an Irish priest was provided as coadjutor to an Irish bishop his provision as coadjutor, as well as the provision to a titular see, was usually mentioned in the nomination by Propaganda and in the written record of the papal approval. But there are cases where only the provision to the titular see is noted in the written record of the

[3] Ibid., pp 49, 53–4, 67, 70, 76–80, 93–4, 98, 100, 102, 105–6.
[4] Ibid., pp 114–16.
[5] Ibid., pp 128–9.

papal approval, and the provision to the coadjutorship is first officially mentioned in the papal brief of provision.

For seventy-eight years another element entered into the formal preliminary stages and was frequently mentioned both in the official records and in the papal brief providing a candidate to an Irish see. This was the *nominatio regis Angliae*, the formal presentation of a candidate by the Stuart monarch. Pope Innocent XI (1676–89) after some hesitation granted an indult at the request of James II, conferring on him the privilege of nominating candidates for bishoprics in his kingdoms. Because his right was upheld at Rome after he had been deprived of his throne, James continued to exercise it; and similar claims by his son, known as James III or the Old Pretender, were also recognised by the holy see. Between 19 March 1687, when James II exercised the privilege of nominating a candidate for an Irish diocese for the first time, and 21 December 1765, when James III made his last nomination, 129 bishops were appointed to the church in Ireland, of whom five were coadjutors and eighteen were instances of translation from one diocese to another. Of those 129 bishops, all except five were nominated by James II or by his son James III; of those five, two were provided in 1711 and three in 1713. Nomination by the Stuarts ceased with the death of the Old Pretender on 1 January 1766; the holy see neither recognised Prince Charles Edward as king nor granted him any say in the selection of Irish bishops.[6]

Since 1908, when appointments to Irish sees ceased to depend on Propaganda, the two important dates are those of appointment or provision by the pope, and issue of the papal bull. These provisions are still made in consistory; but to a great extent this is now a mere legal fiction, for many of the candidates have already been provided and consecrated by the time the next consistory is held and official mention is made in consistorial acts. The abbreviation 'cons.' for 'consecrated' has been used throughout this list, but the term in present usage is 'episcopal ordination', not 'consecration'.

---

[6] See Cathaldus Giblin, 'The Stuart nomination of Irish bishops, 1687–1765' in *Irish Ecclesiastical Record*, 5th ser., cv (1966), pp 35–47.

PROVINCE OF ARMAGH

DIOCESE OF ARMAGH

archbishops	accession	death unless otherwise stated
George Cromer*	prov. 2 Oct. 1521 cons. Apr. 1522	depr. 23 July 1539[1] d. 16 Mar. 1543
Robert Wauchop[2]	admr 23 July 1539 prov. *a.* 23 Mar. 1545	10 Nov. 1551
George Dowdall, O. Cruc.*[3]	prov. 1 Mar. 1553 temp. 23 Oct. 1553	15 Aug. 1558
Donat O'Teige	prov. 7 Feb. 1560 cons. Feb. 1560	1562
Richard Creagh	prov. 22 Mar. 1564 cons. Easter 1564	14/24 Oct. 1585[4]
Edmund Magauran	trs. from Ardagh prov. 21 June/1 July 1587	23 June/3 July 1593
Peter Lombard	prov. 29 June/9 July 1601 cons. 27 Sept./7 Oct. 1601[5]	26 Aug./5 Sept. 1625
Hugh Mac Caghwell, O.F.M.	prov. 17/27 Apr. 1626 cons. 28 May/7 June 1626	12/22 Sept. 1626
Hugh O'Reilly[6]	trs. from Kilmore prov. 11/21 Aug. 1628	Feb. 1653
Edmund O'Reilly	prov. 6/16 Apr. 1657 cons. 16/26 May 1658	26 Feb./8 Mar. 1669
Oliver Plunkett	prov. 4/14 July 1669 brief 24 July/3 Aug. 1669 cons. 21 Nov./1 Dec. 1669	1/11 July 1681
(Edward Drumgoole, vic. ap.)	brief 9/19 Dec. 1681	
Dominic Maguire, O.P.	prov. 11/21 Dec. 1683 brief 2/12 Jan. 1684	10/21 Sept. 1707
Hugh MacMahon[7]	trs. from Clogher prov. 16/27 June 1715 brief 24 June/5 July 1715	2 Aug. 1737†
Bernard MacMahon	trs. from Clogher prov. (brief) 28 Oct./8 Nov. 1737 again (brief amended) 19/30 Sept. 1738[8]	27 May 1747
Ross MacMahon	trs. from Clogher prov. (brief) 23 July/3 Aug. 1747	29 Oct./9 Nov. 1748
Michael O'Reilly	trs. from Derry prov. (brief) 12/23 Jan. 1749	*a.* 19 Apr. 1758

archbishops	accession	death unless otherwise stated
Anthony Blake	trs. from Ardagh prov. (brief) 21 Apr. 1758	11 Nov. 1787
Richard O'Reilly, bp of Oropi[9]	prov. coadj. with succn 17 Feb. 1782 brief 26 Feb. 1782 succ. 11 Nov. 1787	31 Jan. 1818
Patrick Curtis	prov. 8 Aug. 1819 brief 27 Aug. 1819 cons. 28 Oct. 1819	24 July 1832
Thomas Kelly, bp of Dromore[10]	prov. coadj. with succn 7 Dec. 1828 brief 23 Dec. 1828 succ. 24 July 1832	14 Jan. 1835
William Crolly	trs. from Down and Connor prov. 12 Apr. 1835 brief 8 May 1835	6 Apr. 1849
Paul Cullen	prov. 19 Dec. 1849[11] brief 8 Jan. 1850 cons. 24 Feb. 1850	trs. to Dublin 3 May 1852
Joseph Dixon	prov. 3 Oct. 1852[12] brief 4 Oct. 1852 cons. 21 Nov. 1852	29 Apr. 1866
Michael Kieran	prov. 30 Sept. 1866[13] brief 23 Nov. 1866 cons. 3 Feb. 1867	15 Sept. 1869
Daniel MacGettigan	trs. from Raphoe prov. 6 Mar. 1870[14] brief 11 Mar. 1870	3 Dec. 1887
Michael Logue	trs. from Raphoe prov. coadj. with succn (brief) 19 Apr. 1887 succ. 3 Dec. 1887 cardinal 16 Jan. 1893	19 Nov. 1924
Patrick O'Donnell	trs. from Raphoe prov. coadj. with succn 14 Jan. 1922 succ. 19 Nov. 1924 cardinal 14 Dec. 1925	22 Oct. 1927
Joseph MacRory	trs. from Down and Connor prov. 22 June 1928 cardinal 16 Dec. 1929	13 Oct. 1945
John D'Alton	trs. from Meath prov. 25 Apr. 1946 cardinal 12 Jan. 1953	1 Feb. 1963

archbishops	accession	death unless otherwise stated
William Conway	prov. aux. bp 31 May 1958	17 Apr. 1977
	cons. 27 July 1958	
	prov. 10 Sept. 1963	
	cardinal 22 Feb. 1965	
Tomás Ó Fiaich (Thomas Fee)	prov. 22 Aug. 1977	
	cons. 2 Oct. 1977	
	cardinal 30 June 1979	

[1] Cromer was suspended by Paul III in 1539 on a charge of heresy.

[2] Wauchop was app. to administer the see on the suspension of Cromer, and was cons. after Cromer's death.

[3] Dowdall had been app. by Henry VIII, 28 Nov. 1543, and was cons. soon after that date. He abandoned his see in 1551.

[4] Richard Creagh was committed to the Tower of London in 1567, and d. there as a prisoner.

[5] Peter Lombard never came to Ireland, but remained in Rome. David Rothe, who became bp of Ossory in 1618, administered the see of Armagh as vic. gen. 1609-25. The date of Lombard's consecration is given in Fernandus Combaluzier, 'Sacres épiscopaux à Rome de 1565 à 1662; analyse intégrale du MS "Miscellanea XIII, 33" des Archives Vaticanes' in *Sacris Erudiri*, xviii (1967-8), pp 120-305 (hereafter referred to as Combaluzier), pp 156-7.

[6] Hugh O'Reilly was proposed for the vacant see of Armagh 11/21 Aug. 1628, but the exact date of his provision is not known.

[7] Hugh MacMahon was also admr of Dromore 1731-7.

[8] Bernard MacMahon obtained a second brief of provision, since the first brief did not mention his title as primate of all Ire. He was admr of Dromore 1737-47.

[9] Richard O'Reilly had been prov. coadj. to the bp of Kildare 20 May 1781.

[10] Abp Kelly retained Dromore in administration until the provision of Michael Blake to Dromore in Jan. 1833.

[11] Emmet Larkin, *The making of the Roman Catholic church in Ireland, 1850-1860* (Chapel Hill, N.C., 1980), pp 3-4.

[12] Brady, *Episc. succ.*, i, 232.   [13] Ibid.   [14] Ibid., i, 233.

DIOCESE OF ARDAGH

bishops	accession	death unless otherwise stated
Rory O'Malone*	prov. 14 Dec. 1517	1540
Patrick MacMahon, O.F.M.*	prov. 24 Nov. 1541	c. 1572
Richard Brady, O.F.M.	prov. 23 Jan. 1576	trs. to Kilmore 14 Mar. 1580
Edmund Magauran	prov. 11 Sept. 1581	trs. to Armagh 21 June/1 July 1587
(John Gaffney, vic. ap.)[15]	brief 4/14 Jan. 1622	c. 1637
Patrick Plunkett, O. Cist.[16]	prov. 1/11 Mar. 1647	trs. to Meath 21/31 Jan. 1669
	cons. 19 Mar. 1648	
(Gerald Farrell, vic. ap.)	brief 21/31 July 1669	June 1683
(Gregory Fallon, admr)[17]	prov. (bull) 7/17 May 1688	c. 1698
	brief 21 June/1 July 1697	

bishops	accession	death unless otherwise stated
(Charles Tiernan, vic. ap.)[18]	prov. 25 May/4 June 1696 brief 26 June/6 July 1696	a. May 1699
(Bernard Donogher, vic. ap.)	prov. 21/31 July 1699 brief 10/20 Aug. 1699[19]	
Thomas Flynn	prov. (brief) 21 Sept./2 Oct. 1717 cons. p. 4/15 July 1718	29 Jan. 1730
Peter Mulligan, O.S.A.	prov. (brief) 21 Aug./1 Sept. 1730 again (brief) 28 Apr./9 May 1732	23 July 1739
Thomas O'Beirne	prov. coadj. with succn (brief) 15/26 Aug. 1739 direct prov. (brief) 5/16 Sept. 1739	Feb. 1747
Thomas MacDermot Roe	prov. (brief) 27 Apr./8 May 1747	Feb. 1751
Augustine Cheevers, O.S.A.	prov. (brief) 6/17 July 1751	trs. to Meath 7 Aug. 1756

[15] John Gaffney was vic. gen. of Ardagh in 1597, and was probably still vic. gen. in 1622. There is no record of a vicar 1587–1622.

[16] During the years 1637–47 Cornelius Gaffney is named as vic. gen. of Ardagh, though there is no record of a brief appointing him vic. ap. He remained as vic. gen. of the diocese during the episcopate of Patrick Plunkett, who left Ire. c. 1652 and did not return until 1664.

[17] For Gregory Fallon see under Clonmacnoise, n. 36.

[18] Tiernan was vic. gen. at the time of his appointment, and the see was described as devoid of pastoral care for many years, which suggests that Gregory Fallon was not in fact administering the see of Ardagh 1688–96. The date of Tiernan's death is indicated in Brady, Episc. succ., i, 293.

[19] Donogher continued as vic. ap. until 1709 (Brady, Episc. succ., i, 293).

DIOCESE OF ARDAGH AND CLONMACNOISE

bishops	accession	death unless otherwise stated
Anthony Blake[20]	prov. (brief) 11 Aug. 1756	trs. to Armagh 21 Apr. 1758
James Brady	prov. (brief) 21 Aug. 1758	11 Jan. 1788
John Cruise	prov. 18 May 1788 brief 10 June 1788 cons. 17 Aug. 1788	28 June 1812
James Magauran	prov. 12 Mar. 1815 brief 20 Mar. 1815 cons. Aug. 1815	25 June 1829
William O'Higgins	prov. 20 Sept. 1829 brief 2 Oct. 1829 cons. 30 Nov. 1829	3 Jan. 1853

bishops	accession	death unless otherwise stated
(Peter Dawson)	prov. coadj. with succn 27 June 1852[21]	
John Kilduff	prov. 24 Apr. 1853[22] brief 29 Apr. 1853 cons. 29 June 1853	21 June 1867
Neale MacCabe, C.M.	prov. 24 Nov. 1867[23] brief 17 Dec. 1867 cons. 2 Feb. 1868	22 July 1870
George Michael Conroy	prov. 12 Feb. 1871[24] brief 24 Feb. 1871 cons. 11 Apr. 1871	4 Aug. 1878
Bartholomew Woodlock	prov. (brief) 4 Apr. 1879 cons. 1 June 1879	res. 1894[25] d. 13 Dec. 1902
Joseph Hoare	prov. (brief) 8 Feb. 1895 cons. 19 Mar. 1895	14 Apr. 1927
James Joseph MacNamee	prov. 20 June 1927 cons. 31 July 1927	24 Apr. 1966
Cahal Brendan Daly	prov. 26 May 1967 cons. 16 July 1967	trs. to Down and Connor 24 Aug. 1982

[20] On 30 May 1756 Stephen MacEgan, bp of Meath, who had been administering the see of Clonmacnoise, died. On his death the union of Ardagh and Clonmacnoise, which had been proposed in 1709, was carried into effect, and Anthony Blake was app. as the first bp of the united dioceses.

[21] Larkin, *Making of catholic church in Ire.*, p. 163. The provision did not have effect, no brief being issued. It is not mentioned in *Hierarchia catholica.*

[22] Brady, *Episc. succ.*, i, 295.   [23] Ibid., i, 296.   [24] Ibid.

[25] After his resignation in 1894 Bp Woodlock was given the title *in partibus* of bp of Trapozopolis by brief of 12 Feb. 1895. He returned to All Hallows College, Dublin, where he d. in 1902.

DIOCESE OF CLOGHER

bishops	accession	death unless otherwise stated
Patrick O'Cullen, O.S.A.*	prov. 11 Feb. 1517	a. 26 Mar. 1534
Hugh O'Carolan*[26]	prov. 6 Aug. 1535 cons. Jan. 1537	1569
Raymond MacMahon	prov. 27 Aug. 1546	Feb./Mar. 1560[27]
Cornelius MacArdel	prov. 29 May 1560	c. 1592
Eugene Matthews[28] (Eoghan MacMahon)	prov. 21/31 Aug. 1609	trs. to Dublin 22 Apr./2 May 1611
(Patrick Quinn, vic. ap.)	brief 20/30 July 1622	autumn 1626[29]
(Heber MacMahon, vic. ap.)	brief 7/17 Nov. 1627	prov. to Down and Connor 28 Feb./10 Mar. 1642

bishops	*accession*	*death unless otherwise stated*
Heber MacMahon	trs. from Down and Connor prov. (brief) 17/27 June 1643	17 Sept. 1650
(Philip Crolly, vic. ap.)	brief 5/15 Nov. 1651 (again) 7/17 Apr. 1657	
Patrick Duffy, O.F.M.	prov. 6/16 May 1671 brief 3/13 July 1671 cons. Oct. 1671	Aug. 1675
Patrick Tyrrell, O.F.M.[30]	prov. 12/22 Apr. 1676 brief 3/13 May 1676 cons. *a.* 4/14 June 1676	trs. to Meath 14/24 Jan. 1689
Hugh MacMahon[31]	prov. 10/21 Mar. 1707 brief 20/31 Mar. 1707	trs. to Armagh 24 June/5 July 1715
(Bernard MacMahon, vic. ap.)	16/27 Aug. 1718	
Bernard MacMahon	prov. (brief) 27 Mar./7 Apr. 1727	trs. to Armagh 28 Oct./8 Nov. 1737
Ross MacMahon	prov. (brief) 6/17 May 1738 cons. 27 Aug. 1738	trs. to Armagh 23 July/3 Aug. 1747
Daniel O'Reilly	prov. (brief) 31 Aug./11 Sept. 1747	24 Mar. 1778
Hugh O'Reilly	prov. coadj. with succn 27 Apr. 1777 brief 16 May 1777 succ. 24 Mar. 1778	3 Nov. 1801
James Murphy	prov. coadj. with succn 4 May 1798 brief 8 May 1798 succ. 3 Nov. 1801	19 Nov. 1824
Edward Kernan[32]	prov. coadj. with succn (brief) 6 Feb. 1818 cons. 12 Apr. 1818 succ. 19 Nov. 1824	20 Feb. 1844
Charles MacNally	prov. coadj. with succn 9 July 1843 brief 21 July 1843 cons. 5 Nov. 1843 succ. 20 Feb. 1844	21 Nov. 1864
James Donnelly	prov. 11 Dec. 1864 brief 10 Jan. 1865 cons. 26 Feb. 1865	29 Dec. 1893
Richard Owens	prov. (brief) 6 July 1894 cons. 26 Aug. 1894	3 Mar. 1909
Patrick MacKenna	prov. 12 June 1909 cons. 10 Oct. 1909	7 Feb. 1942

bishops	accession	death unless otherwise stated
Eugene O'Callaghan	prov. 17 Feb. 1943	res. 3 Dec. 1969
	cons. 4 Apr. 1943	d. 21 May 1973
Patrick Mulligan	prov. 3 Dec. 1969	res. 2 Sept. 1979
	cons. 18 Jan. 1970	
Joseph Duffy	prov. 7 July 1979	
	cons. 2 Sept. 1979	

[26] O'Carolan was confirmed in possession by Henry VIII, 8 Oct. 1542, and was not mentioned in the provisions of MacMahon and MacArdel. However, he seems to have retained papal recognition. He is said to have shared the administration of the diocese with MacArdel. For more on these matters, and for the dates of his consecration and death, see W. H. G. Flood, 'New light on Hugh O'Carolan, bishop of Clogher, 1535–69' in *Irish Theological Quarterly*, xiv (1919), pp 9–14.

[27] This date for MacMahon's death is given in Flood, loc. cit., p. 11.

[28] There is no record of a vicar 1592–1609 or 1611–22.

[29] Abp Thomas Fleming of Dublin notified Rome on 29 Apr. 1627 that Quinn had d. 6 months earlier; see *Collectanea Hibernica*, xi (1968), p. 14.

[30] Tyrrell was also vic. ap. of Kilmore from 1678. The date of consecration is given in Tomás Ó Fiaich, 'The appointment of Bishop Tyrrell and its consequences' in *Clogher Record*, i, no. 3 (1955), pp 5, 13.

[31] There is no record of a vicar 1689–1707 or 1715–27. MacMahon was admr of Kilmore from 1711.

[32] According to Brady (*Episc. succ.*, i, 259), Kernan was prov. coadj. by the pope 18 Aug. 1816. But according to *Hierarchia catholica*, vii, 154, he was prov. to the titular see of Thabraca 18 Jan. 1818, and in the brief which followed on 6 Feb. 1818 was app. coadj. to the bp of Clogher.

DIOCESE OF CLONMACNOISE

bishops	accession	death unless otherwise stated
Quintin O'Higgins, O.F.M.*	prov. 10 Nov. 1516	a. 16 June 1539
Richard Hogan, O.F.M.	prov. 16 June 1539[33]	1539
Florence Kirwan, O.F.M.*	prov. 5 Dec. 1539[33]	res. 4 May 1556
Peter Wall, O.P.*	prov. 4 May 1556	1568
Alan Sullivan[34]	prov. 19/29 July 1585	—
(Terence Coghlan, vic. ap.)[35]	brief 23 June/3 July 1630	c. 1639
Anthony MacGeoghegan, O.F.M.	prov. 1/11 Mar. 1647	trs. to Meath
	cons. 2 Apr. 1648	6/16 Apr. 1657
(William O'Sheil, vic. ap.)	brief 30 June/10 July 1657	
(Moriarty Kearney, vic. ap.)	brief 17/27 Oct. 1683	
Gregory Fallon	prov. 7/17 May 1688	c. 1698
	(again) 21 June/1 July 1697[36]	
Stephen MacEgan, O.P.[37]	prov. (brief) 9/20 Sept. 1725	trs. to Meath
	cons. 18/29 Sept. 1725	15/26 Sept. 1729

[33] Both these provisions carried with them the administration of Killaloe. During the lifetime of Florence Kirwan (30 Aug. 1549) Roderick Maclean, a priest of the diocese of Ross in Scotland, obtained a provision to Clonmacnoise, and was transferred to Sodor 5 Mar. 1550. See also below, p. 398, n. 8.

[34] There is no record of a vicar 1568–85; and the date of Alan Sullivan's death is unknown.

[35] The situation before 1630 is uncertain. Abp Hugh O'Reilly reported in Sept. 1631 that Fergal Egan had ruled Clonmacnoise as vic. gen. for 16 years and was now in dispute with Coghlan (Brady, *Episc. succ.*, ii, 361–2).

[36] Gregory Fallon obtained a provision to Clonmacnoise with administration of Ardagh 7/17 May 1688; but this provision does not seem to have had effect. Fallon was still dean of Elphin and more than 80 years old when he obtained his second provision 21 June/1 July 1697.

[37] From *c.* 1698 to 1723 the situation in Clonmacnoise is uncertain. On 28 Sept. 1723 John O'Daly was elected vic. gen. in succession to Thady Coghlan deceased (Brady, *Episc. succ.*, i, 249–50). After MacEgan's translation to Meath in 1729 he continued to administer Clonmacnoise to his death in 1756. The see of Clonmacnoise was then united to Ardagh.

DIOCESE OF DERRY

bishops	*accession*	*death unless otherwise stated*
Rory O'Donnell*	prov. 11 Jan. 1520	8 Oct. 1550/51
Eugene O'Doherty*	prov. 25 June 1554	*c.* 1569
Redmond O'Gallagher	trs. from Killala prov. 22 June 1569	15 Mar. 1601†
(Luke Rochford, vic. ap.)[38]	brief 3/13 Mar. 1622	
(Eugene Sweeney, vic. ap.)	brief 31 Aug./10 Sept. 1626	prov. to Kilmore 8/18 Sept. 1629
(Terence O'Kelly, vic. ap.)	brief 31 Dec. 1628/10 Jan. 1629	depr. 1668
(Eugene Conwell, vic. ap.)	brief 20/30 June 1671	
(Bernard O'Cahan, vic. ap.)	brief Jan. 1684	*c.* 1711
Fergus Laurence Lea[39]	prov. (bull) 29 Jan./8 Feb. 1694	9/19 Jan. 1697
Terence O'Donnelly	prov. (brief) 25 Dec. 1719/5 Jan. 1720 cons. 27 Mar. 1720	
Neil Conway	prov. (brief) 27 Mar./7 Apr. 1727	6 Jan. 1738†
Michael O'Reilly	prov. (brief) 13/24 Apr. 1739	trs. to Armagh 12/23 Jan. 1749
John Brullaghan	prov. (brief) 26 Apr./7 May 1749 (not cons.)[40]	res. 30 May/10 June 1750
Patrick Bradley (Ó Brolcháin), O.P.[41]	prov. (brief) 18/29 Jan. 1751 cons. 3 Mar. 1751	res. *a.* 10/21 Mar. 1752 d. May 1760
John MacColgan	prov. (brief) 23 Apr./4 May 1752	*a.* 21 Dec. 1765
Philip MacDevitt	prov. (brief) 14 Jan. 1766	24 Nov. 1797

bishops	accession	death unless otherwise stated
Charles O'Donnell	prov. coadj. with succn 3 Dec. 1797 brief 9 Feb. 1798	a. 23 Oct. 1823
Peter MacLaughlin, bp of Raphoe	prov. admr 6 Dec. 1818 brief 12 Jan. 1819 res. Raphoe 29 July 1819 prov. bp 4 Apr. 1824 brief 11 May 1824	18 Aug. 1840
John MacLaughlin	prov. coadj. with succn 28 Feb. 1837 cons. 16 July 1837 succ. 18 Aug. 1840	18 June 1864
(Edward Maginn)	prov. coadj. with succn 8 Sept. 1845 brief 30 Sept. 1845 cons. 18 Jan. 1846 (did not succeed)	17 Jan. 1849
Francis Kelly	prov. coadj. with succn (brief) 3 Aug. 1849 cons. 21 Oct. 1849 succ. 18 June 1864	1 Sept. 1889
John Keys O'Doherty	prov. (brief) 28 Dec. 1889 cons. 2 Mar. 1890	25 Feb. 1907
Charles MacHugh	prov. 14 June 1907 cons. 29 Sept. 1907	12 Feb. 1926
Bernard Kane	prov. 21 June 1926 cons. 26 Sept. 1926	5 Jan. 1939
Neil Farren	prov. 5 Aug. 1939 cons. 1 Oct. 1939	res. 13 Apr. 1973[42] d. 7 May 1980
Edward Daly	prov. 31 Jan. 1974 cons. 31 Mar. 1974	

[38] There is no record of a vicar 1601–22.

[39] Bp Lea was app. admr of Raphoe 8/18 Feb. 1695; but it seems probable that he never took possession of his see. He d. in Rome. Bernard O'Cahan remained as vic. ap. of Derry until his death c. 1711.

[40] The Irish bps considered Brullaghan unworthy of the episcopal office because of his irregular life, and would not consecrate him.

[41] Bradley, who was chaplain to the Sardinian ambassador in London, went to his diocese, but found it impossible to carry out his duties satisfactorily. His resignation, dated 31 Dec. 1751, was accepted by the pope a. 10/21 Mar. 1752. See also Brady, *Episc. succ.*, i, 321.

[42] Because delay in the provision of a successor was foreseen, Farren was app. temporary admr of the see.

DIOCESE OF DOWN AND CONNOR

bishops	accession	death unless otherwise stated
Robert Blyth, O.S.B.*	prov. 16 Apr. 1520	depr. 1539[43] d. *p.* 19 Oct. 1547
Tiberius?		
Eugene Magennis*[44]	prov. 16 June 1539	*c.* 1563
Miler Magrath,* O.F.M. Conv.	prov. 12 Oct. 1565 cons. 4 Nov. 1565	depr. 14 Mar. 1580[45] d. 14 Nov. 1622
Donat O'Gallagher, O.F.M.	trs. from Killala prov. 23 Mar. 1580	*c.* 1581
Cornelius O'Devany, O.F.M.	prov. 27 Apr. 1582 cons. 2 Feb. 1583†	1 Feb. 1612
(Patrick Hanratty, vic. ap.)	brief 25 Feb./7 Mar. 1614	prov. to Dromore 3/13 Aug. 1625
Edmund Dungan	prov. 30 May/9 June 1625 cons. July 1626	1629
Bonaventure Hugh Magennis, O.F.M.	prov. 12/22 Apr. 1630 cons. 1630	24 Apr. 1640 (?o.s.)
Heber MacMahon	prov. 28 Feb./10 Mar. 1642	trs. to Clogher 17/27 June 1643
Arthur Magennis, O.Cist.	prov. 1/11 Mar. 1647 cons. 1 May 1648	24 Mar. 1653†
(Nicholas O'Bern, vic. ap.)	brief 7/17 Apr. 1657	
Daniel Mackey	prov. 7/17 Mar. 1671 bull 24 Apr./4 May 1671	24 Dec. 1673†
(Terence O'Donnelly, vic. ap.)[46]	brief 11/22 Aug. 1711	prov. to Derry 25 Dec. 1719/ 5 Jan. 1720
James O'Sheil, O.F.M.	prov. 21 Sept./2 Oct. 1717 cons. 24 Nov./5 Dec. 1717	13 Aug. 1724
John Armstrong	prov. (brief) 27 Mar./7 Apr. 1727	Dec. 1739
Francis Stuart, O.F.M.	prov. (brief) 8/19 Sept. 1740 cons. 24 Nov. 1740	6 June 1750 (?o.s.)
Edmund O'Doran	prov. (brief) 19/30 Jan. 1751	18 June 1760
Theophilus MacCartan	prov. (brief) 10 Sept. 1760	16 Dec. 1778
Hugh MacMullan	prov. 18 July 1779 brief 11 Aug. 1779	8 Oct. 1794
Patrick MacMullan	prov. coadj. with succn 16 June 1793 brief 19 July 1793 cons. 21 Sept. 1793 succ. 8 Oct. 1794	25 Oct. 1824

bishops	accession	death unless otherwise stated
William Crolly	prov. 6 Feb. 1825 brief 22 Feb. 1825 cons. 1 May 1825	trs. to Armagh 8 May 1835
Cornelius Denvir	prov. 6 Sept. 1835 brief 22 Sept. 1835 cons. 22 Nov. 1835	res. 4 May 1865 d. 10 July 1866
Patrick Dorrian	prov. coadj. with succn 10 June 1860[47] brief 22 June 1860 cons. 19 Aug. 1860 succ. 4 May 1865	3 Nov. 1885
Patrick MacAllister	prov. (brief) 26 Feb. 1886 cons. 28 Mar. 1886	26 Mar. 1895
Henry Henry	prov. (brief) 6 Aug. 1895 cons. 22 Sept. 1895	8 Mar. 1908
John Tohill	prov. 5 Aug. 1908 cons. 20 Sept. 1908	4 July 1914
Joseph MacRory	prov. 18 Aug. 1915 cons. 14 Nov. 1915	trs. to Armagh 22 June 1928
Daniel Mageean	prov. 31 May 1929 cons. 25 Aug. 1929	17 Jan. 1962
William Philbin	trs. from Clonfert prov. 5 June 1962	res. 24 Aug. 1982
Cahal Brendan Daly	trs. from Ardagh and Clonmacnoise prov. 24 Aug. 1982 cons. 17 Oct. 1982	

[43] Blyth accepted royal supremacy, and is not mentioned in the provision of his successor.

[44] Magennis accepted royal supremacy in 1541, but remained in possession during Mary's reign. He is mentioned in the provision of his successor.

[45] Magrath accepted royal supremacy in 1567, and was finally depr. by Gregory XIII. Elizabeth app. him abp of Cashel in 1571. The date of his consecration is given in Combaluzier, p. 126.

[46] From 1673 to 1711 the two dioceses of Down and Connor seem to have been ruled mainly by separate vics gen. After the death of Michael O'Beirn (Nicholas O'Bern?), probably c. 1670, Patrick Beirn was vic. gen. of Down 1683, while Patrick O'Mulderig was vic. gen. of Connor 1670 and 1683. Quilan, who d. in 1692, was vic. gen. of Connor, and was succ. by Cormac Shiel 1692–1708. Lea was vic. gen. of Down 1704–8, and vic. gen. of both dioceses 1708–10. James Shiel (James O'Shiel, O.F.M.?) was vic. gen. of both dioceses in 1711. Terence O'Donnelly was app. vic. ap. of Down in Aug. 1711, and vic. ap. of both dioceses 24 Jan./4 Feb. 1714. Cf. Brady, *Episc. succ.*, i, 273.

[47] Brady, *Episc. succ.*, i, 275.

DIOCESE OF DROMORE

bishops	accession	death unless otherwise stated
Quintin Cogly, O.P.	prov. 29 May 1536	c. 1539
Roger MacCiadh[48]	prov. 16 June 1539 (not cons.?)	

bishops	*accession*	*death unless otherwise stated*
Arthur Magennis*	prov. 16 Apr. 1540[49]	*c.* 1575
Patrick MacCual (MacCival)	prov. 23 Jan. 1576	*a.* 1598[50]
(Eugene MacGibbon, vic. ap.)	brief 10/20 Feb. 1598	
(Patrick Hanratty, vic. ap.)[51]	brief 3/13 Aug. 1625	*a.* 29 Oct. 1630
Oliver Darcy, O.P.	prov. 1/11 Mar. 1647	Jan./Feb. 1664[52]
	cons. 7 May 1648	
(Ronan Maginn, vic. ap.)	brief 20/30 June 1671	
Patrick Donnelly[53]	prov. (bull) 12/22 June 1697	1716
(Hugh MacMahon, abp of Armagh)[54]	admr (brief) 4/15 Feb. 1731	2 Aug. 1737†
(Bernard MacMahon, abp of Armagh)	admr (brief) 28 Oct./8 Nov. 1737	
Anthony O'Garvey	prov. (brief) 21 Aug./1 Sept. 1747	
Denis Maguire, O.F.M.	prov. 18 Jan. 1767	trs. to Kilmore 25 Mar. 1770
	brief 10 Feb. 1767	brief 7 Apr. 1770
Patrick Brady, O.F.M.	prov. 25 Mar. 1770	4 July 1780
	brief 10 Apr. 1770	
Matthew Lennan	prov. 3 Dec. 1780	22 Jan. 1801
	brief 20 Dec. 1780	
Edmund Derry	prov. 19 July 1801	29 Oct. 1819
	brief 7 Aug. 1801	
Hugh O'Kelly	prov. 30 Jan. 1820	14 Aug. 1825
	brief 1 Feb. 1820	
	cons. 16 Apr. 1820	
Thomas Kelly	prov. 4 June 1826	succ. to Armagh 24 July 1832[55]
	brief 16 June 1826	
	cons. 27 Aug. 1826	
Michael Blake	prov. 13 Jan. 1833	res. 27 Feb. 1860
	brief 22 Jan. 1833	
	cons. 17 Mar. 1833	d. 6 Mar. 1860
John Pius Leahy, O.P.	prov. coadj. with succn 2 July 1854[56]	6 Sept. 1890
	brief 14 July 1854	
	cons. 1 Oct. 1854	
	succ. 27 Feb. 1860	
Thomas MacGivern	prov. coadj. with succn (brief) 18 Jan. 1887	24 Nov. 1900
	cons. 6 May 1887	
	succ. 6 Sept. 1890	
Henry O'Neill	prov. 10 May 1901	9 Oct. 1915
	brief 20 May 1901	
	cons. 7 July 1901	
Edward Mulhern	prov. 19 Jan. 1916	12 Aug. 1943
	cons. 30 Apr. 1916	

bishops	accession	death unless otherwise stated
Eugene O'Doherty	prov. 11 Mar. 1944 cons. 28 May 1944	res. 22 Nov. 1975 d. 24 Mar. 1979
Francis Gerard Brooks	prov. 22 Nov. 1975 cons. 25 Jan. 1976	

[48] Roger MacCiadh is not mentioned in the provision of his successor.

[49] Arthur Magennis had renounced papal authority *a.* 10 May 1550, but he must have been absolved and recognised by Mary, for he continued to hold the see throughout her reign and is mentioned in the provision of his successor.

[50] Brady, *Episc. succ.*, ii, 338-9.

[51] Hanratty had been vic. ap. of Down and Connor 1614-25. Bp Bonaventure Magennis, in a letter of 29 Oct. 1630, informed Propaganda that Hanratty had d.; see *Collectanea Hibernica*, xii (1969), p. 12.

[52] A letter from Dublin dated 1 Mar. 1664 stated that Bp Darcy of Dromore and Bp MacGeoghegan of Meath had died about a month earlier (Benignus Millett, *The Irish Franciscans, 1651-1665* (Rome, 1964), p. 522).

[53] In the provision of Patrick Donnelly his predecessor is named as Daniel Mackey, who was bp of Down and Connor (1671-3). There is no record of Mackey's provision to the see of Dromore, and he is described as a priest in his provision to Down and Connor in 1671. He may perhaps have administered the see of Dromore for some time before 1671. Patrick Donnelly had been vic. gen. of Armagh for some time before his provision in 1697. The position in Dromore at this time is obscure.

[54] No record exists of a vicar after Bp Donnelly's death in 1716.

[55] Kelly had been app. coadj. to the abp of Armagh 7 Dec. 1828, while retaining the see of Dromore. After succeeding to Armagh he retained the administration of Dromore until the provision of Blake in 1833.   [56] Brady, *Episc. succ.*, i, 305.

DIOCESE OF KILMORE

bishops	accession	death unless otherwise stated
Edmund Nugent, can. reg. of St Aug.*	prov. 22 June 1530	depr. 5 Nov. 1540 d. *c.* 1550
John MacBrady*	prov. 5 Nov. 1540	1559
Hugh O'Sheridan	prov. 7 Feb. 1560	1579
Richard Brady, O.F.M.	trs. from Ardagh prov. 14 Mar. 1580	Sept. 1607
Hugh O'Reilly[57]	prov. 30 May/9 June 1625 cons. July 1626†	trs. to Armagh 11/21 Aug. 1628
Eugene Sweeney	prov. 8/18 Sept. 1629 cons. 1630	*a.* 3 Aug. 1669[58]
(Patrick Tyrrell, bp of Clogher)	app. vic. ap. 30 Jan./9 Feb. 1678 brief 11/21 Mar. 1678	1692
(Hugh MacMahon, bp of Clogher)	admr (brief) 11/22 Aug. 1711	
Michael MacDonagh, O.P.	prov. (brief) 21 Nov./2 Dec. 1728 cons. 1/12 Dec. 1728	15/26 Nov. 1746

bishops	accession	death unless otherwise stated
Laurence Richardson, O.P.	prov. (brief) 26 Jan./6 Feb. 1747 cons. 1 May 1747	29 Jan. 1753
Andrew Campbell	prov. (brief) 3 Apr. 1753	23? Dec. 1769
Denis Maguire, O.F.M.	trs. from Dromore prov. 25 Mar. 1770 brief 7 Apr. 1770	23 Dec. 1798
Charles O'Reilly	prov. coadj. with succn 28 Apr. 1793 brief 17 May 1793 succ. 23 Dec. 1798	6 Mar. 1800
James Dillon	trs. from Nilopolis and coadj. to Raphoe prov. 10 Aug. 1800 brief 30 Aug. 1800	19 Aug. 1806
Fergal O'Reilly	prov. 14 Dec. 1806 brief 16 Jan. 1807 cons. 24 Aug. 1807	30 Apr. 1829
(Patrick Maguire, O.F.M.)	prov. coadj. with succn 6 Dec. 1818 brief 12 Jan. 1819 (did not succeed)	1826
James Browne	prov. coadj. with succn 23 Mar. 1827 cons. 10 June 1827 succ. 30 Apr. 1829	11 Apr. 1865
Nicholas Conaty	prov. coadj. with succn 27 Mar. 1863[59] brief 27 Mar. 1863 cons. 24 May 1863 succ. 11 Apr. 1865	17 Jan. 1886
Bernard Finegan	prov. 10 May 1886 brief 18 May 1886 cons. 13 June 1886	11 Nov. 1887
Edward MacGennis	prov. (brief) 21 Feb. 1888 cons. 15 Apr. 1888	15 May 1906
Andrew Boylan, C.SS.R.	prov. 1 Mar. 1907 cons. 19 May 1907	25 Mar. 1910
Patrick Finegan	prov. 4 July 1910 cons. 11 Sept. 1910	25 Jan. 1937
Patrick Lyons	prov. 6 Aug. 1937 cons. 3 Oct. 1937	27 Apr. 1949
Austin Quinn	prov. 19 July 1950 cons. 10 Sept. 1950	res. 10 Dec. 1972 d. 24 Sept. 1974
Francis McKiernan	prov. 11 Oct. 1972 cons. 10 Dec. 1972	

[57] There is no record of a vicar 1607–25. O'Reilly was cons. at Drogheda by the abp of Dublin at the end of July 1626 (Lynch, *De praesulibus Hib.*, i, 143; *Wadding papers, 1614–38*, ed. Brendan Jennings (I.M.C., Dublin, 1953), p. 144).

[58] For Sweeney's death, see A.P.F., Cong. part., 12, ff 31v, 109. In 1666, 3 years before Sweeney's death, Thomas Fitzsimons was app. vic. gen. of Kilmore by Primate Edmund O'Reilly, but was depr. 1677. From 1678 to 1689 or 1692 the diocese was administered by Patrick Tyrrell, bp of Clogher (and later of Meath). No vic. ap. was app. 1689–1711, and the diocese was ruled by vics gen.: a priest named Brady was vic. gen. 1702; James Brady was vic. gen. 1710; Bernard Brady was app. vic. gen. 19 Aug. 1709 (Brady, *Episc. succ.*, i, 284).

[59] Brady, *Episc. succ.*, i, 287.

DIOCESE OF MEATH

bishops	accession	death unless otherwise stated
Edward Staples*[60]	prov. 3 Sept. 1529	depr. 29 June 1554 d. 1560
William Walsh, O. Cist.*[61]	prov. 18 Oct. 1554	4 Jan. 1577
Thomas Dease[62]	prov. 25 Apr./5 May 1621 cons. 12/22 May 1622	1652
Anthony MacGeoghegan, O.F.M.	trs. from Clonmacnoise prov. 6/16 Apr. 1657	Jan./Feb. 1664[63]
(Edmund MacTeige, vic. ap.)	brief 14/24 Nov. 1665	
Patrick Plunkett, O. Cist.	trs. from Ardagh prov. 21/31 Jan. 1669 brief 26 Feb./8 Mar. 1669	18 Nov. 1679
James Cusack	prov. coadj. with succn 16/26 Aug. 1678 brief 25 Sept./5 Oct. 1678 succ. 18 Nov. 1679	1688
Patrick Tyrrell, O.F.M.	trs. from Clogher prov. 14/24 Jan. 1689	1692
(James Fagan)	prov. 10/21 Mar. 1707 brief 1/12 Aug. 1707 (provision not accepted)	
Luke Fagan[64]	prov. 11/22 Aug. 1713 brief 4/15 Sept. 1713 cons. 7/18 Feb. 1714	trs. to Dublin 13/24 Sept. 1729
Stephen MacEgan, O.P.	trs. from Clonmacnoise (brief) 15/26 Sept. 1729	30 May 1756
Augustine Cheevers, O.S.A.	trs. from Ardagh (brief) 7 Aug. 1756	18 Aug. 1778
(Eugene Geoghegan)	prov. coadj. with succn 3 Feb. 1771 brief 8 Mar. 1771 (did not succeed)	26 May 1778[65]
Patrick Joseph Plunkett	prov. 6 Dec. 1778 brief 19 Dec. 1778 cons. 28 Feb. 1779[66]	11 Jan. 1827

bishops	accession	death unless otherwise stated
Robert Logan	prov. coadj. with succn 24 Aug. 1824 cons. 28 Oct. 1824 succ. 11 Jan. 1827	22 Apr. 1830
John Cantwell	prov. 4 July 1830 brief 20 July 1830 cons. 21 Sept. 1830	11 Dec. 1866
Thomas Nulty	prov. coadj. with succn 28 Aug. 1864[67] brief 2 Sept. 1864 cons. 23 Oct. 1864 succ. 11 Dec. 1866	24 Dec. 1898
Matthew Gaffney	prov. (brief) 28 Apr. 1899 cons. 25 June 1899	res. 1906 d. 15 Dec. 1909
Laurence Gaughran	prov. 19 May 1906 cons. 24 June 1906	14 June 1928
Thomas Mulvany	prov. 12 Apr. 1929 cons. 30 June 1929	16 June 1943
John D'Alton	prov. coadj. with succn 7 Apr. 1942 cons. 29 June 1942 succ. 16 June 1943	trs. to Armagh 25 Apr. 1946
John Kyne	prov. 17 May 1946 cons. 29 June 1946	23 Dec. 1966
John McCormack	prov. 29 Jan. 1968 cons. 10 Mar. 1968	

[60] Staples accepted royal supremacy, but no action was taken against him by Paul III (1534–49). He was not depr. till 1554.

[61] Walsh was app. by Cardinal Pole as papal legate in 1554. He was depr. of the temporalities of his see in 1560. His appointment by Cardinal Pole was confirmed in consistory 6 Sept. 1564.

[62] There is no record of any vicar 1577–91. Cornelius Stanley was app. vic. gen. of Meath and Dublin 15 May 1591. No record survives 1591–1621.

[63] See note on Bp Darcy of Dromore, above, p. 349, n. 52. MacGeoghegan did not resign his see in 1661, as Gauchat erroneously states in *Hierarchia catholica*, iv, 236.

[64] There is no record of a vicar 1692–1713.

[65] Anthony Cogan, *The ecclesiastical history of the diocese of Meath* (3 vols, Dublin, 1862–70), ii, 176.

[66] Ibid., iii, 11.

[67] Brady, *Episc. succ.*, i, 243–4.

DIOCESE OF RAPHOE

bishops	accession	death unless otherwise stated
Cornelius O'Cahan*[66]	prov. 6 Feb. 1514	depr. 1534? d. *p.* 1550
Edmund O'Gallagher	prov. 11 May 1534	26 Feb. 1543
Art O'Gallagher*	prov. 28 Nov. 1547	13 Aug. 1561

bishops	accession	death unless otherwise stated
Donald MacGongail	prov. 28 Jan. 1562	29 Sept. 1589
Nial O'Boyle	prov. 30 July/9 Aug. 1591	6 Feb. 1611
(John O'Cullenan, vic. ap.)[67]	brief 21 Nov./1 Dec. 1621	
John O'Cullenan[68]	prov. 30 May/9 June 1625 cons. 1629	1657/8
(Hugh O'Gallagher, vic. ap.)	brief 30 June/10 July 1657	
(Fergus Laurence Lea, bp of Derry)[69]	admr 8/18 Feb. 1695	9/19 Jan. 1697
James Gallagher[70]	prov. (brief) 10/21 July 1725 cons. 14/25 Nov. 1725	trs. to Kildare 7/18 May 1737
Bonaventure O'Gallagher, O.F.M.	prov. (brief) 29 Nov./10 Dec. 1737 cons. 18/29 Dec. 1737	1749
Anthony O'Donnell, O.F.M.	prov. (brief) 8/19 Jan. 1750	20 Apr. 1755
Nathaniel O'Donnell	prov. (brief) 18 July 1755	1758
Philip O'Reilly	prov. (brief) 9 Jan. 1759 cons. 22 Apr. 1759	1782
Anthony Coyle	prov. coadj. with succn 27 Apr. 1777 brief 16 May 1777 cons. 14 Sept. 1777 succ. 1782	22 Jan. 1801
(James Dillon)	prov. coadj. with succn 29 Nov. 1795 brief 19 Jan. 1796 (did not succeed)	trs. to Kilmore 10 Aug. 1800
John McElvoy	prov. coadj. with succn (brief) 30 Jan. 1801 (not cons.)	20 Sept. 1801
Peter MacLaughlin	prov. 25 Apr. 1802 brief 14 May 1802 cons. 24 Aug. 1802[71]	res. 29 July 1819
Patrick MacGettigan	prov. 25 June 1820 brief 11 July 1820 cons. 17 Sept. 1820	1 May 1861
Daniel MacGettigan	prov. coadj. with succn 3 Feb. 1856[72] brief 29 Feb. 1856 cons. 18 May 1856 succ. 1 May 1861	trs. to Armagh 6 Mar. 1870
James MacDevitt	prov. 12 Feb. 1871[73] brief 24 Feb. 1871 cons. 30 Apr. 1871	5 Jan. 1879
Michael Logue	prov. (brief) 13 May 1879 cons. 20 July 1879	trs. to Armagh as coadj. 19 Apr. 1887

bishops	accession	death unless otherwise stated
Patrick O'Donnell	prov. (brief) 21 Feb. 1888 cons. 3 Apr. 1888	trs. to Armagh as coadj. 14 Jan. 1922
William McNeely	prov. 21 Apr. 1923 cons. 22 July 1923	11 Dec. 1963
Anthony Columba MacFeely	prov. 14 May 1965 cons. 27 June 1965	res. 16 Feb. 1982
Seamus Hegarty	prov. 16 Feb. 1982 cons. 28 Mar. 1982	

[66] O'Cahan accepted royal supremacy, and is not mentioned in the provision of his successor.

[67] There is no record of a vicar 1611–21.

[68] Bp O'Cullenan left the country in Mar. 1653, and Hugh O'Gallagher was app. vic. ap. of Raphoe within his lifetime. According to P. F. Moran, *Spicilegium Ossoriense* (Dublin, 1874–84), i, 212, O'Cullenan d. at Brussels 24 Mar. 1661 (N.S.?), but in A.P.F. Atti 27 (1658), ff 186v–187r, no. 17 *bis* of general meeting of 1 July 1658, it is stated that the bp of Raphoe is dead.

[69] No record survives for 1657–95.

[70] There is no record of a vicar 1697–1725.

[71] *Irish Catholic Directory*, 1841, p. 258, quoting obituary in *Londonderry Journal*, n.d. But Brady (*Episc. succ.*, i, 313) gives the date of consecration as 6 Dec. 1802. Bp Maclaughlin was app. admr of Derry 6 Dec. 1818; he was prov. bp of Derry 4 Apr. 1824.

[72] Brady, *Episc. succ.*, i, 314.

[73] Ibid.

PROVINCE OF CASHEL

DIOCESE OF CASHEL

archbishops	accession	death unless otherwise stated
Edmund Butler, O.S.Trin*[1]	prov. 21 Oct. 1524 cons. *p.* 3 Jan. 1525	5 Mar. 1551
(Roland Baron Fitzgerald)*	nom. by Mary 14 Oct. 1553[2] cons. Dec. 1553	28 Oct. 1561
Maurice MacGibbon, O. Cist.[3]	prov. 4 June 1567 cons. 15 June 1567[4]	1578
Dermot O'Hurley	prov. 11 Sept. 1581	20 June 1584
(Maurice MacBrien, bp of Emly)	admr 1584?	
David Kearney[5]	prov. 11/21 May 1603 cons. 21/31 Aug. 1603	4/14 Aug. 1624
Thomas Walsh	prov. 17/27 Apr. 1626 cons. 28 June/8 July 1626	24 Apr./4 May 1654
(John Burke, vic. ap.)	nom. 5/15 Mar. 1657 brief 7/17 Apr. 1657	*a.* 4/14 June 1670[6]
(Gerard Fitzgerald, vic. ap.)	nom. Sept. 1665 (N.S.) brief 14/24 Nov. 1665	withdrawn ?1665

archbishops	accession	death unless otherwise stated
William Burgat	prov. 21/31 Jan. 1669 brief 26 Feb./8 Mar. 1669 cons. *c*. Aug. 1669	27 Apr. 1675†[7]
John Brenan	trs. from Waterford and Lismore[8] prov. 19/29 Jan. 1677 brief 26 Feb./8 Mar. 1677	1693
Edward Comerford[9]	prov. 4/14 Nov. 1695 cons. 28 June 1697	21 Feb. 1710
Christopher Butler[10]	prov. (brief) 9/20 Aug. 1711 cons. 7/18 Oct. 1712	4 Sept. 1757
James Butler I	prov. coadj. with succn 5/16 Jan. 1750 cons. May 1750 succ. 4 Sept. 1757	17 May 1774
James Butler II	prov. coadj. with succn 14 Feb. 1773 brief 15 Mar. 1773 cons. 4 July 1773 succ. 17 May 1774	29 July 1791
(Gerard Teaghan)	trs. from Ardfert prov. 4 Dec. 1791 brief 13 Jan. 1792 (provision not accepted)	
Thomas Bray	prov. 17 June 1792 brief 20 July 1792 cons. 14 Oct. 1792	15 Dec. 1820
Patrick Everard	prov. coadj. with succn (brief) 4 Oct. 1814 cons. 23 Apr. 1815[11] succ. 15 Dec. 1820	31 Mar. 1821
Robert Laffan	prov. 23 Feb. 1823 brief 18 Mar. 1823 cons. 6 July 1823	3 July 1833
Michael Slattery	prov. 5 Dec. 1833 brief 10 Dec. 1833 cons. 24 Feb. 1834	4 Feb. 1857
Patrick Leahy	prov. 3 May 1857[12] brief 15 May 1857 cons. 29 June 1857	26 Jan. 1875
Thomas William Croke[13]	trs. from Auckland prov. 24 June 1875 brief 25 June 1875	22 July 1902
Thomas Fennelly	prov. coadj. with succn 22 Apr. 1901 cons. 9 June 1901 succ. 22 July 1902	res. 6 May 1913 d. 24 Dec. 1927

archbishops	accession	death unless otherwise stated
John Harty	prov. 4 Dec. 1913 cons. 18 Jan. 1914	11 Sept. 1946
Jeremiah Kinane	trs. from Waterford and Lismore prov. coadj. with succn 4 Feb. 1942 succ. 11 Sept. 1946	18 Feb. 1959
Thomas Morris	prov. 24 Dec. 1959 cons. 28 Feb. 1960	

[1] Butler accepted royal supremacy, and is not mentioned in the provision of Maurice MacGibbon.

[2] Fitzgerald was app. by Mary and cons. in 1553, but does not seem to have been confirmed by Julius III. He is not mentioned in the provision of MacGibbon.

[3] Bp Tanner of Cork and Cloyne was given faculties as admr of Cashel in the absence of the abp 10 Apr. 1575 (Brady, *Episc. succ.*, ii, 86–7).

[4] Combaluzier, p. 130.

[5] There is no record of vicars 1584–1603.

[6] John Burke was vic. ap. of Killaloe *c.* 1666–9. His death was reported by the internuncio in Brussels in a letter of 4/14 June 1670; see *Collectanea Hibernica*, xvii (1974–5), p. 22.

[7] For the date of Burgat's consecration, see Brady, *Episc. succ.*, ii, 25–6; for the date of his death, see A.P.F., Atti 45 (1675), ff 176v–177r.

[8] Brenan continued to hold Waterford and Lismore in administration 1677–93.

[9] Comerford was admr of Emly and of Kilfenora 1705–10.

[10] Butler was admr of Ross 1711–30; Emly was united to Cashel May 1718.

[11] John Healy, *Maynooth College* (Dublin, 1895), pp. 698–9; L. F. Renehan, *Collections on Irish church history* (2 vols, Dublin, 1873), ii, 145–6.

[12] Brady, *Episc. succ.*, ii, 31.

[13] Croke had been cons. bp of Auckland in New Zealand 10 July 1870, and had given his resignation in a letter dated 25 June 1874; but his resignation was not accepted prior to his appointment to Cashel (Mark Tierney, *Croke of Cashel* (Dublin, 1976), pp 67–74; *Hierarchia catholica*, viii, 130, 188).

DIOCESE OF ARDFERT[14] (KERRY)

bishops	accession	death unless otherwise stated
James Fitzmaurice, O. Cist.*	prov. 15 May 1536	1583
Michael Fitzwalter	prov. 30 July/9 Aug. 1591	*c.* 1600
(Eugene Egan, vic. ap.)	brief 21 Nov./1 Dec. 1601	
(Richard O'Connell, vic. ap.)	brief 1611 (N.S.)	
Richard O'Connell	prov. 6/16 Sept. 1641 cons. 10 June 1643	13 July 1653 (N.S.?)[15]
(Moriarty O'Brien, vic. ap.)	brief 7/17 Apr. 1657	
(Aeneas O'Leyne, vic. ap.)	brief 1/12 Mar. 1700	
Denis Moriarty	prov. (brief) 25 Feb./7 Mar. 1720	Feb. 1739
Eugene O'Sullivan	prov. (brief) 13/24 Apr. 1739	*a.* 8/19 Sept. 1743
William O'Meara	prov. 21 Sept./2 Oct. 1743	trs. to Killaloe 23 Feb. 1753

bishops	accession	death unless otherwise stated
Nicholas Madgett	prov. (brief) 23 Feb. 1753[16]	Aug. 1774
Francis Moylan	prov. 16 Apr. 1775	trs. to Cork
	brief 8 May 1775	19 June 1787
Gerard Teaghan	prov. 3 June 1787	4 July 1797
	brief 19 June 1787	
Charles Sughrue	prov. 3 Dec. 1797	29 Sept. 1824
	brief 9 Feb. 1798	
	cons. 11 June 1798	
Cornelius Egan	prov. coadj. with succn 14 May 1824	22 July 1856
	cons. 25 July 1824	
	succ. 29 Sept. 1824	
David Moriarty	prov. coadj. with succn 5 Feb. 1854[17]	1 Oct. 1877
	brief 8 Mar. 1854	
	cons. 25 Apr. 1854	
	succ. 22 July 1856	
Daniel McCarthy	prov. 7 June 1878	23 July 1881
	brief 21 June 1878	
	cons. 25 Aug. 1878	
Andrew Higgins	prov. (brief) 23 Dec. 1881	1 May 1889
	cons. 5 Feb. 1882	
John Coffey	prov. (brief) 27 Aug. 1889	14 Apr. 1904
	cons. 10 Nov. 1889	
John Mangan	prov. 8 July 1904	1 July 1917
	cons. 18 Sept. 1904	
Charles O'Sullivan	prov. 10 Nov. 1917	29 Jan. 1927
	cons. 27 Jan. 1918	
Michael O'Brien	prov. 9 May 1927	4 Oct. 1952
	cons. 24 July 1927	
Denis Moynihan	trs. from Ross	res. 17 July
	prov. 10 Feb. 1953	1969
		d. 5 Dec. 1975
Eamonn Casey	prov. 17 July 1969	trs. to Galway
	cons. 9 Nov. 1969	21 July 1976
Kevin MacNamara	prov. 22 Aug. 1976	
	cons. 7 Nov. 1976	

[14] The title 'Ardfert and Aghadoe' has been in common use since the sixteenth century, but is erroneous. There was a medieval archdeaconry of Aghadoe; but there never was a diocese of Aghadoe. See, however, above, p. 293, n. 2.

[15] Lynch, *De praesulibus Hib.*, ii, 201

[16] Nicholas Madgett was prov. to Killaloe on 11 Dec. 1752. But the pope cancelled and annulled the letters of provision and declared them absolutely void (A.V., S. Br. 3270, f. 11).

[17] Brady, *Episc. succ.*, ii, 63.

DIOCESE OF CORK AND CLOYNE

bishops	accession	death unless otherwise stated
John Bennett*	prov. 28 Jan. 1523	1536
(Louis MacNamara, O.F.M.)	prov. 24 Sept. 1540 (not cons.)	Sept. 1540
John O'Heyne[18]	prov. 5 Nov. 1540	a. 1556
Dominic Tirrey*	(app. by Henry VIII in 1536) recognised and prov. 27 Nov. 1556	Aug. 1557
Nicholas Landes[19]	prov. 27 Feb. 1568	c. 1574
Edmund Tanner	prov. 5 Nov. 1574 cons. a. June 1575	4 June 1579
Dermot McGrath	prov. 12 Oct. 1580	p. 1603[20]
(James Miagh, vic. ap.)	brief 24 Aug./3 Sept. 1614	
(Robert Miagh, vic. ap.)	brief 3/13 July 1621	
William Tirry	prov. 14/24 Jan. 1622 cons. 25 Mar./4 Apr. 1623	18 Mar. 1646 (?o.s.)
Robert Barry	prov. 29 Mar./8 Apr. 1647 cons. 25 Mar. 1648	26 June/6 July 1662
Peter Creagh[21]	prov. 12/22 Apr. 1676 brief 3/13 May 1676	trs. to Dublin 27 Feb./9 Mar. 1693
John Baptist Sleyne[22]	prov. (brief) 3/13 Apr. 1693 cons. 8/18 Apr. 1693	res. 11/22 Jan. 1712 d. 5/16 Feb. 1712
Donagh MacCarthy	prov. 5/16 June 1712 brief 5/16 June 1712 second brief 15/26 July 1712 cons. 16/27 Aug. 1713	Mar. 1726
Thaddeus MacCarthy[23]	prov. (brief) 27 Mar./7 Apr. 1727	14 Aug. 1747†

(The separation of Cork from Cloyne was approved by Benedict XIV on 29 Nov./ 10 Dec. 1747)

[18] John O'Heyne was admr of Elphin, 1545–c. 1553/4.

[19] After the death of Tirrey in 1557, Mary ordered the temporalities of Cork and Cloyne to be granted to Roger Skiddy 18 Sept. 1557. Skiddy was cons. *papali ritu* 30 Oct. 1562, but was not recognised in Rome as a catholic bp, is not mentioned in the provision of Nicholas Landes, and resigned his bishopric in 1567.

[20] The date of McGrath's death is not known; he was stated in 1623 to have lived for some years under James I (Brady, *Episc. succ.*, ii, 89–90).

[21] There is no record of a vicar 1662–76.

[22] Sleyne was admr of Ross 1693–1712.

[23] Thaddeus MacCarthy was admr of Ross 1733–47.

DIOCESE OF CORK

bishops	accession	death unless otherwise stated
Richard Walsh[24]	prov. 29 Nov./10 Dec. 1747 brief 30 Dec. 1747/10 Jan. 1748	7 Jan. 1763
John Butler (succ. as Lord Dunboyne c. 24 Dec. 1785[25])	prov. (brief) 16 Apr. 1763 cons. June 1763	res. 3 June 1787 d. 7 May 1800
Francis Moylan	trs. from Ardfert prov. 3 June 1787 brief 19 June 1787	10 Feb. 1815[26]
(Florence MacCarthy)	prov. coadj. with succn 1 Mar. 1803 brief 6 Mar. 1803 (did not succeed)	1810
John Murphy[27]	prov. coadj. with succn 25 Jan. 1815 succ. 10 Feb. 1815 brief 21 Feb. 1815 cons. 23 Apr. 1815	1 Apr. 1847
William Delany	prov. 14 June 1847[28] brief 9 July 1847 cons. 15 Aug. 1847	14 Nov. 1886
Thomas Alphonsus O'Callaghan, O.P.	prov. coadj. with succn (brief) 13 June 1884 cons. 29 June 1884 succ. 14 Nov. 1886	14 June 1916
Daniel Cohalan	prov. aux. bp 25 May 1914 cons. 7 June 1914 prov. bp 29 Aug. 1916	24 Aug. 1952
Cornelius Lucey	prov. coadj. with succn 14 Nov. 1950 cons. 14 Jan. 1951 succ. 24 Aug. 1952	res. 23 Aug. 1980 d. 24 Sept. 1982
Michael Murphy	prov. coadj. with succn 1 Apr. 1976 cons. 23 May 1976 succ. 23 Aug. 1980	

[24] The separation of Cork from Cloyne was approved 29 Nov./10 Dec. 1747, and Walsh was then prov. to the see of Cork (Brady, *Episc. succ.*, ii, 95).

[25] *Dublin Evening Post*, 29 Dec. 1785.

[26] *Cork Advertiser*, 11 Feb. 1815.

[27] Murphy was prov. bp of Jonopolis and coadj. with right of succn to Cork, by papal brief dated 21 Feb. The decree of Propaganda was dated 21 Jan. and approved by the pope on 25 Jan.

[28] Brady, *Episc. succ.*, ii, 98.

DIOCESE OF CLOYNE AND ROSS[29]

bishops	accession	death unless otherwise stated
John O'Brien	prov. 29 Nov./10 Dec. 1747 brief 30 Dec. 1747/10 Jan. 1748	13 Mar. 1769[30]
Matthew MacKenna	prov. 16 July 1769[31] brief 7 Aug. 1769	4 June 1791
(Simon Quin)	prov. coadj. with succn 18 July 1779 brief 17 Aug. 1779 (did not succeed)	a. 3 Dec. 1787
William Coppinger	prov. coadj. with succn 9 Dec. 1787 brief 15 Jan. 1788 succ. 4 June 1791	9 Aug. 1831[32]
Michael Collins	prov. coadj. with succn (brief) 24 Apr. 1827 succ. 9 Aug. 1831	8 Dec. 1832[33]
Bartholomew Crotty	prov. 10 Mar. 1833 brief 22 Mar. 1833 cons. 11 June 1833	3 Oct. 1846
David Walsh	prov. 31 Jan. 1847[34] brief 12 Mar. 1847 cons. 2 May 1847	19 Jan. 1849
Timothy Murphy[35]	prov. (brief) 3 Aug. 1849 cons. 16 Sept. 1849	4 Dec. 1856

(The separation of Ross from Cloyne was authorised by papal brief, 17 Dec. 1850)

[29] The union of Ross with Cloyne was approved on the same day (29 Nov./10 Dec. 1747) as the separation of Cloyne from Cork.
[30] The date of O'Brien's death is given in T.C.D. MS H.1.18, f.3. This MS contains Irish texts gathered together by Bp O'Brien.
[31] Brady erroneously gives the date of provision as 1767.
[32] *Limerick Chronicle*, 13 Aug. 1831.
[33] *Cork Mercantile Chronicle*, 12 Dec. 1832.   [34] Brady, *Episc. succ.*, ii, 102.
[35] Bp Murphy retained Cloyne after the separation of Ross from Cloyne.

DIOCESE OF CLOYNE

bishops	accession	death unless otherwise stated
William Keane	trs. from Ross prov. 3 May 1857[36] brief 15 May 1857	15 Jan. 1874
John MacCarthy	prov. (brief) 1 Sept. 1874 cons. 28 Oct. 1874	9 Dec. 1893

bishops	accession	death unless otherwise stated
Robert Browne	prov. (brief) 26 June 1894 cons. 19 Aug. 1894	23 Mar. 1935
James Roche	trs. from Ross prov. coadj. with succn 26 June 1931 succ. 23 Mar. 1935	31 Aug. 1956
John Ahern	prov. 30 Mar. 1957 cons. 9 June 1957	

[36] Brady, *Episc. succ.*, ii, 103.

DIOCESE OF EMLY

bishops	accession	death unless otherwise stated
Thomas O'Hurley*	prov. 6 Oct. 1505 cons. *c.* 1507	1542
Raymund Burke, O.F.M.*	prov. 20 Oct. 1550	29 July 1562
Maurice MacBrien	prov. 24 Jan. 1567 cons. 7 Oct. 1571	1586[37]
Maurice O'Hurley	prov. 5/15 June 1620 cons. 7 Sept. 1623	Sept. 1646[38]
Terence Albert O'Brien, O.P.	prov. coadj. with succn 1/11 Mar. 1647 cons. 2 Apr. 1648	31 Oct. 1651
(Dermot O'Brien, vic. ap.)	nom. 20/30 July 1652	
(William Burgat, vic. ap.)	brief 7/17 Apr. 1657[39]	prov. to Cashel 21/31 Jan. 1669
(James Stritch)[40]	nom. by Propaganda 20/30 Aug. 1695 (did not take effect)	
(Edward Comerford, abp of Cashel)[41]	admr 1705	21 Feb. 1710
(Christopher Butler, abp of Cashel)[42]	admr (brief) 7/18 May 1718	4 Sept. 1757

(Emly united to Cashel 10 May 1718)

[37] The date of MacBrien's consecration is given in Combaluzier, p. 137. The date of his death is given in Brady, *Episc. succ.*, ii, 36, citing Thomas Burke, *Hibernia Dominicana* (Cologne, 1762), p. 602 fn. No evidence has been found of vicars 1586-1620. Emly was perhaps administered by abps of Cashel for part of this time.

[38] Maurice O'Hurley's bulls, dated 25 July 1620, were lost to pirates; they were re-expedited in 1622 (P. F. Moran, *Spicilegium Ossoriense* (Dublin, 1874-84), i, 132). O'Hurley d. towards the end of Sept. 1646; see Richard O'Ferrall and Robert O'Connell, *Commentarius Rinuccinianus*, ed. Stanislaus Kavanagh (6 vols, Dublin, 1932-49), ii, 491. News of his death cannot have reached Rome before 1/11 Mar. 1647, when Terence Albert O'Brien was app. his coadj. with right of succession.

[39] William Burgat was reapp. vic. ap. 24 Nov. 1665.

[40] The provision of James Stritch (1695) is not recorded by the compilers of *Hierarchia catholica*, no brief (or bull) of provision having been found. From A.P.F., Atti 65 (1695), f. 205, it seems clear that Propaganda had decided to promote him. But from ibid., 69 (1699), ff 359v–362v, a petition presented to Propaganda 4 years later by the abp of Cashel requesting Emly (and Kilfenora) in administration, it seems that Stritch had not been prov. by the pope.

[41] Brady, *Episc. succ.*, ii, 27.

[42] Eustace Browne was vic. gen. of Emly in 1712 at the time of his provision to Killaloe (*Hierarchia catholica*, v, 236). Abp Butler is stated by Ritzler and Sefrin to have been app. admr of Emly 7/18 May 1718 (ibid., v, 147), but according to Brady (*Episc. succ.*, ii, 39), the union of Emly to Cashel was effected at that time.

DIOCESE OF KILFENORA

bishops	*accession*	*death unless otherwise stated*
Maurice O'Kelly, O.F.M.*	prov. 6 Nov. 1514	13 June 1537 × Nov. 1541
John O'Neylan*[43]	prov. 21 Nov. 1541 cons. 29 Dec. 1542	1572
(Donal O'Grioffa, vic. ap.)[44]	brief 22 Mar./1 Apr. 1631	
Andrew Lynch	prov. 1/11 Mar. 1647 cons. 23 Apr. 1648[45]	1681
(Edward Comerford, abp of Cashel)[46]	admr 1705	21 Feb. 1710
William O'Daly[47]	prov. 27 July/7 Aug. 1722	
James Augustine O'Daly	prov. 16/27 July 1726	20 Aug. 1749†

(Kilfenora united to Kilmacduagh Sept. 1750)[48]

[43] John O'Neylan was prov. by Paul III, but seems to have accepted royal supremacy since he was recognised by Henry VIII. His death is recorded by the Four Masters 1572. The date of O'Neylan's consecration, which took place in Rome, is given in the original certificate of consecration in the possession of Mrs R. A. Milne, Shrewsbury (K. W. Nicholls, 'The Lynch Blosse papers' in *Anal. Hib.*, no. 29 (1980), p. 216).

[44] From 1572 to 1647 the see was ruled by vicars (*Hierarchia catholica*, iv, 188). In 1629 O'Grioffa (Gryphaeus, Griffith), who was app. vic. ap. 1631, was vic. gen.

[45] The date of Lynch's consecration is given in *Comment. Rinucc.*, iii, 56; that of his death is in Patrick Power, *A bishop of the penal times* (Cork, 1932), p. 73.

[46] Brady, *Episc. succ.*, ii, 27.

[47] William O'Daly was vic. gen. of Kilfenora before his provision in 1722. But there is no other record of a vicar 1681–1722.

[48] After the death of James O'Daly the union of Kilfenora and Kilmacduagh was decreed by Benedict XIV. The bp of the united dioceses was to be alternately bp of one diocese and admr of the other, since the 2 dioceses were in different provinces. The first bp under this new arrangement was Peter Killikelly, who had been prov. to the see of Kilmacduagh 11/22 Jan. 1744.

DIOCESE OF KILLALOE

bishops	*accession*	*death unless otherwise stated*
James O'Currin*	prov. 24 Aug. 1526	res. 5 May 1542[49] d. *a.* June 1554
(Richard Hogan, O.F.M., admr)[50]	prov. to Clonmacnoise 16 June 1539, and admr of Killaloe	1539
(Florence Kirwan, O.F.M.)[51]	prov. to Clonmacnoise and Killaloe united 5 Dec. 1539	res. *c.* 1542
(Dermot O'Brien, admr)[52]	5 May 1542	res. *c.* 1547? d. 31 Jan. 1552
Turlough O'Brien*	prov. 25 June 1554	1569
Malachy O'Molony	prov. 10 Jan. 1571 cons. 11 Feb. 1571[53]	trs. to Kilmacduagh 22 Aug. 1576
Cornelius O'Mulrian, O.F.M.	prov. 22 Aug. 1576	1616
(Malachy O'Queely, vic. ap.)	brief 20/30 Aug. 1619	prov. to Tuam 12/22 Apr. 1630
John O'Molony I	prov. 2/12 Aug. 1630 cons. Nov. 1630	Oct. 1651
(Denis Harty, vic. ap.)[54]	brief 7/17 Apr. 1657	
John O'Molony II[55]	prov. 6/16 May 1671 brief 14/24 Aug. 1671 cons. 25 Feb./6 Mar. 1672	trs. to Limerick 14/24 Jan. 1689
(John O'Molony II, bp of Limerick)	admr 14/24 Jan. 1689	23 Aug./3 Sept. 1702
Eustace Browne	prov. 5/16 June 1712 brief 5/16 July 1712 cons. 16 Aug. 1713	susp. 23 Sept./4 Oct. 1723 d. *a.* 14/25 Nov. 1724
(Christopher Butler, abp of Cashel)	admr 12/23 Dec. 1723	
Terence MacMahon	prov. (brief) 5/16 Dec. 1724	
Sylvester Louis Lloyd, O.F.M.	prov. (brief) 14/25 Sept. 1728	trs. to Waterford 18/29 May 1739
Patrick MacDonagh	prov. (brief) 3/14 Aug. 1739	25 Feb. 1752†
(Patrick O'Nachten)	prov. (brief) 1/12 May 1752 (provision not accepted)	
(Nicholas Madgett)	prov. (brief) 11 Dec. 1752 (provision annulled and declared void)	prov. to Ardfert 23 Feb. 1753
William O'Meara	trs. from Ardfert (brief) 23 Feb. 1753	*a.* 16 May 1765

bishops	*accession*	*death unless otherwise stated*
Michael Peter MacMahon, O.P.	prov. (brief) 5 June 1765 cons. 4 Aug. 1765	20 Feb. 1807
James O'Shaughnessy	prov. coadj. with succn (brief) 24 Sept. 1798 cons. 13 Jan. 1799 succ. 20 Feb. 1807	5 Aug. 1829
Patrick MacMahon	prov. coadj. with succn 24 Aug. 1819 brief 27 Aug. 1819 cons. 18 Nov. 1819 succ. 5 Aug. 1829	7 June 1836
Patrick Kennedy	prov. coadj. with succn 23 June 1835 cons. 17 Jan. 1836 succ. 7 June 1836	19 Nov. 1850
Daniel Vaughan	prov. 30 Mar. 1851 brief 11 Apr. 1851 cons. 8 June 1851	29 July 1859
Michael Flannery	prov. coadj. with succn (brief) 6 July 1858 cons. 5 Sept. 1858 succ. 29 July 1859	19 June 1891
(Nicholas Power)	prov. coadj. with succn 3 Apr. 1865[56] brief 9 May 1865 cons. 25 June 1865 (did not succeed)	20 Mar. 1871
(James Ryan)	prov. coadj. with succn 8 Oct. 1871[57] brief 21 Nov. 1871 cons. 4 Feb. 1872 (did not succeed)	20 July 1889
Thomas MacRedmond	prov. coadj. with succn (brief) 14 Dec. 1889 cons. 12 Jan. 1890 succ. 19 June 1891	5 Apr. 1904
Michael Fogarty	prov. 8 July 1904 cons. 4 Sept. 1904	25 Oct. 1955
Joseph Rodgers	prov. coadj. with succn 10 Jan. 1948 cons. 7 Mar. 1948 succ. 25 Oct. 1955	10 July 1966
Michael Harty	prov. 28 Sept. 1967 cons. 19 Nov. 1967	

[49] The Roman records do not show that O'Currin was depr. in 1539 but that his resignation was accepted on 5 May 1542 (Brady, *Episc. succ.*, ii, 117).

[50] The pope, when providing Hogan as bp to Clonmacnoise, also app. him admr of Killaloe, said to be

vacant by the death of Turlough O'Brien (Brady, *Episc. succ.*, i, 245). Bp O'Brien, however, had d. before Aug. 1526 when James O'Currin had been prov. Richard Hogan d. a short time after his provision.

[51] Unlike the provision of Hogan, that of Florence Kirwan was to the dioceses of Clonmacnoise and Killaloe, said to be vacant by the deaths of Richard (Hogan) and Turlough (O'Brien), these 2 sees being declared united but only for the lifetime of the said Florence (Brady, *Episc. succ.*, i, 245-6). It is not known whether this provision of Kirwan had any effect in Killaloe. Since there is no mention of him in the consistorial records when Dermot O'Brien was app. admr, it is to be presumed that the holy see had annulled his provision to Killaloe or had told him to resign the provision. Further evidence of the confusion at Rome is the provision of Roderick Maclean to Clonmacnoise 30 Aug. 1549 on a false report of the death of Kirwan. Florence Kirwan, who had accepted royal supremacy, resigned as bp of Clonmacnoise and this resignation was accepted in consistory by the pope 4 May 1556, when he provided Peter Wall, O.P., to Clonmacnoise.

[52] The pope, when accepting the resignation of James O'Currin 5 May 1542, appointed Dermot (later 2nd baron of Inchiquin) admr of Killaloe. Dermot is said to be 22 years of age and is appointed 'until he reaches his twenty-seventh year'. There is no mention of his being prov. bp after five years (Brady, *Episc. succ.*, ii, 117). How long he actually administered Killaloe is not known. On 25 June 1554, when Turlough O'Brien was prov. as bp, the see was said to be vacant by the death of James O'Currin, former bp of Killaloe.

[53] Combaluzier, p. 137.

[54] A certain John O'Molony had been app. vic. ap. 1652 (see below, n. 55). John Burke was vic. ap. of Killaloe in 1666, as well as of Cashel; Denis Harty appears again as vic. ap. in Aug. 1668 (Brady, *Episc. succ.*, ii, 120).

[55] He is probably to be identified as the John O'Molony who was app. vic. ap. 1652. After he was trs. from Killaloe to Limerick in Jan. 1689, O'Molony continued to act as admr of Killaloe until his death in 1702. There is no record of vicars 1702-13.

[56] Brady, *Episc. succ.*, ii, 125.

[57] Ibid.

DIOCESE OF LIMERICK

bishops	*accession*	*death unless otherwise stated*
John Quin (Seaán Ó Cuinn), O.P.*[58]	prov. 21 Oct. 1524 cons. *a.* 3 Jan. 1525	1554/5
Hugh Lacy*[59]	prov. 9 Mar./24 Nov. 1556	1580
Cornelius O'Boyle	prov. 20 Aug. 1582	*p.* 1591
(Richard Cadan, vic. ap.)	brief 13/23 Feb. 1602	
Richard Arthur[60]	prov. 8/18 May 1620 cons. 7 Sept. 1623	23 May 1646
Edmund O'Dwyer	prov. coadj. with succn 27 Jan./6 Feb. 1645 cons. 27 Apr./7 May 1645 succ. 23 May 1646	26 Mar./5 Apr. 1654
(James Dooley, vic. ap.)	brief 7/17 Apr. 1657 (again) 21/31 July 1669	
James Dooley	prov. 19/29 Jan. 1677 brief Feb. 1677 (N.S.)	*c.* Jan. 1685
John O'Molony[61]	trs. from Killaloe (bull) 14/24 Jan. 1689	23 Aug./3 Sept. 1702
Cornelius O'Keeffe[62]	prov. (brief) 25 Feb./7 Mar. 1720	4 May 1737
Robert Lacy	prov. (brief) 19/30 Aug. 1737 cons. 12/23 Feb. 1738	4 Aug. 1759

bishops	accession	death unless otherwise stated
Daniel O'Kearney	prov. (brief) 27 Nov. 1759	24 Jan. 1778
	cons. 27 Jan. 1760	
(John Butler, S.J.)	prov. 23 Mar. 1778	
	brief 10 Apr. 1778	
	(provision not accepted)	
Denis Conway	prov. 17 Jan. 1779	19 June 1796
	brief 25 Feb. 1779	
	cons. 20 June 1779	
John Young	prov. coadj. with succn 2 Dec. 1792	22 Sept. 1813
	brief 4 Jan. 1793	
	cons. 20 May 1793	
	succ. 19 June 1796	
Charles Tuohy	prov. 25 Sept. 1814	17 Mar. 1828
	brief 4 Oct. 1814	
	cons. 23 Apr. 1815	
John Ryan	prov. coadj. with succn (brief) 30 Sept. 1825	6 June 1864
	cons. 11 Dec. 1825	
	succ. 17 Mar. 1828	
George Butler	prov. coadj. with succn 9 June 1861	3 Feb. 1886
	brief 18 June 1861	
	cons. 25 July 1861	
	admr 7 Oct. 1863	
	succ. 6 June 1864	
Edward Thomas O'Dwyer	prov. (brief) 18 May 1886	19 Aug. 1917
	cons. 29 June 1886	
Denis Hallinan	prov. 10 Jan. 1918	2 July 1923
	cons. 10 Mar. 1918	
David Keane	prov. 24 Dec. 1923	12 Mar. 1945
	cons. 2 Mar. 1924	
Patrick O'Neill	prov. 15 Dec. 1945	26 Mar. 1958
	cons. 24 Feb. 1946	
Henry Murphy	prov. 1 July 1958	8 Oct. 1973
	cons. 31 Aug. 1958	
Jeremiah Newman	prov. 17 May 1974	
	cons. 14 July 1974	

[58] Quin was forced to resign by Edward VI 9 Apr. 1551, but was rest. by Mary in 1553.

[59] Hugh Lacy received special faculties 3 May 1575 for the whole province of Cashel in the absence of the abp. The date of provision is given as 9 Mar. 1556 in *Hierarchia catholica*, iii, 225, and as 24 Nov. 1556 in Brady, *Episc. succ.*, ii, 42.

[60] Richard Arthur is named as vic. gen. of Limerick in a report to the government 1613; and he is reported as 'bishop elect and resident in the diocese' in a later report, 1617.

[61] Retained administration of Killaloe 1689-1702.

[62] There is no record of vicars 1702-20.

DIOCESE OF ROSS

bishops	accession	death unless otherwise stated
Dermot MacCarthy, O.S.A.*	prov. 6 June 1526	1552
Maurice O'Fihely, O.F.M.*	prov. 12 Jan. 1554 again 25 May 1555	a. 27 Jan. 1559
Maurice O'Hea	prov. 7 Apr. 1559	c. 1561
Thomas O'Herlihy	prov. 17 Dec. 1561	11 Mar. 1580
Bonaventure Naughten, O.F.M.	prov. 20 Aug. 1582	14 Feb. 1587?
(Eugene Egan, vic. ap.)	brief 20/30 May 1597	
(Florence MacCarthy, vic. ap.)	brief 5/15 July 1619	
(Robert Barry, vic. ap.)	brief 17/27 May 1620	
Boetius MacEgan, O.F.M.	prov. 1/11 Mar. 1647 cons. 25 Mar. 1648	11/21 May 1650
(Eugene Egan, vic. ap.)	brief 7/17 Apr. 1657	
(John Baptist Sleyne, bp of Cork and Cloyne)	admr (brief) 25 Nov./5 Dec. 1693	5/16 Feb. 1712
(Thaddeus MacCarthy, bp of Cork and Cloyne)[63]	admr (brief) 9/20 June 1732	14 Aug. 1747†

(Benedict XIV decreed the union of Ross and Cloyne 29 Nov./10 Dec. 1747. Ross was separated from Cloyne by papal brief 17 Dec. 1850)

William Keane	prov. 24 Nov. 1850 brief 20 Dec. 1850 cons. 2 Feb. 1851	trs. to Cloyne 5 May 1857
Michael O'Hea	prov. 4 Oct. 1857[64] brief 11 Dec. 1857 cons. 7 Feb. 1858	18 Dec. 1876
William Fitzgerald	prov. (brief) 7 Sept. 1877 cons. 11 Nov. 1877	24 Nov. 1896
Denis Kelly	prov. (brief) 29 Mar. 1897 cons. 9 May 1897	18 Apr. 1924
James Roche	prov. 31 Mar. 1926 cons. 30 May 1926	trs. to Cloyne 23 Mar. 1935[65]
Patrick Casey	prov. 22 June 1935 cons. 15 Sept. 1935	19 Sept. 1940
Denis Moynihan	prov. 5 July 1941 cons. 21 Sept. 1941	trs. to Kerry 10 Feb. 1953

(After the translation of Bp Moynihan from Ross to Kerry, Bp Lucey of Cork was app. apostolic admr of Ross, 20 Feb. 1954; bp of Ross, 19 Apr. 1958)

---

[63] Christopher Butler, abp of Cashel, is mentioned as having been admr of Ross 1711–Sept. 1730 (Brady, *Episc. succ.*, ii, 29; *H.B.C.*, p. 393, no. 8), but this has not been substantiated.

[64] Brady, *Episc. succ.*, ii, 113.

[65] James Roche was trs. from Ross to the titular see of Sebastopolis and prov. coadj. with right of succn to Bp Browne of Cloyne 26 June 1931; but from that date until he succ. Browne he was also, by special arrangement of the holy see, apostolic admr of Ross.

DIOCESE OF WATERFORD AND LISMORE

bishops	accession	death unless otherwise stated
Nicholas Comyn*[66]	trs. from Ferns	depr. 1550
	prov. 13 Apr. 1519	d. 12 July 1557
John MacGrath, O.F.M.	prov. 21 July 1550	c. 1551
Patrick Walsh*[67]	app. by Edward VI 9 June 1551	1578
	cons. 23 Oct. 1551	
	recognised and prov. c. 1555/6	
(John White, vic. ap.)[68]	brief 4 Nov. 1578	
(James White, vic. ap.)[69]	brief 14/24 July 1600	
(Peter Lombard, abp of Armagh)	admr (brief) 13/23 Apr. 1623	26 Aug./ 5 Sept. 1625[70]
Patrick Comerford, O.S.A.	prov. 2/12 Feb. 1629	29 Feb./10 Mar.
	cons. 8/18 Mar. 1629	1652
(Patrick Hacket, vic. ap.)	brief 7/17 Apr. 1657	
John Brenan	prov. 6/16 May 1671	trs. to Cashel
	brief 9/19 Aug. 1671	26 Feb./8 Mar.
	cons. 27 Aug./6 Sept. 1671	1677[71]
(John Brenan, abp of Cashel)	admr 26 Feb./8 Mar. 1677[71]	1693
Richard Piers	prov. 11/21 May 1696	a. 29 May 1739
Sylvester Louis Lloyd, O.F.M.	trs from Killaloe brief 18/29 May 1739	1747
(Thomas Stritch)	prov. coadj. with succn (brief) 7/18 Dec. 1743 (did not succeed)	a. 9/20 Feb. 1745[72]
Peter Creagh	prov. coadj. with succn (brief) 1/12 Apr. 1745 succ. 1747	12 Feb. 1775
William Egan	prov. coadj. with succn 3 Feb. 1771 brief 8 Mar. 1771 cons. 19 May 1771[73] succ. 12 Feb. 1775	22 July 1796
Thomas Hussey[74]	prov. 4 Dec. 1796 brief 10 Jan. 1797 cons. 26 Feb. 1797	11 July 1803
John Power I	prov. 1 Jan. 1804 brief 27 Jan. 1804 cons. 25 Apr. 1804	27 Jan. 1816

bishops	accession	death unless otherwise stated
Robert Walsh	prov. 30 May 1817 brief 4 July 1817 cons. 31 Aug. 1817	1 Oct. 1821
Patrick Kelly	trs. from Richmond (Va)[75] prov. 3 Feb. 1822 brief 22 Feb. 1822	8 Oct. 1829
William Abraham	prov. 23 Dec. 1829 brief 12 Jan. 1830	23 Jan. 1837
Nicholas Foran	prov. 28 May 1837 brief 6 June 1837 cons. 24 Aug. 1837	11 May 1855
Dominic O'Brien	prov. 29 July 1855 brief 3 Aug. 1855 cons. 30 Sept. 1855	12 June 1873
John Power II	prov. coadj. with succn (brief) 20 May 1873 succ. 12 June 1873 cons. 20 July 1873	6 Dec. 1887[76]
Piers Power	prov. coadj. with succn (brief) 29 Jan. 1886 cons. 7 Mar. 1886 succ. 6 Dec. 1887	22 May 1889
John Egan	prov. (brief) 19 Nov. 1889 cons. 19 Jan. 1890	10 June 1891
Richard Alphonsus Sheehan	prov. (brief) 15 Jan. 1892 cons. 31 Jan. 1892	14 Oct. 1915
Bernard Hackett, C.SS.R.	prov. 29 Jan. 1916 cons. 19 Mar. 1916	1 June 1932
Jeremiah Kinane	prov. 21 Apr. 1933 cons. 29 June 1933	trs. to Cashel as coadj. 4 Feb. 1942
Daniel Cohalan	prov. 3 Feb. 1943 cons. 4 Apr. 1943	27 Jan. 1965
Michael Russell	prov. 8 Nov. 1965 cons. 19 Dec. 1965	

[66] Comyn accepted royal supremacy, and is not mentioned in the provision of his successor.

[67] Walsh was app. by Edward VI and cons. by royal mandate; but he was recognised as bp in Mary's reign and is mentioned in the provision of his successor.

[68] Brady, *Episc. succ.*, ii, 70.

[69] John White is said to have been vic. ap. 1578–1600 (Patrick Power, *Waterford and Lismore* (Cork, 1937), pp 13, 381), but no consistorial record has been found. James White was active as vic. ap. from July 1600 to some date *p.* 22 Apr. 1610. In 1617 the clergy elected Nicholas Fagan, O.Cist., as bp of Waterford and petitioned the holy see for his provision. But Fagan died in Waterford before the bulls of his provision came.

[70] D. in Rome without coming to Ire.

[71] Brenan retained his administration of Waterford and Lismore after his translation to Cashel 1677–93.

[72] See A. V., Nunz. di Fiandra, 135D, f. 228 rv (*Collectanea Hibernica*, x (1967), p. 104).

[73] W. H. G. Flood, *History of the diocese of Ferns* (Waterford, 1916), p. xix.

[74] Hussey was absent from his see from Apr. or May 1797 until the end of 1802. Leave was granted by Propaganda 12 Mar. 1798, and in his absence the see was governed by Thomas Hearn, vic. gen. This information, with the exact date of Hussey's brief, is given in John Healy, *Maynooth College* (Dublin, 1895), pp. 173, 182-3.

[75] Bp Kelly had been cons. at Kilkenny 24 Aug. 1820.

[76] *Freeman's Journal*, 7 Dec. 1887. The date given in *Hierarchia catholica* is incorrect.

PROVINCE OF DUBLIN

DIOCESE OF DUBLIN

archbishops	accession	death unless otherwise stated
John Alen*	prov. 3 Sept. 1529 cons. 13 Mar. 1530	28 July 1534
Hugh Curwin*[1]	prov. 21 June 1555 cons. 8 Sept. 1555	(suspended?) trs. to Oxford by Elizabeth 1 Sept. 1567 d. Oct. 1568
(Donald)[2]	(date of provision unknown)	
Mateo de Oviedo, O.F.M.	prov. 25 Apr./5 May 1600 cons. *a.* 5 July 1600	31 Dec. 1609/ 10 Jan. 1610
Eugene Matthews	trs. from Clogher prov. 22 Apr./2 May 1611	1 Sept. 1623
Thomas Fleming, O.F.M.	prov. 13/23 Oct. 1623 cons. 21/31 Dec. 1623	2 Aug. 1651 (?o.s.)
(James Dempsey, vic. ap.)[3]	brief 7/17 Apr. 1657	
(Richard Butler, vic. ap.)	brief 14/24 Nov. 1665	(withdrawn ?1665)
Peter Talbot	prov. 1/11 Jan. 1669 brief 26 Feb./8 Mar. 1669 cons. 29 Apr./9 May 1669[4]	15 Nov. 1680
(Gerard Tellin, vic. ap.)	brief 20/30 Sept. 1681	
Patrick Russell	prov. 9/19 July 1683 brief 23 July/2 Aug. 1683	14 July 1692 (?o.s.)
Peter Creagh	trs. from Cork and Cloyne prov. (bull) 27 Feb./9 Mar. 1693	20 July 1705 (?o.s.)
Edmund Byrne	prov. 10/21 Mar. 1707 brief 20/31 Mar. 1707 cons. 31 Aug. 1707	21 Feb. 1724 (?o.s.)[5]
Dominic Edward Murphy[6]	trs. from Kildare prov. (brief) 21 Aug./1 Sept. 1724	*c.* Jan. 1729

archbishops	accession	death unless otherwise stated
Luke Fagan	trs. from Meath prov. (brief) 13/24 Sept. 1729	11 Nov. 1733
John Linegar	prov. (brief) 9/20 Mar. 1734	21 June 1757
Richard Lincoln	prov. coadj. with succn (brief) 21 Nov. 1755 succ. 21 June 1757	18/21 June 1763
Patrick Fitzsimons	prov. (brief) 20 Sept. 1763	24 Nov. 1769
John Carpenter	prov. 25 Mar. 1770 brief 10 Apr. 1770 cons. 3 June 1770	29 Oct. 1786
John Thomas Troy, O.P.	trs. from Ossory prov. 3 Dec. 1786 brief 19 Dec. 1786	11 May 1823
Daniel Murray	prov. coadj. with succn (brief) 30 June 1809 cons. 30 Nov. 1809 succ. 11 May 1823	26 Feb. 1852
Paul Cullen	trs. from Armagh prov. 3 May 1852 cardinal 22 June 1866	24 Oct. 1878
Edward McCabe[7]	prov. aux. bp (brief) 26 June 1877 cons. 25 July 1877 prov. bp (brief) 4 Apr. 1879 cardinal 27 Mar. 1882	11 Feb. 1885
William Joseph Walsh	prov. 23 June 1885[8] brief 3 July 1885 cons. 2 Aug. 1885	9 Apr. 1921
Edward Byrne	prov. coadj. with succn 19 Aug. 1920 cons. 27 Oct. 1920 succ. 9 Apr. 1921	9 Feb. 1940
John Charles McQuaid, C.S.Sp.	prov. 6 Nov. 1940 cons. 27 Dec. 1940	res. 16 Feb. 1972[9] d. 7 Apr. 1973
Dermot Ryan	prov. 29 Dec. 1971 cons. 13 Feb. 1972	

[1] No effort was made by the holy see to fill the see of Dublin 1534–55. Curwin was prov. at Mary's request, but accepted royal supremacy under Elizabeth and was trs. to Oxford in 1567 at his own request.

[2] There is no record of vicars in Dublin 1567–91. On 15 May 1591 Cornelius Stanley was app. vic. gen. of Dublin and Meath, the 2 sees being then vacant. Nothing is known of Donald, who is mentioned as the last abp in the provision of Mateo de Oviedo (bull, not consistorial act). Brady suggests he may have been Donald or Daniel O'Ferrall who kept a school in Dublin in Apr. 1567 (*Episc. succ.*, ii, 335).

[3] James Dempsey was dean of Kildare before Apr. 1657, and was app. vic. ap. of Kildare 1665.

[4] Brady, *Episc. succ.*, i, 337. In a copy in Maynooth College Library this date has been struck out and 2/12 May substituted, but no authority is given.

[5] A. V., Nunz. di Fiandra, vol. 136, f. 202r (*Collectanea Hibernica*, xi (1968), p. 76).

[6] Murphy petitioned the holy see for a coadj. 25 Nov. 1728. His death was announced at Rome 13 Feb. 1729.

[7] McCabe had 30 Jan. 1855 been provided to the titular see of Dardanus and nominated vic. ap. of the eastern district of the Cape of Good Hope, but had declined the appointment.

[8] P. J. Walsh, *William J. Walsh* (Dublin, 1928), p. 166.

[9] Abp McQuaid retained jurisdiction in Dublin until this date by special arrangement.

DIOCESE OF FERNS

bishops	accession	death unless otherwise stated
John Purcell, can. reg. of St Aug.*	prov. 13 Apr. 1519 cons. 6 May 1519	20 July 1539
Bernard O'Donnell, O.F.M.	prov. 30 Mar. 1541	trs. to Elphin 3 June 1541
Gabriel de S. Serio, O.S.B.	trs. from Elphin prov. 3 June 1541	5 May 1542
Alexander Devereux, O. Cist.*	app. by Henry VIII 1539 cons. 14 Dec. 1539 recognised and prov. 1556 (?)	*a.* 19 Aug. 1566[10]
Peter Power	prov. 27 Apr. 1582	1587[11]
(Daniel Drihin, vic. ap.)[12]	brief 17 Nov. 1607	*c.* Sept. 1626[13]
John Roche	prov. 19/29 Apr. 1624 cons. 15/25 Apr. 1627[14]	9 Apr. 1636†
Nicholas French[15]	prov. 27 Jan./6 Feb. 1645 cons. 23 Nov./3 Dec. 1645	13/23 Aug. 1678
Luke Wadding	prov. coadj. with succn 6/16 May 1671 brief 16/26 Aug. 1671 cons. 1683/4	Dec. 1691[16]
Michael Rossiter	prov. 21 June/1 July 1697 cons. 1698	1709(?)[17]
John Verdon	prov. 29 Aug./9 Sept. 1709 brief 3/14 Sept. 1709	*c.* 1728[18]
Ambrose O'Callaghan, O.F.M.	prov. (brief) 15/26 Sept. 1729	13 Aug. 1744[19]
Nicholas Sweetman	prov. (brief) 14/25 Jan. 1745	19 Oct. 1786
(John Stafford)	prov. coadj. with succn 29 Nov. 1772 brief 14 Dec. 1772 (did not succeed)	30 Sept. 1781
James Caulfield	prov. coadj. with succn 17 Feb. 1782 brief 26 Feb. 1782 cons. 7 July 1782 succ. 19 Oct. 1786	12 Jan. 1814[20]

bishops	accession	death unless otherwise stated
Patrick Ryan	prov. coadj. with succn (brief) 2 Oct. 1804 cons. 2 Feb. 1805 succ. 12 Jan. 1814	9 Mar. 1819
James Keating	prov. coadj. with succn (brief) 12 Jan. 1819 succ. 9 Mar. 1819 cons. 21 Mar. 1819	7 Sept. 1849
Myles Murphy	prov. 11 Nov. 1849[21] brief 27 Nov. 1849 cons. 10 Mar. 1850	13 Aug. 1856
Thomas Furlong	prov. 14 Dec. 1856[22] brief 9 Jan. 1857 cons. 22 Mar. 1857	12 Nov. 1875
Michael Warren	prov. (brief) 14 Mar. 1876 cons. 7 May 1876	22 Apr. 1884
James Browne	prov. (brief) 8 July 1884 cons. 14 Sept. 1884	21 June 1917
William Codd	prov. 7 Dec. 1917 cons. 25 Feb. 1918	12 Mar. 1938
James Staunton	prov. 10 Dec. 1938 cons. 5 Feb. 1939	27 June 1963
Donal Herlihy	prov. 30 Oct. 1964 cons. 15 Nov. 1964	

[10] Devereux was app. by Henry VIII in 1539, but was not depr. in Mary's reign. He is mentioned in the provision of his successor. According to Flood (*Ferns*, p. xii), he died in July 1566.

[11] There is no record of vicars 1566–82. Flood (*Ferns*, p. xiv), states that Power 'died as assistant bishop of Compostella on December 15th, 1588'.   [12] There is no record of vicars 1587–1607.

[13] For Drihin's death, see *Collectanea Hibernica*, x (1967), pp 17, 50.   [14] Combaluzier, p. 207.

[15] The name of John Roche II is given by Brady and others as the immediate predecessor of Nicholas French. The name seems to be due to a scribal error, the name John Roche having been written in the brief of provision for French. No brief or provision for Nicholas French has ever been traced, though witnesses were examined as to his suitability for the episcopate on 11/21 Jan. 1645; see the report in Franciscan Fathers (eds), *Father Luke Wadding: a commemorative volume* (Dublin, 1957), p. 568. William Devereux was vic. ap. 1636–45 (Flood, *Ferns*, p. xvi). For the date of French's consecration, see Lynch, *De praesulibus Hib.*, i, 355.

[16] Wadding was app. coadj. to French in 1671, with the title of bp of Zenopolis *in partibus*. But he declined the provision as coadj. in that year. After French's death there was a vacancy for 5 or 6 years, and Wadding was finally cons. bp of Ferns in 1683 or 1684. Flood (*Ferns*, pp xvi–xvii) gives Aug. 1683 as the date, but P. J. Corish ('Bishop Wadding's notebook' in *Archiv. Hib.*, xxix (1970), p. 51), has *a*. 20 June 1684. Both give Dec. 1691 as the date of Wadding's death. He is not to be confused with the famous Luke Wadding, O.F.M., author of *Annales minorum*.

[17] The year of consecration is given by Flood (*Ferns*, p. xvii), who also states that Rossiter died 'in the spring of 1709'.

[18] According to L. F. Renehan, *Collections on Irish church history* (2 vols, Dublin, 1873), ii, 31, Verdon was cons. 'at the close of 1709' and died probably in 1728 and certainly 'some time before Sept. 1729'; but Flood (*Ferns*, p. xvii) gives his date of consecration as Mar. 1711 and death as Feb. 1728.

[19] See letter of abp of Dublin, 15 Aug. 1744, in San Clemente archives, Rome, codex I, vol. 2, f. 306; cited in Hugh Fenning, 'The Irish Dominican province in the final decades of the persecution, 1721–1745' in *Archivum Fratrum Predicatorum*, xlii (1972), p. 346.

[20] *Freeman's Journal*, 1 Feb. 1814.   [21] Brady, *Episc. succ.*, i, 382.   [22] Ibid.

DIOCESE OF KILDARE

bishops	accession	death unless otherwise stated
Walter Wellesley, Can. reg.*	prov. 1 July 1529	Oct. 1539
Donal Ó Boachan, O.F.M.	prov. 16 July 1540[23]	July 1540
Thady Reynolds[24]	prov. 11/15 Nov. 1540	
Thomas Leverous*	trs. from Leighlin[25] prov. 30 Aug. 1555	c. 1577
(James Talbot, vic. ap.)	brief 4/14 Sept. 1617	
(Donatus Doolin, vic. ap.)	brief 4/14 Jan. 1622	
Roch MacGeoghegan, O.P.	prov. 2/12 Feb. 1629	c. May 1644
(James Dempsey, vic. ap.)[26]	brief 14/24 Nov. 1665	(withdrawn ?1665)
(Patrick Dempsey, vic. ap.)	brief 20/30 June 1671	
Mark Forestal, O.S.A.[27]	prov. 31 May/10 June 1676 brief 20/30 June 1676	7 Feb. 1683†
Edward Wesley[28]	prov. 9/19 July 1683 brief 23 July/2 Aug. 1683	1691

(By decree of Propaganda Leighlin was united to Kildare 19/29 Nov. 1694, but John Dempsey, Dominic Edward Murphy, and Bernard Dunne each received a separate provision as admr of Leighlin)

[23] Died a few days after this provision. He is mentioned in the provision of Reynolds.

[24] Reynolds accepted royal supremacy. He was recognised by Henry VIII as a suffragan of Abp Browne in Dublin, but not as bp of Kildare. He is not mentioned in the provision of Leverous.

[25] Leverous had been prov. to Leighlin Nov. 1541, on false news of the death of Sanders. In his provision to Kildare he is given the title 'bp of Leighlin', and may have held the see 1549-55; but it is most likely that the 1541 provision was annulled when the holy see learned that Leighlin was not vacant. In 1560 he refused to take the oath of supremacy and lost the temporalities of Kildare.

[26] James Dempsey had been vic. ap. of Dublin 1657-65. There is no record of vicars in Kildare 1644-65.

[27] Forestal was app. admr of Leighlin 26 Aug./5 Sept. 1678.

[28] Wesley was app. admr of Leighlin 9/19 July 1683.

DIOCESE OF KILDARE AND LEIGHLIN

bishops	accession	death unless otherwise stated
John Dempsey[29]	prov. 19/29 Nov. 1694	c. 1707
Dominic Edward Murphy[30]	prov. 1/12 Sept. 1715 brief 3/14 Sept. 1715 cons. 18 Dec. 1715†	trs. to Dublin 21 Aug./1 Sept. 1724
Bernard Dunne[31]	prov. (brief) 5/16 Dec. 1724	a. 24 Aug./ 4 Sept. 1733

bishops	accession	death unless otherwise stated
Stephen Dowdall	prov. (brief) 11/22 Dec. 1733	a. 21 Apr. 1737
James Gallagher	trs. from Raphoe prov. (brief) 7/18 May 1737	May 1751
James O'Keeffe	prov. (brief) 8/19 Jan. 1752 cons. 12/23 Mar. 1752[32]	18 Sept. 1787
(Richard O'Reilly)	prov. coadj. with succn 20 May 1781 brief 20 June 1781 (did not succeed)	trs. to Armagh as coadj. with succn (brief) 26 Feb. 1782
Daniel Delany	prov. coadj. with succn 13 Apr. 1783 brief 13 May 1783 cons. 31 Aug. 1783 succ. 18 Sept. 1787	9 July 1814
(Arthur Murphy)	prov. 25 Sept. 1814 brief 4 Oct. 1814 (provision not accepted)	
Michael Corcoran	prov. 12 Mar. 1815 brief 20 Mar. 1815 cons. 21 Sept. 1815	22 Feb. 1819
James Warren Doyle, O.S.A.	prov. 8 Aug. 1819 brief 27 Aug. 1819 cons. 14 Nov. 1819	15 June 1834
Edward Nolan	prov. 27 July 1834 brief 8 Aug. 1834 cons. 28 Oct. 1834	14 Oct. 1837
Francis Haly	prov. 28 Dec. 1837 brief 10 Jan. 1838 cons. 25 Mar. 1838	19 Aug. 1855
James Walshe	prov. 3 Feb. 1856[33] brief 29 Feb. 1856 cons. 30 Mar. 1856	5 Mar. 1888
James Lynch, C.M., bp of Arcadiopolis[34]	prov. coadj. with succn 4 Apr. 1869 brief 13 Apr. 1869 succ. 5 Mar. 1888	19 Dec. 1896
(Michael Comerford)	prov. coadj. with succn (brief) 2 Nov. 1888 cons. 1 Jan. 1889 (did not succeed)	19 Aug. 1895
Patrick Foley	prov. coadj. with succn (brief) 18 Mar. 1896 cons. 31 May 1896 succ. 19 Dec. 1896	24 July 1926
Matthew Cullen	prov. 25 Mar. 1927 cons. 5 June 1927	2 Jan. 1936

bishops	accession	death unless otherwise stated
Thomas Keogh	prov. 8 Aug. 1936 cons. 18 Oct. 1936	res. 25 Sept. 1967[35] d. 22 May 1969
Patrick Lennon	prov. aux. bp 14 May 1966 cons. 3 July 1966 prov. bp 25 Sept. 1967	

[29] John Dempsey was app. admr of Leighlin 25 May/4 June 1695.

[30] No record has been found of vicars 1707-12. In 1713 Dominic Edward Murphy was vic. gen. of Kildare and Leighlin. Murphy, having been prov. to Kildare 1715, was app. admr of Leighlin 28 Feb./10 Mar. 1716.

[31] Dunne was app. admr of Leighlin on the same day as his provision.

[32] Flood, *Ferns*, p. xix.   [33] Brady, *Episc. succ.*, i, 359.

[34] Lynch was prov. to the titular see of Arcadiopolis and app. coadj. to the vic. ap. of the western district in Scotland 31 Aug. 1866, and was cons. 4 Nov. 1866. The date of his provision as coadj. to the bp of Kildare and Leighlin is given in Brady, *Episc. succ.*, ii, 372.

[35] First bp in Ire. to go into voluntary retirement following Pope Paul VI's suggestion in 1967 that prelates should not remain in office after the age of 75.

DIOCESE OF LEIGHLIN

bishops	accession	death unless otherwise stated
Matthew Sanders*	prov. 10 Apr. 1527	23 or 24 Dec. 1549[36]
(Thomas Leverous)[37]	prov. 14 Nov. 1541	prov. (trs.) to Kildare 30 Aug. 1555
Thomas O'Fihely*[38]	trs. from Achonry prov. 30 Aug. 1555	21 Mar. 1567
Francis de Ribera, O.F.M.[39]	prov. 1/11 Sept. 1587	31 Aug./10 Sept. 1604
(Luke Archer, O. Cist., vic. ap.)	brief 9/19 Jan. 1609	
(Matthew Roche, vic. ap.)	brief 5/15 Jan. 1622	
Edmund Dempsey, O.P.	prov. 28 Feb./10 Mar. 1642	27 Aug./6 Sept. 1658[40]
(Mark Forestal, bp of Kildare)	admr 16/26 Aug. 1678 brief 26 Aug./5 Sept. 1678	7 Feb. 1683†
(Edward Wesley, bp of Kildare)	admr 9/19 July 1683 brief 27 July/6 Aug. 1683	1691
(John Dempsey, bp of Kildare)	admr (brief) 25 May/4 June 1695	c. 1707
(Dominic Edward Murphy, bp of Kildare)	admr 28 Feb./10 Mar. 1716 brief 9/20 Mar. 1716	trs. to Dublin 21 Aug./1 Sept. 1724
(Bernard Dunne, bp-elect of Kildare)	admr (brief) 5/16 Dec. 1724	a. 24 Aug./4 Sept. 1733

[36] The date 23 Dec. 1549 is given on Sanders's monument in Leighlin cathedral; 24 Dec. is given in Lynch, *De praesulibus Hib.*, i, 408.

[37] Leverous was prov. on false news of the death of Sanders. The provision of Leverous to Kildare bears the same date as the provision of Thomas O'Fihely to Leighlin. Leverous is not mentioned in the provision of O'Fihely, though he is styled bp of Leighlin in his own provision to Kildare; see above, p. 374, n. 25.

[38] O'Fihely submitted to the queen 23 July 1559, but no effort was made to deprive him before his death.

[39] There is no record of a provision to Leighlin 1567–87. In the provision of Francis de Ribera (who never came to Ire.) there is mention of William Ophily as his predecessor. This is most probably an error for Thomas O'Fihely.   [40] Lynch, *De praesulibus Hib.*, i, 410.

DIOCESE OF OSSORY

bishops	accession	death unless otherwise stated
Milo Baron (FitzGerald), can. reg. of St Aug.*	prov. 8 June 1528	1 July × 27 Sept. 1550
John Tonory, O.S.A.*[41]	nom. 14 Oct. 1553 cons. Jan. 1554	?1565
Thomas Strong[42]	prov. 28 Mar. 1582 cons. 5 Apr. 1582	10/20 Jan. 1602
(William Brenan, vic. ap.)[43]	brief 3/13 Nov. 1603	res. *c.* 1609 d. *c.* 1610
David Rothe[44]	prov. 21 Sept./1 Oct. 1618 cons. 1620	20 Apr. 1650
(Terence Fitzpatrick, vic. ap.)	brief 7/17 Apr. 1657	*c.* 1668
James O'Phelan	prov. 21/31 Jan. 1669 brief 26 Feb./8 Mar. 1669 cons. 1/11 Aug. 1669[45]	Jan. 1695(?)
William Daton (Dalton?)	prov. 10/20 Feb. 1696	26 Jan. 1712(?)
Malachy Dulany	prov. 11/22 Aug. 1713 brief 4/15 Sept. 1713 cons. 6/17 Feb. 1715[46]	May 1731
Patrick O'Shea	prov. (brief) 17/28 July 1731	June 1736
Colman O'Shaughnessy, O.P.	prov. (brief) 24 Sept./5 Oct. 1736	2 Sept. 1748†
James Bernard Dunne	prov. (brief) 6/17 Dec. 1748	30 Apr. 1758
Thomas Burke, O.P.	prov. (brief) 9 Jan. 1759 cons. 22 Apr. 1759	26 Sept. 1776
John Thomas Troy, O.P.	prov. 1 Dec. 1776 brief 16 Dec. 1776 cons. 8 June 1777	trs. to Dublin 19 Dec. 1786
John Dunne	prov. 24 June 1787 brief 13 July 1787 cons. 16 Sept. 1787	15 Mar. 1789
James Lanigan	prov. 25 June 1789 brief 10 July 1789 cons. 21 Sept. 1789	11 Feb. 1812

bishops	accession	death unless otherwise stated
Kyran Marum	prov. 25 Sept. 1814 brief 4 Oct. 1814 cons. 5 Mar. 1815	22 Dec. 1827
(Myles Murphy)	prov. 8 June 1828 (provision not accepted)	res. 9 May 1829
William Kinsella	prov. 3 May 1829 brief 15 May 1829 cons. 26 July 1829	12 Dec. 1845
Edward Walsh	prov. 5 Apr. 1846 brief 12 May 1846 cons. 26 July 1846	11 Aug. 1872

Patrick Francis Moran	prov. coadj. with succn
	   17 Dec. 1871
	brief 22 Dec. 1871
	cons. 5 Mar. 1872
	succ. 11 Aug. 1872
		trs. to Sydney
		   14 Mar. 1884
		cardinal 27 July
		   1885
		d. 16 Aug. 1911

Abraham Brownrigg	prov. (brief) 28 Oct. 1884 cons. 14 Dec. 1884	1 Oct. 1928
Patrick Collier	prov. coadj. with succn 18 May 1928 cons. 5 Aug. 1928 succ. 1 Oct. 1928	10 Jan. 1964
Peter Birch	prov. coadj. with succn 24 July 1962 cons. 23 Sept. 1962 succ. 10 Jan. 1964	7 Mar. 1981
Laurence Forristal[48]	trs. from Rotdon prov. 30 June 1981	

[41] John Tonory was nominated by Mary, whose mandate for consecration is dated 14 Oct. 1553. The consecration was valid, and Tonory was confirmed by Cardinal Pole as bp of Ossory. There is doubt about the date of Tonory's death, which may have been in 1567, not 1565 (Brady, *Episc. succ.*, i, 363).

[42] The see was vacant 1565-82. Strong came to Ire. 1583-4, but spent the rest of his life in Spain. George Power, his vic. gen., d. in prison in 1599.

[43] William Brenan was active as vic. ap. 1603-9. In 1609 he entered the Franciscan order, and d. in Flanders, *c.* 1610. Laurence Reneghan was vic. gen. 1609-13. His place was taken by Luke Archer, titular abbot of Holy Cross, who was also vic. ap. of Leighlin.

[44] David Rothe came to Ire. as vic. gen. of Armagh in 1609. He is styled 'titular bishop of Ossory' in some government reports on the state of that diocese 1610-15, but he was most probably vic. gen. at that time. For the evidence, see William Carrigan, *History and antiquities of the diocese of Ossory* (4 vols, Dublin, 1905), i, 86-93.

[45] O'Phelan was cons. in Dublin on Sun., 1 Aug. 1669 (Lynch, *De praesulibus Hib.*, i, 396).

[46] Brady states that Dulany was cons. in Dublin by the abp of Dublin on Sun., 17 Feb. 1714 (*Episc. succ.*, i, 367); but 17 Feb. 1714 (O.S.) was a Wednesday and 17 Feb. 1714 (N.S.) was a Saturday.

[47] Brady, *Episc. succ.*, i, 371.

[48] Forristal had been prov. to the titular see of Rotdon and app. an auxiliary bp of Dublin 3 Dec. 1979, and had been cons. 20 Jan. 1980.

PROVINCE OF TUAM

DIOCESE OF TUAM

archbishops	accession	death unless otherwise stated
Thomas O'Mullally*	trs. from Clonmacnoise prov. 19 June 1514	28 Apr. 1536
Arthur O'Friel[1]	prov. 7 Oct. 1538	*c.* 1573
(Christopher Bodkin)*[2]	trs. from Kilmacduagh by Henry VIII l.p. 15 Feb. 1537 app. admr 1555	1572
Nicholas Skerrett	prov. 17 Oct. 1580	Feb. 1583
Miler O'Higgin	prov. 14/24 Mar. 1586 cons. 15/25 Apr. 1586[3]	*c.* 1590
James O'Hely	prov. 10/20 Mar. 1591	Sept. 1595
Florence Conry, O.F.M.[4]	prov. 20/30 Mar. 1609 cons. 23 Apr./3 May 1609	8/18 Nov. 1629
Malachy O'Queely	prov. 12/22 Apr. 1630 cons. 10 Oct. 1630	26 Oct. 1645[5]
John Burke	trs. from Clonfert prov. 1/11 Mar. 1647	4 Apr. 1667†
James Lynch	prov. 1/11 Jan. 1669 brief 26 Feb./8 Mar. 1669 cons. 6/16 May 1669	21/31 Oct. 1713[6]
Francis Burke	prov. coadj. with succn 11/22 Aug. 1713 brief 9/20 Sept. 1713 succ. 21/31 Oct. 1713 cons. 4 Apr. 1714	*a.* 23 Sept. 1723
Bernard O'Gara	prov. 12/23 Dec. 1723 cons. 24 May 1724	*c.* June 1740
Michael O'Gara	prov. 8/19 Sept. 1740	1748
Marcus Skerrett	trs. from Killala prov. 24 Apr./5 May 1749	19 Aug. 1785
Philip Phillips	trs. from Achonry prov. 25 Sept. 1785 brief 22 Nov. 1785	Sept. 1787
Boetius Egan	trs. from Achonry prov. 9 Dec. 1787 brief 4 Jan. 1788	June/July 1798[7]
Edward Dillon	trs. from Kilmacduagh prov. 19 Nov. 1798	13 Sept. 1809[8]
Oliver Kelly	prov. 25 Sept. 1814 brief 4 Oct. 1814 cons. 12 Mar. 1815	18 Apr. 1834

bishops	accession	death unless otherwise stated
John MacHale	trs. from Killala prov. 21 July 1834 brief 8 Aug. 1834	7 Nov. 1881
John McEvilly, bp of Galway[9]	prov. coadj. with succn (brief) 11 Jan. 1878 succ. 7 Nov. 1881	26 Nov. 1902
John Healy	trs. from Clonfert prov. (brief) 13 Feb. 1903	16 Mar. 1918
Thomas Gilmartin	trs. from Clonfert prov. 10 July 1918	14 Oct. 1939

Joseph Walsh	prov. aux. bp 16 Dec. 1937
	cons. 2 Jan. 1938
	prov. abp 16 Jan. 1940
		res. 31 Jan.
		  1969
		announced 10
		  Feb. 1969
		d. 20 June 1972

Joseph Cunnane	prov. 31 Jan. 1969 cons. 17 Mar. 1969	

[1] O'Friel was unable to get possession as against Bodkin, and it is probable that he resigned when Bodkin was absolved in 1555. He made no effort to get possession of the see when Bodkin d. in 1572, and he is not mentioned in the provision of Skerrett.

[2] Bodkin was app. by Henry VIII 15 Feb. 1537. In 1555 he was absolved from schism by Cardinal Pole, and was app. admr of Tuam. He is mentioned in the provision of Skerrett as the last abp.

[3] Combaluzier, pp 143–4.

[4] Florence Conry spent the years 1609–29 in Flanders and Spain. John Lynch, who was archdeacon of Tuam 1630–52, says that he appointed suitable vics gen. but their names have not been recorded (*De praesulibus Hib.*, ii, 246).

[5] The date of O'Queely's death, which occurred in a skirmish near Sligo, is indicated in a letter from James Dowly, abbot of Kilmannock, to the warden of Galway, 31 Oct. 1645 (James Hardiman, *The history of the town and county of the town of Galway* (Dublin, 1820), pp 122–3). The correct date is given in the article on 'Malachis Quælly' in *D.N.B.*, but Lynch, *De praesulibus Hib.*, ii, 251, has 25 Oct.

[6] Brady gives the date of Lynch's death as Oct. 1714; but the correct date is in Oliver J. Burke, *The history of the catholic archbishops of Tuam* (Dublin, 1882), p. 187.

[7] *Dublin Evening Post*, 10 July 1798.

[8] *Hibernian Journal*, 19 Sept. 1809.

[9] MacEvilly had been bp of Galway since 1857, and admr of Kilmacduagh and Kilfenora since 1866. He retained the see of Galway until he succ. to Tuam in 1881; and he retained the administration of Kilmacduagh and Kilfenora until 1883. See under Galway.

DIOCESE OF ACHONRY

bishops	accession	death unless otherwise stated
Cormac Ó Snighe (?Ó Sniadhaigh)*	prov. 15 June 1522	*a.* June 1547
Thomas O'Fihely, can. reg.*[10]	prov. 15 June 1547	trs. to Leighlin 30 Aug. 1555
Cormac O'Coyn, O.P.*[11]	nom. 1556	*a.* 12 Oct. 1561
Eugene Thadaeus O'Harte, O.P.	prov. 28 Jan. 1562	1603
(Andrew Lynch, vic. ap.)	brief 18/28 Nov. 1629	

bishops	accession	death unless otherwise stated
(James Fallon, vic. ap.)[12]	brief 3/13 Jan. 1631	1662
Louis Dillon, O.F.M.	prov. 6/16 Sept. 1641	a. Nov. 1641[13]
(Maurice Durcan, vic. ap.)[14]	prov. 7/17 July 1677 brief 19/29 July 1677	
Hugh MacDermot	prov. vic. ap. 11/21 Dec. 1683 brief Jan. 1684 (N.S.) prov. bp 31 Mar./11 Apr. 1707 brief 19/30 Apr. 1707	a. Sept. 1725
Dominic O'Daly, O.P.	prov. 9/20 Sept. 1725 cons. 19/30 Nov. 1725	6 Jan. 1735†[15]
John O'Hart	prov. 19/30 Sept. 1735	a. May 1739
Walter Blake	prov. 2/13 Aug. 1739	a. 28 July 1758
Patrick Robert Kirwan	prov. 21 Aug. 1758	Mar.-Apr. 1776[16]
Philip Phillips	trs. from Killala prov. 16 June 1776 brief 1 July 1776	trs. to Tuam 25 Sept. 1785
Boetius Egan	prov. 25 Sept. 1785 brief 22 Nov. 1785	trs. to Tuam 9 Dec. 1787
Thomas O'Connor	prov. 9 Dec. 1787 brief 4 Jan. 1788 cons. Apr. 1788	18 Feb. 1803
Charles Lynagh	prov. 29 Apr. 1803 brief 13 May 1803 cons. a. 4 June 1804	27 Apr. 1808[17]
John O'Flynn	prov. 9 June 1809 brief 30 June 1809 cons. 12 Nov. 1809	17 July 1817
Patrick MacNicholas	prov. 1 Mar. 1818 brief 17 Mar. 1818 cons. 17 May 1818	11 Feb. 1852
Patrick Durcan	prov. 3 Oct. 1852[18] brief 4 Oct. 1852 cons. 30 Nov. 1852	1 May 1875
Francis MacCormack	prov. coadj. with succn 10 Sept. 1871[19] brief 21 Nov. 1871 cons. 4 Feb. 1872 succ. 1 May 1875	trs. to Galway 26 Apr. 1887
John Lyster	prov. (brief) 21 Feb. 1888 cons. 8 Apr. 1888	17 Jan. 1911
Patrick Morrisroe	prov. 13 May 1911 cons. 3 Sept. 1911	27 May 1946
James Fergus	prov. 15 Feb. 1947 cons. 4 May 1947	res. 17 Mar. 1976

bishops	accession	death unless otherwise stated
Thomas Flynn	prov. 30 Dec. 1976 cons. 20 Feb. 1977	

[10] In his provision mention is made of Eugene O'Flanagan as the last bp. O'Flanagan was dead before June 1522 when Cormac Ó Snighe was prov. bp of Achonry. But this Cormac is ignored in the provision of 1547, and there is no record for the years 1522–47.

[11] There is no record of Cormac O'Coyn's provision. He was perhaps app. by Mary, but he is mentioned in the provision of Eugene O'Harte, who was his nephew.

[12] Fallon was active as vic. ap. 1631–52. He was imprisoned in 1652 and was released after 1660 in broken health. There is no record of a vicar 1662–77. The diocese of Achonry was thus under vicars 1603–1707.

[13] Collectanea Hibernica, x (1967), p. 31.

[14] Durcan's brief was repeated 14 Mar. 1678.

[15] Hugh Fenning, 'The Athenry house-chronicle, 1666–1779' in Collectanea Hibernica, xi (1968), p. 52.

[16] Kirwan was reported as having 'died near Galway', but the date of death was not given (Freeman's Journal, 9 Apr. 1776).

[17] Dublin Evening Post, 3 May 1808.

[18] Brady, Episc. succ., ii, 193.

[19] Ibid., ii, 194.

DIOCESE OF ANNAGHDOWN (ENACHDUN)

bishops	accession	death unless otherwise stated
Henry Burke	prov. 16 Apr. 1540	

(After 1555 Abp Bodkin held his see along with Tuam. The union of Tuam and Annaghdown was finally decreed 17 Oct. 1580, when Nicholas Skerrett was prov. to Tuam)

DIOCESE OF CLONFERT

bishops	accession	death unless otherwise stated
Roland Burke*[20]	prov. 18 May 1534 cons. p. 8 June 1537	20 June 1580
Thady Farrell, O.P. (Taddeus Mac Eogha)	prov. 29 May/8 June 1587 cons. 20/30 Aug. 1587[21]	1602
(Dermot Nolan, vic. ap.)	brief 25 Jan./4 Feb. 1609	
(Thady Egan, vic. ap.)	brief 3/13 July 1622	
(John Burke, vic. ap.)	brief 3/13 Oct. 1629	
John Burke	prov. 6/16 Sept. 1641 cons. 29 May 1642	trs. to Tuam 1/11 Mar. 1647
Walter Lynch[22]	prov. 1/11 Mar. 1647 cons. 9 Apr. 1648	4/14 July 1663

bishops	accession	death unless otherwise stated
Thady Keogh, O.P. (Mac Eogha)[23]	prov. 16/26 May 1671 brief 3/13 July 1671 cons. 26 × 30 Nov. 1671†	1684/5
Maurice Donnellan[24]	prov. (bull) 4/14 Nov. 1695	2 July 1706 (?o.s.)
Ambrose Madden[25]	prov. 17/28 Aug. 1711 again 9/20 Sept. 1713 cons. 4/15 Apr. 1714	July 1715
Edmund Kelly	prov. (brief) 1/12 Feb. 1718 cons. a. 14 May 1718	a. 23 July/3 Aug. 1733
Peter O'Donnellan	prov. (brief) 31 July/11 Aug. 1733	7 May 1778
Andrew Donnellan	prov. coadj. with succ. 1 Dec. 1776 brief 20 Dec. 1776 succ. 7 May 1778	a. 6 July 1786
Thomas Costello	prov. titular bp of Enos 30 June 1786 nom. coadj. with succn (brief) 4 July 1786	9 Oct. 1831
Thomas Coen	prov. coadj. with succ. 26 Jan. 1816 cons. 5 May 1816 succ. 9 Oct. 1831	25 Apr. 1847
John Derry	prov. 20 June 1847[26] brief 9 July 1847 cons. 21 Sept. 1847	28 June 1870
(Hugh O'Rorke)	prov. 12 Feb. 1871[27] brief 24 Feb. 1871 (provision not accepted)	19 Oct. 1885
Patrick Duggan	prov. 10 Sept. 1871[28] brief 2 Oct. 1871 cons. 14 Jan. 1872	15 Aug. 1896
John Healy	prov. coadj. with succn 26 June 1884 brief 27 June 1884 cons. 31 Aug. 1884 succ. 15 Aug. 1896	trs. to Tuam 13 Feb. 1903
Thomas O'Dea	prov. 12 June 1903 brief 16 June 1903 cons. 30 Aug. 1903	trs. to Galway 29 Apr. 1909
Thomas Gilmartin	prov. 3 July 1909 cons. 13 Feb. 1910	trs. to Tuam 10 July 1918
Thomas O'Doherty	prov. 3 July 1919 cons. 14 Sept. 1919	trs. to Galway 13 July 1923
John Dignan	prov. 24 Mar. 1924 cons. 1 June 1924	12 Apr. 1953

bishops	accession	death unless otherwise stated
William Philbin	prov. 22 Dec. 1953 cons. 14 Mar. 1954	trs. to Down and Connor 5 June 1962
Thomas Ryan	prov. 9 May 1963 cons. 16 June 1963	res. 1 May 1982
Joseph Cassidy	prov. coadj. with succn 24 Aug. 1979 cons. 23 Sept. 1979 succ. 1 May 1982	

[20] The exact date of Burke's provision is given in Lynch, *De praesulibus Hib.*, ii, 313. He accepted royal supremacy, and received the temporalities 24 Oct. 1541. In Mary's reign he was pardoned, but again accepted royal supremacy under Elizabeth. He is mentioned in the provision of his successor. See list of bps of established church, below.

[21] Combaluzier, p. 145.

[22] Lynch came to Ireland in 1647, but left *c.* 1648 and spent the rest of his life in Hungary. There were vicars 1648–71. Daniel Kelly was vic. gen. 1664; Gildas Bruoder was app. vic. gen. 1 Sept. 1664; Kelly appears again as vic. gen. Oct. 1668 (Brady, *Episc. succ.*, ii, 217).

[23] The date of Keogh's provision is given in Brady, *Episc. succ.*, ii, 219; his consecration in *Collectanea Hibernica*, xxi–xxii (1979–80), p. 56, n. 64; his death in A.P.F., Atti 55 (1685), ff 92–4.

[24] Donnellan was vic. gen. of Clonfert 1685–95 (Brady, *Episc. succ.*, ii, 219–20).

[25] Madden had been prov. to Killala in 1695, and to Kilmacduagh 1707 but had never been cons.

[26] Brady, *Episc. succ.*, ii, 223.   [27] Ibid.   [28] Ibid.

DIOCESE OF ELPHIN

bishops	accession	death unless otherwise stated
John Maxey, O. Praem., abbot of Welbeck*	prov. 7 Apr. 1525	15 Aug. 1536
William Magennis (Maginn)[29]	prov. 16 June 1539	
Gabriel de S. Serio, O.S.B.	prov. 27 Aug. 1539	trs. to Ferns 3 June 1541
Bernard O'Donnell, O.F.M.	trs. from Ferns prov. 3 June 1541	*a.* 5 May 1542
Bernard O'Higgin, O.S.A.[30]	prov. 5 May 1542 cons. 7 Sept. 1542	res. 1561 d. 1564
(John O'Heyne, bp of Cork and Cloyne)[31]	admr (brief) 20 Feb. 1545	
Andrew O'Crean, O.P.	prov. 28 Jan. 1562	1594
(Nicholas a S. Patritio, O.S.A., vic. ap.)[32]	brief 19/29 Aug. 1620	
Raymund Galvin	prov.?	
Boetius Egan, O.F.M.[33]	prov. 30 May/9 June 1625 cons. 1626	19 Apr. 1650 (?o.s.)
(William Burgat, vic. ap.)	prov. 14/24 Nov. 1665[34]	
Dominic Burke, O.P.	prov. 6/16 May 1671 brief 3/13 July 1671 cons. 12/22 Nov. 1671	21 Dec. 1703/1 Jan. 1704

bishops	accession	death unless otherwise stated
Ambrose MacDermott, O.P.	prov. 10/21 Mar. 1707 brief 20/31 Mar. 1707 cons. *c.* Aug. 1707[35]	Sept. 1717
Carbry O'Kelly	prov. (brief) 15/26 Mar. 1718 cons. 8 June 1718	4 Aug. 1731
Patrick French, O.F.M.	prov. (brief) 12/23 Nov. 1731	*a.* Aug. 1748
John Brett, O.P.	trs. from Killala prov. (brief) 17/28 Aug. 1748	22 June 1756
James O'Fallon	prov. (brief) 4 Aug. 1756	2 Dec. 1786
Edmund French	prov. (brief) 13 Feb. 1787	29 Apr. 1810
George Thomas Plunket	prov. 25 Sept. 1814 brief 4 Oct. 1814 cons. 24 Feb. 1815	8 May 1827
Patrick Burke	prov. coadj. with succn 6 Dec. 1818 brief 12 Jan. 1819 cons. 27 June 1819 succ. 8 May 1827	16 Sept. 1843
George Joseph Plunket Browne	trs. from Galway prov. 10 Mar. 1844 brief 26 Mar. 1844	1 Dec. 1858
Laurence Gillooly, C.M.	prov. coadj. with succn (brief) 26 Feb. 1856 cons. 7 Sept. 1856 succ. 1 Dec. 1858	15 Jan. 1895
John Clancy	prov. (brief) 8 Feb. 1895 cons. 24 Mar. 1895	19 Oct. 1912
Bernard Coyne	prov. 18 Jan. 1913 cons. 30 Mar. 1913	17 July 1926
Edward Doorly	prov. coadj. with succn 5 Apr. 1923 cons. 24 June 1923 succ. 17 July 1926	4 Apr. 1950
Vincent Hanly	prov. 19 July 1950 cons. 24 Sept. 1950	9 Nov. 1970
Dominic Joseph Conway	prov. aux. bp 16 Oct. 1970 cons. 8 Nov. 1970 prov. bp 12 Mar. 1971	

[29] Eugene Magennis was prov. to Down and Connor on the same day (16 June 1539), and it is possible that there is some confusion here. Nothing further is known of William Magennis (Maginn).

[30] Bernard O'Higgin left Ire. during the last years of the reign of Henry VIII, but returned under Mary. During his absence, from 1545 to *c.* 1553/4, the diocese was administered by John O'Heyne, bp of Cork and Cloyne; but O'Heyne was never bp of Elphin.

[31] O'Heyne ceased to be admr of Elphin, *c.* 1553/4.

[32] There is no record of vicars 1594–1620.

³³ Elphin was ruled by vicars 1650–71. William Burgat was vic. ap. 1665. Thomas Higgin was vic. gen. 1666 and James Ferrall 1669 (Brady, *Episc. succ.*, ii, 202).

³⁴ This provision and similar ones to Dublin and Meath 14/24 Nov. 1665 were probably annulled shortly afterwards (see *Collectanea Hibernica*, vi–vii (1963–4), p. 24). Burgat was provided to Cashel 1669.

³⁵ Hugh Fenning, 'Ambrose MacDermott, O.P.' in *Archivum Fratrum Praedicatorum*, xl (1970), p. 248.

DIOCESE OF GALWAY

(Gregory XVI erected the collegiate church of St Nicholas, Galway, into a cathedral, separating the wardenship of Galway from the archdiocese of Tuam and creating the new suffragan see of Galway, by a bull of 26 Apr. 1831.)

bishops	accession	death unless otherwise stated
(Nicholas Foran)	prov. 20 Mar. 1831 brief 27 Apr. 1831 (provision not accepted)[36]	
George Joseph Plunket Browne	prov. 31 July 1831 brief 26 Aug. 1831 cons. 23 Oct. 1831	trs. to Elphin 10 Mar. 1844 brief 26 Mar. 1844
Laurence O'Donnell	prov. 25 Sept. 1844 brief 27 Sept. 1844 cons. 28 Oct. 1845	29 June 1855
John McEvilly[37]	prov. 14 Dec. 1856 brief 9 Jan. 1857 cons. 22 Mar. 1857	prov. coadj. of Tuam 11 Jan. 1878; succ. 7 Jan. 1881

³⁶ Foran fell ill and did not accept the provision. He became bp of Waterford and Lismore 1837.

³⁷ For the date of his provision to Galway, see Brady, *Episc. succ.*, ii, 233. Bp McEvilly was admr of Kilmacduagh and Kilfenora from 1866 to 1883. When he was prov. to Tuam as coadj. in 1878, he retained Galway, but vacated it when he succ. to Tuam in 1881. He did not vacate the administration of Kilmacduagh and Kilfenora until 1883, when Carr was prov. to the united sees of Galway and Kilmacduagh and app. admr of Kilfenora.

DIOCESE OF GALWAY, KILMACDUAGH, AND KILFENORA

bishops	accession	death unless otherwise stated
Thomas Joseph Carr[38]	prov. (brief) 12 June 1883 cons. 26 Aug. 1883	trs. to Melbourne 16 Nov. 1886 d. 6 May 1917

bishops	accession	death unless otherwise stated
Francis MacCormack	trs. from Achonry prov. (brief) 26 Apr. 1887	res. 21 Oct. 1908[39] d. 14 Nov. 1909
Thomas O'Dea	trs. from Clonfert prov. 29 Apr. 1909	9 Apr. 1923
Thomas O'Doherty	trs. from Clonfert prov. 13 July 1923	15 Dec. 1936
Michael Browne	prov. 6 Aug. 1937 cons. 10 Oct. 1937	res. 21 July 1976 d. 23 Feb. 1980
Eamonn Casey	trs. from Ardfert prov. 21 July 1976	

[38] Galway and Kilmacduagh were united 5 June 1883, and the bp of the 2 united dioceses was also app. apostolic admr of Kilfenora, which is in the province of Cashel.

[39] MacCormack was provided to the titular archiepiscopal see of Nisibis 21 June 1909.

DIOCESE OF KILLALA

bishops	accession	death unless otherwise stated
Richard Barrett*	prov. 7 Jan. 1513	a. Nov. 1545
Redmond O'Gallagher*	prov. 6 Nov. 1545	trs. to Derry 22 June 1569
Donat (Donagh) O'Gallagher, O.F.M.	prov. 4 Sept. 1570 cons. 5 Nov. 1570[40]	trs. to Down and Connor 23 Mar. 1580
John O'Cahasy, O.F.M.	prov. 27 July 1580	Oct. 1583
(Miler Cawell, vic. ap.)[41]	brief 5/15 May 1591	
(Andrew Lynch, vic. ap.)	brief 18/28 Nov. 1629	
Francis Kirwan	prov. (bull) 27 Jan./6 Feb. 1645 cons. 27 Apr./7 May 1645	16/26 Aug. 1661[42]
(John Burke, vic. ap.)[43]	prov. 6/16 May 1671 brief 20/30 June 1671	
(John Dooley, vic. ap.)	prov. 12/22 Apr. 1676	
(Ambrose Madden)[44]	nom. by Propaganda 20/30 Aug. 1695 (did not take effect)	
Thadeus Francis O'Rourke, O.F.M.[45]	prov. 4/15 Nov. 1703 (again) 3/14 Feb. 1707 brief 4/15 Mar. 1707 cons. 24 Aug. 1707	a. Sept. 1735
Peter Archdekin, O.F.M.	prov. (brief) 19/30 Sept. 1735 cons. 25 Jan./5 Feb. 1736	1738[46]
Bernard O'Rourke	prov. (brief) 13/24 Apr. 1739	a. 27 June/8 July 1743

bishops	accession	death unless otherwise stated
John Brett, O.P.	prov. (brief) 16/27 July 1743 cons. 28 Aug./8 Sept. 1743	trs. to Elphin 17/28 Aug. 1748
Marcus Skerrett	prov. (brief) 12/23 Jan. 1749	trs. to Tuam 24 Apr./5 May 1749
Bonaventura MacDonnell, O.F.M.	prov. (brief) 26 Apr./7 May 1749	a. 16 Sept. 1760
Philip Phillips	prov. (brief) 24 Nov. 1760	trs. to Achonry 16 June 1776; brief 1 July 1776
Alexander Irwin	prov. 16 June 1776 brief 1 July 1776	a. 25 Sept. 1779
Dominic Bellew	prov. 5 Dec. 1779 brief 18 Dec. 1779 cons. 1780	c. 1812
Peter Waldron	prov. 25 Sept. 1814 brief 4 Oct. 1814 cons. 24 Feb. 1815	27 May 1834
John MacHale	prov. coadj. with succn 20 Feb. 1825 brief 8 Mar. 1825 cons. 5 June 1825 succ. 27 May 1834	trs. to Tuam 2 Aug. 1834
Francis Joseph O'Finan, O.P.	prov. 1 Feb. 1835 brief 13 Feb. 1835 cons. 21 Mar. 1835[47]	27 Nov. 1847
Thomas Feeny	prov.tit.bp of Ptolemais and papal admr of Killala 18 July 1839 brief 30 July 1839 cons. 13 Oct. 1839 prov. bp 12 Dec. 1847[48] brief 11 Jan. 1848	9 June 1873
Hugh Conway	prov. coadj. with succn 10 Sept. 1871[49] brief 21 Nov. 1871 cons. 4 Feb. 1872 succ. 9 June 1873	23 Apr. 1893
John Conmy	prov. coadj. with succn (brief) 25 June 1892 cons. 24 Aug. 1892 succ. 23 Apr. 1893	26 Aug. 1911
James Naughton	prov. 27 Nov. 1911 cons. 7 Jan. 1912	16 Feb. 1950

bishops	accession	death unless otherwise stated
Patrick O'Boyle	prov. 12 Dec. 1950 cons. 25 Feb. 1951	res. 12 Oct. 1970 d. 25 Nov. 1971
Thomas McDonnell	prov. 12 Oct. 1970 cons. 13 Dec. 1970	

[40] Combaluzier, p. 136.

[41] Duald Mac Firbis names a Bp Edmond Og O'Gallagher, O.F.M., as successor to John O'Cahasy and states that, like the latter, he died on his way to Rome (B.L., Add. MS 4799, f. 21).

[42] Lynch, *De praesulibus Hib.*, ii, 334.

[43] Bp Kirwan went into exile and Killala was probably ruled by vicars until 1703. John Burke was vic. gen. in Jan. 1654 when he was replaced by John Dooley; Richard Lee was vic. gen. in 1666 (Brady, *Episc. succ.*, ii, 177). Burke, as vic. ap., was imprisoned 1674. For his imprisonment and subsequent adventures up to 1682, cf. ibid., ii, 177–8.

[44] Brady, *Episc. succ.*, ii, 165, 178. Madden was also admr of Kilmacduagh. See also under Clonfert.

[45] Thadeus O'Rourke was bp of Killala 1707–35. The situation before 1703, the date of his first provision, is not clear. Madden's provision in 1695 did not take effect, and the diocese was probably ruled by a vicar.

[46] A. V., Nunz. di Fiandra, vol. 135, f. 32r.

[47] On 19 Nov. 1838 Gregory XVI approved the decree of Propaganda to allow O'Finan to retain the title of bp but to deprive him of all jurisdiction in Killala. For his death, see *Irish Catholic Directory*, 1849, pp 246–7.   [48] Brady, *Episc. succ.*, ii, 182.   [49] Ibid.

DIOCESE OF KILMACDUAGH

bishops	accession	death unless otherwise stated
Christopher Bodkin*	prov. 3 Sept. 1533 cons. 4 Nov. 1533	trs. to Tuam 15 Feb. 1537[50]
Cornelius O'Dea[51]	prov. 5 May 1542	1568 × 1576
Christopher Bodkin*	prov. (again) 7 Oct. 1555	1572
Malachy O'Molony	trs. from Killaloe prov. 22 Aug. 1576	1603 × 1610
(Oliver Burke, O.P., vic. ap.)	brief 18/28 Nov. 1629	
Hugh Burke, O.F.M.	prov. 1/11 Mar. 1647	c. 1654
(Michael Lynch, vic. ap.)	prov. 6/16 May 1671 brief 20/30 June 1671	
(Ambrose Madden)[52]	prov. 3/14 Feb. 1707 brief 4/15 Mar. 1707 (not cons.)	trs. to Clonfert 17/28 Aug. 1711; again 9/20 Sept. 1713
Francis Burke, O.F.M.[53]	prov. (brief) 25 Dec. 1719/ 5 Jan. 1720 cons. 1 May 1720	a. 16 Aug. 1732
Martin (Milo) Burke	prov. (brief) 11/22 Nov. 1732 cons. 25 Feb./8 Mar. 1733	1743

bishops	accession	death unless otherwise stated
Peter Killikelly, O.P.	prov. (brief) 11/22 Jan. 1744 cons. 14 Oct. 1744†	

[50] Bodkin accepted royal supremacy; he was trs. to Tuam by Henry VIII and retained Kilmacduagh in administration.

[51] O'Dea may have been opposed by Bodkin, but he was still styled bp of Kilmacduagh on 10 July 1568 (*The Inchiquin manuscripts*, ed. John Ainsworth (Dublin, 1961), no. 890), and he was mentioned in the provision of O'Molony.

[52] In 1677 Michael Lynch was still vic. ap. of Kilmacduagh. The situation 1677–95 is uncertain. Madden was nom. by Propaganda as bp of Killala and admr of Kilmacduagh 20/30 Aug. 1695 but the provision did not take effect. He was prov. to the see of Kilmacduagh 4/15 Nov. 1703 but again his provision did not take effect. It seems likely that Madden acted as admr of Kilmacduagh 1695–1713 (Brady, *Episc. succ.*, ii, 165–6, 178).

[53] Kilmacduagh was probably ruled by vicars 1713–19. Edmund Lynch was vic. gen. 1716 and 1717 (Brady, *Episc. succ.*, ii, 166). The date of Francis Burke's death is indicated in A.V., Nunz. di Fiandra, vol. 153A, f. 165v (*Collectanea Hibernica*, xiv (1971), p. 46).

DIOCESE OF KILMACDUAGH AND KILFENORA

(On 12 Nov. 1750 Pope Benedict XIV united Kilmacduagh and Kilfenora, prescribing that the bp be alternately bp of Kilmacduagh and adm of Kilfenora and vice versa.)

bishops	accession	death unless otherwise stated
Peter Killikelly, O.P.	prov. Sept. 1750 (N.S.) brief 1/12 Nov. 1750	29 May 1783
Laurence Nihill	prov. 7 Dec. 1783 brief 23 Dec. 1783 (again) 16 July 1784	29 June 1795
Edward Dillon	prov. coadj. with succn 8 Dec. 1793 brief 21 Jan. 1794 succ. 29 June 1795	trs. to Tuam 19 Nov. 1798
(Richard Luke Concanon, O.P.)	prov. (brief) 19 Nov. 1798 (provision not accepted)[54]	
Nicholas Joseph Archdeacon	prov. (brief) 31 May 1800 prov. 12 Oct. 1800	27 Nov. 1823
Edmund French, O.P.	prov. 1 Aug. 1824 brief 24 Aug. 1824 cons. 13 Mar. 1825	14 July 1852
Patrick Fallon[55]	prov. 5 Dec. 1852 brief 28 Jan. 1853 cons. 1 May 1853	res. 31 Aug. 1866 d. 13 May 1879
(John McEvilly, bp of Galway)[56]	admr (brief) 31 Aug. 1866	

(On 5 June 1883 Kilmacduagh was united to Galway; from that date Kilfenora, which is in the province of Cashel, was administered by the bp of Galway.)

[54] Concanon was prov. to the newly established bishopric of New York 4 Mar. 1808, cons. in Rome 24 Apr. 1808, but d. in Naples without going to his diocese, 19 June 1810.

[55] The date of Fallon's provision is given in Brady, *Episc. succ.*, ii, 169. On 31 Aug. 1866 John McEvilly, bp of Galway, was app. apostolic admr of Kilmacduagh and Kilfenora *sede plena*, because of the infirmity of Bp Fallon who went to live in Mount Argus, Dublin.

[56] McEvilly was prov. to Tuam as coadj. in 1878; he retained Galway but vacated it when he succeeded to Tuam 1881. He vacated the administration of Kilmacduagh and Kilfenora 1883.

DIOCESE OF MAYO

bishops	accession	death unless otherwise stated
John Bell, O.F.M.*	prov. 4 Nov. 1493	*c.* 1541
Eugene MacBrehon, O.Carm.*[57]	prov. 21 Nov. 1541	*c.* 1559
Dermot Odiera (O'Cleara), O.F.M.	prov. 12 Feb. 1574 cons. 12 Mar. 1574[58]	
Patrick O'Healy, O.F.M.	prov. 4 July 1576	mid-Aug. 1579
Adam Magauran	prov. 19/29 July 1585 cons. 5/15 Sept. 1585[59]	

(Mayo united to Tuam after 1631)[60]

[57] MacBrehon cannot have got possession, since the diocese was held by Abp Bodkin 1537-72.

[58] Fernandus Combaluzier, 'Sacres épiscopaux à Rome de 1566 à 1602' in *Sacris Erudiri*, xix (1969-70), p. 446.

[59] Combaluzier, pp 142-3.

[60] There is no record of any bp of Mayo after 1585. The diocese may have been administered by bps of Achonry. On 12 Mar. 1631 the earl of Tyrconnell wrote recommending the appointment of Nicholas Lynch to the see of Mayo and Achonry in Connacht, which is stated to have been long vacant. On 20 May 1631 Abp O'Queely wrote to Cardinal Ludovisi, petitioning for the union of Tuam and Mayo. Brady (*Episc. succ.*, ii, 156) says that 'Mayo was subsequently united to Achonry'; and this statement was repeated in the first edition of *H.B.C.* But Mayo was united to Tuam, probably in response to the petition of Abp O'Queely, though the exact date of the union is not known.

BISHOPS OF THE CHURCH
OF IRELAND FROM 1534

BRENDAN BRADSHAW, J. G. SIMMS, AND C. J. WOODS

INTRODUCTION

THE lists for 1534–1957 are primarily based on those compiled by J. G. Simms for *H.B.C.*, pp 351–79, with minor corrections. The section 1534–1603 has been revised by Brendan Bradshaw. From 1957 the lists have been compiled by C. J. Woods from information supplied by Miss Geraldine Willis, librarian of the representative church body, and Mr John Buttimore, assistant secretary of the general synod.

1534 has been taken as the year in which the reformation was extended to Ireland. By May of that year Henry VIII had issued instructions to the Dublin government to ignore papal provisions and jurisdiction. The bishops then in office continued to be recognised by the crown. The term 'Church of Ireland' seems first to have been used for the established church in the act of supremacy, 28 Hen. VIII, c. 5 (1536). In the period 1801–70 the official term was 'the United Church of England and Ireland'. Since 1871 the title of the disestablished church has been the Church of Ireland.

All bishops recognised or appointed by the crown from 1534 to 1870 have been included in these lists, which begin with the bishops in office in 1534, who are also shown in the lists of bishops of Ireland up to 1534 (above, pp 264–332). In addition, some sixteenth-century bishops who are also in the lists of Roman Catholic bishops (above, pp 333–91) are included here if they were recognised by the crown as well as by the pope, and are marked with an asterisk. All bishops in office during the Marian period are presumed to have been recognised by the crown.

Up to the time of disestablishment, which came into effect on 1 January 1871, the dates given for the accession of new bishops are ordinarily those of nomination (i.e. the first letter from the crown relating to the appointment) and of consecration. If either of these is not available, the date of the letters patent of appointment, if known, has been given. For translations the dates of nomination and of the patent of translation have been given whenever possible.

From 1871 onwards archbishops and bishops have been elected. The election of the archbishops of Armagh is made by the house of bishops. For vacancies occurring up to 30 November 1959 the archbishops of Dublin and the bishops were elected either by the diocesan synods or, if a two-thirds majority was not gained in the synod election, by the house of bishops. Elections by diocesan synods required confirmation by the house of bishops. For vacancies since 1 December 1959 elections have been made by an electoral college containing representatives of the house of bishops and of the clergy and laity of each diocese of the province concerned, subject to confirmation by the house of bishops. For the accession of new bishops since 1871, the dates of election and consecration have been given. For translations the dates are those of election and, for those elected by a diocesan synod or by an electoral college, of confirmation.

Amalgamations and divisions of dioceses have been recorded at appropriate places in the lists. In particular the church temporalities act of 1833 (3 & 4 Will IV, c. 37) provided for a number of amalgamations, which were to take effect as vacancies occurred. That act also reduced the number of provinces to two, Cashel and Tuam ceasing to be archbishoprics. In recent years there have also been a number of amalgamations and divisions of dioceses.

PROVINCE OF ARMAGH

DIOCESE OF ARMAGH

archbishops	accession	death unless otherwise stated
George Cromer*	papal prov. 2 Oct. 1521 cons. Apr. 1522	16 Mar. 1543
George Dowdall, O.Cruc.*	nom. 19 Apr. 1543 cons. Dec. 1543	deemed to have abandoned see a. 28 July 1551
Hugh Goodacre	nom. 28 Oct. 1552 cons. 2 Feb. 1553	1 May 1553
George Dowdall*	reinstated 23 Oct. 1553	15 Aug. 1558
Adam Loftus	nom. 30 Oct. 1562[1] cons. 2 Mar. 1563	trs. to Dublin 9 Aug. 1567
Thomas Lancaster[2]	nom. 12 Mar. 1568 cons. 13 June 1568	1584
John Long	nom. 7 July 1584 cons. 13 July 1584	a. 16 Jan. 1589
John Garvey	trs. from Kilmore nom. 24 Mar. 1589 l.p. 10 May 1589	2 Mar. 1595

archbishops	accession	death unless otherwise stated
Henry Ussher	nom. 24 May 1595 cons. Aug. 1595	2 Apr. 1613
Christopher Hampton	nom. 16 Apr. 1613 cons. 8 May 1613	3 Jan. 1625
James Ussher[3]	trs. from Meath nom. 29 Jan. 1625 l.p. 21 Mar. 1625	21 Mar. 1656
John Bramhall	trs. from Derry nom. 1 Aug. 1660 l.p. 18 Jan. 1661	25 June 1663
James Margetson	trs. from Dublin nom. 25 July 1663 l.p. 20 Aug. 1663	28 Aug. 1678
Michael Boyle	trs. from Dublin nom. 21 Jan. 1679 l.p. 27 Feb. 1679	10 Dec. 1702
Narcissus Marsh	trs. from Dublin nom. 26 Jan. 1703 l.p. 18 Feb. 1703	2 Nov. 1713
Thomas Lindsay	trs. from Raphoe nom. 22 Dec. 1713 l.p. 4 Jan. 1714	13 July 1724
Hugh Boulter	trs. from Bristol nom. 12 Aug. 1724 l.p. 31 Aug. 1724	27 Sept. 1742
John Hoadly	trs. from Dublin nom. 6 Oct. 1742 l.p. 21 Oct. 1742	16 July 1746
George Stone	trs. from Derry nom. 28 Feb. 1747 l.p. 13 Mar. 1747	19 Dec. 1764
Richard Robinson (cr. Baron Rokeby 26 Feb. 1777)	trs. from Kildare nom. 8 Jan. 1765 l.p. 8 Feb. 1765	10 Oct. 1794
William Newcome	trs. from Waterford nom. 16 Jan. 1795 l.p. 27 Jan. 1795	11 Jan. 1800
Hon. William Stuart	trs. from St David's nom. 30 Oct. 1800 l.p. 22 Nov. 1800	6 May 1822
Lord John George Beresford	trs. from Dublin nom. 17 June 1822 l.p. 17 June 1822	18 July 1862

(Clogher united to Armagh, 1850–86)

Marcus Gervais Beresford	trs. from Kilmore l.p. 15 Oct. 1862	26 Dec. 1885

archbishops	accession	death unless otherwise stated
Robert Bent Knox	trs. from Down el. 11 May 1886	23 Oct. 1893
Robert Samuel Gregg	trs. from Cork el. 14 Dec. 1893	10 Jan. 1896
William Alexander	trs. from Derry el. 25 Feb. 1896	res. 1 Feb. 1911 d. 12 Sept. 1911
John Baptist Crozier	trs. from Down el. 2 Feb. 1911	11 Apr. 1920
Charles Frederick D'Arcy	trs. from Dublin el. 17 June 1920	1 Feb. 1938
John Godfrey Fitzmaurice Day	trs. from Ossory el. 27 Apr. 1938	26 Sept. 1938
John Allen Fitzgerald Gregg	trs. from Dublin el. 15 Dec. 1938	res. 18 Feb. 1959 d. 2 May 1961
James McCann	trs. from Meath el. 19 Feb. 1959	res. 16 July 1969
George Otto Simms	trs. from Dublin el. 17 July 1969	res. 11 Feb. 1980
John Ward Armstrong	trs. from Cashel el. 25 Feb. 1980	

[1] *Congé d'élire*, in spite of the act 2 Eliz. I, c.4; the chapter refused to elect and the crown proceeded to appoint directly.
[2] Former bp of Kildare, depr. 1554.
[3] Held Carlisle *in commendam* from 16 Feb. 1642.

DIOCESE OF ARDAGH

bishops	accession	death unless otherwise stated
Rory O'Malone (Ruaidhrí Ó Maoileóin, Roger O'Melline)*	papal prov. 14 Dec. 1517	1540
Richard O'Ferrall	nom. 2 May 1541	1553
Patrick MacMahon*	papal prov. 24 Nov. 1541 obtained possession 1553	c. 1572
John Garvey[4]	nom. 6 Nov. 1572 (never cons.)	
Lysach O'Ferrall	nom. 4 Nov. 1583	a. 26 Apr. 1601
(Held with Kilmore, 1604–33)		
John Richardson	nom. 8 Apr. 1633 cons. Sept. 1633	11 Aug. 1654
(Held with Kilmore, 1661–92)		

bishops	*accession*	*death unless otherwise stated*
Ulysses Burgh	nom. 7 Apr. 1692 cons. 11 Sept. 1692	1692

(Held with Kilmore, 1693–1742; held with Tuam, 1742–1839; since 1839 united to Kilmore)

[4] Later bp of Kilmore (27 Jan. 1585) and abp of Armagh (10 May 1589).

DIOCESE OF CLOGHER

Patrick O'Cullen (Pádraig Ó Cuilín), O.S.A.*	papal prov. 11 Feb. 1517	*a.* 26 Mar. 1534
Hugh O'Carolan (Aodh Ó Cearbhalláin)*[5]	papal prov. 6 Aug. 1535 cons. Jan. 1537 conf. by crown 8 Oct. 1542	1569
Miler Magrath[6]	l.p. 18 Sept. 1570	trs. to Cashel 3 Feb. 1571

(See not filled by crown 1571–1604)

George Montgomery[7]	nom. 15 Feb. 1605 l.p. 13 June 1605	15 Jan. 1621
James Spottiswood	nom. 20 Jan. 1621 mandate for cons. 22 Oct. 1621	Mar. 1645
Henry Jones	nom. 29 Sept. 1645 cons. 9 Nov. 1645	trs. to Meath 25 May 1661
John Leslie	trs. from Raphoe nom. 29 Apr. 1661 l.p. 17 June 1661	8 Sept. 1671
Robert Leslie	trs. from Raphoe l.p. 26 Oct. 1671	10 Aug. 1672
Roger Boyle	trs. from Down nom. 29 Aug. 1672 l.p. 19 Sept. 1672	26 Nov. 1687
Richard Tennison	trs. from Killala nom. 4 Dec. 1690 l.p. 28 Feb. 1691	trs. to Meath 25 June 1697
St George Ashe	trs. from Cloyne nom. 1 June 1697 l.p. 25 June 1697	trs. to Derry 25 Feb. 1717
John Stearne	trs. from Dromore nom. 28 Feb. 1717 l.p. 30 Mar. 1717	6 June 1745
Robert Clayton	trs. from Cork nom. 3 Aug. 1745 l.p. 26 Aug. 1745	26 Feb. 1758

bishops	accession	death unless otherwise stated
John Garnett	trs. from Ferns nom. 14 Mar. 1758 l.p. 4 Apr. 1758	1 Mar. 1782
John Hotham (succ. as bt, 25 Jan. 1794)	trs. from Ossory nom. 11 Apr. 1782 l.p. 17 May 1782	3 Nov. 1795
William Foster	trs. from Kilmore nom. 26 Dec. 1795 l.p. 21 Jan. 1796	a. 4 Nov. 1797
John Porter	trs. from Killala nom. 18 Dec. 1797 l.p. 30 Dec. 1797	27 July 1819
Lord John George Beresford	trs. from Raphoe nom. 29 Aug. 1819 l.p. 25 Sept. 1819	trs. to Dublin 21 Apr. 1820
Hon. Percy Jocelyn	trs. from Ferns nom. 3 Apr. 1820 l.p. 3 Apr. 1820	depr. 21 Oct. 1822 d. 2 Dec. 1843
Lord Robert Ponsonby Tottenham Loftus	trs. from Ferns nom. 26 Nov. 1822 l.p. 21 Dec. 1822	26 Apr. 1850

(See united to Armagh 1850–86)

Charles Maurice Stack	el. 4 June 1886 cons. 29 June 1886	res. 31 Dec. 1902 d. 9 Jan. 1914
Charles Frederick D'Arcy	el. 21 Jan. 1903 cons. 24 Feb. 1903	trs. to Ossory 6 Nov. 1907
Maurice Day	el. 19 Dec. 1907 cons. 25 Jan. 1908	27 May 1923
James MacManaway	el. 9 July 1923 cons. 6 Aug. 1923	res. 30 Sept. 1943 d. 29 Nov. 1947
Richard Tyner	el. 9 Nov. 1943 cons. 6 Jan. 1944	6 Apr. 1958
Alan Alexander Buchanan	el. 17 June 1958 cons. 29 Sept. 1958	trs. to Dublin 14 Oct. 1969
Richard Patrick Crosland Hanson	el. 9 Dec. 1969 cons. 17 Mar. 1970	res. 31 Mar. 1973
Robert William Heavener	el. 4 May 1973 cons. 29 June 1973	res. 31 May 1980
Gordon McMullan	el. 13 June 1980 cons. 7 Sept. 1980	

[5] Renounced provision 1 Oct. 1542. See above, p. 343, n. 26.
[6] Papal bp of Down; accepted royal supremacy.
[7] Held Clogher with Derry and Raphoe to 1610; from 1612 held Clogher with Meath.

DIOCESE OF CLONMACNOISE

bishops	accession	death unless otherwise stated
Quintin O'Higgins (Quintinus Ó hUiginn), O.F.M.*	papal prov. 10 Nov. 1516	a. 16 June 1539
Florence Kirwan*	papal prov. 5 Dec. 1539 conf. by crown 23 Sept. 1541	res. 4 May 1556[8]
Peter Wall, O.P.*	papal prov. 4 May 1556	1568

(See united to Meath 1569)

[8] Appears to have res. in 1554 (Lynch, *De praesulibus Hib.*, i, 276).

DIOCESE OF CONNOR

(See united to Down 1442? to 1944; see above, p. 281, n. 19)

bishops	accession	death unless otherwise stated
Charles King Irwin[9]	1 Jan. 1945	res. 31 May 1956 d. 15 Jan. 1960
Robert Cyril Hamilton Glover Elliott	el. 28 June 1956 cons. 21 Sept. 1956	res. 31 July 1969 d. 3 Apr. 1977
Arthur Hamilton Butler	trs. from Tuam el. 16 Sept. 1969 conf. 14 Oct. 1969	res. 30 Sept. 1981
William McCappin	el. 28 Oct. 1981 cons. 30 Nov. 1981	

[9] Bp of united diocese of Down, Connor, and Dromore; retained Connor on the separation of the see.

DIOCESE OF DERRY

bishops	accession	death unless otherwise stated
Rory O'Donnell (Ruaidhrí Ó Domhnaill)*	papal prov. 11 Jan. 1520 conf. by crown, 23 Sept. 1541	8 Oct. 1550/51
Eugene O'Doherty*	papal prov. 25 June 1554	c. 1569

(See not filled by crown until 1605)

George Montgomery[10]	nom. 15 Feb. 1605 l.p. 13 June 1605	trs. to Meath 8 July 1609
Brutus Babington	nom. 11 Aug. 1610 cons. 1610	10 Sept. 1611

bishops	accession	death unless otherwise stated
John Tanner	nom. 16 Apr. 1613 cons. May 1613	14 Oct. 1615
George Downham	nom. 28 Oct. 1616 cons. Jan. 1617	17 Apr. 1634
John Bramhall	nom. 9 May 1634 cons. 26 May 1634	trs. to Armagh 18 Jan. 1661
George Wild	nom. 6 Aug. 1660 cons. 27 Jan. 1661	29 Dec. 1665
Robert Mossom	nom. 11 Jan. 1666 cons. 1 Apr. 1666	21 Dec. 1679
Michael Ward	trs. from Ossory nom. 6 Jan. 1680 l.p. 22 Jan. 1680	3 Oct. 1681
Ezekiel Hopkins	trs. from Raphoe nom. 21 Oct. 1681 l.p. 11 Nov. 1681	22 June 1690
William King	nom. 7 Dec. 1690 cons. 25 Jan. 1691	trs. to Dublin 11 Mar. 1703
Charles Hickman	nom. 17 Feb. 1703 cons. 11 June 1703	28 Nov. 1713
John Hartstonge	trs. from Ossory nom. 7 Feb. 1714 l.p. 3 Mar. 1714	30 Jan. 1717
St George Ashe	trs. from Clogher nom. 16 Feb. 1717 l.p. 25 Feb. 1717	27 Feb. 1718
William Nicolson	trs. from Carlisle l.p. 2 May 1718	trs. to Cashel 28 Jan. 1727
Henry Downes	trs. from Meath nom. 11 Jan. 1727 l.p. 8 Feb. 1727	14 Jan. 1735
Thomas Rundle	nom. 20 Feb. 1735 cons. 3 Aug. 1735	15 Apr. 1743
Carew Reynell	trs. from Down nom. 25 Apr. 1743 l.p. 6 May 1743	1 Jan. 1745
George Stone	trs. from Kildare nom. 26 Apr. 1745 l.p. 11 May 1745	trs. to Armagh 13 Mar. 1747
William Barnard	trs. from Raphoe nom. 28 Feb. 1747 l.p. 19 Mar. 1747	10 Jan. 1768
Hon. Frederick Augustus Hervey (earl of Bristol 23 Sept. 1779)	trs. from Cloyne nom. 28 Jan. 1768 l.p. 18 Feb. 1768	8 July 1803

bishops	accession	death unless otherwise stated
Hon. William Knox	trs. from Killaloe nom. 27 Aug. 1803 l.p. 9 Sept. 1803	10 July 1831
Hon. Richard Ponsonby	trs. from Killaloe nom. 14 Sept. 1831 l.p. 21 Sept. 1831	27 Oct. 1853

(Raphoe united to Derry 1834)

William Higgin	trs. from Limerick nom. 18 Nov. 1853 l.p. 7 Dec. 1853	12 July 1867
William Alexander	nom. 27 July 1867 cons. 6 Oct. 1867	trs. to Armagh 25 Feb. 1896
George Alexander Chadwick	el. 18 Feb. 1896 cons. 25 Mar. 1896	res. 31 Jan. 1916 d. 27 Dec. 1923
Joseph Irvine Peacocke	el. 15 Mar. 1916 cons. 25 Apr. 1916	res. 31 Dec. 1944 d. 31 Jan. 1962
Robert McNeil Boyd	trs. from Killaloe el. 18 Mar. 1945 conf. 20 Mar. 1945	d. 1 July 1958
Charles John Tyndall	trs. from Kilmore el. and conf. 14 Oct. 1958	res. 30 Sept. 1969 d. 3 Apr. 1971
Cuthbert Irvine Peacocke	el. 16 Oct. 1969 cons. 6 Jan. 1970	res. 31 Mar. 1975
Robert Henry Alexander Eames	el. 9 May 1975 cons. 9 June 1975	trs. to Down 20 May 1980
James Mehaffey	el. 27 June 1980 cons. 7 Sept. 1980	

[10] Also bp of Clogher and Raphoe.

DIOCESE OF DOWN AND CONNOR

bishops	accession	death unless otherwise stated
Robert Blyth, O.S.B.*	papal prov. 16 Apr. 1520	res. c. 1541 d. p. 19 Oct. 1547
Eugene Magennis*	papal prov. 16 June 1539 l.p. 8 May 1542	c. 1563
James McCawell	nom. 6 June 1565 (did not obtain possession)	nom. to Cashel 12 Feb. 1567
John Merriman	temp. 20 Dec. 1568 cons. 19 Jan. 1569	a. 6 July 1571

bishops	accession	death unless otherwise stated
Hugh Allen	l.p. 21 Nov. 1572	trs. to Ferns 24 May 1582
Edward Edgeworth	nom. 31 July 1593 cons. 1593	1595
John Charden	cons. 4 May 1596	1601
Robert Humpston	nom. 17 July 1601 cons. 5 Apr. 1602	a. 14 Jan. 1607
John Todd[11]	nom. 24 Jan. 1607 l.p. 16 May 1607	res. 20 Jan. 1612
James Dundas	nom. 23 Feb. 1612 cons. July 1612	a. 29 Nov. 1612
Robert Echlin	nom. 29 Nov. 1612 l.p. 4 Mar. 1613	17 July 1635
Henry Leslie	nom. 8 Aug. 1635 cons. 4 Oct. 1635	trs. to Meath 19 Jan. 1661
Jeremy Taylor	nom. 6 Aug. 1660 cons. 27 Jan. 1661	13 Aug. 1667
Roger Boyle	nom. 26 Aug. 1667 cons. 18 Oct. 1667	trs. to Clogher 19 Sept. 1672
Thomas Hacket	nom. 29 Aug. 1672 cons. 28 Sept. 1672	depr. 21 Mar. 1694 d. Aug. 1697
Samuel Foley	nom. 17 Aug. 1694 cons. 2 Sept. 1694	22 May 1695
Edward Walkington	nom. 10 July 1695 cons. 4 Aug. 1695	Jan. 1699
Edward Smyth	nom. 21 Jan. 1699 cons. 2 Apr. 1699	16 Oct. 1720
Francis Hutchinson	nom. 30 Nov. 1720 cons. 22 Jan. 1721	23 June 1739
Carew Reynell	nom. 4 Sept. 1739 cons. 18 Nov. 1739	trs. to Derry 6 May 1743
John Ryder	trs. from Killaloe nom. 25 Apr. 1743 l.p. 1 Aug. 1743	trs. to Tuam 19 Mar. 1752
John Whitcombe	trs. from Clonfert nom. 24 Feb. 1752 l.p. 21 Mar. 1752	trs. to Cashel 1 Sept. 1752
Robert Downes	trs. from Ferns nom. 12 Aug. 1752 l.p. 13 Oct. 1752	trs. to Raphoe 16 Jan. 1753
Arthur Smyth	trs. from Clonfert nom. 28 Dec. 1752 l.p. 24 Jan. 1753	trs. to Meath 28 Oct. 1765
James Traill	nom. 27 Sept. 1765 cons. 3 Nov. 1765	12 Nov. 1783
William Dickson	nom. 19 Nov. 1783 cons. 1 Feb. 1784	19 Sept. 1804

bishops	accession	death unless otherwise stated
Nathaniel Alexander	trs. from Killaloe nom. 2 Nov. 1804 l.p. 21 Nov. 1804	trs. to Meath 21 Mar. 1823
Richard Mant	trs. from Killaloe nom. 13 Mar. 1823 l.p. 23 Mar. 1823	2 Nov. 1848

(Dromore united to Down 1842)

Robert Bent Knox	nom. 2 Apr. 1849 cons. 1 May 1849	trs. to Armagh 11 May 1886
William Reeves	el. 18 Mar. 1886 cons. 29 June 1886	12 Jan. 1892
Thomas James Welland	el. 19 Feb. 1892 cons. 25 Mar. 1892	29 July 1907
John Baptist Crozier	trs. from Ossory el. 3 Sept. 1907 conf. 26 Sept. 1907	trs. to Armagh 2 Feb. 1911
Charles Frederick D'Arcy	trs. from Ossory el. 27 Mar. 1911 conf. 29 Mar. 1911	trs. to Dublin 15 Oct. 1919
Charles Thornton Primrose Grierson	el. 9 Oct. 1919 cons. 28 Oct. 1919	res. 30 Nov. 1934 d. 9 July 1935
John Frederick McNeice	trs. from Cashel el. 11 Dec. 1934 conf. 12 Dec. 1934	14 Apr. 1942
Charles King Irwin	trs. from Limerick el. 6 Aug. 1942 conf. 17 Nov. 1942	relinquished diocese 1 Jan. 1945[12]

(Connor separated from Down 1944)

[11] Also held Dromore. Sir James Ware (*Works*, rev. Walter Harris, i (Dublin, 1739)) says he was depr. and did not resign. *Cal. S.P. Ire., 1611–14*, p. 248, shows that he res.

[12] Retained Connor on the division of the united diocese 1 Jan. 1945.

DIOCESE OF DOWN

bishops	accession	death unless otherwise stated
William Shaw Kerr[13]	el. 9 Dec. 1944 cons. 25 Jan. 1945	res. 31 July 1955 d. 2 Feb. 1960
Frederick Julian Mitchell	trs. from Kilmore el. and conf. 18 Oct. 1955	res. 7 Nov. 1969 d. 3 June 1979

bishops	accession	death unless otherwise stated
George Alderson Quin	el. 26 Nov. 1969 cons. 6 Jan. 1970	res. 31 Mar. 1980
Robert Henry Alexander Eames	trs. from Derry el. 23 Apr. 1980 conf. 20 May 1980	

[13] Bp of Down and Dromore.

DIOCESE OF DROMORE

(See vacant 1526-40)

bishops	accession	death unless otherwise stated
Arthur Magennis*	papal prov. 16 Apr. 1540 conf. by crown 10 May 1550	c. 1575

(See not filled by crown until 1607)

John Todd[14]	nom. 24 Jan. 1607 l.p. 16 May 1607	res. 20 Jan. 1612
John Tanner	nom. 9 Feb. 1612 l.p. 7 Jan. 1613 (never cons.)	nom. to Derry 16 Apr. 1613
Theophilus Buckworth	nom. 16 Apr. 1613 cons. May 1613	a. 8 Sept. 1652[15]
Robert Leslie	nom. 6 Aug. 1660 cons. 27 Jan. 1661	trs. to Raphoe 20 June 1661

(Diocese administered by Jeremy Taylor, bp of Down, 1661-7)

George Rust	nom. 27 Sept. 1667 cons. 15 Dec. 1667	Dec. 1670
Essex Digby	nom. 6 Jan. 1671 cons. 27 Feb. 1671	12 May 1683
Capel Wiseman	nom. 23 June 1683 cons. 23 Sept. 1683	Sept. 1694
Tobias Pullein	trs. from Cloyne nom. 17 Mar. 1695 l.p. 7 May 1695	22 Jan. 1713
John Stearne	nom. 23 Apr. 1713 cons. 10 May 1713	trs. to Clogher 30 Mar. 1717
Ralph Lambert	nom. 14 Mar. 1717 cons. 23 Apr. 1717	trs. to Meath 10 Feb. 1727

bishops	accession	death unless otherwise stated
Charles Cobbe	trs. from Killala nom. 13 Jan. 1727 l.p. 16 Feb. 1727	trs. to Kildare 16 Mar. 1732
Henry Maule	trs. from Cloyne nom. 18 Feb. 1732 l.p. 20 Mar. 1732	trs. to Meath 24 May 1744
Thomas Fletcher	nom. 10 May 1744 cons. 10 June 1744	trs. to Kildare 14 May 1745
Jemmett Browne	trs. from Killaloe nom. 26 Apr. 1745 l.p. 16 May 1745	trs. to Cork 27 Aug. 1745
George Marlay	nom. 3 Aug. 1745 cons. 15 Sept. 1745	12 Apr. 1763
John Oswald	trs. from Clonfert nom. 19 Apr. 1763 l.p. 7 May 1763	trs. to Raphoe 25 Aug. 1763
Edward Young	nom. 19 July 1763 cons. 16 Oct. 1763	trs. to Ferns 4 Mar. 1765
Hon. Henry Maxwell	nom. 8 Feb. 1765 cons. 10 Mar. 1765	trs. to Meath 15 Apr. 1766
William Newcome	nom. 28 Feb. 1766 cons. 27 Apr. 1766	trs. to Ossory 13 Apr. 1775
James Hawkins	nom. 23 Mar. 1775 cons. 29 Apr. 1775	trs. to Raphoe 1 Apr. 1780
Hon. William Beresford	nom. 20 Mar. 1780 cons. 8 Apr. 1780	trs. to Ossory 21 May 1782
Thomas Percy	nom. 17 Apr. 1782 cons. 26 May 1782	30 Sept. 1811
George Hall	nom. 10 Oct. 1811 cons. 17 Nov. 1811	23 Nov. 1811
John Leslie	nom. 5 Dec. 1811 cons. 26 Jan. 1812	trs. to Elphin 16 Nov. 1819
James Saurin	nom. 2 Nov. 1819 cons. 19 Dec. 1819	9 Apr. 1842

(See united to Down)

[14] Held Dromore with Down.   [15] Bur. 8 Sept. 1652.

DIOCESE OF KILMORE

bishops	accession	death unless otherwise stated
Edmund Nugent, can. reg.*	papal prov. 22 June 1530	c. 1550
John MacBrady*	papal prov. 5 Nov. 1540	1559

(See not filled by crown 1559–85)

bishops	accession	death unless otherwise stated
John Garvey	nom. 20 Jan. 1585	trs. to Armagh
	l.p. 27 Jan. 1585	10 May 1589

(See not filled by crown 1589-1603)

Robert Draper[16]	nom. 9 Dec. 1603	Aug. 1612
	l.p. 2 Mar. 1604	
Thomas Moigne	nom. 6 Dec. 1612	1 Jan. 1629
	cons. 12 Jan. 1613	
William Bedell	nom. 16 Apr. 1629	7 Feb. 1642
	cons. 13 Sept. 1629	
Robert Maxwell	nom. 17 Nov. 1642	1 Nov. 1672
	cons. 24 Mar. 1643	
Francis Marsh	trs. from Limerick	trs. to Dublin
	nom. 4 Dec. 1672	14 Feb. 1682
	l.p. 10 Jan. 1673	
William Sheridan	nom. 14 Jan. 1682	depr. 1691
	cons. 19 Feb. 1682	d. 1 Oct. 1711
William Smyth	trs. from Raphoe	24 Feb. 1699
	l.p. 5 Apr. 1693	
Edward Wetenhall	trs. from Cork	12 Nov. 1713
	nom. 19 Mar. 1699	
	l.p. 18 Apr. 1699	
Timothy Godwin	nom. 7 Oct. 1714	trs. to Cashel
	cons. 16 Jan. 1715	3 July 1727
Josiah Hort	trs. from Ferns	trs. to Tuam
	l.p. 27 July 1727	27 Jan. 1742
Joseph Story	trs. from Killaloe	22 Sept. 1757
	nom. 7 Jan. 1742	
	l.p. 29 Jan. 1742	
John Cradock	nom. 14 Oct. 1757	trs. to Dublin
	cons. 4 Dec. 1757	5 Mar. 1772
Denison Cumberland	trs. from Clonfert	a. 22 Nov.
	nom. 27 Jan. 1772	1774[17]
	l.p. 6 Mar. 1772	
George Lewis Jones	nom. 21 Nov. 1774	trs. to Kildare
	cons. 22 Jan. 1775	5 June 1790
William Foster	trs. from Cork	trs. to Clogher
	nom. 7 May 1790	21 Jan. 1796
	l.p. 11 June 1790	
Hon. Charles Broderick	trs. from Clonfert	trs. to Cashel
	nom. 28 Dec. 1795	9 Dec. 1801
	l.p. 19 Jan. 1796	
George de la Poer Beresford	trs. from Clonfert	15 Oct. 1841
	nom. 12 Jan. 1802	
	l.p. 1 Mar. 1802	

(Ardagh and Elphin united to Kilmore 1841)

bishops	accession	death unless otherwise stated
John Leslie	15 Oct. 1841	22 July 1854
Marcus Gervais Beresford	nom. 14 Aug. 1854	trs. to Armagh
	cons. 24 Sept. 1854	15 Oct. 1862
Hamilton Verschoyle	l.p. 24 Oct. 1862	28 Jan. 1870
	cons. 26 Oct. 1862	
Charles Leslie	nom. 8 Apr. 1870	8 July 1870
	cons. 24 Apr. 1870	
Thomas Carson	nom. 9 Sept. 1870	7 July 1874
	cons. 2 Oct. 1870	
John Richard Darley	el. 23 Sept. 1874	20 Jan. 1884
	cons. 25 Oct. 1874	
Samuel Shone	el. 26 Mar. 1884	res. *c.* 1 Sept.
	cons. 25 Apr. 1884	1897
		d. 5 Oct. 1901
Alfred George Elliott	el. 2 Sept. 1897	28 Sept. 1915
	cons. 17 Oct. 1897	
William Richard Moore	el. 10 Nov. 1915	23 Feb. 1930
	cons. 30 Nov. 1915	
Arthur William Barton	el. 4 Apr. 1930	trs. to Dublin
	cons. 1 May 1930	15 Feb. 1939
Albert Edward Hughes	el. 14 Dec. 1938	res. 12 May 1950
	cons. 25 Apr. 1939	d. 12 May 1954
Frederick Julian Mitchell	el. 28 July 1950	trs. to Down
	cons. 21 Sept. 1950	18 Oct. 1955
Charles John Tyndall	el. 16 Dec. 1955	trs. to Derry
	cons. 2 Feb. 1956	14 Oct. 1958
Edward Francis Butler Moore	el. 28 Nov. 1958	res. 31 May 1981
	cons. 6 Jan. 1959	
William Gilbert Wilson	el. 11 June 1981	
	cons. 21 Sept. 1981	

[16] The bps of Kilmore held Ardagh in addition 1604–33, 1661–92, and 1693–1742.
[17] Bur. 22 Nov. 1774.

DIOCESE OF MEATH

bishops	accession	death unless otherwise stated
Edward Staples*	papal prov. 3 Sept. 1529	depr. 29 June 1554
		d. 1560
William Walsh[18]	l.p. 22 Nov. 1554	depr. 1560
		d. 4 Jan. 1577
Hugh Brady	nom. 21 Oct. 1563	14 Feb. 1584
	cons. 19 Dec. 1563	

(Clonmacnoise united to Meath 1569)

bishops	*accession*	*death unless otherwise stated*
Thomas Jones	nom. 18 Apr. 1584 cons. 12 May 1584	trs. to Dublin 8 Nov. 1605
Roger Dod	l.p. 13 Nov. 1605	27 July 1608
George Montgomery[19]	trs. from Derry nom. 8 July 1609 l.p. 24 Jan. 1612	15 Jan. 1621
James Ussher	nom. 16 Jan. 1621 cons. 2 Dec. 1621	trs. to Armagh 21 Mar. 1625
Anthony Martin	nom. 22 Feb. 1625 cons. 25 July 1625	July 1650
Henry Leslie	trs. from Down nom. 3 Aug. 1660 l.p. 19 Jan. 1661	7 Apr. 1661
Henry Jones	trs. from Clogher nom. 9 Apr. 1661 l.p. 25 May 1661	5 Jan. 1682
Anthony Dopping	trs. from Kildare nom. 14 Jan. 1682 l.p. 11 Feb. 1682	25 Apr. 1697
Richard Tennison	trs. from Clogher nom. 1 June 1697 l.p. 25 June 1697	29 July 1705
William Moreton	trs. from Kildare nom. 27 Aug. 1705 l.p. 18 Sept. 1705	21 Nov. 1715
John Evans	trs. from Bangor nom. 19 Jan. 1716 l.p. 10 Feb. 1716	2 Mar. 1724
Henry Downes	trs. from Elphin nom. 17 Mar. 1724 l.p. 9 Apr. 1724	trs. to Derry 8 Feb. 1727
Ralph Lambert	trs. from Dromore nom. 12 Jan. 1727 l.p. 10 Feb. 1727	6 Feb. 1732
Welbore Ellis	trs. from Kildare nom. 18 Feb. 1732 l.p. 13 Mar. 1732	1 Jan. 1734
Arthur Price	trs. from Ferns nom. 18 Jan. 1734 l.p. 2 Feb. 1734	trs. to Cashel 7 May 1744
Henry Maule	trs. from Dromore nom. 10 May 1744 l.p. 24 May 1744	13 Apr. 1758
Hon. William Carmichael	trs. from Ferns nom. 30 May 1758 l.p. 8 June 1758	trs. to Dublin 12 June 1765

bishops	accession	death unless otherwise stated
Richard Pococke	trs. from Ossory nom. 22 June 1765 l.p. 16 July 1765	15 Sept. 1765
Arthur Smyth	trs. from Down nom. 27 Sept. 1765 l.p. 28 Oct. 1765	trs. to Dublin 14 Apr. 1766
Hon. Henry Maxwell	trs. from Dromore nom. 28 Feb. 1766 l.p. 15 Apr. 1766	7 Oct. 1798
Thomas Lewis O'Beirne	trs. from Ossory nom. 1 Dec. 1798 l.p. 18 Dec. 1798	17 Feb. 1823
Nathaniel Alexander	trs. from Down nom. 12 Mar. 1823 l.p. 21 Mar. 1823	21 Oct. 1840
Charles Dickinson	nom. 21 Dec. 1840 cons. 27 Dec. 1840	12 July 1842
Edward Stopford	nom. 20 Oct. 1842 cons. 6 Nov. 1842	17 Sept. 1850
Thomas Stewart Townsend	nom. 9 Oct. 1850 cons. 1 Nov. 1850	1 Sept. 1852
Joseph Henderson Singer	nom. 2 Nov. 1852 cons. 28 Nov. 1852	16 July 1866
Samuel Butcher	l.p. 21 Aug. 1866 cons. 14 Oct. 1866	29 July 1876
William Conyngham Plunket, Baron Plunket	el. 18 Oct. 1876 cons. 10 Dec. 1876	trs. to Dublin 23 Dec. 1884
Charles Parsons Reichel	el. 19 Aug. 1885 cons. 29 Sept. 1885	29 Mar. 1894
Joseph Ferguson Peacocke	el. 15 May 1894 cons. 11 June 1894	trs. to Dublin 19 May 1897
James Bennett Keene	el. 10 Sept. 1897 cons. 17 Oct. 1897	5 Aug. 1919
Hon. Benjamin John Plunket	trs. from Tuam el. 3 Oct. 1919 conf. 15 Oct. 1919	res. 31 Mar. 1925 d. 26 Jan. 1947
Thomas Gibson George Collins	el. 4 Feb. 1926 cons. 17 Mar. 1926	3 July 1927
John Orr	trs. from Tuam el. 22 Sept. 1927 conf. 15 Nov. 1927	21 July 1938
William Hardy Holmes	trs. from Tuam el. 14 Oct. 1938 conf. 19 Oct. 1938	res. 31 May 1945 d. 26 May 1951
James McCann	el. 4 July 1945 cons. 24 Aug. 1945	trs. to Armagh 19 Feb. 1959

bishops	accession	death unless otherwise stated
Robert Bonsall Pike	el. 14 Apr. 1959 cons. 19 May 1959	27 Dec. 1973

(The see was transferred from the province of Armagh to that of Dublin, and Kildare was separated from the see of Dublin and united with Meath to form the see of Meath and Kildare, in accordance with a statute of the general synod of 13 May 1976)

Donald Arthur Richard Caird	trs. from Limerick el. 9 Sept. 1976 conf. 14 Sept. 1976	

[18] Nom. by *congé d'élire* (N.D.) Cardinal Pole gave Walsh a conditional provision 18 Oct. 1554, subject to papal confirmation, which was not given until 1564. See above, p. 352, n. 61.

[19] Bp of Clogher, which he continued to hold in addition.

DIOCESE OF RAPHOE

bishops	accession	death unless otherwise stated
Cornelius O'Cahan (Conn Ó Catháin)*	papal prov. 6 Feb. 1514	p. 1550
Art (Arthur) O'Gallagher*	papal prov. 28 Nov. 1547	13 Aug. 1561

(See not filled by crown 1561–1605)

George Montgomery[20]	nom. 15 Feb. 1605 l.p. 13 June 1605	trs. to Meath 8 July 1609
Andrew Knox	trs. from the Isles nom. 7 May 1610 l.p. 26 June 1611	17 Mar. 1633
John Leslie	trs. from the Isles nom. 8 Apr. 1633 l.p. 1 June 1633	trs. to Clogher 17 June 1661
Robert Leslie	trs. from Dromore nom. 29 Apr. 1661 l.p. 20 June 1661	trs. to Clogher 26 Oct. 1671
Ezekiel Hopkins	nom. 6 Sept. 1671 cons. 29 Oct. 1671	trs. to Derry 11 Nov. 1681
William Smyth	trs. from Killala nom. 16 Jan. 1682 l.p. 17 Feb. 1682	trs. to Kilmore 5 Apr. 1693
Alexander Cairncross	former abp of Glasgow depr. 13 Jan. 1687 nom. 22 Mar. 1693 l.p. 16 May 1693	14 May 1701

bishops	accession	death unless otherwise stated
Robert Huntington	nom. 7 June 1701	2 Sept. 1701
	cons. 20 July 1701	
John Pooley	trs. from Cloyne	16 Oct. 1712
	nom. 14 May 1702	
	l.p. 12 Sept. 1702	
Thomas Lindsay	trs. from Killaloe	trs. to Armagh
	nom. 23 Apr. 1713	4 Jan. 1714
	l.p. 6 June 1713	
Edward Synge	nom. 7 Oct. 1714	trs. to Tuam
	cons. 7 Nov. 1714	8 June 1716
Nicholas Forster	trs. from Killaloe	5 June 1743
	nom. 22 May 1716	
	l.p. 8 June 1716	
William Barnard	nom. 20 Apr. 1744	trs. to Derry
	cons. 19 Aug. 1744	19 Mar. 1747
Philip Twysden	nom. 28 Feb. 1747	2 Nov. 1752
	cons. 29 Mar. 1747	
Robert Downes	trs. from Down	30 June 1763
	nom. 28 Dec. 1752	
	l.p. 16 Jan. 1753	
John Oswald	trs. from Dromore	4 Mar. 1780
	nom. 18 July 1763	
	l.p. 25 Aug. 1763	
James Hawkins	trs. from Dromore	23 June 1807
	nom. 20 Mar. 1780	
	l.p. 1 Apr. 1780	
Lord John George Beresford	trs. from Cork	trs. to Clogher
	nom. 23 July 1807	25 Sept. 1819
	l.p. 10 Aug. 1807	
William Magee	l.p. 22 Sept. 1819	trs. to Dublin
	cons. 24 Oct. 1819	24 June 1822
William Bissett	nom. 17 June 1822	5 Sept. 1834
	cons. 21 July 1822	

(See then united to Derry)

[20] Also bp of Clogher and Derry.

PROVINCE OF CASHEL
DIOCESE OF CASHEL

archbishops	accession	death unless otherwise stated
Edmund Butler, O.S.Trin.*	prov. 21 Oct. 1524 cons. *p.* 3 Jan. 1525	5 Mar. 1551
Roland Baron (Fitzgerald)*	nom. 14 Oct. 1553 cons. Dec. 1553	28 Oct. 1561
James MacCawell	nom. 12 Feb. 1567 l.p. 2 Oct. 1567	1570
Miler Magrath[1]	trs. from Clogher app. 3 Feb. 1571	14 Nov. 1622
Malcolm Hamilton	nom. 8 Mar. 1623 cons. 29 June 1623	25 Apr. 1629
Archibald Hamilton	trs. from Killala nom. 14 Nov. 1629 l.p. 20 Apr. 1630	1659
Thomas Fulwar	trs. from Ardfert nom. 2 Aug. 1660 l.p. 1 Feb. 1661	31 Mar. 1667
Thomas Price	trs. from Kildare nom. 20 Apr. 1667 l.p. 30 Mar. 1667	4 Aug. 1685
Narcissus Marsh	trs. from Ferns nom. 25 Dec. 1690 l.p. 26 Feb. 1691	trs. to Dublin 24 May 1694
William Palliser	trs. from Cloyne nom. 10 Apr. 1694 l.p. 26 June 1694	1 Jan. 1727
William Nicolson	trs. from Derry nom. 10 Jan. 1727 l.p. 28 Jan. 1727	14 Feb. 1727
Timothy Godwin	trs. from Kilmore nom. 20 June 1727 l.p. 3 July 1727	13 Dec. 1729
Theophilus Bolton	trs. from Elphin nom. 26 Dec. 1729 l.p. 6 Jan. 1730	31 Jan. 1744
Arthur Price	trs. from Meath nom. 20 Apr. 1744 l.p. 7 May 1744	17 July 1752
John Whitcombe	trs. from Down nom. 12 Aug. 1752 l.p. 1 Sept. 1752	22 Sept. 1753
Michael Cox	trs. from Ossory nom. 3 Jan. 1754 l.p. 22 Jan. 1754	28 May 1779

archbishops	accession	death unless otherwise stated
Charles Agar[2]	trs. from Cloyne nom. 26 July 1779 l.p. 6 Aug. 1779	trs. to Dublin 7 Dec. 1801
Hon. Charles Brodrick	trs. from Kilmore nom. 21 Nov. 1801 l.p. 9 Dec. 1801	6 May 1822
Richard Laurence	nom. 28 June 1822 cons. 21 July 1822	28 Dec. 1838

(Waterford and Lismore united to Cashel 1833; on death of Abp Laurence province united to Dublin and see ceased to be archbishopric)

bishops		
Stephen Creagh Sandes	trs. from Killaloe nom. 23 Jan. 1839 l.p. Feb. 1839	13 Nov. 1842
Robert Daly	nom. 28 Dec. 1842 cons. 29 Jan. 1843	16 Feb. 1872
Maurice Fitzgerald Day	el. 19 Mar. 1872 cons. 14 Apr. 1872	res. 30 Sept. 1899 d. 13 Dec. 1904
Henry Stewart O'Hara	el. 6 Feb. 1900 cons. 24 Feb. 1900	res. 31 Mar. 1919 d. 11 Dec. 1923
Robert Miller	el. 12 May 1919 cons. 11 June 1919	13 Mar. 1931
John Frederick McNeice	el. 29 Apr. 1931 cons. 24 June 1931	trs. to Down 12 Dec. 1934
Thomas Arnold Harvey	el. 25 Jan. 1935 cons. 25 Mar. 1935	res. 15 May 1958 d. 25 Dec. 1966
William Cecil de Pauley	el. 18 June 1958 cons. 29 Sept. 1958	30 Mar. 1968
John Ward Armstrong	el. 22 May 1968 cons. 21 Sept. 1968	trs. to Armagh 25 Feb. 1980
Noel Vincent Willoughby	el. 28 Mar. 1980 cons. 25 Apr. 1980	

(Emly was separated from Cashel and united with Limerick in accordance with a statute of the general synod of 13 May 1976)

[1] Also held Waterford and Lismore 1582–9 and 1592–1608; held Killala 1613–22 and Achonry 1607–22.

[2] Created Baron Somerton 12 June 1795; Viscount Somerton 30 Dec. 1800; earl of Normanton 4 Feb. 1806.

DIOCESE OF ARDFERT

bishops	accession	death unless otherwise stated
James (fitz Richard) Fitzmaurice, O.Cist.*[3]	papal prov. 15 May 1536	1583
Nicholas Keenan	nom. 26 June 1588 l.p. 22 Oct. 1588	c. 1599
John Crosbie	nom. 2 Oct. 1600 l.p. 15 Dec. 1600	Sept. 1621
John Steere	trs. from Kilfenora nom. 8 Dec. 1621 l.p. 20 July 1622	May 1628
William Steere	nom. 21 July 1628 cons. Oct. 1628	21 Jan. 1638
Thomas Fulwar	nom. 27 June 1641 cons. 1641	trs. to Cashel 1 Feb. 1661

(See united to Limerick)

[3] Fitzmaurice is shown as bishop in May 1534 by R. D. Edwards, 'The Irish bishops and the anglican schism, 1534-1547' in *Irish Ecclesiastical Record*, 5th ser., xlv (1935), p. 198, although it is noted there that he was not app. by the pope until 1536.

DIOCESE OF CLOYNE

(See united to Cork 1429-1638)

George Synge	nom. 21 June 1638 cons. 11 Nov. 1638	Aug. 1652

(See held with Cork 1661-78)

Patrick Sheridan	nom. 11 Feb. 1679 cons. 27 Apr. 1679	22 Nov. 1682
Edward Jones	nom. 22 Dec. 1682 cons. 11 Mar. 1683	trs. to St Asaph 13 Dec. 1692 d. 10 May 1703
William Palliser	nom. 20 Jan. 1693 cons. 5 Mar. 1693	trs. to Cashel 26 June 1694
Tobias Pullein	nom. 29 Sept. 1694 cons. Nov. 1694	trs. to Dromore 7 May 1695
St George Ashe	nom. 17 Mar. 1695 cons. 18 July 1695	trs. to Clogher 25 June 1697
John Pooley	nom. 1 June 1697 cons. 5 Dec. 1697	trs. to Raphoe 12 Sept. 1702

bishops	accession	death unless otherwise stated
Charles Crow	nom. 18 May 1702	26 June 1726
	cons. 18 Oct. 1702	
Henry Maule	nom. 28 July 1726	trs. to Dromore
	cons. 11 Sept. 1726	20 Mar. 1732
Edward Synge	trs. from Clonfert	trs. to Ferns
	nom. 18 Feb. 1732	8 Feb. 1734
	l.p. 22 Mar. 1732	
George Berkeley	nom. 18 Jan. 1734	14 Jan. 1753
	cons. 19 May 1734	
James Stopford	nom. 19 Jan. 1753	24 Aug. 1759
	cons. 11 Mar. 1753	
Robert Johnson	nom. 19 Sept. 1759	16 Jan. 1767
	cons. 21 Oct. 1759	
Hon. Frederick Augustus Hervey	nom. 2 Feb. 1767	trs. to Derry
	cons. 31 May 1767	18 Feb. 1768
Charles Agar	nom. 12 Feb. 1768	trs. to Cashel
	cons. 20 Mar. 1768	6 Aug. 1779
George Chinnery	trs. from Killaloe	13 Aug. 1780
	nom. 29 Jan. 1780	
	l.p. 15 Feb. 1780	
Richard Woodward	nom. 17 Jan. 1781	12 May 1794
	cons. 4 Feb. 1781	
William Bennet	trs. from Cork	16 July 1820
	nom. 20 May 1794	
	l.p. 27 June 1794	
Charles Mongan Warburton	trs. from Limerick	9 Aug. 1826
	nom. 26 Aug. 1820	
	l.p. 18 Sept. 1820	
John Brinkley	nom. 13 Sept. 1826	14 Sept. 1835
	cons. 8 Oct. 1826	

(See united to Cork)

DIOCESE OF CORK AND CLOYNE

bishops	accession	death unless otherwise stated
John Bennett*	papal prov. 28 Jan. 1523	1536
Dominic Tirrey*	nom. 11 June 1536	Aug. 1557
	l.p. 25 Sept. 1536	
Roger Skiddy	temp. 2 Nov. 1557	res. 18 Mar.
	l.p. 1562	1567
	cons. 30 Oct. 1562	
Richard Dixon	nom. 17 May 1570	depr. 8 Nov.
	l.p. 6 June 1570	1571

bishops	accession	death unless otherwise stated
Mathew Sheyn	nom. 2 Jan. 1572 l.p. 29 May 1572	1582 or 1583
William Lyon[4]	nom. Nov. 1583	4 Oct. 1617
John Boyle	nom. 22 Apr. 1618 l.p. 25 Aug. 1618	10 July 1620
Richard Boyle	nom. 23 Aug. 1620 cons. Nov. 1620	trs. to Tuam 30 May 1638

[4] Bp of Ross; granted Cork *in commendam*. Cork and Ross have since been held by the same bp.

DIOCESE OF CORK

bishops	accession	death unless otherwise stated
William Chappell	nom. 30 Aug. 1638 cons. 11 Nov. 1638	13 May 1649
Michael Boyle[5]	nom. 6 Aug. 1660 cons. 27 Jan. 1661	trs. to Dublin 27 Nov. 1663
Edward Synge[5]	trs. from Limerick nom. 24 Aug. 1663 l.p. 21 Dec. 1663	22 Dec. 1678
Edward Wetenhall	nom. 3 Feb. 1679 cons. 23 Mar. 1679	trs. to Kilmore 18 Apr. 1699
Dive Downes	nom. 9 Mar. 1699 cons. 4 June 1699	13 Nov. 1709
Peter Browne	nom. 26 Dec. 1709 cons. 8 Apr. 1710	25 Aug. 1735
Robert Clayton	trs. from Killala nom. 22 Nov. 1735 l.p. 19 Dec. 1735	trs. to Clogher 26 Aug. 1745
Jemmett Browne	trs. from Dromore nom. 3 Aug. 1745 l.p. 27 Aug. 1745	trs. to Elphin 6 Mar. 1772
Isaac Mann	nom. 27 Jan. 1772 cons. 15 Mar. 1772	10 Dec. 1788
Euseby Cleaver	nom. 21 Mar. 1789 cons. 28 Mar. 1789	trs. to Ferns 13 June 1789
William Foster	nom. 5 June 1789 cons. 14 June 1789	trs. to Kilmore 11 June 1790
William Bennet	nom. 7 May 1790 cons. 13 June 1790	trs. to Cloyne 27 June 1794
Hon. Thomas Stopford	nom. 20 May 1794 cons. 29 June 1794	24 Jan. 1805
Lord John George Beresford	nom. 13 Feb. 1805 cons. 24 Mar. 1805	trs. to Raphoe 10 Aug. 1807

bishops	accession	death unless otherwise stated
Hon. Thomas St Lawrence	nom. 3 Sept. 1807 cons. 27 Sept. 1807	10 Feb. 1831
Samuel Kyle	nom. 2 Mar. 1831 cons. 27 Mar. 1831	18 May 1848

(Cloyne united to Cork from 14 Sept. 1835)

[5] Also held Cloyne.

DIOCESE OF CORK AND CLOYNE

bishops	accession	death unless otherwise stated
James Wilson	nom. 24 June 1848 cons. 30 July 1848	5 Jan. 1857
William Fitzgerald	nom. 27 Jan. 1857 cons. 8 Mar. 1857	trs. to Killaloe 3 Feb. 1862
John Gregg	nom. 15 Jan. 1862 cons. 16 Feb. 1862	26 May 1878
Robert Samuel Gregg	trs. from Ossory el. 27 June 1878 conf. 4 July 1878	trs. to Armagh 14 Dec. 1893
William Edward Meade	el. 5 Dec. 1893 cons. 6 Jan. 1894	12 Oct. 1912
Charles Benjamin Dowse	trs. from Killaloe el. 22 Nov. 1912 conf. 23 Dec. 1912	res. 15 Sept. 1933 d. 13 Jan. 1934
William Edward Flewett	el. 6 Oct. 1933 cons. 30 Nov. 1933	5 Aug. 1938
Robert Thomas Hearn	el. 19 Oct. 1938 cons. 13 Nov. 1938	14 July 1952
George Otto Simms	el. 2 Oct. 1952 cons. 28 Oct. 1952	trs. to Dublin 11 Dec. 1956
Richard Gordon Perdue	trs. from Killaloe el. 31 Jan. 1957 conf. 19 Feb. 1957	res. 20 May 1978
Samuel Greenfield Poyntz	el. 21 June 1978 cons. 17 Sept 1978	

DIOCESE OF EMLY

bishops	accession	death unless otherwise stated
Thomas O'Hurley (Tomás Ó hUrthaile)*	papal prov. 6 Oct. 1505 cons. c. 1507	1542

bishops	accession	death unless otherwise stated
Aonghus (Aeneas) O'Hernan	nom. 8 Oct. 1542 l.p. 6 Apr. 1543	1553
Raymund Burke, O.F.M.*	papal prov. 20 Oct. 1550	29 July 1562

(See united to Cashel 1569; separated from Cashel and united with Limerick in accordance with a statute of the general synod of 13 May 1976)

DIOCESE OF KILFENORA

bishops	accession	death unless otherwise stated
Maurice O'Kelly (Mauricius Ó Ceallaigh), O.F.M.*	papal prov. 6 Nov. 1514	a. Nov. 1541
?Matthaeus[6]	fl. 1537	
John O'Neylan (Ó Nialláin)	papal prov. 21 Nov. 1541 conf. by crown a. 1552	1572

(See apparently not filled by crown 1572-1606;[7] see held with Limerick 1606-17)

John Steere	nom. 9 July 1617	trs. to Ardfert 20 July 1622
William Murray	nom. 15 Mar. 1622 cons. 18 Dec. 1622	trs. to Llandaff 24 Dec. 1627 d. 1640
James Heygate	nom. 28 Feb. 1630 cons. 9 May 1630	30 Apr. 1638
Robert Sibthorp	nom. 19 June 1638 cons. 11 Nov. 1638	trs. to Limerick 7 Apr. 1643

(See held with Tuam 1661-1741; with Clonfert 1742-52; since 1752 united to Killaloe)

[6] Took part in consecration of Richard Nangle as bp of Clonfert 13 June 1537; possibly identical with Bp O'Kelly.
[7] 'Daniel' is mentioned as bp-elect in 1585.

DIOCESE OF KILLALOE

bishops	accession	death unless otherwise stated
James O'Currin (Séamus Ó Cuirrín)*	papal prov. 24 Aug. 1526	res. 5 May 1542 d. a. June 1554
Con (Cornelius) O'Dea[8]	nom. 30 May 1546 cons. 12 July 1546	1568 × 1576
Turlough (Terence) O'Brien*[9]	papal prov 25 June 1554	1569
Murrough (Maurice, Murtagh) O'Brien-Arra[10]	nom. 17 May 1570 cons. 1576	res. 1612 d. 30 Apr. 1613

bishops	*accession*	*death unless otherwise stated*
John Rider	nom. 5 July 1612	12 Nov. 1632
	cons. 12 Jan. 1613	
Lewis Jones	nom. 14 Dec. 1632	2 Nov. 1646
	cons. 12 Apr. 1633	
Edward Parry	nom. 29 Dec. 1646	20 July 1650
	cons. 28 Mar. 1647	
Edward Worth	nom. 7 Aug. 1660	2 Aug. 1669
	cons. 27 Jan. 1661	
Daniel Wytter	nom. 4 Aug. 1669	16 Mar. 1675
	cons. Sept. 1669	
John Roan	nom. 28 Mar. 1675	5 Sept. 1692
	cons. June 1675	
Henry Ryder	nom. 13 May 1693	30 Jan. 1696
	cons. 11 June 1693	
Thomas Lindsay	nom. 12 Feb. 1696	trs. to Raphoe
	cons. 22 Mar. 1696	6 June 1713
Sir Thomas Vesey, bt	nom. 11 May 1713	trs. to Ossory
	cons. 12 July 1713	28 Apr. 1714
Nicholas Forster	nom. 7 Oct. 1714	trs. to Raphoe
	cons. 7 Nov. 1714	8 June 1716
Charles Carr	nom. 26 May 1716	26 Dec. 1739
	cons. June 1716	
Joseph Story	nom. 16 Jan. 1740	trs. to Kilmore
	cons. 10 Feb. 1740	29 Jan. 1742
John Ryder	nom. 18 Jan. 1742	trs. to Down
	cons. 21 Feb. 1742	1 Aug. 1743
Jemmett Browne	nom. 29 Aug. 1743	trs. to Dromore
	cons. 9 Oct. 1743	16 May 1745
Richard Chenevix	nom. 26 Apr. 1745	trs. to Waterford
	cons. 28 July 1745	15 Jan. 1746
Nicholas Synge	nom. 23 Dec. 1745	19 Jan. 1771
	cons. 26 Jan. 1746	

(Kilfenora united to Killaloe 1752)

Robert Fowler	nom. 13 June 1771	trs. to Dublin
	cons. 28 July 1771	8 Jan. 1779
George Chinnery	nom. 21 Dec. 1778	trs. to Cloyne
	cons. 7 Mar. 1779	15 Feb. 1780
Thomas Barnard	nom. 29 Jan. 1780	trs. to Limerick
	cons. 20 Feb. 1780	12 Sept. 1794
Hon. William Knox	nom. 14 Aug. 1794	trs. to Derry
	cons. 21 Sept. 1794	9 Sept. 1803
Hon. Charles Dalrymple Lindsay	nom. 27 Aug. 1803	trs. to Kildare
	cons. 13 Nov. 1803	14 May 1804
Nathaniel Alexander	trs. from Clonfert	trs. to Down
	nom. 15 May 1804	21 Nov. 1804
	l.p. 22 May 1804	

bishops	accession	death unless otherwise stated
Lord Robert Ponsonby Tottenham Loftus	nom. 3 Nov. 1804 cons. 16 Dec. 1804	trs. to Ferns 5 May 1820
Richard Mant	nom. 10 Apr. 1820 cons. 7 May 1820	trs. to Down 23 Mar. 1823
Alexander Arbuthnot	nom. 13 Mar. 1823 cons. 11 May 1823	9 Jan. 1828
Hon. Richard Ponsonby	nom. 22 Feb. 1828 cons. 16 Mar. 1828	trs. to Derry 21 Sept. 1831
Hon. Edmund Knox	nom. 23 Sept. 1831 cons. 9 Oct. 1831	trs. to Limerick 29 Jan. 1834
Christopher Butson[11]	29 Jan. 1834	23 Mar. 1836
Stephen Creagh Sandes	nom. 27 Apr. 1836 cons. 12 June 1836	trs. to Cashel 23 Jan. 1839
Hon. Ludlow Tonson (succ. as Baron Riversdale 3 Apr. 1848)	nom. 23 Jan. 1839 cons. 17 Feb. 1839	13 Dec. 1861
William Fitzgerald	trs. from Cork nom. 15 Jan. 1862 l.p. 3 Feb. 1862	24 Nov. 1883
William Bennett Chester	el. 16 Jan. 1884 cons. 24 Feb. 1884	27 Aug. 1893
Frederick Richard Wynne	el. 15 Nov. 1893 cons. 10 Dec. 1893	3 Nov. 1896
Mervyn Archdall	el. 8 Jan. 1897 cons. 2 Feb. 1897	res. 31 Mar. 1912 d. 18 May 1913
Charles Benjamin Dowse	el. 17 May 1912 cons. 11 June 1912	trs. to Cork 23 Dec. 1912
Thomas Sterling Berry	el. 18 Feb. 1913 cons. 25 Mar. 1913	res. 6 Mar. 1924 d. 25 Feb. 1931
Henry Edmund Patton	el. 4 Apr. 1924 cons. 1 May 1924	28 Apr. 1943
Robert McNeil Boyd	el. 23 June 1943 cons. 21 Sept. 1943	trs. to Derry 20 Mar. 1945
Hedley Webster	el. 19 June 1945 cons. 25 July 1945	res. 30 Sept. 1953 d. 28 June 1954
Richard Gordon Perdue	el. 11 Nov. 1953 cons. 2 Feb. 1954	trs. to Cork 19 Feb. 1957
Henry Arthur Stanistreet	el. 5 Apr. 1957 cons. 11 June 1957	res. 1 Nov. 1971 d. 4 Sept. 1981
Edwin Owen	el. 1 Dec. 1971 cons. 25 Jan. 1972	res. 6 Jan. 1981

(Killaloe united to Limerick, 9 Sept. 1976)

[8] Papal bp of Kilmacduagh, see above, p. 389.   [9] In succession to O'Currin.

[10] The queen ordered the revenues of the see to be allowed to him until he should be old enough to be cons. In 1575 she considered that he was still too young.

[11] Bp of Clonfert; became bp of the united diocese of Killaloe, Kilfenora, Clonfert, and Kilmacduagh.

DIOCESE OF LIMERICK

bishops	accession	death unless otherwise stated
John Quin (Seaán Ó Cuinn), O.P.*	papal prov. 21 Oct. 1524 cons. *a.* 3 Jan. 1525	res. 9 Apr. 1551 d. 1554/5
William Casey	nom. 6 July 1551	depr. 1556
Hugh Lacy*	papal prov. 9 Mar./24 Nov. 1556[12]	depr. 8 May 1571 d. 1580
William Casey	reinstated 8 May 1571	7 Feb. 1591
John Thornburgh	nom. 20 Sept. 1593 l.p. 9 Jan. 1594	trs. to Bristol 4 July 1603 to Worcester 17 Feb. 1617 d. 9 July 1641
Bernard Adams[13]	nom. 5 Aug. 1603 cons. Apr. 1604	22 Mar. 1626
Francis Gough	nom. 18 Apr. 1626 cons. 17 Sept. 1626	29 Aug. 1634
George Webb	nom. 6 Oct. 1634 cons. 18 Dec. 1634	22 June 1642
Robert Sibthorp	trs. from Kilfenora nom. 7 Apr. 1643	Apr. 1649
Edward Synge	nom. 6 Aug. 1660 cons. 27 Jan. 1661	trs. to Cork 21 Dec. 1663

(Ardfert united to Limerick 1661)

William Fuller	nom. 4 Mar. 1664 cons. 20 Mar. 1664	trs. to Lincoln Sept. 1667 d. 22 Apr. 1675
Francis Marsh	nom. 27 Sept. 1667 cons. 22 Dec. 1667	trs. to Kilmore 10 Jan. 1673
John Vesey	l.p. 11 Jan. 1673 cons. 22 Dec. 1673	trs. to Tuam 18 Mar. 1679
Simon Digby	nom. 24 Jan. 1679 cons. 23 Mar. 1679	trs. to Elphin 12 Jan. 1692
Nathaniel Wilson	nom. 7 Dec. 1690 cons. 8 May 1692	3 Nov. 1695
Thomas Smyth	nom. 15 Nov. 1695 cons. 8 Dec. 1695	4 May 1725
William Burscough	nom. 29 May 1725 cons. 20 June 1725	*a.* 3 Apr. 1755[14]
James Leslie	nom. 30 Sept. 1755 cons. 16 Nov. 1755	24 Nov. 1770
John Averill	nom. 14 Dec. 1770 cons. 6 Jan. 1771	14 Sept. 1771

bishops	accession	death unless otherwise stated
William Gore	trs. from Elphin nom. 27 Jan. 1772 l.p. 5 Mar. 1772	25 Feb. 1784
William Cecil Pery (cr. Baron Glentworth 2 June 1790)	trs. from Killala nom. 29 Apr. 1784 l.p. 13 May 1784	4 July 1794
Thomas Barnard	trs. from Killaloe nom. 14 Aug. 1794 l.p. 12 Sept. 1794	7 June 1806
Charles Mongan Warburton	nom. 28 June 1806 cons. 12 July 1806	trs. to Cloyne 18 Sept. 1820
Thomas Elrington	nom. 1 Sept. 1820 cons. 8 Oct. 1820	trs. to Ferns 21 Dec. 1822
John Jebb	nom. 26 Nov. 1822 cons. 12 Jan. 1823	9 Dec. 1833
Hon. Edmund Knox	trs. from Killaloe nom. 18 Dec. 1833 l.p. 29 Jan. 1834	3 May 1849
William Higgin	nom. 21 May 1849 cons. 15 July 1849	trs. to Derry 7 Dec. 1853
Henry Griffin	nom. 18 Nov. 1853 cons. 1 Jan. 1854	5 Apr. 1866
Charles Graves	nom. 14 Apr. 1866 cons. 29 June 1866	17 July 1899
Thomas Bunbury	el. 6 Oct. 1899 cons. 1 Nov. 1899	19 Jan. 1907
Raymond D'Audemar Orpen	el. 28 Feb. 1907 cons. 2 Apr. 1907	res. 31 Dec. 1920 d. 9 Jan. 1930
Harry Vere White	el. 20 Sept. 1921 cons. 18 Oct. 1921	res. 31 Oct. 1933 d. 20 Jan. 1941
Charles King Irwin	el. 12 Dec. 1933 cons. 2 Feb. 1934	trs. to Down 6 Aug. 1942
Evelyn Charles Hodges	el. 17 Nov. 1942 cons. 2 Feb. 1943	res. 30 Sept. 1960 d. 18 Mar. 1980
Robert Wyse Jackson	el. 2 Nov. 1960 cons. 6 Jan. 1961	res. 12 July 1970 d. 21 Oct. 1976
Donald Arthur Richard Caird	el. 31 July 1970 cons. 29 Sept. 1970	trs. to Meath and Kildare 9 Sept. 1976

(On the translation of Caird to Meath and Kildare, Killaloe united to Limerick.)

Edwin Owen	9 Sept. 1976	res. 6 Jan. 1981
Walton Newcombe Francis Empey	el. 14 Jan. 1981 cons. 25 Mar. 1981	

[12] Both dates ultimately derive from the consistorial acts: 9 Mar. is given in *Hierarchia catholica*, iii, 225; 24 Nov. is given by Brady, *Episc. succ.*, ii, 42.
[13] Held Kilfenora in addition 1606–17.
[14] Buried 3 Apr. 1755.

DIOCESE OF ROSS

bishops	accession	death unless otherwise stated
Dermot Mac Carthy (Diarmaid Mac Carthaigh), O.S.A.*	papal prov. 6 June 1526	1552
Maurice O'Fihely, O.F.M. Conv.*	papal prov. 12 Jan. 1554 (again 25 May 1555)	a. 27 Jan. 1559

(See not filled by crown until 1582)

William Lyon[15]	nom. 30 Mar. 1582 l.p. 12 May 1582	4 Oct. 1617

[15] Granted Cork in commendam 1583; since then Cork and Ross have been held by the same bp.

DIOCESE OF WATERFORD AND LISMORE

bishops	accession	death unless otherwise stated
Nicholas Comyn*	trs. from Ferns papal prov. 13 Apr. 1519	res. July 1551 d. 12 July 1557
Patrick Walsh*	nom. 9 June 1551 cons. 23 Oct. 1551	1578
Marmaduke Middleton	nom. 11 Apr. 1579 l.p. 31 May 1579	trs. to St David's 30 Nov. 1582 d. 1593
Miler Magrath[16]		
Thomas Weatherhead (Walley)	nom. 21 Mar. 1589 l.p. 20 July 1589	a. 15 Mar. 1592
John Lancaster	nom. 5 Jan. 1608 l.p. 26 Feb. 1608	1619
Michael Boyle	nom. 7 Aug. 1619	29 Dec. 1635
John Atherton	nom. 5 Apr. 1636 l.p. 4 May 1636	executed 5 Dec. 1640
Archibald Adair	trs. from Killala nom. 7 June 1641 l.p. 13 July 1641	c. 1647
George Baker	nom. 6 Aug. 1660 cons. 27 Jan. 1661	13 Nov. 1665
Hugh Gore	nom. 8 Feb. 1666 cons. 25 Mar. 1666	a. 27 Mar. 1691 [17]
Nathaniel Foy	nom. 16 Apr. 1691 cons. 9 Aug. 1691	31 Dec. 1707
Thomas Mills	nom. 17 Jan. 1708 cons. 18 Apr. 1708	13 May 1740

bishops	accession	death unless otherwise stated
Charles Este	trs. from Ossory nom. 10 July 1740 l.p. 4 Oct. 1740	29 Nov. 1745
Richard Chenevix	trs. from Killaloe nom. 23 Dec. 1745 l.p. 15 Jan. 1746	11 Sept. 1779
William Newcome	trs. from Ossory nom. 22 Oct. 1779 l.p. 5 Nov. 1779	trs. to Armagh 27 Jan. 1795
Richard Marlay	trs. from Clonfert nom. 11 Mar. 1795 l.p. 21 Mar. 1795	1 July 1802
Hon. Power Le Poer Trench	nom. 18 Aug. 1802 cons. 21 Nov. 1802	trs. to Elphin 30 Apr. 1810
Joseph Stock	trs. from Killala nom. 12 Apr. 1810 l.p. 1 May 1810	14 Aug. 1813
Hon. Richard Bourke	nom. 25 Aug. 1813 cons. 10 Oct. 1813	15 Nov. 1832

(See united to Cashel, 1833)

[16] See granted *in commendam* to Miler Magrath, abp of Cashel, 1582–9, 1592–1608.
[17] Buried 27 Mar. 1691.

PROVINCE OF DUBLIN

DIOCESE OF DUBLIN

archbishops	accession	death unless otherwise stated
John Alen*	papal prov. 3 Sept. 1529 cons. 13 Mar. 1530	murdered 28 July 1534
George Browne	nom. 11 Jan. 1536 cons. 19 Mar. 1536	depr. 10 May × 10 July 1554 d. *a.* 1558
Hugh Curwin*	papal prov. 21 June 1555 cons. 8 Sept. 1555	trs. to Oxford 1 Sept. 1567 d. Oct. 1568
Adam Loftus	trs. from Armagh nom. 5 June 1567 l.p. 9 Aug. 1567	5 Apr. 1605
Thomas Jones	trs. from Meath nom. 8 Oct. 1605 l.p. 8 Nov. 1605	10 Apr. 1619

archbishops	*accession*	*death unless otherwise stated*
Lancelot Bulkeley	nom. 30 Apr. 1619 cons. 3 Oct. 1619	8 Sept. 1650
James Margetson	nom. 3 Aug. 1660 cons. 27 Jan. 1661	trs. to Armagh 20 Aug. 1663
Michael Boyle	trs. from Cork nom. 24 Aug. 1663 l.p. 27 Nov. 1663	trs. to Armagh 27 Feb. 1679
John Parker	trs. from Tuam nom. 22 Jan. 1679 l.p. 28 Feb. 1679	28 Dec. 1681
Francis Marsh	trs. from Kilmore nom. 10 Jan. 1682 l.p. 14 Feb. 1682	16 Nov. 1693
Narcissus Marsh	trs. from Cashel nom. 9 Apr. 1694 l.p. 24 May 1694	trs. to Armagh 18 Feb. 1703
William King	trs. from Derry nom. 16 Feb. 1703 l.p. 11 Mar. 1703	8 May 1729
John Hoadly	trs. from Ferns nom. 26 Dec. 1729 l.p. 13 Jan. 1730	trs. to Armagh 21 Oct. 1742
Charles Cobbe	trs. from Kildare l.p. 4 Mar. 1743	14 Apr. 1765
Hon. William Carmichael	trs. from Meath nom. 29 May 1765 l.p. 12 June 1765	15 Dec. 1765
Arthur Smyth	trs. from Meath nom. 28 Feb. 1766 l.p. 14 Apr. 1766	14 Dec. 1771
John Cradock	trs. from Kilmore nom. 27 Jan. 1772 l.p. 5 Mar. 1772	10 Dec. 1778
Robert Fowler	trs. from Killaloe nom. 21 Dec. 1778 l.p. 8 Jan. 1779	10 Oct. 1801
Charles Agar, Viscount Somerton (cr. earl of Normanton 4 Feb. 1806)	trs. from Cashel nom. 7 Nov. 1801 l.p. 7 Dec. 1801	14 July 1809
Euseby Cleaver[1]	trs. from Ferns nom. 29 July 1809 l.p. 25 Aug. 1809	Dec. 1819
Lord John George Beresford	trs. from Clogher nom. 21 Mar. 1820 l.p. 21 Apr. 1820	trs. to Armagh 17 June 1822

archbishops	accession	death unless otherwise stated
William Magee	trs. from Raphoe nom. 17 June 1822 l.p. 24 June 1822	18 Aug. 1831
Richard Whately	nom. 20 Oct. 1831 cons. 23 Oct. 1831	8 Oct. 1863

(Kildare united to Dublin 8 Aug. 1846)

Richard Chenevix Trench	nom. 18 Dec. 1863 cons. 1 Jan. 1864	res. 28 Nov. 1884 d. 28 Mar. 1886
William Conyngham Plunket, Baron Plunket	trs. from Meath el. 18 Dec. 1884 conf. 23 Dec. 1884	1 Apr. 1897
Joseph Ferguson Peacocke	trs. from Meath el. 19 May 1897	res. 3 Sept. 1915 d. 26 May 1916
John Henry Bernard	trs. from Ossory el. 7 Oct. 1915	res. 30 June 1919 d. 29 Aug. 1927
Charles Frederick D'Arcy	trs. from Down el. 6 Aug. 1919 conf. 15 Oct. 1919	trs. to Armagh 17 June 1920
John Allen Fitzgerald Gregg	trs. from Ossory el. 10 Sept. 1920	trs. to Armagh 1 Jan. 1939
Arthur William Barton	trs. from Kilmore el. 7 Feb. 1939 conf. 15 Feb. 1939	res. 15 Nov. 1956 d. 22 Sept. 1962
George Otto Simms	trs. from Cork el. 4 Dec. 1956 conf. 11 Dec. 1956	trs. to Armagh 17 July 1969
Alan Alexander Buchanan	trs. from Clogher el. 10 Sept. 1969 conf. 14 Oct. 1969	res. 10 Apr. 1977
Henry Robert McAdoo	trs. from Ossory el. 15 Apr. 1977 conf. 19 Oct. 1977	

[1] Found to be of unsound mind; abp of Cashel app. coadj. 27 Aug. 1811.

DIOCESE OF FERNS

bishops	accession	death unless otherwise stated
John Purcell, can. reg.*	papal prov. 13 Apr. 1519 cons. 6 May 1519	20 July 1539
Alexander Devereux*	nom. 1539 cons. 14 Dec. 1539	a. 19 Aug. 1566

bishops	accession	death unless otherwise stated
John Devereux	nom. 10 Oct. 1566 l.p. 19 Oct. 1566	1578
Hugh Allen	trs. from Down l.p. 24 May 1582	1599

(Leighlin united to Ferns 1597)

Robert Grave	nom. 30 Apr. 1600 cons. Aug. 1600	1 Oct. 1600
Nicholas Stafford	nom. 16 Jan. 1601 cons. 18 Mar. 1601	15 Nov. 1604
Thomas Ram	nom. 6 Feb. 1605 cons. 2 May 1605	24 Nov. 1634
George Andrews	nom. 11 Jan. 1635 cons. 14 May 1635	Oct. 1648
Robert Price	nom. 6 Aug. 1660 cons. 27 Jan. 1661	26 Mar. 1666
Richard Boyle	nom. 2 May 1666 cons. 10 Jan. 1667	c. Jan. 1683
Narcissus Marsh	nom. 9 Feb. 1683 cons. 6 May 1683	trs. to Cashel 26 Feb. 1691
Bartholomew Vigors	nom. 25 Dec. 1690 cons. 8 Mar. 1691	3 Jan. 1722
Josiah Hort	nom. 17 Jan. 1722 cons. 25 Feb. 1722	trs. to Kilmore 27 July 1727
John Hoadly	nom. 22 June 1727 cons. 3 Sept. 1727	trs. to Dublin 13 Jan. 1730
Arthur Price	trs. from Clonfert nom. 26 May 1730 l.p. 26 May 1730	trs. to Meath 2 Feb. 1734
Edward Synge	trs. from Cloyne nom. 18 Jan. 1734 l.p. 8 Feb. 1734	trs. to Elphin 15 May 1740
George Stone	nom. 12 May 1740 cons. 3 Aug. 1740	trs. to Kildare 19 Mar. 1743
William Cottrell	nom. 15 Feb. 1743 cons. 19 June 1743	21 June 1744
Robert Downes	nom. 14 July 1744 cons. 19 Aug. 1744	trs. to Down 13 Oct. 1752
John Garnet	nom. 12 Aug. 1752 cons. 12 Nov. 1752	trs. to Clogher 4 Apr. 1758
Hon. William Carmichael	trs. from Clonfert nom. 17 Mar. 1758 l.p. 5 Apr. 1758	trs. to Meath 8 June 1758
Thomas Salmon	nom. 30 May 1758 cons. 11 June 1758	19 Mar. 1759

bishops	accession	death unless otherwise stated
Richard Robinson	trs. from Killala nom. 27 Mar. 1759 l.p. 19 Apr. 1759	trs. to Kildare 13 Apr. 1761
Charles Jackson	nom. 20 Mar. 1761 cons. 19 Apr. 1761	trs. to Kildare 25 Feb. 1765
Edward Young	trs. from Dromore nom. 8 Feb. 1765 l.p. 4 Mar. 1765	29 Aug. 1772
Joseph Deane Bourke[2]	nom. 7 Sept. 1772 cons. 11 Oct. 1772	trs. to Tuam 8 Aug. 1782
Walter Cope	trs. from Clonfert nom. 26 July 1782 l.p. 9 Aug. 1782	31 July 1787
William Preston	trs. from Killala nom. 10 Sept. 1787 l.p. 9 Nov. 1787	19 Apr. 1789
Euseby Cleaver	trs. from Cork nom. 5 June 1789 l.p. 13 June 1789	trs. to Dublin 25 Aug. 1809
Hon. Percy Jocelyn	nom. 31 July 1809 cons. 13 Sept. 1809	trs. to Clogher 3 Apr. 1820
Lord Robert Ponsonby Tottenham Loftus	trs. from Killaloe nom. 3 Apr. 1820 l.p. 5 May 1820	trs. to Clogher 21 Dec. 1822
Thomas Elrington	trs. from Limerick nom. 26 Nov. 1822 l.p. 21 Dec. 1822	12 July 1835

(See then united to Ossory)

[2] Styled hon. 1 Aug. 1776, later third earl of Mayo.

DIOCESE OF KILDARE

bishops	accession	death unless otherwise stated
Walter Wellesley, can. reg.*	papal prov. 1 July 1529	a. 18 Oct. 1539
William Miagh	app. 1540	15 Dec. 1548
Thomas Lancaster	nom. 20 Apr. 1550 cons. July 1550	depr. 1554 nom. to Armagh, 12 Mar. 1568
Thomas Leverous*	trs. from Leighlin papal prov. 30 Aug. 1555	depr. 1560 d. c. 1577
Alexander Craik	nom. 17 May 1560 cons. Aug. 1560	a. 3 Mar. 1564

bishops	*accession*	*death unless otherwise stated*
Robert Daly	nom. 16 Apr. 1564	*a.* 3 July 1583
	cons. May 1564	
Daniel Neylan	nom. 3 July 1583	18 May 1603
	cons. Nov. 1583	
William Pilsworth	nom. 23 July 1604	9 May 1635
	cons. 11 Sept. 1604	
Robert Ussher	nom. 19 Oct. 1635	7 Sept. 1642
	cons. 25 Feb. 1636	
William Golborne	nom. 17 May 1644	1650
	cons. 1 Dec. 1644	
Thomas Price	nom. 8 Oct. 1660	trs. to Cashel
	cons. 10 Mar. 1661	30 May 1667
Ambrose Jones	nom. 20 Apr. 1667	15 Dec. 1678
	cons. 29 June 1667	
Anthony Dopping	nom. 3 Jan. 1679	trs. to Meath
	cons. 2 Feb. 1679	11 Feb. 1682
William Moreton	nom. 14 Jan. 1682	trs. to Meath
	cons. 19 Feb. 1682	18 Sept. 1705
Welbore Ellis	nom. 28 Aug. 1705	trs. to Meath
	cons. 11 Nov. 1705	13 Mar. 1732
Charles Cobbe	trs. from Dromore	trs. to Dublin
	nom. 18 Feb. 1732	4 Mar. 1743
	l.p. 16 Mar. 1732	
George Stone	trs. from Ferns	trs. to Derry
	nom. 15 Feb. 1743	11 May 1745
	l.p. 10 Mar. 1743	
Thomas Fletcher	trs. from Dromore	18 Mar. 1761
	nom. 26 Apr. 1745	
	l.p. 14 May 1745	
Richard Robinson	trs. from Ferns	trs. to Armagh
	nom. 26 Mar. 1761	8 Feb. 1765
	l.p. 13 Apr. 1761	
Charles Jackson	trs. from Ferns	29 Mar. 1790
	nom. 8 Feb. 1765	
	l.p. 25 Feb. 1765	
George Lewis Jones	trs. from Kilmore	9 Mar. 1804
	nom. 7 May 1790	
	l.p. 5 June 1790	
Hon. Charles Dalrymple Lindsay	trs. from Killaloe	8 Aug. 1846
	nom. 9 May 1804	
	l.p. 14 May 1804	

(See united to Dublin 1846; separated from Dublin and united to Meath 1976)

DIOCESE OF LEIGHLIN

bishops	accession	death unless otherwise stated
Matthew Sanders*	papal prov. 10 Apr. 1527	23/4 Dec. 1549
Robert Travers	nom. 5 Aug. 1550	depr. 1554
Thomas O'Fihely*	trs. from Achonry papal prov. 30 Aug. 1555	21 Mar. 1567
Daniel Cavanagh	nom. 10 Apr. 1567 l.p. 7 May 1567	4 Apr. 1587
Richard Meredith	nom. 11 Jan. 1589 cons. Apr. 1589	3 Aug. 1597

(See united to Ferns)

DIOCESE OF OSSORY

bishops	accession	death unless otherwise stated
Milo Baron (FitzGerald),* can. reg.	papal prov. 8 June 1528	1 July × 27 Sept. 1550
John Bale	nom. 22 Oct. 1552 cons. 2 Feb. 1553	abandoned see Sept. 1553[3] d. 17 Nov. 1563
John Tonory*[4]	nom. 14 Oct. 1553 cons. Jan. 1554	?1565
Christopher Gaffney	nom. 4 Dec. 1566 cons. May 1567	3 Aug. 1576
Nicholas Walsh	l.p. 23 Jan. 1578 cons. Feb. 1578	14 Dec. 1585
John Horsfall	nom. 1 Aug. 1586 l.p. 15 Sept. 1586	13 Feb. 1610
Richard Deane	nom. 7 Mar. 1610 l.p. 18 Apr. 1610	20 Feb. 1613
Jonas Wheeler	nom. 14 Mar. 1613 cons. 8 May 1613	19 Apr. 1640
Griffith Williams	nom. 19 July 1641 cons. 26 Sept. 1641	29 Mar. 1672
John Parry	nom. 5 Apr. 1672 cons. 28 Apr. 1672	21 Dec. 1677
Benjamin Parry	nom. 29 Dec. 1677 cons. 27 Jan. 1678	4 Oct. 1678
Michael Ward	nom. 25 Oct. 1678 cons. 24 Nov. 1678	trs. to Derry 22 Jan. 1680
Thomas Otway	trs. from Killala nom. 6 Jan. 1680 l.p. 7 Feb. 1680	6 Mar. 1693

bishops	*accession*	*death unless otherwise stated*
John Hartstonge	nom. 16 Mar. 1693	trs. to Derry
	cons. 2 July 1693	3 Mar. 1714
Sir Thomas Vesey, bt	trs. from Killaloe	6 Aug. 1730
	nom. 18 Feb. 1714	
	l.p. 28 Apr. 1714	
Edward Tennison	nom. 11 Sept. 1730	29 Nov. 1735
	cons. 4 July 1731	
Charles Este	nom. 17 Dec. 1735	trs. to Waterford
	cons. 1 Feb. 1736	4 Oct. 1740
Anthony Dopping	nom. 19 June 1741	1 Feb. 1743
	cons. 19 July 1741	
Michael Cox	nom. 15 Feb. 1743	trs. to Cashel
	cons. 29 May 1743	22 Jan. 1754
Edward Maurice	nom. 3 Jan. 1754	10 Feb. 1756
	cons. 27 Jan. 1754	
Richard Pococke	nom. 5 Mar. 1756	trs. to Meath
	cons. 21 Mar. 1756	16 July 1765
Charles Dodgson	nom. 22 June 1765	trs. to Elphin
	cons. 11 Aug. 1765	12 Apr. 1775
William Newcome	trs. from Dromore	trs. to Waterford
	nom. 23 Mar. 1775	5 Nov. 1779
	l.p. 13 Apr. 1775	
John Hotham	nom. 22 Oct. 1779	trs. to Clogher
	cons. 14 Nov. 1779	17 May 1782
Hon. William Beresford	trs. from Dromore	trs. to Tuam
	nom. 11 Apr. 1782	10 Oct. 1794
	l.p. 21 May 1782	
Thomas Lewis O'Beirne	nom. 17 Jan. 1795	trs. to Meath
	cons. 1 Feb. 1795	18 Dec. 1798
Hugh Hamilton	trs. from Clonfert	1 Dec. 1805
	nom. 15 Jan. 1799	
	l.p. 24 Jan. 1799	
John Kearney	nom. 4 Jan. 1806	22 May 1813
	cons. 2 Feb. 1806	
Robert Fowler	nom. 7 June 1813	31 Dec. 1841
	cons. 20 June 1813	

(Ferns united to Ossory 1835)

James Thomas O'Brien	nom. 24 Feb. 1842	12 Dec. 1874
	cons. 20 Mar. 1842	
Robert Samuel Gregg	el. 4 Mar. 1875	trs. to Cork
	cons. 30 Mar. 1875	4 July 1878
William Pakenham Walsh	el. 30 Aug. 1878	res. 30 Sept.
	cons. 29 Sept. 1878	1897
		d. 30 July 1902

bishops	accession	death unless otherwise stated
John Baptist Crozier	el. 20 Oct. 1897 cons. 30 Nov. 1897	trs. to Down 26 Sept. 1907
Charles Frederick D'Arcy	trs. from Clogher el. 6 Nov. 1907	trs. to Down 29 Mar. 1911
John Henry Bernard	el. 14 June 1911 cons. 25 July 1911	trs. to Dublin 7 Oct. 1915
John Allen Fitzgerald Gregg	el. 20 Nov. 1915 cons. 28 Dec. 1915	trs. to Dublin 10 Sept. 1920
John Godfrey Fitzmaurice Day	el. 15 June 1920 cons. 1 Nov. 1920	trs. to Armagh 27 Apr. 1938
Forde Tichborne	el. 1 Mar. 1938 cons. 24 June 1938	18 Feb. 1940
John Percy Phair	el. 13 Mar. 1940 cons. 11 June 1940	res. 31 Dec. 1961 d. 28 Dec. 1967
Henry Robert McAdoo	el. 31 Jan. 1962 cons. 11 Mar. 1962	trs. to Dublin 19 Apr. 1977

(Ossory united to Cashel, in accordance with a statute of the general synod of 13 May 1976)

[3] *Harleian miscellany*, vi (London, 1810), pp 453-4.
[4] His position under Elizabeth is uncertain. See referred to as vacant *c.* 1561.

PROVINCE OF TUAM

DIOCESE OF TUAM

archbishops	accession	death unless otherwise stated
Thomas O'Mullally (Tomás Ó Maolalaidh)*	trs. from Clonmacnoise papal prov. 19 June 1514	28 Apr. 1536
Christopher Bodkin*[1]	l.p. 15 Feb. 1537	1572
William O'Mullally	nom. 11 Nov. 1572 cons. Apr. 1573	1595
Nehemiah Donnellan	nom. 24 May 1595 l.p. 17 Aug. 1595	res. 1609
William Daniel (O'Donnell)	nom. 28 June 1609 cons. Aug. 1609	11 July 1628
Randolph Barlow	nom. 6 Feb. 1629 cons. Apr. 1629	22 Feb. 1638
Richard Boyle	trs. from Cork nom. 2 Apr. 1638 l.p. 30 May 1638	19 Mar. 1645
John Maxwell	trs. from Killala l.p. 30 Aug. 1645	14 Feb. 1647

archbishops	*accession*	*death unless otherwise stated*
Samuel Pullen	nom. 3 Aug. 1660 cons. 27 Jan. 1661	24 Jan. 1667
John Parker	trs. from Elphin nom. 26 Feb. 1667 l.p. 9 Aug. 1667	trs. to Dublin 28 Feb. 1679
John Vesey	trs. from Limerick nom. 23 Jan. 1679 l.p. 18 Mar. 1679	28 Mar. 1716
Edward Synge	trs. from Raphoe nom. 19 May 1716 l.p. 8 June 1716	23 July 1741
Josiah Hort[2]	trs. from Kilmore nom. 5 Jan. 1742 l.p. 27 Jan. 1742	14 Dec. 1751
John Ryder	trs. from Down nom. 24 Feb. 1752 l.p. 19 Mar. 1752	4 Feb. 1775
Jemmett Browne	trs. from Elphin l.p. 11 Apr. 1775	15 June 1782
Hon. Joseph Deane Bourke (succ. as earl of Mayo 20 Apr. 1792)	trs. from Ferns l.p. 8 Aug. 1782	17 Aug. 1794
Hon. William Beresford (cr. Baron Decies, 22 Dec. 1812)	trs. from Ossory l.p. 10 Oct. 1794	8 Sept. 1819
Hon. Power Le Poer Trench	trs. from Elphin l.p. 10 Nov. 1819	25 Mar. 1839

(Killala united to Tuam from 13 Apr. 1834. On death of Abp Trench province united to Armagh and see ceased to be archbishopric)

bishops

Hon. Thomas Span Plunket (succ. as Baron Plunket 5 Jan. 1854)	nom. 5 Apr. 1839 cons. 14 Apr. 1839	19 Oct. 1866
Hon. Charles Brodrick Bernard	l.p. 30 Nov. 1866 cons. 30 Jan. 1867	31 Jan. 1890
James O'Sullivan	el. 14 Apr. 1890 cons. 15 May 1890	res. Feb. 1913 d. 10 Jan. 1915
Hon. Benjamin John Plunket	el. 13 Apr. 1913 cons. 10 May 1913	trs. to Meath 15 Oct. 1919
Arthur Edwin Ross	el. 15 Jan. 1920 cons. 24 Feb. 1920	24 May 1923
John Orr	el. 18 July 1923 cons. 6 Aug. 1923	trs. to Meath 29 Sept. 1927
John Mason Harden	el. 15 Nov. 1927 cons. 6 Jan. 1928	2 Oct. 1931

bishops	accession	death unless otherwise stated
William Hardy Holmes	el. 15 Dec. 1931 cons. 2 Feb. 1932	trs. to Meath 19 Oct. 1938
John Winthrop Crozier	el. 23 Nov. 1938 cons. 2 Feb. 1939	res. 31 Dec. 1957 d. 14 Feb. 1966
Arthur Hamilton Butler	el. 9 Apr. 1958 cons. 27 May 1958	trs. to Connor 14 Oct. 1969
John Coote Duggan	el. 27 Nov. 1969 cons. 2 Feb. 1970	

¹ Bp of Kilmacduagh, which he continued to hold in addition to Tuam.
² Ardagh, which had been held by bp of Kilmore, was held by abp of Tuam 1742-1839.

DIOCESE OF ACHONRY

bishops	accession	death unless otherwise stated
Cormac Ó Snighe (?Ó Sniadhaigh)*	papal prov. 15 June 1522	a. June 1547
Thomas O'Fihely,* can. reg.	papal. prov. 15 June 1547	trs. to Leighlin 30 Aug. 1555
Cormac O'Coyne,* O.P.	nom. 1556	a. 12 Oct. 1561

(See not filled by crown 1561-91; held with Killala 1591-1607; held with Cashel 1607-22; united to Killala 1622)

DIOCESE OF ANNAGHDOWN

bishop	accession	death unless otherwise stated
John O'More³	papal prov. c. 1539 ?	p. 1553

(No royal appointee before see united to Tuam c. 1555)

³ No papal record of provision. He was imprisoned on the ground that he had accepted the bishopric from Rome; he was released in 1540 and then appears to have been recognised by the crown. In 1551 and 1553 he was officially referred to as the bp of the see.

DIOCESE OF CLONFERT

bishops	accession	death unless otherwise stated
Denis O'More (Moore) (Dionysius Ó Mórdha), O.P.	papal prov. 7 Nov. 1509	1534
Roland Burke (de Burgo)*⁴	papal prov. 18 May 1534 cons. p. 8 June 1537	20 June 1580

bishops	accession	death unless otherwise stated
Richard Nangle	nom. 1536 cons. 13 June 1537	expelled *a.* 19 July 1538
Stephen Kirwan	trs. from Kilmacduagh nom. 30 Mar. 1582 l.p. 24 May 1582	*a.* 4 Nov. 1601

(See granted *in commendam* to Roland Lynch, bp of Kilmacduagh 1602; after his death in 1625 Kilmacduagh was held by the bp of Clonfert until 1834, when both sees were united to Killaloe)

Robert Dawson	nom. 29 Aug. 1626 cons. 4 May 1627	13 Apr. 1643
William Baily	nom. 22 Dec. 1643 cons. 2 May 1644	11 Aug. 1664
Edward Wolley	nom. 5 Nov. 1664 cons. 16 Apr. 1665	1684
William Fitzgerald	nom. 9 Dec. 1690 cons. 26 July 1691	1722
Theophilus Bolton	nom. 17 Aug. 1722 cons. 30 Sept. 1722	trs. to Elphin 16 Apr. 1724
Arthur Price	nom. 19 Mar. 1724 cons. 3 May 1724	trs. to Ferns 26 May 1730
Edward Synge	nom. 14 May 1730 cons. 7 June 1730	trs. to Cloyne 22 Mar. 1732
Mordecai Cary	nom. 18 Feb. 1732 cons. 26 Mar. 1732	trs. to Killala 20 Dec. 1735
John Whitcombe	nom. 22 Nov. 1735 cons. 4 Jan. 1736	trs. to Down 21 Mar. 1752
Arthur Smyth	nom. 24 Feb. 1752 cons. 5 Apr. 1752	trs. to Down 24 Jan. 1753
Hon. William Carmichael	nom. 28 Dec. 1752 cons. 1 Apr. 1753	trs. to Ferns 5 Apr. 1758
William Gore	nom. 17 Mar. 1758 cons. 16 Apr. 1758	trs. to Elphin 3 May 1762
John Oswald	nom. 1 Apr. 1762 cons. 4 July 1762	trs. to Dromore 7 May 1763
Denison Cumberland	nom. 19 Apr. 1763 cons. 19 June 1763	trs. to Kilmore 6 Mar. 1772
Walter Cope	nom. 27 Jan. 1772 cons. 15 Mar. 1772	trs. to Ferns 9 Aug. 1782
John Law	nom. 26 July 1782 cons. 21 Sept. 1782	trs. to Killala 10 Nov. 1787
Richard Marlay	nom. 10 Sept. 1787 cons. 30 Dec. 1787	trs. to Waterford 21 Mar. 1795
Hon. Charles Brodrick	nom. 11 Mar. 1795 cons. 22 Mar. 1795	trs. to Kilmore 19 Jan. 1796

bishops	accession	death unless otherwise stated
Hugh Hamilton	nom. 31 Dec. 1795 cons. 31 Jan. 1796	trs. to Ossory 24 Jan. 1799
Matthew Young	nom. 15 Jan. 1799 cons. 3 Feb. 1799	28 Nov. 1800
George de la Poer Beresford	nom. 23 Dec. 1800 cons. 1 Feb. 1801	trs. to Kilmore 1 Mar. 1802
Nathaniel Alexander	nom. 13 Jan. 1802 cons. 21 Mar. 1802	trs. to Killaloe 22 May 1804
Christopher Butson	nom. 5 May 1804 cons. 29 July 1804	c. 23 Mar. 1836

(See united to Killaloe 1834)

[4] Roland Burke was prov. by the pope, 18 May 1534 (Lynch, *De praesulibus Hib.*, ii, 313), but delayed his consecration until 1537 (*Hierarchia catholica*, iii, 170) and does not appear to have gone to Clonfert before then. Nangle was nominated by Henry VIII in 1536 and was cons. in 1537 (Lynch, loc. cit.), but was expelled in 1538 by Burke, who was conf. by the crown 24 Oct. 1541 (*Cal. pat. rolls Ire., Hen. VIII–Eliz.*, p. 82).

DIOCESE OF ELPHIN

bishops	accession	death unless otherwise stated
John Maxey*	papal prov. 7 Apr. 1525	15 Aug. 1536
Conach O'Shiel	nom. 23 Sept. 1541	a. 28 July 1551
Roland Burke (de Burgo)[5]	nom. 23 Nov. 1551 l.p. 10 Apr. 1552	20 June 1580
Thomas Chester	nom. 25 May 1582	1583
John Lynch	nom. 4 Nov. 1583	res. 19 Aug. 1611
Edward King	nom. 6 July 1611 cons. Dec. 1611	8 Mar. 1639
Henry Tilson	nom. 7 Aug. 1639 cons. 23 Sept. 1639	31 Mar. 1655
John Parker	nom. 6 Aug. 1660 cons. 27 Jan. 1661	trs. to Tuam 9 Aug. 1667
John Hodson	nom. 17 July 1667 cons. 8 Sept. 1667	18 Feb. 1686
Simon Digby	trs. from Limerick nom. 4 Dec. 1690 l.p. 12 Jan. 1691	7 Apr. 1720
Henry Downes	trs. from Killala nom. 1 May 1720 l.p. 12 May 1720	trs. to Meath 9 Apr. 1724
Theophilus Bolton	trs. from Clonfert nom. 18 Mar. 1724 l.p. 16 Apr. 1724	trs. to Cashel 6 Jan. 1730

bishops	accession	death unless otherwise stated
Robert Howard	trs. from Killala nom. 26 Dec. 1729 l.p. 13 Jan. 1730	3 Apr. 1740
Edward Synge	trs. from Ferns nom. 30 Apr. 1740 l.p. 15 May 1740	27 Jan. 1762
William Gore	trs. from Clonfert nom. 21 Apr. 1762 l.p. 3 May 1762	trs. to Limerick 5 Mar. 1772
Jemmett Browne	trs. from Cork nom. 27 Jan. 1772 l.p. 6 Mar. 1772	trs. to Tuam 11 Apr. 1775
Charles Dodgson	trs. from Ossory nom. 23 Mar. 1775 l.p. 12 Apr. 1775	7 Mar. 1795
John Law	trs. from Killala nom. 11 Mar. 1795 l.p. 27 Mar. 1795	19 Mar. 1810
Hon. Power Le Poer Trench	trs. from Waterford nom. 12 Apr. 1810 l.p. 30 Apr. 1810	trs. to Tuam 10 Nov. 1819
John Leslie	trs. from Dromore nom. 16 Nov. 1819	18 July 1854

(See united to Kilmore 1841)

[5] Bp of Clonfert; granted Elphin in addition.

DIOCESE OF ENACHDUN

(See Annaghdown)

DIOCESE OF KILLALA

bishops	accession	death unless otherwise stated
Richard Barrett (Risdeárd Bairéad)*	papal prov. 7 Jan. 1513	a. Nov. 1545
Redmond O'Gallagher*[6]	papal prov. 6 Nov. 1545	papal trs. to Derry 22 June 1569
Owen O'Connor	nom. 18 Oct. 1591 cons. a. 25 Mar. 1592	14 Jan. 1607

bishops	accession	death unless otherwise stated
Archibald Hamilton[7]	nom. 8 Mar. 1623 cons. 29 May 1623	trs. to Cashel 20 Apr. 1630
Archibald Adair	nom. 23 Nov. 1629 cons. 9 May 1630	depr. 18 May 1640 trs. to Waterford 13 July 1641
John Maxwell	trs. from Ross (Scot.) nom. 13 Jan. 1641 l.p. 26 Feb. 1641	trs. to Tuam 30 Aug. 1645
Henry Hall	nom. 7 Aug. 1660 cons. 27 Jan. 1661	19 July 1663
Thomas Bayly	nom. 17 Dec. 1663 cons. 5 June 1664	20 July 1670
Thomas Otway	nom. 19 Oct. 1670 cons. 29 Jan. 1671	trs. to Ossory 7 Feb. 1680
John Smith	nom. 6 Jan. 1680 l.p. 13 Feb. 1680	2 Mar. 1681
William Smyth	nom. 15 Apr. 1681 cons. June 1681	trs. to Raphoe 17 Feb. 1682
Richard Tennison	nom. 16 Jan. 1682 cons. 19 Feb. 1682	trs. to Clogher 28 Feb. 1691
William Lloyd	nom. 7 Dec. 1690 cons. 23 Aug. 1691	11 Dec. 1716
Henry Downes	nom. 24 Jan. 1717 cons. 12 May 1717	trs. to Elphin 12 May 1720
Charles Cobbe	nom. 20 May 1720 cons. 14 Aug. 1720	trs. to Dromore 16 Feb. 1727
Robert Howard	nom. 14 Jan. 1727 cons. 19 Mar. 1727	trs. to Elphin 13 Jan. 1730
Robert Clayton	nom. 26 Dec. 1729 cons. 10 May 1730	trs. to Cork 19 Dec. 1735
Mordecai Cary	trs. from Clonfert l.p. 20 Dec. 1735	2 Oct. 1751
Richard Robinson	nom. 31 Oct. 1751 cons. 19 Jan. 1752	trs. to Ferns 19 Apr. 1759
Samuel Hutchinson	nom. 27 Mar. 1759 cons. 22 Apr. 1759	27 Oct. 1780
William Cecil Pery	nom. 7 Jan. 1781 cons. 18 Feb. 1781	trs. to Limerick 13 May 1784
William Preston	nom. 13 Oct. 1784 cons. 11 Nov. 1784	trs. to Ferns 9 Nov. 1787
John Law	trs. from Clonfert nom. 10 Sept. 1787 l.p. 10 Nov. 1787	trs. to Elphin 27 Mar. 1795
John Porter	nom. 6 May 1795 cons. 7 June 1795	trs. to Clogher 30 Dec. 1797

bishops	accession	death unless otherwise stated
Joseph Stock	nom. 1 Jan. 1798 cons. 28 Jan. 1798	trs. to Waterford 1 May 1810
James Verschoyle	nom. 12 Apr. 1810 cons. 6 May 1810	13 Apr. 1834

(See united to Tuam)

[6] Papal nominee, presumably recognised by crown in Mary's reign. There is no record of his recognition by Elizabeth.

[7] See held *in commendam* by Miler Magrath, abp of Cashel, 1613-22.

DIOCESE OF KILMACDUAGH

bishops	accession	death unless otherwise stated
Christopher Bodkin*[8]	papal prov. 3 Sept. 1533 cons. 4 Nov. 1533	1572
Stephen Kirwan	nom. 6 Nov. 1572 l.p. 13 Apr. 1573	trs. to Clonfert 24 May 1582
Roland Lynch[9]	nom. 9 Jan. 1587 cons. Aug. 1587	Dec. 1625

[8] Became abp of Tuam in 1537 but continued to hold Kilmacduagh in addition.

[9] Thomas Burke was *custos* on behalf of the crown 26 Jan. 1585 (Charles McNeill, 'The Perrot papers' in *Anal. Hib.*, xii (1943), pp 14-15, 46). Roland Lynch held Clonfert *in commendam* 1602-25; thereafter Kilmacduagh was held by bps of Clonfert.

DIOCESE OF MAYO

bishops	accession	death unless otherwise stated
John Bell, O.F.M.*	papal prov. 4 Nov. 1493	c. 1541
Eugene MacBrehon, O. Carm.*	papal prov. 21 Nov. 1541	c. 1559

(See united to Tuam)

MODERATORS OF PRESBYTERIAN CHURCHES FROM 1690

JOHN M. BARKLEY

INTRODUCTION

THE president of John Calvin's *Compagnie des pasteurs* in Geneva (a body corresponding exactly to Bucer's *Kirchenconvent* in Strasbourg) was called 'modérateur', a title which has been adopted in the reformed churches for the annually elected president of all the church courts.

The records of the general synod of Ulster are not sufficiently detailed to warrant a definite statement about election procedure prior to 1698, but then it becomes clear. The moderator of the previous year, having constituted the synod, proposed the leet of candidates. This consisted of one name (occasionally two) nominated by each presbytery from its own membership. From this, by plurality of votes in the synod, a moderator was elected. This continued to be the method of nomination in the synod and its continuation from 1840, the assembly, up to the latter's code of 1859, which removed the requirement for each presbytery to nominate a candidate from among its own members. Voting on each nomination continued as heretofore. This is still the practice in theory, though in fact the person receiving the nomination of the greatest number of presbyteries is usually (but not necessarily) elected as a sole nominee. Up to 1865 moderators were elected in July; from 1866 onwards they have been elected in June.

Originally the moderator was nothing more than a chairman, who, after election, chaired the meeting and closed it with prayer. The 'Discipline' of the reformed church in France stated that 'the office of the moderator shall expire with the synod'. The same practice was followed in Scotland and Ireland. At the next meeting of the synod or the assembly, the moderator of the previous year opened it with a sermon and prayer (though this was not laid down in Scotland until 1570) and, having constituted the court, then called upon it to elect his successor. He had no status during the time between meetings. The 1887 code of the general assembly enacts that 'he shall continue in office one year', that is, from the date of his election (for example, in June 1950) until his successor is chosen at the next annual meeting (for example, in June 1951). This change probably arose from legal necessities, such as the signing of documents, as a result of the disestablishment act of 1869. Even so, the moderator has no authority to make pronouncements in the name of the church; this can only be done by the general assembly itself, or by a commission or committee it has authorised to do so. He is simply first among equals.

The first regular presbytery in Ireland was established at Carrickfergus in 1642. From then until 1649 the presbytery of Ulster, or 'army presbytery', met regularly; the minutes, however, have not survived. From 1649 to 1654 presbyterianism was suppressed, and meetings could only be held clandestinely. In 1654 the original presbytery was divided into the 'meetings or presbyteries' of Antrim, Down, and Route; these were further divided, the presbytery of Laggan being formed out of Route in 1657, and the presbytery of Tyrone out of Down in 1659. In 1659, 1660, and 1661 these five met in 'general presbytery or synod', but no minutes survive. From 1661 to 1690 presbyterianism was again suppressed; and, while clandestine meetings of the presbyteries continued, there was no meeting of the synod. From 1690 there is an unbroken succession of synods until 1840, and from then of general assemblies.

The letters 'O.C.' in the second column stand for 'Old Congregation'.

MODERATORS OF THE SYNOD OF ULSTER, 1690–1840

Records of the general synod of Ulster, 1691–1820 (3 vols, Belfast, 1890–98); printed records of the general synod for 1821–40, Library of the Presbyterian Historical Society, Church House, Belfast.

	congregation	year of election
Thomas Hall, M.A.	Inver (Larne)	1690
John Abernethy	Moneymore	1691
Alexander Hutcheson	Capel Street, Dublin	1692
William Leggat, M.A.	Dromore	1693
Robert Campbell	Ray	1694
Thomas Kennedy, M.A.	Carland	1696[1]
John McBride, M.A.	First Belfast	1697
William Adair	Ballyeaston	1698
Hugh Kirkpatrick	Lurgan	1699
John Campbell, M.A.	Cairncastle	1700
Francis Iredell	Capel Street	1701
Matthew Haltbridge, M.A.	Ahoghill	1702
James Bruce, M.A.	Killyleagh	1703
Alexander Sinclair, M.A.	Plunket Street, Dublin	1704
John Mairs, M.A.	Corboy (Longford)	1705
Thomas Futt	Ballyclare	1706
John Hutcheson, M.A.	Armagh	1707

[1] The moderator for 1695 is unknown, as the minutes for 1695–6 have not survived.

	congregation	*year of election*
William Holmes	Strabane	1708
Thomas Orr, M.A.	Comber	1709
William Taylor	Randalstown O.C.	1710
Archibald Maclaine, M.A.	Markethill	1711
James Kirkpatrick, M.A., D.D.	Second Belfast (All Souls)	1712
Alexander Colvil, M.A.	Dromore, Co. Down	1713
Fulk White, M.A.	Braid (Broughshane)	1714
John Abernethy, M.A.	Antrim	1715
Samuel Shannon	Portaferry	1716
George Lang, M.A.	Loughbrickland	1717
William Biggar, M.A.	Bangor	1718
Robert Craghead, M.A.	Capel Street	1719
Gilbert Kennedy	Tullylish	1720
William Gray	Taughboyne (Monreagh)	1721
Thomas Kennedy	Ballyclug (Brigh)	1722
Charles Masterson, M.A.	Third Belfast	1723
James Tate	Killeshandra	1724
John Stirling	Ballykelly	1725
Francis Laird, M.A.	Donoughmore, Co. Donegal	1726
William Livingstone, M.A.	Templepatrick	1727
Robert McBride	Ballymoney	1728
Samuel Ross, M.A.	Derry	1729
William Boyd, M.A.	Taughboyne	1730
James Cobham	Broadisland (Ballycarry)	1731
Alexander Brown, M.A.	Donegore	1732
Charles Lynd, M.A.	New Row, Coleraine	1733
John Alexander, M.A.	Plunket Street	1734
James Johnston, M.A.	Donaghmore, Co. Down	1735
Samuel Delap, M.A.	Letterkenny	1736
James White, M.A.	Braid	1737
James Cochran	Greyabbey	1738
Robert McMaster	Ussher's Quay, Dublin	1739
Robert Wirling	Boveedy	1740
Hugh Wallace	Magherafelt	1741
James Fraser, M.A.	Carrickfergus	1742
Timothy White, M.A.	Ballyeaston	1743
John Carlisle, M.A.	Clogher	1744
John Moorhead	Dunmurry O.C.	1745
Robert Higginbotham, M.A.	Coleraine	1746
James McCurdy	Clough, Co. Antrim	1747
John Brown, M.A.	Ballymena	1748
John Kennedy	Benburb	1749
John Gibson, M.A.	Keady	1750
William Patton, M.A.	Plunket Street	1751
Victor Ferguson, M.A.	Strabane	1752
John Maxwell, M.A.	Armagh	1753
John Menogh, M.A.	Lurgan	1754
John Marshall	Ballindrait	1755

	congregation	*year of election*
William Ambrose, M.A.	Kinnaird (Lislooney)	1756
George Cherry	Clare, Co. Armagh	1757
Andrew Ferguson, M.A.	Burt	1758
John Hood	Derry	1759
Charles McCollum	Capel Street	1760
Alexander Macomb	Creggan	1761
Charles Caldwell, M.A.	Moneymore	1762
Gilbert Kennedy, M.A.	Second Belfast	1763
John White, M.A.	Ballyclug	1764
James Huey, M.A.	Newtownards	1765
William Warnock	Donaghadee	1766
James Armstrong, M.A.	Portaferry	1767
John Cameron	Dunluce	1768
James Hull	Cookstown	1769
James Caldwell	Ussher's Quay	1770
Andrew Alexander, M.A.	Urney	1771
John Strong	Ballynahinch	1772
William Campbell, M.A., D.D.	Armagh	1773
John Rankin	Antrim	1774
Henry Jackson	Banbridge O.C.	1775
Hugh Mulligan, M.A.	Aughnacloy and Ballygawley	1776
Robert Smith	Ballee	1777
James Bryson, M.A.	Second Belfast	1778
Robert McClure	Anahilt	1779
Joseph Osborne, M.A.	Limavady O.C.	1780
John McClelland	Coagh	1781
Thomas Reid	Glenarm O.C.	1782
William Wilson	Magherafelt	1783
William Crawford, M.A.	Strabane	1784
George Murray	Cookstown	1785
Benjamin McDowell, M.A., D.D.	Mary's Abbey, Dublin	1786
John Thompson	Carnmoney	1787
William Kennedy	Carland	1788
Joseph Douglass	Clough, Co. Antrim	1789
Samuel Barber, M.A.	Rathfriland	1790
James Jackson Birch, M.A.	Dromara	1791
William Stitt, M.A.	Dungannon	1792
William Steel Dickson, M.A., D.D.	Portaferry	1793
James Cochrane	Ballywalter	1794
Alexander Marshall	Ballymoney	1795
Isaac Patrick	Magherally	1796
Moses Neilson, M.A., D.D.	Kilmore	1797
Thomas Cuming	Armagh	1798
Andrew Millar	Clogher	1799
John Bankhead, M.A.	Ballycarry	1800
Joseph Hay	Donaghmore, Co. Down	1801
Nathaniel Shaw	Banbridge O.C.	1802

	congregation	*year of election*
Thomas Henry, M.A., D.D.	Randalstown O.C.	1803
James Horner, D.D.	Mary's Abbey	1804
Robert Rentoul, M.A.	Lurgan	1805
William Neilson, M.A., D.D.	Dundalk	1806
Henry Henry	Connor	1807
Joseph Denham	Killeshandra	1808
Samuel Hanna, M.A., D.D.	Third Belfast	1809
William Dunlop	Strabane	1810
James Bankhead, M.A.	Dromore O.C.	1811
Thomas McKay, M.A.	Ballyclug	1812
James Morell, M.A.	Ballybay	1813
George Hay	Derry	1814
John McCance, M.A.	Comber	1815
Robert Stewart, M.A.	Broughshane	1816
Nathaniel Alexander, M.A.	Crumlin	1817
Henry Montgomery, M.A.	Dunmurry O.C.	1818
Alexander Patterson	Magherally	1819
Andrew George Malcolm, M.A.	Newry O.C.	1820
Edward Reid	Ramelton	1821
John Mitchel	Derry	1822
Robert Hogg	Loughgall	1823
Henry Cooke, LL.D., D.D.	Killyleagh	1824
James Carlile, M.A., D.D.	Mary's Abbey	1825
William Wright	Anahilt	1826
James Seaton Reid, M.A., D.D.	Carrickfergus	1827
Patrick White, M.A.	Corglass (Bailieborough)	1828
Robert Park, M.A.	Ballymoney	1829
Robert Winning, M.A.	Ervey and Corvalley	1830
James Morgan, D.D.	Fisherwick Place, Belfast	1831
John Brown, D.D.	Aghadowey	1832
Moses Finlay	Donaghmore, Co. Down	1833
William McClure	Derry	1834
John Barnett, D.D.	Moneymore	1835
Hugh Walker Rodgers	Kilrea	1836
William Craig, M.A.	Dromara	1837
Henry Wallace, M.A.	First Derry	1838
James Denham, M.A., D.D.	Great James Street, Derry	1839
James Elder	Finvoy	1840

MODERATORS OF THE SECESSION SYNOD, 1818-40

MS minutes of the secession synod, Library of the Presbyterian Historical Society, Church House, Belfast.

The original secession occurred in 1733 within the Church of Scotland, in protest against the enforced system of patronage appointments; a further division among the seceders into 'burgher' and 'anti–burgher' synods in Scotland occurred in 1747. A 'burgher' synod was formed in Ireland in 1779 and an 'anti–burgher' in 1788. On 9 July 1818 these united to form 'The Presbyterian Synod of Ireland, distinguished by the name Seceders'.

	congregation	*year of election*
James Rentoul[1]	Ray	1818
David Stuart, D.D.	Union Chapel, Dublin	1819
Thomas Millar, M.A.	Cookstown	1820
James Thompson, M.A.	Drum	1821
William Carr, M.A.	Berry Street, Belfast (Crescent)	1822
Samuel Campbell, M.A., D.D.	Ramelton	1823
William Bell	Bailieborough	1824
Thomas Heron	Ballygoney	1825
William Reid	Scarva	1826
James Rankin, M.A.	Monaghan (Ballyalbany)	1827
John Edgar, LL.D., D.D.	Alfred Place, Belfast (Fitzroy)	1828
John Coulter, D.D.	Gilnahirk	1829
Robert McMahon	Tyrone's Ditches	1830
Isaiah Steen	Ballycopeland	1831
Thomas Reid	Randalstown	1832
Joseph Lowry, M.A.	Lissara	1833
Robert Morrison	Markethill	1834
James Porter	Drumlee	1835
James Crawford	Strand, Derry	1836
Thomas McKee	Castlewellan	1837
Samuel Craig	Crossroads	1838
Samuel Dunlop	Hillhall	1839
Alexander Rentoul, M.A., D.D.	Ray	1840

[1] The two synods met separately in Cookstown and conducted business separately; they then met at the synod of Ulster church, where Rentoul was elected moderator. He constituted them as one synod, but appears to have transacted no other business.

MODERATORS OF THE GENERAL ASSEMBLY OF THE PRESBYTERIAN CHURCH FROM 1840

Minutes of the proceedings of the general assembly of the Presbyterian Church in Ireland, 1840– (Belfast, 1840–).

In 1840 the general synod of Ulster and the secession synod united to form the Presbyterian Church in Ireland, with the general assembly as its supreme court.

	congregation	*year of election*
Samuel Hanna, M.A., D.D.	Rosemary Street, Belfast	1840
Henry Cooke, LL.D., D.D.	May Street, Belfast	1841
John Edgar, LL.D., D.D.	Fitzroy, Belfast	1842

	congregation	*year of election*
Robert Stewart, D.D.	First Broughshane	1843
John Brown, D.D.	Aghadowey	1844
James Carlile, D.D.	Mary's Abbey, Dublin	1845
James Morgan, D.D.	Fisherwick Place, Belfast	1846
William McClure	First Derry	1847
Henry Jackson Dobbin, D.D.	First Ballymena	1848
John Barnett, D.D.	First Moneymore	1849
William Bailey Kirkpatrick, D.D.	Mary's Abbey	1850
John Coulter, D.D.	Gilnahirk	1851
John Bleckley, A.M.	First Monaghan	1852
Henry William Molyneaux, D.D.	First Larne	1853
David Hamilton	York Street, Belfast	1854
Robert Allen, A.M.	Ballina	1855
Robert Wilson, D.D.	professor, Belfast	1856
Alexander Porter Gowdy, D.D.	First Strabane	1857
John Johnston, A.M., D.D.	Tullylish	1858
William Gibson, D.D.	professor, Belfast	1859
Samuel Marcus Dill, D.D.	First Ballymena	1860
John Macnaughtan, A.M.	Rosemary Street	1861
Henry Cooke, LL.D., D.D.	May Street	1862
John Rogers, D.D.	Second Comber	1863
John Rogers, D.D.	Second Comber	1864
David Wilson, D.D.	Limerick	1865
David Wilson, D.D.	Limerick	1866
Robert Montgomery	missionary, India	1867
Charles Lucas Morell, D.D.	First Dungannon	1868
Richard Smyth, D.D.	professor, Derry	1869
Richard Smyth, D.D.	professor, Derry	1870
Lowry Edmonds Berkeley	First Lurgan	1871
William Johnston, D.D.	Townsend Street, Belfast	1872
William Johnston, D.D.	Townsend Street	1873
William Magill, D.D.	Trinity, Cork	1874
Josias Leslie Porter, LL.D., D.D.	professor, Belfast	1875
John Meneely, D.D.	First Ballymacarrett, Belfast	1876
George Bellis, D.D.	Cliftonville, Belfast	1877
Thomas Witherow D.D., LL.D.	professor, Derry	1878
Robert Watts, D.D., LL.D.	professor, Belfast	1879
Jackson Smyth, D.D.	First Armagh	1880
William Fleming Stevenson, D.D.	Rathgar, Dublin	1881
Thomas Young Killen, D.D.	Duncairn, Belfast	1882
Hamilton Brown Wilson, D.D.	First Cookstown	1883
James Maxwell Rogers, M.A., D.D.	Gt James Street, Derry	1884
James Weir Whigham, D.D.	Ballinasloe	1885
Robert Ross, D.D.	Carlisle Road, Derry	1886
John Henry Orr, D.D.	High Street, Antrim	1887
Robert John Lynd, B.A., D.D.	May Street	1888

	congregation	*year of election*
William Clarke, B.A.	Trinity, Bangor	1889
William Park, M.A., LL.D., D.D.	Rosemary Street	1890
Nathaniel Macauley Brown, D.D., LL.D.	Drumachose	1891
Robert McCheyne Edgar, M.A., D.D.	Adelaide Road, Dublin	1892
William Todd Martin, M.A., D. Litt., D.D.	professor, Belfast	1893
William Todd Martin, M.A., D. Litt., D.D.	professor, Belfast	1894
George Raphael Buick, M.A., LL.D.	Cullybackey	1895
Henry McIlree Williamson, D.D.	Fisherwick Place	1896
Matthew Leitch, M.A., D. Litt., D.D.	professor, Belfast	1897
William Beatty, B.A., D.D.	missionary, India	1898
David Alexander Taylor, M.A., D.D.	Second Comber	1899
John McCurdy Hamilton, A.M., D.D.	Donore, Dublin	1900
James Heron, B.A., D.D.	professor, Belfast	1901
John Edgar Henry, M.A., D.D.	professor, Derry	1902
John MacDermott, M.A., D.D.	Belmont, Belfast	1903
Samuel Prenter, M.A., LL.D., D.D.	Ormond Quay, Dublin	1904
William McMordie, M.A., D.D.	Mourne	1905
William McKean, D.D.	First Ballymacarrett	1906
John Davidson, M.A., D.D.	Glennan	1907
John McIlveen, B.A., D.D.	Crescent, Belfast	1908
John Courtenay Clarke, B.A., D.D.	Galway	1909
John Howard Murphy, M.A., D.D.	Trinity, Cork	1910
John Macmillan, B.A., D.D.	Cooke Centenary, Belfast	1911
Henry Montgomery, M.A., D.D.	Shankill Road, Belfast	1912
William John Macaulay, B.A., D.D.	First Portadown	1913
James Bingham, M.A., D.D.	Dundonald	1914
Thomas Macafee Hamill, M.A., D.D.	professor, Belfast	1915
Thomas West, B.A., D.D.	First Antrim	1916
John Irwin, M.A., D.D.	Windsor, Belfast	1917
James McGranahan, B.A., D.D.	First Derry	1918
John Morrow Simms, C.B., C.M.G., LL.D., D.D., K.H.C.	chaplain to forces	1919
Henry Patterson Glenn, A.B.	Bray	1920
William James Lowe, M.A., LL.D., D.D.	clerk of assembly	1921

	congregation	*year of election*
William Gordon Strahan, D.D.	First Newry	1922
George Thompson, D.D.	convener, foreign mission	1923
Robert Wilson Hamilton, M.A., D.D.	Railway Street, Lisburn	1924
Thomas Haslett, M.A., D.D.	First Ballymena	1925
Robert Kennedy Hanna, M.A., D.D.	Adelaide Road	1926
James Thompson, B.A., D.D.	Gt James Street	1927
Thomas Alexander Smyth, M.A., LL.B., D.D.	Gt Victoria Street, Belfast	1928
John Love Morrow, M.A., D.D.	Clontarf, Dublin	1929
Edward Clarke, M.A., D.D.	Strabane	1930
James Gilbert Paton, M.C., M.A., D.D.	Malone, Belfast	1931
James Jordan Macauley, B.A., D.D.	Rathgar	1932
William Corkey, M.A., D.D.	Windsor	1933
Thomas McGimpsey Johnstone, B.A., D.D.	Newington, Belfast	1934
Andrew Frederick Moody, M.A., D.D.	Cliftonville	1935
Frederick William Scott O'Neill, M.A., D.D.	missionary, China	1936
John Waddell, M.A., D.D.	Fisherwick	1937
William John Currie, B.A., D.D.	First Bangor	1938
James Haire, M.A., D.D.	professor, Belfast	1939
James Barkley Woodburn, M.A., D.D.	Fitzroy	1940
William Alexander Watson, M.A., D.D.	clerk of assembly	1941
Wilson Moreland Kennedy, B.A., D.D.	First Derry	1942
Phineas McKee, B.A., D.D.	Downshire Road, Newry	1943
Andrew Gibson, M.C., B.A., D.D.	Trinity, Cork	1944
Robert Corkey, P.C., M.A., Ph.D.	professor, Belfast	1945
Thomas Byers, M.A., D.D.	Ormond Quay and Scots	1946
Robert Boyd, B.A., D.D.	convener, foreign mission	1947
Alfred William Neill, M.A., D.D.	First Armagh	1948
Gordon Douglas Erskine, B.A., D.D.	Rosemary Street	1949
Joseph Hugh Rush Gibson, O.B.E., M.A., D.D.	clerk of assembly	1950
Hugh McIlroy, B.A., D.D.	Ryans	1951
John Knox Leslie McKean, M.A., D.D.	First Comber	1952
James Ernest Davey, M.A., D.D.	professor, Belfast	1953
John Knowles, B.A., D.D.	Tullylish	1954
James Carlile Breakey, B.A., D.D.	Fortwilliam, Belfast	1955

	congregation	*year of election*
Thomas McCurdy Barker, M.A., D.D.	Donegal	1956
Robert John Wilson, M.A., B.D., D.D.	professor, Belfast	1957
William McAdam, M.A., D.D.	First Newry	1958
Thomas Alexander Byers Smith, B.A., D.D.	Rathgar	1959
Austin Alfred Fulton, M.A., Ph.D., D.D.	St Enoch's, Belfast	1960
William Alexander Albert Park, M.A., D.D.	Ballygilbert	1961
John Higginson Davey, B.A., D.D.	missionary, India	1962
William Alexander Montgomery, M.A., D.D.	Strand, Derry	1963
James Dunlop, M.A., D.D.	Oldpark, Belfast	1964
Samuel James Park, M.A., D.D.	Dún Laoghaire	1965
Alfred Martin, B.A., D.D.	Finaghy, Belfast	1966
William Boyd, M.A., D.D.	First Lisburn	1967
John Herbert Withers, B.A., D.D.	Fisherwick	1968
John Talbot Carson, B.A., D.D.	Trinity, Bangor	1969
James Loughridge Mitchell Haire, M.A., M.Th., D.D.	professor, Belfast	1970
Frederick Rupert Gibson, B.A., D.D.	superintendent, Irish mission	1971
Robert Victor Alexander Lynas, B.A., D.D.	Gardenmore, Larne	1972
John Whiteford Orr, B.A., D.D.	Bloomfield, Belfast	1973
George Temple Lundie, M.A., LL.B., D.D.	First Armagh	1974
George Frederick Hampton Wynne, B.A., D.D.	Gt James Street	1975
Andrew John Weir, M.Sc., D.D.	clerk of assembly	1976
Thomas Algeo Patterson, B.A., D.D.	Portaferry	1977
David Burke, B.A., D.D.	Hamilton Road, Bangor	1978
William Magee Craig, B.A., D.D.	First Portadown	1979
Ronald Gavin Craig, B.A., D.D.	First Carrickfergus	1980
John Girvan, B.A., D.D.	Hill Street, Lurgan	1981
Eric Paul Gardner, B.A., D.D.	First Ballymena	1982

VICE-PRESIDENTS OF THE CONFERENCE AND PRESIDENTS OF THE METHODIST CHURCH IN IRELAND FROM 1868

ERNEST W. GALLAGHER

R. Lee Cole, *A history of methodism in Ireland, 1860–1960* (Belfast, 1960), ch. XII, appendix I; Frederick Jeffery, *Irish methodism: an historical account of its traditions, theology and influence* (Belfast, 1964), p. 82.

The president of the Methodist Church in Ireland is the elected head of the church, from one meeting of the annual conference to the next. He presides over all committees of the whole church of which he is a member, but the conference itself is presided over by the president of the British conference, and the Irish president is its vice-president. During his year of office he has the authority vested in him by the constitution of the church to take action in specified areas, and he acts as spokesman and representative of the church in the community. By extensive travel throughout the church during the year he gives help, guidance, and inspiration to its members.

Each year, at the annual conference, one minister is chosen by ballot to be president designate, to take office from the following conference. He must be a minister of at least twenty years' service, who is not retired or about to retire. Nominations for the election are made by a nomination committee of the conference, and from the floor of the house, and balloting continues until one person has a clear majority. The conference consists of 125 ministers and 125 lay persons, representing the whole church. At the next conference, in a special service, his election is formally confirmed and he is installed as president of the Methodist Church in Ireland. The dates given below are of these formal elections.

	year of election
Henry Price	1868
James Tobias	1869
Joseph W. McKay	1870
Robinson Scott, D.D.	1871
William P. Appelbe, LL.D.	1872
George Vance	1873
Wallace McMullen	1874
Gibson McMillen	1875

year of election

Joseph W. McKay	1876
James Tobias	1877
Wallace McMullen	1878
William Guard Price	1879
William P. Appelbe, LL.D.	1880
James Tobias	1881
Oliver McCutcheon	1882
William Crook, D.D.	1883
James Donnelly	1884
Thomas A. McKee, D.D.	1885
Joseph W. McKay, D.D.	1886
John Donor Powell	1887
Wallace McMullen	1888
William Guard Price	1889
Oliver McCutcheon	1890
John Woods Ballard	1891
William Gorman	1892
Wesley Guard	1893
William Nicholas, D.D.	1894
Wallace McMullen, D.D.	1895
William Crook, D.D.	1896
James Robertson	1897
R. Crawford Johnson, D.D.	1898
Charles H. Crookshank, M.A.	1899
William Crawford, M.A.	1900
John O. Park	1901
Wesley Guard	1902
William Nicholas, M.A., D.D.	1903
Thomas Knox	1904
George R. Wedgewood	1905
James Robertson, D.D.	1906
William Crawford, M.A.	1907
James D. Lamont	1908
Joseph W. R. Campbell, M.A.	1909
John O. Park, B.A.	1910
Wesley Guard	1911
George R. Wedgewood	1912
Samuel T. Boyd, B.A.	1913
William R. Budd	1914
John O. Price	1915
Pierce Martin	1916
William Maguire	1917
Hugh McKeag	1918
James Kirkwood	1919
Henry Shire	1920
William H. Smyth, M.A.	1921
James M. Alley	1922
James W. Parkhill	1923

	year of election
William Corrigan	1924
Edward B. Cullen	1925
Robert M. Ker	1926
William H. Smyth, M.A.	1927
Randall C. Phillips	1928
John C. Robertson, M.A., B.D.	1929
William Moore	1930
Frederick E. Harte, M.A.	1931
John A. Duke, B.A.	1932
R. Lee Cole, M.A., B.D.	1933
John A. Walton, M.A.	1934
Thomas J. Irwin, D.Litt.	1935
William H. Massey	1936
C. Henry Crookshank	1937
Thomas J. Allen	1938
Alexander McCrea, M.A.	1939
Hugh M. Watson, M.A.	1940
John N. Spence	1941
Beresford S. Lyons	1942
George A. Joynt, M.A.	1943
William L. Northridge, M.A., D.D., Ph.D.	1944
Edward Whittaker	1945
Robert H. Gallagher, B.A.	1946
John England	1947
W. E. Morley Thompson	1948
John W. Stutt	1949
J. R. Wesley Roddie	1950
Henry N. Medd	1951
John Montgomery	1952
Richard M. L. Waugh, M.A., B.D.	1953
Ernest Shaw	1954
Albert Holland, D.D.	1955
Samuel E. McCaffrey	1956
J. Wesley McKinney, M.A.	1957
Robert J. Good	1958
R. Ernest Ker, M.A.	1959
Robert W. McVeigh	1960
Charles W. Ranson, B.Litt., D.Theol., S.T.D.	1961
James Wisheart	1962
Frederick E. Hill, B.A.	1963
Samuel H. Baxter, M.A., D.D.	1964
Robert A. Nelson	1965
Samuel J. Johnston	1966
Robert David Eric Gallagher, M.A., D.D.	1967
Gerald G. Myles, M.A.	1968
George E. Good, M.A.	1969
James Davison, O.B.E.	1970
Charles H. Bain, B.D.	1971

RULERS OF ENGLAND, SCOTLAND, WALES, AND MAN FROM *a.* 500

KINGS OF NORTHUMBRIA, *c.* 588–*c.* 878

H.B.C., pp 12–14.

	accession	death unless otherwise stated
?Ethelric	*c.* 588	*c.* 592
Ethelfrith	*c.* 592	616
Edwin	616	12 Oct. 632
Oswald	633	5 Aug. 641
Oswiu	654[1]	15 Feb. 670
Ecgfrith	Feb. 670	20 May 685
Aldfrith	May 685	14 Dec. 704
Eadwulf	?late 704	?early 705
Osred I	705	716
Coenred	716	718
Osric	718	9 May 729
Ceolwulf	729	abd. 737
		d. 760/64
Eadbert	737	abd. 757/8
		d. 19/20 Aug. 768
Oswulf	757/8	24/5 July 757/8
Ethelwald Moll	5 Aug. 758/9	dep. 30 Oct. 765
Alchred	765	dep. 774
Ethelred I	774	dep. 778–90
		rest. 790
		d. 18/19/29 Apr. 796
Elfwald I	778/9	23 Sept. 788
Osred II	788	dep. 790
		d. 14 Sept. 792
Osbald	796	dep. 796
Eardwulf	14 May 796	dep. 806/8
	(cor. 26 May)	?rest. 808
Elfwald II	806/8	808/10
Eanred	808/10	840/41
Ethelred II	840/41	dep. and rest. 844
		d. 848/50
Redwulf	844	?dep. 844

	accession	*death unless otherwise stated*
Osbert	848/49/50	dep. ?862/3
		rest. 867
		d. 21 Mar. 867
Aelle	862/3/7	21 Mar. 867
Egbert I	867	dep. 872
		d. 873
Ricsige	873	876
Egbert II	876	?878

¹ Kg of Bernicia from 641; Deira, the other kingdom incorporated in Northumbria, was under separate rule 641–54.

MONARCHS OF WESSEX, 519–955

H.B.C., pp 22–6.

	accession	*death unless otherwise stated*
Cerdic	519	534
Cynric	534¹	560
Ceawlin	560	?abd. 591
		d. 593
Ceol (Ceolric)	591	597
Ceolwulf	597	611
Cynegils	611	643
Cenwalh	643	674
Seaxburh (queen)	?672	?674
Cenfus	?	?
Aescwine	674	676
Centwine	676	685
Caedwalla	685	abd. 688
		d. 20 Apr. 689
Ine	688	*c.* 726
Aethelheard	726	?740
Cuthred	740	756
Sigeberht	756	?757
Cynewulf	757	786
Beorhtric	786	802
Egbert	802	839
Ethelwulf	839	13 Jan. 858²
Ethelbald	855²	860
Ethelbert	860	865/6
Ethelred	865/6	Apr. 871
Alfred	Apr. 871	26 Oct. 899
Edward the Elder	Oct. 899	17 July 924/5
	(cor. 8 June 900)	

	accession	death unless otherwise stated
Athelstan	?summer 924/5	27 Oct. 939
Edmund	Oct. 939	26 May 946
Edred	May 946	23 Nov. 955

[1] May have ruled jointly with Cerdic since 519.

[2] From 855 Ethelwulf's rule was confined to the recently-annexed kingdoms of Kent, Sussex, and Essex, of which (with Surrey) he had been sub-king, 825-39.

MONARCHS OF ENGLAND FROM 955

H.B.C., pp 28-45.

Henry VIII was the first English sovereign to adopt the custom of formally appending a number to his name (from 1525). The enumeration of English monarchs conventionally starts after the Norman conquest, but medieval chroniclers occasionally numbered the Edwards from Edward the Elder of Wessex (see preceding list). So, for instance, Friar Clyn calls Edward III *Eduardus Sextus* (Richard Butler (ed.), *The Annals of Ireland, by Friar John Clyn, etc.* (Dublin, 1849), p. 18).

	accession	death unless otherwise stated
Edwy	Nov. 955	1 Oct. 959
Edgar	Oct. 959	8 July 975
Edward the Martyr	?July 975	18 Mar. 978/9
Ethelred 'the unready'	soon *p.* 18 Mar. 978/9	dispossessed 1013-14 d. 23 Apr. 1016
Svein Forkbeard[1]	autumn 1013	3 Feb. 1014
Edmund Ironside	Apr. 1016[2]	30 Nov. 1016
Cnut	Nov. 1016	12 Nov. 1035
Harold Harefoot	1037[3]	17 Mar. 1040
Harthacnut	late 1035[3]	10 June 1042
Edward the Confessor	1042 cor. 3 Apr. 1043	5 Jan. 1066
Harold Godwinson	6 Jan. 1066	14 Oct. 1066
William I	25 Dec. 1066	9 Sept. 1087
William II	26 Sept. 1087	2 Aug. 1100
Henry I	el. 3 Aug. 1100 cor. 5 Aug. 1100	1 Dec. 1135
Stephen	22 Dec. 1135	in captivity 2 Feb.- 1 Nov. 1141 recrowned 25 Dec. 1141 d. 25 Oct. 1154
Henry II	19 Dec. 1154	6 July 1189
Richard I	3 Sept. 1189	6 Apr. 1199

	accession	*death unless otherwise stated*
John	27 May 1199	18/19 Oct. 1216
Henry III	28 Oct. 1216[4]	16 Nov. 1272
Edward I	20 Nov. 1272	7 July 1307
Edward II	8 July 1307	dep. 20 Jan. 1327
		d. 21 Sept. 1327
Edward III	25 Jan. 1327[5]	21 June 1377
Richard II	22 June 1377	dep. 29 Sept. 1399
		d. ?14 Feb. 1400
Henry IV	30 Sept. 1399	20 Mar. 1413
Henry V	21 Mar. 1413	31 Aug./1 Sept. 1422
Henry VI	1 Sept. 1422[6]	dep. 4 Mar. 1461
		rest. 3 Oct. 1470
		dep. 11 Apr. 1471
		d. 21 May 1471
Edward IV	4 Mar. 1461	in captivity Aug.-Sept. 1469
		fled abroad 3 Oct. 1470
		rest. 11 Apr. 1471
		d. 9 Apr. 1483
Edward V	9 Apr. 1483	dep. 25 June 1483
		d. probably July × Sept. 1483
Richard III	26 June 1483	22 Aug. 1485
Henry VII	22 Aug. 1485	21 Apr. 1509
Henry VIII	22 Apr. 1509	28 Jan. 1547
Edward VI	28 Jan. 1547	6 July 1553
Jane	6 July 1553	dep. 19 July 1553
		executed 12 Feb. 1554
Mary I[7]	19 July 1553[8]	17 Nov. 1558
Elizabeth I	17 Nov. 1558	24 Mar. 1603
James I	24 Mar. 1603	27 Mar. 1625
Charles I	27 Mar. 1625	executed 30 Jan. 1649[9]
Oliver Cromwell, lord protector	16 Dec. 1653	3 Sept. 1658
Richard Cromwell, lord protector	3 Sept. 1658	abd. 24 May 1659
		d. 12 July 1712
Charles II	29 May 1660[10]	6 Feb. 1685
James II	6 Feb. 1685	fled abroad 11 Dec. 1688[11]
		d. 6 Sept. 1701[12]
William III & Mary II	13 Feb. 1689[13]	Mary, 28 Dec. 1694; William, 8 Mar. 1702
Anne	8 Mar. 1702	1 Aug. 1714
George I	1 Aug. 1714	11 June 1727

	accession	death unless otherwise stated
George II	11 June 1727	25 Oct. 1760
George III	25 Oct. 1760	29 Jan. 1820
George IV	29 Jan. 1820	26 June 1830
William IV	26 June 1830	20 June 1837
Victoria	20 June 1837	22 Jan. 1901
Edward VII	22 Jan. 1901	6 May 1910
George V	6 May 1910	20 Jan. 1936
Edward VIII	20 Jan. 1936	abd. 11 Dec. 1936 d. 28 May 1972
George VI	11 Dec. 1936	6 Feb. 1952
Elizabeth II	6 Feb. 1952	

[1] Kg of Denmark, 987–1014.   [2] Chosen kg at London.

[3] Harold Harefoot acted as regent until assuming sole kingship in 1037; Harthacnut became effective kg in 1040.

[4] Assumed personal rule, Jan. 1227.   [5] Assumed personal rule, 19/20 Oct. 1330.

[6] John, duke of Bedford, and Humphrey, duke of Gloucester, acted successively as protector from 5 Dec. 1422 to Henry's coronation on 5 Nov. 1429. Henry was declared of age, 12 Nov. 1437.

[7] On 25 July 1554 Mary married Philip, kg of Naples and Jerusalem (kg of Spain from 16 Jan. 1556), who was styled, but not crowned, kg of England.

[8] Mary's second regnal year began on 6 July 1554, ignoring Jane's reign.

[9] Government by council of state was established, 14 Feb. 1649; kingship abolished, 16 Mar.; council dissolved, 20 Apr. 1653; another council set up, 29 Apr.

[10] Regnal years date from death of Charles I.

[11] Deemed by his opponents to have abdicated on fleeing from England. The peers in London assumed the executive functions, 24 Dec. 1688; a convention parliament offered William and Mary the crown of England and Ire., 13 Feb. 1689, and a Scottish convention ordered their proclamation, Mar. 1689.

[12] Jacobites acknowledged his son as James III (the 'Old Pretender') from this date until the son's own death, 1 Jan. 1766. The 'Young Pretender', Charles Edward Louis Philip Casimir, was not, however, acknowledged as kg by the pope; he d. 31 Jan. 1788.

[13] Made kg and queen for their joint and separate lives; William, however, possessed sole and full exercise of the regal power.

KINGS OF DÁL RIATAI (SCOTS), *a.* 500–858

F. J. BYRNE

Based on A. O. Anderson, *Early sources of Scottish history,* A.D. *500 to 1286* (2 vols, Edinburgh and London, 1922); M. O. Anderson, *Kings and kingship in early Scotland* (Edinburgh and London, 1973); John Bannerman, *Studies in the history of Dalriada* (Edinburgh and London, 1974).

	accession	death unless otherwise stated
Fergus mac Eirc	—	—
Domangart 'Réti' mac Fergusso[1]	—	*c.* 503/7
Comgall mac Domangairt Riatai[2]	*c.* 503/7	*c.* 538/41

	accession	death unless otherwise stated
Gabrán mac Domangairt[3]	c. 538/41	c. 558/60
Conall mac Comgaill	c. 558/60	c. 574
Áedán mac Gabráin	c. 574	17 Apr. 608/9
Eochaid Buide mac Áedáin	608/9	629/31
Connad Cerr mac Conaill	629/31	629/31
Domnall Brecc mac Echdach	629/31	Dec. 642/3
Ferchar mac Connaid[4]	?637	?abd. 650 ?d. 694
Conall Crandomnae mac Echdach	?650	659/60
Dúnchad mac Dubáin (?mac Eóganáin)[5]	?650	?abd. 659/60 ?d. 680
Domangart mac Domnaill	659/60	673
Máel Dúin mac Conaill	673	689
Domnall Donn mac Conaill	689	696
Ferchar Foto mac Feradaig[6]	?696	697
Eochaid mac Domangairt	697	697
Ainbchellach mac Ferchair[7]	697	dep. 698
Fiannamail ua Dúnchado	698	700
Selbach mac Ferchair[7]	700	abd. 723 d. 730
Dúngal mac Selbaig[7]	723	dep. 726 d. p. 734
Eochaid mac Echdach	726	733
Ailpín mac Echdach Muiredach mac Ainbchellaig[7] }	733	?736
Áed Find mac Echdach[8]	?750	778
Fergus mac Echdach	778	781
Domnall 'mac Causantín'[9]	?781	?805
Donn Coirci[10]	?781	792
Conall mac Taidg[11]	?805	807
Conall mac Áedáin[12]	807	?811
Causantín mac Fergusso[13]	?811	820
Óengus mac Fergusso[14]	820	834
Áed mac Boanta[15]	?834	839
Eóganán mac Óengusso[16]	?826	839
Ailpín mac Echdach	839	?840
Eóganán[17]	?840	?840
Cináed mac Ailpín[18]	840	858

---

[1] *Réti* is archaic for Old Irish *Riatai*; M. O. Anderson, *Kings*, pp 137 ff, suggests that *A.U.* 507 refers to his abdication.

[2] Ancestor of Cenél Comgaill.

[3] Ancestor of Cenél nGabráin.

[4] Last known Cenél Comgaill kg; M. O. Anderson, *Kings*, pp 110, 153, suggests that he shared the kingship with Domnall Brecc 637–642/3 and that his obit in the Irish annals belongs to a group of Scottish entries misplaced by about 40 years.

[5] Identity uncertain; apparently joint kg with Conall Crandomnae; see M. O. Anderson, *Kings*, p. 155.

[6] First known Cenél Loairn kg; descended from Loarn, brother of Fergus mac Eirc; he is mentioned in the annals as early as 677, but the reign of 21 years assigned him in the regnal lists is probably an error.

[7] Of the Cenél Loairn.

[8] The conquest of Dál Riatai by Óengus mac Forggusso, kg of the Picts in 736, apparently caused an interregnum until his power declined in 750.

[9] Ancestry unknown; his patronymic may be an error (M. O. Anderson, *Kings*, pp 191–3); not mentioned in the annals.

[10] Ancestry unknown; not mentioned in the regnal lists; possibly to be identified with Domnall.

[11] Ancestry unknown; had been kg of the Picts *c.* 783/4–9.

[12] Ancestry unknown; not mentioned in the annals.

[13] Kg of the Picts since 789.

[14] Kg of the Picts and Scots.

[15] Ancestry unknown.

[16] Kg of the Picts since *c.* 837; he is assigned a reign of 13 years as kg of Dál Riatai, which may, if correct, imply a period as sub-king under his father.

[17] Ancestry unknown; not mentioned in the annals.

[18] Succ. to the kingship of the Picts 842/3.

KINGS OF THE PICTS *c.* 553–842/3

F. J. BYRNE

Based on A. O. Anderson, *Early sources*; F. T. Wainwright (ed.), *The problem of the Picts* (Edinburgh and London, 1955); M. O. Anderson, *Kings*; D. P. Kirby, '... per universas Pictorum provincias' in Gerald Bonner (ed.), *Famulus Christi: essays in commemoration of the thirteenth centenary of the birth of the Venerable Bede* (London, 1976), pp 286–324.

Succession to the Pictish kingship was matrilinear, hence several kings of the Picts were sons of Anglian, British, or Gaelic princes. It would appear that Conall mac Taidg, Causantín mac Fergusso, Óengus mac Fergusso, and Eóganán mac Óengusso all succeeded to the kingdom of the Picts by mother–right and independently to that of Dál Riatai by the Gaelic *derbfhine* system of agnatic succession. When Cináed mac Ailpín similarly effected such a personal union in 842/3 matrilinear succession was abandoned and the Pictish kingdom was merged in that of the Scots. The Pictish language, a P-Celtic dialect akin to but not identical with Old Welsh, also disappeared, but the native names of the kings have been preserved in the later medieval Latin regnal lists: the Gaelic forms by which they are known in the Irish annals and Gaelic regnal lists are given here in brackets. The Latin lists indicate relationship by the terms *filius* 'son of' (abbreviated below as 'f.'), *nepos* 'grandson of', and *frater eius, frater eorum* 'his/their brother'. In the absence of knowledge of the native Pictish words, the Latin terminology has been retained here.

	accession	death unless otherwise stated
Galam Cennaleph (Cennalath)[1]	?c. 553	abd ? c. 557 d. 580
Bridei filius Mailcon (Bruide mac Máelchon)	a. 558	584/6
Gartnait f. Domelch	584/6	c. 597/9
Nectu nepos Uerb (Nechtan mac Canonn)	c. 597/9	621
Cinioth f. Lutrin (Cináed mac Lugthrin)[2]	?612	631
Gartnait f. Uuid (Gartnán mac Foith)	631	635
Bridei f. Uuid (Bruide mac Foith)	635	641
Talorc frater eorum (Tolargg mac Foith)	641	653
Talorcen f. Enfret (Tolarggan mac Ainfrith)[3]	653	657
Gartnait f. Donuel (Gartnaid mac Domnaill)	657	663/4
Drest frater eius (Drust mac Domnaill)[4]	?665/6	dep. 671/2 d. 678
Bridei f. Bili (Bruide mac Bili)[5]	671/2	692/3
Tarain f. Entifidich (Tarachain mac Ainbthig)	692/3	dep. 696/7 d. p. 699
Bridei f. Derilei (Bruide mac Derili)	696/7	706
Nechton f. Derilei (Nechtan mac Derili)[6]	706	dep. c. 724 rest. 728 dep. 729 d. 732
Drest (Drust)	c. 724	dep. 726 d. 12 Aug. 729
Elpin (Ailpín)[7]	726	dep. 728
Onuist f. Uurguist (Óengus mac Forggusso)	729	761
Bridei f. Uurguist (Bruide mac Forggusso)	761	763
Ciniod f. Uuredech (Cináed mac Feradaig)	763	775
Elpin f. Uuroid	775/6	780
Drest f. Talorcen (Drust mac Talarggan)	?780	?781
Talorcen f. Drostan (Talarggan mac Drostan)[8]	—	—
Talorcen f. Onuist (Talarggan mac Óengusso)[8]	—	—
Canaul f. Tang (Conall mac Taidg)[9]	?783/4	dep. 789 d. 807
Constantinus f. Uurguist (Causantín mac Fergusso)[10]	789	820
Unuist f. Uurguist (Óengus mac Fergusso)[11]	820	834
Drest f. Constantini (Drust mac Causantín) ⎫ Talorcen f. Uuthoil (Talarggan mac Fothoil) ⎭	834	c. 836/7
Uuen f. Unuist (Eóganán mac Óengusso)[12]	c. 836/7	839
Uurad f. Bargoit (Ferat mac Barot)	839	c. 841/2
Bred (Bruide mac Ferat)[13]	c. 841/2	c. 841/2

[1] Said to have reigned 4 years, the last year jointly with Bridei; Kirby, p. 323, dates his reign 579-80.

[2] On Kirby's hypothesis Cinioth was of a rival northern line (as were Bridei f. Mailcon, and Gartnait and Drest sons of Donuel) and reigned jointly with or in opposition to Nectu 612-21.

[3] Son of Eanfrith of Bernicia, kg of Bernicia 633-4.

[4] The apparent interregnum 663/4-665/6 may reflect the dominance of Oswiu, kg of Northumbria 654-70.

⁵ Son of Beli map Neithon, British kg of Strathclyde.

⁶ The form *Nechton* may be an archaism; Bede calls him *Naiton* (cf. Welsh *Neithon*).

⁷ Probably identical with Ailpín mac Echdach, who became joint-king of Dál Riatai in 733 (see above, p. 458).

⁸ One of these kgs is probably to be identified with the Dubtholargg, kg of the southern Picts (*citra Monoth*), whose obit is recorded *A.U.* 782.

⁹ Became kg of Dál Riatai *c.* 805 (see above, p. 458).

¹⁰ Became kg of Dál Riatai *c.* 811 (see above, p. 458); sometimes reckoned as Constantine I, kg of Picts and Scots.

¹¹ Kg of Picts and Scots (see above, p. 458).

¹² Kg of Dál Riatai since 834 or earlier (see above, p. 458).

¹³ Some versions of the regnal list add 3 further names: Cináed mac Ferat (1 year); Bruide mac Fothoil (2 years); Drust mac Ferat (3 years).

KINGS OF ALBA, *c.* 842/3–1124

F. J. BYRNE

Based on A. O. Anderson, *Early sources*, and William Croft Dickinson, *Scotland from the earliest times to 1603* (*A new history of Scotland*, i; 2nd ed., London and Edinburgh, 1965), pp 52–8.

With the accession of Cináed mac Ailpín to the Pictish kingdom, matrilinear succession was replaced by the Gaelic *derbfhine* system of eligibility within the agnatic kindred, thus permanently uniting Picts and Scots under the rule of the Dál Riatai dynasty of Cenél nGabráin. The reigns of Eochaid and Giric, Donnchad mac Crínáin, Mac Bethad mac Findlaích, and Lulach mac Gilla Comgáin are, however, notable exceptions to the rules of agnatic succession, and with the successive reigns of the three sons of Malcolm III, Edgar, Alexander I, and David I, it was displaced by filiogeniture on the English model. Throughout the ninth century the style 'king of the Picts' remained in use, Domnall mac Causantín being the first to style himself 'king of Alba'. In the reign of Máel Coluim mac Cináeda, both Anglian Lothian and the old British kingdom of Strathclyde–Cumbria were finally incorporated into the realm of Scotland.

	accession	death unless otherwise stated
Cináed mac Ailpín (Kenneth I)	842/3	858
Domnall mac Ailpín (Donald I)	858	862
Causantín mac Cináedon (Constantine I)¹	862	876
Áed mac Cináedon	876	878
Eochaid² Giric mac Dúngaile² }	*c.* 878	dep. *c.* 889 ?
Domnall mac Causantín (Donald II)	*c.* 889	900
Custantín mac Áeda (Constantine II)	*c.* 900	abd. *c.* 943 d. 952
Máel Coluim mac Domnaill (Malcolm I)	*c.* 943	954
Illulb mac Custantín (Indulf)	954	962

	accession	death unless otherwise stated
Dub mac Máel Coluim	962	966/7
Cuilén mac Illuilb	966/7	971
Cináed mac Máel Coluim (Kenneth II)	971	995
Custantín mac Cuiléin (Constantine III)	995	997
Cináed mac Duib (Kenneth III)	997	1005
Máel Coluim mac Cináeda meic Máel Coluim (Malcolm II)	1005	25 Nov. 1034
Donnchad mac Crínáin (Duncan I)[3]	1034	15 Aug. 1040
Mac Bethad mac Findlaích (Macbeth)[4]	1040	15 Aug. 1057
Lulach mac Gilla Comgáin[5]	1057	17 Mar. 1058
Máel Coluim mac Donnchada (Malcolm III 'Canmore')	1058	13 Nov. 1093
Domnall Bán mac Donnchada (Donaldbane)	1093	dep. 1094 rest. 1094 dep. 1097 bld 1099
Donnchad mac Máel Coluim (Duncan II)	1094	1094
Étgar mac Máel Coluim (Edgar)	1097	7 Jan. 1107
Alaxandair mac Máel Coluim (Alexander I)	1107	25 Apr. 1124

[1] Or Constantine II, counting Causantín mac Fergusso (d. 820) as the first of that name to be kg of Picts and Scots.

[2] Eochaid was son of Rhun, British kg of Strathclyde, and grandson through his mother of Cináed mac Ailpín; Giric is said to have been his foster-father; neither are mentioned in the Irish annals.

[3] Son of the abbot of Dunkeld, and grandson, through his mother Bethóc, of Máel Coluim mac Cináeda.

[4] Of the Cenél Loairn; his father, Findláech mac Ruaidrí, *mormáer* of Moray (d. 1020), is styled 'kg of Alba' by the Irish annals, as is Findláech's nephew and successor, Máel Coluim mac Máel Brigte (d. 1029); Mac Bethad may have been grandson, through his mother, of Cináed mac Máel Coluim.

[5] Stepson of Mac Bethad through his mother Gruoch, granddaughter of Cináed mac Duib, and cousin through his father, Gilla Comgáin mac Máel Brigte, of the Cenél Loairn *mormáer* of Moray (d. 1032). His son, Máel Snechta mac Lulaig (d. 1085), is styled 'kg of Moray' by the Irish annals and 'kg of Alba' in the twelfth-century genealogical collections (see O'Brien, *Corpus geneal. Hib.*, p. 329). The rival 'kingship' of Moray lasted until the defeat and death of Óengus 'son of the daughter of Lulach, kg of the Men of Moray' (*A.U.*) at the hands of David I in 1130.

MONARCHS OF SCOTLAND, 1124–1603

H.B.C., pp 53–8.

	accession	death
David I	?25 Apr. 1124	24 May 1153
Malcolm IV	24 May 1153	9 Dec. 1165
William I	9 Dec. 1165	4 Dec. 1214
Alexander II	4 Dec. 1214	8 July 1249
Alexander III	8 July 1249	19 Mar. 1286
Margaret	19 Mar. 1286	26 Sept. 1290

	accession	death
John (Balliol)	17 Nov. 1292	abd. 10 July 1296[1]
		d. Apr. 1313
Robert I	25 Mar. 1306	7 June 1329
David II	7 June 1329	22 Feb. 1371
Edward (Balliol)	24 Sept. 1332	exp. 1332
		rest. 1333[2]
		abd. 20 Jan. 1356
		d. Jan. 1364
Robert II	22 Feb. 1371	19 Apr. 1390
Robert III	19 Apr. 1390	4 Apr. 1406
James I	4 Apr. 1406	21 Feb. 1437
James II	21 Feb. 1437	3 Aug. 1460
James III	3 Aug. 1460	11 June 1488
James IV	11 June 1488	9 Sept. 1513
James V	9 Sept. 1513	14 Dec. 1542
Mary	14 Dec. 1542	abd. 24 July 1567
		executed 8 Feb. 1587
James VI	24 July 1567	succ. to English throne,
		24 Mar. 1603

[1] On 10 July 1296 Edward I of England took the government of the kingdom into his own hands.
[2] Acknowledged Edward III of England as his lord, Nov. 1333; on abdication he surrendered his claim to the Scottish crown to Edward.

WELSH RULERS, 844–1283

H.B.C., pp 46–52.

	accession	death unless otherwise stated	area ruled
Rhodri Mawr (the Great) ap Merfyn Frych	844	878	Gwynedd from 844; Powys from 855; Seisyllwg from 872
Anarawd ap Rhodri	878	916	Gwynedd
Cadell ap Rhodri	878	909	Seisyllwg
Hywel Dda (the Good) ap Cadell	904	949/950	Dyfed from *c.* 904; Seisyllwg from *c.* 920; Gwynedd from 942
Idwal Foel (the Bald) ap Anarawd	916	942	Gwynedd
Iago ap Idwal	950	dep. 979	Gwynedd
Owain ap Hywel	954	988	Deheubarth[1]
Hywel ap Idwal Ieuaf	979	985	Gwynedd
Cadwallon ap Idwal Ieuaf	985	986	Gwynedd

	accession	*death unless otherwise stated*	*area ruled*
Maredudd ap Owain	986	999	Gwynedd from 986; Deheubarth from 988
Cynan ap Hywel	999	1005	Gwynedd
Llywelyn ap Seisyll	1005	1023	Gwynedd from 1005; Deheubarth from 1018
Rhydderch ap Iestyn	1023	1033	Deheubarth
Iago ap Idwal	prob. 1023	1039	Gwynedd
Hywel ap Edwin	*c.* 1035	1044	Deheubarth
Gruffydd ap Llywelyn[2]	1039	5 Aug. 1063	Gwynedd and Powys from 1039; Deheubarth from 1055
Gruffydd ap Rhydderch	*c.* 1044	1055	Deheubarth
Maredudd ap Owain	*c.* 1063	1072	Deheubarth
Bleddyn ap Cynfyn	1063	1075	Gwynedd and Powys
Rhys ap Owain	1072	1078	Deheubarth
Trahaearn ap Caradog[3]	1075	1081	Gwynedd
Rhys ap Tewdwr	*c.* 1078	1093	Deheubarth
Gruffydd ap Cynan	1081	1137	Gwynedd
Maredudd ap Bleddyn	*c.* 1116	1132	Powys
Madog ap Maredudd	1132	1160	Powys
Gruffydd ap Rhys[4]	1135	1137	Cantref Mawr (part of Deheubarth)
Owain Gwynedd ap Gruffydd[5]	1137	23 Nov. 1170	Gwynedd
Rhys ap Gruffydd[6] (Yr Arglwydd Rhys 'the Lord Rhys')	1155	28 Apr. 1197	Cantref Mawr from 1155; Ceredigion (Deheubarth) from 1165
Owain Cyfeiliog	1160	abd. 1195 d. 1197	S. Powys
Gruffydd Maelor I	1160	1191	N. Powys
Cynan ap Owain	*c.* 1170	1174	Gwynedd
Dafydd ap Owain	1175	dep. 1195 d. 1203	E. Gwynedd
Rhodri ap Owain	1175	1195	W. Gwynedd
Madog ap Gruffydd	1191	1236	N. Powys
Llywelyn Fawr ap Iorwerth (Llywelyn the Great)	1195	11 Apr. 1240	E. Gwynedd from 1195; W. Gwynedd from 1200; S. Gwynedd from 1202; S. Powys from 1208; overlord of Deheubarth from 1216

	accession	death unless otherwise stated	area ruled
Gwenwynwyn	1195	dep. 1208 d. 1216	S. Powys
Gruffydd ap Rhys	1197	25 July 1201	Cantref Mawr
Rhys Gryg	1204	1234	Cantref Mawr
Maelgwn ap Rhys	1216	1231	parts of Deheubarth
Gruffydd Maelor II	1236	1269	N. Powys
Gruffydd ap Gwenwynwyn	1240	dep. 1257 rest. 1263 dep. 1274 rest. 1277 d. 1286	S. Powys
Dafydd (David) ap Llywelyn[7]	1240	25 Feb. 1246	Gwynedd
Llywelyn ap Gruffydd[7]	1246	11 Dec. 1282	part of Gwynedd from 1246; all Gwynedd from 1256; overlordship of all Welsh lords, 1258
Dafydd (David) ap Gruffydd[7]	1282	executed 3 Oct. 1283	

[1] Seisyllwg and Dyfed.
[2] The only native ruler to exercise power throughout Wales.
[3] Kg of Arwystli.
[4] Exiled in Ire. to 1116.
[5] Son of Gruffydd ap Cynan.
[6] Son of Gruffydd ap Rhys.
[7] The title 'prince of Wales' was used by Dafydd ap Llywelyn at the close of his reign, assumed by Llywelyn ap Gruffydd on his becoming overlord, recognised by Henry III in 1267, and assumed by Dafydd ap Gruffydd in 1282.

RULERS OF MAN TO 1765

F. J. BYRNE

Based on A. O. Anderson, *Early sources*; *Chronicle of the kings of Mann and the Isles*, pt 1, ed. and trans. George Broderick (Edinburgh, 1973); *Brut y Tywysogion*, trans. Thomas Jones (Cardiff, 1952). From the beginning of Scottish rule (1266/7), the list follows *H.B.C.*, pp 62–4.

Possession of the Isle of Man was disputed between the Ulaid of Ulster and the Scots of Dál Riatai, *c.* 577–83. Although invaded by Edwin of Northumbria, *c.* 630, it seems to have been occupied by British rulers (probably of Rheged) in the seventh and eighth centuries: the ancestors of Merfyn Frych (d. 844), founder of the Gwynedd dynasty (see Welsh rulers, above, p. 463), apparently came from Man. It may have come under the control of Ketil Flatnef, first Norwegian jarl of the

Hebrides, in the mid-ninth century, and thus later under the nominal suzerainty of the kings of Norway from the reign of Harald Fairhair *c.* 890. But from 914 until 980 Man lay within the sphere of influence of the kings of Dublin (see above, pp 208-10). A new Danish dynasty briefly established itself in the Hebrides *a.* 971, led by Maccus or Magnus mac Arailt and Gofraid mac Arailt (d. 989) and Gofraid's son Ragnall (d. 1004/5); the former may have been sons of Harald Bluetooth, king of Denmark (d. *c.* 986), and brothers of Svein Forkbeard (king of Denmark 987-1014), who ravaged Man in 995. Claims over Man may have been exercised by Sigurd, jarl of Orkney (*c.* 989-1014), and by his son and successor Thorfinn (d. 1065/6), but by the mid-eleventh century the Dublin Norse had successfully reasserted their suzerainty. The kingdom of Man and the Isles dates from this period, and included at various times most or all of the Hebrides (until the establishment of an independent lordship of Argyll and the southern Hebrides by Sumarlaide in 1156), and in the eleventh century also part of Galloway (*Gallgaídil* or *Na Renna*, the Rhinns of Galloway).[1] The kings of the dynasty founded by Godred Crovan owed allegiance to Norway.

---

[1] The Irish annals record in 1034 the obit of Suibne mac Cináeda, kg of Galloway, who may have been a brother of Máel Coluim mac Cináeda (Malcolm II, kg of Scotland 1005-34), or possibly a son of Cináed mac Duib (Kenneth III, 997-1005).

	accession	death unless otherwise stated
Echmarcach mac Ragnaill, kg of Dublin 1036-8, 1046-52	1052	abd. 1064 d. 1065[2]
Godred Sitricsson	*a.* 1066	1070/75[3]
Fingal Godredsson[4]	1070/75	dep. 1075/9
Godred I Crovan[5]	1075/9	1095
Lagmann Godredsson	1095	abd. 1096 d. 1096/7[6]
?Domnall mac Muirchertaig Ua Briain, kg of Dublin ?1094-1118[7]	?1096	dep. 1098 d. 1135
Magnus Bareleg, kg of Norway 1093-1103	1098	24 Aug. 1103
Sigurd Magnusson, kg of Norway 1103-30	1099/1102[8]	?dep. 1103 d. 26 Mar. 1130
Olaf I Godredsson[7]	?1103	29 June 1153
Domnall mac Taidg Ua Briain[7]	1111	dep. ?1114 d. 1115
Godred II Olafsson (Godfrey)	1153	dep. 1158 rest. 1164 d. 10 Nov. 1187
Sumerled, lord of Argyll (Somarlaide mac Gilla Brigte)	1158	1164
Reginald I Haraldsson[9]	1164	dep. 1164
Reginald II Godredsson (Ragnall mac Gofraid)	1187	dep. 1226 rest. 1228 d. 14 Feb. 1229

	accession	death unless otherwise stated
Olaf II Godredsson	1126	dep. 1228
		rest. 1229
		d. 21 May 1237
Harald I Olafsson	1237	Oct./Nov. 1248
Reginald III Olafsson	6 May 1249	30 May 1249
Harald II Godredsson[10]	1249	1250/52
Magnus Olafsson[11]	1252	24 Nov. 1265

Scottish rule

Alexander III, kg of Scots	1266/7	19 Mar. 1286
Margaret, queen of Scots ('Maid of Norway')	1286	26 Sept. 1290

English suzerainty

Richard de Burgh, earl of Ulster	1290	relq. 1290
Walter de Huntrecumbe	4 June 1290	?
John Balliol, kg of Scots	1293	forfeited 1296
Anthony Bek, bp of Durham	*a.* 11 Apr. 1298	3 Mar. 1311
Henry de Beaumont	1 May 1310	depr. 1310
		rest. 1312.
		depr. 1312
Gilbert Makaskyl ⎫	1310	remvd 1311
Robert de Leiburn ⎭		Makaskyl rest. 1312[12]
Piers de Gaveston	1311	1312

Scottish suzerainty

Thomas Randolph, earl of Moray	Dec. 1313	?[13]

English suzerainty

William Montague (cr. earl of Salisbury 16 Mar. 1337)	1333	30 Jan. 1344
William Montague, 2nd earl of Salisbury	1344	sold lordship 1393
		d. 3 June 1397
William le Scrope (cr. earl of Wiltshire 29 Sept. 1397)	1393	30 July 1399
Henry Percy, 9th earl of Northumberland	19 Oct. 1399	fled Apr. 1405
		d. 19 Feb. 1408
Sir John Stanley I	4 Oct. 1405	1414
Sir John Stanley II	1414	1437
Thomas I, lord Stanley	1437	1459
Thomas II (cr. earl of Derby 27 Oct. 1485)	1459	29 July 1504
Thomas III, 2nd earl of Derby	1504	23 May 1521
Edward, 3rd earl of Derby	1521	24 Oct. 1572
Henry, 4th earl of Derby	1572	25 Sept. 1593

	accession	death unless otherwise stated
Ferdinando, 5th earl of Derby	1593	16 Apr. 1594
William I, 6th earl of Derby	1610[14]	29 Sept. 1642
Elizabeth, countess of Derby	1612	10 Mar. 1627
James I, 7th earl of Derby	1627[15]	15 Oct. 1651
Thomas, lord Fairfax	1649[16]	depr. 1660
Charles, 8th earl of Derby	1660	21 Dec. 1672
William II, 9th earl of Derby	1672	5 Nov. 1702
James II, 10th earl of Derby	1702	1 Feb. 1736
James III, 2nd duke of Atholl	1736	8 Jan. 1764
John, 3rd duke of Atholl	1764	bought out 1765[17]

[2] Died in Rome; styled kg of Man and Na Renna by Marianus Scottus; had probably ruled Man from Dublin before 1052; defeated in 1061 by Murchad mac Diarmata meic Máel na mBó, kg of Dublin, who made Man tributary to Dublin.

[3] *Chron. Mann.*, whose chronology is very confused, records his obit *s.a.* 1051, which apparently means 1070, but records Godred Crovan's conquest *s.a.* 1056 (? = 1075); Broderick identifies the former year with 1075 and the latter with 1079, as the Chronicle states that Godred Crovan reigned 16 years. It is possible that the Chronicle is mistaken as to Godred Sitricsson's patronymic: he may have been identical with Gofraid mac Amlaíb meic Ragnaill, kg of Dublin *c.* 1070/72-4 (d. 1075); a Gofraid son of Sitric Silkbeard was killed in Wales in 1036.

[4] 'Fingal' in MS of *Chron. Mann.*, in place of an erased 'Sytric'; perhaps we should read 'Congal', as *Ann. Inisf.* record the obit of a Mac Congail as kg of Na Renna in 1094.

[5] Almost certainly identical with Gofraid Méránach, kg of Dublin, *a.* 1091-1094; a fugitive from the defeated army of Harald Hardrada at Stamford Bridge in 1066, he claimed to be the son of a Harald the Black of 'Ysland' (Iceland or Islay ?); died in Islay.

[6] Died on crusade 'in Jerusalem'.

[7] *Chron. Mann.*, records *s.a.* 1075 (? = 1095) that Muirchertach Ua Briain sent Domnall mac Taidg Ua Briain at the request of the Manxmen to act as regent during the minority of Olaf Godredsson, but that he was expelled after 3 years; *Ann. Inisf.* record that Domnall mac Taidg took the kingship of the Isles in 1111; *Chron. Mann.* further records the beginning of Olaf Godredsson's reign *s.a.* 1102 (? = 1112) and states that he reigned 40 years. It is here assumed that 2 periods of rule by 2 distinct Ua Briain princes named Domnall have been confused, and that Olaf's effective reign began *c.* 1114.

[8] In 1102 Sigurd was married to the daughter of Muirchertach Ua Briain.

[9] Grandson of Godred Crovan; Harald had been blinded and castrated by his brother Lagmann *c.* 1095.

[10] Son of Godred Don son of Reginald II; he was deprived of Man by Haakon IV, kg of Norway, in 1250; the knight Ivar, who had killed Reginald III with Harald's connivance, may have ruled Man 1250-52.

[11] Became vassal of Alexander III of Scotland *c.* 1264; his son Godred was proclaimed kg of the Manx in their unsuccessful rebellion, 1275.

[12] In succession to de Beaumont.

[13] Man was in English hands in July 1317 but was recovered by the Scots, whose claim was recognised by treaty in 1328.

[14] Ferdinando died leaving three daughters but no son, and was succeeded as earl by his brother William. While the claims of William and his nieces were in dispute, Man was resumed by the crown and governed 1594-1610 by crown appointees. At the Stanleys' request, Henry Howard, earl of Northampton, and Robert Sidney, earl of Leicester, acted as governors 1607-10. By royal grant of 7 July 1609 (ratified by parliament 1610) the lordship was confirmed to William, his wife Elizabeth (who appears to have ruled Man 1612-27) and his son James (who ruled from 1627 onwards).

[15] See note 14 above.

[16] Man granted to Fairfax by parliament, 29 Sept. 1649; commonwealth recognised in Man, Oct./Nov. 1651; Fairfax proclaimed lord of Man, 23 Feb. 1652.

[17] Man resumed to crown by proclamation, 21 June 1765.

PRINCIPAL OFFICERS OF THE CENTRAL GOVERNMENT IN IRELAND, 1172-1922

CHIEF GOVERNORS, 1172-1922

THE term 'chief governor' has been adopted as a convenient designation for the representatives of lord or monarch who, under various titles, were placed at the head of the Irish administration. The following abbreviations are used throughout this list: L. = lieutenant, D. = deputy, J. = justiciar or lord justice.

Throughout the thirteenth century, and for most of the fourteenth, the chief governor was normally styled 'justiciar'. However, in the later medieval period the normal style was 'lieutenant' or 'deputy to the lieutenant', and in this context the term 'justiciar' was applied to a temporary or emergency appointment. The term 'lord justice', a translation of *justiciarius*, originally had the same connotation.

(A) 1172-1534

ART COSGROVE

In this section of the list an additional abbreviation is used: C. = *custos* or keeper, the term normally applied to an emergency appointment in the earlier medieval period. Up to the late fourteenth century the term 'deputy justiciar' (D.J.) is also used. From 1398 the title 'deputy lieutenant' appears, abbreviated here as D.L. to distinguish the post from that of deputy (D.), appointed directly by the king from 1494 onwards. For the significance of the different titles, see H. G. Richardson and G. O. Sayles, *The administration of Ireland, 1172-1377* (Dublin, 1963), pp 8-14, and A. J. Otway-Ruthven, 'The chief governors of medieval Ireland' in *Journal of the Royal Society of Antiquaries of Ireland*, xcv (1965), pp 227-36.

A list of chief governors for the period 1172-1509 was compiled by Herbert Wood, appearing as 'The office of chief governor of Ireland, 1172-1509' in *R.I.A. Proc.*, xxxvi, sect. C, no. 12 (1923), pp 206-38. For the period up to 1377 Wood's list has been superseded by that given in Richardson and Sayles, *Admin. Ire.*, pp 73-91, but Wood's article remains useful for the later period and can be corrected in some instances by reference to A. J. Otway-Ruthven, *History of medieval Ireland* (London, 2nd ed., 1981). The list given in *H.B.C.* has now been superseded.

The present list has been substantially improved by the generous contributions of Miss Elizabeth Sykes and Dr Steven Ellis. The sequence of chief governors for the period 1413-61 is based on the list prepared by Miss Sykes for her University of Durham thesis 'The governing of the Lancastrian lordship of Ireland in the time of

James Butler, fourth earl of Ormond, *c.* 1420–52'. Miss Sykes hopes to publish the list, along with the evidence on which it is based, in the near future. Dr Ellis produced the section of the list and the accompanying footnotes covering the period 1485–1534, and has also made a number of valuable suggestions for the Yorkist period. Dr Otway-Ruthven and Dr Robin Frame kindly read a draft of the list, and a number of amendments suggested by them have been incorporated.

In the present list dates of appointment and period of office are given. For the period 1272–1377 reasonably accurate dates for the latter can be garnered from the issue rolls of the Irish exchequer, where the payments to chief governors are recorded. Before and after this period, however, such detailed guidance is lacking and the datings are necessarily tentative. In the later medieval period the evidence for the term of office is drawn from a variety of sources, as the footnotes indicate, but there are still many gaps in our knowledge. There is not sufficient information to make it practicable to include dates of swearing-in for this period. Names of persons who did not take up their appointments are shown in square brackets.

	appointment	*period of office*
Hugh de Lacy		1172–3
William fitz Audelin, C.[1]		1173
Richard de Clare, earl of Pembroke ('Strongbow'), C.[2]		1173–6
Raymond le Gros, deputy to the earl of Pembroke, *procurator*[3]		1173–*p*. 20 Apr. 1176[4]
William fitz Audelin, *procurator*[5]		1176–Mar. 1177
Hugh de Lacy, *procurator generalis*[6]		1177–81
John de Lacy, constable of Chester ⎱ C.		1181
Richard of the Peak ⎰		
Hugh de Lacy		1181/2–Sept. 1184
Philip of Worcester, *procurator*[7]		*c*. 1 Sept. 1184–25 Apr. 1185

(John, lord of Ire., in Ire. 25 Apr. 1185–mid-Dec. 1185)

John de Courcy, J.		1185–?1192
Peter Pipard ⎱ J.		?1192–4[8]
William le Petit ⎰		
Walter de Lacy ⎱ J.		1194–5
John de Courcy ⎰		
Hamo de Valognes, J.		1195–8
Meiler fitz Henry, J.		?1198–1200
Meiler fitz Henry, J.		early 1200–late Oct. 1200[9]
Meiler fitz Henry, J.	late Oct. 1200	late Oct. 1200–*p*. 19 June 1208
John de Grey, bp of Norwich, J.		1208–13

[[1] *Footnotes for this section begin on p. 480.*]

(King John, in Ire., 20 June 1210–24/5 Aug. 1210)

	appointment	*period of office*
William le Petit, J. (during de Grey's absence)		1211
Henry of London, abp of Dublin, J.	23 July 1213	1213–15
Geoffrey de Marisco, J.	6 July 1215	1215–4 Oct. 1221
Henry of London, abp of Dublin, J.	3 July 1221	4 Oct. 1221–*p.* 19 June 1224
William Marshal the Younger, J.	2 May 1224	*p.* 19 June 1224[10]–22 June 1226
Geoffrey de Marisco, J.	25 June 1226	July 1226–13 Feb. 1228
Richard de Burgh, J.	13 Feb. 1228	?Mar. 1228–1232
[Hubert de Burgh, J.]	16 June 1232[11]	
Maurice FitzGerald, J.	2 Sept. 1232	1232–Oct. 1245
John fitz Geoffrey, J.	4 Nov. 1245	?Aug. 1246–1256
Geoffrey de Tourville, bp of Ossory, D.J.	Nov. 1245	Nov. 1245–?Aug. 1246
[Edward, son of Henry III, lord of Ire.]	14 Feb. 1254	
Richard de la Rochelle, D.J.		1254–5
Richard de la Rochelle, J.		1256
Alan de la Zouche, J.		1256–8
Stephen Longespée, J.		1258–60
William of Dene, J.		1260–61
Richard de la Rochelle, J.		autumn 1261–6 Dec. 1264[12]
Geoffrey de Geneville, acting J.		6 Dec. 1264–19 Apr. 1265[12]
Richard de la Rochelle, J.		19 Apr. 1265–1266
[Fulk de Sandford, abp of Dublin, J.]	16 Feb. 1265[13]	
[Roger Waspayl, C.]	6 May 1265[14]	
[Hugh of Taghmon, bp of Meath, J.]	10 June 1265[15]	
David de Barry, J.		*a.* Mich. 1266–1268
Robert d'Ufford, J.		1268–70
James de Audley, J.		Mich. 1270–11 June 1272
Maurice fitz Maurice FitzGerald, J.		*p.* 11 June 1272–mid-Apr. 1273
Geoffrey de Geneville, J.		Mich. 1273–Mich. 1276
Richard d'Exeter, D.J.		6 Mar. 1270–6 Nov. 1276[16]
Robert d'Ufford, J.	17 June 1276	Mich. 1276–Mich. 1281
Stephen de Fulbourn, bp of Waterford, D.J. (during d'Ufford's absence)		mid-1280
Stephen de Fulbourn, J.	21 Nov. 1281	21 Nov. 1281–3 July 1288
William fitz Roger, prior of Kilmainham, D.J.		Easter 1284–29 July 1285

	appointment	*period of office*
John de Sandford, abp of Dublin, C., J., D.J.[17]		7 July 1288–10 Nov. 1290
William de Vesci, J.	12 Sept. 1290	11 Nov. 1290–5 Mar. 1294
Walter de la Haye, C. and acting J.		5 Mar. 1294–?4 June 1294
William fitz Roger, prior of Kilmainham, C. and acting J.		4 June 1294–19 Oct. 1294
William de Oddingeseles, J.	18 Oct. 1294	19 Oct. 1294–3 Apr. 1295
Thomas fitz Maurice FitzGerald, C. and D.J.		19 Apr. 1295–2 Dec. 1295
Walter de la Haye, D.J.		13 Nov. 1295
John Wogan, J.	18 Oct. 1295	3 Dec. 1295–30 Sept. 1308
Richard de Burgh, 3rd earl of Ulster, D.J.		Mich. 1299–Hilary 1300
William de Ros, prior of Kilmainham, D.J.		23 Aug. 1301–31 Mar. 1302
Maurice Rochfort, D.J.		30 June 1302–29 Sept. 1302
Edmund Butler, C. and D.J.		4 Nov. 1304–23 May 1305
[Richard de Burgh, earl of Ulster, L.]	15 June 1308[18]	
Piers Gaveston, L.	16 June 1308	*p.* 25 June 1308–15 May 1309
William de Burgh, D.J.		1 Oct. 1308–15 May 1309
John Wogan, J.		16 May 1309–6 Aug. 1312
Edmund Butler, C. and acting J.		7 Aug. 1312–18 June 1314
Theobald de Verdun, J.	30 Apr. 1313	19 June 1314–27 Feb. 1315
Edmund Butler, J.	4 Jan. 1315	28 Feb. 1315–4 Apr. 1318[19]
Roger Mortimer, L.	23 Nov. 1316	7 Apr. 1317–5 May 1318
William FitzJohn, abp of Cashel, C.	6 May 1318	6 May 1318–3 Nov. 1318
Alexander Bicknor, abp of Dublin, C. and J.	11 Aug. 1318	23 Sept. 1318–23 June 1319
Roger Mortimer, J.	15 Mar. 1319	12 June 1319–12 Dec. 1320
Thomas fitz John FitzGerald, 2nd earl of Kildare, D.J.		30 Sept. 1320–30 June 1321
[Sir Ralph de Gorges, J.]	1 Feb. 1321[20]	
Earl of Kildare, J.	23 Apr. 1321	30 June 1321–1 Oct. 1321[21]
John de Bermingham, earl of Louth, J.	21 May 1321	28 Aug. 1321[21]–Feb. 1324[22]
William de Bermingham, D.J.		18 Aug. 1322–18 Feb. 1323[23]
John Darcy, J.	18 Nov. 1323	1 Feb. 1324–1 May 1327[24]
Roger Outlaw, prior of Kilmainham, D.J.		*c.* July–Oct. 1324
Roger Outlaw, D.J.		1 May 1327–12 May 1327

	appointment	*period of office*
Earl of Kildare, J.	12 Mar. 1327[25]	12 May 1327–5 Apr. 1328
Roger Outlaw, acting J.[26]		6 Apr. 1328–May 1329
John Darcy, J.	19 Feb. 1329	*c*. May 1329–12 Feb. 1331
Roger Outlaw, D.J.	31 May 1330[27]	17 July 1330–2 June 1331
William de Burgh, 4th earl of Ulster, L.	3 Mar. 1331	17 July 1331–*p*. 5 Nov. 1331[28]
Anthony de Lucy, J.	27 Feb. 1331	3 June 1331–3 Dec. 1332
Thomas de Burgh, D.J.		3 Dec. 1332–12 Feb. 1333
John Darcy, J.	30 Sept. 1332	13 Feb. 1333–29 Sept. 1333
Thomas de Burgh, D.J.		29 June 1333–18 Jan. 1334
John Darcy, J.		19 Jan. 1334–14 Mar. 1335
Thomas de Burgh, D.J.	16 July 1334[29]	
Roger Outlaw, D.J.	15 Mar. 1335	15 Mar. 1335–26 June 1335
John Darcy, J.		27 June 1335–27 Aug. 1335
Roger Outlaw, D.J.		28 Aug. 1335–18 Sept. 1335
John Darcy, J.		18 Sept. 1335–14 Nov. 1336
Roger Outlaw, D.J.		15 Nov. 1336–15 Oct. 1337
John de Charleton, J.	28 July 1337	15 Oct. 1337–16 June 1338
Thomas de Charleton, bp of Hereford, C. and acting J.	15 May 1338	19 June 1338–7 Apr. 1340
John Darcy, J.	3 Mar. 1340	8 Apr. 1340–14 July 1344
Roger Outlaw, D.J.		8 Apr. 1340–5 Feb. 1341[30]
Alexander Bicknor, abp of Dublin, C. and acting J.[31]		22 Feb. 1341–16 May 1341
John Morice, D.J.	16 Mar. 1341	16 May 1341–14 July 1344
Ralph d'Ufford, J.	10 Feb. 1344	14 July 1344–9 Apr. 1346
Roger Darcy, J.	10 Apr. 1346[32]	10 Apr. 1346–15 May 1346
John Morice, J.	7 Apr. 1346	16 May 1346–28 June 1346
Walter de Bermingham, J.	10 May 1346	29 June 1346–27 Nov. 1347
John Larcher, prior of Kilmainham, D.J.		28 Nov. 1347–26 Apr. 1348
Walter de Bermingham, J.		27 Apr. 1348–27 Oct. 1349[33]
John de Carew, D.J.		3 Oct. 1349–19 Dec. 1349
Thomas de Rokeby, J.	17 July 1349	20 Dec. 1349–4 Mar. 1352
Maurice Rochfort, bp of Limerick, D.J.		5 Mar. 1352–14 June 1352
Thomas de Rokeby, J.		15 June 1352–9 Aug. 1355
Maurice fitz Thomas FitzGerald, 4th earl of Kildare, D.J.		11 Aug. 1355–20 Aug. 1355[34]
Maurice fitz Thomas FitzGerald, 1st earl of Desmond, J.	8 July 1355	17 Aug. 1355–25 Jan. 1356
Earl of Kildare, J.	30 Mar. 1356[35]	26 Jan. 1356–17 Oct. 1356
Thomas de Rokeby, J.	24 July 1356	31 Oct. 1356–23 Apr. 1357[36]
John de Boulton, J.		24 Apr. 1357–5 Sept. 1357
Earl of Kildare, D.J.	30 Aug. 1357	5 Sept. 1357–26 Nov. 1357

	appointment	*period of office*
Amaury de St Amand, J.	14 July 1357	27 Nov. 1357–17 Mar. 1359
James Butler, 2nd earl of Ormond, J.	16 Feb. 1359	18 Mar. 1359–18 Sept. 1360
Earl of Kildare D.J.		9 Oct. 1360–31 Mar. 1361
Earl of Kildare, J.	16 Mar. 1361	1 Apr. 1361–15 Sept. 1361
Lionel, 5th earl of Ulster (cr. duke of Clarence, 13 Nov. 1362), L.	1 July 1361	15 Sept. 1361–22 Apr. 1364
Earl of Ormond, C.		25 Apr. 1364–25 Jan. 1365
Duke of Clarence, L.	25 Sept. 1364	mid Dec. 1365–7 Nov. 1366
Thomas de la Dale, C.		7 Nov. 1366–22 Apr. 1367
Gerald fitz Maurice FitzGerald, 3rd earl of Desmond, J.	20 Feb. 1367	*c.* 23 Apr. 1367–20 June 1369
William of Windsor, L.	3 Mar. 1369	20 June 1369–9 Apr. 1372
James Pickering, J.		29 Apr. 1370
[Richard of Pembridge, L.]	*a.* 26 Jan. 1372[37]	
Earl of Kildare, C.	22 Mar. 1372[38]	6 Apr. 1372–16 July 1372
Robert of Ashton, J.		16 July 1372–2 Dec. 1373
Ralph Cheyne, D.J.		Oct.–Nov. 1373[39]
William Tany, prior of Kilmainham, J.		3 Dec. 1373–18 Apr. 1374
William of Windsor, governor and C.	20 Sept. 1373	19 Apr. 1374–20 June 1376
John Keppok, governor and C.		15 Nov. 1373–31 Oct. 1375
Earl of Kildare, J.	16 Feb. 1376	21 June 1376–21 Sept. 1376
Earl of Ormond, J.	24 July 1376	Mich. 1376–Mich. 1379[40]
Alexander Petit (de Balscot), bp of Ossory, J.	13 Oct. 1379[41]	13 Oct. 1379–Dec. 1379
John de Bromwych, J.	22 Sept. 1379	Dec. 1379–May 1380
Edmund Mortimer, 3rd earl of March, L.	22 Oct. 1379	May 1380–26 Dec. 1381[42]
John Colton, abp of Armagh, J.	10 Jan. 1382[43]	10 Jan. 1382–3 Mar. 1382
Roger Mortimer, 4th earl of March, L.	24 Jan. 1382	3 Mar. 1382–autumn 1383[44]
Thomas Mortimer, D. to earl of March	3 Mar. 1382	3 Mar. 1382–autumn 1383[44]
Philip de Courtenay, L.	1 July 1383	Sept. 1383–26 Nov./1 Dec. 1384[45]
James Butler, 3rd earl of Ormond, J.	26 Nov./1 Dec. 1384	26 Nov./1 Dec. 1384–6 May 1385
Philip de Courtenay, L.	1 Mar. 1385	6 May 1385–Easter 1386[46]
Robert de Vere, marquis of Dublin (cr. duke of Ire., Oct. 1386)	1 Dec. 1385[47]	(did not go to Ire.)

	appointment	period of office
Richard White, prior of Kilmainham, J. of marquis of Dublin	Easter 1386	Easter 1386–30 Aug. 1386[48]
John Stanley, L. of marquis of Dublin	8 June 1386	30 Aug. 1386–?Nov. 1387[49]
Alexander Petit (de Balscot), bp of Meath, J. of duke of Ire., J. of the kg		?Nov. 1387–Feb. 1388
Alexander Petit (de Balscot), J. of the king		Feb. 1388–autumn 1389[50]
[Thomas Mortimer, J.]	5 Mar. 1389[51]	
John Stanley, J.	1 Aug. 1389	25 Oct. 1389[52]–?3 Oct. 1391[53]
Robert Sutton, J.	31 Jan. 1390[54]	
Alexander Petit (de Balscot), bp of Meath, J.	11 Sept. 1391	3 Oct. 1391–8 Oct. 1392[55]
[Thomas, duke of Gloucester, L.]	May 1392[56]	
Earl of Ormond, J.	24 July 1392	8 Oct. 1392–15 May 1395[57]

(Richard II in Ire. 2 Oct. 1394–15 May 1395)

Earl of March, L.	c. May 1395[58]	15 May 1395–23 Jan. 1397[59]
William le Scrope, J.		?15 May 1395–Apr. 1397[59]
Edmund Mortimer, L.	23 Jan. 1397	23 Jan. 1397–?18 July 1397
Earl of March, L.	24 Apr. 1397	p. 18 July 1397–20 July 1398[60]
Edmund Mortimer, D.L.		Apr. 1398[61]
Reginald de Grey, J.[62]	c. 20 July 1398	c. 20 July 1398–7 Oct. 1398
Thomas Holland, duke of Surrey, L.	26 July 1398[63]	7 Oct. 1398– ?

(Richard II in Ire. 1 June 1399–27 July 1399)

Edmund Holland, ?D. to duke of Surrey		autumn 1399
Alexander Petit (de Balscot), bp of Meath, J.		a. Jan. 1400–Mar. 1400
John Stanley, L.	10 Dec. 1399	10/13 Mar. 1400–May 1401
William Stanley, D.L.	May 1401	May 1401–Aug. 1401[64]
Thomas of Lancaster, L.	18 July 1401	13 Nov. 1401–7 Nov. 1403[65]
Stephen le Scrope, D.L.	19 Dec. 1401[66]	23 Aug. 1401–2 Feb. 1404
Earl of Ormond, J.[67]	3 Mar. 1404	3 Mar. 1404–Oct. 1404
Stephen le Scrope, D.L.	18/26 Oct. 1404	?Oct. 1404–June 1405
Earl of Ormond, D. to Stephen le Scrope	25 June 1405	4 July 1405–7 Sept. 1405
Gerald fitz Maurice FitzGerald, 5th earl of Kildare, J.	7 Sept. 1405	7 Sept. 1405– ?autumn 1406
Stephen le Scrope, D.L.		autumn 1406–8 Dec. 1407

	appointment	*period of office*
James Butler, 4th earl of Ormond, D. to Stephen le Scrope	8 Dec. 1407[68]	8 Dec. 1407–2 Aug. 1408
Thomas of Lancaster, L.[69]		2 Aug. 1408–Mar. 1409[70]
Thomas Butler, prior of Kilmainham, D.L.	4 Mar. 1409[71]	9 Mar. 1409–25 Sept. 1413
John de Stanley, L.	8 June 1413	25 Sept. 1413–18 Jan. 1414
Thomas Cranley, abp of Dublin, J.[72]	18 Jan. 1414	18 Jan. 1414–13 Nov. 1414
John Talbot, Lord Furnival, L.	24 Feb. 1414	13 Nov. 1414–7 Feb. 1416
Thomas Cranley, abp of Dublin, D.L.	5 Feb. 1416	8 Feb. 1416[73]–summer or autumn 1416[74]
Lord Furnival, L.		summer or autumn 1416–late 1417 or early 1418
Thomas Talbot, D.L.		*a.* Mar. 1418–mid-June 1418
Lord Furnival, L.		*a.* 29 June 1418–22 July 1419[75]
Richard Talbot, abp of Dublin, D.L.	prob. 22 July 1419	22 July 1419–6 Mar. 1420
Richard Talbot, J.	6 Mar. 1420	9 Mar. 1420–22 Apr. 1420
Earl of Ormond, L.	10 Feb. 1420	22 Apr. 1420–10 Apr. 1422
William fitz Thomas Butler, prior of Kilmainham, J.	*c.* 10 Apr. 1422	*a.* 10 May 1422–10 Oct. 1422[76]
Richard Talbot, abp of Dublin, J.	4 Oct. 1422	10/11 Oct. 1422–*p.* 24 Sept. 1423
Edmund Mortimer, 5th earl of March, L.	9 May 1423	*c.* 29 Sept. 1424–18 Jan. 1425
Edward Dantsey, bp of Meath, D.L.	4 Aug. 1423	2 Oct. 1423–*p.* 3 May 1424
Earl of Ormond, D.L.		*a.* 11 May 1424–*p.* 2 Sept. 1424
John Talbot, Lord Talbot and Furnival, J.		*a.* 22 Jan. 1425–28 Apr. 1425
Earl of Ormond, L.	1 Mar. 1425	28 Apr. 1425–13 Apr. 1426
Earl of Ormond, J.[77]	15 Apr. 1426	15 Apr. 1426–31 July 1427
John de Grey, L.	15 Mar. 1427	1 Aug. 1427–*p.* 16 Dec. 1427
Edward Dantsey, bp of Meath, D.L.		*a.* 22 Dec. 1427–*p.* 19 July 1428
John Sutton, Lord Dudley, L.	23 Mar. 1428	*a.* 17 Sept. 1428–*p.* 5 Nov. 1429
Thomas Strange, D.L.	*a.* 5 Nov. 1429	*a.* 11 Nov. 1429–*p.* 26 Apr. 1430
Richard Talbot, abp of Dublin, J.		8 May 1430–30 Sept. 1431
Thomas Stanley, L.	29 Jan. 1431[78]	30 Sept. 1431–autumn 1432
Christopher Plunket, D.L.		*a.* 10 Dec. 1432–*p.* 9 Apr. 1434
Thomas Stanley, L.		*a.* 4 Nov. 1434–*p.* 6 Oct. 1435

	appointment	*period of office*
Richard Talbot, abp of Dublin, D.L.		*a.* 22 Nov. 1435–*p.* 11 Apr. 1437[79]
Richard Talbot, J.	19 Apr. 1437	19 Apr. 1437–29 May 1438
Lionel Welles, Lord Welles, L.	12 Feb. 1438	*c.* 29 May 1438–*a.* mid Feb. 1439
William Welles, D.L.		*a.* 13 Apr. 1439–*p.* 11 May 1440
Lord Welles, L.		*a.* 10 June 1440–*p.* 15 Mar. 1441
Earl of Ormond, D.L.	on or *a.* 15 Mar. 1441	Mar. 1441–late 1441 or early 1442[80]
Earl of Ormond, L.	27 Feb. 1442	*a.* 15 May (prob. early Apr.) 1442–*p.* 28 Aug. 1444[81]
Richard Nugent, baron of Delvin, D.L.	28 Aug. 1444	*p.* 28 Aug. 1444–*p.* 22 Oct. 1444
Richard Talbot, abp of Dublin, J.		*a.* 5 Feb. 1445–*p.* 15 Oct. 1446
John Talbot, earl of Shrewsbury, L.	12 Mar., revised 21 May 1445	*a.* 18 Nov. 1446–*p.* 20 Oct. 1447[82]
Richard, duke of York, L.	9 Dec. 1447[83] renewed 11 Feb. 1451, 1 Dec. 1454, 6 Mar. 1457	*c.* 6 July 1449–*c.* 8 Sept. 1450
Richard Talbot, abp of Dublin, D.L.		?late 1447–1448[84]
Richard Nugent, baron of Delvin, D.L.		*a.* 23 Dec. 1448–*p.* 1 Apr. (prob. 6 July) 1449
Earl of Ormond, D.L.	22 Aug., revised 23 Aug. 1450	*c.* 8 Sept. 1450–23 Aug. 1452
Edward FitzEustace, D.L.		*p.* 23 Aug. 1452–*p.* 25 May 1453
James Butler, 2nd earl of Wiltshire and 5th earl of Ormond, L.	12 May 1453	(did not go to Ire.)
John Mey, abp of Armagh, D.L.	on or *a.* 25 June 1453	*a.* 14 Sept. 1453–*p.* 8 Mar. 1454[85]
Edward FitzEustace, D.L. of duke of York	23 Apr. 1454	22 May 1454–25 Oct. 1454
Thomas 'fitz Maurice' FitzGerald, 7th earl of Kildare, J.	on or *p.* 25 Oct. 1454[86]	*a.* 6 Nov. 1454–*p.* 13 Feb. 1455
Earl of Kildare, D.L. of duke of York		*a.* 18 Apr. 1455–*p.* 20 Nov. 1456 (prob. until autumn 1459)[87]
Richard, duke of York, L.	6 Mar. 1457 (renewal from 8 Dec. 1457)	mid or late Oct. 1459–early Sept. 1460

	appointment	*period of office*
James Butler, earl of Wiltshire and earl of Ormond, L.	4 Dec. 1459	}
Thomas Bathe, baron of Louth, D.L.	12 Dec. 1459	appointments apparently ineffective in Ire.
John Bole, abp of Armagh, D.L.	13 Dec. 1459	
Earl of Kildare, D.L.		prob. Sept.–Dec. 1460
Earl of Kildare, J.	*p.* 31 Dec. 1460, conf. 30 Apr. 1461	Jan. 1461– ?June 1462
George, duke of Clarence, L.	28 Feb. 1462[88]	
Roland FitzEustace, Lord Portlester, D.L.	16 May 1462	12 June 1462–Apr. 1463[89]
Thomas fitz James Fitz-Gerald, 8th earl of Desmond, D.L.	1 Apr. 1463	Apr. 1463–Oct. 1467
Earl of Kildare, D. to earl of Desmond		summer 1464[90]
[John Tiptoft, earl of Worcester, D.L.]	May 1465[91]	
Earl of Worcester, D.L.	spring 1467	Oct. 1467–?early 1470[92]
Earl of Worcester, L.	23 Mar. 1470[93]	
Edmund[94] Dudley, D.L.		?early 1470–summer 1470
Earl of Kildare, J.		*a.* 13 Oct. 1470[95]–?Feb. 1471
Duke of Clarence, L.	18 Feb. 1471 (app. by Henry VI)[96]	
Earl of Kildare, D.L.		Feb. 1471–?Apr. 1471
Earl of Kildare, J.		?Apr. 1471–22 × 28 Dec. 1471[97]
Duke of Clarence, L.	16 Mar. 1472 (app. by Edward IV)[98]	
Earl of Kildare, D.L.		22 × 28 Dec. 1471– ?July 1475
William Sherwood, bp of Meath, D.L.	*a.* 18 Apr. 1475	?May 1475–Feb. 1478[99]
Robert Preston, Lord Gormanston, D. to bp of Meath		1477[100]
Earl of Kildare, J.		Feb. 1478–25 Mar. 1478[101]
[John de la Pole, duke of Suffolk, L.]	10 Mar. 1478[102]	
Gerald FitzGerald, 8th earl of Kildare, J.		*c.* 25 Mar. 1478–Sept. 1478[103]
George, son of Edward IV, L.[104]	6 July 1478	
Henry Grey, Lord Grey, D.L.		*a.* 15 Sept. 1478–*p.* 15 Dec. 1478[105]

	appointment	period of office
Robert Preston, Viscount (since 7 Aug. 1478) Gormanston, D. to Lord Grey		*a.* 14 Jan. 1479-*p.* Mar. 1479[106]
Richard, duke of York, L.	5 May 1479[107]	
Viscount Gormanston, D.L.	7 May 1479[108]	?1 June 1479-*p.* 18 Oct. 1479[109]
Earl of Kildare, D.L.	*a.* 5 Oct. 1479[110]	Oct. 1479-*p.* 9 Apr. 1483[111]
Earl of Kildare, J.		*p.* 9 Apr. 1483-Aug. 1483[112]
Edward, son of Richard III, L.	19 July 1483[113]	
Earl of Kildare, D.L.	31 Aug. 1483[114]	31 Aug. 1483-Mar. 1484[115]
Earl of Kildare, J.		?Mar. 1484-*p.* 15 Oct. 1484[116]
John de la Pole, earl of Lincoln, L.	21 Aug. 1484	
Earl of Kildare, D.L.	*c.* 22 Sept. 1484[117]	*p.* 22 Oct. 1484- ?24 Oct. 1485[118]
Earl of Kildare, J.		*a.* 18 Dec. 1485-?Mar. 1486[119]
Jasper Tudor, duke of Bedford, L.	11 Mar. 1486	
Earl of Kildare, D.L.		?Mar. 1486[120]-20 May 1492[121]
[Earl of Kildare, L.]		*a.* 24 May 1487-*p.* 13 Aug. 1487[122]
Walter FitzSimons, abp of Dublin, D.L.	20 May 1492[123]	20 May 1492-*p.* 3 Sept. 1493
James Ormond, governor		*a.* 6 July 1492-*p.* 3 Sept. 1493[124]
Viscount Gormanston, D.L.	*a.* 12 Sept. 1493[125]	*a.* 12 Sept. 1493-Oct. 1494
William Preston, D. to Viscount Gormanston		*c.* Nov. 1493-*a.* 20 Feb. 1494[126]
Henry Tudor, duke of York, L.	12 Sept. 1494	
Edward Poynings, D.	13 Sept. 1494	*a.* 12 Oct. 1494-*p.* 20 Dec. 1495[127]
Henry Deane, bp of Bangor, J.	1 Jan. 1496[128]	*a.* 2 Jan. 1496-*p.* 4 July 1496[129]
Gilbert Nugent, Lord Delvin, commr		6 July 1496-21 Sept. 1496[130]
Earl of Kildare, D.	6 Aug. 1496	21 Sept. 1496-*p.* 21 Apr. 1509[131]
Walter FitzSimons, abp of Dublin, D. to earl of Kildare		Apr. 1503-Aug. 1503[132]
Earl of Kildare, J.		*a.* 1 June 1509-Nov. 1510[133]
Earl of Kildare, D.	8 Nov. 1510	Nov. 1510-3 Sept. 1513

	appointment	*period of office*
Gerald FitzGerald, 9th earl of Kildare, J.	4 Sept. 1513	4 Sept. 1513–*p.* 26 Nov. 1513
Earl of Kildare, D.	26 Nov. 1513	*a.* 13 Jan. 1514–*p.* 5 May 1515[134]
William Preston, Viscount Gormanston, J.	13 Apr. 1515	*a.* 14 May 1515–*a.* 20 Sept. 1515[135]
Earl of Kildare, D.		*a.* 20 Sept. 1515–*p.* 10 Sept. 1519[136]
Maurice FitzGerald, D. to earl of Kildare		*a.* 20 Dec. 1519–23 May 1520[137]
Thomas Howard, earl of Surrey, L.	10 Mar. 1520	24 May 1520–*p.* 21 Mar. 1522[138]
Piers Butler, 8th earl of Ormond, D.L.		*p.* 21 Dec. 1521–*a.* 9 Mar. 1522[139]
Earl of Ormond, D.	6 Mar. 1522	26 Mar. 1522–4 Aug. 1524[140]
Earl of Kildare, D.	13 May 1524	4 Aug. 1524–*p.* 20 Dec. 1526[141]
Thomas FitzGerald, D. to earl of Kildare		*p.* 20 Dec. 1526– ?*a.* 14 Sept. 1527[142]
Richard Nugent, Lord Delvin, D. to earl of Kildare		?*p.* 14 Sept. 1527–*p.* 10 June 1528[143]
Thomas FitzGerald, captain	15 May 1528[144]	15 May–Oct. 1528
Piers Butler, earl of Ossory, D.	4 Aug. 1528	*a.* 14 Oct. 1528–*a.* 4 Sept. 1529[145]
Henry FitzRoy, duke of Richmond and Somerset, L.	22 June 1529	
John Alen, abp of Dublin Patrick Bermingham John Rawson }	secret council as D.	*a.* 4 Sept. 1529–24 Aug. 1530[146]
William Skeffington, D.	22 June 1530	24 Aug. 1530–18 Aug. 1532[147]
Earl of Kildare, D.	5 July 1532	18 Aug. 1532–11 June 1534[148]
Thomas FitzGerald, Lord Offaly, D. to earl of Kildare		mid-Feb. 1534–11 June 1534[149]
Lord Delvin, governor		?11 June 1534–?early Aug. 1534[150]

---

[1] It is unlikely that his authority extended beyond Dublin. He is entitled bailiff of Dublin (G. H. Orpen, *Ireland under the Normans, 1169–1333* (4 vols, Oxford, 1911–20; reprint, Oxford, 1968), i, 285).

[2] So described in Giraldus Cambrensis, *Expugnatio Hibernica*, ed. A. B. Scott and F. X. Martin (Dublin, 1978), p. 134. He termed himself 'vices regis Angliae in Hibernia agens' (*Rotulorum patentium et clausorum cancellariae Hiberniae calendarium* (Dublin, 1828) hereafter cited as *Rot. pat. Hib.*), 4, no. 52).

[3] So termed in *Expugnatio*, p. 166.

[4] He continued to act after the earl of Pembroke's death. For the dating of the earl's death to 20 Apr., see G.E.C., *Peerage*, x, 356, n. e. Ralph de Diceto (i, 407) has 5 Apr. and *Expugnatio*, p. 164, gives 'circa Kalendas Junii'.

[5] *Expugnatio*, p. 168.

[6] Ibid., p. 182.

[7] Ibid., p. 198.

[8] Their authority ceased on John's forfeiture in Apr. 1194.

[9] It is not known what arrangements were made for the administration of Ire. after Meiler's recall in 1200.

[10] He arrived in Waterford on 19 June 1224 and journeyed thence to Dublin (W. W. Shirley (ed.), *Royal and other historical letters illustrative of the reign of Henry III* (2 vols, London, 1862-6), i, 500).

[11] Hubert de Burgh held the office formally until his deprivation in Aug. 1232, but never came to Ire.; the functions continued to be exercised by Richard de Burgh. See Richardson and Sayles, *Admin. Ire.*, p. 77.

[12] De Geneville took de la Rochelle's place as justiciar when the latter was captured by the Geraldines in Dec. 1264. See *Admin. Ire.*, p. 79.

[13] Appointment ineffective.

[14] Appointment ineffective.

[15] Appointment ineffective.

[16] He served as deputy throughout this period.

[17] All three terms seem to have been applied to him.

[18] Appointment ineffective.

[19] Butler continued to serve as justiciar under Mortimer throughout this period. See G. J. Hand, *English law in Ireland, 1290-1324* (Cambridge, 1967), pp 230-32.

[20] Appointment ineffective.

[21] Payments to Kildare continued until 1 Oct. 1321, although John de Bermingham received payment from 28 Aug. 1321.

[22] De Bermingham acted until Feb. 1324, although there is no record of payment to him after 25 Aug. 1323. He held pleas as J. 25 Nov. 1323-10 Feb. 1324 (P.R.O.I., M.2750; for this and subsequent references to this source, I am indebted to Miss Philomena Connolly).

[23] During this period William de Bermingham was paid as 'justiciar's lieutenant'. Payment to his brother, John, began again on 25 Feb. 1323 (P.R.O., E101/238/6). This information was kindly supplied by Dr Robin Frame.

[24] He was absent in England in the late summer of 1324 (*Cal. close rolls, 1323-7*, pp 215, 308). Richardson and Sayles, *Admin. Ire.*, p. 85, n. 1, err in supposing that he did not leave the country during Outlaw's term as D.J. This point I also owe to Dr Frame.

[25] His impending appointment had been announced on 14 Feb. 1327 (*Cal. close rolls, 1327-30*, pp 106-7).

[26] App. by the council on Kildare's death. He held pleas as J. 11 Apr. 1328-23 May 1329 (P.R.O.I., M.2750).

[27] Outlaw held pleas as D.J. 30 Nov. 1329-13 May 1331 (P.R.O.I., M.2750).

[28] I have followed Dr Frame's suggested alteration in dates. De Burgh was sworn in at Dublin on 17 July (H. G. Richardson and G. O. Sayles, *The Irish parliament in the middle ages* (Philadelphia 1952; reissue, 1964), p. 29) and his summons to England was issued on 5 Nov. 1331 (*Cal. pat. rolls, 1330-34*, p. 220; *Cal. close rolls, 1330-33*, p. 400).

[29] Thomas de Burgh was app. to deputise for Darcy in the latter's absence (*Cal. pat. rolls, 1330-34*, p. 568), but Darcy held pleas as J. 10 Apr. 1334-14 Mar. 1335 (P.R.O.I., M.2750).

[30] P.R.O.I., M.2750.

[31] App. by the council on Outlaw's death when the justiciar, John Darcy, was out of the country.

[32] He was app. justiciar by the council in Ire. on d'Ufford's death (*Rot. pat. Hib.*, p. 49, no. 44).

[33] Payment continued until that date though de Carew was acting from 3 Oct. 1349.

[34] P.R.O.I., M.2750.

[35] He was app. by the council in Ire. on 26 Jan. 1356, after Desmond's death. The kg ratified the appointment on 30 Mar. 1356. He was still holding pleas on 17 Oct. 1356 (P.R.O.I., M.2750).

[36] P.R.O.I., M.2750.

[37] Appointment ineffective (*Cal. close rolls, 1369-74*, p. 420).

[38] He took the oath as keeper on 22 Mar. 1372 (*Rot. pat. Hib.*, p. 82, no. 53), but payment to him did not begin until 9 Apr. 1372. He held pleas as keeper 6 Apr.-16 July 1372 (P.R.O.I., M.2750).

[39] Mentioned on 8 June 1374 as Tany's predecessor in office (*Rot. pat. Hib.*, p. 86, no. 41).

[40] His appointment was renewed on 21 July 1377 and again on 20 Aug. 1378. He was permitted to resign on 24 Aug. 1379 but continued to act until 13 Oct. 1379 (*Cal. pat. rolls, 1377-81*, pp 14, 269, 385; *Rot. pat. Hib.*, p. 106, no. 26).

[41] App. to act until de Bromwych arrived in Dec. 1379.

[42] *H.B.C.* wrongly gives 29 Dec. as date of Mortimer's death.

[43] The hiatus which occurred in the aftermath of Mortimer's death was ended by the emergency appointment of Colton by the council in Ire. (Otway-Ruthven, *Med. Ire.*, p. 316). The appointment was confirmed on 20 Jan. 1382 (*Rot. pat. Hib.*, p. 111, no. 75).

[44] He was still acting on 27 July 1383 (*Rot. pat. Hib.*, p. 122, no. 26). Presumably his uncle, Sir Thomas Mortimer, continued to act for the same period.

[45] He arrived in Ire. on 11 Sept. 1383 and returned to England between 26 Nov. and 1 Dec. 1384 (Otway-Ruthven, *Med. Ire.*, p. 317).

[46] He returned to Ire. on 6 May 1385 and continued to act until his formal discharge at Easter 1386 (ibid., pp 318–19).

[47] *Cal. pat. rolls, 1385–9*, pp 112, 115. The duke had been granted the land and lordship of Ire. (*Cal. close rolls, 1385–9*, p. 232).

[48] Otway-Ruthven, *Med. Ire.*, p. 319.

[49] He arrived in Ire. on 30 Aug. 1386 and his letters patent, enrolled in Dublin on 18 Sept., dated his appointment from his time of arrival (*Rot. pat. Hib.*, p. 131, no. 31). According to Wood, he was holding pleas as late as 4 Nov. 1387.

[50] According to Wood, he began to hold pleas on 13 Nov. 1387. The grant of Ire. to de Vere was annulled by the parliament of Feb. 1388, but de Balscot was continued as justiciar until the autumn of 1389 (Otway-Ruthven, *Med. Ire.*, pp 320–21).

[51] *Cal. pat. rolls, 1388–92*, p. 20. Appointment ineffective.

[52] *Rot. pat. Hib.*, p. 144, nos 76–7.

[53] Presumably Stanley continued to act until de Balscot took office on 3 Oct. 1391 (*Rot. pat. Hib.*, p. 148, nos. 42–3).

[54] He was to conduct parliament at Kilkenny because Stanley was unable to attend in person (ibid., p. 146, no. 202).

[55] Otway-Ruthven, *Med. Ire.*, p. 323.

[56] Did not come to Ire.; patent cancelled 23 July 1392 (ibid., p. 323). On the same day the kg announced that he had ordered Roger Mortimer, earl of March, to prepare to undertake the government of Ire. (*A roll of the proceedings of the king's council in Ireland for a portion of the sixteenth year of the reign of Richard II, 1392–93*, ed. James Graves (London, 1877), pp 255–6). The earl of Ormond was to act as J. until March's arrival. See Anthony Tuck, 'Anglo-Irish relations, 1382–93' in *R.I.A. Proc.*, lxix, sect. C, no. 2 (1970), pp 28–9.

[57] The appointment was renewed on 31 May 1393 (*Cal. pat. rolls, 1391–6*, p. 275) and he seems to have remained in office until the king left Ire. on 15 May 1395 (Otway-Ruthven, *Med. Ire.*, p. 334).

[58] *H.B.C.* gives 28 Apr. 1395 as date of March's appointment, but cites no authority.

[59] Authority was divided between March and Scrope. See Otway-Ruthven, *Med. Ire.*, p. 335. Their appointments were renewed on 25 Apr. 1396 and again on 25 Sept. 1396 when March was made king's lieutenant in Ulster, Connacht, and Meath, and Scrope justiciar in Leinster, Munster, and Louth (*Cal. pat. rolls, 1391–6*, pp 710–11; *1396–9*, p. 29).

[60] His appointment was renewed on 24 Apr. 1398 (*Cal. pat. rolls, 1396–9*, p. 336) and he remained in office until his death on 20 July 1398. Sir Edward Perrers was to govern in Munster and Leinster during the lieutenant's absence (Otway-Ruthven, *Med. Ire.*, p. 335).

[61] During March's absence in England.

[62] App. by the council in Ire. on March's death.

[63] His appointment was to date from 1 Sept. 1398 (*Cal. pat. rolls, 1396–9*, p. 402).

[64] Otway-Ruthven, *Med. Ire.*, pp 340–41.

[65] Le Scrope was formally app. Lancaster's deputy on that date (*Rot. pat. Hib.*, p. 177, no. 34), and Lancaster left Ire. shortly afterwards.

[66] He was formally app. as Lancaster's deputy in Dec. 1401 (*Rot. pat. Hib.*, p. 162, no. 84), but he seems to have been acting in that capacity since his arrival on 23 Aug. 1401 (Otway-Ruthven, *Med. Ire.*, p. 341).

[67] The great council granted a subsidy to Ormond as 'soldier and governor of the wars' (*soldario et gubernatori guerrarum*) rather than as justiciar, so that the grant might not set a precedent for future justiciars (*A roll of the proceedings of the king's council in Ireland for a portion of the sixteenth year of the reign of Richard II, 1392–93*, ed. James Graves (London, 1877), pp 269–72). But it seems clear that Ormond was app. justiciar. See Richardson and Sayles, *Ir. parl. in middle ages*, p. 155, n. 72.

[68] *Calendar of Ormond deeds, 1350–1413*, ed. Edmund Curtis (Dublin, 1934), no. 391, pp 282–3.

[69] Lancaster's appointment was renewed in 1404, 1405, and 1406, and he was to retain the office until June 1413 (*Cal. pat. rolls, 1401–5*, p. 456; *1405–8*, pp 143, 237).

[70] Arrival and departure dates.

[71] *Rot. pat. Hib.*, p. 191, no. 75. The letter making the appointment is dated 4 Mar. 1409.

[72] He was elected by the council after Stanley's death (*Rot. pat. Hib.*, p. 221, no. 111).

[73] Ibid., p. 212, nos 101-2.

[74] Preparations for Talbot's return to Ire. were being made in June 1416 (*Cal. pat. rolls, 1416-22*, p. 31).

[75] Henry Marleburrough, 'The chronicle of Ireland' in Sir James Ware (ed.), *Ancient Irish histories* (2 vols, Dublin, 1809), ii, pt 2, p. 28, states that he left Ire. on 22 July 1419. Professor Otway-Ruthven thinks that he may not have departed until Feb. 1420 (*Med. Ire.*, pp 356-7), but Sykes accepts Marleburrough's dating, and her evidence suggests that Richard Talbot was acting as deputy in Sept. 1419, Jan. and Feb. 1420 (cf. *Calendar of ancient records of Dublin*, ed. J. T. Gilbert, i (Dublin, 1889), p. 28).

[76] He held office for 40 days after the death of Henry V on 31 Aug. 1422 (*Rot. pat. Hib.*, p. 240, no. 52).

[77] App. by the council in Ire.

[78] He was to take up office on 12 Apr. 1431 (*Cal. pat. rolls, 1429-36*, p. 105), but was not sworn until 30 Sept. 1431 (*Rot. pat. Hib.*, p. 253, nos 12, 13, 14, 16).

[79] Sykes thinks it unlikely that Stanley returned to Ire. in the autumn of 1436, as suggested by Wood.

[80] Sykes believes that Ormond was absent in England for some months in late 1441-early 1442 but does not know who was in charge in Ire. while he was away.

[81] Ormond was summoned in Aug. 1442 to appear before the English council in the following February, but Sykes thinks it unlikely that he went to England before 1444. Otway-Ruthven, *Med. Ire.*, pp 372-3, suggests that Ormond was in England in the summer of 1442.

[82] Talbot was still in Ire. on 20 Oct. 1447 for a great council held at Naas (*Statute rolls of the parliament of Ireland, reign of King Henry VI*, ed. H. F. Berry (Dublin, 1910), pp 150-54). Otway-Ruthven, *Med. Ire.*, p. 375, dates his departure to the summer of 1447.

[83] York had originally signed an indenture on 30 July 1447 undertaking the office from 29 Sept. 1447. See P.R.O., E101/71/4, 921 and 922; E404/63/160; E404/65/59 and 104. These references were supplied by Mr Vincent Gorman.

[84] Wood suggests that Richard Talbot acted as deputy both for his brother John and later for Richard, duke of York, but Sykes has been unable to date his term of office. Professor Otway-Ruthven states that Richard Talbot was made justiciar in Nov. 1447 (*Med. Ire.*, p. 375).

[85] Mey continued to claim the deputyship even after FitzEustace had been sworn in. For the dispute between York and Wiltshire about the lieutenancy, see Otway-Ruthven, *Med. Ire.*, pp 385-6, and Herbert Wood, 'Two chief governors of Ireland at the same time' in *R.S.A.I. Jn.*, lxiii (1928), pp 156-7.

[86] Edward FitzEustace d. on 25 Oct. 1454. Thomas 'fitz Maurice' was not recognised as earl of Kildare until 1456.

[87] Kildare was still in office on 3 Apr. 1459 (*Anal. Hib.*, xxiii (1966), p. 169).

[88] He was to take office on 6 Mar. 1462 (*Cal. pat. rolls, 1461-7*, p. 142), but he never came to Ire. His appointment as lieutenant was renewed on 10 May 1465 (ibid., p. 437).

[89] I have found no evidence to support the statement in J. T. Gilbert, *History of the viceroys of Ireland* (Dublin, 1865), p. 377, that William Sherwood, bp of Meath, acted as deputy after FitzEustace in 1462.

[90] During Desmond's absence in England. Desmond was still in Ire. on 24 June 1464 (*Anal. Hib.*, x (1941), p. 18). William Lynch, *A view of the legal institutions, honorary hereditary offices, and feudal baronies, established in Ireland during the reign of Henry II* (London, 1830), p. 272, states that Christopher Plunket, Lord Killeen, 'was deputy to the earl of Desmond in the government of Ireland'. Possibly this was in 1466, during the period that Desmond was held captive by O'Connor Faly.

[91] The indenture made with the king on 11 May 1465 bound him to act as deputy for 6 years from 14 June 1465 (P.R.O., E404/73, 18 May 1465), but the appointment seems to have been ineffective.

[92] He arrived in Ire. early in October (9 Oct., according to Wood) and departed, apparently, early in 1470. See Otway-Ruthven, *Med. Ire.*, p. 394. Desmond was still acting as deputy on 13 Oct. 1467 (St Peter's College, Wexford, Hore MS 1, p. 1109, mem. roll, 8 Edw. IV, m. 16d). I owe this reference to Dr Steven Ellis.

[93] *Cal. pat. rolls, 1467-77*, p. 205. He did not return to Ire. and was executed on 18 Oct. 1470 after the restoration of Henry VI.

[94] *H.B.C.* gives Edmund Dudley, Wood gives Rowland Dudley. He is termed Edmund Dudley in *Cal. close rolls, 1468-76*, no. 536, p. 138.

[95] *Statute rolls of the parliament of Ireland, 1st to the 12th years of the reign of King Edward IV*, ed. H. F. Berry (Dublin, 1914) (hereafter cited as *Stat. Ire., 1-12 Edw. IV*), pp 814-17. As justiciar, he held parliament on 26 Nov. 1470 (ibid., pp 650-51).

[96] *Cal. pat. rolls, 1467-77*, p. 243. He was app. for 20 years from the previous Michaelmas.

[97] Kildare was deputy to Clarence by 7 Feb. 1471 (Hore MS 1, pp 1127-9, mem. roll, 12 Edw. IV, m. 6; reference from Dr Steven Ellis), which suggests that the Lancastrian appointment of Clarence was accepted in Ire. Presumably that appointment lapsed with the deposition of Henry VI on 11 Apr. 1471. Kildare was certainly styled justiciar in Sept. 1471 (*Anal. Hib.*, xxiii (1966), p. 186) and, as such, held parliament in Dec. 1471 (*Stat. Ire., 1-12 Edw. IV*, pp 712-13). He was still justiciar on 22 Dec. 1471 but had become deputy to Clarence by 28 Dec. 1471 (ibid., pp 814-15, and B.L., Add. MS 4793, f. 157v; reference from Dr Ellis).

[98] *Cal. pat. rolls, 1467-77*, p. 335. In view of Kildare's title in Dec. 1471, Clarence must already have been acting as lieutenant prior to this appointment.

[99] Sherwood was app. before 18 Apr. 1475 (*Anal. Hib.*, x (1941), pp 47-8), and his tenure presumably ended with the attainder and execution of Clarence in Feb. 1478.

[100] During Sherwood's absence in England (cf. *Statute rolls of the parliament of Ireland, 12th and 13th to the 21st and 22nd years of the reign of King Edward IV*, ed. James F. Morrissey (Dublin, 1939) (hereafter cited as *Stat. Ire., 12-22 Edw. IV*), pp 548-53). He was acting at various dates between 14 Jan. and 13 Oct. 1477 (ibid., pp 461, 465, 476-7, 490-91).

[101] App. justiciar by the council on the lapse of Sherwood's patent, he died shortly afterwards.

[102] *Cal. pat. rolls, 1476-85*, p. 90. The appointment was ineffective.

[103] He was still acting as justiciar at the session of parliament which opened on 14 Sept. 1478 (*Stat. Ire., 12-22 Edw. IV*, pp 628-9).

[104] The infant son of the king; he died within a year.

[105] P.R.O.I., RC 8-42, p. 57, mem. roll, 19 Edw. IV, m. 18. Cf. *Stat. Ire., 12-22 Edw. IV*, pp 636, 664-6; B.L. Add. MS 4791, f. 197 (references from Dr Ellis).

[106] Calendar to Christ Church deeds, no. 1014, in *Twenty-fourth report of the deputy keeper of the public records in Ireland* (Dublin, 1892), appendix VIII, pp 107-8.

[107] *Cal. pat. rolls, 1476-85*, p. 153. Richard was then only 4 years old. He was reappointed on 9 Aug. 1480 (Gilbert, *Viceroys*, pp 600-01).

[108] Thomas Rymer (ed.), *Foedera, conventiones, litterae et cujuscunque generis acta publica . . .* (20 vols, London, 1704-35), v, pt 2, p. 102.

[109] *Anal. Hib.*, x (1941), pp 18, 31-2.

[110] *Cal. pat. rolls, 1476-85*, p. 164. He was reappointed from 5 May 1481 (Gilbert, *Viceroys*, pp 600-01). [111] His appointment lapsed with the death of Edward IV.

[112] Kildare was probably app. justiciar twice—firstly on the death of Edward IV and then on the succession of Richard III. [113] *Cal. pat. rolls, 1476-85*, p. 403.

[114] Kildare was originally app. for 1 year from that date (*Letters and papers illustrative of the reigns of Richard III and Henry VII*, ed. James Gairdner (2 vols, London, 1861-3) (hereafter cited as *L. & P. Rich. III & Hen. VII*), i, 44).

[115] Presumably Kildare's appointment as deputy lapsed with the death of Edward, the king's son and lieutenant of Ire., on 9 Mar. 1484.

[116] Kildare was still acting as justiciar on 15 Oct. 1484 (*Calendar of Archbishop Alen's register, c. 1172-1534*, ed. Charles McNeill (Dublin, 1950) p. 248; Richardson and Sayles, *Ir. parl. in middle ages*, p. 363; references from Dr Ellis).

[117] *L. & P. Rich. III & Hen. VII*, i, 74-5.

[118] Richard's second Irish parliament was dissolved by Kildare only after the session on 24 Oct. 1485 (P.R.O.I., MS transcript of parliament roll, 2-3 Rich. III; heading printed in Richardson and Sayles, *Ir. parl. in middle ages*, p. 330); the courts of king's bench and exchequer, however, were held in Henry's name from 6 Oct. (*Reports from the commissioners appointed by his majesty to execute the measures recommended . . . respecting the public records of Ireland* (3 vols, [London, 1815-25]), ii, 538).

[119] Mem. roll, 1 Hen. VII, m. 19 (R.I.A., MS 24 H 17, p. 191).

[120] Kildare was certainly D.L. by 14 July 1486 (*Anal. Hib.*, x (1941), p. 78).

[121] FitzSimons was app. D. L., 20 May 1492 (Patent roll, 7 Hen. VII; B.L., Add. MS 4787, f. 53).

[122] Lambert Simnel was crowned Edward VI in Dublin on 24 May; Kildare was still acting as his lieutenant on 13 August (*Calendar of Ormond deeds, 1413-1509* (Dublin, 1935), no. 272). Henry VII ignored proceedings in the name of the pretender.

[123] Patent roll, 7 Hen. VII (B.L., Add. MS 4787, f. 53). The king confirmed FitzSimons as D.L. on 11 June (*Cal. pat. rolls, 1485-94*, p. 376).

[124] The viceroyalty was exercised jointly at this time by FitzSimons and Ormond. See especially patent roll, 7 Hen. VII (B.L., Add. MS 4787, f. 53), mem. roll, 9 Hen. VII, m. 6 (B.L., Add. MS 4793, f. 149v), parliament roll, 8 Hen. VII, cc 19, 21 (P.R.O.I. MS RC13/19). They were still acting on 3 Sept. 1493; *Calendar of ancient records of Dublin*, ed. J. T. Gilbert, i (Dublin, 1889), p. 142; *Calendar of Ormond deeds, 1413-1509* (Dublin, 1935), no. 285.

125 *Rot. pat. Hib.*, p. 270b, nos 1–2.

126 Mem. roll, 9 Hen. VII, m. 8 (B.L., Add. MS 4793, f. 150v); letters patent attested by Gormanston on 20 Feb. 1494.

127 D. B. Quinn, 'The Irish parliamentary subsidy in the fifteenth and sixteenth centuries' in *R.I.A. Proc.*, xlii, sect. C, no. 11 (1935), p. 232.

128 *Cal. pat. rolls, 1494–1509*, p. 65: Deane must, however, have been elected justiciar by the council prior to this, probably on instructions from the king, since he was signing warrants as such by 2 Jan. (B.L., Royal MS, 18C, xiv, f. 32v).

129 B.L., Royal MS, 18C, xiv, f. 63v.

130 Delvin was elected 'commissionarius generalis ac capitalis capitaneus sub justiciario Hibernie' by the council on 25 June 1496 (Sir James Ware, *The antiquities and history of Ireland* (ed. R. Ware, Dublin, 1705), p. 33; B.L., Royal MS 18C, xiv, ff 63v, 64), but his commission and indenture did not pass the great seal until 6 July.

131 Kildare took his oath on 21 Sept. 1496 (P.R.O., SC1/58/70; printed in Agnes Conway, *Henry VII's relations with Scotland and Ireland 1485–1498* (Cambridge, 1932), p. 232). He would cease to act on news of Henry VII's death on 21 Apr. 1509.

132 FitzSimons attested as Kildare's deputy on 17 June 1503: patent roll, 17 & 18 Hen. VII (Bodleian Library, Oxford, Rawl. MS B 502, f. 18v).

133 Mem. roll, 1 Hen. VIII, m. 3 (P.R.O.I., MS 1A 49 136, f. 6): attestation by Kildare as justiciar, 1 June 1509.

134 Mem. roll, 4 & 5 Hen. VIII, m. 24; 8 & 9 Hen. VIII, m. 17d (P.R.O.I., MS 1A 49 136, f. 19; BL. Add. MS 4791, f. 198: patents attested by Kildare on 13 Jan. 1514 and 5 May 1515 respectively).

135 Christ Church deed, attested by Gormanston, 14 Mar. 1515 (Bodleian Library, Oxford, Rawl. MS B 484, f. 76; cf. calendar to Christ Church deeds, no. 403, in *Twentieth report of the deputy keeper of the public records in Ireland* (Dublin, 1888), appendix VII, p. 111; mem. roll, 6 & 7 Hen. VIII, m. 18 (P.R.O.I., MS 1A 49 136, f. 35), patent attested by Kildare, 20 Sept. 1515).

136 *The 'Dignitas decani' of St Patrick's cathedral, Dublin*, ed. Newport B. White, with introduction by Aubrey Gwynn (Dublin, 1957) (hereafter cited as *Dignitas decani*), no. 141; William Monck Mason, *The history and antiquities of the collegiate and cathedral church of St Patrick . . .* (Dublin, 1820), appendix, pp xxxv–xxxvi.

137 *Calendar of Ormond deeds, 1509–47* (Dublin, 1937), no. 61.

138 'The bills and statutes of the Irish parliaments of Henry VII and Henry VIII', ed. D. B. Quinn, in *Anal. Hib.*, x (1941), p. 116; T.C.D., MS 543/2.

139 *State papers, Henry VIII* (11 vols, London, 1830–52) (hereafter cited as *S.P. Hen. VIII*), ii, 91–3, 96.   140 Ibid., ii, 97.   141 *Dignitas decani*, no. 52.

142 The changeover of vice-deputies from FitzGerald to Delvin may have occurred about 14 Sept. 1527, when the chancellor, apparently in temporary charge of the administration, attested a grant (N.L.I., D.2146 (*Calendar of Ormond deeds, 1509–47* (Dublin, 1937), no. 130).

143 Delvin was taken prisoner by O'Connor Faly on 12 May 1528, and effectively ceased to act from that date. He remained, however, nominally in charge of the administration under the earl of Kildare. See *S.P. Hen. VIII*, ii, 127, 133–4.

144 Elected by the council in response to the emergency (*S.P. Hen. VIII*, ii, 127–30). It is possible that FitzGerald may only have had responsibility for defence, with the chancellor (Hugh Inge, abp of Dublin) remaining in overall charge of the administration.

145 *S.P. Hen. VIII*, ii, 143; P.R.O., MS SP1/67, f. 35 (letter signed by the secret council on the latter date).

146 See D. B. Quinn, 'Henry Fitzroy, duke of Richmond, and his connexion with Ireland, 1529–30' in *Bulletin of the Institute of Historical Research*, xii (1935), pp 175–7. The secret council, Skeffington (1530–32, 1534–5), Kildare (1532–4), and Grey (until mid-1536) were apparently styled deputies both to the king and to his lieutenant, the duke of Richmond (d. 22 July 1536); see especially mem. roll, 23 Hen. VIII, m. 29 (P.R.O.I., Ferguson collection, iv, f. 160), and *S.P. Hen. VIII*, ii, 367.

147 Kildare took his oath as deputy on 18 Aug. 1532 (*Cal. pat. rolls, Ire., Hen. VIII–Eliz.*, plate I).

148 Kildare was summoned to England, leaving his son, Lord Offaly ('Silken Thomas'), as deputy (Feb. 1534); imprisoned in Tower of London (29 June); died there, 2 Sept. 1534 (Steven Ellis, 'Tudor policy in Ireland, 1490–1534' in *I.H.S.*, xx, no. 79 (Mar. 1977), p. 257). Kildare's deputyship lapsed with the resignation of his deputy on 11 June; see P.R.O., MS SP 65/1/2; *Letters and papers, foreign and domestic, Henry VIII* (21 vols, London, 1862–1932) (hereafter cited as *L. & P. Hen. VIII*), xii (ii), 1310, II (2).   149 T.C.D., MS 543/2, *s.a.* 1534.

150 Delvin held office for 8 weeks in June, July and August (P.R.O., MS SP 65/1/2; *L. & P. Hen. VIII*, xii (ii), 1310, II (2)).

(B) *1534–1800*

J. G. SIMMS

This list generally follows *H.B.C.*, pp 156–67. For this period the principal source is Rowley Lascelles, *Liber munerum publicorum Hiberniae* (2 vols, London, 1824–30; 2nd ed., 1852) (hereafter cited as *Liber mun. pub. Hib.*), based on the manuscript collections of John Lodge, deputy keeper of the rolls, 1754–74, which has been used to correct or supplement *H.B.C.* Other sources are cited in the footnotes. The date of appointment shown is generally that of the patent; but in the case of appointments made in England and patented in Dublin, the date is that of the English privy seal (as in *Liber mun.*). The date of swearing-in has also been shown; it was not until a governor was sworn in that he assumed the exercise of his office. If the date of swearing-in is not ascertainable the date shown is that of arrival in Ireland or of the Dublin patent. Unless otherwise indicated, the period of a governor's tenure ended with the swearing-in of his successor.

H.B.C. shows in a separate column the names of lords justices appointed during the absence of a chief governor. In this list the names have been arranged in a single column to show who was in effective charge of the administration at any time. For much of the eighteenth century the viceroy came to Ireland for only a few months in alternate years for the parliamentary session. Lords justices held office during his absence. From 1767 to 1800 the viceroys were almost continuously resident.

The editors gratefully acknowledge help received from Dr Christopher Woods.

	appointment	swearing-in
Sir William Skeffington, D.	30 July 1534[1]	24 Oct. 1534[2]
Lord Leonard Grey, J.	1 Jan. 1536[3]	
Lord Leonard Grey, D.	23 Feb. 1536	
Sir William Brereton, J.	1 Apr. 1540[4]	2 May 1540
Sir Anthony St Leger, D.	7 July 1540	c. 12 Aug. 1540[5]
Sir William Brabazon, J.	12 Oct. 1543	10 Feb. 1544
Sir Anthony St Leger, D.	3 July 1544[6]	11 Aug. 1544[7]
Sir William Brabazon, J.	16 Feb. 1546	1 Apr. 1546
Sir Anthony St Leger, D.	7 Nov.1546[8]	16 Dec. 1546[9]
Sir Edward Bellingham, D.	22 Apr. 1548	21 May 1548[10]
Sir Francis Bryan, J.	27 Dec. 1549[11]	29 Dec. 1549
Sir William Brabazon, J.	2 Feb. 1550[12]	
Sir Anthony St Leger, D.	4 Aug. 1550	10 Sept. 1550
Sir James Croft, D.	29 Apr. 1551	23 May 1551[13]
Sir Thomas Cusack ⎱ J. Sir Gerald Aylmer ⎰	7 Nov. 1552[14]	9 Dec. 1552
Sir Anthony St Leger, D.	1 Sept. 1553[15]	19 Nov. 1553
Thomas Radcliffe, Viscount Fitzwalter (earl of Sussex, 17 Feb. 1557), D.	27 Apr. 1556	26 May 1556
Hugh Curwin, abp of Dublin ⎱ J. Sir Henry Sidney ⎰	12 Nov. 1557	5 Dec. 1557

[¹ *Footnotes for this section begin on p. 495.*]

	appointment	swearing-in
Sir Henry Sidney, J.	18 Jan. 1558	6 Feb. 1558
Earl of Sussex, D.	9 Mar. 1558	1 May 1558[16]
Sir Henry Sidney, J.	4 Aug. 1558	18 Sept. 1558[17]
Sir Henry Sidney, J.	12 Dec. 1558[18]	13 Dec. 1558
Earl of Sussex, D.	3 July 1559	30 Aug. 1559
Sir William Fitzwilliam, J.	18 Jan. 1560	15 Feb. 1560
Earl of Sussex, L.	6 May 1560	25 June 1560
Sir William Fitzwilliam, J.	10 Jan. 1561	2 Feb. 1561
Earl of Sussex, L.	24 May 1561	5 June 1561
Sir William Fitzwilliam, J.	20 Dec. 1561	22 Jan. 1562
Earl of Sussex, L.	4 July 1562	29 July 1562
Sir Nicholas Arnold, J.	2 May 1564	25 May 1564
Sir Henry Sidney, D.	13 Oct. 1565	20 Jan. 1566
Robert Weston, L.C. Sir William Fitzwilliam } J.	12 Aug. 1567[19]	14 Oct. 1567
Sir Henry Sidney, D.	17 Apr. 1568	28 Oct. 1568
Sir William Fitzwilliam, J.	1 Apr. 1571[20]	1 Apr. 1571
Sir William Fitzwilliam, D.	11 Dec. 1571	13 Jan. 1572
Sir Henry Sidney, D.	5 Aug. 1575	18 Sept. 1575
Sir William Drury, J.	27 Apr. 1578	14 Sept. 1578
Sir William Pelham, J.	11 Oct. 1579[21]	11 Oct. 1579
Arthur Grey, 14th Baron Grey de Wilton, D.	15 July 1580	7 Sept. 1580
Adam Loftus, abp of Dublin Sir Henry Wallop } J.	14 July 1582[22]	31 Aug. 1582
Sir John Perrot, D.	7 Jan. 1584	21 June 1584
Sir William Fitzwilliam, D.	17 Feb. 1588	30 June 1588
Sir William Russell, D.	16 May 1594	11 Aug. 1594
Thomas, Lord Burgh, D.	5 Mar. 1597	22 May 1597
Sir Thomas Norris, J.	29 Oct. 1597[23]	30 Oct. 1597
Abp Loftus Richard Gardiner } J.	15 Nov. 1597[24]	27 Nov. 1597
Robert Devereux, 2nd earl of Essex, L.	12 Mar. 1599	15 Apr. 1599
Abp Loftus Sir George Cary } J.	24 Sept. 1599[25]	25 Sept. 1599
Charles Blount, Lord Mountjoy, D.	21 Jan. 1600	28 Feb. 1600[26]
Lord Mountjoy, J.[27]	9 Apr. 1603	9 Apr. 1603
Lord Mountjoy, D.	12 Apr. 1603	
Lord Mountjoy (cr. earl of Devonshire, 21 July 1603[28]), L.	25 Apr. 1603[29]	c. 26 May 1603
Sir George Carey, D.	30 May 1603	1 June 1603
Sir Arthur Chichester (cr. Baron Chichester of Belfast 23 Feb. 1613), D.	15 Oct. 1604[30]	3 Feb. 1605
Thomas Jones, abp of Dublin Sir Richard Wingfield } J.	7 Feb. 1614[30]	4 Mar. 1614
Lord Chichester, D.		26 July 1614[31]

	appointment	*swearing-in*
Abp Jones Sir John Denham } J.	29 Nov. 1615[30]	11 Feb. 1616
Sir Oliver St John (cr. Viscount Grandison of Limerick, 3 Jan. 1621), D.	2 July 1616	30 Aug. 1616
Sir Adam Loftus, L.C. Richard Wingfield, 1st Viscount } J. Powerscourt	18 Apr. 1622[30]	4 May 1622
Henry Cary, 1st Viscount Falkland, D.	4 Feb. 1622[32]	8 Sept. 1622
Adam Loftus, 1st Viscount Loftus of Ely, L.C. Richard Boyle, 1st earl of Cork } J.	10 Aug. 1629[30]	26 Oct. 1629
Thomas Wentworth, Viscount Wentworth	3 July 1633	25 July 1633
Viscount Loftus Christopher Wandesford } J.	4 Apr. 1636[30]	3 July 1636
Viscount Wentworth (cr. earl of Strafford, 12 Jan. 1640), D. (on return)		23 Nov. 1636
Lord Robert Dilion Christopher Wandesford } J.	19 Aug. 1639[30]	12 Sept. 1639
Earl of Strafford, L.	13 Jan. 1640[33]	18 Mar. 1640
Christopher Wandesford, D.[34]	1 Apr. 1640	3 Apr. 1640
Lord Robert Dillion Sir William Parsons } J.	15 Dec. 1640[30]	30 Dec. 1640
Sir William Parsons Sir John Borlase } J.	30 Dec. 1640[35]	10 Feb. 1641
Robert Sydney, 2nd earl of Leicester, L.[36]	14 June 1641	
Sir John Borlase Sir Henry Tichborne } J.[37]	31 Mar. 1643	12 May 1643
James Butler, 1st marquis of Ormond, L.[37]	13 Nov. 1643	21 Jan. 1644
Philip Sidney, Viscount Lisle, L.	21 Jan. 1646[38]	
Arthur Annesley; Col. Michael Jones; Sir Robert King; Sir Robert Meredith; Col. John Moore (commrs of parliament)	19 June 1647[39]	28 July 1647
Marquis of Ormond, L. (on return)		30 Sept. 1648[40]
Oliver Cromwell, L.	22 June 1649[41]	15 Aug. 1649[42]
Henry Ireton, D.[43]	26 May 1650[44]	29 May 1650
Ulick Burke, 1st marquis of Clanricard, D.[45]	6 Dec. 1650	

	appointment	*swearing-in*
Edmund Ludlow, parliamentary commr, app. (after Ireton's death) commander-in-chief by fellow-commrs (Miles Corbet, John Jones, John Weaver)[46]	2 Dec. 1651[47]	
John Lambert, D.[48]	30 Jan. 1652	
Charles Fleetwood, app. by parliament as commander-in-chief of forces in Ireland and one of parliamentary commrs	9 July 1652[49]	*c.* 10 Sept. 1652[50]
Charles Fleetwood, D.	*c.* 27 Aug. 1654[51]	
Henry Cromwell; Matthew Tomlinson; Miles Corbet; Robert Goodwin (commrs)[52]	Aug. 1655	
Henry Cromwell, D.	17 Nov. 1657	
Henry Cromwell, L.[53]	6 Oct. 1658	
John Jones; William Steele; Robert Goodwin; Matthew Tomlinson; Miles Corbet (commrs)	7 July 1659[54]	
Roger Boyle, 1st Baron Broghill (cr. earl of Orrery, 5 Sept. 1660); Sir Charles Coote (cr. earl of Mountrath, 6 Sept 1660); William Bury (commrs)	Jan. 1660	
George Monck, Baron Monck (cr. duke of Albemarle, 7 July 1660), L.[55]	June 1660	
John Robartes, 2nd Baron Robartes, D.[56]	25 July 1660	
Sir Maurice Eustace, L.C. ⎫ Earl of Orrery ⎬ J. Earl of Mountrath[57] ⎭	26 Oct. 1660[58]	31 Dec. 1660[59]
James Butler, 1st duke of Ormond, L.	21 Feb. 1662	27 July 1662
Thomas Butler, earl of Ossory, D.	6 May 1664[60]	21 May 1664
Duke of Ormond, L. (on return)		3 Sept. 1665
Earl of Ossory, D.	7 Feb. 1668[60]	25 Apr. 1668
Lord Robartes, L.	3 May 1669	18 Sept. 1669
John Berkeley, 1st Baron Berkeley of Stratton, L.	4 Feb. 1670	21 Apr. 1670[61]
Michael Boyle, abp of Dublin, L.C. ⎫ ⎬ J. Sir Arthur Forbes ⎭	11 May 1671[60]	12 June 1671
Lord Berkeley, L. (on return)		23 Sept. 1671
Arthur Capell, earl of Essex, L.	21 May 1672	5 Aug. 1672
Abp Boyle ⎫ Sir Arthur Forbes (cr. ⎬ J. Viscount Granard, 22 Nov. 1675) ⎭	25 June 1675[62]	5 July 1675
Earl of Essex, L. (on return)		*c.* 3 May 1676[63]
Duke of Ormond, L.	24 May 1677	24 Aug. 1677

	appointment	swearing-in
Richard Butler, 1st earl of Arran, D.	13 Apr. 1682	2 May 1682
Duke of Ormond, L. (on return)		19 Aug. 1684[64]
Abp Boyle ⎫ J. Arthur Forbes, earl of Granard ⎭	24 Feb. 1685	20 Mar. 1685
Henry Hyde, 2nd earl of Clarendon, L.	1 Oct. 1685	9 Jan. 1686
Richard Talbot, earl of Tyrconnell, D.	8 Jan. 1687[60]	12 Feb. 1687
Sir Alexander Fitton, L.C. ⎫ William Burke, 7th earl of ⎬ J. Clanricard ⎭	6 Aug. 1687[60]	18 Aug. 1687

Earl of Tyrconnell (cr. duke of
   Tyrconnell, 30 Mar. 1689), D. (on
   return)
		4 Sept. 1687[65]

(James II in Ire. 12 Mar. 1689–4 July 1690)

(William III in Ire. 14 June–5 Sept. 1690)

	appointment	swearing-in
Duke of Tyrconnell, D. (Jacite)		c. 4 July 1690[66]
Henry, Viscount Sidney ⎫ J. (Wmite) Thomas Coningsby ⎭	4 Sept. 1690	15 Sept. 1690
Viscount Sidney ⎫ Sir Charles Porter, L.C. ⎬ J. (Wmite)[67] Thomas Coningsby ⎭	4 Dec. 1690	24 Dec. 1690
Duke of Tyrconnell, L. (Jacite)		14 Jan. 1691[68]
Alexander Fitton, Baron ⎫ Gawsworth, L.C. ⎪ Sir Richard Nagle ⎬ J. (Jacite) Francis Plowden ⎭	c. 14 Aug. 1691[69]	c. 14 Aug. 1691
Viscount Sidney, L.	18 Mar. 1692	4 Sept. 1692
Sir Charles Porter ⎫ J. Sir Cyril Wyche ⎭	13 June 1693[70]	3 July 1693
Henry Capell, Baron Capell ⎫ of Tewkesbury ⎪ Sir Cyril Wyche ⎬ J. William Duncombe ⎭	26 June 1693[71]	28 July 1693
Lord Capell, D.	9 May 1695	27 May 1695
Murrough Boyle, 1st ⎫ Viscount Blessington ⎬ J.[72] William Wolseley ⎭	16 May 1696	18 May 1696
Sir Charles Porter, J.[73]	2 June 1696	2 June 1696

Sir Charles Porter ⎫
Charles Coote, 3rd earl of ⎪
   Mountrath ⎬ J.
Henry Moore, 3rd earl of ⎪
   Drogheda ⎭
	10 July 1696	29 July 1696

Henry Massue de Ruvigny, Viscount
   Galway (cr. earl of Galway, 12 May
   1697), J.[74]
	21 Jan. 1697[75]	6 Feb. 1697

		appointment	*swearing-in*
Charles Powlett, 7th marquis of Winchester (2nd duke of Bolton, 27 Feb. 1699) Earl of Galway Edward Villiers, 1st Viscount Villiers (cr. earl of Jersey, 13 Oct. 1697)[76]	J.	14 May 1697	31 May 1697
Duke of Bolton Earl of Galway Earl of Jersey Narcissus Marsh, abp of Dublin	J.[77]	9 Apr. 1699[70]	18 May 1699
Duke of Bolton Charles Berkeley, 2nd earl of Berkeley Earl of Galway	J.[78]	29 June 1699	23 Aug. 1699
Laurence Hyde, earl of Rochester, L.		28 Dec. 1700	18 Sept. 1701
Abp Marsh Earl of Drogheda Hugh Montgomery, 2nd earl of Mountalexander	J.	28 Mar. 1701[79]	4 Apr. 1701
Abp Marsh Earl of Drogheda	J.	9 Dec. 1701[79]	4 Jan. 1702
Earl of Mountalexander Thomas Erle Thomas Keightley	J.	30 Mar. 1702[79]	11 Apr. 1702
James Butler, 2nd duke of Ormond, L.		19 Feb. 1703	4 June 1703
Sir Richard Cox, L.C. Earl of Mountalexander Thomas Erle	J.	10 Feb. 1704[79]	23 or 24 Mar. 1704
Duke of Ormond, L. (on return)			16 Nov. 1704
Sir Richard Cox John Cutts, Baron Cutts of Gowran	J.	21 May 1705[79]	27 June 1705
Narcissus Marsh, abp of Armagh, J.[80]		8 Feb. 1707[79]	15 Feb. 1707
Thomas Herbert, earl of Pembroke and Montgomery, L.		30 Apr. 1707	24 June 1707
Abp Marsh Richard Freeman, L.C.	J.	13 Nov. 1707[79]	27 Nov. 1707
Thomas Wharton, 1st earl of Wharton, L.		4 Dec. 1708	21 Apr. 1709
Richard Freeman Richard Ingoldsby	J.	5 Sept. 1709[79]	19 Sept. 1709
Earl of Wharton, L. (on return)			7 May 1710
Richard Freeman Richard Ingoldsby	J.	15 Aug. 1710[79]	c. 29 Aug. 1710
Duke of Ormond, L.		26 Oct. 1710	3 July 1711

	appointment	swearing-in
Abp Marsh ⎫ J. Richard Ingoldsby ⎭	22 Nov. 1710[79]	28 Nov. 1710
Sir Constantine Phipps, L.C.[81]	30 Dec. 1710[79]	22 Jan. 1711
Sir Constantine Phipps, L.C. ⎫ J. Richard Ingoldsby ⎭	29 Oct. 1711[79]	3 Dec. 1711
John Vesey, abp of Tuam, J.[82]	4 Feb. 1712[79]	13 Mar. 1712
Charles Talbot, duke of Shrewsbury, L.	22 Sept. 1713	27 Oct. 1713
Thomas Lindsay, abp of Armagh ⎫ Sir Constantine Phipps ⎬ J. Abp Vesey ⎭	7 Feb. 1714[79]	7 June 1714[83]
William King, abp of Dublin ⎫ Abp Vesey ⎪ Robert Fitzgerald, 19th earl ⎬ J. of Kildare ⎭	4 Sept. 1714	21 Sept. 1714[84]
Charles Spencer, earl of Sunderland, L.	21 Sept. 1714[84]	
Charles Fitzroy, 2nd duke ⎫ of Grafton ⎬ J. Earl of Galway ⎭	6 Sept. 1715	1 Nov. 1715
Charles, Viscount Townshend, L.[85]	13 Feb. 1717	

Alan Brodrick, 1st Baron ⎫
  Brodrick (cr. Viscount ⎪
  Midleton, 15 Aug. 1717), ⎬ J.
  L.C. ⎪
Abp King ⎪
William Conolly, speaker ⎭
	22 Feb. 1717[86]	20 Mar. 1717[87]

Duke of Bolton, L.	27 Apr. 1717	7 Aug. 1717
Viscount Midleton ⎫ Abp King ⎬ J. William Conolly ⎭	25 Nov. 1717[86]	9 Jan. 1718[88]
Duke of Bolton, L. (on return)		31 May 1719
Viscount Midleton ⎫ J. William Conolly ⎭	8 Oct. 1719[86]	20 Nov. 1719
Duke of Grafton, L.	18 June 1720[89]	28 Aug. 1721
Abp King ⎫ Richard Boyle, Viscount ⎪ Shannon ⎬ J. William Conolly ⎭	31 Jan. 1722[86]	24 Feb. 1722
Viscount Midleton, J. (in addition)	30 Dec. 1722[86]	13 June 1723
Duke of Grafton, L. (on return)		13 Aug. 1723[90]
Viscount Midleton ⎫ Viscount Shannon ⎬ J. William Conolly ⎭	7 Apr. 1724[86]	9 May 1724
John Carteret, 2nd Baron Carteret, L.	6 May 1724	22 Oct. 1724
Hugh Boulter, abp of Armagh ⎫ Richard West, L.C. ⎬ J. William Conolly ⎭	9 Mar. 1726[86]	2 Apr. 1726
Thomas Wyndham, L.C., J.[91]	15 Dec. 1726[86]	23 Dec. 1726
Lord Carteret, L.	26 Oct. 1727	19 Nov. 1727

	appointment	*swearing-in*
Abp Boulter		
Thomas Wyndham (cr. Baron Wyndham, 17 Sept. 1731), L.C. } J.	27 Feb. 1730[86]	22 Apr. 1730
Sir Ralph Gore, speaker		
Lionel Cranfield Sackville, 1st duke of Dorset, L.	23 June 1730	11 Sept. 1731
Abp Boulter		
Lord Wyndham } J.	16 Mar. 1732[92]	24 Apr. 1732
Sir Ralph Gore		
Duke of Dorset, L. (on return)		17 Sept. 1733
Abp Boulter		
Lord Wyndham } J.	23 Mar. 1734[93]	3 May 1734
Henry Boyle, speaker		
Duke of Dorset, L. (on return)		23 Sept. 1735
Abp Boulter		
Lord Wyndham } J.	15 Apr. 1736[93]	19 May 1736
Henry Boyle		
William Cavendish, 3rd duke of Devonshire, L.	9 Apr. 1737	7 Sept. 1737
Abp Boulter		
Lord Wyndham } J.	16 Feb. 1738[93]	28 Mar. 1738
Henry Boyle		
Duke of Devonshire, L. (on return)		27 Sept. 1739
Abp Boulter		
Robert Jocelyn, L.C. } J.	26 Mar. 1740[93]	18 Apr. 1740[94]
Henry Boyle		
Duke of Devonshire, L. (on return)		23 Sept. 1741
Abp Boulter		
Robert Jocelyn (cr. Baron Newport, 29 Nov. 1743) } J.	20 Jan. 1742[93]	18 Feb. 1742
Henry Boyle		
John Hoadly, abp of Armagh, J.[95]	25 Nov. 1742[93]	3 Dec. 1742
Duke of Devonshire, L. (on return)		29 Sept. 1743
Abp Hoadly		
Lord Newport } J.	19 Jan. 1744[93]	12 Apr. 1744
Henry Boyle		
Philip Dormer Stanhope, 4th earl of Chesterfield, L.	8 Jan. 1745	31 Aug. 1745
Abp Hoadly		
Lord Newport } J.	26 Mar. 1746[93]	25 Apr. 1746
Henry Boyle		
William Stanhope, 1st earl of Harrington, L.	15 Nov. 1746	13 Sept. 1747
George Stone, abp of Armagh, J.[96]	31 Mar. 1747[93]	10 Apr. 1747
Abp Stone		
Lord Newport } J.	15 Mar. 1748[93]	20 Apr. 1748
Henry Boyle		
Earl of Harrington, L. (on return)		20 Sept. 1749

	appointment	*swearing-in*
Abp Stone ⎫		
Lord Newport ⎬ J.	8 Mar. 1750	20 Apr. 1750
Henry Boyle ⎭		
Duke of Dorset, L.	15 Dec. 1750	19 Sept. 1751
Abp Stone ⎫		
Lord Newport ⎬ J.	24 Mar. 1752[93]	27 May 1752
Henry Boyle ⎭		
Duke of Dorset, L. (on return)		21 Sept. 1753
Abp Stone ⎫		
Lord Newport (cr. Viscount		
Jocelyn, 6 Dec. 1755) ⎬ J.	11 Apr. 1754[97]	11 May 1754
Brabazon Ponsonby, 1st earl		
of Bessborough ⎭		
William Cavendish, marquis of	2 Apr. 1755	5 May 1755
Hartington (4th duke of Devonshire,		
5 Dec. 1755), L.		
Viscount Jocelyn ⎫		
James Fitzgerald, 20th ⎬ J.	20 Apr. 1756[97]	11 May 1756
earl of Kildare ⎪		
Earl of Bessborough ⎭		
John Russell, 4th duke of Bedford, L.	3 Jan. 1757	25 Sept. 1757
Abp Stone ⎫		
Henry Boyle, 1st earl of Shannon ⎬ J.	17 Mar. 1758[97]	10 May 1758
John Ponsonby, speaker ⎭		
Duke of Bedford, L. (on return)		7 Oct. 1759
Abp Stone ⎫		
Earl of Shannon ⎬ J.	15 Apr. 1760[97]	20 May 1760
John Ponsonby ⎭		
George Montague-Dunk, earl of	3 Apr. 1761	6 Oct. 1761
Halifax, L.		
Abp Stone ⎫		
Earl of Shannon ⎬ J.	24 Mar. 1762[97]	3 May 1762
John Ponsonby ⎭		
Hugh Percy, 2nd duke of	27 Apr. 1763	22 Sept. 1763
Northumberland, L.		
Abp Stone ⎫		
Earl of Shannon ⎬ J.	9 Apr. 1764	15 May 1764[98]
John Ponsonby ⎭		
John Bowes, 1st Baron Bowes of	8 Feb. 1765[97]	22 Feb. 1765
Clonlyon, L.C., J[99]		
Thomas Thynne, 3rd Viscount	5 June 1765	
Weymouth, L.[100]		
Francis Seymour-Conway, earl of	7 Aug. 1765	19 Oct. 1765
Hertford, L.		
Lord Bowes ⎫		
Charles Moore, 6th earl ⎬ J.	10 Apr. 1766[97]	11 June 1766
of Drogheda ⎪		
John Ponsonby ⎭		

	appointment	swearing-in
George William Hervey, 2nd earl of Bristol, L.[100]	6 Oct. 1766	
George Townshend, 4th Viscount Townshend, L.	19 Aug. 1767	14 Oct. 1767
Simon Harcourt, 1st Earl Harcourt, L.	29 Oct. 1772	30 Nov. 1772
John Hobart, 2nd earl of Buckinghamshire, L.	7 Dec. 1776	25 Jan. 1777
Frederick Howard, 5th earl of Carlisle, L.	29 Nov. 1780	23 Dec. 1780
William Henry Cavendish Bentinck, 3rd duke of Portland, L.	8 Apr. 1782	14 Apr. 1782
George Nugent-Temple-Grenville, 3rd Earl Temple, L.	15 Aug. 1782	15 Sept. 1782
Robert Henley, 2nd earl of Northington, L.	3 May 1783	3 June 1783
Charles Manners, 4th duke of Rutland, L.[101]	12 Feb. 1784	24 Feb. 1784
Richard Robinson, 1st Baron Rokeby, abp of Armagh James Hewitt, 1st Viscount Lifford, L.C. } J. John Foster, speaker	27 Oct. 1787	3 Nov. 1787
George Nugent-Temple-Grenville, marquis of Buckingham, L.	6 Nov. 1787	16 Dec. 1787
Abp Lord Rokeby John Fitzgibbon (cr. Baron Fitzgibbon, 6 July 1789), } J. L.C. John Foster	19 June 1789[102]	30 June 1789[103]
John Fane, 10th earl of Westmorland, L.	24 Oct. 1789	5 Jan. 1790
William Wentworth Fitzwilliam, 2nd Earl Fitzwilliam, L.	13 Dec. 1794	4 Jan. 1795
William Newcome, abp of Armagh John Fitzgibbon, 1st Viscount Fitzgibbon (cr. earl of Clare, 12 June 1795), L.C. } J.[104]	24 Mar. 1795	25 Mar. 1795
John Jeffreys Pratt, 2nd Earl Camden, L.	13 Mar. 1795	31 Mar. 1795
Charles Cornwallis, 1st Marquis Cornwallis, L.	14 June 1798	20 June 1798

---

[1] *Liber mun. pub. Hib.* (date of patent); *H.B.C.* has 23 July.

[2] *H.B.C.* does not show the date; *Liber mun. pub. Hib.* has 11 Oct., which appears to be erroneous, as Skeffington did not reach Dublin till 23 Oct. (*L. & P. Hen. VIII*, vii, 527–8).

[3] By council, after death of Skeffington (31 Dec. 1535).

[4] By council, on recall of Grey; Grey executed 28 June 1541 (*L. & P. Hen. VIII*, xvi, 466); *H.B.C.* has 28 July.

[5] *S. P. Hen. VIII*, iii, 235; *H.B.C.* has 25 July.

⁶ *L. & P. Hen. VIII*, xix (1), 619; *H.B.C.* has 3 July 1545.

⁷ Date of arrival (*Liber mun. pub. Hib.*).

⁸ *L. & P. Hen. VIII*, xxi (2) 233; *H.B.C.* omits. Appointment renewed 7 Apr. 1547 (after death of Henry VIII).

⁹ Date of arrival (*Liber mun. pub. Hib.*); *H.B.C.* omits, but notes that Brabazon acted to 1 Dec. 1546.

¹⁰ Whit Monday (21 May) (*Liber mun. pub. Hib.*); *H.B.C.* has 20 May.

¹¹ By council, on departure of Bellingham.

¹² By council, on death of Bryan.

¹³ *Liber mun. pub. Hib.*; *H.B.C.* has 23 May or 1 June.

¹⁴ Privy seal 7 Nov. 1552, ordering election of Cusack and Aylmer by council; election took place 6 Dec., date shown in *H.B.C.*

¹⁵ *Cal. pat. rolls, 1553-4.* p. 165; *H.B.C.* has Oct.

¹⁶ *Calendar of patent and close rolls of chancery in Ireland, Henry VIII to 18th Elizabeth*, ed. James Morrin (Dublin, 1861), p. 371; *H.B.C.* has 26 May.

¹⁷ On departure of Sussex for Scotland; Sussex resumed office 10 Nov.

¹⁸ By council, in vacancy caused by death of Mary; Sussex left on 13 Dec.

¹⁹ Privy seal; *H.B.C.* has 9 Oct., date of Dublin patent.

²⁰ By council, on departure of Sidney.

²¹ By council, *vice* Drury (d. 3 Oct.).

²² Privy seal, ordering Grey to hand over to Loftus and Wallop; *H.B.C.* has 25 Aug., date of Dublin patent.

²³ By council, *vice* Burgh (d. 13 Oct.).

²⁴ Privy seal, ordering council to elect Loftus and Gardiner: election took place 26 Nov.

²⁵ By council, on departure of Essex.

²⁶ See *Cal. S.P. Ire, 1599-1600*, p. 499; *H.B.C.* has 27 Feb.

²⁷ Elected by council after death of Elizabeth.

²⁸ *H.B.C.*, mistakenly, has July 1604; Devonshire d. 3 Apr. 1606.

²⁹ *Liber mun. pub. Hib.* (date of patent); *H.B.C.* has 23 Apr.

³⁰ Privy seal; *H.B.C.* has date of Dublin patent.

³¹ Date of arrival (*Anal. Hib.*, viii (1938), p. 164).

³² Patent renewed by Charles I, 29 Mar. 1625.

³³ Executed 12 May 1641.

³⁴ Died 3 Dec. 1640.

³⁵ King's letter (*Cal. S.P. Ire., 1633-47*, p. 248); *H.B.C.* has date of Dublin patent.

³⁶ Did not come to Ire.

³⁷ App. by Charles I.

³⁸ App. by parliament (*Journal of the house of commons* (hereafter cited as *Commons' jn.*), iv, 413), commn issued 9 Apr. (ibid., p. 504); landed in Munster 21 Feb. 1647 (*Sydney papers*, ed. R. W. Blencowe (London, 1825), pp. 13, 17); commn expired 15 Apr. 1647.

³⁹ Patent issued on day that Ormond agreed to hand Dublin over to parliament; Ormond left Ire. 28 July.

⁴⁰ Date of landing at Cork (Thomas Carte, *An history of the life of James, duke of Ormonde* (3 vols, London, 1735-6), i, 39); *H.B.C.* has 29 Sept.

⁴¹ App. by parliament for 3 years (*Commons' jn.*, vi, 239).

⁴² Date of landing in Dublin (S. R. Gardiner, *History of the commonwealth and protectorate, 1649-1656* (3 vols, London, 1894-1901), i, 118); *H.B.C.* has 14 Aug. as date of appointment.

⁴³ *H.B.C.* notes that Ireton d. 20 Nov. 1650; correct date is 26 Nov. 1651 (*Ireland under the commonwealth*, ed. R. Dunlop (2 vols, Manchester, 1913) i, 94).

⁴⁴ *H.B.C.* has 29 May (date of Dublin patent) as date of appointment; appointment was made by Cromwell, who left Ire. 26 May.

⁴⁵ *H.B.C.* notes that appointment was made by Charles II; it was made by Ormond (Carte, *Ormonde*, ii, 137). Clanricard submitted to parliamentary authority 28 June 1652.

⁴⁶ *H.B.C.* shows parliamentary commrs as deputies (13 Sept. 1650); *Commons' jn.* vi, 479 (4 Oct. 1650) makes it clear that they were to act with advice and approbation of Cromwell or Ireton. After Ireton's death the commrs acted as chief governors until Fleetwood's appointment as deputy.

⁴⁷ See Edmund Ludlow, *Memoirs*, ed. C. H. Firth (2 vols, Oxford, 1894), i, 496-7.

⁴⁸ *Commons' jn.* vii, 79; *H.B.C.* has Mar. He did not come to Ire.; appointment lapsed with lord lieutenancy, 22 June 1652.

⁴⁹ *Commons jn.* vii, 152; *H.B.C.* has 24 Aug. (confirmatory order).

⁵⁰ Date of landing (Edmund Ludlow, *Memoirs*, ed. C. H. Firth (2 vols, Oxford, 1894), i, 330.

[51] *H.B.C.* suggests July; parliamentary commrs were abolished 22 Aug. (Gardiner, *Commonwealth & protectorate*, iii, 314); instructions for deputy and council 27 Aug. (*Fourteenth report of the deputy keeper of the public records in Ireland* (Dublin, 1882), p. 28).

[52] Fleetwood left 6 Sept. 1655; William Steele added Aug. 1656.

[53] Recalled, following commons' resolution of 7 June 1659 that Ire. should no longer be under a single governor; he left 27 June 1659.

[54] *Acts and ordinances of the interregnum, 1642–1660*, ed. C. H. Firth and R.S. Rait (3 vols, London, 1911) ii, 1298–9.

[55] Did not come to Ire.

[56] Leopold von Ranke, *A history of England, principally in the seventeenth century* (6 vols, Oxford, 1875), v, 526 (minutes of Secretary Nicholas); Robartes did not come to Ire. till his reappointment in 1669.

[57] *H.B.C.* omits Mountrath, who died 18 Dec. 1661.

[58] Date of king's order (*Cal. S.P. Ire., 1660–62*, p. 68); *H.B.C.* has date of Dublin patent.

[59] Orrery was sworn in 17 Jan. 1661 (*Liber mun. pub. Hib.*).

[60] Privy seal; *H.B.C.* has date of Dublin patent.

[61] *Cal. S.P. Ire., 1669–70*, p. 111; *H.B.C.* has 21 May.

[62] King's order (*Cal. S.P. dom., 1675–6*, p. 180); *H.B.C.* has date of Dublin patent.

[63] *Cal. S.P. dom., 1676–7*, p. 101.

[64] *Calendar of the manuscripts of the marquess of Ormonde, preserved at Kilkenny Castle* (London, 1895–1920), new ser., vii, 267.

[65] Ibid., new ser., viii, 351.

[66] Date of James's departure; Tyrconnell left Ire. *c.* 12 Sept. 1690, entrusting civil government to 12 commrs and command of army to James FitzJames, duke of Berwick (Charles O'Kelly, *Macariae excidium*, ed. J. C. O'Callaghan (Dublin, 1850), p. 72).

[67] Sidney left Ire., 15 Dec.; Porter sworn in 24 Dec. (*Liber mun. pub. Hib.*).

[68] Date of Tyconnell's return; he d. 14 Aug. 1691.

[69] J. T. Gilbert, *A Jacobite narrative of the war in Ireland, 1688–1691* (Dublin, 1892), p. 282.

[70] Privy seal; *H.B.C.* has date of Dublin patent.

[71] *Liber mun. pub. Hib. H.B.C.* has June/26 July.

[72] During Capell's illness.

[73] By council, after Capell's death (20 May 1696).

[74] *Vice* Porter (d. 8 Dec. 1696).

[75] Warrant (*Cal. S.P. dom., 1697*, p. 19); *H.B.C.* has 6 Feb.

[76] Villiers did not come to Ire.

[77] Bolton left Ire.; Jersey did not come. Only Galway and Marsh were sworn in.

[78] Bolton did not come to Ire.

[79] Privy seal; *H.B.C.* has date of Dublin patent.

[80] *Vice* Cutts (d. 25 Jan. 1707).

[81] *Vice* Marsh (resigned).

[82] *Vice* Ingoldsby (d. 29 Jan. 1712).

[83] *H.B.C.* gives 20 Apr. for swearing-in of abps, 7 June for Phipps; all 3 were sworn in 7 June (*Dublin Gazette*, 5–8 June 1714) after departure of Shrewsbury (5 June).

[84] Patent (*Liber. mun. pub. Hib.*); *H.B.C.* has 4 Oct. Sunderland did not come to Ire.

[85] Did not come to Ire.

[86] Privy seal; *H.B.C.* has date of Dublin patent.

[87] Abp King not sworn in till 20 July.

[88] Midleton not sworn till 22 May; *H.B.C.*, mistakenly, says it was Conolly who was not sworn in till that date.

[89] *Liber mun. pub. Hib.*; *H.B.C.* has 8 June.

[90] P.R.O., S.P. 63/381, p. 77; *H.B.C.* has Aug. or Sept.

[91] *Vice* West (d. 3 Dec. 1726).

[92] Warrant (P.R.O., S.P. 67/20, ff 131–2); *H.B.C.* has 24 Apr. (date of Dublin patent).

[93] Privy seal; *H.B.C.* has date of Dublin patent.

[94] Jocelyn and Boyle sworn-in 18 Apr.; Boulter 13 May.

[95] *Vice* Boulter (d. 27 Sept. 1742).

[96] *Vice* Hoadly (d. 16 July 1746).

[97] Privy seal; *H.B.C.* has date of Dublin patent.

[98] Shannon and Ponsonby sworn-in 15 May; Stone not sworn—(d. 19 Dec.).

[99] *Vice* Shannon (d. 27 Sept. 1764).

[100] Did not assume office.
[101] Died 24 Oct. 1787.
[102] Privy seal; *H.B.C.* has date of Dublin patent.
[103] Fitzgibbon and Foster sworn-in; Rokeby was ill in England (*Dublin Chronicle*, 30 June–2 July 1789).
[104] Appointed by Fitzwilliam; sworn-in next day (*Faulkner's Dublin Journal*, 26 Mar. 1795).

(C) 1801–1922

C. J. WOODS

This list is based on that in *H.B.C.* Names have been checked in *D.N.B.* and *G.E.C., Peerage.* Dates of appointment and swearing-in have been checked in *London Gazette* and *Dublin Gazette.* The date of appointment given below is that of the monarch's making an order in council; that given in *H.B.C.*, in most cases, is later, and is apparently that of letters patent being issued or passing under the great seal.

All the names given here are of lords lieutenant. No lord deputy was appointed. Lords justices were appointed occasionally in the lord lieutenant's absence, but so briefly and infrequently as to make their inclusion here unnecessary.

In accordance with the provisions of the Irish Free State Constitution Act, 1922, and the Irish Free State (Consequential Provisions) Act, 1922 (13 Geo. V, sess. 2, cc 1 and 2), the powers of the lord lieutenant in the Irish Free State and in Northern Ireland lapsed on 6 and 8 December 1922 respectively.[1]

	appointment	swearing-in
Philip Yorke, 3rd earl of Hardwicke	17 Mar. 1801	25 May 1801
Edward Clive, 1st earl of Powis[2]	21 Nov. 1805	
John Russell, 6th duke of Bedford	12 Feb. 1806	28 Mar. 1806
Charles Lennox, 4th duke of Richmond	1 Apr. 1807	19 Apr. 1807
Charles Whitworth, 1st Baron Whitworth (cr. Viscount Whitworth, 14 June 1813; Earl Whitworth, 25 Nov. 1815)	3 June 1813	26 Aug. 1813
Charles Chetwynd Talbot, 2nd Earl Talbot	17 Sept. 1817	9 Oct. 1817
Richard Wellesley, 1st Marquis Wellesley	10 Dec. 1821	29 Dec. 1821
Henry William Paget, 1st marquis of Anglesey	27 Feb. 1828	1 Mar. 1828
Hugh Percy, 3rd duke of Northumberland	2 Feb. 1829	6 Mar. 1829
Marquis of Anglesey	22 Nov. 1830	23 Dec. 1830
Marquis Wellesley	11 Sept. 1833	26 Sept. 1833
Thomas Hamilton, 9th earl of Haddington	29 Dec. 1834	6 Jan. 1835
Constantine Henry Phipps, 6th earl of Mulgrave (cr. marquis of Normanby, 25 June 1838)	23 Apr. 1835	11 May 1835
Hugh Fortescue, Viscount Ebrington (2nd Earl Fortescue, 16 June 1841)	1 Mar. 1839	3 Apr. 1839

	appointment	*swearing-in*
Thomas Philip de Grey, 2nd Earl de Grey	3 Sept. 1841	15 Sept. 1841
William A'Court, 1st Baron Heytesbury	10 July 1844	26 July 1844
John William Ponsonby, 4th earl of Bessborough	6 July 1846	11 July 1846
George William Frederick Villiers, 4th earl of Clarendon	20 May 1847	26 May 1847
Archibald William Montgomerie, 13th earl of Eglinton	27 Feb. 1852	10 Mar. 1852
Edward Granville Eliot, 3rd earl of St Germans	4 Jan. 1853	6 Jan. 1853
George William Frederick Howard, 7th earl of Carlisle	28 Feb. 1855	13 Mar. 1855
Earl of Eglinton (cr. earl of Winton, 17 June 1859)	26 Feb. 1858	12 Mar. 1858
Earl of Carlisle	18 June 1859	13 July 1859
John Wodehouse, 3rd Baron Wodehouse (cr. earl of Kimberley, 1 June 1866)	1 Nov. 1864	8 Nov. 1864
James Hamilton, 2nd marquis of Abercorn (cr. duke, 10 Aug. 1868)	6 July 1866	20 July 1866
John Poyntz Spencer, 5th Earl Spencer	12 Dec. 1868	23 Dec. 1868
Duke of Abercorn	2 Mar. 1874	3 Mar. 1874
John Winston Spencer Churchill, 7th duke of Marlborough	28 Nov. 1876	12 Dec. 1876
Francis Thomas de Grey Cowper, 7th Earl Cowper	3 May 1880	5 May 1880
Earl Spencer	3 May 1882	6 May 1882
Henry Howard Molyneux Herbert, 4th earl of Carnarvon	27 June 1885[3]	30 June 1885
John Campbell Hamilton Gordon, 7th earl of Aberdeen	6 Feb. 1886	10 Feb. 1886
Charles Stewart Vane-Tempest-Stewart, 6th marquis of Londonderry	3 Aug. 1886[3]	5 Aug. 1886
Lawrence Dundas, 3rd earl of Zetland	30 July 1889[3]	5 Oct. 1889
Robert Offley Ashburton Milnes, 2nd Baron Houghton (assumed surname Crewe-Milnes, 8 June 1894)	18 Aug. 1892	22 Aug. 1892
George Henry Cadogan, 6th Earl Cadogan	29 June 1895	8 July 1895
William Humble Ward, 3rd earl of Dudley	11 Aug. 1902	16 Aug. 1902
Earl of Aberdeen	11 Dec. 1905	14 Dec. 1905
Ivor Churchill Guest, 2nd Baron Wimborne	16 Feb. 1915	18 Feb. 1915[4]
John Denton Pinkstone French, 1st Viscount French of Ypres and of High Lake	7 May 1918	11 May 1918

	appointment	*swearing-in*
Lord Edmund Bernard Talbot (cr. Viscount Fitzalan of Derwent, 28 Apr. 1921; resumed paternal surname, Fitzalan-Howard, 9 June 1921)	22 Apr. 1921	2 May 1921

[1] Sir Arthur S. Quekett, *The constitution of Northern Ireland*, pt 1 (Belfast, 1928), p. 34; R. B. McDowell, *The Irish administration 1801-1914* (London and Toronto, 1964; Studies in Irish History, 2nd ser., II), p. 294.
[2] Did not come to Ire.
[3] *H.B.C.*; not found in *London Gazette* or *Dublin Gazette*.
[4] Wimborne res. on or shortly before 10 May 1916 (*The Times*, 11 May 1916), and was reapp. 18 Aug. 1916.

CHANCELLORS AND KEEPERS OF THE GREAT SEAL, 1232-1922

(A) 1232-1534

PAUL BRAND

Except where otherwise indicated, this list is based on the same sources as those cited by Richardson and Sayles in *Admin. Ire.*, pp 92-7, for the period 1232-1377, and by A. J. Otway-Ruthven, in 'The medieval Irish chancery' in *Album Helen Maud Cam*, ii (Louvain and Paris, 1961), pp 131-5, for the period 1377-1485.

Unless otherwise indicated, all persons listed bore the title of chancellor; exceptionally, in this period, a few men were appointed as chancellor and/or keeper of the great seal, but as this seems to have had no practical significance, the second title has not been noted below. Other titles are indicated as follows.

D.C. denotes a deputy chancellor (or equivalent), i.e. a temporary substitute for a chancellor while the latter was out of Ireland or otherwise prevented from fulfilling his duties; each person so designated was deputy to the chancellor immediately preceding him in the list.

J. denotes a justiciar who is known to have had temporary custody of the seal during the interval between the end of one officeholder's period of tenure and his successor's assumption of the duties of his office.

K. denotes a keeper of the seal or, from the later fourteenth century, a keeper of the 'great seal' (a term which appears to have been adopted in imitation of English practice, as there seems to have been no Irish privy seal), i.e. someone given responsibility for the custody of the seal (usually as a temporary measure pending the appointment of a new chancellor) without himself being appointed chancellor.

D.K. denotes a deputy keeper of the great seal; each person so designated was deputy to the keeper immediately preceding him in the list.

Considerable time often elapsed between the date of an officeholder's formal appointment (frequently made in England) and the date on which he took custody of the seal, thereby assuming the duties and responsibilities of his office; between the death of an officeholder and the appointment of his replacement; or (where an officeholder was superseded) between the date of appointment of his replacement and the date on which he relinquished custody of the seal. As many of these dates as are ascertainable have consequently been shown. Unless otherwise noted, all appointments were to hold during pleasure. In this list app. = formal appointment; cust. = took custody of the seal; d. = death (where the officeholder's term of office appears to have ended with his own death); relq. = custody of the seal relinquished; remvd = formally removed from office (this normally occurred at the formal appointment of the successor); ter. = appointment formally terminated by the death or removal of the monarch in whose name the officeholder had been appointed.

My thanks are due to Miss Elizabeth Sykes of the University of Durham for assistance in compiling that part of the list which relates to the period 1413-61.

	beginning of term of office	*end of term of office*
Ralph de Neville, bp of Chichester, chancellor of England	app. 28 Sept. 1232[1] app. 4 May 1233[1]	d. 1/4 Feb. 1244
Geoffrey de Tourville, archdeacon of Dublin, D.C.	app. 28 Sept. 1232 app. 21 May 1234	
Robert Luterel, treasurer of St Patrick's, Dublin, D.C.	cust. *a.* 23 Feb. 1234	
Robert Luterel	cust. *a.* 18 Nov. 1245[2]	remvd 20 Apr. 1246
Geoffrey of Wolford (Wuleward)	app. 20 Apr. 1246	d. *a.* 15 Mar. 1249[3]
Ralph of Norwich	app. 9 July 1249	remvd 16 May 1256 relq. *a.* 25 July 1256
John of Burningfold (Bruningfald)	cust. *a.* 26 June 1257	relq. *p.* 23 Oct. 1258
Fromund de Brun	cust. *a.* 1261	d. 6 June 1283
Stephen de Fulbourn, bp of Waterford, J.	cust. *a.* 24 Jan. 1284[4]	
Adam de Fulbourn, K. or D.C.[5]	cust. 6 June 1283	relq. Lent 1284
Walter de Fulbourn, bp-elect of Meath	app. 13 Aug. 1283 cust. Lent 1284	relq. *p.* Easter 1285
William of Beverley	cust. on or *a.* Easter 1287	d. 8 Apr. 1289
John de Sandford, abp of Dublin, J.	cust. 13 Apr. 1289	relq. 9 Mar. 1291[6]
William de Vesci, J.	cust. 9 Mar. 1291	remvd 28 Oct. 1291 relq. 10 Dec. 1291
Thomas Quantok (Cantok), bp of Emly (from 1306)	app. 28 Oct. 1291	ter. 7 July 1307
John de Quantok, D.C.	cust. Mich. 1300 cust. *a.* 22 Sept. 1302 cust. Mich. 1305	relq. Easter 1301 relq. *a.* 7 Mar. 1305[7] relq. Easter 1306

	beginning of term of office	*end of term of office*
Bp Quantok	app. 5 June 1308	d. 4 Feb. 1309
John de Quantok, D.C.	cust. Easter 1308	relq. Mich. 1308
Piers Gaveston, J.	cust. *p.* 8 Feb. 1309[8]	relq. *a.* 20 Feb. 1309[9]
Walter of Thornbury, K.	cust. *a.* 20 Feb. 1309[9]	
Walter of Thornbury[10]	app. 4 Mar. 1309	d. *a.* 28 Jan. 1314
William FitzJohn, bp of Ossory	cust. 8 Feb. 1314	relq. 10 May 1314
Richard of Barford	app. 1 Apr. 1314	relq. 23 Feb. 1316
	cust. 11 May 1314	remvd *a.* 26 June 1316[11]
Bp FitzJohn	cust. 24 Feb. 1316	remvd 2 June 1317[12]
	app. 8 Aug. 1316	
Nicholas de Balscot	app. 2 June 1317[12]	
William FitzJohn, abp of Cashel	app. 4 Aug. 1317	remvd 4 Jan. 1322
		relq. 16 Apr. 1322
Roger Outlaw, prior of Kilmainham	app. 4 Jan. 1322	relq. 20 Jan. 1327
	cust. 16 Apr. 1322	
Roger Outlaw	app. 6 Apr. 1327	remvd 26 Feb. 1331
		relq. 13 May 1331
Adam of Limber	app. 26 Feb. 1331	remvd 30 Sept. 1332
	cust. 14 May 1331	relq. 14 Nov. 1332
Roger Outlaw	app. 30 Sept. 1332	remvd 16 July 1334[13]
	cust. 14 Nov. 1332	relq. *p.* 14 Aug. 1334[14]
Adam of Limber	app. 16 July 1334[13]	
Roger Outlaw	cust. on or *a.* 14 Nov. 1334[14]	remvd 28 July 1337
		relq. 14 Aug. 1337
Thomas de Charleton, bp of Hereford	app. 28 July 1337	remvd 15 May 1338
	cust. 15 Oct. 1337	relq. 1 Sept. 1338
Roger Outlaw	app. 15 May 1338	d. 6 Feb. 1341
	cust. 2 Sept. 1338	
Hugh de Burgh, K.	cust. on or *a.* 23 Feb. 1341	relq. 23 May 1341
Robert of Ashby (Askeby)	app. 14 Mar. 1341	remvd 10 Mar. 1342
	cust. 19 May 1341	relq. *a.* 15 May 1342
Thomas of Newnham, D.C.[15]	cust. *p.* 19 Nov. 1341	relq. *a.* 15 May 1342
John Larcher, prior of Kilmainham	app. 10 Mar. 1342	relq. 15 Aug. 1342
	cust. *p.* 18 Apr. 1342[16]	
	cust. on or *a.* 15 May 1342	
John de la Bataille, K.	cust. 15 Aug. 1342	relq. *p.* 15 Nov. 1342 and *a.* 15 Nov. 1343
John Larcher	cust. on or *a.* 15 Nov. 1343	remvd 20 May 1346
		relq. 17 Aug. 1346
John Morice	app. 20 May 1346	remvd 26 July 1346
	cust. 18 Aug. 1346	relq. 8 Dec. 1346
John Darcy, K.	app. 8 Dec. 1346	relq. 24 Mar. 1347

	beginning of term of office	*end of term of office*
John Larcher	app. 26 July 1346 app. 16 Nov. 1346 cust. 26 Mar. 1347	relq. 26 Mar. 1348
John Darcy, K.	cust. 20 Apr. 1349	relq. 20 Jan. 1350
William of Bromley, K.	cust. 21 Jan. 1350	relq. 21 July 1350
Thomas of Bowes, K.	cust. 8 June 1350	relq. 12 Sept. 1350
John of St Paul, abp of Dublin	app. 20 July 1350 cust. 13 Sept. 1350	remvd 24 July 1356 relq. 13 Sept. 1356
John of Frowick, prior of Kilmainham	app. 24 July 1356 cust. 24 Sept. 1356	
Brother John of the Moor } William of Drayton } D.C.	app. 5 June 1359 cust. 24 June 1359	relq. 4 Aug. 1359
Thomas of Burley, prior of Kilmainham	cust. 5 Aug. 1359	remvd 24 Oct. 1364
Robert of Ashton	app., cust. 24 Oct. 1364	remvd 20 Feb. 1367
Thomas le Reve, bp of Waterford	app. 20 Feb. 1367	remvd 25 May 1368
Thomas of Burley	app. 25 May 1368	remvd 20 June 1368 relq. *p.* 12 Aug. 1368[17]
Bp le Reve	app. 20 June 1368	remvd 5 July 1370
John of Boothby	app. 5 July 1370	relq. on or *p.* 16 Mar. 1372
William Tany, prior of Kilmainham	cust. on or *a.* 2 Sept. 1372	ter. 21 June 1377
John Keppok, D.C.	app. 13 Apr. 1375	
Robert of Wikeford, abp of Dublin	app. 18 July 1376[18]	
Alexander Petit (de Balscot), bp of Ossory	app. 20 Aug. 1377[19]	
Abp Wikeford	app. 26 Sept. 1377	remvd 15 Dec. 1378
Robert of Sutton, keeper of the rolls, K.	app. 15 Dec. 1378	remvd 8 Apr./8 May 1380
John Gilbert, bp of Hereford	app. 8 Apr. 1380[20]	
John Colton, dean of St Patrick's, Dublin (abp of Armagh, 1381)	app. 8 May 1380	remvd 26 Nov. 1381 relq. 19 Feb. 1382
William Tany	app. 26 Nov. 1381 cust. 19 Feb. 1382	
Ralph Cheyny	app. 27 June 1383	relq. 8 Nov. 1384
Abp Wikeford	app. 10 Sept. 1384 cust. 8 Nov. 1384	relq. 12 Apr. 1385
Bp Petit	app. 8 Mar. 1385 cust. 12 Apr. 1385	remvd 26 Apr. 1388
Robert of Sutton, D.C.	app. 13 Nov. 1385[21]	
Thomas of Everdon, D.C.	app. 12 Jan. 1386 cust. 20 Jan. 1386	

	beginning of term of office	*end of term of office*
Robert of Preston, K.	app. 26 Apr. 1388	relq. 25 Oct. 1389
Christopher of Preston } D.K. Robert of Sutton	cust. on or *a.* 21 May 1389	
Alexander Petit (de Balscot), bp of Meath	app. 27 Aug. 1389 cust. 25 Oct. 1389	relq. 3 Oct. 1391
Robert of Preston, K.	app. 11 Sept. 1391 cust. 3 Oct. 1391	relq. *p.* 13 Feb. 1392[22]
Robert of Waldeby, abp of Dublin	app. 28 Feb. 1392 app. 24 July 1392	
Robert of Sutton, keeper of the rolls, D.C.	cust *a.* 26 Nov. 1392	relq. *p.* 13 Apr. 1393
Richard Northalis, bp of Ossory	app. 29 May 1393	
Robert of Sutton, K.	app. 1 July 1394	
Abp Waldeby	cust. *a.* 11 Apr. 1395	relq. *p.* 18 Apr. 1395
Robert of Farington, keeper of the rolls, D.C.	app., cust. 11 Apr. 1395	relq. 18 Apr. 1395
Thomas of Everdon } K. John of Kirkby	app., cust. 19 June 1395	relq. 1 Aug. 1395
Bp Petit	app. 10 June 1395 cust. 1 Aug. 1395	relq. *p.* 3 Feb. 1396[23]
Robert Braybrooke, bp of London	app. 15 Oct. 1397[24]	
Robert of Sutton, K.	app. 17 Oct. 1397	
Thomas Cranley, abp of Dublin	app. 24 Apr. 1398	ter. 29 Sept. 1399 relq. 4 Jan. 1400
Thomas Bache, arch-deacon of Meath, D.C.	app. 25 May 1398	
Bp Petit	app. 18 Nov. 1399	d. 10 Sept. 1400
John of Kirkby, keeper of the rolls, D.C.	app., cust., 7 May 1400	
Abp Cranley	app. 4 July 1401	
Thomas of Everdon, keeper of the rolls, D.C.	app. 9 Nov. 1402	
Robert of Sutton, keeper of the rolls, D.C.	app. 7 Mar. 1405	relq. 5 Sept. 1406
Laurence Marbury (Merbury)	app. 14 July 1406 cust. 5 Sept. 1406	
Robert of Sutton, keeper of the rolls, K.	app. 28 June 1407	relq. *p.* 8 Dec. 1407[25]
Patrick Barrett, bp of Ferns	app. 18 Mar. 1410	ter. 20 Mar. 1413
Robert of Sutton, keeper of the rolls, D.C.	cust. *a.* Trinity term 1410	
Robert of Sutton, keeper of the rolls, D.C.	app. 4 May 1412	

	beginning of term of office	*end of term of office*
Abp Cranley	app. 20 Apr. 1413 cust. on or *p.* 8 Aug. 1413[26]	relq. 18 Sept. 1414
Laurence Marbury	app. 21 Mar. 1414 cust. 18 Sept. 1414	remvd 1 Aug. 1421[27]
Hugh Bavent (Banent), D.C.	app. 21 Mar. 1421 cust. 22 Mar. 1421	relq. 21 Aug. 1421
William FitzThomas, prior of Kilmainham	app. 21 Aug. 1421 cust. 28 Aug. 1421	
Laurence Marbury	app. 16 Aug. 1421	ter. 31 Aug. 1422
William Young (Yonge), archdeacon of Meath	cust. 19 Oct. 1422[28]	relq. 7 Dec. 1422
Laurence Marbury	app. 4 Oct. 1422 cust. 7 Dec. 1422[29]	
Richard Sydgrove, D.C.	app. 8 Apr. 1423	relq. *p.* 2 June 1423[30]
Richard Talbot, abp of Dublin	app. 19 May 1423 cust. 13 July 1423[31]	relq. 25 Apr. 1426[32]
William FitzThomas	app. 25 Apr. 1426[33] cust. 26 Apr. 1426	relq. 5 Aug. 1426
William FitzThomas	app. 8 Aug. 1426[34] cust. 8 Aug. 1426[35]	relq. 10 Sept. 1426[35]
Richard FitzEustace	app. 10 Sept. 1426[36] cust. 15 Sept. 1426[36]	relq. 27 Dec. 1426[36]
Abp Talbot	app. 23 Oct. 1426 cust. 12 Jan. 1427	
Thomas Chace, chancellor of Oxford University	app. 26 Feb. 1430 cust. 23 Oct. 1430[37]	remvd 27 May 1436[38]
Thomas Strange (Straunge), D.C.	app. 12 Feb. 1435 cust. *a.* 6 Oct. 1436[39]	d. 27 May 1436[40]
Robert Dyke, archdeacon of Dublin, keeper of the rolls, K.	cust. 22 June 1436[41]	
Thomas Chace	app. 15 Nov. 1436	relq. *p.* 3 May 1442[42]
James Cornewalsh, D.C.	cust *a.* 4 Feb. 1440	
Richard Wogan	app. 27 Feb. 1441[43] cust. *a.* 5 June 1442[44]	relq. 16 July 1442[45] remvd 21 July 1442[45]
Richard FitzEustace	app. 21 July 1442[46] cust. 2 Aug. 1442	remvd *a.* 27 Oct. 1442[47]
Abp Talbot	app. 7 Aug. 1442[48]	remvd 21 Nov. 1442[49]
Richard FitzEustace, K.	cust. *a.* 25 Apr. 1443[50]	
Richard Wogan	app. 4 Mar. 1443 cust. *a.* 21 June 1444[51]	relq. *p.* 28 Aug. 1444[52]
William Chevir, D.C.	cust. *a.* 28 Aug. 1444	relq. *p.* 4 Jan. 1446[53]
John Talbot (earl of Shrewsbury from July 1453)	app. 12 Aug. 1446[54] or 13 Aug. 1446[55] or 2 Sept. 1446[56]	
Robert Dyke, keeper of the rolls, D.C.	cust. *a.* 13 Jan. 1447[57]	

	beginning of term of office	*end of term of office*
Thomas Talbot, prior of Kilmainham, D.C.	app. 6 Nov. 1451	
William Welles, D.C.	app. 7 Aug. 1454[58] cust. on or *a.* 6 Nov. 1454[59]	relq. *p.* 5 Nov. 1456[59]
Michael Tregury, abp of Dublin, D.C.	app. 5 Apr. 1458	
Thomas FitzGerald, prior of Kilmainham	app. 5 Apr. 1448[60]	
Edmund Ouldhall, bp of Meath	cust. *a.* 26 Mar. 1451[61]	
Edmund Plantagenet, earl of Rutland	app. 24 Feb. 1460	d. 30 Dec. 1460
John Dinham	app. 5 Nov. 1460[62] app. 2 May 1461[63]	ter. 4 Mar. 1461
Robert Preston, Lord Gormanston, D.C.	app. 2 May 1461 cust. 2 May 1461	
William Welles	app. 18 July 1461[62]	d. 1463
Thomas 'fitz Maurice' FitzGerald, 7th earl of Kildare	app. 25 Jan. 1464[62]	
John Tiptoft, earl of Worcester	app. 31 Jan. 1464[62]	d. 18 Oct. 1470
William Sherwood, bp of Meath, D.C.	app. 26 Jan. 1464[64]	
Roland FitzEustace, Lord Portlester John Tapton	app. 16 Apr. 1472[65]	remvd Nov. 1478[66] Tapton d. *a.* 29 May 1478[65]
Gilbert Debenham	app. 5 Aug. 1474[62]	remvd. Nov. 1478[67]
Richard Martin (Martyn)	app. 15 Feb. 1478[62]	remvd Nov. 1478[67]
Bp Sherwood	app. 5 Oct. 1479[67] app. 4 Nov. 1480[68] app. 25 Aug. 1482[68]	d. 3 Dec. 1482
Walter de Champfleur, abbot of St Mary's, Dublin, K.	cust. *a.* 31 Dec. 1482	
Robert St Lawrence, lord of Howth	app. 11 Jan. 1483 app. 20 May 1483 app. 12 July 1483	ter. 9 Apr. 1483 ter. 25 June 1483
Thomas FitzGerald	cust. *a.* 31 Dec. 1483	ter. 22 Aug. 1485
Roland FitzEustace, Lord Portlester	cust. *a.* 31 Dec. 1486[69]	
Alexander Plunket	app. 11 June 1492[70]	
Henry Dean, prior of Llanthony and bp of Bangor	app. 13 Sept. 1494[71] app. 20 Nov. 1494[71]	
Walter Fitzsimon, abp of Dublin	app. 6 Aug. 1496[72]	ter. 22 Apr. 1509

	beginning of term of office	*end of term of office*
Nicholas St Lawrence, lord of Howth	app. 10 June 1509[73]	
Abp Fitzsimon	cust. *a*. 31 Dec. 1509[73]	d. 14 May 1511
William Rokeby, abp of Dublin	app. 21 May 1512[74]	
William Compton	app. 6 Nov. 1513[75]	
Abp Rokeby	app. 24 Mar. 1516[76]	d. 29 Nov. 1521
Hugh Inge, bp of Meath (abp of Dublin, 27 Feb. 1523)	app. 6 Mar. 1522[77]	d. 3 Aug. 1528
John Alen, abp of Dublin	app. 19 Sept. 1528[78]	remvd 5 July 1532
George Cromer, abp of Armagh	app. 5 July 1532[79]	remvd 16 Aug. 1534

[1] Granted for life.

[2] *Cal. pat. rolls, 1232–47*, p. 467.

[3] *Close rolls of the reign of Henry III, 1247–51*, (London, 1922), p. 147.

[4] Stephen de Fulbourn is addressed as justiciar and chancellor in a writ from England of this date (P.R.O., C47/10/15, no. 7).

[5] Described as executing the office of chancellor; possibly acting as deputy to his brother Stephen.

[6] De Sandford kept custody of the seal after the appointment of de Vesci as his successor as justiciar.

[7] Thomas de Quantok was then in Ireland and acting as chancellor (P.R.O., C47/10/17, no. 4).

[8] *Rot. pat. Hib.*, p. 11, no. 273.

[9] Ibid.

[10] The deed of 3 Mar. 1309 which describes Alexander of Bicknor, treasurer of Ireland, as deputy chancellor should probably be construed as meaning that he was then deputy chancellor of the exchequer.

[11] Described then as former chancellor (*Cal. pat. rolls, 1313–17*, p. 486).

[12] Nicholas de Balscot's appointment in place of William FitzJohn was probably not effective: there is no interruption in the payments to the latter.

[13] Probably not effective.

[14] Outlaw may have been paid without any break; there is a gap in the records.

[15] Newnham deputised for Ashby for a quarter-year at least.

[16] *Cal. pat. rolls, 1341–3*, p. 411.

[17] *Rot. pat. Hib.*, p. 80, no. 5.

[18] This appointment does not seem to have been effective, as Tany was paid as chancellor from 3 June 1376 to 20 June 1377 (*Liber mun. pub. Hib.*, pt ii, p. 201).

[19] Probably not effective, as it was Tany who was ordered to hand over custody of the seal to Wikeford.

[20] Probably not effective, as it was Sutton who was ordered to hand over custody of the seal to Colton.

[21] Probably not effective.

[22] Preston answered a writ from England of this date as keeper; P.R.O., C47/10/24, no. 11.

[23] Balscot answered a writ from England of this date as chancellor; P.R.O., C47/10/24, no. 12.

[24] *Cal. pat. rolls, 1396–9*, p. 218: ineffective and subsequently cancelled.

[25] *Cal. pat. rolls Ire., Eliz.*, p. 454.

[26] Cranley returned to Ireland on this date after being away on official business for sixteen months (P.R.O.I., R.C. 8/34, pp 98–102).

[27] Marbury was declared by lieutenant and council to have vacated his post.

[28] *Liber mun. pub. Hib.*, pt ii, p. 203.

[29] Ibid.

[30] *Rot. pat. Hib.*, p. 226, no. 18.

[31] *Liber mun. pub. Hib.*, pt ii, p. 203.

[32] P.R.O., E101/248/2.

[33] Ibid.; *Rot. pat. Hib.*, p. 239, no. 5; p. 243, no. 8.

[34] P.R.O., E101/247/20, no. 38.

35 *Rot. pat. Hib.*, p. 244, no. 35.

36 *Liber mun. pub. Hib.*, pt ii, p. 203.

37 But note that Chace's predecessor Talbot seems to have been paid as chancellor down to 27 July 1431 (P.R.O., E101/248/8).

38 *Cal. pat. rolls, 1436-41*, p. 28; the deputy whose death, during Chace's absence, was said to have caused Chace's office to be vacated must have been Strange.

39 *Rot. pat. Hib.*, p. 260, no. 26.   40 P.R.O., E364/73 m.2.

41 *Rot. pat. Hib.*, p. 261, no. 40.

42 Ibid., p. 263, no. 21.   43 *Cal. pat. rolls, 1436-41*, p. 514.

44 *A roll of the proceedings of the king's council in Ireland for a portion of the sixteenth year of the reign of Richard II, 1392-93*, ed. James Graves (London, 1877) (hereafter cited as *Proc. king's council, Ire., 1392-3*), p. 276.

45 Ibid., pp 288-94.   46 Ibid., p. 294.

47 Ibid., p. 295; after which custody of the seal may have been in the hands of the king's lieutenant, James Butler, earl of Ormond (ibid., pp 295-6).

48 This appointment seems never to have become effective; ibid., pp 295-303.

49 Ibid., pp 300-03.

50 *Proceedings and ordinances of the privy council of England, 1436-43* (London, 1835), pp 325-7.

51 *Proc. king's council, Ire., 1392-3*, p. 311. The seal may already have been in his custody on 30 Mar. 1444 (*Ormond deeds, 1413-1509*, p. 140).

52 Ibid., p. 158.   53 *Cal. pat. rolls Ire., Eliz.*, p. 455.

54 Granted during good behaviour (*Cal pat. rolls, 1441-6*, p. 455).

55 Granted during good behaviour (*Cal. close rolls, 1454-61*, p. 289).

56 Granted during good behaviour (*Cal. pat. rolls, 1446-52*, p. 560; *Cal. pat. rolls, 1452-61*, pp 163, 179; *Statute rolls of the parliament of Ireland, reign of King Henry VI*, ed. H. F. Berry (Dublin, 1910), p. 55; *Rotuli parliamentorum* (London, 1783), v, 167.

57 Dyke was also said (30 Mar. 1444) to have acted as deputy chancellor on a number of occasions.

58 *Cal. pat. rolls, 1452-61*, p. 163.

59 *Stat. Ire., Hen. VI.*, pp 457-9.

60 Granted for life in reversion on the death, surrender or forfeiture of John Talbot. He may have had custody of the seal for a short period prior to Feb. 1449, when Talbot petitioned the English parliament for a remedy against FitzGerald's usurpation of his office (*Rotuli parliamentorum*, v, 166-7).

61 *Registrum Johannis Mey*, p. 433; but since the punctuation is uncertain, the chancellor may not be intended to be the same man as the bishop.

62 Granted for life.

63 This Irish ratification of Dinham's previous grant of the office of chancellor was, in effect, declared to be null and void by a royal mandate of 7 Sept. 1461, which voided any instruments passed under the great seal in his nominal custody since 4 Mar. 1461, and ordered that only those instruments passed under the great seal which was in Welles's custody should be regarded as valid: *Rot. pat. Hib.*, p. 269, no. 67.

64 P.R.O., P.S.O. 1/25/1341.

65 For life of both and of survivor; confirmed to FitzEustace alone at Naas parliament of May 1478 (*Stat. Ire., 12-22 Edw. IV*, pp 591-2).

66 Ibid., pp 663, 675, 680.

67 If ever effective, cancelled by a general act of resumption of the Drogheda parliament (*Stat. Ire., 12-22 Edw. IV*, p. 675), or by a further act of resumption at the Dublin parliament of Feb. 1480 (ibid., p. 685).

68 *Cal. pat. rolls, 1476-85*, pp 237, 312.

69 W. Harris, *Whole works of Sir James Ware*, ii (Dublin, 1745), p. 108; 1496 seems to be an error for 1486.

70 *Cal. pat. rolls, 1485-94*, p. 376.

71 Ibid., *1494-1509*, pp 15, 38.

72 Ibid., pp 60, 64.

73 Harris, *Works of Ware*, ii. 109.

74 *L. & P. Hen. VIII*, i, no. 3212.

75 Ibid., no. 4542; app. for life.

76 Ibid., ii, no. 1705.

77 Ibid., iii, no. 2088; Harris, *Works of Ware*, ii, 109, says that in 1527 he was made chancellor for life.

78 *L. & P. Hen. VIII*, iv, no. 4758.

79 Ibid., v, no. 1207 (14).

(B) 1534-1922

J. G. SIMMS

The lists from 1534 to 1826 are based on *Liber mun. pub. Hib.*, and thereafter on *Dublin Gazette*. K. indicates keepers who were not also chancellors. Keepers appointed during the temporary absences of chancellors have not been included, except for special reasons, stated in the notes. Dates refer to letters patent, unless otherwise stated. The office of chancellor was abolished under schedule 2, pt II, of the Irish Free State (Consequential Provisions) Act, 1922 (13 Geo. V, sess. 2, c. 2).

	appointment
John Barnewall, Baron Trimleston	16 Aug. 1534
John Alen[1]	18 Oct. 1538
Sir Thomas Cusack, K.[2]	1 May 1546
Sir Richard Rede	6 Nov. 1546
Sir John Alen	22 Apr. 1548
Sir Thomas Cusack	5 Aug. 1550[3]
Sir William Fitzwilliam, K.[4]	7 Aug. 1555
Hugh Curwin, abp of Dublin	13 Sept. 1555
Robert Weston	10 June 1567
Adam Loftus, abp of Dublin, K.[5]	25 May 1573
William Gerrard (kt 11 Oct. 1579)	23 Apr. 1576
Abp Loftus	16 Aug. 1581
Thomas Jones, bp of Meath ⎫ Sir James Ley ⎬ K.[6] Sir Edmund Pelham ⎪ Sir Anthony St Leger ⎭	6 Apr. 1605
Thomas Jones, abp of Dublin	8 Nov. 1605
Sir William Jones ⎫ Sir William Methwold ⎬ K.[7] Sir Francis Aungier ⎭	10 Apr. 1619
Sir Adam Loftus (cr. Viscount Loftus of Ely, 20 May 1622)	13 May 1619
James Ussher, abp of Armagh ⎫ Henry, Baron Docwra ⎬ K.[8] Sir William Parsons ⎪ Viscount Loftus ⎭	30 May 1627
Lord Robert Dillon ⎫ Sir Adam Loftus ⎬ K.[9] Christopher Wandesford ⎪ Sir Philip Mainwaring ⎭	26 May 1638
Sir Richard Bolton	15 Jan. 1640
Richard Pepys; Sir Gerard Lowther; Miles Corbet (commrs of the great seal)[10]	14 June 1655
William Steele[11]	20 Aug. 1656
Sir Maurice Eustace	9 Oct. 1660
Michael Boyle, abp of Dublin (abp of Armagh, 27 Feb. 1679)[12]	17 July 1665

appointment

Sir Charles Porter	16 Apr. 1686
Sir Alexander Fitton (cr. Baron Gawsworth 1 May 1689)	12 Feb. 1687
Richard Pyne }	
Sir Richard Ryves } K.[13]	1 Aug. 1690
Robert Rochfort }	
Sir Charles Porter[13]	29 Dec. 1690
Francis Marsh, abp of Dublin }	
Edward Brabazon, earl of Meath } K.[14]	31 Oct. 1693
William Hill }	
Sir John Jeffryson }	
Thomas Coote } K.[15]	12 Jan. 1697
Nehemiah Donnellan }	
John Methuen	11 Mar. 1697
Sir Richard Cox	6 Aug. 1703
Richard Freeman	30 June 1707
William King, abp of Dublin }	
Robert Fitzgerald, 19th earl of Kildare } K.[16]	28 Nov. 1710
Thomas Keightley }	
Sir Constantine Phipps	22 Jan. 1711
Alan Brodrick (cr. Baron Brodrick of Midleton, 13 Apr. 1715; Viscount Midleton, 15 Aug. 1717)	11 Oct. 1714
Richard West[17]	23 July 1725
Thomas Wyndham (cr. Baron Wyndham, 17 Sept. 1731)	21 Dec. 1726
Robert Jocelyn (cr. Baron Newport, 29 Nov. 1743, Viscount Jocelyn, 6 Dec. 1755)	7 Sept. 1739
John Bowes (cr. Baron Bowes of Clonlyon, 15 Aug. 1758)	22 Mar. 1757
Arthur Smyth, abp of Dublin }	
Frederick Augustus Hervey, bp of Cloyne } K.[18]	3 Aug. 1767
Thomas St Laurence, Lord Howth (cr. earl of Howth, 3 Sept. 1767) }	
James Hewitt, Baron Lifford (cr. Viscount Lifford, 8 Jan. 1781)	9 Jan. 1768
Robert Fowler, abp of Dublin }	
Hugh Carleton } K.[19]	5 May 1789
Sir Samuel Bradstreet }	
John Fitzgibbon (cr. Baron Fitzgibbon, 6 July 1789; Viscount Fitzgibbon, 6 Dec. 1793; earl of Clare, 12 June 1795)	20 June 1789
John Mitford, Baron Redesdale	15 Mar. 1802
George Ponsonby	25 Mar. 1806
Thomas Manners-Sutton, Baron Manners	1 May 1807
Sir Anthony Hart	5 Nov. 1827
William Conyngham Plunket, Baron Plunket	23 Dec. 1830
Sir Edward Burtenshaw Sugden	13 Jan. 1835
Lord Plunket	30 Apr. 1835
Sir John Campbell (cr. Baron Campbell, 30 June)	28 June 1841
Sir Edward Burtenshaw Sugden	28 Sept. 1841
Maziere Brady	16 July 1846
Francis Blackburne	10 Mar. 1852
Maziere Brady	13 Jan. 1853

	appointment
Joseph Napier	10 Mar. 1858
Maziere Brady	27 June 1859
Francis Blackburne	24 July 1866
Abraham Brewster	29 Mar. 1867
Thomas O'Hagan (cr. Baron O'Hagan, 14 June 1870)	18 Dec. 1868
Sir Joseph Napier ⎱	
James Lewis ⎰ K.[20]	11 Mar. 1874
William Brook ⎰	
John Thomas Ball	1 Jan. 1875
Lord O'Hagan	10 May 1880[21]
Hugh Law	11 Nov. 1881
Sir Edward O'Sullivan, bt	11 Dec. 1883[21]
John Naish	23 May 1885[21]
Edward Gibson (cr. Baron Ashbourne, 4 July 1885)	1 July 1885[21]
John Naish	11 Feb. 1886[21]
Lord Ashbourne	5 Aug. 1886[21]
Samuel Walker	22 Aug. 1892[21]
Lord Ashbourne	8 July 1895[21]
Samuel Walker (bt, 12 July 1906)	14 Dec. 1905[21]
Redmond John Barry	5 Sept. 1911
Ignatius John O'Brien (bt, 15 Jan. 1916; cr. Baron Shandon, 1 July 1918)	26 Mar. 1913[21]
Sir James Henry Mussen Campbell, bt (cr. Baron Glenavy, 1 July 1921)	19 June 1918
Sir John Ross, bt	27 June 1921[21]

[1] Had been app. keeper by L.D. and council on 31 July after Trimleston's death (25 July).

[2] During absence of Alen, summoned to England in connection with dispute involving L.D. St Leger.

[3] Date of privy seal.   [4] After Cusack's resignation (3 July).

[5] By L.D. and council after Weston's death (20 May).

[6] By L.D. and council after Loftus's death (5 Apr.).

[7] By L.D. and council after Jones's death (10 Apr.).

[8] During absence in England of Viscount Loftus, summoned to answer charges; Loftus ordered to be reinstated 1 Aug. 1628.

[9] Viscount Loftus removed and charged with misdemeanours, 1 Apr. 1638.

[10] App. by Cromwell by writ of privy seal.

[11] App. by Cromwell to be chancellor and keeper of the great seal by writ of privy seal.

[12] Had been app. keeper by L.D. and council on 24 June after Eustace's death (22 June).

[13] App. by William III, Fitton remaining Jacobite chancellor.

[14] During Porter's absence in England, where he was accused of high treason; the charges were dropped 29 Jan. 1694 (*Journals of the house of commons*, xi, 72). After the deaths of Marsh and Hill, Francis Aungier, earl of Longford, and Murrough Boyle, Viscount Blessington, were app. in their places (17 Nov. 1693).

[15] After Porter's death (8 Dec. 1696).

[16] After Freeman's death (20 Nov. 1710).

[17] Died 3 Dec. 1726.

[18] After Bowes's death (22 July 1767).

[19] After Lifford's death (28 Apr. 1789).

[20] Seal temporarily entrusted to commrs while services of John Thomas Ball, attorney general, were required in house of commons in connection with judicature bill. *Dublin Gazette* does not give date of appointment, which is taken from *Thom's directory, 1875*.

[21] Date of swearing-in.

ATTORNEY GENERALS, SOLICITOR GENERALS, AND SERJEANTS AT LAW, TO 1922

These offices originated in the appointment of legal representatives of the monarch. Their order in the above title reflects their relative importance under the union, when the attorney general and solicitor general were pivotal members of the administration, and the term 'law officers of the crown' meant, for nearly all practical purposes, these two officers with the chancellor. In origin, however, throughout the medieval period in practice, and up to 1805 in dignity, the serjeants took precedence.

The older practice of one of the friends or advisers of a litigant being allowed to speak on his behalf in court had developed, by the later thirteenth century, in Ireland as well as England, into the use, in all important litigation, of the services of a professional pleader (*narrator*) or serjeant (*serviens*). A different professional lawyer, the attorney, would normally represent the litigant during the purely procedural stages of a case, the serjeant only representing the litigant at the stage at which tentative, oral pleading took place between the parties. In Ireland, as in England, the king employed both attorneys and serjeants in his service, although his legal privileges rendered this less necessary than it was for other litigants. The division of function between them was probably much the same as that between the two kinds of legal representative when acting for other litigants.

In the fourteenth century a few cases occur in which 'attorney' and 'serjeant' are used to refer to the same individual, but the 'king's pleaders' ('king's serjeants' in contemporary English usage) formed a distinct group whose superior status over the king's attorneys was reflected in their higher remuneration and underlined by their frequent elevation to judicial rank.[1]

The assistance of Dr Paul Brand in compiling these lists and the introductory notes is gratefully acknowledged.

[1] Richardson & Sayles, *Admin. Ire.*, pp 41–2.

KING'S ATTORNEYS AND ATTORNEY GENERALS, 1313-1921

For 1313-77 this list is drawn from Richardson and Sayles, *Admin. Ire.*, pp 174-80. Subsequently, down to 1839, it is based on *Liber mun. pub. Hib.*, pt ii, pp 73-4, pt iii, pp 68-9, and Constantine J. Smyth, *Chronicle of the law officers of Ireland* (London, 1839), pp 161-71; the section 1378-1553 has been revised and corrected by Dr Paul Brand. From 1840 the main source is the *Dublin Gazette*. The dates of appointment shown are those of letters patent unless otherwise stated.

To the end of the fourteenth century (and to some extent even to the middle of the fifteenth) the king's attorney was particularly associated with the courts of common pleas and of the exchequer, whereas the king's pleaders acted in any court as required. There was a rise in the status of the king's attorney in the early sixteenth century, probably reflecting a similar rise in the status of the king's attorney in England. The term 'attorney general' was probably not used in Ireland before *c.* 1534.

Before 1554 it is often not possible to ascertain the conditions of tenure of those appointed. Where these are known, they have been noted. After 1554 all appointments were during pleasure, unless otherwise stated.

T. W. Brown left office on 16 November 1921. No further appointment was made. Under the Government of Ireland Act, 1920 (10 & 11 Geo. V, c. 67), Richard Best was appointed attorney general for Northern Ireland on 24 September 1921 by warrant of the lord lieutenant. On 22 March 1922 Hugh Kennedy was appointed law officer of the provisional government, exercising in the Irish Free State the functions previously discharged by the attorney general and solicitor general for Ireland. The title 'law officer' was changed to 'attorney general' in 1923. For the office and its holders in both parts of Ireland since 1921, see J. P. Casey, *The office of the attorney general in Ireland* (Dublin, 1980).

	beginning of term of office	end of term of office
Richard Manning	Mich. 1313	*p.* Mich. 1328
William of Woodworth	*p.* Mich. 1328	24 June 1334
Thomas of·Westham	19 Oct. 1334[1]	29 Oct. 1347
Thomas of Crowland[2]	11 Dec. 1348	11 Dec. 1350
Thomas Keppok	15 Oct. 1351	23 Nov. 1352
John of Leicester	23 Nov. 1352	12 Feb. 1359
William Lynnore	12 Feb. 1359	10 July 1362
Henry Michel	10 July 1362	10 April 1376
Robert Hore	*a.* 6 May 1378[3]	*p.* 8 June 1381[4]
Thomas Malalo	15 Jan. 1382[5]	—
Robert Hemyngborgh	28 July 1384[6]	—
Robert Hore[7]	*a.* 8 Nov. 1384	*p.* 29 Oct. 1385
Alan Furlong	18 May 1394[8]	—
John Barry	16 Aug. 1398[9]	—
William Tynbagh	20 Jan. 1400	—
John Barry	16 Feb. 1400	—
	30 Oct. 1403[10]	—
John White	4 Oct. 1413	*p.* 13 Mar. 1432[11]

	beginning of term of office	*end of term of office*
William Sutton	—	3 Dec. 1445[12]
Stephen Roche	late Feb. 1449[13]	—
Robert FitzRery	10 Oct. 1450[14]	*p.* 5 July 1454[15]
Thomas Dowedall	?1463[16]	—
Robert FitzRery	?1467[17]	—
Nicholas Sutton	22 May 1471[18]	1473
Thomas Cusake	1480[19]	*p.* 25 May 1488[20]
Walter St Lawrence	1491[21]	?1496[22]
Clement FitzLeones	?1502[23]	?1504[24]
John Barnewall, Lord Trimleston	1504[25]	1504[26]
Nicholas Fitzsimons	1504[27]	—
Thomas St Lawrence	19 Aug. 1532[28]	—
Robert Dillon	9 June 1534[29]	*p.* 20 Nov. 1553[30]

	appointment
Barnaby Scurloke (Scurlog)	1554[31]
James Barnewall	3 Sept. 1559
Lucas Dillon	8 Nov. 1566
Edward Fitzsimons	4 June 1570
John Bathe of Drumcondra	21 Feb. 1574
Thomas Snagg	13 Sept. 1577
Christopher Fleming	9 Sept. 1580[32]
Edward Butler	28 Aug. 1582
Charles Calthrope (cr. kt 24 Mar. 1604)	22 June 1584[33]
Sir John Davies	29 May 1606[34]
Sir William Ryves	30 Oct. 1619[35]
Richard Osbaldstone	7 Dec. 1636
Thomas Tempest	1 Oct. 1640
William Basil	18 July 1649[36]
Sir William Domville	23 June 1660[37]
Sir Richard Nagle	15 Feb. 1686
Sir John Temple ·	21 Mar. 1690
Robert Rochfort	6 June 1695[38]
Alan Brodrick	30 June 1707
John Forster	5 Jan. 1710
Sir Richard Levinge	5 July 1711
George Gore	3 Dec. 1714
John Rogerson	23 May 1720
Thomas Marlay	4 May 1727
Robert Jocelyn	22 Oct. 1730
John Bowes	11 Sept. 1739
St George Caulfield	15 Jan. 1742
Warden Flood	2 Oct. 1751
Philip Tisdall	27 Aug. 1760
John Scott	1 Nov. 1777
Barry Yelverton	12 July 1782
John Fitzgibbon	20 Dec. 1783

	appointment
Arthur Wolfe	12 Aug. 1789
John Toler	10 July 1798
John Stewart	23 Dec. 1800
Standish O'Grady	8 June 1803
William Conyngham Plunket	23 Oct. 1805
William Saurin	21 May 1807
William Conyngham Plunket	22 Jan. 1822[39]
Henry Joy	18 June 1827
Francis Blackburne	11 Jan. 1831
Louis Perrin	29 Apr. 1835
Michael O'Loghlen	31 Aug. 1835
John Richards	10 Nov. 1836
Stephen Woulfe	3 Feb. 1837
Nicholas Ball	11 July 1838
Maziere Brady	23 Feb. 1839
David Richard Pigot	14 Aug. 1840[40]
Francis Blackburne	28 Sept. 1841
Thomas Berry Cusack Smith	4 Nov. 1842
Richard Wilson Greene	2 Feb. 1846
Richard Moore	16 July 1846
James Henry Monahan	24 Dec. 1847
John Hatchell	22 Oct. 1850
Joseph Napier	12 Mar. 1852
Abraham Brewster	13 Jan. 1853
William Nicholas Keogh	2 Mar. 1855[41]
John David Fitzgerald	10 Apr. 1856[41]
James Whiteside	1 Mar. 1858[41]
John David Fitzgerald	27 June 1859
Rickard Deasy	22 Feb. 1860
Thomas O'Hagan	14 Feb. 1861
James Anthony Lawson	3 Feb. 1865
John Edward Walsh	25 July 1866
Michael Morris	1 Nov. 1866
Hedges Eyre Chatterton	29 Mar. 1867
Robert Richard Warren	23 Aug. 1867
John Thomas Ball	7 Dec. 1868
Edward Sullivan	21 Dec. 1868
Charles Robert Barry	26 Jan. 1870
Richard Dowse	13 Jan. 1872
Christopher Palles	5 Nov. 1872
Hugh Law	23 Feb. 1874[42]
John Thomas Ball	12 Mar. 1874
Henry Ormsby	21 Jan. 1875
George Augustus Chichester May	27 Nov. 1875
Edward Gibson	15 Feb. 1877
Hugh Law	10 May 1880
William Moore Johnson	17 Nov. 1881
Andrew Marshall Porter	3 Jan. 1883

appointment

John Naish	19 Dec. 1883
Samuel Walker	3 June 1885[43]
Hugh Holmes	2 July 1885
Samuel Walker	12 Feb. 1886
Hugh Holmes	9 Aug. 1886
John George Gibson	30 July 1887[43]
Peter O'Brien	19 Jan. 1888
Dodgson Hamilton Madden	6 Dec. 1889[43]
John Atkinson	1 July 1892
Hugh Hyacinth O'Rorke MacDermot (The MacDermot)	24 Aug. 1892
John Atkinson	8 July 1895
James Henry Mussen Campbell	8 Dec. 1905
Richard Robert Cherry	23 Dec. 1905
Redmond John Barry	6 Dec. 1909[44]
Charles Andrew O'Connor	29 Sept. 1911[44]
Ignatius John O'Brien	4 July 1912[44]
John Francis Moriarty	24 June 1913[44]
Jonathan Pim	6 July 1914[44]
John Gordon	17 June 1915[44]
James Henry Mussen Campbell	15 April 1916[44]
James O'Connor	11 Jan. 1917[44]
Arthur Warren Samuels	23 Apr. 1918[44]
Denis Stanislaus Henry	11 July 1919[44]
Thomas Watters Brown	15 Aug. 1921[44]

[1] During good behaviour.

[2] On 18 Mar. 1348 Robert of Embleton was app. king's attorney, but without effect.

[3] H. G. Richardson and G. O. Sayles, *Parliaments and councils of medieval Ireland* (Dublin, 1947), i, 98.

[4] *Rot. pat. Hib.* p. 108b, no. 49.

[5] Ibid., p. 111b, no. 77. App. during pleasure.

[6] Ibid., p. 124, nos 39–40. App. for life.

[7] Hore may have been reapp., or the appointments of Malalo and Hemyngborgh may not have been effective; he was still being paid on 8 Nov. 1384, and again on 29 Oct. 1385 (ibid., p. 122, no. 11; p. 129, nos 38–9).

[8] During good behaviour; ibid., p. 150b, no. 11.

[9] *Cal. pat. rolls, 1396–9*, p. 374.

[10] Original grant to last during good behaviour; second grant for life, with power to appoint deputies (*Rot. pat. Hib.*, p. 176b, no. 12).

[11] White's first appointment was during pleasure, and was renewed during good behaviour on 18 Mar. 1414; he was reapp. on 19 Oct. 1422 and 19 Oct. 1429 (*Rot. pat. Hib.*, p. 202b, no. 23; p. 202, no. 4; p. 257b, no. 13).

[12] App. 3rd baron of the exchequer; *Cal. pat. rolls, 1441–6*, p. 392.

[13] Appointment confirmed by parliament; *Statute rolls of the parliament of Ireland, reign of King Henry VI*, ed. H. F. Berry (Dublin, 1910), p. 123.

[14] Granted during good behaviour, ratified by the great council of Nov. 1450; ibid., pp 275–7.

[15] Ibid., p. 349.

[16] Dowedall was in office at the Wexford session of the 1463–4 parliament, which exempted him from a general resumption; *Statute rolls of the parliament of Ireland, 1st to the 12th years of the reign of King Edward IV*, ed. H. F. Berry (Dublin, 1914), p. 111.

[17] FitzRery was in office at the time of the 1467–8 parliament, which exempted him from resumption; ibid., p. 555.

[18] App. for life, confirmed by 1471–2 parliament; ibid., p. 893.

¹⁹ Ibid., p. 187. In F. Elrington Ball, *The judges in Ireland, 1221-1921* (2 vols, London, 1926), i, 185, Thomas Archbold is described as king's attorney in 1478; but this probably derives from *Liber mun. pub. Hib.*, where Archbold is called king's attorney, although the original document cited describes him as *narrator regis*, i.e. king's serjeant.

²⁰ In office at this date, *Cal. pat. rolls, 1485-94*, p. 227; presumably vacated it on or before becoming chief justice of king's bench, 1490.

²¹ Ball, *Judges*, i, 190.

²² App. chief baron of exchequer, 1496.

²³ In office, 1502; Ball, *Judges*, i, 188.

²⁴ App. king's serjeant, 1505.

²⁵ Ball, *Judges*, i, 193.

²⁶ App. king's serjeant, 1504.

²⁷ Ball, *Judges*, i, 193.

²⁸ During pleasure.

²⁹ *L. & P. Hen. VIII*, vii, no. 922(2).

³⁰ *Calendar of patent and close rolls of chancery in Ireland, Henry VIII to 18th Elizabeth*, ed. James Morrin (Dublin, 1861), p. 306.

³¹ Appointment renewed, 15 June 1556, 4 June 1558, 26 Jan. 1559.

³² During good behaviour.

³³ Appointment renewed, 19 Apr. 1603. His name is spelled Calthrope in *D.N.B.*, Calthorpe in Smyth, *Law officers of Ire.*, and Culthorpe in *Liber mun. pub. Hib.*

³⁴ New patent issued, 29 May 1609.

³⁵ New patent issued.

³⁶ During good behaviour.

³⁷ During good behaviour; new patent (during pleasure) issued 4 Mar. 1684.

³⁸ New patent issued, 4 June 1702.

³⁹ King's letter (Smyth, *Law officers of Ire.*, p. 171).

⁴⁰ As the *Dublin Gazette* gives the l.p. date in only a few cases, dates in this column are henceforth those of the announcement that the l.p. has passed the great seal of Ireland, as printed in the *Gazette*, unless otherwise stated.

⁴¹ Queen's letter (State Paper Office, Dublin Castle, Chief Secretary's Office Registered Papers; hereafter cited as C.S.O., R.P.).

⁴² Sworn in as member of privy council.

⁴³ Sworn in as member of privy council.

⁴⁴ Date of l.p.

PRINCIPAL SOLICITORS AND SOLICITOR GENERALS, 1504-1921

Liber mun. pub. Hib., pt ii, pp 74-6, pt iii, p. 69; Smyth, *Law officers of Ire.*, pp 172-82; *Dublin Gazette*, 1840-1919. The section 1504-74 has been compiled by Dr Paul Brand.

The office of king's solicitor appeared in England first in 1461, and seems to have been from the outset junior and auxiliary to the office of attorney general. The position in Ireland is more complicated, and from 1504 to 1574, except for an interval in 1554-67, the post of solicitor general was concurrently held by the king's serjeant. The post of principal or chief solicitor was instituted in 1537, and corresponded more closely to the role of the solicitor general in England. From 1554 to 1565 the posts of solicitor general and principal solicitor were held in conjunction, and from 1574 they were in effect unified, the holder of the combined post ranking below the attorney general. In the following list, principal solicitors, as distinct from solicitor generals, are shown in brackets. To 1840, dates of appointment are those of letters patent unless otherwise stated. All appointments were during pleasure unless otherwise stated.

No further appointment was made when T. W. Brown became attorney general on 15 August 1921.

	appointment
John Barnewall, Lord Trimleston	1504[1]
Clement FitzLeones	1505[2]
Thomas Rochfort	1511[3]
Thomas Lutterell	9 Sept. 1532
Patrick Barnewall of Fieldstown	17 Oct. 1534[4]
(Walter Cowley	7 Sept. 1537)[5]
(John Bathe of Athcarne	7 Feb. 1547)[6]
John Bathe of Athcarne	16 Oct. 1550[7]
(Richard Finglas	17 Oct. 1550)[8]
James Dowdall	20 July 1554[9]
(Luke Dillon	17 Apr. 1565)
(Nicholas Nugent	5 Dec. 1566)[10]
Richard Finglas	28 Feb. 1567[11]
(John Bathe of Drumcondra	20 Oct. 1570)
(Richard Bealing	Feb. 1574)
Richard Bealing	*a.* Dec. 1576[12]
Jesse Smythes	7 July 1584[13]
Roger Wilbraham	19 Apr. 1586
Sir John Davies	18 Sept. 1603
Sir Robert Jacobe	29 May 1606
Sir Richard Bolton	10 Feb. 1619[14]
Sir Edward Bolton	20 Jan. 1623[15]
Sir William Sambach	24 June 1640
William Ellis[16]	—
Robert Shapcott	Hilary term 1658
Sir John Temple	10 July 1660[17]
Sir Theobald Butler	25 July 1689
Sir Richard Levinge	29 Dec. 1690
Alan Brodrick	6 June 1695[18]
Sir Richard Levinge	15 Apr. 1704
John Forster	8 Sept. 1709
William Whitshed	5 Jan. 1710
Francis Bernard	3 July 1711
John Rogerson	3 Dec. 1714
Thomas Marlay	26 Dec. 1720
Robert Jocelyn	4 May 1727[19]
John Bowes	23 Oct. 1730
St George Caulfield	6 Oct. 1739
Warden Flood	15 Jan. 1742
Philip Tisdall	2 Oct. 1751
John Gore	27 Aug. 1760[20]
Marcus Paterson	24 Sept. 1764
Godfrey Lill	4 July 1770

appointment

John Scott	15 Dec. 1774
Robert Hellen	2 Nov. 1777
Hugh Carleton	4 May 1779
Arthur Wolfe	10 May 1787
John Toler	12 Aug. 1789
John Stewart	16 July 1798
William Cusack Smith	23 Dec. 1800
James McClelland	9 Jan. 1802
William Conyngham Plunket	5 Nov. 1803
Charles Kendal Bushe	24 Oct. 1805
Henry Joy	1 Mar. 1822
John Doherty	18 June 1827
Philip Cecil Crampton	23 Dec. 1830
Michael O'Loghlen	21 Oct. 1834
Edward Pennefather	27 Jan. 1835
Michael O'Loghlen	29 Apr. 1835
John Richards	21 Sept. 1835
Stephen Woulfe	10 Nov. 1836
Maziere Brady	3 Feb. 1837
David Richard Pigot	11 Feb. 1839
Richard Moore	14 Aug. 1840
Edward Pennefather	28 Sept. 1841[21]
Joseph Devonsher Jackson	11 Nov. 1841
Thomas Berry Cusack Smith	22 Sept. 1842
Richard Wilson Greene	4 Nov. 1842
Abraham Brewster	2 Feb. 1846
James Henry Monahan	16 July 1846
John Hatchell	24 Dec. 1847
Henry George Hughes	22 Oct. 1850
James Whiteside	12 Mar. 1852[22]
William Nicholas Keogh	13 Jan. 1853
John David Fitzgerald	2 Mar. 1855[23]
Jonathan Christian	15 Apr. 1856[23]
Henry George Hughes	26 Jan. 1858
Edmund Hayes	31 Mar. 1858
John George	8 Feb. 1859
Rickard Deasy	14 July 1859
Thomas O'Hagan	?22 Feb. 1860[24]
James Anthony Lawson	14 Feb. 1861
Edward Sullivan	10 Feb. 1865
Michael Morris	3 Aug. 1866
Hedges Eyre Chatterton	8 Nov. 1866
Robert Richard Warren	4 Apr. 1867
Michael Harrison	19 Sept. 1867
John Thomas Ball	4 Nov. 1868
Henry Ormsby	?7 Dec. 1868[25]
Charles Robert Barry	21 Dec. 1868
Richard Dowse	14 Feb. 1870

appointment

Christopher Palles	6 Feb. 1872
Hugh Law	18 Nov. 1872
Henry Ormsby	12 Mar. 1874
Hon. David Robert Plunket	29 Jan. 1875
Gerald Fitzgibbon	3 Mar. 1877
Hugh Holmes	14 Dec. 1878
William Moore Johnson	24 May 1880
Andrew Marshall Porter	17 Nov. 1881
John Naish	9 Jan. 1883
Samuel Walker	19 Dec. 1883
Hugh Hyacinth O'Rorke MacDermot (The MacDermot)	? June 1885[26]
John Monroe	3 July 1885
John George Gibson	5 Dec. 1885[27]
The MacDermot	12 Feb. 1886
John George Gibson	9 Aug. 1886
Peter O'Brien	11 July 1887
Dodgson Hamilton Madden	19 Jan. 1888
John Atkinson	6 Dec. 1889[28]
Edward Carson	1 July 1892[29]
Charles Hare Hemphill	24 Aug. 1892
William Kenny	28 Aug. 1895
Dunbar Plunket Barton	1 Jan. 1898
George Wright	2 Feb. 1900
James Henry Mussen Campbell	30 Oct. 1901
Redmond John Barry	23 Dec. 1904
Charles Andrew O'Connor	6 Dec. 1909[30]
Ignatius John O'Brien	28 Oct. 1911[30]
Thomas Francis Molony	4 July 1912[30]
John Francis Moriarty	1 May 1913[30]
Jonathan Pim	24 June 1913[30]
James O'Connor	6 July 1914[30]
Arthur Warren Samuels	17 Sept. 1917[30]
John Blake Powell	24 Apr. 1918[30]
Denis Stanislaus Henry	3 Dec. 1918[30]
Daniel Martin Wilson	11 July 1919[30]
Thomas Watters Brown	16 June 1921[30]

[1] Ball, *Judges*, i, 193. Terms of appointment not known.

[2] Ibid., i, 188. Terms of appointment not known.

[3] Ibid., i, 192. Terms of appointment not known.

[4] For life.

[5] During good behaviour.

[6] Reapp. 15 Mar. 1547.

[7] App. for life; reapp. 1553 during pleasure.   [8] Reapp. 12 Feb. 1554.

[9] App. during good behaviour; also principal solicitor.

[10] 'Calendar to fiants of the reign of Elizabeth' in *Eleventh* [etc.] *report of the deputy keeper of the public records in Ireland* (Dublin, 1879–90) (hereafter cited as *Fiants Ire., Eliz.*), no. 962.

[11] According to his appointment, he was to replace John Bathe; ibid., no. 988.

[12] Bealing was holding office as solicitor general on 1 Dec. 1576 and apparently still held it on 26 Nov. 1584; *Cal. pat. rolls Ire., Eliz.*, pp 3, 71.

¹³ As 'chief or principal solicitor general'; confirmed as 'solicitor at laws', 18 Jan. 1585 (*Fiants Ire.*, *Eliz.*, nos 4478, 4577).

¹⁴ New patent issued 3 Apr. 1619.

¹⁵ New patent issued 16 Apr. 1625.

¹⁶ *Liber mun. Hib.* and Smyth state only that he was in office in 1657; he was solicitor general for England at this time.

¹⁷ New patents issued, 1 Feb. 1661, 4 Mar. 1685.

¹⁸ New patent issued, 4 June 1702.

¹⁹ New patent issued, 28 Oct. 1727.

²⁰ New patent issued, 6 Feb. 1761.

²¹ Dates in this column are henceforth those of the announcements printed in the *Dublin Gazette*, unless otherwise stated.

²² Date of issue of *Dublin Gazette* (hereafter cited as *D.G.*), in which undated notice appeared.

²³ No notice in *D.G.*; date of queen's letter (C.S.O., R.P.).

²⁴ No notice in *D.G.*; O'Hagan, formerly third serjeant, presumably became solicitor general on or after Deasy's elevation to attorney general.

²⁵ No notice in *D.G.*; although Ormsby presumably succeeded Ball when the latter became attorney general, he can have had only a few days in office before the change of administration.

²⁶ No notice in *D.G.*; cf. the case of Ormsby in 1868.

²⁷ No notice in *D.G.*, but the queen's letter appointing Gibson bore the same date (30 Nov.) as that appointing Monroe a judge (C.S.O., R.P. 1885/22682); the date in *D.G.* for the latter is 5 Dec.

²⁸ No notice in *D.G.*, but the C.S.O. applied in the same letter for Madden to be app. attorney general and Atkinson solicitor general (C.S.O., R.P. 1889/22617).

²⁹ No notice in *D.G.*, but the queen's letter appointing Carson bore the same date (30 June) as that appointing Atkinson attorney general (C.S.O., R.P. 1892/8817).

³⁰ Date of l.p.

SERJEANTS AT LAW, c. 1261-1632, AND PRIME OR FIRST SERJEANTS, 1632-1922

For the period *c.* 1261-1377, this list is based on Richardson and Sayles, *Admin. Ire.*, pp 174-81. The sections for 1377-1836 are based on *Liber mun. pub. Hib.*, pt ii, pp 71-3, 219, pt iii, pp 68-71, and Smyth, *Law officers of Ire.*, pp 192, 199-200, 202-3; the main source thereafter is the *Dublin Gazette*. Dr Paul Brand has thoroughly revised the list for the period *c.* 1261-1511, and contributed corrections to the later part.

From *c.* 1261 to *c.* 1400, the king was served in his courts in Ireland by one, two, or (exceptionally) three serjeants at law, but the surviving evidence gives no indication of their relative precedence, nor even, with rare exceptions, of any division of labour between them. Before the late fourteenth century, it is rare to find any record of their appointment, and normally it is only possible to fix this approximately from the financial records which record some, though not all, of the payments made to them. Similarly it is often difficult to fix the date on which they ceased to hold office, in the absence of any record of the appointment of a successor. From shortly before 1400 to 1632 there was normally only a single king's serjeant at law in Ireland. In 1632 a second serjeant was appointed, and in 1682 a third; the prime, second, and third serjeants seem all to have taken precedence over the attorney general and solicitor general. When in 1805 this precedence was abolished, the title 'first serjeant' replaced that of 'prime serjeant'. Second and third serjeants have been omitted from the present list.

From 1532 the dates of appointment shown are those of letters patent unless otherwise stated. Before 1532, it is often not possible to ascertain the conditions of tenure of those appointed. Where these are known, they have been noted. After 1532 all appointments were during pleasure, unless otherwise stated.

The office of serjeant came to an end for all practical purposes on the transfer of power to the Irish Free State government in 1922, but A. M. Sullivan continued to use the title by courtesy until his death on 9 January 1959.

	beginning of term of office	*end of term of office*
Roger Owen	*c.* 1261 × 1266	*c.* 1275 × 1280
Robert of St Edmund	1270	*p.* Sept. 1285
John FitzWilliam	on or *a.* Mich. 1281	—
John de Ponz	on or *a.* 22 July 1292	on or *p.* Oct. 1297[1]
John de Neville	on or *a.* 25 Dec. 1293	?Trinity 1297[2]
William of Bardfield	?Trinity 1297[2]	on or *p.* Mich. 1307[3]
Richard le Blond of Arklow	on or *a.* Mich. 1297	21 Mar. 1322
Matthew of Hanwood	on or *a.* Mich. 1310	on or *p.* Mich. 1314
John of Staines	21 Aug. 1319	20 Aug. 1327
Simon fitz Richard	21 Mar. 1322	2 June 1331
John Gernoun	on or *a.* 29 Sept. 1327	6 June 1338[4]
John of Cardiff	on or *a.* 29 Sept. 1327	on or *p.* 22 Nov. 1330
Hugh Brown	on or *a.* 3 June 1331	on or *p.* 3 June 1346[5]
Thomas of Dent	on or *a.* 3 June 1331	on or *p.* 3 Mar. 1334
William Petit	17 July 1338	21 Mar. 1350[6]
Edmund of Barford	on or *a.* 19 Nov. 1347	on or *p.* 19 Feb. 1360
Robert of Preston	on or *a.* 11 Dec. 1348	17 July 1358
Richard Plunket	on or *a.* Easter 1358	?7 Aug. 1376[7]
John Keppok	19 Aug. 1358	8 Feb. 1365[8]
John Tyrell	8 Feb. 1366	*p.* 24 Apr. 1381 and *a.* 24 Oct. 1385[9]
Walter Coterell	20 Jan. 1378[10]	*p.* 20 July 1388[11]
Peter Rowe	on or *a.* 5 May 1381[12]	*p.* 20 Sept. 1386[13]
Richard Glynyon	on or *a.* 16 Feb. 1386[14]	—
John Bermingham	24 Sept. 1388[15]	on or *p.* 4 Oct. 1392[16]
	16 Jan. 1400[17]	*a.* 13 June 1402[18]
Christopher Barnewell	20 Oct. 1422[19]	*a.* 6 Apr. 1434[20]
Thomas son of Christopher Plunket	8 Nov. 1434[21]	—
Robert Dowedall	20 June 1435[22]	—
Edward Somerton	4 Feb. 1438[23]	*a.* 18 Jan. 1447[24]
Thomas Sneterby	21 June 1447[25]	*p.* Nov. 1450[26]
Peter Trevers	*a.* Feb. 1460[27]	—
Thomas Dowedall	4 Mar. 1462[28]	*p.* Dec. 1467[29]
Philip Bermingham	*a.* Nov. 1463–Feb. 1464[30]	—
Henry Duffe of Drogheda	3 Dec. 1471[31]	*p.* Dec. 1476[32]

	beginning of term of office	*end of term of office*
Thomas Archbold	1478 or *a.* 1478[33]	—
John Barnewall, Lord Trimleston	1504[34]	—
Clement FitzLeones	1505[35]	—
Thomas Rochfort	1511[36]	—

	appointment
Thomas Luttrell	9 Sept. 1532
Patrick Barnewall	17 Oct. 1534[37]
John Bathe	16 Oct. 1550[37]
Richard Finglas	11 Sept. 1554[38]
Edward Fitzsimons	21 Feb. 1575
Arthur Corye	9 May 1594
Edward Loftus	1 Nov. 1597
Nicholas Kerdiffe	8 June 1601[39]
John Beere	9 Feb. 1609[40]
John Brereton, kt	13 May 1617[41]
James Barry*	6 Oct. 1629
Sir Maurice Eustace	Aug. 1634[42]
Sir Audley Mervyn	21 Mar. 1661[43]
Sir William Davies	26 Oct. 1675[43]
John Osborne	29 Aug. 1676[44]
Gerald Dillon	15 Feb. 1687
John Osborne	29 Sept. 1690[45]
Nehemiah Donnellan	8 Feb. 1693
Sir Thomas Pakenham	5 Nov. 1695[46]
Robert Saunders	28 Feb. 1703
William Neave	1 Dec. 1708
Robert Blennerhassett	11 Aug. 1711
Morley Saunders	9 Feb. 1713
William Caulfield	8 Dec. 1714
Godfrey Boate	13 June 1715
Robert Fitzgerald	23 June 1717
Francis Bernard	26 Jan. 1724
Henry Singleton	22 June 1726[47]
Arthur Blennerhassett	14 Jan. 1742
Anthony Malone	9 May 1743
Eaton Stannard	24 Jan. 1754
William Scott	6 Oct. 1757
Thomas Tenison	27 July 1759[48]
John Hely Hutchinson	11 Dec. 1761
James Dennis	18 July 1774
Walter Hussey Burgh	24 July 1777
Thomas Kelly	13 July 1782
John Scott	31 Dec. 1783
James Browne	21 May 1784
James Fitzgerald	21 June 1787
St George Daly	28 Jan. 1799

* From 1632 he and his successors to 1805 were styled 'prime serjeant'.

appointment

Edmund Stanley	1 July 1801
Arthur Browne	29 Dec. 1802[49]
Arthur Moore	25 July 1805
William Johnson	25 July 1816
Henry Joy	28 Oct. 1817
Thomas Langlois Lefroy	13 May 1822
Thomas Goold	Apr. 1830[50]
Edward Pennefather	Feb. 1832[50]
Louis Perrin	Feb. 1835[50]
Richard Wilson Greene	23 May 1835
Joseph Stock	4 Nov. 1842[51]
John Howley (kt 14 Aug. 1865)	10 June 1851[52]
Richard Armstrong	*p.* 13 Feb. 1866[53]
David Sherlock	25 Oct. 1880[51]
James Robinson	20 May 1884[51]
Charles Hare Hemphill	18 July 1885[51]
William Bennett Campion	17 Nov. 1892[51]
Charles Andrew O'Connor	5 Dec. 1907[54]
John Francis Moriarty	15 Mar. 1910[54]
Charles Louis Matheson	1 July 1913[54]
Alexander Martin Sullivan	29 Oct. 1919[54]

[1] William Prynne, *An exact chronological vindication . . .*, iii (London, 1668), pp 813–16.

[2] De Neville was paid for half the twenty-fifth regnal year: in the second half of the year he was replaced by Bardfield.

[3] He was only paid to Mich. 1307, but may have remained king's serjeant at law till appointed a justice of common pleas on 5 June 1308.

[4] There is a gap in recorded payments to him from 22 Nov. 1330 to 2 Nov. 1334. He was paid as justice of common pleas from 15 June 1338.

[5] There is a gap in recorded payments to him from 24 June to 2 Nov. 1334.

[6] There is a gap in recorded payments to him from 21 Sept. 1348 to 21 Sept. 1349. He was a temporary justice in the court of the jcr from 26 Nov. 1347 to 27 Apr. 1348.

[7] There are several gaps in the recorded payments to him, but he probably remained in office till becoming a justice in the court of the jcr on 8 Aug. 1376. Richard White of Clonegall acted as his deputy during his absence in England on the king's service, 19 June 1359–19 July 1359.

[8] There is a gap in recorded payments to him from 19 Feb. 1360 to 30 May 1362.

[9] *Rotulorum patentium et clausorum cancellariae Hiberniae calendarium* (Dublin, 1828), p. 107b, nos 15, 16; p. 129, no. 35.

[10] To act in Munster and Counties Kilkenny and Wexford only; ibid., p. 105b, no. 103.

[11] Ibid., p. 141b, no. 200.

[12] At this time Rowe was apparently only acting in the court of the jcr; ibid., p. 108, no. 45.

[13] Ibid., p. 136, no. 183. On 23 Sept. 1388 he became chief justice of the court of the jcr.

[14] Ibid., p. 129, no. 27.

[15] App. during pleasure, to act in Counties Dublin, Meath, Kildare, Louth and Carlow only; ibid., p. 139, no. 63.

[16] Licensed to study law in England; ibid., p. 149b, no. 100.

[17] App. during pleasure, ibid., p. 156, no. 29; no geographical limitation noted.

[18] When he became a justice of the court of king's bench.

[19] Ibid., p. 239b, no. 19. His appointment was renewed during good behaviour on 22 Sept. 1430 (ibid., p. 250, no. 15) and again renewed on 20 June 1432 (ibid., p. 259, no. 9).

[20] When he became a justice of the court of king's bench.

[21] App. during pleasure, ibid., p. 256, nos 5–6.

[22] App. during pleasure, ibid., p. 257b, no. 63.

[23] Ibid., p. 261b, no. 3; life appointment.

[24] When he became a justice of the court of king's bench.

[25] *Cal. pat. rolls, 1446-1452*, p. 115: confirmed by the king on 20 July 1448. Appointment during good behaviour.

[26] When confirmed in office: *Stat. Ire., Hen. VI*, p. 275.

[27] When licensed to go to England: ibid., p. 793.

[28] *Cal. pat. rolls, 1461-1467*, p. 184; appointed for life.

[29] He still held the office when confirmed in the parliament which began then: *Stat. Ire., 1-12 Edw. IV*, p. 549.

[30] Ibid., p. 111.

[31] *Stat. Ire., 1-12 Edw. IV*, pp 792-3: appointment for life, confirmed by parliament.

[32] *Stat. Ire., 12-22 Edw. IV*, pp 507-9.

[33] App. as deputy by the master of the rolls. *Liber mun. pub. Hib.*, pt ii, p. 204, gives his description as *narrator regis*, but translates this as 'king's attorney'.

[34] Ball, *Judges* i, 193.

[35] Ibid., p. 188.

[36] Ibid., p. 192.

[37] For life.

[38] During good behaviour.

[39] New patent issued, 19 Apr. 1603.

[40] Patent later surrendered; new patent issued, 22 Jan. 1617.

[41] New patent issued, 15 Apr. 1625.

[42] Not enrolled; terms of appointment not stated.

[43] During good behaviour.

[44] In reversion. Osborne took office in 1681 when Davies became chief justice of king's bench (2 Mar. 1681), holding during good behaviour. A new patent (at pleasure) was issued on 18 Mar. 1685, after the accession of James II.

[45] During good behaviour.

[46] New patent issued, 8 Aug. 1702.

[47] New patent issued, 28 Oct. 1727.

[48] New patent issued, 19 Feb. 1761.

[49] Browne was the last to hold the title 'prime serjeant'. His successors were styled 'first serjeant'.

[50] Precise dates are given neither in Smyth, *Law officers of Ire.*, nor in *D.G.*

[51] Date of announcement in *D.G.*

[52] Date of issue of *D.G.* in which undated notice appeared.

[53] No notice in *D.G.*; Howley d. 13 Feb. 1866, and Armstrong was presumably app. soon after.

[54] Date of l.p.

SECRETARIES OF STATE FOR IRELAND AND KEEPERS OF THE SIGNET OR PRIVY SEAL, 1560–1829

Herbert Wood, 'The offices of secretary of state for Ireland and keeper of the signet or privy seal' in *R.I.A. Proc.*, xxxviii, sect. C, no. 4 (1928), pp 51–68; *Liber mun. pub. Hib.*, pt ii, p. 82; pt iii, p. 106. The assistance of Dr Ciaran Brady is gratefully acknowledged.

A clear distinction must be made between the secretary of state (often referred to as 'principal secretary') and the secretary to the chief governor (generally referred to as 'chief secretary' from the late seventeenth century onwards; see below, p. 528). The secretary of state—appointed by letters patent from the crown as an officer of the Irish establishment, communicating regularly with the crown, and directing the clerks of the Irish privy council, of which he was a member—was always in theory, and until the end of the seventeenth century in practice, a far more important official than the secretary to the chief governor. The secretary of state acted as the English government's chief link with the administration in Dublin, and took part in formulating policy. Other important functions were attached to the office, and its holder was usually also a member of parliament. The purpose of the office was to provide a permanent and continuous leadership to the Irish administration as distinct from the occasional presence of the viceroys, who were often mainly concerned with special objectives. Fenton's appointment in 1580, to supplement the infirm Challoner, set a precedent of joint tenure which was followed for much of the seventeenth century (and even echoed in the eighteenth); the patent appointing Cooke, in view of Fenton's infirmity, observed that 'heretofore there have been for like cause usually two secretaries of that estate'. The junior appointee was normally granted the reversion to the office. As early as 1622, however, a commission of inquiry into the ecclesiastical and temporal state of Ireland was instructed to examine 'the duties and practice of the principal secretaries of state's offices, as no such use is made of the secretaries as is proper to their place'.* With the decline of the Irish privy council as an instrument of government, the office became a sinecure by the eighteenth century, most of its duties being performed by the chief governors and their secretaries. It retained a superior status to the chief secretaryship, however, and for this reason was granted to Pelham and Abbot during their tenure of the latter office. No further appointment was made after Abbot's resignation in 1802.

The office of keeper of the signet or privy seal was of great importance in the issuing of fiants, warrants, and commissions. Up to the death of Hely Hutchinson in 1794, it was always held by the secretary of state, being granted in the same letters patent. Abbot, to whom it was granted for life, retained it after his resignation as secretary of state and chief secretary; after his death, the chief secretary became keeper of the privy seal.

The dates of appointment shown below are those of letters patent unless otherwise stated.

	appointment	end of term of office
John Challoner	May 1560	d. a. 13 May 1581
Edward Waterhouse	1579	relq. early 1580[1]
Geoffrey Fenton (kt 1588)	July 1580	
	14 Nov. 1581[2]	d. 19 Oct. 1608
Sir Richard Cooke	25 Oct. 1603	d. 8 Sept. 1616
[Dudley Carleton][3]		
Sir Dudley Norton	22 Jan. 1613	
	25 Sept. 1615[4]	retired 1634
Sir Francis Annesley (cr. Baron Mountnorris, 8 Feb. 1629)	31 Oct. 1616[5]	
Philip Mainwaring (kt 13 July 1634)	12 July 1634[6]	
Viscount Valentia (formerly Lord Mountnorris)	1 June 1648[7]	d. a. 23 Nov. 1660

* *Cal. S.P. Ire., 1615–25*, p. 347.

	appointment	end of term of office
Sir Philip Mainwaring	1660[8]	d. 2 Aug. 1661[9]
Sir Paul Davis	6 July 1661	d. 1672
Sir George Lane (cr. Viscount Lanesborough, 31 July 1676)	16 Sept. 1665	d. 11 Dec. 1682
Sir John Davis	19 July 1678	d. 1689
Sir Robert Southwell	25 July 1690	d. 11 Sept. 1702
Edward Southwell, sr	13 July 1702[10]	d. 4 Dec. 1730
Edward Southwell, jr	20 July 1720[11]	d. 1755
Thomas Carter	13 Nov. 1755	d. 3 Sept. 1763
Philip Tisdall	18 Feb. 1760	d. 11 Sept. 1777
John Hely Hutchinson	10 July 1766	d. 4 Sept. 1794
Edmond Henry Pery, 2nd Baron Glentworth of Mallow	22 June 1795[12]	patent revoked 17 July 1797
Thomas Pelham	24 June 1796[13]	
Robert Stewart, Viscount Castlereagh	24 July 1797[14]	patents revoked 26 May and 1 June 1801
Charles Abbot (cr. Baron Colchester, 3 June 1817)[15]	12 June 1801	d. 7 May 1829[16]

[1] Waterhouse was acting as secretary of state in 1579 and asked to be relieved of the post in Jan. 1580, but no formal appointment is recorded.

[2] New patent issued after Challoner's death; renewed patents were issued, 22 Apr. 1584 and 20 Apr. 1603.

[3] On 10 Jan. 1610 the king ordered Carleton (Cooke's nephew) to be made secretary of state, but no patent has been found, and Carleton took up another post.

[4] New patent issued. The first had granted Norton the reversion to the office, but on 19 Jan. 1615 the king ordered him to take up his duties because of Cooke's infirmity (*Cal. S.P. Ire., 1615-25*, p. 2).

[5] Date of privy seal warrant; *Liber mun. pub. Hib.* gives no date for l.p.

[6] On Norton's retirement Mountnorris should have become principal secretary of state, but the post was given instead to Mainwaring, a political associate of Wentworth.

[7] Mountnorris had been deprived of office soon after Mainwaring was app., and was reinstated on this date by order of the H.C.

[8] Wood and *Liber mun. pub. Hib.* say only that Mainwaring was reinstated on the accession of Charles II. He appears as principal secretary in the Irish privy council that was ordered to be sworn, 19 Dec. 1660 (*Cal. S.P. Ire., 1660-62*, p. 142).

[9] *D.N.B.*; Wood says Mainwaring died in 1662.

[10] New patent issued, 22 Dec. 1714. Southwell, who was twice C.S. (1703-7 and 1710-13; see below, (p. 530), was also clerk of the English privy council and absent from Ireland during most of his term of office.

[11] Joint patent granted to both Edward Southwells, granting the son the reversion to the office, which he assumed on his father's death.

[12] As keeper of the signet or privy seal, not secretary of state.

[13] As secretary of state, the seal remaining with Glentworth. Pelham was C.S. since 13 Mar. 1795.

[14] Wood states that Pelham continued as secretary of state, and that Castlereagh merely succeeded Glentworth as keeper of the signet or privy seal; but *Liber mun. pub. Hib.*, recording Abbot's separate appointments as secretary and keeper, mentions in each case a revocation of patents previously issued to Castlereagh. Castlereagh (acting C.S. from 29 Mar. 1798) became C.S., 3 Nov. 1798.

[15] C.S. since 25 May 1801.

[16] Retired as C.S. and secretary of state on becoming speaker of H.C., 11 Feb. 1802; retained privy seal till his death.

SECRETARIES TO CHIEF GOVERNORS, AND CHIEF SECRETARIES, 1566–1922

C. J. WOODS AND CIARAN BRADY

This list is based on J. L. J. Hughes, 'The chief secretaries in Ireland, 1566–1921' in *I.H.S.*, viii, no. 29 (Mar. 1952), pp 59–72, where further particulars are to be found. Minor corrections have been made. Hughes's promised treatment of the interregnum in a supplementary list has not appeared, and this remains a period in which further research is needed. Nor did Hughes's original list include chief secretaries to lords justices. In the present list these have been added for 1690–1717 (marked with an asterisk) from J. C. Sainty, 'The secretariat of the chief governors of Ireland, 1690–1800' in *R.I.A. Proc.*, lxxvii, sect. C, no. 1 (1977), p. 13. The date 1566 remains the earliest point from which a continuous list can be compiled.

A continuous list runs the risk of obscuring the great difference in importance between the secretary to a sixteenth-century lord deputy and the 'chief secretary to the lord lieutenant' of three centuries later. In the sixteenth century the secretary was essentially a member of the chief governor's household: a personal clerical assistant with minor executive duties, uninvolved in policy, and often referred to simply as the chief governor's 'man'. He was not a member of the Irish establishment, not appointed by patent, and not salaried from the civil list. He was usually not of high social origin; he was appointed and paid by the chief governor, and his tenure of office, informal influence, and future career were all subject to his employer's discretion. Few secretaries served for long; most held a patent office during their period of tenure; some, but by no means all, progressed to higher positions. Despite the great increase in the practical importance of the office during the seventeenth and eighteenth centuries, this dependent position was not formally altered until the union.[1] Up to that date, appointment was made by a verbal communication to the chief secretary's office from the chief governor; and up to that date, therefore, the dates of appointment given below generally correspond with those of the entry into office of the chief governors, although in the early part of the list this is not a completely accurate guide to the secretary's period of office. The title 'chief secretary' or 'first secretary' was adopted in the late seventeenth century when chief governors took to appointing a second secretary; the division of responsibility between secretaries is described in Sainty, loc. cit.[2] The post of second secretary was terminated in 1777.

[1] 'There is no country probably in Europe where such various powers and departments are in one man and that man unknown to the constitution' (John Hely Hutchinson to Lord Loughborough, 18 Mar. 1793, *H.M.C. rep. 12*, app. ix, p. 328). The appointment of Pelham and Abbot as secretary of state, while each held the chief secretaryship, was intended to remove this anomaly by giving them a dignity commensurate with their practical importance.

[2] Mountjoy employed Francis Mitchell and George Cranmer concurrently in 1600, without apparently establishing a precedent; it is notable that the division of labour between them was arranged by the superintendent of the lord deputy's household (*Calendar of the manuscripts of the ... marquess of Salisbury ... preserved at Hatfield House*, xi (H.M.C., 1906), p. 552). Cranmer is described as 'chief about his lord' (*Cal. S.P. Ire., 1600*, p. 39). Holcroft is mentioned in 1617 as 'one of the lord deputy's secretaries' (*Cal. S.P. Ire., 1615–25*, p. 195). Earlier, it is possible that Molyneux and Tremayne may have both served Sidney at the same time. In such circumstances the title 'chief secretary' may be found long before its regular use began.

After the union, the chief secretary's status was enhanced by his bearing the main parliamentary responsibility for Irish administration and legislation; his term of office ceased to correspond with that of the viceroy, and lasted until the appointment of his successor. From 1801 the date of appointment shown is that of the official notification issued from the chief secretary's office, and is the date from which the emoluments of office begin.

After the Anglo-Irish treaty of 6 December 1921, the chief secretary's responsibilities were confined to the running-down of the British administration in Ireland. No further appointment was made when Greenwood vacated the office on 25 October 1922.

	appointment
Edward Waterhouse	20 Jan. 1566
	28 Oct. 1568[1]
Edmund Tremayne	15 July 1569[2]
Philip Williams	*p*. Mar. 1571
Edmund Molyneux	18 Sept. 1575[3]
Edmund Spenser	7 Sept. 1580
Philip Williams	21 June 1584
	30 June 1588[4]
Richard Cooke	11 Aug. 1594
Philip Williams	22 May 1597
Henry Wotton	15 Apr. 1599
Francis Mitchell	28 Feb. 1600
George Cranmer	Mar. 1600
Fynes Moryson	14 Nov. 1600
John Bingley	1 June 1603
Henry Piers	3 Feb. 1605
Henry Holcroft	30 Aug. 1616
John Veele	8 Sept. 1622
George Lane	21 Jan. 1644[5]
Mathew Lock	June 1660
Thomas Page	27 July 1662
Henry Ford	18 Sept. 1669
Sir Ellis Leighton	21 Apr. 1670
Sir Henry Ford	5 Aug. 1672
Sir William Harbord	11 Dec. 1673
Sir Cyril Wyche[6]	24 Aug. 1677
William Ellis	2 May 1682
Sir Paul Rycaut	9 Jan. 1686
Thomas Sheridan	12 Feb. 1687
Patrick Tyrrell[7]	2 Feb. 1688
John Davis*	Sept. 1690
Sir Cyril Wyche	4 Sept. 1692
Richard Aldworth*[8]	July 1693
William Palmer*	30 July 1696
Matthew Prior*	May 1697
Humphrey May*	Nov. 1699
Francis Gwyn	28 Dec. 1700

Edward Southwell[9]	19 Feb. 1703
George Dodington	30 Apr. 1707
Joseph Addison	4 Dec. 1708
Edward Southwell[9]	26 Oct. 1710
Sir John Stanley	22 Sept. 1713
Joseph Addison[10]	4 Oct. 1714
Martin Bladen* } Charles Delafaye* }	Sept. 1715[11]
Edward Webster	27 Apr. 1717
Horatio Walpole	18 June 1720
Edward Hopkins	Aug. 1721
Thomas Clutterbuck	6 May 1724
Walter Cary	23 June 1730
Sir Edward Walpole	9 Apr. 1737
Thomas Townshend	12 May 1739
Henry Bilson Legge	14 Oct. 1739
William Ponsonby, Viscount Duncannon	8 June 1741
Richard Liddell[12]	8 Jan. 1745
Sewallis Shirley	5 July 1746
Edward Weston	15 Nov. 1746
Lord George Sackville	15 Dec. 1750
Henry Seymour-Conway	2 Apr. 1755
Richard Rigby	3 Jan. 1757
William Gerard Hamilton	3 Apr. 1761
Charles Moore, 6th earl of Drogheda	3 July 1764
Sir Charles Bunbury	5 June 1765
Francis Seymour-Conway, Viscount Beauchamp	7 Aug. 1765
Augustus John Hervey[13]	6 Oct. 1766
Theophilus Jones	9 July 1767
Lord Frederick Campbell	19 Aug. 1767
Sir George Macartney	1 Jan. 1769
Sir John Blaquiere	30 Nov. 1772
Richard Heron (cr. bt, 25 July 1778)	13 Dec. 1776
William Eden	29 Nov. 1780
Richard Fitzpatrick	8 Apr. 1782
William Wyndham Grenville	15 Aug. 1782
William Windham	3 May 1783
Thomas Pelham	27 Aug. 1783
Thomas Orde	12 Feb. 1784
Alleyne Fitzherbert	6 Nov. 1787
Robert Hobart[14]	6 Apr. 1789
Sylvester Douglas	16 Dec. 1793
George Damer, Viscount Milton	13 Dec. 1794
Thomas Pelham[9,15]	13 Mar. 1795
Robert Stewart, Viscount Castlereagh	3 Nov. 1798[16]
Charles Abbot[9]	25 May 1801
William Wickham	13 Feb. 1802
Sir Evan Nepean	6 Feb. 1804

	appointment
Nicholas Vansittart	23 Mar. 1805
Charles Long	21 Sept. 1805
William Elliot	28 Mar. 1806
Sir Arthur Wellesley	19 Apr. 1807
Robert Dundas	13 Apr. 1809
William Wellesley-Pole	18 Oct. 1809
Robert Peel	4 Aug. 1812
Charles Grant	3 Aug. 1818
Henry Goulburn	29 Dec. 1821
William Lamb	29 Apr. 1827
Lord Francis Leveson-Gower	21 June 1828
Sir Henry Hardinge	17 July 1830
Edward George Geoffrey Smith Stanley	29 Nov. 1830
Sir John Cam Hobhouse	29 Mar. 1833
Edward John Littleton	17 May 1833
Sir Henry Hardinge	16 Dec. 1834
George William Frederick Howard, Viscount Morpeth	22 Apr. 1835
Edward Granville Eliot, Lord Eliot	6 Sept. 1841
Sir Thomas Francis Fremantle	1 Feb. 1845
Henry Pelham Pelham-Clinton, earl of Lincoln	14 Feb. 1846
Henry Labouchere	6 July 1846
Sir William Meredyth Somerville	22 July 1847
Richard Southwell Bourke, Lord Naas	1 Mar. 1852
Sir John Young	6 Jan. 1853
Edward Horsman	1 Mar. 1855
Henry Arthur Herbert	27 May 1857
Lord Naas	4 Mar. 1858
Edward Cardwell	24 June 1859
Sir Robert Peel	29 July 1861
Chichester Samuel Parkinson-Fortescue	7 Dec. 1865
Lord Naas (6th earl of Mayo, 12 Aug. 1867)	10 July 1866
John Wilson-Patten	29 Sept. 1868
Chichester Samuel Parkinson-Fortescue	23 Dec. 1868
Spencer Compton Cavendish, marquis of Hartington	12 Jan. 1871
Sir Michael Edward Hicks Beach	27 Feb. 1874
James Lowther	15 Feb. 1878
William Edward Forster	30 Apr. 1880
Lord Frederick Charles Cavendish	6 May 1882[17]
George Otto Trevelyan	9 May 1882
Henry Campbell-Bannerman	23 Oct. 1884
Sir William Hart Dyke	25 June 1885
William Henry Smith	23 Jan. 1886
John Morley	6 Feb. 1886
Sir Michael Edward Hicks Beach	5 Aug. 1886
Arthur James Balfour	7 Mar. 1887
William Lawies Jackson	9 Nov. 1891
John Morley	22 Aug. 1892
Gerald William Balfour	4 July 1895

George Wyndham	9 Nov. 1900
Walter Hume Long[18]	12 Mar. 1905
James Bryce	14 Dec. 1905
Augustine Birrell[19]	29 Jan. 1907
Henry Edward Duke	3 Aug. 1916
Edward Shortt	4 May 1918
James Ian Macpherson	13 Jan. 1919
Sir Hamar Greenwood	12 Apr. 1920

[1] On returning to Ire. with Sidney, lord deputy, after an interval in which the administration was under lords justices (see above, p. 487).

[2] Tremayne to Cecil, 12 Apr. 1570 (P.R.O., State papers, Eliz. I–Geo. III, xxx, no. 42).

[3] *Report on the manuscripts of Lord de L'Isle and Dudley*, i (H.M.C., 1925), p. 355.

[4] As secretary to Fitzwilliam; he had served the previous term under Perrot, who, however, had dismissed and imprisoned him in Sept. 1586 (Williams to Burghley, 12 May 1587; *Cal. S.P. Ire.*, *1586-8*, p. 348).

[5] Hughes's list includes Sir George Radcliffe from 25 July 1633, but although Radcliffe had been Wentworth's secretary in England there is no evidence that he, or anyone else, held this office in Ire.

[6] Wyche was in London throughout his term of office; William Ellis was acting in his place in Dublin.

[7] Tyrrell was catholic bp of Clogher, was trs. to Meath on 14/24 Jan. 1689, and d. 1692.

[8] Aldworth was probably app. by the lords justices on 28 July 1693; he was continued in office by Capel, 27 May 1695 (Sainty, loc. cit., p. 17).

[9] Also secretary of state; see above, p. 527.

[10] Neither Addison nor the lord lieutenant (Sunderland) came to Ire.

[11] Delafaye had previously been second secretary. On the appointment of lords justices in 1715, Bladen and Delafaye were app. 'joint secretaries', and this arrangement appears to have continued on Townshend's becoming lord lieutenant in Feb. 1717.

[12] Died 22 June 1746.

[13] Res. 6 July 1767.

[14] Continued in office by Westmorland, 24 Oct. 1789.

[15] Continued in office by Cornwallis, 14 June 1798.

[16] Castlereagh had been app. temporarily, owing to Pelham's illness, on 29 Mar. 1798 (H. M. Hyde, *The rise of Castlereagh* (London, 1933), p. 209).

[17] Assassinated same day.

[18] Edward Carson held office for a day in succession to Wyndham, and was then relieved of it at his own request without a formal appointment being made (A. T. Q. Stewart, *Edward Carson* (Dublin, 1981), p. 62).

[19] Birrell res. as from 3 May 1916, and Herbert Samuel, home secretary, acted as chief secretary pending the appointment of a successor.

UNDER-SECRETARIES, 1777–1922

C. J. WOODS

Appointment of an under-secretary was not by letters patent or any other instrument, but was informal. In most cases the source of information is the number of the *Dublin Gazette* which followed the appointment. For the period 1777–1800 a definitive list exists in J. C. Sainty, 'The secretariat of the chief governors of Ireland, 1690–1800' in *R.I.A. Proc.*, lxxvii, sect. C, no. 1 (1977), pp 1–33. For the later period there is no comparable list, but information has been gleaned from proclamations bearing the signature of the under-secretary (*Dublin*

Gazette), and from the *Dublin Evening Post*. Also helpful, though not always reliable, is Joseph Haydn, *The book of dignities* (3rd ed., London, 1894), p. 563.

The title 'under-secretary' was in use before 1777 to denote the officials directly below the chief and second secretaries but little evidence exists for this period. In 1777 the post of second secretary was terminated and the chief secretary's office was reorganised into a civil and a military department, each headed by an under-secretary. The post of military under-secretary lapsed in 1819; its occupants are not listed here. The under-secretary in the civil department was from 1819 entitled simply 'under-secretary', and was responsible to the chief secretary for the routine working of the whole Irish administration. See Edith M. Johnston, *Great Britain and Ireland, 1760-1800: a study in political administration* (Edinburgh, 1963), pp 57-64, and R. B. McDowell, *The Irish administration, 1801-1914* (London, 1964), pp 62-5.

	appointment
Thomas Waite	June 1777
Sackville Hamilton	7 Feb. 1780[1]
Lodge Evans Morres	7 Feb. 1795
Sackville Hamilton	15 May 1795
Edward Cooke	6 June 1796[2]
Alexander Marsden	21 Oct. 1801
James Trail	8 Sept. 1806
Charles Saxton (succ. as bt, 11 Nov. 1808)	6 Sept. 1808
William Gregory	5 Oct. 1812
Lt-col. Sir William Gosset	1 Jan. 1831[3]
Thomas Drummond	25 July 1835[4]
Norman Hilton Macdonald	28 May 1840[5]
Edward Lucas	15 Sept. 1841[6]
Richard Pennefather	Aug. 1845[7]
Thomas Nicholas Redington (K.C.B., 28 Aug. 1849)	11 July 1846[8]
John Arthur Wynne	Mar. 1852[9]
Major Thomas Aiskew Larcom (major-gen., 1 Apr. 1858; K.C.B., 19 June 1860	Jan. 1853[10]
Sir Edward Robert Wetherall	1 Dec. 1868
Thomas Henry Burke	20 May 1869
Robert George Crookshank Hamilton	9 May 1882[11]
Major-gen. Sir Redvers Henry Buller	10 Dec. 1886
Col. Sir Joseph West Ridgeway	15 Oct. 1887
David Harrel (kt bach., 19 Jan. 1893)	12 Jan. 1893[12]
Sir Antony Patrick MacDonnell	8 Nov. 1902
Sir James Brown Dougherty	14 July 1908
Lt-col. Sir Matthew Nathan	12 Oct. 1914
Sir Robert Chalmers	6 May 1916
Sir William Patrick Byrne	23 Oct. 1916
James MacMahon	15 July 1918
Sir John Anderson[13]	28 May 1920

[1] Sainty, loc. cit., p. 16, has 7 Feb.; Haydn, op. cit., has 17 Feb.
[2] *D.G.* has 6 June; Sainty, ibid., has 5 June.
[3] Haydn, op. cit.

⁴ *D.G.* publishes proclamations signed by Gosset on 24 July and Drummond on 28 July. According to *D.E.P.* (28 July) Drummond dined with the lord lieutenant on 25 July. Haydn has 25 July.

⁵ *D.E.P.*, 2 June 1840.

⁶ Haydn. op. cit. But *D.E.P.* states (14 Sept.) 'we understand that Mr Lucas, having accepted the office, is now attending to his duties at the Castle'.

⁷ Haydn, op. cit., states 21 Aug. 1845. But *D.E.P.* reported him (9 Aug.) as about to vacate the chief clerkship for the under-secretaryship; on 16 Aug. it reported him as promoted; on 21 Aug. it published a letter from him as under-secretary dated 18 Aug.

⁸ Haydn, op. cit. On the same day *D.E.P.* reported 'Thomas N. Redington, M.P., under-secretary for Ireland, has arrived at the Gresham Hotel'.

⁹ The latest proclamation signed by Redington is dated 8 Mar., the earliest by Wynne 11 Mar. Haydn, op. cit., states Feb.

¹⁰ 'Major Larcom has received the appointment of under-secretary and, we believe, has already entered upon the duties of that office' (*D.E.P.*, 29 Jan. 1853).

¹¹ As acting under-secretary; app. permanently, 23 Apr. 1883.

¹² App. temporarily during Ridgeway's absence in Morocco; app. permanently, 12 Dec. 1893.

¹³ Additional under-secretary.

LORDS PRESIDENT OF MUNSTER AND CONNACHT, 1569–1672

LIAM IRWIN

Acts of the privy council of England, 1542–1631 (46 vols, London, 1890–1964); B.L., Egerton MS 2551, Harleian MS 697; *Calendar of the Carew manuscripts preserved in the archiepiscopal library at Lambeth, 1515–1624* (6 vols, London, 1867–73); *Calendar of patent and close rolls of chancery in Ireland, Elizabeth, 19 year to end of reign*, ed. James Morrin (Dublin, 1862); *Irish patent rolls of James I: facsimile of the Irish record commissioners' calendar prepared prior to 1830*, with foreword by M. C. Griffith (I.M.C., Dublin, 1966); *Cal. S.P. Ire.*; *Journal of the house of commons* [England], iv; [John Lodge (ed.)], *Desiderata curiosa Hibernica: or a select collection of state papers* (2 vols, Dublin, 1772); *Liber mun. pub. Hib.*

The system of effectively governing distant and difficult areas through the appointment of a lord president and council, which Thomas Cromwell had developed in England and Wales, was extended to Ireland by Sir Henry Sidney. Each of the three outlying Irish provinces was intended to be so governed, but despite its implementation in Connacht (1569) and Munster (1570) the proposal for Ulster was repeatedly deferred and ultimately abandoned. While subject to the chief governor, who appointed the provincial council, the lord president had full authority within his province. His commissions gave extensive powers, embracing civil, criminal, and ecclesiastical jurisdiction and the invocation of martial law. He commanded all forces in the province, appointed the large range of officials needed for his administration, and had freedom to develop the scope and character of the office. This facility was successfully used by the Munster presidents in the seventeenth century to further the social and economic development of the province. In the Tudor period English military men were invariably appointed and the martial dimension predominated. Under the Stuarts the conciliatory character of the system was developed, particularly through the courts' providing popular and impartial justice. Apart from an inevitable reversion to its military role in the 1640s this benign approach continued until the suppression of the system in 1672.

The dates of appointment shown are those of letters patent unless otherwise stated. The privy seal warrant for appointment often preceded the letters patent by weeks or months; hence, in some cases, the term of office appears to begin before the date of appointment.

LORDS PRESIDENT OF MUNSTER

	appointment	period of office
Sir John Perrot	13 Dec. 1570[1]	Mar. 1571–Sept. 1573[2]
Sir William Drury	20 June 1576	July 1576–Oct. 1579[3]
John Norris (kt 26 Apr. 1586)	24 June 1584	July 1584–Sept. 1597[4]
Sir Thomas Norris	3 Nov. 1597	Sept. 1597–Aug. 1599
Sir George Carew	6 Mar. 1600	April 1600–Sept. 1603
Sir Henry Brouncker	4 June 1604	July 1604–June 1607
Henry Danvers, 1st Baron Danvers of Dantsey	12 Jan. 1608	Jan. 1608–Mar. 1615[5]
Donnchadh (Donough) O'Brien, 4th earl of Thomond	6 May 1615	Mar. 1615–Sept. 1624
Sir Edward Villiers	27 May 1625[6]	Aug. 1625–Sept. 1626
Sir William St Leger	14 Apr. 1627	Mar. 1627–July 1642
[Jerome Weston, 2nd earl of Portland]	1 Mar. 1644 (royalist)[7]	
Murrough O'Brien, 6th Baron Inchiquin	Jan. 1645 (parliamentarian) 1649 (royalist)	Jan. 1645–Apr. 1648[8]
Henry Ireton	Jan. 1650[9]	Jan. 1650–Nov. 1651
Roger Boyle (cr. earl of Orrery, 5 Sept. 1660)	10 Oct. 1660	Mar. 1663–Aug. 1672[10]

LORDS PRESIDENT OF CONNACHT

	appointment	period of office
Sir Edward Fitton	1 June 1569	Dec. 1569–27 Sept. 1575
Sir Nicholas Malby	31 Mar. 1579	May 1579–d. 4 Mar. 1584
Sir Richard Bingham	Mar. 1584	Mar. 1584–Sept. 1596[11]
Sir Conyers Clifford	4 Sept. 1597[12]	Sept. 1597–d. 5 Aug. 1599
Ricard Burke, 4th earl of Clanricard	1 Sept. 1604	Sept. 1604– ?Sept. 1616
Sir Charles Wilmot (cr. Viscount Wilmot of Athlone, 4 Jan. 1621)	20 Sept. 1616[13]	Sept. 1616–Aug. 1630
Viscount Wilmot Roger Jones, 1st Viscount Ranelagh	} 11 Sept. 1630	Sept. 1630–Apr. 1644

	appointment	*period of office*
Henry Wilmot, 2nd Viscount Wilmot Thomas Dillon, 4th Viscount Dillon	Apr. 1644 (royalist)	Apr. 1644–June 1651[14]
Sir Charles Coote	12 May 1645 (parliamentarian)	May 1645–July 1660[15]
Sir Charles Coote (cr. earl of Mountrath, 6 Sept. 1660)	30 July 1660	July 1660–Dec. 1661
John Berkeley, 1st Baron Berkeley of Stratton	13 Jan. 1662	Jan. 1662–Mar. 1666[16]
Lord Berkeley John King, 1st Baron Kingston	2 Apr. 1666	Apr. 1666–Aug. 1672

[1] Date of privy seal warrant.

[2] On Perrot's resignation, Sept. 1573, Munster was ruled by commrs until July 1576.

[3] Officially in office until his death, Oct. 1579, but from Sept. 1578 he was J. and absent from the province.

[4] Norris remained in England for most of his term of office; his brother Thomas, app. vice-president Dec. 1585, acted in his place.

[5] Sir Richard Moryson app. vice-president Apr. 1609 on Danvers's departure.

[6] Named as president Jan. 1625; confirmed by Charles I, 6 May 1625.

[7] Never took up office; unsuccessfully petitioned for the presidency again after the restoration.

[8] Vice-president under St Leger; joint commr. for civil government and sole commr for army, July 1642–Mar. 1644. Joined parliamentary side on being refused presidency by the king, but reverted to royalist side in 1648 and was named as president by Charles II in 1649; cr. earl of Inchiquin, 21 Oct. 1654.

[9] App. by parliament, 4 Jan. 1650 (*Commons' jn.*, vi, 343).

[10] App. president by interim council of state in England, May 1660. From his return to Ire. on 31 Dec. 1660 until Mar. 1663 he remained in Dublin as lord justice, preparing the land settlement.

[11] Suspended from office, Sept. 1596, owing to his unauthorised departure for England (*D.N.B.*).

[12] Date of privy seal warrant.

[13] Granted new patent 16 Apr. 1625, in context of charges of misconduct made by Sir Charles Coote in 1621.

[14] Dillon surrendered to Coote, the parliamentary president, on 18 June 1651. In 1662 he formally resigned the presidency to Charles II.

[15] Coote is referred to as lord president on 4 Aug. 1656 in commonwealth state accounts (*Anal. Hib.*, xv (1944), p. 305), despite the official abandonment of the presidency system.

[16] Berkeley never performed his duties as president. The 1666 arrangement with Kingston was to remedy this: Berkeley retained all the financial benefits of the office, while Kingston received a reversion of it solely to himself on Berkeley's death.

SPEAKERS OF THE IRISH HOUSE OF COMMONS
c. 1415/16–1800

C. J. WOODS

This list is based on one compiled by C. L. Falkiner and published in his 'The parliament of Ireland under the Tudor sovereigns: with some notices of the speakers of the Irish house of commons' in *R.I.A. Proc.*, xxv, sect. C, no. 10 (1905), pp 533–4, and, after revision, republished in 'Irish parliamentary antiquities' in his posthumous *Essays relating to Ireland, biographical, historical and topographical*, ed. Edward Dowden (London, 1909), pp 223-4. Further information, including the exact dates of election, has been obtained for the period up to 1450 from H. G. Richardson and G. O. Sayles, *The Irish parliament in the middle ages* (Philadelphia, 1952), for the period 1560-1613 from T. W. Moody, 'The Irish parliament under Elizabeth and James I: a general survey' in *R.I.A. Proc.*, xlv, sect. C, no. 6 (1939), pp 41-81, and for the period 1634-1800 from *Commons' jn. Ire.* The exact dates of election of some of the early speakers have merely been inferred from the dates of the meeting of parliament (see below, pp 599-600).

speaker	*date of election*
Maurice Stafford[1]	*fl.* 1415 or 1416
Robert Plunket[2]	6 July (?) 1442
James Alleyn[3]	26 June 1444
John Chever[4]	28 Feb. 1449
John Chever[5]	24 Apr. (?) 1450
Sir Thomas Cusake	13 June (?) 1541
James Stanihurst	1 June (?) 1557
	11 or 12 Jan. (?) 1560
	17 Jan. 1569
Sir Nicholas Walsh	26 Apr. 1585
Sir John Davies	18 May 1613
Sir Nathaniel Catelyn	15 July 1634
Sir Maurice Eustace	16 Mar. 1639/40
Sir Audley Mervyn	8 May 1661
Sir Richard Nagle	7 May 1689[6]
Sir Richard Levinge	5 Oct. 1692
Robert Rochfort	27 Aug. 1695
Alan Brodrick	21 Sept. 1703
Hon. John Forster	19 May 1710
Alan Brodrick	25 Nov. 1713
William Conolly	12 Nov. 1715
	28 Nov. 1727
Sir Ralph Gore	13 Oct. 1729
Henry Boyle	4 Oct. 1733
John Ponsonby	26 Apr. 1756
	22 Oct. 1761
	17 Oct. 1769
Edmund Sexton Pery	7 Mar. 1771
	18 June 1776
	14 Oct. 1783
John Foster	5 Sept. 1785
	9 July 1790
	9 Jan. 1798

[1] Richardson & Sayles, *Ir. parl. in middle ages*, pp 159-60, 350-51. Speaker of a great council.
[2] Ibid., pp 185, 354. Speaker of a great council.
[3] Ibid., pp 189, 354. Speaker of an afforced council.
[4] Ibid., pp 191, 318-20, 355.   [5] Ibid., pp 318, 355.
[6] *The journal of the proceedings of the parliament in Ireland* (London, 1689), p. 3.

PRIME MINISTERS AND SECRETARIES OF STATE OF THE UNITED KINGDOM

PRIME MINISTERS FROM 1730

H.B.C., pp 107–110.

Footnote references are given where dates differ from those in the *H.B.C.* list. After 1957 the dates given are those of kissing hands, as recorded in the 'Court circular' in *The Times*.

In all cases a prime minister in office at the death of a monarch was continued in office under the successor.

	appointment
Sir Robert Walpole	15 May 1730
Spencer Compton, 1st earl of Wilmington	16 Feb. 1742
Henry Pelham	27 Aug. 1743
Thomas Pelham-Holles, 4th duke of Newcastle-upon-Tyne (cr. duke of Newcastle-under-Line, 17 Nov. 1756)	16 Mar. 1754
William Cavendish, 4th duke of Devonshire	16 Nov. 1756
Duke of Newcastle	2 July 1757
John Stuart, 3rd earl of Bute	26 May 1762
George Grenville	16 Apr. 1763
Charles Watson-Wentworth, 2nd marquis of Rockingham	13 July 1765
William Pitt (cr. earl of Chatham, 4 Aug. 1766)	30 July 1766
Augustus Henry Fitzroy, 3rd duke of Grafton	14 Oct. 1768
Frederick North, styled Lord North	28 Jan. 1770
Marquis of Rockingham	28 Mar. 1782
William Petty, 3rd earl of Shelburne	4 July 1782
William Henry Cavendish Cavendish-Bentinck, 3rd duke of Portland	2 Apr. 1783
William Pitt	19 Dec. 1783
Henry Addington	17 Mar. 1801
William Pitt	10 May 1804
William Wyndham Grenville, 1st Baron Grenville	11 Feb. 1806
Duke of Portland	31 Mar. 1807
Spencer Perceval	4 Oct. 1809[1]
Robert Banks Jenkinson, 2nd earl of Liverpool	8 June 1812
George Canning	10 Apr. 1827
Frederick John Robinson, 1st Viscount Goderich	31 Aug. 1827
Arthur Wellesley, 1st duke of Wellington	22 Jan. 1828
Charles Grey, 2nd Earl Grey	22 Nov. 1830
William Lamb, 2nd Viscount Melbourne	16 July 1834
Duke of Wellington	17 Nov. 1834
Sir Robert Peel	10 Dec. 1834
Viscount Melbourne	18 Apr. 1835

appointment

Sir Robert Peel	30 Aug. 1841
Lord John Russell (cr. Earl Russell, 30 July 1861)	30 June 1846
Edward George Geoffrey Smith Stanley, 14th earl of Derby	23 Feb. 1852
George Hamilton-Gordon, 4th earl of Aberdeen	19 Dec. 1852
Henry John Temple, 3rd Viscount Palmerston	6 Feb. 1855
Earl of Derby	26 Feb. 1858[2]
Viscount Palmerston	12 June 1859
Earl Russell	29 Oct. 1865
Earl of Derby	28 June 1866
Benjamin Disraeli	27 Feb. 1868
William Ewart Gladstone	3 Dec. 1868
Benjamin Disraeli (cr. earl of Beaconsfield, 21 Aug. 1876)	20 Feb. 1874
William Ewart Gladstone	23 Apr. 1880
Robert Arthur Talbot Gascoyne-Cecil, 3rd marquis of Salisbury	23 June 1885
William Ewart Gladstone	1 Feb. 1886
Marquis of Salisbury	25 July 1886
William Ewart Gladstone	15 Aug. 1892
Archibald Philip Primrose, 5th earl of Rosebery	5 Mar. 1894
Marquis of Salisbury	25 June 1895
Arthur James Balfour	12 July 1902
Sir Henry Campbell-Bannerman	5 Dec. 1905
Herbert Henry Asquith	8 Apr. 1908[3]
David Lloyd George	7 Dec. 1916
Andrew Bonar Law	23 Oct. 1922
Stanley Baldwin	22 May 1923
James Ramsay MacDonald	22 Jan. 1924
Stanley Baldwin	4 Nov. 1924
James Ramsay MacDonald	5 June 1929
Stanley Baldwin	7 June 1935
Arthur Neville Chamberlain	28 May 1937
Winston Leonard Spencer Churchill	10 May 1940
Clement Richard Attlee	26 July 1945
Winston Leonard Spencer Churchill (K.G., 24 Apr. 1953)	26 Oct. 1951
Sir Robert Anthony Eden	6 Apr. 1955
Maurice Harold Macmillan	10 Jan. 1957
Alexander Frederick Douglas-Home, 14th earl of Home[4]	19 Oct. 1963
James Harold Wilson	16 Oct. 1964
Edward Richard George Heath	19 June 1970
James Harold Wilson	4 Mar. 1974
Leonard James Callaghan	5 Apr. 1976
Margaret Hilda Thatcher	4 May 1979

[1] Assassinated, 11 May 1812.

[2] Kissed hands; *The Times*, 27 Feb. 1858.

[3] Kissed hands at Biarritz; *The Times*, 9 Apr. 1908.

[4] Disclaimed title for life, 23 Oct. 1963; as P.M., known by his knighthood (Order of the Thistle, 1962).

SECRETARIES OF STATE FOR THE HOME
DEPARTMENT FROM 1782

H.B.C., pp 115–16.

Footnote references are given where dates differ from those in the *H.B.C.* After 1957 the dates are those of kissing hands, as recorded in the 'Court circular' in *The Times*.

The secretary of state for the home department, as minister with general responsibility for the internal government of Britain and all British possessions, was the constitutional superior of the lord lieutenant and chief secretary. From 1922 till 1972 the home secretary acted as the medium of communication between the governments of the United Kingdom and Northern Ireland. A secretaryship of state for Northern Ireland was instituted in 1972 (see below, p. 546).

	appointment
William Petty, 3rd earl of Shelburne and 2nd Baron Wycombe	27 Mar. 1782
Thomas Townshend (cr. Baron Sydney of Chislehurst, 6 Mar. 1783)	10 July 1782
Frederick North, styled Lord North	2 Apr. 1783
George Nugent-Temple-Grenville, 3rd Earl Temple	19 Dec. 1783
Lord Sydney	23 Dec. 1783
William Wyndham Grenville (cr. Baron Grenville, 25 Nov. 1790)	5 June 1789
Henry Dundas	8 June 1791
William Henry Cavendish Cavendish-Bentinck, 3rd duke of Portland	11 July 1794
Thomas Pelham, 3rd Baron Pelham of Stanmer	30 July 1801
Charles Philip Yorke	17 Aug. 1803
Robert Banks Jenkinson, 2nd Baron Hawkesbury	12 May 1804
George John Spencer, 2nd Earl Spencer	5 Feb. 1806
Lord Hawkesbury	25 Mar. 1807
Richard Ryder	1 Nov. 1809
Henry Addington, 1st Viscount Sidmouth	11 June 1812
Robert Peel	17 Jan. 1822
William Sturges-Bourne	30 Apr. 1827
Henry Petty-Fitzmaurice, 3rd marquis of Landsdowne	16 July 1827
Robert Peel	26 Jan. 1828
William Lamb, 2nd Viscount Melbourne	22 Nov. 1830
John William Ponsonby (cr. Baron Duncannon, 19 July 1834)	19 July 1834
Henry Goulburn	15 Dec. 1834
Lord John Russell	18 Apr. 1835
Constantine Henry Phipps, 1st marquis of Normanby	30 Aug. 1839
Sir James Robert George Graham, bt	3 Sept. 1841[1]
Sir George Grey, bt	6 July 1846
Spencer Horatio Walpole	27 Feb. 1852
Henry John Temple, 3rd Viscount Palmerston	28 Dec. 1852
Sir George Grey	?8 Feb. 1855[2]

appointment

Spencer Horatio Walpole	26 Feb. 1858
Thomas Henry Sutton Sotheron Estcourt	3 Mar. 1859
Sir George Cornewall Lewis, bt	18 June 1859
Sir George Grey	25 July 1861
Spencer Horatio Walpole	6 July 1866
Gathorne Hardy	17 May 1867
Henry Austin Bruce	9 Dec. 1868
Robert Lowe	9 Aug. 1873
Richard Assheton Cross (G.C.B., 20 Apr. 1880)	21 Feb. 1874
Sir William George Granville Venables Vernon Harcourt	28 Apr. 1880
Sir Richard Assheton Cross	24 June 1885
Hugh Culling Eardley Childers	6 Feb. 1886
Henry Matthews	3 Aug. 1886
Herbert Henry Asquith	18 Aug. 1892
Sir Matthew White Ridley	29 June 1895
Charles Thomson Ritchie	12 Nov. 1900
Aretas Akers-Douglas	11 Aug. 1902[3]
Herbert John Gladstone	11 Dec. 1905
Winston Leonard Spencer Churchill	19 Feb. 1910
Reginald McKenna	24 Oct. 1911
Sir John Allsebrook Simon	27 May 1915
Herbert Louis Samuel	12 Jan. 1916
Sir George Cave	11 Dec. 1916
Edward Shortt	14 Jan. 1919
William Clive Bridgeman	25 Oct. 1922
Arthur Henderson	23 Jan. 1924
Sir William Joynson-Hicks	7 Nov. 1924
John Robert Clynes	8 June 1929
Sir Herbert Louis Samuel[4]	26 Aug. 1931
Sir John Gilmour	1 Oct. 1932
Sir John Allsebrook Simon	7 June 1935
Sir Samuel John Gurney Hoare, bt	28 May 1937
Sir John Anderson	4 Sept. 1939
Herbert Stanley Morrison	4 Oct. 1940
Sir Donald Bradley Somervell	28 May 1945
James Chuter Ede	3 Aug. 1945
Sir David Patrick Maxwell Fyfe	27 Oct. 1951
Gwilym Lloyd George	19 Oct. 1954
Richard Austen Butler	14 Jan. 1957
Henry Brooke	16 July 1962
Sir Frank Soskice	19 Oct. 1964
Roy Harris Jenkins	23 Dec. 1965
Leonard James Callaghan	29 Nov. 1967
Reginald Maudling	22 June 1970
Leonard Robert Carr	19 July 1972
Roy Harris Jenkins	5 Mar. 1974
Merlyn Rees	15 Sept. 1976
William Stephen Ian Whitelaw	7 May 1979[5]

[1] *The Times*, 4 Sept. 1841.

[2] Grey attended the privy council on this day when other ministers were appointed, and it is almost certain that he was; he is reported as having acted as home secretary on 9 Feb. (*The Times*, 10 Feb.).

[3] *The Times*, 12 Aug. 1902.

[4] Samuel had received the G.B.E. in 1920 and the G.C.B. in 1926.

[5] Information kindly supplied by House of Commons library.

SECRETARIES OF STATE FOR THE COLONIES, 1921–5, FOR DOMINION AFFAIRS, 1925–47, AND FOR COMMONWEALTH RELATIONS, 1947–50

H.B.C., pp 119–20.

After the conclusion of the Anglo-Irish treaty in December 1921, relations with the provisional government in Dublin, and later with the Irish Free State, were the responsibility of the colonial secretary. On 1 July 1925 the office of secretary of state for dominion affairs was created by executive act, with responsibility for 'the autonomous communities within the empire', including the Irish Free State. On 3 July 1947 the title of the office was changed to 'secretary of state for commonwealth relations'. Ireland ceased to belong to the commonwealth on 18 April 1949.

	appointment
Winston Leonard Spencer Churchill	14 Feb. 1921
Victor Christian William Cavendish, 9th duke of Devonshire	25 Oct. 1922
James Henry Thomas	23 Jan. 1924
Leopold Charles Maurice Stennett Amery	7 Nov. 1924[1]
Sidney James Webb (cr. Baron Passfield, 22 June 1929)	8 June 1929[2]
James Henry Thomas	13 June 1930[3]
Malcolm MacDonald	27 Nov. 1935
Edward Montagu Cavendish Stanley, Lord Stanley	16 May 1938
Malcolm MacDonald	4 Nov. 1938[4]
Sir Thomas Walker Hobart Inskip (cr. Viscount Caldecote, 6 Sept. 1939)	2 Feb. 1939
Robert Anthony Eden	4 Sept. 1939
Viscount Caldecote	15 May 1940
Robert Arthur James Gascoyne-Cecil, Viscount Cranborne[5]	4 Oct. 1940
Clement Richard Attlee[6]	23 Feb. 1942
Viscount Cranborne[5]	28 Sept. 1943
Christopher Addison, Viscount Addison	3 Aug. 1945
Philip John Noel-Baker	14 Oct. 1947[7]

[1] As colonial secretary; also secretary of state for dominion affairs from 1 July 1925.

[2] As colonial secretary and secretary of state for dominion affairs; remained colonial secretary until Aug. 1931.

[3] As secretary of state for dominion affairs; also colonial secretary from 26 Aug. 1931.

[4] As secretary of state for dominion affairs; he had been colonial secretary from 16 May 1938 and continued to hold both offices.

[5] Summoned to parliament as Lord Cecil of Essendon, 1941.

[6] Also deputy prime minister.

[7] Held office until Mar. 1950.

HEADS OF STATE AND HEADS OF GOVERNMENT IN IRELAND FROM 1922

GOVERNORS GENERAL OF THE IRISH FREE STATE, 1922-37

H.B.C., p. 168.

The office of governor general was established by the Irish Free State Constitution Act, 1922 (session 2) (15 Geo. V, c. 1 [U.K.]) and abrogated on 11 Dec. 1936 by the Constitution (Amendment no. 27) Act, 1936 (57/1936 [I.F.S.]), confirmed on 8 June 1937 by the Executive Powers (Consequential Provisions) Act, 1937 (20/1937 [I.F.S.]).

	appointment	*swearing-in*
Timothy Michael Healy	6 Dec. 1922	6 Dec. 1922
James McNeill	15 Dec. 1927	1 Feb. 1928[1]
Domhnall Ua Buachalla (Donal Buckley)	26 Nov. 1932	26 Nov. 1932

[1] Dismissed 1 Nov. 1932.

PRESIDENTS OF IRELAND FROM 1938

H.B.C., p. 168; *Irish Times*.

The office of president was established by article 10 of the constitution of Ireland, which became operative on 29 Dec. 1937. Tenure of the office is for seven years, and the outgoing president is eligible for re-election for a second term.

	election	*installation*
Douglas Hyde	4 May 1938	25 June 1938
Seán Thomas O'Kelly	18 June 1945[1]	25 June 1945
Eamon de Valera	19 June 1959[2]	25 June 1959
Erskine Hamilton Childers[3]	31 May 1973	25 June 1973
Cearbhall Ó Dálaigh[4]	3 Dec. 1974	19 Dec. 1974
Patrick John Hillery	9 Nov. 1976	3 Dec. 1976

[1] Re-elected, 16 May 1952. [2] Re-elected, 1 June 1966.
[3] Died, 17 Nov. 1974. [4] Resigned, 22 Oct. 1976.

HEADS OF IRISH GOVERNMENT, 1919-22

Except in the case of Cosgrave (see note 5 below), appointment was by the vote of Dáil Éireann. After de Valera's resignation, the office of chairman of the provisional government was of greater practical importance than the presidency of Dáil Éireann.

	appointment
Cathal Brugha, president of the ministry *pro tem.*[1]	22 Jan. 1919
Eamon de Valera, president of Dáil Éireann[2]	1 Apr. 1919
Arthur Griffith, president of Dáil Éireann[3]	10 Jan. 1922
Michael Collins, chairman of provisional government[4]	14 Jan. 1922
William Thomas Cosgrave, chairman of provisional government	25 Aug. 1922[5]

[1] Brugha is so described in the dáil proceedings at the time of his election. At his resignation on 1 Apr. he is described as *priomh-aire*; de Valera on election was given the same title, and described as English as 'president of dáil'.

[2] Resigned, 9 Jan. 1922.

[3] On 17 June 1919 the dáil ratified the appointment of Griffith as 'deputy president' during de Valera's absence in America; Griffith is referred to in subsequent dáil proceedings as 'acting president'. He died on 12 Aug. 1922.

[4] Killed, 22 Aug. 1922.

[5] Cosgrave was appointed chairman at the meeting of the provisional government on 25 Aug., and again, more formally, in a resolution dealing with the general reallocation of ministerial posts, adopted at the meeting of 30 Aug. (State Paper Office of Ireland, Dublin Castle; minutes of provisional government G1/3, P.G. 100, 104). Cosgrave had often previously been acting chairman in Collins's absence and was acting president of Dáil Éireann after Griffith's death; he was elected president by the third dáil at its assembly on 9 Sept. 1922.

PRIME MINISTERS OF THE IRISH FREE STATE AND ITS SUCCESSORS FROM 1922

Under the constitution of the Irish Free State the president of the executive council was appointed by the governor general on the nomination of the dáil; similarly, under the constitution of Ireland the taoiseach is appointed by the president after election by the dáil.

	appointment
William Thomas Cosgrave, president of executive council	6 Dec. 1922
Eamon de Valera, president of executive council[1]	9 Mar. 1932
John Aloysius Costello, taoiseach	18 Feb. 1948
Eamon de Valera, taoiseach	13 June 1951
John Aloysius Costello, taoiseach	2 June 1954
Eamon de Valera, taoiseach	20 Mar. 1957
Seán Lemass, taoiseach[2]	23 June 1959
John Mary Lynch, taoiseach	10 Nov. 1966
Liam Cosgrave, taoiseach	14 Mar. 1973
John Mary Lynch, taoiseach[3]	5 July 1977

	appointment
Charles James Haughey, taoiseach	11 Dec. 1979
Garret FitzGerald, taoiseach	30 June 1981
Charles James Haughey, taoiseach	9 Mar. 1982
Garret FitzGerald, taoiseach	14 Dec. 1982

[1] Taoiseach as from 29 Dec. 1937, when the constitution of Ireland came into operation.
[2] Resigned, 10 Nov. 1966.
[3] Resigned, 11 Dec. 1979.

GOVERNORS OF NORTHERN IRELAND, 1922-73

Belfast Gazette.

The office of governor of Northern Ireland was abolished on 18 July 1973 under the Northern Ireland Constitution Act, 1973, c. 36, s. 32, § 1.

	appointment	swearing-in
James Albert Edward Hamilton, 3rd duke of Abercorn	11 Dec. 1922	12 Dec. 1922
William Spencer Leveson Gower, 4th Earl Granville	7 Sept. 1945	7 Sept. 1945
John de Vere Loder, 2nd Baron Wakehurst	1 Dec. 1952	3 Dec. 1952
John Maxwell Erskine, 1st Baron Erskine of Rerrick	1 Dec. 1964	3 Dec. 1964
Ralph Francis Alnwick Grey, Baron Grey of Naunton	2 Dec. 1968	3 Dec. 1968

PRIME MINISTERS OF NORTHERN IRELAND, 1921-72, AND CHIEF EXECUTIVE OF NORTHERN IRELAND, 1974

The prime minister was formally appointed by the governor general, and official announcement was made in the next number of the *Belfast Gazette*.

	appointment
Sir James Craig (cr. Viscount Craigavon, 20 Jan. 1927)	7 June 1921[1]
John Miller Andrews	25 Nov. 1940
Sir Basil Stanlake Brooke (cr. Viscount Brookeborough, 4 July 1952)	1 May 1943
Terence Marne O'Neill	25 Mar. 1963
James Dawson Chichester-Clark	1 May 1969
Arthur Brian Deane Faulkner[2]	23 Mar. 1971
Arthur Brian Deane Faulkner, chief executive[3]	1 Jan. 1974

[1] Under 10 & 11 Geo. V, c. 67, sect. 8, the lord lieutenant established various departments including that of the prime minister, which was officially notified in the *Belfast Gazette*, 7 June 1921. Craig was named as prime minister. See also *Belfast News Letter*, 7 and 8 June 1921.

[2] Suspended 24 Mar. 1972. Under the Northern Ireland (Temporary Provisions) Act, 1972 (c. 22), enacted on 30 Mar. 1972, the office of prime minister was abolished.

[3] On 22 November 1973 William Whitelaw, then secretary of state for Northern Ireland, announced in the house of commons the formation of a power-sharing government, with Faulkner as chief executive. On 1 Jan. 1974 the government took up the powers devolved to it under part II of the Northern Ireland Constitution Act, 1973 (c. 36). Faulkner resigned on 28 May 1974, and on 17 July 1974 the Northern Ireland Act, 1974 (c. 28), provided for the discharge of all executive functions under the secretary of state.

SECRETARIES OF STATE FOR NORTHERN IRELAND FROM 1972

The date of effective appointment is given in the left-hand column, and that of kissing hands, as given in the 'Court circular' in *The Times*, is shown on the right.

William Stephen Ian Whitelaw	24 Mar. 1972	30 Mar. 1972
Francis Leslie Pym	2 Dec. 1973	3 Dec. 1973
Merlyn Rees	5 Mar. 1974	6 Mar. 1974
Roy Mason	10 Sept. 1976	15 Sept. 1976
Humphrey Edward Atkins	5 May 1979	7 May 1979[1]
James Michael Leathes Prior	14 Sept. 1981	23 Sept. 1981

[1] Information kindly supplied by House of Commons library.

MAYORS AND LORD MAYORS OF
DUBLIN FROM 1229

JACQUELINE HILL

This list is based upon the two most comprehensive lists previously published: that compiled by Patrick Meehan and published in Dublin corporation's *Diary for the year ending 30 June 1932*, pp 46-66, giving mayors and lord mayors for almost all years between 1229 and 1931; and that in *Dublin Corporation Yearbook, 1978*, pp 42-3, giving lord mayors for 1932-77. Meehan's list, in turn, was largely based upon Henry F. Berry, 'Catalogue of the mayors, provosts, and bailiffs of Dublin city, A.D. 1229 to 1447' in *R.I.A. Proc.*, xxviii, sect. C, no. 2 (1910), pp 47-61, and upon *Calendar of ancient records of Dublin, in the possession of the municipal corporation . . .*, ed. Sir J. T. Gilbert and Lady Gilbert (19 vols, Dublin, 1889-1944) (referred to below as *Anc. rec. Dublin*). Amendments and additions to these lists have been indicated by footnotes. Thanks are due to Dr A. J. Otway-Ruthven, who supplied many amendments to Berry's list; and to Councillor James Mitchell (lord mayor 1976-7), Mr James Molloy, city manager, Mr John Lalor, public relations officer, and the muniments department, City Hall, Dublin, for their assistance.

A number of surnames in this list appear to be variants of the same name, and in many cases may refer to the same person or family. The spellings here printed are those given by Berry and Gilbert, neither of whom investigated the problems involved, though Berry was aware of them. The following is a concordance of these presumed variants.

Cromp	Crompe		Newbery	Newberry	Newebery
Crompe	Cromp		Newberry	Newbery	Newebery
FitzSimon	FitzSymon		Newebery	Newberry	Newbery
FitzSymon	FitzSimon		Oeyn	Owain	Owen
Fian	Fiand	Fyane	Owain	Oeyn	Owen
Fiand	Fian	Fyane	Owen	Oeyn	Owain
Fyane	Fian	Fiand	Seriaunt	le Seriaunt	
Gaydon	Geydoun		Stackbold	Stakebold	
Geydoun	Gaydon		Stakebold	Stackbold	
la Ware	le Warre		Tanner	le Tanner	
le Seriaunt	Seriaunt		Tirrell	Tyrrell	Tyrell
le Tanner	Tanner		Tyrell	Tyrrell	Tirrell
le Warre	la Ware		Tyrrell	Tyrell	Tirrell

Variant spellings, supplied by Berry, Gilbert, and other sources, of a few individual mayors are shown in parentheses. 'Sampson' in 'David (Sampson) de Callan' (mayor, 1277-9) is the family name of the de Callans, as noted by Berry.

(A) 1229-1447

On 15/18 June 1229 Henry III issued a charter empowering 'the citizens' of Dublin to elect a mayor annually, to hold office for one year; it seems most likely that up to 1760 the exercise of this right was always confined to the council of aldermen, membership of which was restricted to members of the city guilds. During this period both election and inauguration appear to have taken place at Michaelmas, on St Michael's day, 29 September.[1]

mayors	term of office	
Richard Muton (Multon, Motoun)	1229-30	
Henry de Exeter	c. 1230-31	
Thomas de la Corner	c. 1231-2	
Robert Pollard	c. 1232-3	
Gilbert de Lyvet (del Ivet)	c. 1233-4	
Roger Owain	c. 1234-5	
Gilbert de Lyvet	c. 1235-7	re-elected 1236
Elias Burel (Burell)	c. 1237-8	
Robert Pollard	1238- ?1240	?re-elected 1239
Edward Palmer[2]	c. 1239-40	
Henry de Exeter	c. 1240-41	
William Flamstede	c. 1241-2	
John le Warre	c. 1242-3	
Philip de Dureham[3]	c. 1243-4	
John le Warre[4]	c. 1244-5	
Roger Owen[4]	c. 1245-6	
John le Warre	1246-c. 1249	re-elected 1247, 1248
Roger Oeyn	c. 1249-50	
Elias Burel	c. 1250-52	re-elected 1251
John le Warre	c. 1252-6[5]	re-elected 1253, 1254, 1255
Richard Olof	1256-7	
Sir John la Ware	c. 1257-8	
Peter Abraham	c. 1258-9	
Elias Burel	c. 1259-60	
Thomas de Winchester	1260-61	
Roger de Asshebourne	1261-3	re-elected 1262
Thomas de Winchester	c. 1263-4	
Vincent Taverner	1264-5	
Thomas de Winchester	c. 1265-7	?re-elected 1266
Vincent Taverner	1267-8	
Roger Asshebourne	c. 1268-9	
Vincent Taverner	c. 1269-70	
Thomas de Winchester	c. 1270-71	
William de Bristol	c. 1271-2	
John Garget	1272-5	re-elected 1273, 1274

(City in king's hands 1275-6)

mayors	*term of office*	
Walter Unred	*c.* 1276–7	
David (Sampson) de Callan	1277–9	re-elected 1278
Henry le Mareschall	1279–80	
David de Callan	1280–83[6]	re-elected 1281, 1282
Walter Unred	1283–6	re-elected 1284, 1285
Thomas de Coventry	1286–8	re-elected 1287
William de Bristol	1288–92[7]	re-elected 1289, 1290, 1291
Robert de Bray	1292–4	re-elected 1293
John le Seriaunt	1294–5	
Robert de Wyleby	1295–6	
Thomas Colys	1296–9[8]	re-elected ?1297, 1298
John le Seriaunt	*c.* 1299–1301	re-elected 1300

(City in king's hands, 1301–2)

John le Decer	1302–3	
Geoffrey de Morton	1303–4	
John le Seriaunt	1304–5	
John le Decer	*c.* 1305–6	
John le Seriaunt	1306–7	
John le Decer	1307–9	re-elected 1308

(City in king's hands to Dec. 1309)

Robert de Nottingham	1309–10[9]	
John Seriaunt	1310–11	
Richard Lawles	1311–14	re-elected 1312, 1313
Robert de Nottingham	1314–15	
Richard Lawles	1315–16	
Robert de Nottingham	1316–19	re-elected 1317, 1318
Robert de Moenes	1319–20	
Robert de Nottingham	1320–22	re-elected 1321
William Douce	1322–4	re-elected 1323
John le Decer	1324–6[10]	re-elected 1325
Robert le Tanner	1326–7	
William le Mareschal	1327–8	
Robert Tanner	1328–9[11]	
Philip Cradok	1329–30[11]	
William Douce	1330–31	
John de Moenes	1331–2	
William Beydyn (Beydin, Geydyn)	1332–3[12]	
Geoffrey Cromp	1333–4	
William Beydin	1334–5	
John de Moenes	1335–6	
Philip Cradok	1336–7	
John de Moenes	1337–8	
Robert le Tanner	1338–9	
Kenewrek Scherman	1339–41	re-elected 1340
John le Seriaunt	1341–7	re-elected 1342, 1343, 1344, 1345, 1346

mayors	*term of office*	
Geoffrey Crompe	1347–8	
Kenewrek Scherman	1348–9	
Geoffrey Crompe	1349–50	
John Seriaunt	1349–50	
John Bathe	1350–51	
Robert de Moenes	1351–2	
Adam Louestoc	1352–3	
John Seriaunt	1353–6	re-elected 1354, 1355
Robert Burnell	1356–7	
Peter Barfot	1357–8	
John Taylor	1358–9	
Peter Barfot	1359–61	re-elected 1360
Richard Heygrewe	1361–2	
John Beke	1362–4	re-elected 1363
David Tyrrell	1364–5	
Richard Heygrewe	1365–6	
David Tyrrell	1366–7	
Peter Woder	1367–8	
John Wydon	1368–9	
John Passavaunt	1369–71	re-elected 1370
John Wydon	1371–4	re-elected 1372, 1373
Nicholas Seriaunt	1374–5	
Edmund Berle	1375–6[13]	
Nicholas Seriaunt	1376–8	re-elected 1377
Robert Stakebold	1378–9	
John Wydon	1379–80	
John Hull	1380–82	re-elected 1381
Edmond Berle	1382–3	
Robert Burnel	1383–4	
Roger Bekeford	1384–5	
Edmond Berle	1385–6	
Robert Stackbold	1386–7	
John Bermingham	1387–8	
John Passavaunt	1388–9	
Thomas Mareward	1389–90	
Thomas Cusake	1390–91	
Richard Chamberlain	1391–2	
John Mareward[14]	1392–3	
Thomas Cusake	1393–6	re-elected 1394, 1395
Geoffrey Gallane	1396–7	
Thomas Cusake	1397–8	
Nicholas Fynglas	1398–9	
Ralph Ebbe	1399–1400	
Thomas Cusake	1400–01	
John Drake	1401–3	re-elected 1402
Thomas Cusake	1403–4	
John Drake	1404–6[15]	re-elected 1405
Thomas Cusake	1406–8[16]	

mayors	term of office	
William Wade	1407-8[16]	
Thomas Cusake	1408-10	re-elected 1409
Robert Gallane	1410-12[17]	re-elected 1411
John Drake	1411-12[17]	
Thomas Cusake	1412-13	
Luke Dowdall	1413-14	
Thomas Cusake	1414-16	re-elected 1415
Walter Tyrell	1416-17	
Thomas Cusake	1417-19	re-elected 1418
Walter Tyrrell	1419-20	
John Burnell	1420-22	re-elected 1421
Thomas Cusake	1422-3	
John White	1423-4	
Thomas Cusake	1424-5	
Sir Walter Tyrrell	1425-6	
John Walshe	1426-7	
Thomas Shortall	1427-9	re-elected 1428
Thomas Cusake	1429-30	
John White	1430-32	re-elected 1431
John Hadsor	1432-3	
Nicholas Woder	1433-4	
Ralph Pembroke	1434-5	
John Kylbery	1435-6	
Robert Chambre	1436-7	
Thomas Newberry	1437-8	
Nicholas Woder	1438-9	
John FitzRobert	1439-40	
Nicholas Woder	1440-41	
Ralph Pembroke	1441-2	
Nicholas Woder	1442-3	
Nicholas Woder, jr.	1443-7	re-elected 1444, 1445, 1446

[1] However, see below, p. 552, n. 17.

[2] *Register of the hospital of S. John the Baptist without the Newgate, Dublin*, ed. Eric St John Brooks (Dublin, 1936), p. 158. Not otherwise known; may have been acting as deputy mayor.

[3] Ibid., p. 247.

[4] Le Warre and Owen may have held office in the reverse order to that shown; *Reg. St John, Dublin*, p. 197.

[5] *Twenty-third report of the deputy keeper of the public records of Ireland* (Dublin, 1891) (referred to below as *P.R.I. rep. D.K. 23*), p. 82; *Chartulary of St Mary's abbey, Dublin, . . . and annals of Ireland, 1162-1370*, ed. J. T. Gilbert (2 vols, London, 1884-6), p. 56.

[6] At some time between 1280 and 1282 Thomas de Winchester was deputy mayor; *Reg. St John, Dublin*, pp 78, 124, 130-31.

[7] Robert de Wyleby appears, June 1290.

[8] Berry's list gives no entry for 1297-8.

[9] John le Decer acted as deputy mayor in Nottingham's absence.

[10] In a T.C.D. deed of *c.* 1324-5 Elias de Assheborne appears as mayor.

[11] *P.R.I. rep. D.K. 23*, p. 98, indicates that Cradok was mayor by 27 June 1329.

[12] Berry gives the variants 'Beydyn' and 'Geydyn', while 'Beidin' appears in H. G. Richardson and G. O. Sales (ed.), *Parliaments and councils of medieval Ireland*, i (Dublin, 1947), p. 15.

[13] J. Gilbart Smyly (ed.), 'Old deeds in the library of Trinity College' in *Hermathena*, lxix (1947), p. 41.

[14] *A roll of the proceedings of the king's council in Ireland for a portion of the sixteenth year of the reign of Richard II, 1392–93*, ed. James Graves (London, 1877), pp 53–4.

[15] Drake seems to have continued in office until Oct. 1406 (*P.R.I. rep. D.K. 23*, p. 133).

[16] Berry's list shows both Cusake and Wade under the year 1407–8; Wade's name appears from 27 Oct. 1407 (*P.R.I. rep. D.K. 23*, p. 134).

[17] Drake's name first appears on 23 Nov. 1411 (ibid., p. 137). Together with other evidence (above, notes 11 and 15), this suggests that the date of election may have changed.

(*B*) *1447–1841*

This section of the list is based upon the assembly rolls of the city, which begin in 1447 and are published in *Anc. rec. Dublin*. These, however, do not give an unbroken record, and it has been impossible to avoid leaving gaps.

During this period the mayor was usually selected at the quarterly meeting of the council held after Easter, but inauguration continued to take place at Michaelmas—usually on the day after St Michael's day unless that fell on a Saturday, in which case the inauguration would be deferred until the Monday.[18] In 1641 Charles I authorised the mayor of Dublin to assume the title of 'lord mayor', but this was not done until the council, on 14 October 1665, resolved that Sir Daniel Bellingham should take the title.

In September 1672 new regulations for the election of the lord mayor and other municipal officers—'Essex's rules'—were issued by the viceroy; they included the requirements that the lord mayor should be elected by lord mayor and council, and that his election should be subject to the viceroy's approval.[19] From the assembly rolls of the early eighteenth century it can be seen that the lord mayor and aldermen made the choice of lord mayor from among the aldermen; in 1711 some council members claimed that it was an ancient custom for the most senior alderman to be elected, but this was contested.[20]

Sir Samuel Cooke (lord mayor 1712–13) claimed that the lord mayor had the right to nominate three aldermen for election to the mayoralty. The lords justices and Irish privy council upheld this view, but George I's first Irish parliament rejected it. The assembly rolls indicate that by 1718 the lord mayor was able to recommend three aldermen for election, but that the other aldermen could object to his nominees before the election took place.[21]

In 1760 the common council of Dublin drew up a set of recommendations for constitutional changes in the corporation, including the proposal that the election of the lord mayor should be subject to the commons' approval. The lord mayor and aldermen favoured the proposal, and it and others eventually became law on 17 May 1760 in 33 Geo. II, c. 16. From 1761 to 1840 the name of the lord mayor elect, chosen by the lord mayor and aldermen, was submitted to the commons for approval.[22] In general, approval was automatic; but in 1820 the commons rejected twelve successive names proposed to them; and after application to the Irish privy council and the lord lieutenant the commons' choice, Abraham Bradley King, became the next lord mayor.[23]

mayors	*term of office*	
Thomas Newebery	1447–8	
Sir Robert Burnell	1449–51 [24]	re-elected 1450
Thomas Newbery	1451–3	re-elected 1452

mayors	*term of office*	
Sir Nicholas Woder	1453-4	
Sir Robert Burnell	1454-5	
Philip Bellewe	1455-6	
John Bennet	1456-7	
Thomas Newbery	1457-8	
Sir Robert Burnell	1458-9	
Thomas Walshe	1459-60	
Thomas Newbery	1460-61	
Sir Robert Burnell	1461-2	
Thomas Newbery	1463-5[25]	re-elected 1464; kt *a.* 29 Sept. 1464
Simon FitzRery	1465-6	
William Crampe	1466-7	
Sir Thomas Newbery	1467-9	re-elected 1468 d. 21 Jan. 1469
William Grauntpe	1469[26]	
Arland Ussher	1469-70	
Thomas Walton	1470-71	
Simon FitzRery	1471-2	
John Fyan	1472-3	
Nicholas Bourke	1474-5[27]	
Thomas FitzSimon	1475-7	re-elected 1476
Patrick FitzLeones	1477-8	
John Weste	1478-9	
John Fyane	1479-80	
William Donewith	1480-81	
Thomas Mulghan	1481-2	
Patrick FitzLeones	1482-3	
John West	1483-5	re-elected 1484
John Serjeant	1485-6	
Janico Marcus	1486-7	
Thomas Meyler	1487-8	
William Tue	1488-9	
Richard Stanyhurst	1489-90	
John Serjaunt	1490-91	
Thomas Benet	1491-2	
John Serjaunt	1492-3	
Richard Arlon[28]	1493	
John Savage	1493-4	
Patrick FitzLeones	1494-5	
Thomas Brymigham	1495-6	
John Geydoun	1496-7	
Reginald Talbot	1498-9[29]	
James Barby	1499-1500	
Robert Forster	1500-01	
Hugh Talbot	1501-2	
Richard Tyrell	1502-3	
John Blake	1503-4	

mayors	*term of office*
William Cauterell	1507–8[30]
Christopher Usher	1516–17[31]
Nicholas Queytrot	1523–4[32]
Richard Talbot	1525–6[33]
Walter Ewstas	1526–7
Thomas Barbe	1530–31[34]
John Sarsewell	1531–2
Nicholas Gaydon	1532–3
Walter FitzSymon	1533–4
Robert Shillyngford	1534–5
Thomas Stephens	1535–6
John Shilton	1536–7
John Scuyr	1537–8
James FitzSymond	1538–9
Nicholas Bennet	1539–40
Walter Tirrell	1540–41 .
Nicholas Umfre	1541–2
Nicholas Stanyhurst	1542–3
Henry Plunket	1546–7[35]
Thady Duff	1547–8
James Hancoke	1548–9
Richard Fyane (Fian)	1549–50
John Money	1550–51
Michael Penteny	1551–2
Robert Cusake	1552–3
Bartholomew Ball	1553–4
Patrick Sarsfeld	1554–5
Thomas Rogers	1555–6
John Challyner	1556–7
John Spensfelde	1557–8
Robert Golding	1558–9
Christopher Sedgrave	1559–60
Thomas FitzSymon	1560–61
Robert Ussher	1561–2
Thomas Fininge	1562–3
Robert Cusake	1563–4
Richard Fiand (Fian)	1564–5
Nicholas FitzSimon	1565–6
Sir William Sarsfeld	1566–7
John FitzSymon	1567–8
Michael Bea	1568–9
Walter Cusake	1569–70
Henry Browne	1570–71
Patrick Dowdall	1571–2
James Bellewe (Bedlow)	1572–3
Christopher Fagan	1573–4
John Ussher	1574–5
Patrick Goghe (Googhe)	1575–6

mayors	*term of office*	
John Goughe	1576-7	
Giles Allen	1577-8	
Richard Rownsell	1578-9	
Nicholas Duffe	1579-80	
Walter Ball	1580-81	
John Gaydon	1581-2	
Nicholas Ball	1582-3	
John Lennan	1583-4	
Thomas Cosgrave	1584-5	
William Piccott	1585-6	
Richard Rounsell	1586-7	
Richard Fagan	1587-8	
Walter Sedgrave	1588-9	
John Forster	1589-90	
Edmond Devnish	1590-91	
Thomas Smith	1591-2	
Philip Conran	1592-3	
James Janes	1593-4	
Thomas Gerrald	1594-5	
Francis Tayllor	1595-6	
Michael Chamberlen	1596-7	
Nicholas Weston	1597-8	
James Bellewe (Bedlow)	1598-9	
Gerrald Yonge	1599-1600	
Nicholas Barran	1600-01	
Mathew Handcocke	1601-2	
John Terrell	1602-3	
William Goughe	1603-4	d. 1604
John Elliott[36]	1604	
Robert Ball[37]	1604-5	
John Brice	1605-6	
John Arthore	1606-7	
Nicholas Barran	1607-8	
John Cusake	1608-9	
Robert Ball	1609-10	
Richard Barrye	1610-11	
Thomas Buyshoppe	1611-12	
Sir James Carroll	1612-13	
Richard Forster	1613-14	
Richard Brown (Browne)	1614-16	re-elected 1615[38]
John Bennes	1616-17	
Sir James Carroll	1617-18	
John Lany	1618-19	
Richard Forster	1619-20	
Richard Browne	1620-21	
Edward Ball	1621-2	
Richard Wiggett	1622-3	
Thadee Duffe	1623-4	

mayors	*term of office*	
William Bushopp	1624–5	
Sir James Carroll	1625–6	
Thomas Evans	1626–7	
Edward Jans	1627–8	
Robert Bennett	1628–9	
Christopher Forster	1629–30	
Thomas Evans	1630–31	
George Jones	1631–2	
Robert Bennett	1632–3	
Robert Dixon	1633–4	
Sir James Carroll	1634–5	
Sir Christopher Forster	1635–7[39]	
James Watson	1637–8	
Sir Christopher Forster	1638–9	
Charles Forster	1639–40	
Thomas Wakefield	1640–42	re-elected 1641
William Smith	1642–7	re-elected 1643, 1644, 1645, 1646
William Bladen	1647–8	
John Pue	1648–9	
Thomas Pemberton	1649–50	d. ?1650
Sankey Sullyard	1650[40]	
Raphael Hunt	1650–51	
Richard Tighe	1651–2	
Daniel Hutchinson	1652–3	
John Preston	1653–4	
Thomas Hooke	1654–5	
Richard Tighe	1655–6	
Ridgley Hatfield	1656–7	
Thomas Waterhouse	1657–8	
Peter Wybrants	1658–9	
Robert Deey	1659–60	
Hubart Adryan Verneer	1660–61	
George Gilbert	1661–2	
John Cranwell	1662–3	
William Smyth	1663–5	re-elected 1664
lord mayors		
Sir Daniel Bellingham	1665–6	
John Desmynieres	1666–7	
Mark Quinn	1667–8	
John Forrest	1668–9	
Lewis Desmynieres	1669–70	
Enoch Reader	1670–71	
Sir John Totty	1671–2	
Robert Deey	1672–3	
Sir Joshua Allen	1673–4	
Sir Francis Brewster	1674–5	

lord mayors	term of office	
William Smith	1675-6	
Christopher Lovet	1676-7	
John Smith	1677-8	
Peter Ward	1678-9	
John Eastwood	1679-80	
Luke Lowther	1680-81	
Sir Humphrey Jervis	1681-3	re-elected 1682
Sir Elias Best	1683-4	
Sir Abel Ram	1684-5	
Sir John Knox	1685-6	
Sir John Castleton	1686-7	
Sir Thomas Hackett	1687-8	
Sir Michael Creagh	1688-9	
Terence McDermott	1689-90	
John Otrington	1690-91	
Sir Michael Mitchell	1691-3	re-elected 1692
Sir John Rogerson	1693-4	
George Blackhall	1694-5	
William Watts	1695-6	
Sir William Billington	1696-7	
Bartholomew Vanhomrigh	1697-8	
Thomas Quinn	1698-9	
Sir Anthony Percy	1699-1700	
Sir Mark Rainsford	1700-01	
Samuel Walton	1701-2	
Thomas Bell	1702-3	
John Page	1703-4	
Sir Francis Stoyte	1704-5	
William Gibbons	1705-6	
Benjamin Burton	1706-7	
John Pearson	1707-8	
Sir William Fownes	1708-9	
Charles Forrest	1709-10	
Sir John Eccles	1710-11	
Ralph Gore	1711-12	
Sir Samuel Cooke	1712-13[41]	
Sir James Barlow	1714-15	
John Stoyte	1715-16	
Thomas Bolton	1716-17	
Anthony Barkey	1717-18	
William Quaill	1718-19	
Thomas Wilkinson	1719-20	
George Forbes	1720-21	
Thomas Curtis	1721-2	
William Dickson	1722-3	
John Porter	1723-4	
John Reyson	1724-5	
Joseph Kane	1725-6	

lord mayors	term of office	
William Empson	1726-7	
Sir Nathaniel Whitwell	1727-8	
Henry Burrowes	1728-9	res. 17 June 1729
John Page	1729[42]	
Sir Peter Verdoen	1729-30	
Nathaniel Pearson	1730-31	
Joseph Nuttall	1731-2	
Humphrey French	1732-3	
Thomas How	1733-4	
Nathaniel Kane	1734-5	
Sir Richard Grattan	1735-6	d. 1736
George Forbes	1736[43]	
James Somerville	1736-7	
William Walker	1737-8	
John Macarroll	1738-9	
Daniel Falkiner	1739-40	
Sir Samuel Cooke	1740-41	
William Aldrich	1741-2	
Gilbert King	1742-3	
David Tew	1743-4	d. 1744
William Aldrich	1744[44]	
John Walker	1744-5	
Daniel Cooke	1745-6	
Richard White	1746-7	d. 1747
William Walker	1747[45]	
Sir George Ribton	1747-8	
Robert Ross	1748-9	
John Adamson	1749-50	
Thomas Taylor	1750-51	
John Cooke	1751-2	
Sir Charles Barton	1752-3	
Andrew Murray	1753-4	
Hans Bailie	1754-5	
Percival Hunt	1755-6	
John Forbes	1756-7	
Thomas Meade	1757-8	
Philip Crampton	1758-9	
John Tew	1759-60	
Sir Patrick Hamilton	1760-61	
Sir Timothy Allen	1761-2	
Charles Rossell	1762-3	
William Forbes	1763-4	
Benjamin Geale	1764-5	
Sir James Taylor	1765-6	
Edward Sankey	1766-7	
Francis Fetherston	1767-8	
Benjamin Barton	1768-9	
Sir Thomas Blackhall	1769-70	

lord mayors	*term of office*	
George Reynolds	1770-71	
Francis Booker	1771-2	d. 1772
William Forbes	1772[46]	
Richard French	1772-3	
William Lightburne	1773-4	
Henry Hart	1774-5	
Thomas Emerson	1775-6	
Henry Bevan	1776-7	
William Dunne	1777-8	
Sir Anthony King	1778-9	
James Hamilton	1779-80	
Kilner Swettenham	1780-81	
John Darragh	1781-2	
Nathaniel Warren	1782-3	
Thomas Green	1783-4	
James Horan	1784-5	
James Sheil	1785-6	
George Alcock	1786-7	
William Alexander	1787-8	
John Rose	1788-9	
John Exshaw	1789-90	
Henry Hewison	1790-91	
Henry Gore Sankey	1791-2	
John Carleton	1792-3	
William James	1793-4	
Richard Moncrieff	1794-5	
Sir William Worthington	1795-6	
Samuel Reed	1796-7	
Thomas Fleming	1797-8	
Thomas Andrews	1798-9	
John Sutton	1799-1800	d. 9 Feb. 1800
John Exshaw	1800[47]	
Charles Thorp	1800-01	
Richard Manders	1801-2	
Jacob Poole	1802-3	
Henry Hutton	1803-4	
Meredith Jenkins	1804-5	
James Vance	1805-6	
Joseph Pemberton	1806-7	
Hugh Trevor	1807-8	
Frederick Darley	1808-9	
Sir William Stamer, bt	1809-10	
Nathaniel Hone	1810-11	
William Henry Archer	1811-12	
Abraham Bradley King	1812-13	
John Cash	1813-14	
John Claudius Beresford	1814-15	
Robert Shaw	1815-16	

lord mayors	term of office
Mark Bloxham	1816–17
John Alley	1817–18
Sir Thomas McKenny	1818–19
Sir William Stamer, bt	1819–20
Sir Abraham Bradley King, bt	1820–21
Sir John Kingston James, bt	1821–2
John Smith Fleming	1822–3
Richard Smyth	1823–4
Drury Jones	1824–5
Thomas Abbott	1825–6
Samuel Wilkinson Tyndall	1826–7
Sir Edmond Nugent	1827–8
Alexander Montgomery	1828–9
Jacob West	1829–30
Sir Robert Way Harty, bt	1830–31
Richard Smyth	1831[48]
Sir Thomas Whelan	1831–2
Charles Palmer Archer	1832–3
Sir George Whiteford	1833–4
Arthur Perrin	1834–5
Arthur Morrison	1835–6
William Hodges	1836–7
Samuel Warren	1837–8
George Hoyte	1838–9
Sir Nicholas William Brady	1839–40
Sir John Kingston James, bt	1840–41

[18] *Anc. rec. Dublin*, ii, 10; iii, preface, p. xx; vii, appendix 1, p. 559.

[19] *Anc. rec. Dublin*, v, preface, p. vi.

[20] Ibid., vii, appendix 1, pp 521–8.

[21] Ibid., vii, preface, p. xxii, appendix 1, pp 536–7; viii, appendix 1, pp 398–9.

[22] Ibid., x, 406; xi, 8; xvi, 134–5.

[23] Ibid., xvii, appendix 1, pp 512–19.   [24] No entry for 1448–9.

[25] No entry for 1462–3.

[26] Elected for remainder of Newbery's term.

[27] No entry for 1473–4.

[28] Elected in place of Serjaunt, who was imprisoned *a.* end of July 1493.

[29] No entry for 1497–8.

[30] No entry for 1504–7.

[31] No entry for 1508–16.

[32] No entry for 1517–23.

[33] No entry for 1524–5.

[34] No entry for 1527–30.

[35] No entry for 1543–6.

[36] Elected *vice* Goughe, deceased.

[37] John Shelton, mayor-elect, refused to take the oath of supremacy. On 20 Nov. 1604 the council decided that Ball should take his place (*Anc. rec. Dublin*, ii, 430; cf. ibid., iii, 577).

[38] The council resolved in Oct. 1615 that henceforth no mayor should serve two consecutive terms (ibid., iii, 60), but this restriction appears to have lasted only twenty years.

[39] On 19 June 1635 the council censured Carroll for violating a regulation on coals, and replaced him by Forster. Although Forster was originally to hold office only to Michaelmas 1635, he appears to have continued as mayor to 1637 despite the recorded elections of Robert Arthur in 1635 and Christopher White in 1636 (ibid., iii, 305–6, 313, 321).

[40] Elected *vice* Pemberton, deceased.

[41] Cooke appears to have retained office illegitimately, without election, during 1713-14 (*Anc. rec. Dublin*, vi, 506-9).

[42] Elected 17 June 1729 for remainder of Burrowes's term.

[43] Elected 22 June 1736 *vice* Grattan, deceased.

[44] Elected 21 Aug. 1744 *vice* Tew, deceased.

[45] Elected 19 Mar. 1747 *vice* White, deceased.

[46] Elected 11 Feb. 1772 *vice* Booker, deceased.

[47] Elected locum tenens for remainder of Sutton's term, under 11 & 12 Geo. III, c. 11.

[48] Mentioned as locum tenens in early 1831 in *Anc. rec. Dublin*, xviii, 504, but not included in Meehan's list of mayors.

(C) 1841-1924

The Municipal Corporations (Ireland) Act, 1840 (3 & 4 Vict., c. 108), placed the Dublin corporation on an entirely new footing; under the act the council, previously restricted to members of the guilds, was to be elected by all ten-pound householders, and anyone with the necessary property qualification could stand for membership. Section 83 provided that 'on the first day of November in every year the council . . . shall elect out of the aldermen or councillors . . . a fit person to be the mayor . . . , who shall continue in his office for one whole year and until his successor shall have accepted the office of mayor, and shall have made and subscribed the declaration required . . .; and in the case of an equality of votes in any election of mayor, the alderman who shall have been elected by the greatest number of votes shall have a second or casting vote'.[49] Daniel O'Connell was accordingly elected lord mayor of Dublin, in the first elections under the act, on 1 November 1841, and George Roe succeeded him on 1 November 1842. However, section 5 of 6 & 7 Vict., c. 93 (1843), changed the date of election to 1 December and the date of coming into office to 1 January; thus Roe continued in office until succeeded by Sir Timothy O'Brien on 1 January 1844. These dates remained unchanged until 1898, when section 94 of the Local Government (Ireland) Act (61 & 62 Vict., c. 37) changed the date of election to 23 January and stipulated that the new lord mayor should take office then or on 23 February. In 1899 Daniel Tallon took office on 23 January, but from 1900 it became customary for the lord mayor to enter office on 23 February.

lord mayors	term of office
Daniel O'Connell	1841-2
George Roe	1842-3
Sir Timothy O'Brien, bt	1844
John L. Arabin	1845
John Keshan	1846
Michael Staunton	1847
Jeremiah Dunne	1848
Sir Timothy O'Brien, bt	1849
John Reynolds	1850
Benjamin Lee Guinness	1851
John D'Arcy	1852
Robert Henry Kinahan	1853
Sir Edward McDonnell	1854
Joseph Boyce	1855
Fergus Farrell	1856

lord mayors	*term of office*	
Richard Atkinson	1857	
John Campbell	1858	
James Lambert	1859	
Redmond Carroll	1860	
Richard Atkinson	1861	
Denis Moylan	1862	
John Prendergast Vereker	1863	
Peter Paul McSwiney	1864	
Sir John Barrington	1865	
James William Mackey	1866	
William Lane Joynt	1867	
Sir William Carroll	1868–9	re-elected 1868
Edward Purdon	1870	
Patrick Bulfin	1871	d. 12/13 June 1871
John Campbell	1871[50]	
Robert Garde Durdin	1872	
Sir James William Mackey	1873	
Maurice Brooks	1874	
Peter Paul McSwiney	1875	
Sir George Bolster Owens, bt	1876	
Hugh Tarpey	1877–8	re-elected 1877
Sir John Barrington	1879	
Edmund Dwyer Gray	1880	
George Moyers	1881	
Charles Dawson	1882–3	re-elected 1882
William Meagher	1884	
John O'Connor	1885	
Timothy Daniel Sullivan	1886–7	re-elected 1886
Thomas Sexton	1888–9	re-elected 1888
Edward Joseph Kennedy	1890	
Joseph Michael Meade	1891–2	re-elected 1891
James Shanks	1893	
Valentine Blake Dillon	1894–5	re-elected 1894
Richard F. McCoy	1896–7	re-elected 1896
Daniel Tallon	1897–1900[51]	
Sir Thomas Devereux Pile, bt	1900–01[52]	
Timothy Charles Harrington	1901–4	re-elected 1902, 1903
Joseph Hutchinson	1904–6	re-elected 1905
Joseph Patrick Nannetti	1906–8	re-elected 1907
Gerald O'Reilly	1908–9	
William Coffey	1909–10	
Michael Doyle	1910–11	
John J. Farrell	1911–12	
Lorcan G. Sherlock	1912–15	re-elected 1913, 1914
James Mitchell Gallagher	1915–17[53]	re-elected 1916
Laurence O'Neill	1917–24[54]	re-elected 1918, 1919, 1920, 1921, 1922, 1923, 1924

[49] The final sentence on procedure in the event of an equality of votes was repealed by the Local Government Act, 1941 (1941/23 [Éire]).

[50] Elected 21 June 1871 for the remainder of Bulfin's term.

[51] App. lord mayor, 1 Dec. 1897; re-elected 1898; took office for second term on 23 Jan. 1899.

[52] Pile and subsequent lord mayors down to 1924 came into office on 23 Feb.

[53] John Clancy was elected 23 Jan. 1915 but d. 29 Jan.

[54] Thomas Kelly was elected 30 Jan. 1920 but was prevented by ill health from taking office.

(D) FROM 1924

Following an official inquiry into the administration of Dublin, the municipal council was dissolved at 6 p.m. on 20 May 1924 by an order of the minister for local government under section 12 of the Local Government (Temporary Provisions) Act, 1923 (1923/9 [I.F.S.]), and the administration of the county borough of Dublin was vested in commissioners until 13 Oct. 1930. The Local Elections Act (1927/39 [I.F.S.]), section 10, stipulated that mayors should be elected at the quarterly meeting of the council held next after 22 June; that the mayor-elect should come into office as soon as he had made the declaration accepting it; and that he should continue in office until the declaration was made by his successor. The dates on which lord mayors of Dublin have taken office from 1930 have therefore varied from year to year, as shown below. Electoral procedure was further regulated by section 43 of the Local Government Act, 1941 (1941/23 [Éire]). Dates of election for 1930–68 are as given in the council minutes, and from 1974 are taken from the *Irish Times*.

lord mayors	term of office	took office
Senator Alfred Byrne	1930–31	14 Oct. 1930
Senator Alfred Byrne	1931–2	1 July 1931
Senator Alfred Byrne	1932–3	1 Sept. 1932
Senator Alfred Byrne	1933–4	7 July 1933
Senator Alfred Byrne	1934–5	25 June 1934
Senator Alfred Byrne	1935–6	1 July 1935
Senator Alfred Byrne	1936–7	10 July 1936
Senator Alfred Byrne	1937–8	28 June 1937
Senator Alfred Byrne	1938–9	27 June 1938
Caitlín Bean Uí Chléirigh	1939–40	27 June 1939
Caitlín Bean Uí Chléirigh	1940–41	1 July 1940
Peadar Seán Ua Dubhghaill (Doyle)	1941–2	30 June 1941
Peadar Seán Ua Dubhghaill (Doyle)	1942–3	29 June 1942
Martin O'Sullivan	1943–4	28 June 1943
Martin O'Sullivan	1944–5	26 June 1944
Peadar Seán Ua Dubhghaill (Doyle)	1945–6	26 June 1945
John McCann	1946–7	1 July 1946
Patrick Joseph Cahill	1947–8	30 June 1947

lord mayors	term of office	took office
John Breen	1948–9	28 June 1948
Cormac Breathnach	1949–50	27 June 1949
John Belton	1950–51	30 Sept. 1950
Andrew S. Clarkin	1951–2	25 June 1951
Andrew S. Clarkin	1952–3	30 June 1952
Bernard Butler	1953–4	30 June 1953
Alfred Byrne	1954–5	28 June 1954
Denis Larkin	1955–6	4 July 1955
Robert Briscoe	1956–7	25 June 1956
James Carroll	1957–8	1 July 1957
Catherine Byrne	1958–9	30 June 1958
Philip A. Brady	1959–60	29 June 1959
Maurice Edward Dockrell	1960–61	4 July 1960
Robert Briscoe	1961–2	26 June 1961
James O'Keefe	1962–3	25 June 1962
Seán Moore	1963–4	24 June 1963
John McCann	1964–5	1 July 1964
Eugene Timmons	1965–6	1 July 1965
Eugene Timmons	1966–7	27 June 1966
Thomas Strafford	1967–8	8 July 1967
Frank Cluskey	1968–9	8 July 1968

On 25 April 1969 the lord mayor and the city council were removed from office by the minister for local government, and until 28 June 1974 their duties were performed by commissioners for the corporation. Under the Local Elections Regulations (1965), part VI, the election of the lord mayor was to take place at the first annual or quarterly meeting following polling day (in a local election year) and in every other year at a meeting held not more than fourteen days before or after the anniversary of the first annual or quarterly meeting. In 1974 the corporation resumed its powers, and its first quarterly meeting was held on 28 June.

James O'Keefe	1974–5	28 June 1974
Patrick Dunne	1975–6	30 June 1975
James Mitchell	1976–7	5 July 1976
Michael Collins	1977–8	4 July 1977
Patrick Belton	1978–9	3 July 1978
William Cumiskey	1979–80	18 June 1979
Fergus O'Brien	1980–81	30 June 1980
Alexis Fitzgerald	1981–2	29 June 1981
Daniel Browne	1982–3	28 June 1982

FOREIGN RULERS

ROMAN EMPERORS, 27 B.C.–A.D. 802

EDWARD JAMES

E. J. Bickermann, *Chronology of the ancient world* (London, 1968), pp 193–5; A. H. M. Jones, *The decline of the ancient world* (London, 1966), pp 372–4; Fergus Millar, *The Roman empire and its neighbours* (London, 1967), pp 321–2; G. A. Ostrogorsky, *History of the Byzantine state* (Oxford, 1968), p. 578.

The three procedures of hereditary succession (either by actual or adopted sons), election by the senate, and acclamation by the army were often in conflict with each other. In order to prevent succession disputes, emperors would occasionally nominate colleagues (as Marcus Aurelius did in 161 and Septimius Severus in 193) or have their sons acclaimed emperor in their own lifetime (as Marcus Aurelius did in 176). Diocletian attempted to formalise the succession procedure: there were to be two senior emperors (Augusti), one in the east and one in the west, and each was to nominate a successor (the Caesar). This experiment broke down after the reign of Constantius II.

ROMAN EMPERORS, 27 B.C.–A.D. 284

	accession	end of reign
Augustus	27 B.C.	A.D. 14
Tiberius	A.D. 14	37
Gaius (Caligula)	37	41
Claudius I	41	54
Nero	54	68
Galba	68	69
Otho	69	69
Vitellius	69	69
Vespasian	69	79
Titus	79	81
Domitian	81	96
Nerva	96	98
Trajan	98	117
Hadrian	117	138
Antoninus Pius	138	161
Marcus Aurelius	161	180
Lucius Verus	161	169
Commodus	176	192
Pertinax	193	193
Didius Julianus	193	193
Septimius Severus	193	211
Clodius Albinus	193	197

	accession	end of reign
Pescennius Niger	193	194
Caracalla	198	217
Geta	209	212
Macrinus	217	218
Diadumenianus	218	218
Elagabalus (Heliogabalus)	218	222
Severus Alexander	222	235
Maximinus	235	238
Gordian I	238	238
Gordian II	238	238
Balbinus	238	238
Pupienus (Maximus)	238	238
Gordian III	238	244
Philip the Arab	244	249
Decius	249	251
Trebonianus Gallus	251	251
Volusianus	251	253
Aemilianus	253	253
Valerian	253	260
Gallienus	253	268
Claudius II Gothicus	268	270
Quintillus	270	270
Aurelian	270	275
Tacitus	275	276
Florianus	276	276
Probus	276	282
Carus	282	283
Carinus	283	285
Numerianus	283	284
Diocletian	284	—[1]

WESTERN ROMAN EMPERORS, 284–480

		accession	end of reign
Diocletian		284	286 (in west)
Maximian	Caesar	285	
	Augustus	286	305[2]
	Augustus	307[2]	310
Constantius I	Caesar	293	
	Augustus	305	306
Constantine I	Caesar	306	
	Augustus	308	337
Severus	Augustus	306	307
Maxentius	Augustus	307	312
Crispus	Caesar	317	325
Constantine II	Caesar	317	
	Augustus	337	340

	accession		end of reign
Constans	Caesar	333	
	Augustus	337	350
Dalmatius	Caesar	335	337
Constantius II	Augustus	351	361
Julian	Caesar	355	
	Augustus	360	363
Jovian	Augustus	363	364
Valentinian I		364	375
Gratian		375	383
Valentinian II		383	392
Maximus[3]		383	388
Theodosius I		392	395
Honorius		395	423
Constantius III[3]		421	421
Valentinian III		425	455
Petronius Maximus		455	455
Avitus		455	456
Majorian		457	461
Libius Severus		461	465
Anthemius		467	472
Olybrius		472	472
Glycerius		473	473
Julius Nepos		473	475[4]
Romulus (Augustulus)		475	476

EASTERN ROMAN EMPERORS, 284–802

	accession		end of reign
Diocletian	Augustus	284	305
Galerius	Caesar	293	
	Augustus	305	311
Maximin	Caesar	305	
	Augustus	308	313
Licinius	Augustus	308	324
Licinianus	Caesar	317	323
Martinianus	Caesar	324	324
Constantine I	Augustus	324	337
Constantius II	Caesar	324	
	Augustus	337	361
Gallus	Caesar	350	354
Julian	Augustus	361	363
Jovian	Augustus	363	364
Valens	Augustus	364	378
Theodosius I		379	395
Arcadius		395	408
Theodosius II		408	450
Marcian		450	457

		accession	end of reign
Leo I		457	474
Leo II		474	474
Zeno		474	491[5]
Basiliscus		475	476
Anastasius		491	518
Justin I		518	527
Justinian		527	565
Justin II		565	578
Tiberius I Constantine	Caesar	574	
	Augustus	578	582
Maurice		582	602
Phocas		602	610
Heraclius		610	641
Constantine III and Heraclonas		641	641
Heraclonas		641	641
Constans II		641	668
Constantine IV		668	685
Justinian II		685	711[6]
Leontius		695	698
Tiberius II		698	705
Philippicus		711	713
Anastasius II		713	715
Theodosius III		715	717
Leo III		717	741
Constantine V		741	775
Leo IV		775	780
Constantine VI		780	797
Irene		797	802

[1] See pp 566, 567.
[2] Maximian abdicated in 305, but returned in 307 to support his son Maxentius.
[3] Usurper.
[4] Deposed; killed, 480.
[5] Dep. by Basiliscus, brother-in-law of Leo I, 475; rest., 476.
[6] Dep., 695; rest., 705.

MEROVINGIAN KINGS OF THE FRANKS, 481–751

EDWARD JAMES

Bruno Krusch, 'Chronologica regum Francorum stirpis Merovingicae' in *Monumenta Germaniae historia: scriptores rerum Merovingicarum*, vii (Hanover, 1920), pp 468–516.

	accession	end of reign	area ruled
Clovis I	481	511	
Theuderic I	511	533	kingdom of Metz
Theudebert I	533	547/8	kingdom of Metz

	accession	end of reign	area ruled
Theudebald I	547/8	555	kingdom of Metz
Clodomer	511	524	kingdom of Orleans
Childebert I	511	558	kingdom of Paris
Clothar I	511	561	kingdom of Soissons; kingdom of Metz after 555; all kingdom, 558–61
Charibert I	561	567	kingdom of Paris
Guntram	561	592	Burgundy
Sigibert I	561	575	Austrasia
Childebert II	575	595	Austrasia; Burgundy, 592–5
Theudebert II	595	612	Austrasia
Theuderic II	595	613	Burgundy; Austrasia, 612–13
Sigibert II	613	613	Austrasia
Chilperic I	561	584	Neustria
Clothar II	584	629	Neustria; all kingdom, 612–23
Dagobert I	623	639	Austrasia; all kingdom, 629–39
Charibert II	629	632	Aquitaine
Sigibert III	634	656	Austrasia
Dagobert II	656	661 }	Austrasia
	676	679 }	
Childebert, son of Grimoald	661	662	Austrasia
Clovis II	639	657	Neustria and Burgundy
Clothar III	657	673	Neustria and Burgundy
Childeric II	662	675	Austrasia; Neustria, 673–5
Clovis, son of Clothar III	676	676	Austrasia
Theuderic III	673	690	whole kingdom
Clovis III	690	694	whole kingdom
Childebert III	694	711	whole kingdom
Dagobert III	711	715/16	whole kingdom
Chilperic II	715/16	721	whole kingdom
Clothar IV	718	719	Austrasia
Theuderic IV	721	737	whole kingdom
Childeric III	743	751	whole kingdom

CAROLINGIAN KINGS AND EMPERORS, 751–905

MICHAEL RICHTER

Meyers enzyklopädisches Lexikon (Jubilee edition, Mannheim, 1971–   ), vi, 535; ix, 278; xii, 481; by courtesy of the publishers, Bibliographisches Institut A.G.

The history of the possession and transmission of power in the Carolingian empire and its successor states is extremely complex, and this list does not attempt more than a sketch of the main lines of the dynasty. For the successions in West Francia (France) and East Francia (Germany) from 843, see below, pp 570–72.

	accession	co-emp.	emp.	end of reign
Pepin III the Short	751			768
Charles (Charlemagne)	768		800	814
Carloman	768			771
Louis the Pious	781	813	814	840
Kings of Italy				
Pepin	781			810
Bernard	810/13			818
Lothar	817	817	840	855
Louis II	844	850	855	875
Louis III the Blind	900		901	905
				d. ?928
Kings of Aquitaine				
Pepin I	817			838
Pepin II	838			848

GERMAN KINGS AND HOLY ROMAN EMPERORS, 843–1806

MICHAEL RICHTER

Meyers enzyklopädisches Lexikon (Jubilee edition, Mannheim, 1971–   ), vi, 535; ix, 278; xiii, 481; by courtesy of the publishers, Bibliographisches Institut A.G.

German kings who did not receive the imperial crown should not strictly be counted as emperors.

	accession	emp.	end of reign
Louis II the German	843		876
Charles II the Bald	875	875	877
Carloman of Bavaria	876		880
Louis III the Younger	876		882
Charles III the Fat	876	881	887
Arnulf of Carinthia	887	896	899
Louis IV the Child	900		911
Conrad I	911		918
Henry I the Fowler	919		936
Otto I the Great	936	962	973
Otto II	973	967[1]	983
Otto III	983	996	1002
Henry II	1002	1014	1024
Conrad II	1024	1027	1039
Henry III	1039	1046	1056
Henry IV	1056	1084	1106
Rudolf of Rheinfelden[2]	1077		1080
Hermann of Salm[2]	1081		1088
Conrad (s. of Henry IV)[2]	1087		1093
Henry V	1106	1111	1125

	accession	emp.	end of reign
Lothar III of Saxony	1125	1133	1137
Conrad III	1138		1152
Frederick I Barbarossa	1152	1155	1190
Philip of Swabia	1198[3]		1208
Otto IV	1198[3]	1209	1218
Frederick II	1212	1220	1250
Henry (VII)[4]	1220		1235
Henry Raspe[2]	1246		1247
Conrad IV	1250		1254
William of Holland	1248[5]		1256
Richard of Cornwall	1257[3]		1272
Alfonso X of Castile and León	1257[3]		1273
Rudolf I	1273		1291
Adolf	1292		1298
Albrecht I	1298		1308
Henry VII	1308	1312	1313
Frederick III	1314[6]		1330
Louis IV of Bavaria	1314[6]	1328	1347
Charles IV	1346	1355	1378
Günther[7]	1349		
Wenceslas	1378		1400
Ruprecht of the Palatinate	1400		1410
Jobst of Moravia	1410[6]		1411
Sigismund	1410[6]	1433	1437
Albrecht II	1438		1438
Frederick III	1440	1452	1493
Maximilian I	1486	1508	1519
Charles V	1519	1530	1556
Ferdinand I	1531	1556	1564
Maximilian II[8]	1564		1576
Rudolf II	1576		1612
Matthias Corvinus	1612		1619
Ferdinand II	1619		1637
Ferdinand III	1637		1657
Leopold I	1657		1705
Joseph I	1705		1711
Charles VI	1711		1740
Charles VII Albrecht	1742		1745
Francis I Stephen[9]	1745		1765
Joseph II	1765		1790
Leopold II	1790		1792
Francis II	1792		1806

[1] Otto was crowned emperor during the lifetime of his father, whom he succeeded as kg of Germany.
[2] Anti-king.   [3] Double election.   [4] Sub-king.   [5] Elected kg of the Romans.
[6] Double election.   [7] Anti-king.
[8] From Maximilian II onwards, dates of accession and dates of imperial coronation are identical.
[9] Husband of Maria Theresa, archduchess of Austria 1740, queen of Hungary 1741, queen of Bohemia 1743; d. 1780.

WEST FRANKISH KINGS, 843-987

MICHAEL RICHTER

Meyers enzyklopädisches Lexikon (Jubilee edition, Mannheim 1971-   ), vi, 535; ix, 278; xiii, 481; by courtesy of the publishers, Bibliographisches Institut A.G.

	accession	end of reign
Charles the Bald[1]	843	877
Louis II the Stammerer	877	879
Louis III	879	882
Carloman	879	884
Charles the Fat[1]	885	887
Odo of Paris	888	898
Charles III the Simple	898	923
Robert I	922	923
Rudolph of Burgundy	923	936
Louis IV d'Outremer	936	954
Lothar	954	986
Louis V	986	987

[1] Both Charles the Bald and Charles the Fat were crowned as emperor by Pope John VIII, in 875 and 881 respectively.

KINGS OF FRANCE, 987-1792

IAN ROBINSON

Hermann Grotefend, *Taschenbuch der Zeitrechnung des deutschen Mittelalters und der Neuzeit* (8th ed., Hanover, 1941).

Dates of death are given only where they differ from the date of the next accession. Hugh Capet had his son Robert crowned kg of France in association with him; this practice was followed until the reign of Philip Augustus.

		accession	death
Hugh Capet		3 July 987	24 Oct. 996
Robert II	cor.	1 Jan. 988	
	sole kg	24 Oct. 996	20 July 1031
Henry I	cor.	14 May 1027	
	sole kg	20 July 1031	29 Aug. 1060
Philip I	cor.	23 May 1059	
	sole kg	29 Aug. 1060	29 July 1108
Louis VI	cor.	end of 1098	
	sole kg	29 July 1108	1 Aug. 1137
Philip	cor.	14 Apr. 1129	13 Oct. 1131
Louis VII	cor.	25 Oct. 1131	
	sole kg	1 Aug. 1137	18 Sept. 1180

		accession	*death*
Philip II Augustus	cor.	29 Mar. 1180	
	sole kg	18 Sept. 1180	
Louis VIII		14 July 1223	
Louis IX		8 Nov. 1226	
Philip III		25 Aug. 1270	
Philip IV		6 Oct. 1285	
Louis X		29 Nov. 1314	8 June 1316
John I		15 Nov. 1316[1]	19 Nov. 1316
Philip V		6 Jan. 1317	
Charles IV		3 Jan. 1322	1 Feb. 1328
Philip VI		27 May 1328	
John II		22 Aug. 1350	
Charles V		8 Apr. 1364	
Charles VI		16 Sept. 1380	21 Oct. 1422
Charles VII		28 Oct. 1422	
Louis XI		22 July 1461	
Charles VIII		30 Aug. 1483	
Louis XII		7 Apr. 1498	
Francis I		1 Jan. 1515	
Henry II		31 Mar. 1547	
Francis II		10 July 1559	
Charles IX		5 Dec. 1560	
Henry III		30 May 1574	
Henry IV		23 July/2 Aug. 1589[2]	
Louis XIII		4/14 May 1610	
Louis XIV		4/14 May 1643	
Louis XV		21 Aug./1 Sept. 1715	
Louis XVI		10 May 1774	abd., 21 Sept. 1792
			executed, 21 Jan. 1793

[1] The birthdate of John I is taken also as the date of his accession.
[2] Recognised as successor by the dying Henry III; not crowned until 17/27 Feb. 1594.

VISIGOTHIC KINGS IN SPAIN, 395-?720

EDWARD JAMES

E. A. Thompson, *The Goths in Spain* (Oxford, 1969); Dietrich Claude, *Adel, Kirche und Königtum im Westgotenreich* (Sigmaringen, 1971), p. 211.

	accession	*end of reign*
Alaric I	395	410
Athaulf	410	415
Sigeric	415	415
Wallia	415	418
Theodoric I	418	451
Thurismund	451	453

	accession	end of reign
Theodoric II	453	466
Euric	466	484
Alaric II	484	507
Gesalic	507	511
Theodoric the Great[1]	511	526
Amalaric	526	531
Theudis	531	548
Theudegisel	548	549
Agila I	549	555
Athanagild	555	567
Liuva I	567	571/2
Leovigild	568	586
Reccared I	586	601
Liuva II	601	603
Witteric	603	610
Gundemar	610	612
Sisebut	612	621
Reccared II	621	621
Suinthila	621	631
Sisenand	631	636
Chintila	636	639
Tulga	639	642
Chindasuinth	642	653
Reccesuinth	653	672
Wamba	672	680
Erwig	680	687
Egica	687	702
Wittiza	702	710
Roderic	710	711
Agila II	711	?714
Ardo	?714	?720

[1] Regent on behalf of Amalaric.

MONARCHS OF SPAIN, 1474–1808

IAN ROBINSON

Diccionario de historia de España. Desde sus origenes hasta el fin del reinado de Alfonso XIII (2 vols., Madrid, 1952).

	accession
Ferdinand V and Isabella I	13 Dec. 1474 (Castile)[1]
Charles I	23 Jan. 1516[2]
Philip II	16 Jan. 1556
Philip III	3/13 Sept. 1598
Philip IV	21/31 Mar. 1621

	accession
Charles II	7/17 Sept. 1665
Philip V	21 Oct./1 Nov. 1700
Ferdinand VI	28 June/9 July 1746
Charles III	10 Aug. 1759
Charles IV	14 Dec. 1788[3]

[1] On 20 Jan. 1479 Ferdinand also became kg of Aragon (as Ferdinand II), following the death of his father John II. Isabella I d. 26 Nov. 1504, whereupon Ferdinand's title as kg of Castile lapsed. Thereafter he administered Castile in the name of his daughter, Juana 'the mad', the 'queen proprietress'.

[2] Elected Holy Roman Emperor (as Charles V), 28 June 1519; resigned kingdom of Spain to his son Philip, 16 Jan. 1556; d. 24 Sept. 1558.

[3] Abd. 19 Mar. 1808; d. 20 Jan. 1819.

KINGS OF NORWAY, *c.* 890–1263

DENIS BETHELL

H.B.C.; G. M. Gathorne-Hardy, *A royal impostor: King Sverre of Norway* (Oslo, 1956); Knut Gjerset, *History of the Norwegian people* (New York, 1932; reprint, 1969); Lucien Musset, *Les peuples scandinaves au moyen-âge* (Paris, 1951).

Claimants who were not proclaimed king are shown in square brackets. Junior co-kings, of whom little is known, are marked with an asterisk.

	accession	death unless otherwise stated
Harald I Fairhair	872/*c.* 890[1]	933
Eric Bloodaxe	930	exp. 934;[2] d. 954
Haakon I the Good (Athelstansfosterling)[3]	934	960/961
Harald II Greycloak[4]	961	970
Jarl Haakon of Lade[5]	970	995
Olaf I Tryggvason	995	Sept. 1000
Jarl Eric of Lade[6]	*p.* Sept. 1000	
Olaf II (St Olaf)[7]	1016	exp. 1028; d. 29 July 1030
Cnut the Great[8]	1028	12 Nov. 1035
Magnus I the Good[9]	1035	25 Oct. 1047
Harald III Hardrada[10]	1047	25 Sept. 1066
Olaf III Kyrre (the Quiet)[11]	1066	22 Sept. 1093
Magnus II*		1069
Magnus III Bareleg[12]	1093	24 Aug. 1103
Haakon II*		1095
Sigurd I the Crusader[13]	1103	26 Mar. 1130
Olaf IV*		d. 1115
Eystein I*		d. 1123
Magnus IV the Blinded[14]	1130	dep. and bld Jan. 1135; d. Nov. 1139

	accession	*death unless otherwise stated*
Harald IV Gillechrist*[15]	1130	14 Dec. 1136
[Sigurd II Slembediakn (the Mock Deacon)[16]		Nov. 1139]
Inge I Crookback[17]	1136	3 Feb. 1161
Sigurd III Mund*		1155
Eystein II*		1157
['Haakon II' Herdebred the Broadshouldered[18]		spring 1162]
Magnus V Erlingsson[19]	1161	15 June 1184
Sverre[19]	1177	exp. 1180; rest. 1184; d. 9 Mar. 1202
Haakon III[20]	1202	1 Jan. 1204
Guttorm[21]	1204	Aug. 1204
Inge II Baardson[22]	1204	23 Apr. 1217
[Erling Steinvaeg[23]		25 Dec. 1206]
[Philip Simonsson[23]		made peace, summer 1208]
Haakon IV[24]	1217	15 Dec. 1263

[1] 872 is the traditional date, but *c.* 890 is probably correct.

[2] Kg of York 947-8, 952-4.

[3] Son of Harald I.

[4] Son of Eric Bloodaxe; ruled conjointly with his brothers, and in south-west Norway only; successfully opposed by (among others) Jarl Sigurd of Lade and Kg Tryggve Olafson, grandson of Harald I.

[5] Effective ruler of Norway under suzerainty of Harald Bluetooth, kg of Denmark (d. *c.* 986).

[6] Accepted suzerainty of Svein (Swegn) Forkbeard, kg of Denmark (d. 3 Feb. 1014), after death of Olaf I Tryggvason.

[7] Great-great-grandson of Harald I.

[8] See list of kgs of England, above, p. 455.

[9] Son of Olaf II.

[10] Half-brother of Olaf II.

[11] Son of Harald III; reigned jointly with his brother Magnus II.

[12] Son of Olaf III; reigned jointly with his brother Haakon II.

[13] Son of Magnus III; reigned jointly with his brothers Olaf IV and Eystein I.

[14] Son of Sigurd I; reigned jointly with Harald IV, who deposed and blinded him.

[15] Claimed to be son of Magnus III.

[16] Claimed to be son of Magnus III; killed Harald IV and released Magnus IV, but was not proclaimed kg.

[17] Son of Harald IV; reigned jointly with his brothers Sigurd III Mund and Eystein II.

[18] Son of Sigurd III.

[19] Magnus V and Sverre (who claimed to be son of Sigurd III) reigned together 1177-80. Sverre returned from expulsion and killed Magnus.

[20] Son of Sverre.

[21] Son of Sverre's brother Sigurd.

[22] Son of Sverre's sister Cecilia.

[23] Rival of Inge Baardson.

[24] Son of Haakon III.

PRESIDENTS OF THE UNITED STATES OF AMERICA FROM 1789

DONALD R. MCCOY

Burke's presidential families of the United States of America (London, 1975).

In the case of elected presidents, the date shown for entering office is that of inauguration. No constitutional provision for a standard date for beginning and end of terms was made until the twentieth amendment (1933), which established that terms should begin at noon on 20 January, and first took effect in 1937. 4 March had previously been the statutory inaugural date, beginning with the start of Washington's second term in 1793, and it is therefore consistently shown as such, even though in a few cases the inauguration or taking of the oath took place a day earlier or later.

In nine cases (indicated by 'v.p.' in the list) a vice-president became president on the death or resignation of his predecessor. In such circumstances, succession is immediate, although the successor is not supposed to exercise presidential powers before taking the oath; nor has any vice-president exercised presidential powers before his predecessor vacated office, although (as in the cases of Garfield and McKinley) a president might be incapacitated for a considerable time before death.

	presidency begins	
George Washington	30 Apr. 1789	re-elected 1793
John Adams	4 Mar. 1797	
Thomas Jefferson	4 Mar. 1801	re-elected 1805
James Madison	4 Mar. 1809	re-elected 1813
James Monroe	4 Mar. 1817	re-elected 1821
John Quincy Adams	4 Mar. 1825	
Andrew Jackson	4 Mar. 1829	re-elected 1833
Martin Van Buren	4 Mar. 1837	
William Henry Harrison	4 Mar. 1841	d. 4 Apr. 1841
John Tyler, v.p.	4 Apr. 1841	
James Knox Polk	4 Mar. 1845	
Zachary Taylor	4 Mar. 1849	d. 9 July 1850
Millard Fillmore, v.p.	9 July 1850	
Franklin Pierce	4 Mar. 1853	
James Buchanan	4 Mar. 1857	
Abraham Lincoln	4 Mar. 1861	re-elected 1865
		shot 14 Apr. 1865
		d. 15 Apr.
Andrew Johnson, v.p.	15 Apr. 1865	
Hiram Ulysses Simpson Grant[1]	4 Mar. 1869	re-elected 1873
Rutherford Birchard Hayes	4 Mar. 1877	
James Abram Garfield	4 Mar. 1881	shot 2 July 1881
		d. 19 Sept.
Chester Alan Arthur, v.p.	19 Sept. 1881	
Stephen Grover Cleveland	4 Mar. 1885	

	presidency begins	
Benjamin Harrison	4 Mar. 1889	
Stephen Grover Cleveland	4 Mar. 1893	
William McKinley	4 Mar. 1897	re-elected 1901
		shot 6 Sept. 1901
		d. 14 Sept.
Theodore Roosevelt, v.p.	14 Sept. 1901	re-elected 1905
William Howard Taft	4 Mar. 1909	
Thomas Woodrow Wilson	4 Mar. 1913	re-elected 1917
Warren Gamaliel Harding	4 Mar. 1921	d. 2 Aug. 1923
John Calvin Coolidge, v.p.	2 Aug. 1923	re-elected 1925
Herbert Clark Hoover	4 Mar. 1929	
Franklin Delano Roosevelt	4 Mar. 1933	re-elected 1937, 1941, 1945
		d. 12 Apr. 1945
Harry S. Truman, v.p.	12 Apr. 1945	re-elected 1949
Dwight David Eisenhower	20 Jan. 1953	re-elected 1957
John Fitzgerald Kennedy	20 Jan. 1961	shot and d. 22 Nov. 1963
Lyndon Baines Johnson, v.p.	22 Nov. 1963	re-elected 1965
Richard Milhous Nixon	20 Jan. 1969	re-elected 1973
		res. 9 Aug. 1974
Gerald Rudolph Ford, v.p.[2]	9 Aug. 1974	
James Earl Carter, Jr	20 Jan. 1977	
Ronald Reagan	20 Jan. 1981	

[1] Christened Hiram Ulysses; known as Ulysses S. (for Simpson, his mother's maiden name) at West Point and thereafter.

[2] Christened Leslie King, Jr; subsequently took step-father's surname and changed forenames.

POPES FROM 422

The following list is derived, as far as Pelagius II, from that in *Annuario pontificio per l'anno 1976* (Vatican City, 1976), collated with those in P. B. Gams, *Series episcoporum ecclesiae catholicae* (1866 and 1873; reprinted Leipzig, 1931); Louis Duchesne (ed.), *Le liber pontificalis: texte, introduction et commentaire*, i (Paris, 1886; reprinted, 1955); and Philippus Jaffé (ed.), *Regesta pontificum Romanorum ad annum 1198*, i (2nd ed., Berlin, 1885); and with the biographies of individual popes in the *New catholic encyclopaedia* (15 vols; San Francisco, London, Toronto and Sydney, 1967). The editors are grateful to Dr Michael Haren for preparing this section of the list. From Gregory I to the accession of Paul VI, the list is based on C. R. Cheney (ed.), *Handbook of dates for students of English history* (corrected reprint; London, 1970), by courtesy of the Royal Historical Society. Additional information for the early fifteenth century has been provided by the editors, with reference to Hermann Grotefend, *Taschenbuch der Zeitrechnung des deutschen Mittelalters und der Neuzeit* (10th ed., Hanover, 1960). Particulars of the last three popes have been kindly supplied by Dr Haren.

This list begins with Celestine I, in whose pontificate the association of the papacy with Ireland begins. All dates from the death of Gregory XIII onwards are given in New Style; Old Style dates are also given for 1582-1752. Antipopes and those of doubtful status are shown in square brackets.

	accession	death unless otherwise stated
Celestine I	cor. ?10 Sept. 422	?27 July 432
Sixtus III	cor. ?31 July 432	18/19 Aug. 440
Leo I	el. Aug. 440 cor. 29 Sept. 440	bur. 10 Nov. 461
Hilary	cor. ?12/19 Nov. 461	21/29 Feb. 468
Simplicius	cor. 25 Feb./3 Mar. 468	2/10 Mar. 483
Felix III (II)[1]	cor. 6/13 Mar. 483	25 Feb./1 Mar. 492
Gelasius I	cor. ?1 Mar. 492	19/21 Nov. 496
Anastasius II	cor. ?24 Nov. 496	d. 17/19 Nov. 498 bur. 19 Nov. 498
Symmachus	cor. 22 Nov. 498	bur. 19 July 514
[Laurentius	cor. ?22 Nov. 498	?505]
Hormisdas	cor. 20 July 514	d. ?6 Aug. 523 bur. 7 Aug. 523
John I	cor. 13 Aug. 523	18 May 526
Felix IV (III)	cor. 12 July 526	15/22 Sept. 530
Boniface II	el. ?17/22 Sept. 530 cor. 22 Sept. 530	bur. 17 Oct. 532
[Dioscorus	el. ?17/22 Sept. 530 cor. 22 Sept. 530	14 Oct. 530]
John II	el. and cor. late Dec./early Jan. 532/3 or cor. 2 Jan. 533	d. ?8 May 535 bur. 27 May 535

	accession	*death unless otherwise stated*
Agapetus I	cor. ?13 May 535	22 Apr. 536
Silverius	cor. 1/8 June 536	dep. Mar. 537
		?res. 11 Nov. 537
		d. 2 Dec. 537 ?
Vigilius	cor. ?29 Mar. 537/Apr. × May 537	7 June 555
Pelagius I	cor. *p.* 7 June 555/16 Apr. 556	3 Mar. 560/61
John III	cor. 14/17 July 560/61	bur. 13 July 573/4
Benedict I	cor. 3 June 574/5	bur. 31 July 578/9
Pelagius II	cor. 26/7 Nov. 578/9	bur. 6 Feb. or
		d. 7 Feb. 590
Gregory I	el. ? Feb. 590	12 Mar. 604
	cor. 3 Sept. 590	
Sabinian	cor. 13 Sept. 604	22 Feb. 606
Boniface III	cor. 19 Feb. 607	12 Nov. 607
Boniface IV	cor. 15 Sept. 608	25 May 615
Deusdedit	cor. 19 Oct. 615	8 Nov. 618
Boniface V	cor. 23 Dec. 619	25 Oct. 625
Honorius I	cor. ?27 Oct. 625	12 Oct. 638
Severinus	el. ? Oct. 638	2 Aug. 640
	cor. 28 May 640	
John IV	cor. 24 Dec. 640	12 Oct. 642
Theodore I	cor. 24 Nov. 642	14 May 649
Martin I	cor. 5 July 649	exiled 17 June 653
		d. 26 Sept. 655
Eugenius I	cor. 10 Aug. 654	2 June 657
Vitalian	cor. 30 July 657	27 Jan. 672
Adeodatus	cor. 11 Apr. 672	17 June 676
Donus	el. Aug. 676	11 Apr. 678
	cor. 2 Nov. 676	
Agatho	cor. 27 June 678	10 Jan. 681
Leo II	el. *a.* Dec. 681	3 July 683
	cor. 17 Aug. 682	
Benedict II	el. summer 683	8 May 685
	cor. 26 June 684	
John V	cor. 23 July 685	2 Aug. 686
Conon	cor. 21 Oct. 686	21 Sept. 687
[Theodore	el. *p.* 21 Sept. 687	res. Oct. × Dec. 687]
[Paschal	el. *p.* 21 Sept. 687	dep. *p.* 15 Dec. 687
		d. ?692]
Sergius I	el. Oct. × Dec. 687	8 Sept. 701
	cor. 15 Dec. 687	
John VI	cor. 30 Oct. 701	11 Jan. 705
John VII	cor. 1 Mar. 705	18 Oct. 707
Sisinnius	cor. 15 Jan. 708	4 Feb. 708
Constantine I	cor. 25 Mar. 708	9 Apr. 715

	accession	death unless otherwise stated
Gregory II	cor. 19 May 715	11 Feb. 731
Gregory III	el. 11 Feb. 731 cor. 18 Mar. 731	29 Nov. 741
Zacharias	cor. 10 Dec. 741	15 Mar. 752
Stephen II (III)[2]	el. 18 × 25 Mar. 752 cor. 26 Mar. 752	?26 Apr. 757
Paul I	el. ?26 Apr. 757 cor. 29 May 757	28 June 767
Constantine II	el. 28 June 767 cor. 5 July 767	dep. 6 Aug. 768
[Philip	el. 31 July 768	dep. 31 July 768]
Stephen III (IV)	el. 1 Aug. 768 cor. 7 Aug. 768	24 Jan. 772
Adrian I	el. 1 Feb. 772 cor. 9 Feb. 772	25 Dec. 795
Leo III	el. 26 Dec. 795 cor. 27 Dec. 795	12 June 816
Stephen IV (V)	cor. 22 June 816	24 Jan. 817
Paschal I	cor. 25 Jan. 817	?11 Feb. 824
Eugenius II	cor. a. 6 June 824	Aug. 827
Valentine	cor. ? Aug. 827	? Sept. 827
Gregory IV	el. Dec. 827 cor. 5 Jan. 828	25 Jan. 844
[John	? Jan. 844]	
Sergius II	cor. ? Jan. 844	a. 27 Jan. 847
Leo IV	cor. 10 Apr. 847	17 July 855
Benedict III	el. 17 July 855 cor. ?6 Oct. 855	?17 Apr. 858
[Anastasius	el. Aug. 855	expelled 24 Sept. 855]
Nicholas I	cor. 24 Apr. 858	13 Nov. 867
Adrian II	cor. 14 Dec. 867	?14 Dec. 872
John VIII	cor. 14 Dec. 872	15 Dec. 882
Marinus I (Martin II)	cor. Dec. 882	15 May 884
Adrian III	cor. 17 May 884	Sept. 885
Stephen V (VI)	cor. ? Sept. 885	14 Sept. 891
Formosus	el. ?late Sept. 891 cor. ?6 Oct. 891	4 Apr. 896
[Boniface VI	el. Apr. 896	? May 896]
Stephen VI (VII)	el. ? May 896	expelled ? July 897
Romanus	cor. early Aug. 897	? Nov. 897
Theodore II	cor. ? Nov. 897	? Dec. 897
John IX	cor. ? June 898	? May 900
Benedict IV	cor. 900	?late July 903
Leo V	el. ?late July 903	? Sept. 903
Christopher	cor. ? Sept. 903	expelled Jan. 904
Sergius III	cor. 29 Jan. 904	14 Apr. 911

	accession	*death unless otherwise stated*
Anastasius III ?	cor. ? Apr. 911	? June 913
Lando	cor. ?late July 913	? Feb. 914
John X	cor. Mar. 914	dep. ? May 928
Leo VI	cor. ? May 928	? Dec. 928
Stephen VII (VIII)	cor. ? Jan. 929	? Feb. 931
John XI	cor. Feb./Mar. 931	Dec. 935/Jan. 936
Leo VII	cor. ?3 Jan. 936	July 939
Stephen VIII (IX)	cor. ?14 July 939	?late Oct. 942
Marinus II (Martin III)	cor. ?30 Oct. 942	early May 946
Agapitus II	cor. 10 May 946	Dec. 955
John XII	cor. ?16 Dec. 955	dep. 4 Dec. 963
		d. 14 May 964
Leo VIII	el. 4 Dec. 963	? Mar. 965
	cor. 6 Dec. 963	
Benedict V	cor. ?22 May 964	dep. 23 June 964
		d. 4 July 966
John XIII	cor. 1 Oct. 965	6 Sept. 972
Benedict VI	cor. 19 Jan. 973	? June 974
[Boniface VII	el. ? June 974	exp. ? July 974
		returned Aug. 984
		d. July 985]
Benedict VII	cor. Oct. 974	10 July 983
John XIV	cor. ? Aug./Dec. 983	dep. Apr. 984
		d. 20 Aug. 984
John XV	cor. ? Aug. 985	? Apr. 996
Gregory V	cor. 3 May 996	18 Feb. 999
[John XVI	cor. ? Apr. 997	dep. ?Feb. 998]
Silvester II	el. ?early Apr. 999	12 May 1003
	cor. ?2/9 Apr. 999	
John XVII	cor. ? June 1003	? Dec. 1003
John XVIII	cor. ? Jan. 1004	? July 1009
Sergius IV	cor. ?31 July 1009	12 May 1012
Benedict VIII	el. ?17 May 1012	7/9 Apr. 1024
	cor. 18 May 1012	
[Gregory	el. ? May 1012	exp. late 1012]
John XIX	cor. Apr./May 1024	?6 Nov. 1032
Benedict IX	el. ?12 Dec. 1032	res. 1 May 1045
	cor. ?17 Dec. 1032	dep. 20 Dec. 1046
		returned 8 Nov. 1047
		exp. 17 July 1048
[Silvester III	el. 10 Jan. 1045	dep. 10 Mar. 1045]
	cor. 13/20 Jan. 1045	
Gregory VI	el. 1 May 1045	dep. 20 Dec. 1046
	cor. ?5 May 1045	
Clement II	el. 24 Dec. 1046	9 Oct. 1047
	cor. 25 Dec. 1046	
Damasus II	el. Dec. 1047	9 Aug. 1048
	cor. 17 July 1048	

	accession	*death unless otherwise stated*
Leo IX	el. Dec. 1048 cor. 12 Feb. 1049	19 Apr. 1054
Victor II	el. late 1054 cor. 16 Apr. 1055	28 July 1057
Stephen IX (X)	el. 2 Aug. 1057 cor. 3 Aug. 1057	29 Mar. 1058
Benedict X	el. 4/5 Apr. 1058 cor. 5 Apr. 1058	dep. 24 Jan. 1059
Nicholas II	el. late Dec. 1058 cor. 24 Jan. 1059	?22 July 1061
Alexander II	el. 29/30 Sept. 1061 cor. 30 Sept. 1061	21 Apr. 1073
[Honorius II	cor. 28 Oct. 1061	late 1072]
Gregory VII	el. 22 Apr. 1073 cor. 29/30 June 1073	25 May 1085
[Clement III	el. 25 June 1080 cor. 24 Mar. 1084	Sept. 1100]
Victor III	el. 24 May 1086 cor. 9 May 1087	16 Sept. 1087
Urban II	el. and cor. 12 Mar. 1088	29 July 1099
Paschal II	el. 13 Aug. 1099 cor. 14 Aug. 1099	21 Jan. 1118
[Theodoric	cor. Sept. 1100	exp. late 1100]
[Albert	el. and dep. Feb. × Mar. 1102]	
[Silvester IV	el. 18 Nov. 1105	dep. 13 Apr. 1111]
Gelasius II	el. 24 Jan. 1118 cor. 10 Mar. 1118	29 Jan. 1119
[Gregory VIII	el. and cor. 8 Mar. 1118	dep. Apr. 1121]
Calixtus II	el. 2 Feb. 1119 cor. 9 Feb. 1119	13 Dec. 1124
Honorius II	el. 16 Dec. 1124 cor. 21 Dec. 1124	13/14 Feb. 1130
Innocent II	el. 14 Feb. 1130 cor. 23 Feb. 1130	24 Sept. 1143
[Anacletus II	el. 14 Feb. 1130 cor. 23 Feb. 1130	25 Jan. 1138]
[Victor IV	el. ?15 Mar. 1138	res. 29 May 1138]
Celestine II	el. and cor. 26 Sept. 1143	8 Mar. 1144
Lucius II	el. 12 Mar. 1144	15 Feb. 1145
Eugenius III	el. 15 Feb. 1145 cor. 18 Feb. 1145	8 July 1153
Anastasius IV	el. or cor. 12 July 1153	3 Dec. 1154
Adrian IV	el. 4 Dec. 1154 cor. 5 Dec. 1154	1 Sept. 1159
Alexander III	el. 7 Sept. 1159 cor. 20 Sept. 1159	30 Aug. 1181
[Victor IV	el. 7 Sept. 1159 cor. 4 Oct. 1159	20 Apr. 1164]

	accession	*death unless otherwise stated*
[Paschal III	el. 22 Apr. 1164 cor. 26 Apr. 1164	Sept. 1168]
[Calixtus III	el. ? Sept. 1168	res. 29 Aug. 1178]
[Innocent III	el. ?29 Sept. 1179	dep. Jan. 1180]
Lucius III	el. 1 Sept. 1181 cor. 6 Sept. 1181	25 Nov. 1185
Urban III	el. 25 Nov. 1185 cor. 1 Dec. 1185	20 Oct. 1187
Gregory VIII	el. 21 Oct. 1187 cor. 25 Oct. 1187	17 Dec. 1187
Clement III	el. 19 Dec. 1187 cor. 20 Dec. 1187	late Mar. 1191
Celestine III	el. 30 Mar. 1191 cor. 14 Apr. 1191	8 Jan. 1198
Innocent III	el. 8 Jan. 1198 cor. 22 Feb. 1198	16 July 1216
Honorius III	el. 18 July 1216 cor. 24 July 1216	18 Mar. 1227
Gregory IX	el. 19 Mar. 1227 cor. 21 Mar. 1227	22 Aug. 1241
Celestine IV	el. 25 Oct. 1241 cor. ?27 Oct. 1241	10 Nov. 1241
Innocent IV	el. 25 June 1243 cor. 28 June 1243	7 Dec. 1254
Alexander IV	el. 12 Dec. 1254 cor. 20 Dec. 1254	25 May 1261
Urban IV	el. 29 Aug. 1261 cor. 4 Sept. 1261	2 Oct. 1264
Clement IV	el. 5 Feb. 1265 cor. 15 Feb. 1265	29 Nov. 1268
Gregory X	el. 1 Sept. 1271 cor. 27 Mar. 1272	10 Jan. 1276
Innocent V	el. 21 Jan. 1276 cor. 22 Feb. 1276	22 June 1276
Adrian V	el. 11 July 1276	18 Aug. 1276
John XXI[3]	el. ?8 Sept. 1276 cor. 20 Sept. 1276	20 May 1277
Nicholas III	el. 25 Nov. 1277 cor. 26 Dec. 1277	22 Aug. 1280
Martin IV	el. 22 Feb. 1281 cor. 23 Mar. 1281	28 Mar. 1285
Honorius IV	el. 2 Apr. 1285 cor. 20 May 1285	3 Apr. 1287
Nicholas IV	el. 15/22 Feb. 1288 cor. 22 Feb. 1288	4 Apr. 1292
Celestine V	el. 5 July 1294 cor. 29 Aug. 1294	res. 13 Dec. 1294

	accession	*death unless otherwise stated*
Boniface VIII	el. 24 Dec. 1294 cor. 23 Jan. 1295	12 Oct. 1303
Benedict XI	el. 22 Oct. 1303 cor. 27 Oct. 1303	7 July 1304
Clement V	el. 5 June 1305 cor. 14 Nov. 1305	20 Apr. 1314
John XXII	el. 7 Aug. 1316 cor. 5 Sept. 1316	4 Dec. 1334
[Nicholas V	el. 12 May 1328 cor. 22 May 1328	res. 25 July 1330]
Benedict XII	el. 20 Dec. 1334 cor. 8 Jan. 1335	25 Apr. 1342
Clement VI	el. 7 May 1342 cor. 19 May 1342	6 Dec. 1352
Innocent VI	el. 18 Dec. 1352 cor. 30 Dec. 1352	12 Sept. 1362
Urban V	el. 28 Sept. 1362 cor. 6 Nov. 1362	19 Dec. 1370
Gregory XI	el. 30 Dec. 1370 cor. 5 Jan. 1371	27 Mar. 1378
Urban VI	el. 8 Apr. 1378 cor. 18 Apr. 1378	15 Oct. 1389
[Clement VII	el. 20 Sept. 1378 cor. 31 Oct. 1378	16 Sept. 1394]
Boniface IX	el. 2 Nov. 1389 cor. 9 Nov. 1389	1 Oct. 1404
[Benedict XIII	el. 28 Sept. 1394 cor. 11 Oct. 1394	dep. by Council of Pisa 5 June 1409, and by Council of Constance 26 July 1417 d. 29 Nov. 1422/ ?23 May 1423]
Innocent VII	el. 17 Oct. 1404 cor. 11 Nov. 1404	6 Nov. 1406
Gregory XII	el. 30 Nov. 1406 cor. 19 Dec. 1406	dep. by Council of Pisa 5 June 1409 res. 4 July 1415 d. 18 Oct. 1417
[Alexander V	el. 26 June 1409 cor. 7 July 1409	3 May 1410]
[John XXIII	el. 17 May 1410 cor. 25 May 1410	dep. by Council of Constance 29 May 1415 d. 22 Nov. 1419]
Martin V	el. 11 Nov. 1417 cor. 21 Nov. 1417	20 Feb. 1431

	accession	*death unless otherwise stated*
[Clement VIII	el. 10 June 1423	res. 26 July 1429 d. 28 Dec. 1447]
[Benedict XIV	el. 12 Nov. 1425	1430]
Eugenius IV	el. 3 Mar. 1431 cons. 11 Mar. 1431	suspended by Council of Basel 24 Jan. 1438 and dep. by Council 25 June 1439 d. 23 Feb. 1447
[Felix V (IV)	el. 5 Nov. 1439 cor. 24 July 1440	res. 7 Apr. 1449]
Nicholas V	el. 6 Mar. 1447 cor. 19 Mar. 1447	24 Mar. 1455
Calixtus III	el. 8 Apr. 1455 cor. 20 Apr. 1455	6 Aug. 1458
Pius II	el. 19 Aug. 1458 cor. 3 Sept. 1458	15 Aug. 1464
Paul II	el. 30 Aug. 1464 cor. 16 Sept. 1464	26 July 1471
Sixtus IV	el. 9 Aug. 1471 cor. 25 Aug. 1471	12 Aug. 1484
Innocent VIII	el. 29 Aug. 1484 cor. 12 Sept. 1484	25 July 1492
Alexander VI	el. 11 Aug. 1492 cor. 26 Aug. 1492	18 Aug. 1503
Pius III	el. 22 Sept. 1503 cons. 1 Oct. 1503 cor. 8 Oct. 1503	18 Oct. 1503
Julius II	el. 1 Nov. 1503 cor. 26 Nov. 1503	20/21 Feb. 1513
Leo X	el. 9 Mar. 1513 cons. 17 Mar. 1513 cor. 19 Mar. 1513	1 Dec. 1521
Adrian VI	el. 9 Jan. 1522 cor. 31 Aug. 1522	14 Sept. 1523
Clement VII	el. 19 Nov. 1523 cor. 26 Nov. 1523	25 Sept. 1534
Paul III	el. 13 Oct. 1534 cor. 3 Nov. 1534	10 Nov. 1549
Julius III	el. 7 Feb. 1550 cor. 22 Feb. 1550	23 Mar. 1555
Marcellus II	el. 9 Apr. 1555 cor. 10 Apr. 1555	1 May 1555
Paul IV	el. 23 May 1555 cor. 26 May 1555	18 Aug. 1559
Pius IV	el. 25 Dec. 1559 cor. 6 Jan. 1560	9 Dec. 1565

	accession	*death unless otherwise stated*
Pius V	el. 7 Jan. 1566 cor. 17 Jan. 1566	1 May 1572
Gregory XIII	el. 13 May 1572 cor. 25 May 1572	31 Mar/10 Apr. 1585
Sixtus V	el. 14/24 Apr. 1585 cor. 21 Apr./1 May 1585	17/27 Aug. 1590
Urban VII	el. 5/15 Sept. 1590	17/27 Sept. 1590
Gregory XIV	el. 25 Nov./5 Dec. 1590 cor. 28 Nov./8 Dec. 1590	6/16 Oct. 1591
Innocent IX	el. 19/29 Oct. 1591 cor. 24 Oct./3 Nov. 1591	20/30 Dec. 1591
Clement VIII	el. 20/30 Jan. 1592 cor. 30 Jan./9 Feb. 1592	21 Feb./3 Mar. 1605
Leo XI	el. 22 Mar./1 Apr. 1605 cor. 31 Mar./10 Apr. 1605	17/27 Apr. 1605
Paul V	el. 6/16 May 1605 cor. 19/29 May 1605	18/28 Jan. 1621
Gregory XV	el. 30 Jan./9 Feb. 1621 cor. 4/14 Feb. 1621	28 June/8 July 1623
Urban VIII	el. 27 July/6 Aug. 1623 cor. 19/29 Sept. 1623	19/29 July 1644
Innocent X	el. 5/15 Sept. 1644 cor. 24 Sept./4 Oct. 1644	28 Dec. 1654/7 Jan. 1655
Alexander VII	el. 28 Mar./7 Apr. 1655 cor. 8/18 Apr. 1655	12/22 May 1667
Clement IX	el. 10/20 June 1667 cor. 16/26 June 1667	29 Nov./9 Dec. 1669
Clement X	el. 19/29 Apr. 1670 cor. 1/11 May 1670	12/22 July 1676
Innocent XI	el. 11/21 Sept. 1676 cor. 24 Sept./4 Oct. 1676	2/12 Aug. 1689
Alexander VIII	el. 26 Sept./6 Oct. 1689 cor. 6/16 Oct. 1689	22 Jan./1 Feb. 1691
Innocent XII	el. 2/12 July 1691 cor. 5/15 July 1691	16/27 Sept. 1700
Clement XI	el. 12/23 Nov. 1700 cons. 19/30 Nov. 1700 cor. 27 Nov./8 Dec. 1700	8/19 Mar. 1721
Innocent XIII	el. 27 Apr./8 May 1721 cor. 7/18 May 1721	25 Feb./7 Mar. 1724
Benedict XIII	el. 18/29 May 1724 cor. 24 May/4 June 1724	10/21 Feb. 1730
Clement XII	el. 1/12 July 1730 cor. 5/16 July 1730	26 Jan./6 Feb. 1740
Benedict XIV	el. 6/17 Aug. 1740 cor. 11/22 Aug. 1740	3 May 1758

	accession	death unless otherwise stated
Clement XIII	el. 6 July 1758 cor. 16 July 1758	2 Feb. 1769
Clement XIV	el. 19 May 1769 cons. 28 May 1769 cor. 4 June 1769	22 Sept. 1774
Pius VI	el. 15 Feb. 1775 cor. 22 Feb. 1775	29 Aug. 1799
Pius VII	el. 14 Mar. 1800 cor. 21 Mar. 1800	20 Aug. 1823
Leo XII	el. 28 Sept. 1823 cor. 5 Oct. 1823	10 Feb. 1829
Pius VIII	el. 31 Mar. 1829 cor. 5 Apr. 1829	30 Nov. 1830
Gregory XVI	el. 2 Feb. 1831 cor. 6 Feb. 1831	1 June 1846
Pius IX	el. 16 June 1846 cor. 21 June 1846	7 Feb. 1878
Leo XIII	el. 20 Feb. 1878 cor. 3 Mar. 1878	20 July 1903
Pius X	el. 4 Aug. 1903 cor. 9 Aug. 1903	20 Aug. 1914
Benedict XV	el. 3 Sept. 1914 cor. 6 Sept. 1914	22 Jan. 1922
Pius XI	el. 6 Feb. 1922 cor. 12 Feb. 1922	10 Feb. 1939
Pius XII	el. 2 Mar. 1939 cor. 12 Mar. 1939	9 Oct. 1958
John XXIII	el. 28 Oct. 1958 cor. 4 Nov. 1958	3 June 1963
Paul VI	el. 21 June 1963 cor. 30 June 1963	6 Aug. 1978
John Paul I	el. 26 Aug. 1978 inaug. 3 Sept. 1978[4]	28 Sept. 1978
John Paul II	el. 16 Oct. 1978 inaug. 22 Oct. 1978	

[1] The dual numbering in this case, and in those of subsequent popes of this name, arises from the erroneous inclusion of a Felix II in the list of fourth-century popes. As the wrong numbering is still customarily used, the correct numbering is given in parentheses.

[2] The dual numbering in this case, and in those of subsequent popes of this name, arises from the election on 15 × 22 Mar. 752 of a Stephen who died 18 × 25 Mar. 752 before consecration; thus, although considered as 'Stephen II' in some later lists, he was not in the middle ages, and is not now, reckoned in the sequence.

[3] In the thirteenth century, the period of John XIV's pontificate (983–4) was erroneously ascribed to two popes, 'John XIV' and 'John XV', with consequential error in the numbering of subsequent popes of this name, John XIX (1024–32) being reckoned as John XX. Pietro Giuliani, therefore, became pope in 1276 under the title John XXI.

[4] John Paul I chose a ceremony of inauguration instead of coronation, and his successor followed this example.

IV

PARLIAMENTS
FROM 1264

CONTENTS

PARLIAMENT IN IRELAND, 1264-1800

(A) 1264-1586

ART COSGROVE

THE following list is based, up to 1482, on that given in H. G. Richardson and G. O. Sayles, *The Irish parliament in the middle ages* (2nd ed., Philadelphia, 1964), pp 332-65, and incorporates the corrections and additions made by Dr A. J. Otway-Ruthven in *I.H.S.*, xvi, no. 62 (Sept. 1968), p. 214. For the period 1494-1586 it is based on the list of parliaments and great councils published by Professor D. B. Quinn in *I.H.S.*, iii, no. 9 (Mar. 1942), pp 60-77. Footnotes indicate any variation from these authorities. Dr Steven Ellis has thoroughly revised the list for 1483-94 and provided the corresponding footnotes, and has also furnished additional information on the parliament of 1469. Further evidence relating to these changes appears in his doctoral thesis, 'The administration of the lordship of Ireland under the early Tudors' (Queen's University, Belfast, 1978). See also his 'Parliaments and great councils, 1483-99: addenda et corrigenda' in *Anal. Hib.*, no. 29 (1980), pp 95-111.

There is some evidence to suggest that the word 'parliament' may have been in use in Ireland as early as 1234-5,[1] but the earliest known Irish parliament for which there is a definite record met in 1264. In origin, parliament was not a representative assembly but a meeting of the chief governor's council to which were summoned various magnates or their delegates, i.e. an afforced council. There is no certain evidence of the presence of elected representatives in parliament before 1297, when two knights were summoned from each of ten counties and five liberties, and a number of towns were represented for the first time in the 1299 parliament; but these elected representatives were not essential to the working of parliament, and for much of the fourteenth century it could and did function without them.

From the later fourteenth century onwards, elected representatives, the commons, had an established place in parliament and a distinction emerged between them and the lords, those peers of parliament who were summoned by individual writ. The Irish parliament, unlike its contemporary English counterpart, also contained a third element, representatives or proctors of the diocesan clergy, who continued to form part of the assembly until their formal exclusion in 1537.

---

[1] J. A. Watt, 'The first recorded use of the word "parliament" in Ireland?' in *Irish Jurist*, iv (1969), pp 123-6.

The conciliar origins of parliament are underlined by the application of the term 'great council' to assemblies which in the fifteenth century differed little in composition or function from those styled 'parliaments'. Afforced councils also continued to meet. These varied in composition and differed from great councils in that they were summoned not under the Irish great seal but under the lieutenant's privy seal.[2] In this list, parliaments have been denoted by the letter P, great councils by G.C., and other afforced meetings of the council by C. Distinctions between these types of assembly are not easily drawn, and the classification used here is taken from the sources cited above, in which it is based upon the terminology (not always consistent) of contemporary documents.[3] After 1494, as a result of Poynings' law, much of the administrative and judicial business of government that had previously been transacted in parliaments or great councils was dealt with by the council. Parliaments, from this date, were accordingly summoned much less frequently. Great councils and afforced councils continued to be held to give force to certain administrative decisions; although the evidence is incomplete before 1534, by the mid–Tudor period afforced sessions of the council were being held about twice a year.[4] As a result of this separation of functions, great councils and afforced councils do not appear in this list after 1493.

Up to 1459, only the beginnings of sessions are dated. From 1460, the closing date of each session has been given where possible; whether the session was adjourned or prorogued has not been indicated, since the terms appear to have been used interchangeably in this period, and the word 'session' is not used in the headings of any statute roll before that for the parliament of 1585-6.[5] The terminal dates shown below from 1464 onwards are identical with the dates of dissolution given in Professor Quinn's list except for the period revised by Dr Ellis.

[2] H. G. Richardson and G. O. Sayles, *Ir. parl. in middle ages*, esp. pp 8, 61, 188-9, 332.
[3] See ibid., pp 101-9, 187-8, 332.
[4] D. B. Quinn (ed.), 'Calendar of the Irish council book, 1 Mar. 1581 to 1 July 1586' in *Anal. Hib.*, xxiv (1967), p. 97.
[5] D. B. Quinn, 'Parliaments and great councils in Ireland, 1461-1586' in *I.H.S.*, iii, no. 9 (Mar. 1942), p. 62; Professor Quinn's list, however, indicates whether 'adjournment' or 'prorogation' was used in the contemporary documents.

year	regnal year	date of opening	place	
1264	48 Hen. III	18 June	Castledermot	P
1269	53-4 Hen. III	*p.* 29 Sept.(?)		P(?)
1276	4-5 Edw. I	between 29 Sept. 1276 and 29 Sept. 1277	Kildare	P
1277			Kilkenny	P
1278	6 Edw. I	Easter (?)		P

year	regnal year	date of opening	place	
1279	7 Edw. I	22 Sept.	Dublin	P
1281	9 Edw. I	*p.* 13 Apr.	Dublin	P
1289	17 Edw. I	*p.* 29 Sept.	Dublin	P
1290	18 Edw. I	*a.* 13 Jan.	Dublin	P
1290	18 Edw. I	3 × 8 Apr.	Kilkenny	P
1291	19 Edw. I	6 May	Dublin	P
1292	20 Edw. I	28 Jan.	Dublin	C
1295	23 Edw. I	12 Mar.	Kilkenny	P
1296	24 Edw. I	7 Jan.	Kilkenny	P
1297	25 Edw. I	*a.* May	Dublin	P
1298	26 Edw. I	27 Jan.	Dublin	P
1298	26 Edw. I	Apr. × May		P
1299	27 Edw. I	20 × 27 Jan.	Dublin	P
1299	27 Edw. I	3 May	Dublin	P
1300	28 Edw. I	24 Apr.	Dublin	P
1302	30 Edw. I	13 × 20 May	Dublin	P
1302	30–31 Edw. I	*p.* 1 Oct.	Dublin	P
1302	31 Edw. I	3 Dec.	Kilkenny	P
1307	35 Edw. I	9 Apr.	Dublin	P
1310	3 Edw. II	9 Feb.	Kilkenny	P
1310	3 Edw. II	*p.* 24 Mar.	Kildare	P
1312	6 Edw. II	8 July	Dublin	P
1315	8 Edw. II	beginning of June	Kilkenny	P
1315	9 Edw. II	27 Oct.	Dublin	P
1316	9 Edw. II	14 Feb.		P
1316	10 Edw. II	8 July	Kilkenny	P
1317	10 Edw. II	8 May	Dublin	P
1317	10 Edw. II	27 June	Kilmainham	P
1320	13 Edw. II	27 Apr.	Dublin	P
1324	17 Edw. II	13 May	Dublin	P
1325	19 Edw. II	8 July	Kilkenny	P
1326	19 Edw. II	11 May	Kilkenny	P
1326	20 Edw. II	*p.* 8 July	Dublin	P
1327	1 Edw. III	10 May	Dublin	P
1328	2 Edw. III	2 Feb.	Kilkenny	P
1328	2 Edw. III	15 Aug.	Dublin	P
1329	2 Edw. III	20 Jan.	Dublin	P

year	regnal year	date of opening	place	
1329	3 Edw. III	2 Apr.	Dublin	P
1330	4 Edw. III	8 July	Kilkenny	P
1331	4 Edw. III	21 Jan.	Dublin	P
1331	5 Edw. III	1 July adjourned to 1 Aug.	Dublin Kilkenny	P
1332	6 Edw. III	17 Aug.	Dublin	P
1333	7 Edw. III	6 June	Dublin	P
1335	8–9 Edw. III	uncertain		
1338	11 Edw. III	14 Jan.	Dublin	
1338	12 Edw. III	Mar.		P
1341	15 Edw. III	Oct. adjourned to Nov.	Dublin Kilkenny	P
1345	19 Edw. III	24 Apr.	Dublin	P
1345	19 Edw. III	5 June	Dublin	P
1346	20 Edw. III	16 Oct.	Kilkenny	C
1348	22 Edw. III	May	Kilkenny	C
1350	24 Edw. III	25 June	Kilkenny	G.C.
1351	25 Edw. III	17 Oct.	Dublin	G.C.
1351	25 Edw. III	31 Oct.	Kilkenny	G.C.
1353	27 Edw. III	Oct.	Dublin	P
1355	29 Edw. III	19 May	Naas	C
1356	30 Edw. III	June		P
1358	32 Edw. III	a. Apr.		P(?)
1359	32 Edw. III	14 Jan.	Kilkenny	P
1359	33 Edw. III	1 Apr.	Dublin	C
1359	33 Edw. III	8 Apr.	Waterford	C
1359	33 Edw. III	5 Aug.	Dublin	C
1360	34 Edw. III	27 July	Kilkenny	G.C.
1362	35 Edw. III	7 Jan.	Dublin	P
1363	37 Edw. III	late in year		
1366	40 Edw. III	19 Feb.	Kilkenny	P
1367	41 Edw. III	14 June	Kilkenny	P
1368	42 Edw. III	1 May	Dublin	P
1369	43 Edw. III	30 July	Dublin	P
1370	43 Edw. III	2 Jan.	Dublin	C
1370	44 Edw. III	22 Apr.	Dublin	G.C.
1371	44 Edw. III	7 Jan.	Kilkenny	P

year	regnal year	date of opening	place	
1371	45 Edw. III	Apr.	Ballydoyle/ Cashel[6]	G.C.
1371	45 Edw. III	8 June	Ballydoyle/ Cashel[7]	P
1372	45 Edw. III	14 Jan.	Kilkenny	P
1372	46 Edw. III	25 Feb.	Dublin	G.C.
1372	46 Edw. III	8 June	Ballyhea	C
1373	46 Edw. III	7 Jan.	Kilkenny	P
1374	48 Edw. III	29 Mar.	Dublin	C
1374	48 Edw. III	27 May	Dublin	G.C.
1375	48 Edw. III	20 Jan.	Dublin	P
1375	49 Edw. III	18 June	Kilkenny	P
1375	49 Edw. III	6 Oct.	Kilkenny	P
1377	50 Edw. III	8 Jan.	Dublin	P
1378	1 Rich. II	14 Jan.	Castledermot	G.C.
1378	1 Rich. II	8 Mar.	Castledermot	P
1379	2 Rich. II	30 Apr.	Castledermot	C
1380	3 Rich. II	early in year		P(?)
1380	3 Rich. II	30 Apr.	Castledermot	P
1380	4 Rich. II	3 Nov.	Dublin	P
1381	5 Rich. II	5 Aug.	Clonmel	G.C.
1382	5 Rich. II	9 Jan.	Cork	C
1382	5 Rich. II	3 Mar.	Naas	C
1382	5 Rich. II	16 June	Dublin	P
1383	6 Rich. II	16 Jan.	Naas	C
1384	8 Rich. II	late in year		P
1385	9 Rich. II	17 July	Kilkenny	C
1385	9 Rich. II	23 Oct.	Dublin	G.C.
1388	12 Rich. II	6 July	Castledermot	G.C.
1388	12 Rich. II	20 July	Clonmel	C
1389	13 Rich. II	3 Dec.	Kilkenny	P
1390		adjourned to 3 Feb. further adjourned to unspecified dates	Castledermot Ballymore Naas	
1390	13 Rich. II	12 Mar.	Castledermot	P
1391	15 Rich. II	late in year	Castledermot	C

[⁶ *Footnotes for this section begin on p. 604.*]

year	regnal year	date of opening	place	
1392	15 Rich. II	29 Jan.	Trim	P
1392	16 Rich. II	Oct.	Castledermot	C
1393	16 Rich. II	13 Jan.	Kilkenny	P
1394	17 Rich. II	19 Feb.	Castledermot	P
1394	17 Rich. II	30 Mar.	Kilkenny	G.C.
1394	18 Rich. II	1 Dec.	Dublin	P
1395	18 Rich. II	19 Apr.	Kilkenny	C
1396	19–20 Rich. II	summer	Dublin	P
1398	21 Rich. II	10 June	Naas	C
1398	22 Rich. II	1 Aug. adjourned to 12 Aug.	Dunboyne Naas	C
1401	2 Hen. IV	spring		P
1401	3 Hen. IV	Dec.	Ross	P
1402	3 Hen. IV	13 Apr.	Dublin	P
1402	3–4 Hen. IV	Sept.	Dublin	P
1403	4 Hen. IV	*a.* 24 Feb. adjourned to *a.* 24 Feb. further adjourned to 5 Mar. further adjourned to 18 June	Dublin Waterford Waterford Kilkenny	P
1404	5 Hen. IV	3 Mar.	Castledermot	C
1404	5 Hen. IV	28 Apr.	Dublin	P
1404	5 Hen. IV	*a.* 4 Aug.	Castledermot	G.C.
1404	5 Hen. IV	12 Aug.	Dublin	G.C.
1407	8 Hen. IV	13 Jan.	Dublin Trim	P
1408	9 Hen. IV	*p.* 25 Mar.	Dublin	P
1409	10 Hen. IV	14 Jan.	Kilkenny	P
1409	10 Hen. IV	22 Apr.	Dublin	C
1409	11 Hen. IV	14 Oct.	Dublin	C
1410	11 Hen. IV	14 May	Dublin	P
1411	12–13 Hen. IV	Sept.	Naas	C
1412	13 Hen. IV	4 Feb.	Drogheda	C
1414	1 Hen. V	25 Feb.	Dublin	P
1415	3 Hen. V	13 May	Naas	C
1416	4 Hen. V	late in Mar. adjourned to 11 May	Dublin Trim	P
1417	4 Hen. V	27 Jan.	Dublin	P

year	regnal year	date of opening	place	
1417	5 Hen. V	26 June		C
1417	5 Hen. V	23 Oct.	Naas	C
1417	5 Hen. V	20 Nov. adjourned to 14 Dec.	Naas	G.C.
1418	5–6 Hen. V	14 Feb. adjourned to 30 May[8]	Dublin Trim	P
1419	7 Hen. V	May	Naas	C
1420	8–9 Hen. V	7 June adjourned to 2 Dec. further adjourned to	Dublin Dublin	P
1421		7 Apr.	Dublin	
1421	9 Hen. V	10 Oct.	Dublin	G.C.
1422	10 Hen. V	summer		
1423	2 Hen. VI	3 Nov.		G.C.
1425	3–4 Hen. VI	uncertain	Kilkenny	P
1426	5 Hen. VI	30 Nov.	Naas	G.C.
1427	5–6 Hen. VI	21 Mar. adjourned to 22 Sept.	Dublin Dublin	P
1427	6 Hen. VI	3 Nov.	Dublin	G.C.
1428	7 Hen. VI	5 Nov.	Dublin	P
1429	8 Hen. VI	9 Dec.	Dublin	G.C.
1430	8 Hen. VI	19 May	Dublin	P
1430	9 Hen. VI	30 Sept.	Dublin	G.C.
1431	9 Hen. VI	25 May	Dublin	P
1431	10 Hen. VI	23 Nov.		P
1433	11 Hen. VI	spring		
1433	12 Hen. VI	16 Oct.	Dublin	G.C.
1435	13 Hen. VI	7 Mar.	Dublin	P
1436	14 Hen. VI	16 Jan.		G.C.
1436	15 Hen. VI	16 Nov.	Dublin	P
1437	16 Hen. VI	15 Nov.	Dublin	P
1438	17 Hen. VI	17 Nov.	Dublin	P
1440	19 Hen. VI	11 Nov.	Drogheda	P
1441	19 Hen. VI	23 June	Naas	G.C.
1441	20 Hen. VI	17 Nov.	Dublin	P
1442	20 Hen. VI	6 July adjourned to 30 July	Naas Dublin	G.C.
1443	21 Hen. VI	25 Jan.	Drogheda	P
1443	22 Hen. VI	25 Oct.	Naas	G.C.

year	regnal year	date of opening	place	
1444	22 Hen. VI	24 Jan.	Dublin	P
1444	22 Hen. VI	26 June	Drogheda	C
1444	22 Hen. VI	21 Aug.	Drogheda	G.C.
1445	23 Hen. VI	5 Feb.	Dublin	P
1446	24 Hen. VI	4 Feb.	Dublin	G.C.
1447	25 Hen. VI	13 Jan.	Trim	P
1447	26 Hen. VI	20 Oct.	Naas	G.C.
1449	27 Hen. VI	28 Feb.	Dublin	P
1449	28 Hen. VI	17 Oct.	Dublin	G.C.
1450	28 Hen. VI	24 Apr.	Drogheda	P
1450	29 Hen. VI	27 Nov. adjourned to 14 Dec.	Drogheda Dublin	G.C.
1451	29 Hen. VI	26 Mar.	Drogheda	P
1451/2	30 Hen. VI	uncertain	Dublin	P
1453	31 Hen. VI	25 May	Dublin	G.C.
1454	·32 Hen. VI	5 July	Dublin	P
1455	33 Hen. VI	14 Feb.	Dublin	P
1455	33 Hen. VI	18 Apr.	Dublin	G.C.
1455	34 Hen. VI	17 Oct.	Dublin	P
1456	35 Hen. VI	5 Nov.	Naas	P
1457	35 Hen. VI	28 Jan.	Dublin	P
1458	36 Hen. VI	3 Feb.	Dublin	P
1459	37 Hen. VI	9 Feb.	Dublin	P

year	regnal year	dates of session	place	
1460	38 Hen. VI	8 Feb.–[ ]	Drogheda	P
		23 Feb.–[ ]	Dublin	
		3 Mar.–7 Mar.		
		28 Apr.–28 Apr.		
		9 June–11 June		
		21 July–[ ]		
1461	1 Edw. IV	12 June–[ ]	Naas	P
1462	1–2 Edw. IV	8 Jan.–[ ]	Dublin	G.C.
		8 Mar.–[ ]		
		3 May–[ ]		
1462	2 Edw. IV	15 Oct.–[ ]	Dublin	P
1463	3 Edw. IV	4 Nov.–10 Nov.	Wexford	P
		14 Nov.–19 Nov.	Waterford	
1464		20 Feb.–24 Feb.	Naas	
		27 Feb.–3 Mar.	Dublin	

year	regnal year	dates of session	place	
1465	5 Edw. IV	12 Aug.-17 Aug.	Trim	P
		14 Oct.-22 Oct.	Dublin	
		18 Nov.-[ ]	Drogheda	
1467	7-8 Edw. IV	11 Dec.-23 Dec.	Dublin	P
1468		4 Feb.-22 or 23 Feb.	Drogheda	
		2 May-3 May		
		30 May-31 May		
		20 June-28 June		
		11 July-13 July		
		26 or 27 July[9]-29 or 30 July		
		1 Sept.-3 Sept.		
		3 Oct.-5 Oct.		
		3 or 7 Nov.[10]-15 Nov.		
1469	8 Edw. IV	27 Jan.-[ ]	Drogheda	P
		adjourned to un-	Dublin	
		specified dates	Bray	
		diss. *a.* 10 Jan. 1470[11]	Dublin	
1470	10 Edw. IV	26 Nov.-[ ]	Dublin	P
1471	11-12 Edw. IV	29 Nov.-10 Dec.	Dublin	P
1472		2 Mar.-6 Mar.		
		25 May-29 May		
		13 July-17 July		
		12 Oct.-22 Oct.		
1472	12-13 Edw. IV	4 Dec.-[ ]	Naas	P
1473		11 Mar.-16 Mar.	Dublin	
		12 July[12]-[ ]		
		25 Oct.-29 Oct.		
1474	14 Edw. IV	18 Mar.-[ ]	Dublin	P
		[ ]-[ ]	Kilmainham	
1475	15-16 Edw. IV	21 July-[ ]	Dublin	P
		23 Oct.-[ ]	Drogheda	
1476		5 Feb.-[ ]	Dublin	
		6 May-[ ]		
		17 June-[ ]		
1476	16-17 Edw. IV	6 Dec.-[ ]	Drogheda	P
1477		14 Jan.-[ ]	Dublin	
		13 Oct.-[ ]		
1478	18 Edw. IV	29 May-[ ]	Naas	P
		6 July-[ ]	Dublin	
		14 Sept.-[ ]	Connell, Co. Kildare	
1478	18-19 Edw. IV	6 Nov.-[ ]	Trim	P
		19 Nov.-[ ]	Drogheda	
1479		31 May-[ ]	Dublin	

year	regnal year	dates of session	place	
1479	19–20 Edw. IV	10 Dec.-[ ]	Dublin	P
1480		7 Feb.-[ ]	Dublin	
		8 May–8 May[13]	Naas	
		15 May-[ ]		
		10 July-[ ]	Dublin	
1481		15 Jan.-[ ]		
1481	21–2 Edw. IV	19 Oct.-[ ]	Dublin	P
1482		4 Feb.-[ ]		
		3 June-[ ]		
1483	22–3 Edw. IV	7 Feb.-[ ]	Limerick	P
1483	1 Rich. III	[c. Aug.][14]	?	G.C.
1484	1–2 Rich. III	19 Mar.-[ ]	Dublin	P
		30 Aug.-[ ]	Naas	
1484	2 Rich. III	15 Oct.[15]-[ ]	Naas	G.C.
1485	2–3 Rich. III	18 Mar.-[ ]	Dublin	P
		6 June-[ ]	Trim	
		8 Aug.–8 Aug.	Trim	
		24 Oct.-[ ]	Dublin	
1486	1–2 Hen. VII	14 July-[ ]	Dublin	P
		24 Nov.-[ ]	Dublin	
[1487	1 Edw. VI	[May or June][16]	[? Dublin]	P]
[1487	1 Edw. VI	[June–Oct.][17]	[? Dublin]	G.C.]
1488	3 Hen. VII	11 Jan.-[ ]	Drogheda	P
1488	3 Hen. VII	17 July–30 July	Dublin	C or G.C.[18]
1489	4 Hen. VII	[?16] Jan.[19]-[ ]	Drogheda	P
1490	5 Hen. VII	8 Jan.-[ ]	Trim	P[20]
		2 Mar.-[ ]	Dublin	
1491	6–7 Hen. VII	14 Jan.-[ ]	Dublin	P
		4 June[21]-[ ]	Dublin	
		[ ]–8 Nov.	[? Dublin]	
1492	7 Hen. VII	13 Jan.-[ ]	Trim	P
1493	8 Hen. VII	28 June-[ ]	Dublin	P
		5 Aug.-[ ]		
1493	9 Hen. VII	12 Sept.-[ ]	Trim	C
1494	10 Hen. VII	[c. Sept.][22]	Drogheda	P
1494	10 Hen. VII	1 Dec.-[ ]	Drogheda	P
1495		[ ]–c. Apr.		
1499	14–15 Hen. VII	1 Mar.-[ ]	Dublin	P
		26 Aug.-[ ]	Castledermot	
1508	24 Hen. VII	6 Oct.-[ ]	Dublin	P
		23 Oct.-[ ]		
1509		26 Feb.-[ ]		
		26 July-[ ]	Castledermot	

year	regnal year	dates of session	place	
1516	7–8 Hen. VIII	25 Feb.–7 Mar. 1 July–1 July 25 Sept.–2 Oct.	Dublin	P
1521	13 Hen. VIII	4 June–14 June 5 Aug.–5 Aug. 17 Oct.–[ ]	Dublin	P
1522		25 Jan.–29 Jan. 13 Feb.–13 Feb. 17 Feb.–17 Feb. 21 Mar.–21 Mar.		
1531	23 Hen. VIII	15 Sept.–13 Oct. 27 Oct.–31 Oct.	Dublin Drogheda	P
1533	25 Hen. VIII	19 May–[ ] 5 June–[ ] 2 Oct.–[ ]	Dublin	P
1536	28–9 Hen. VIII	1 May–31 May 25 July–26 July 28 July–28 July 2 Aug.–19 Aug. 15 Sept.–28 Sept.	Dublin Kilkenny Cashel Limerick Dublin	P
1537		20 Jan.–5 or 6 Feb.[23] 1 May–8 May 20 July–21 July 13 Oct.–20 Dec.[24]		
1541	33–5 Hen. VIII	13 June–20 or 23 July 7 Nov.–7 Nov. 22 Dec.–22 Dec.	Dublin	P
1542		15 Feb.–7 or 10 Mar. 12 June–21 June 6 Nov.–18 Nov.	Limerick Trim Dublin	
1543		17 Apr.–2 May 6 Nov.–19 Nov.		
1557	3–5 Philip & Mary	1 June–2 July 10 Nov.–10 Nov.	Dublin Limerick	P
1558		1 Mar.–1 Mar.	Drogheda	
1560	2 Eliz. I	11 or 12 Jan.–1 Feb.	Dublin	P
1569	11–13 Eliz. I	17 Jan.–17 Jan. 20 Jan.–17 Feb. 21 Feb.–21 Feb. 23 Feb.–11 Mar. 10 Oct.–31 Oct.	Dublin	P
1570		13 Feb.–15 Feb. 26 May–26 June 6 Nov.–2 Dec. 5 Dec.–12 Dec.	Drogheda Dublin	
1571		25 Apr.–25 Apr.		

year	regnal year	dates of session	place	
1585	27–8 Eliz. I	26 Apr.–25 May	Dublin	P
		27 May–27 May		
		29 May–29 May		
		3 Nov.–3 Nov.	Drogheda	
1586		17 Feb.–17 Feb.		
		21 Mar.–21 Mar.	Dublin	
		26 Apr.–14 May		

[6] A writ of summons specifically mentions a great council at 'Balydoille' (either the modern Ballydoyle or Ballyduagh, a few miles nearer Cashel), but a later account implies that the assembly met at Cashel (H. G. Richardson and G. O. Sayles, *Parliaments and councils of medieval Ireland*, i (Dublin, 1947), pp 38–9, 43–4).

[7] Similarly the site of the parliament of June 1371 is given as both 'Balidoyl' and Cashel (ibid., pp 38–9, 40, 44, 45, 48).

[8] On 1 June Sir Christopher Preston declared that the parliament had been dissolved because the deputy, Sir Thomas Talbot, had failed to attend. The chancellor and the other councillors departed, but the lords and commons remained behind and arranged to meet again in Dublin on 6 June, a meeting subsequently adjourned to 14 June. See A. J. Otway-Ruthven, 'The background to the arrest of Sir Christopher Preston in 1418' in *Anal. Hib.*, xxix (1980), pp 79–80.

[9] *Statute rolls of the parliament of Ireland, 1st to the 12th years of the reign of King Edward IV*, ed. H. F. Berry (Dublin, 1914), pp 429–31, 587.

[10] Ibid., pp 429, 626.

[11] Gearóid Mac Niocaill, *Na buirgéisí* (Dublin, 1964), ii, 583.

[12] *Statute rolls of the parliament of Ireland, 12th and 13th to the 21st and 22nd years of the reign of King Edward IV*, ed. James F. Morrissey (Dublin, 1939), pp 95, 123.

[13] It was prorogued on the same day, 'no act, ordinance or statute then published' (ibid., p. 761).

[14] See Parliament roll, 1 Rich. III c. 8 (P.R.O.I., MS RC 13/8). Cf. D. B. Quinn, 'Guide to English financial records for Irish history, 1461–1558, with illustrative extracts, 1461–1509' in *Anal. Hib.*, x (1941), pp 23–4.

[15] 'Liber niger Alani', ff 49–50v; the published version of this passage in *Calendar of Archbishop Alen's register*, c. *1172–1534*, ed. Charles McNeill (Dublin, 1950), pp 248–9, contains inaccuracies.

[16] See Parliament roll, 8 Hen. VII c. 22 (P.R.O.I., MS RC 13/9); M. T. Hayden, 'Lambert Simnel in Ireland' in *Studies*, iv (1915), p. 629, and J. T. Gilbert, *History of the viceroys of Ireland* (Dublin, 1865), p. 606 and n. 3, both based on Statute roll 10 Henry VII c. 14 (since destroyed).

[17] *Letters and papers illustrative of the reigns of Richard III and Henry VII*, ed. James Gairdner (2 vols, London, 1861–3) (cited below as *L. & P. Rich. III & Hen. VII*), i, 383–4; Hayden, loc. cit., p. 629; Gilbert, *Viceroys*, p. 606 and n. 3.

[18] 'The voyage of Sir Richard Edgecombe into Ireland, in the year 1488' in Walter Harris (ed.), *Hibernica* (Dublin, 1770), pp 64–73. Edgecombe styled the assembly a great council, but he probably had English usage in mind.

[19] See Memoranda roll, 15 Hen. VIII m. 20 (P.R.O.I., Ferguson coll., iv, f. 78); 'The bills and statutes of the Irish parliaments of Henry VII and Henry VIII', ed. D. B. Quinn, in *Anal. Hib.*, x (1941) (cited below as *Stat. Ire., Hen. VII & VIII*), pp 84, 85 (two acts, one of which from internal evidence must be of 1489; the other dated 5 Hen. VII (1490), probably in error in view of the known sessions of the 1490 parliament, but the only indication of the exact date of the parliament).

[20] See *Dowdall deeds*, ed. Charles McNeill and A. J. Otway-Ruthven (Dublin, 1960), no. 503.

[21] *L. & P., Rich. III & Hen. VII*, i, 377–9. There may have been other sessions of the parliament: see *Stat. Ire., Hen. VII & VIII*, p. 85.

[22] Placed in 1493 by *Stat. Ire., Hen. VII & VIII*, p. 91, but an act of Poynings' parliament which declared the parliament void (10 Hen. VII c. 40; *The statutes at large passed in the parliaments held in Ireland . . .* (20 vols, Dublin, 1786–1801), i, 57), states that the parliament was summoned after the duke of Bedford had surrendered his letters patent as lieutenant: this must have been about the beginning of September 1494.

[23] The heading on the roll gives 'die Martis, viz. quinto die Februarii', but 5 Feb. 1537 was Monday not Tuesday (*The statutes at large passed in the parliaments held in Ireland*, i, 66).

[24] There were probably further prorogations between 13 Oct. and the closing of parliament on 20 Dec.

(B) *1613-1800*

C. J. WOODS

Journals of the house of commons of the kingdom of Ireland (19 vols, Dublin, 1796-1800; cited below as *Commons' jn. Ire.*), and sources cited in footnotes.

Sessions of parliament were held at irregular intervals until the reign of Anne. From 1703 they were usually held every second year. After 1782 they were annual. There was no legal limitation on the duration of parliaments, other than the death of the monarch, until the octennial act of 1768.[1]

Until 1661 meetings of parliament were held at Dublin castle, and after that date at Chichester House in College Green, Dublin,[2] except that James II's parliament (unrecognised by William III) met in the King's Inns, Dublin.[3] Chichester House was demolished in 1728, and Parliament House was built on the same site between 1729 and 1731.[4] During the interval, parliament met in the Bluecoat School, Dublin.[5] Parliament House was the seat of the Irish parliament until the union.

Sessions were terminated by prorogation unless otherwise stated. A new parliament is indicated by a preceding blank line.

[1] 7 Geo. III, c. 3 [Ire.].
[2] J. T. Gilbert, *An account of the Parliament House, Dublin* (Dublin, 1896), pp 4 ff.
[3] J. G. Simms, *Jacobite Ireland* (London, 1969), p. 77.   [4] Gilbert, op. cit., pp 23-5.
[5] Frederick R. Falkiner, *The foundation of the hospital and free school of King Charles II, Oxmantown, Dublin, commonly called the Blue-coat School* (Dublin, 1906), p. 167.

year	regnal year	dates of session
1613	11 Jas I	18 May–5 June[6]
1614	12 Jas I	11 Oct.–29 Nov.
1615	13 Jas I	18 Apr.[7]–16 May
		24 Oct. diss.
1634	10 Chas I	14 July–2 Aug.
1634	10 Chas I	4 Nov.–14 Dec.[8]
1635	10 Chas I	26 Jan.–21 Mar.[9]
1635	10 & 11 Chas I	24 Mar.–18 Apr. diss.
1640	15 & 16 Chas I	16 Mar.[10]–17 June
1640	16 Chas I	1 Oct.–12 Nov.
1641	16 Chas I	26 Jan.–5 Mar.
1641	17 Chas I	11 May–17 Nov.
1641–7	17–22 Chas I	11 Jan. 1642–9 Feb. 1647[11]
1647–8	22 & 23 Chas I	26 Mar. 1647–15 June 1647[12]
		30 Jan. 1649 diss.[13]

[[6] *Footnotes for this section continue on p.* 607.]

year	*regnal year*	*dates of session*
1661	13 Chas II	8 May–31 July
1661–2	13 & 14 Chas II	6 Sept. 1661–22 Mar. 1662[14]
1662–3	14 & 15 Chas II	17 Apr. 1662–16 Apr. 1663[15]
1665–6	17 & 18 Chas II	26 Oct. 1665–7 Aug. 1666 diss.[16]
1689[17]	5 Jas. II	7 May[18]–18 July[19]
1692	4 Will. & Mary	5 Oct.–3 Nov.
		26 June 1693 diss.[20]
1695–7	7, 8 & 9 Will. III	27 Aug. 1695–3 Dec. 1697
1698–9	10 Will. III	27 Sept. 1698–26 Jan. 1699
		14 June 1699 diss.
1703–4	2 Anne	21 Sept. 1703–4 Mar. 1704
1705	3 & 4 Anne	10 Feb.–16 June[21]
1707	6 Anne	1 July–30 Oct.
1709	8 Anne	5 May–30 Aug.
1710	9 Anne	19 May–28 Aug.
1711	10 Anne	9 July–9 Nov.
		6 May 1713 diss.
1713	12 Anne	25 Nov.–24 Dec.
		1 Aug. 1714 diss.
1715–16	2 Geo. I	12 Nov. 1715–20 June 1716
1717	4 Geo. I	27 Aug.–23 Dec.
1719	5 & 6 Geo. I	26 June–2 Nov.
1721–2	8 Geo. I	12 Sept. 1721–18 Jan. 1722
1723–4	10 Geo. I	29 Aug. 1723–10 Feb. 1724
1725–6	12 Geo. I	7 Sept. 1725–8 Mar. 1726
		11 June 1727 diss.
1727–8	1 Geo. II	28 Nov. 1727–6 May 1728
1729–30	3 Geo. II	23 Sept. 1729–15 Apr. 1730
1731–2	5 Geo. II	5 Oct. 1731–10 Mar. 1732
1733–4	7 Geo. II	4 Oct. 1733–29 Apr. 1734
1735–6	9 Geo. II	7 Oct. 1735–30 Mar. 1736
1737–8	11 Geo. II	4 Oct. 1737–23 Mar. 1738
1739–40	13 Geo. II	9 Oct. 1739–31 Mar. 1740
1741–2	15 Geo. II	6 Oct. 1741–15 Feb. 1742
1743–4	17 Geo. II	4 Oct. 1743–9 Feb. 1744
1745–6	19 Geo. II	8 Oct. 1745–11 Apr. 1746
1747–8	21 Geo. II	6 Oct. 1747–9 Apr. 1748
1749–50	23 Geo. II	10 Oct. 1749–14 Apr. 1750
1751–2	25 Geo. II	8 Oct. 1751–7 May 1752
1753–4	27 Geo. II	9 Oct. 1753–15 Jan. 1754[22]
1755–6	29 Geo. II	7 Oct. 1755–8 May 1756

year	regnal year	dates of session
1757-8	31 Geo. II	11 Oct. 1757-29 Apr. 1758
1759-60	33 Geo. II	16 Oct. 1759-17 May 1760
		25 Nov. 1760 diss.[23]
1761-2	1 & 2 Geo. III	22 Oct. 1761-30 Apr. 1762
1763-4	3 & 4 Geo. III	11 Oct. 1763-12 May 1764
1765-6	5 & 6 Geo. III	22 Oct. 1765-7 June 1766
1767-8	7 & 8 Geo. III	20 Oct. 1767-27 May 1768
		28 May 1768 diss.
1769	9 & 10 Geo. III	17 Oct.-26 Dec.
1771	11 Geo. III	26 Feb.-18 May
1771-2	11 & 12 Geo. III	8 Oct. 1771-2 June 1772
1773-4	13 & 14 Geo. III	12 Oct. 1773-2 June 1774
1775-6	15 & 16 Geo. III	10 Oct. 1775-4 Apr. 1776
		5 Apr. 1776 diss.[24]
1776	16 Geo. III	18 June-20 June
1777-8	17 & 18 Geo. III	14 Oct. 1777-14 Aug. 1778
1779-80	19 & 20 Geo. III	12 Oct. 1779-2 Sept. 1780
1781-2	21 & 22 Geo. III	9 Oct. 1781-27 July 1782
		25 July 1783 diss.
1783-4	23 & 24 Geo. III	14 Oct. 1783-14 May 1784
1785	25 Geo. III	20 Jan.-7 Sept.
1786	26 Geo. III	19 Jan.-8 May
1787	27 Geo. III	18 Jan.-28 May
1788	28 Geo. III	17 Jan.-18 Apr.
1789	29 Geo. III	5 Feb.-25 May
1790	30 Geo. III	21 Jan.-5 Apr.
		8 Apr. diss.
1790	30 Geo. III	2 July-24 July
1791	31 Geo. III	20 Jan.-5 May
1792	32 Geo. III	19 Jan.-18 Apr.
1793	33 Geo. III	10 Jan.-16 Aug.
1794	34 Geo. III	21 Jan.-25 Mar.
1795	35 Geo. III	22 Jan.-5 June
1796	36 Geo. III	21 Jan.-15 Apr.
1796-7	36 & 37 Geo. III	13 Oct. 1796-3 July 1797
		11 July 1797 diss.
1798	38 Geo. III	9 Jan.-6 Oct.
1799	39 Geo. III	22 Jan.-1 June
1800	40 Geo. III	15 Jan.-2 Aug.
		31 Dec. diss.[25]

[6] There is some difficulty about the dating of this first session owing to the tumultuous circumstances attending it. T. W. Moody ('The Irish parliament under Elizabeth and James I' in *R.I.A. Proc.*, xlv, sect. C, no. 6 (1939), p. 60) states that the session ended on 22 May, the date on which the recusant body withdrew from parliament. This was the effective, but not the formal, end of the session. Parliament was

adjourned from 22 May to 27 May (*Anal. Hib.*, no. 8, p. 99), when, it appears, there was technically a sitting, though the recusants refused to attend (*Cal. S.P. Ire., 1611-14*, p. 398; [John Lodge (ed.)], *Desiderata curiosa Hibernica: or a select collection of state papers* (2 vols, Dublin, 1772), i, 427-9). Parliament was then adjourned to 17 June, but on 5 June it was prorogued (*Anal. Hib.*, no. 8, p. 105). The date of the termination is incorrectly given as 17 June in *Commons' jn. Ire.*, i, 11, and in *The statutes at large passed in the parliaments held in Ireland* (20 vols, Dublin, 1786-1801) (cited below as *Stat. Ire.*), i, 431.

[7] This session is incorrectly described as 'secunda sessio parliamenti' in *Commons' jn. Ire.*, i, 31.

[8] 15 Dec. 1634 according to *Stat. Ire.*, ii, 21.

[9] Adjourned.

[10] 20 Mar. 1640 according to *Stat. Ire.*, ii, 185.

[11] Between these two dates there were forty-one prorogations or lengthy adjournments (*Commons' jn. Ire.*, i, 353). The intervening sessions or meetings were very short and little legislative business was transacted.

[12] Adjournment to 27 Mar. 1648. However, the title page for the relevant section in *Commons' jn. Ire.* gives the terminal date as 15 June 1648.

[13] Date of the king's death. Ire. was represented by 6 members in the Little or 'Barebones' Parliament which met at Westminster, 4 July–12 Dec. 1653, and by 30 members in the first protectorate parliament which met on 3 Sept. 1654 and was dissolved on 22 Jan. 1655.

[14] There were seven formal sessions between these two dates, but they were very short, and little business was transacted.

[15] Ninth session.

[16] The tenth session was not prorogued but parliament was dissolved at the end of business on this date (*Lords' jn. Ire.*, i (1779), p. 466).

[17] The English parliament of William and Mary passed an act declaring this to be 'an unlawful and rebellious assembly' and all its acts and proceedings 'absolutely null and void' (1 Will. & Mary, sess. 2, c. 9); William's second Irish parliament passed an act endorsing this declaration and moreover ordering the destruction of all records (7 Will. III, c. 3). *Commons' jn. Ire.* and *Lords' jn. Ire.*, therefore, contain no record of its proceedings.

[18] *Calendar of the manuscripts of the marquess of Ormonde, preserved at Kilkenny castle* (new series, London, 1902-20), viii, 364.

[19] Ibid., p. 367.

[20] *Lords' jn. Ire.*, i (1779), p. 478.

[21] However, the title page of the relevant section gives 17 Feb. 1706.

[22] Adjournment; prorogation, 20 Jan. 1754.

[23] By proclamation of the lords justices. The king had died, 25 Oct. 1760.

[24] *Lords' jn. Ire.*, iv, 856. The date is incorrectly stated as 5 Aug. 1776 in *Commons' jn. Ire.*, ix, 289.

[25] By the acts for the union of Great Britain and Ireland (39 & 40 Geo. III, c. 67 [G.B.] and 40 Geo. III, c. 38 [Ire.]), which received royal assent on 2 July and 1 Aug. 1800 respectively, the parliaments of the two kingdoms were united on 1 Jan. 1801; see below, p. 610.

GENERAL ASSEMBLY OF THE CONFEDERATION OF KILKENNY, 1642-9

C. J. WOODS

Donal F. Cregan, 'The confederation of Kilkenny: its organisation, personnel and history' (Ph.D. thesis, University College, Dublin, 1947), pp 75–6. See also John Lowe, 'Charles I and the confederation of Kilkenny, 1643–9' in *I.H.S.*, xiv, no. 53 (Mar. 1964), p. 16, n. 43.

The first meeting of the assembly was held at the house of Robert Shee in Coal Market (now Parliament Street), Kilkenny. All others were held in Kilkenny (the sixth in Kilkenny castle), except the third, which was held in Waterford.

year	dates of assembly
(1) 1642	24 Oct.–21 Nov.
(2) 1643	20 May–19 June
(3) 1643	*c.* 7 Nov.–1 Dec.
(4) 1644	20 July–31 Aug.
(5) 1645	15 May–*p.* 31 Aug.[1]
(6) 1646	*c.* 7 Feb.–4 Mar.
(7) 1647	10 Jan.–4 Apr.
(8) 1647	12 Nov.–24 Dec.
(9) 1648–9	4 Sept. 1648–17 Jan. 1649

[1] Adjourned 5 July 1645; reassembled 27 Aug. 1645; diss. soon *p.* 31 Aug. 1645.

PARLIAMENT OF THE
UNITED KINGDOM, 1801–1982

C. J. WOODS

Journals of the house of commons [of the United Kingdom].

With the union, the British parliament, with its seat at the Palace of Westminster, became the parliament of the United Kingdom of Great Britain and Ireland. British representation was unchanged. As provided under the 4th article of the act of union (40 Geo. III, c. 38 [Ire.]), Ireland was represented by 4 spiritual peers, 28 temporal peers and 100 commoners (64 for counties, 35 for boroughs and 1 for Dublin University).[1] Under 40 Geo. III, c. 29, s. 6 [Ire.], the sitting members for the 32 counties and the 2 boroughs of Dublin and Cork in the old Irish parliament were to retain their seats as members of the new United Kingdom parliament. In fact before the union came into effect on 1 January 1801 one such member succeeded to a peerage and another died, necessitating by-elections in the counties of Londonderry and Wicklow respectively.[2] Under the same section, for those constituencies which returned two members to the Irish parliament but were to return only one to the United Kingdom parliament (31 boroughs and the university), a choice between the sitting members was to be made by lot, except that in cases where in the meantime a member resigned or died the remaining member was to be returned and in cases where both members either resigned or died a by-election was to be held. In fact when, on 2 December 1800, the deputy clerk of the crown and hanaper came to make the selection, it was found that in 15 constituencies one member had resigned and in 2 constituencies (Clonmel and Dundalk) both members, so that lots were drawn for only 15 of the 32 constituencies.[3]

Sessions were terminated by prorogation unless otherwise stated. Meetings held solely for the purpose of prorogation are ignored throughout. A new parliament is indicated by a preceding blank line.

In 1922 the number of Irish members was reduced to 13, representing Northern Ireland (see below, p. 642).

---

[1] Irish representation in the U.K. house of commons was later increased (see below, p. 634).

[2] B. M. Walker, *Parliamentary election results in Ireland, 1801–1922* (Dublin, 1978), pp 3, 4, 5.

[3] *Hibernian Magazine*, Dec. 1800, pp 376–7. A list is given here of the 32 constituencies, showing the result of the resignation or draw in each case.

year	regnal year	dates of session
1801	41 Geo. III	22 Jan.–2 July
1801–2	42 Geo. III	29 Oct. 1801–28 June 1802
		29 June 1802 diss.
1802–3	43 Geo. III	16 Nov. 1801–12 Aug. 1803
1803–4	44 Geo. III	22 Nov. 1803–31 July 1804
1805	45 Geo. III	15 Jan.–12 July
1806	46 Geo. III	21 Jan.–23 July
		24 Oct. diss.
1806–7	47 Geo. III	15 Dec. 1806–27 Apr. 1807
		29 Apr. 1807 diss.
1807	47 Geo. III	22 June–14 Aug.
1808	48 Geo. III	21 Jan.–4 July
1809	49 Geo. III	19 Jan.–21 June
1810	50 Geo. III	23 Jan.–21 June
1810–11	51 Geo. III	1 Nov. 1810–24 July 1811
1812	52 Geo. III	7 Jan.–30 July
		29 Sept. diss.
1812–13	53 Geo. III	24 Nov. 1812–22 July 1813
1813–14	54 Geo. III	4 Nov. 1813–30 July 1814
1814–15	55 Geo. III	8 Nov. 1814–12 July 1815
1816	56 Geo. III	1 Feb.–2 July
1817	57 Geo. III	28 Jan.–12 July
1818	58 Geo. III	27 Jan.–10 June diss.[4]
1819	59 Geo. III	14 Jan.–13 July
1819–20	60 Geo. III & 1 Geo. IV	23 Nov. 1819–28 Feb. 1820
		29 Feb. 1820 diss.
1820	1 Geo. IV	21 Apr.–23 Nov.
1821	1 & 2 Geo. IV	23 Jan.–11 July
1822	3 Geo. IV	5 Feb.–6 Aug.
1823	4 Geo. IV	4 Feb.–19 July
1824	5 Geo. IV	3 Feb.–25 June
1825	6 Geo. IV	3 Feb.–6 July
1826	7 Geo. IV	2 Feb.–31 May
		2 June diss.
1826–7	7 & 8 Geo. IV	14 Nov. 1826–2 July 1827
1828	9 Geo. IV	29 Jan.–28 July
1829	10 Geo. IV	5 Feb.–24 June
1830	11 Geo. IV & 1 Will. IV	4 Feb.–23 July
		24 July diss.
1830–31	1 Will. IV	26 Oct. 1830–22 Apr. 1831
		23 Apr. 1831 diss.

---

[4] Sixth session was not prorogued, but parliament was dissolved at the end of business on this date.

year	regnal year	dates of session
1831	1 & 2 Will. IV	14 June–20 Oct.
1831–2	2 & 3 Will. IV	6 Dec. 1831–16 Aug. 1832
		3 Dec. 1832 diss.
1833	3 & 4 Will. IV	29 Jan.–29 Aug.
1834	4 & 5 Will. IV	4 Feb.–15 Aug.
		29 Dec. diss.
1835	5 & 6 Will. IV	19 Feb.–10 Sept.
1836	6 & 7 Will. IV	4 Feb.–20 Aug.
1837	7 Will. IV & 1 Vict.	31 Jan.–17 July
		17 July diss.
1837–8	1 & 2 Vict.	15 Nov. 1837–16 Aug. 1838
1839	2 & 3 Vict.	5 Feb.–27 Aug.
1840	3 & 4 Vict.	16 Jan.–11 Aug.
1841	4 & 5 Vict.	26 Jan.–22 June
		23 June diss.
1841	5 Vict.	19 Aug.–7 Oct.
1842	5 & 6 Vict.	3 Feb.–12 Aug.
1843	6 & 7 Vict.	2 Feb.–19 Dec.
1844	7 & 8 Vict.	1 Feb.–5 Sept.
1845	8 & 9 Vict.	4 Feb.–9 Aug.
1846	9 Vict.	22 Jan.–28 Aug.
1847	10 Vict.	19 Jan.–23 July
		23 July diss.
1847–8	11 & 12 Vict.	18 Nov. 1847–5 Sept. 1848
1849	12 & 13 Vict.	1 Feb.–1 Aug.
1850	13 & 14 Vict.	31 Jan.–15 Aug.
1851	14 & 15 Vict.	4 Feb.–8 Aug.
1852	15 & 16 Vict.	3 Feb.–1 July
		1 July diss.
1852–3	16 & 17 Vict.	4 Nov. 1852–20 Aug. 1853
1854	17 & 18 Vict.	31 Jan.–12 Aug.
1854–5	18 & 19 Vict.	12 Dec. 1854–14 Aug. 1855
1856	19 & 20 Vict.	31 Jan.–29 July
1857	20 Vict.	3 Feb.–21 Mar.
		21 Mar. diss.
1857	20 & 21 Vict.	30 Apr.–28 Aug.
1857–8	21 & 22 Vict.	3 Dec. 1857–2 Aug. 1858
1859	22 Vict.	3 Feb.–19 Apr.
		23 Apr. diss.
1859	22 & 23 Vict.	31 May–13 Aug.
1860	23 & 24 Vict.	24 Jan.–28 Aug.
1861	24 & 25 Vict.	5 Feb.–6 Aug.
1862	25 & 26 Vict.	6 Feb.–7 Aug.

year	regnal year	dates of session
1863	26 & 27 Vict.	5 Feb.–28 July
1864	27 & 28 Vict.	4 Feb.–29 July
1865	28 & 29 Vict.	7 Feb.–6 July
		6 July diss.
1866	29 & 30 Vict.	1 Feb.–10 Aug.
1867	30 & 31 Vict.	5 Feb.–21 Aug.
1867-8	31 & 32 Vict.	19 Nov. 1867–31 July 1868
		11 Nov. 1868 diss.
1868-9	32 & 33 Vict.	10 Dec. 1868–11 Aug. 1869
1870	33 & 34 Vict.	8 Feb.–10 Aug.
1871	34 & 35 Vict.	9 Feb.–21 Aug.
1872	35 & 36 Vict.	6 Feb.–10 Aug.
1873	36 & 37 Vict.	6 Feb. 1873–5 Aug. 1873
		26 Jan. 1874 diss.
1874	37 & 38 Vict.	5 Mar.–7 Aug.
1875	38 & 39 Vict.	5 Feb.–13 Aug.
1876	39 & 40 Vict.	8 Feb.–15 Aug.
1877	40 & 41 Vict.	8 Feb.–14 Aug.
1878	41 & 42 Vict.	17 Jan.–16 Aug.
1878-9	42 & 43 Vict.	5 Dec. 1878–15 Aug. 1879
1880	43 Vict.	5 Feb.–24 Mar.
		24 Mar. diss.
1880	43 & 44 Vict.	29 Apr.–7 Sept.
1881	44 & 45 Vict.	6 Jan.–27 Aug.
1882	45 & 46 Vict.	7 Feb.–2 Dec.
1883	46 & 47 Vict.	15 Feb.–25 Aug.
1884	47 & 48 Vict.	5 Feb.–14 Aug.
1884-5	48 & 49 Vict.	23 Oct. 1884–14 Aug. 1885
		18 Nov. 1885 diss.
1886	49 Vict.	12 Jan.–25 June
		26 June diss.
1886	50 Vict.	5 Aug.–25 Sept.
1887	50 & 51 Vict.	27 Jan.–16 Sept.
1888	51 & 52 Vict.	9 Feb.–24 Dec.
1889	52 & 53 Vict.	21 Feb.–30 Aug.
1890	53 & 54 Vict.	11 Feb.–18 Aug.
1890-91	54 & 55 Vict.	25 Nov. 1890–5 Aug. 1891
1892	55 & 56 Vict.	9 Feb.–28 June
		28 June diss.
1892	56 Vict.	4 Aug.–18 Aug.
1893-4	56 & 57 Vict.	31 Jan. 1893–5 Mar. 1894
1894	57 & 58 Vict.	12 Mar.–25 Aug.
1895	58 & 59 Vict.	5 Feb.–6 July
		8 July diss.

year	regnal year	dates of session
1895	59 Vict.	12 Aug.–5 Sept.
1896	59 & 60 Vict.	11 Feb.–14 Aug.
1897	60 & 61 Vict.	19 Jan.–6 Aug.
1898	61 & 62 Vict.	8 Feb.–12 Aug.
1899	62 & 63 Vict.	7 Feb.–9 Aug.
1899	63 Vict.	17 Oct.–27 Oct.
1900	63 & 64 Vict.	30 Jan.–8 Aug.
		17 Sept. diss.
1900	64 Vict.	3 Dec.–15 Dec.
1901	1 Edw. VII	23 Jan.–17 Aug.
1902	1 & 2 Edw. VII	16 Jan.–18 Dec.
1903	3 Edw. VII	17 Feb.–14 Aug.
1904	4 Edw. VII	2 Feb.–15 Aug.
1905	5 Edw. VII	14 Feb.–11 Aug.
		8 Jan. 1906 diss.
1906	6 Edw. VII	13 Feb.–21 Dec.
1907	7 Edw. VII	12 Feb.–28 Aug.
1908	8 Edw. VII	29 Jan.–21 Dec.
1909	9 Edw. VII	16 Feb.–3 Dec.
		10 Jan. 1910 diss.
1910	10 Edw. VII–1 Geo. V	15 Feb.–28 Nov.
		28 Nov. diss.
1911	1 & 2 Geo. V	31 Jan.–16 Dec.
1912–13	2 & 3 Geo. V	14 Feb. 1912–7 Mar. 1913
1913	3 & 4 Geo. V	10 Mar.–15 Aug.
1914	4 & 5 Geo. V	10 Feb.–18 Sept.
1914–16	5 & 6 Geo. V	11 Nov. 1914–27 Jan. 1916
1916	6 & 7 Geo. V	15 Feb.–22 Dec.
1917–18	7 & 8 Geo. V	7 Feb. 1917–6 Feb. 1918
1918	8 & 9 Geo. V	12 Feb.–21 Nov.
		25 Nov. diss.
1919	9 & 10 Geo. V	4 Feb.–23 Dec.
1920	10 & 11 Geo. V	10 Feb.–23 Dec.
1921 ·	11 & 12 Geo. V	15 Feb.–10 Nov.
1921	12 Geo. V	14 Dec.–19 Dec.
1922	12 & 13 Geo. V	7 Feb.–4 Aug.[5]
		26 Oct. diss.
1922	13 Geo. V	20 Nov.–15 Dec.
1923	13 & 14 Geo. V	13 Feb.–16 Nov.
		16 Nov. diss.

[5] Adjourned.

year	regnal year	dates of session
1924	14 & 15 Geo. V	8 Jan.–9 Oct.
1924–5	15 & 16 Geo. V	2 Dec. 1924–22 Dec. 1925
1926	16 & 17 Geo. V	2 Feb.–15 Dec.
1927	17 & 18 Geo. V	8 Feb.–22 Dec.
1928	18 & 19 Geo. V	7 Feb.–3 Aug.
1928–9	19 & 20 Geo. V	6 Nov. 1928–10 May 1929
		10 May diss.
1929–30	20 & 21 Geo. V	25 June 1929–1 Aug. 1930
1930–31	21 & 22 Geo. V	28 Oct. 1930–7 Oct. 1931
		7 Oct. diss.
1931–2	22 & 23 Geo. V	3 Nov. 1931–17 Nov. 1932
1932–3	23 & 24 Geo. V	22 Nov. 1932–17 Nov. 1933
1933–4	24 & 25 Geo. V	21 Nov. 1933–16 Nov. 1934
1934–5	25 & 26 Geo. V	20 Nov. 1934–25 Oct. 1935
		25 Oct. diss.
1935–6	26 Geo. V & 1 Edw. VIII	26 Nov. 1935–30 Oct. 1936
1936–7	1 Edw. VIII & 1 Geo. VI	3 Nov. 1936–22 Oct. 1937
1937–8	1 & 2 Geo. VI	26 Oct. 1937–4 Nov. 1938
1938–9	2 & 3 Geo. VI	8 Nov. 1938–23 Nov. 1939
1939–40	3 & 4 Geo. VI	28 Nov. 1939–20 Nov. 1940
1940–41	4 & 5 Geo. VI	21 Nov. 1940–11 Nov. 1941
1941–2	5 & 6 Geo. VI	12 Nov. 1941–10 Nov. 1942
1942–3	6 & 7 Geo. VI	11 Nov. 1942–23 Nov. 1943
1943–4	7 & 8 Geo. VI	24 Nov. 1943–28 Nov. 1944
1944–5	8 & 9 Geo. VI	29 Nov. 1944–15 June 1945
		15 June diss.
1945–6	9 & 10 Geo. VI	1 Aug. 1945–6 Nov. 1946
1946–7	10 & 11 Geo. VI	12 Nov. 1946–20 Oct. 1947
1947–8	11 & 12 Geo. VI	21 Oct. 1947–13 Sept. 1948
1948	12 Geo. VI	14 Sept.–25 Oct.
1948–9	12 & 13 Geo. VI	26 Oct. 1948–16 Dec. 1949
		3 Feb. 1950 diss.
1950	14 Geo. VI	1 Mar.–26 Oct.
1950–51	14 & 15 Geo. VI	31 Oct. 1950–4 Oct. 1951
		5 Oct. diss.
1951–2	15 Geo. VI & 1 Eliz. II	31 Oct. 1951–30 Oct. 1952
1952–3	1 & 2 Eliz. II	4 Nov. 1952–29 Oct. 1953
1953–4	2 & 3 Eliz. II	3 Nov. 1953–25 Nov. 1954
1954–5	3 & 4 Eliz. II	30 Nov. 1954–6 May 1955
		6 May diss.
1955–6	4 & 5 Eliz. II	7 June 1955–5 Nov. 1956
1956–7	5 & 6 Eliz. II	6 Nov. 1956–1 Nov. 1957

year	regnal year	dates of session
1957–8	6 & 7 Eliz. II	5 Nov. 1957–23 Oct. 1958
1958–9	7 & 8 Eliz. II	28 Oct. 1958–18 Sept. 1959
		18 Sept. diss.
1959–60	8 & 9 Eliz. II	20 Oct. 1959–27 Oct. 1960
1960–61	9 & 10 Eliz. II	1 Nov. 1960–24 Oct. 1961
1961–2	10 & 11 Eliz. II	31 Oct. 1961–25 Oct. 1962
1962–3	11 & 12 Eliz. II	30 Oct. 1962–24 Oct. 1963
1963–4	12 & 13 Eliz. II	12 Nov. 1963–31 July 1964[6]
		25 Sept. diss.
1964–5	13 & 14 Eliz. II	27 Oct. 1964–8 Nov. 1965
1965–6	14 & 15 Eliz. II	9 Nov. 1965–10 Mar. 1966
		10 Mar. diss.
1966–7	15 & 16 Eliz. II	18 Apr. 1966–27 Oct. 1967
1967–8	16 & 17 Eliz. II	31 Oct. 1967–25 Oct. 1968
1968–9	17 & 18 Eliz. II	30 Oct. 1968–22 Oct. 1969
1969–70	18 & 19 Eliz. II	28 Oct. 1969–29 May 1970
		29 May diss.
1970–71	19 & 20 Eliz. II	29 June 1970–28 Oct. 1971
1971–2	20 & 21 Eliz. II	2 Nov. 1971–26 Oct. 1972
1972–3	21 & 22 Eliz. II	31 Oct. 1972–25 Oct. 1973
1973–4	22 & 23 Eliz. II	30 Oct. 1973–8 Feb. 1974
		8 Feb. diss.
1974	23 Eliz. II	6 Mar.–31 July[6]
		20 Sept. diss.
1974–5	23 & 24 Eliz. II	22 Oct. 1974–12 Nov. 1975
1975–6	24 & 25 Eliz. II	19 Nov. 1975–17 Nov. 1976
1976–7	25 & 26 Eliz. II	24 Nov. 1976–26 Oct. 1977
1977–8	26 & 27 Eliz. II	3 Nov. 1977–24 Oct. 1978
1978–9	27 & 28 Eliz. II	1 Nov. 1978–4 Apr. 1979[6]
		7 Apr. diss.
1979–80	28 & 29 Eliz. II	9 May 1979–13 Nov. 1980
1980–81	29 & 30 Eliz. II	20 Nov. 1980–30 Oct. 1981
1981–2	30 & 31 Eliz. II	4 Nov. 1981–28 Oct. 1982
1982–3	31 & 32 Eliz. II	3 Nov. 1982–13 May 1983 diss.[7]

[6] Adjourned.
[7] Fourth session was not prorogued, but parliament was dissolved at the end of business on this date.

PARLIAMENT AND PARLIAMENTARY ASSEMBLIES OF NORTHERN IRELAND, 1921-82

C. J. WOODS

(A) *PARLIAMENT OF NORTHERN IRELAND, 1921-73*

The parliamentary debates, official report . . . first [etc.] *parliament of Northern Ireland . . . house of commons, session 1921* [etc.] (Belfast, 1921-72).[1]

For its first three meetings (7 June, 22 June, and 23 June 1921) the parliament met in the council chamber of the City Hall, Belfast. Subsequent meetings were held at the Presbyterian College, Belfast, until the summer recess of 1932. On 30 September 1932 parliament met again at City Hall. From 22 November 1932 all meetings were held at Parliament Buildings, Stormont, Belfast.

Sessions were terminated by prorogation unless otherwise stated. A new parliament is indicated by a preceding blank line.

The assistance of Mr Thomas Hamilton, formerly librarian of the Northern Ireland assembly, is acknowledged with thanks.

[1] From 1958 the series is entitled *Parliamentary debates (Hansard) . . . house of commons, official report . . . .*

year	regnal year	dates of session
1921	12 Geo. V	7 June–14 Dec.
1922	12 & 13 Geo. V	14 Mar.–14 Dec.
1923	13 & 14 Geo. V	27 Feb.–27 Nov.
1924	14 & 15 Geo. V	11 Mar.–7 Nov.
1925	15 Geo. V	10 Mar.–13 Mar.
		14 Mar. diss.
1925	15 & 16 Geo. V	14 Apr.–22 Dec.
1926	16 & 17 Geo. V	9 Mar.–30 Dec.
1927	17 & 18 Geo. V	15 Mar.–21 Dec.
1928	18 & 19 Geo. V	6 Mar.–18 Dec.
1929	19 Geo. V	26 Feb.–16 Apr.
		2 May diss.[2]
1929–30	20 Geo. V	29 May 1929–24 Feb. 1930
1930	20 & 21 Geo. V	11 Mar.–25 Nov.

[2 *Footnotes for this section continue on p. 619.*]

year	regnal year	dates of session
1931–2	21 & 22 Geo. V	3 Mar. 1931–18 Feb. 1932
1932	22 & 23 Geo. V	8 Mar.–30 Sept.
1932–3	23 & 24 Geo. V	22 Nov. 1932–9 Nov. 1933 diss.[3]
1933–4	24 & 25 Geo. V	18 Dec. 1933–14 Nov. 1934
1934–5	25 & 26 Geo. V	20 Nov. 1934–13 Nov. 1935
1935–6	26 Geo. V–1 Edw. VIII	26 Nov. 1935–12 Nov. 1936
1936–7	1 Edw. VIII–1 Geo. VI	24 Nov. 1936–9 Nov. 1937
1937–8	1 & 2 Geo. VI	23 Nov. 1937–17 Dec. 1937[4]
		20 Jan. 1938 diss.
1938	2 Geo. VI	1 Mar.–24 Nov.
1938–9	3 Geo. VI	6 Dec. 1938–6 Dec. 1939
1939–41	4 & 5 Geo. VI	19 Dec. 1939–18 Feb. 1941
1941–2	5 Geo. VI	25 Feb. 1941–27 Jan. 1942
1942–3	6 & 7 Geo. VI	3 Feb. 1942–16 Feb. 1943
1943–4	7 & 8 Geo. VI	23 Feb. 1943–25 Jan. 1944
1944–5	8 & 9 Geo. VI	1 Feb. 1944–13 Feb. 1945
1945	9 Geo. VI	20 Feb.–24 May
		25 May diss.
1945–6	9 & 10 Geo. VI	17 July 1945–28 Feb. 1946
1946–7	10 & 11 Geo. VI	5 Mar. 1946–31 Mar. 1947
1947–8	11 & 12 Geo. VI	29 Apr. 1949–4 Feb. 1948
1948–9	12 & 13 Geo. VI	10 Feb. 1948–20 Jan. 1949
		21 Jan. 1949 diss.
1949–50	13 & 14 Geo. VI	1 Mar. 1949–14 Feb. 1950
1950–51	14 & 15 Geo. VI	28 Feb. 1950–13 Feb. 1951
1951–2	15 & 16 Geo. VI	20 Feb. 1951–11 Feb. 1952
1952–3	1 & 2 Eliz. II	19 Feb. 1952–17 Feb. 1953
1953	2 Eliz. II	24 Feb.–29 Sept.
		2 Oct. diss.
1953–5	2 & 3 Eliz. II	9 Nov. 1953–1 Feb. 1955
1955–6	4 & 5 Eliz. II	8 Feb. 1955–9 Feb. 1956
1956–7	5 & 6 Eliz. II	14 Feb. 1956–29 Jan. 1957
1957–8	6 & 7 Eliz. II	5 Feb. 1957–27 Feb. 1958
		27 Feb. 1958 diss.[5]
1958–9	7 Eliz. II	31 Mar. 1958–3 Feb. 1959
1959–60	8 Eliz. II	10 Feb. 1959–2 Feb. 1960
1960–61	9 Eliz. II	9 Feb. 1960–31 Jan. 1961
1961–2	10 & 11 Eliz. II	7 Feb. 1961–10 May 1962
		11 May 1962 diss.[6]
1962–3	11 & 12 Eliz. II	19 June 1962–15 Oct. 1963
1963–4	12 & 13 Eliz. II	22 Oct. 1963–20 Oct. 1964
1964–5	13 & 14 Eliz. II	27 Oct. 1964–4 Nov. 1965
		5 Nov. 1965 diss.[7]

year	regnal year	dates of session
1965-6	14 & 15 Eliz. II	13 Dec. 1965-6 Dec. 1966
1966-7	15 & 16 Eliz. II	13 Dec. 1966-14 Dec. 1967
1967-8	16 & 17 Eliz. II	19 Dec. 1967-12 Dec. 1968
1968-9	17 Eliz. II	17 Dec. 1968-30 Jan. 1969[8]
		4 Feb. 1969 diss.
1969-70	18 Eliz. II	3 Mar. 1969-5 Feb. 1970
1970-71	19 & 20 Eliz. II	10 Feb. 1970-15 June 1971
1971-2	20 & 21 Eliz. II	22 June 1971-28 Mar. 1972[9]

[2] *Belfast Gazette*, 2 May 1929.

[3] Ibid., 10 Nov. 1933.

[4] Adjournment.

[5] *Belfast Gazette*, 27 Feb. 1958.

[6] Ibid., 11 May 1962.

[7] Ibid., 5 Nov. 1965.

[8] Adjournment.

[9] Adjournment. Under the Northern Ireland (Temporary Provisions) Act, 1972 (1972, c. 22 [U.K.]), which received the royal assent on 30 Mar., the parliament was prorogued for one year. Under the same act, by means of Statutory Instrument 1973 no. 602, dated 29 Mar. 1973, it was further prorogued for one year. Under the Northern Ireland Constitution Act, 1973 (1973, c. 36, s. 31 [U.K.]), which received royal assent on 18 July 1973, it was abolished.

(B) *NORTHERN IRELAND ASSEMBLY, 1973–5*

Northern Ireland assembly: official report of debates (3 vols, Belfast, 1974–5).

The assembly was established by the Northern Ireland Assembly Act, 1973 (1973, c. 17 [U.K.]), which received the royal assent on 3 May. A general election to the assembly was held on 28 June, and the assembly sat at Parliament Buildings, Stormont, on the following dates.

1973	*1974*
31 July	22–4 Jan.
15–18 Oct.	29–31 Jan.
24–5 Oct.	5–7 Feb.
30 Oct.–1 Nov.	12–14 Feb.
7 Nov.	19–21 Feb.
14 Nov.	26–7 Feb.
21 Nov.	5–7 Mar.
28 Nov.	12–14 Mar.
5 Dec.	19–21 Mar.
14 Dec.	26–7 Mar.
19 Dec.	2–4 Apr.
	30 Apr.–2 May
	7–9 May
	14–16 May
	21–3 May
	28–9 May[1]

[1] Adjourned and prorogued, 29 May 1974. Dissolved, 28 Mar. 1975, by means of Statutory Instrument 1975 no. 422.

(C) *NORTHERN IRELAND CONSTITUTIONAL CONVENTION, 1975̄-6*

Northern Ireland constitutional convention: report, together with the proceedings of the convention (London, 1975); printed reports of proceedings (plenary sessions 1-34), library of Parliament Buildings, Stormont; *Northern Ireland constitutional convention: report of debates, 8 May 1975 to 7 November 1975* (Belfast, 1975). The assistance of Mr Thomas Hamilton, formerly librarian of the Northern Ireland assembly, is acknowledged with thanks.

The Northern Ireland Act, 1974 (1974, c. 28 [U.K.]), which received the royal assent on 17 July, provided for the holding of a constitutional convention, similar to the Northern Ireland assembly in number of seats and manner of election. A general election to the convention was held on 1 May 1975, and the convention sat on the following dates.

1975	*1976*[2]
8 May	3 Feb.
22 May	2 Mar.
27-9 May	3 Mar.[3]
3-4 June	
10-12 June	
17-19 June	
24-6 June	
1-3 July	
11 Sept.	
17 Sept.	
30 Sept.-3 Oct.	
23 Oct.	
29-30 Oct.	
4 Nov.	
6-7 Nov.[1]	

[1] On 7 Nov. the convention resolved to submit its report to the secretary of state for Northern Ireland.

[2] On 28 Jan. 1976 the secretary of state issued an order reconvening the convention.

[3] On 3 Mar. the convention adjourned to 9 Mar., but this meeting was not held, as the convention was dissolved by Statutory Instrument 1976 no. 349 with effect from 6 Mar. 1976.

(D) *NORTHERN IRELAND ASSEMBLY, 1982-*

Northern Ireland assembly: official report, iv (Belfast, 1982). The assistance of Mr Patrick Melvin, assistant librarian of the Oireachtas, and Mr George Woodman, librarian of the Northern Ireland assembly, is acknowledged with thanks.

The assembly was established by the Northern Ireland Act, 1982 (1982, c. 38 [U.K.]), which received the royal assent on 23 July. A general election to the assembly was held on 20 October, and to the end of 1982 the assembly sat on the following dates.

1982
11 Nov.
22 Nov.
23 Nov.
25 Nov.
30 Nov.
1 Dec.
2 Dec.
7 Dec.
8 Dec.
9 Dec.
14 Dec.
15 Dec.
22 Dec.

DÁIL ÉIREANN, 1919-82

C. J. WOODS

Dáil Éireann . . . minutes of proceedings of the first parliament of the Republic of Ireland, 1919-21 . . . (Dublin, [1923]); *Dáil Éireann: tuairisg oifigiúil (official report) for periods 16th August 1921 to 26th August 1921, and 28th February 1922 to 8th June 1922* (Dublin, [? 1923]); *Dáil Éireann . . . private sessions of second dáil . . . minutes of proceedings, 18 August 1921 to 14 September 1921, and reports of debates 14 December 1921 to 6 January 1922* (Dublin, [1973]); *Iris Dháil Éireann: . . . debate on the treaty between Great Britain and Ireland signed in London on 6 December 1921* (Dublin, [? 1923]); *Dáil Éireann . . ., díosbóireachtaí páirliminte (parliamentary debates); tuairisg oifigiúil (official report)* (Dublin, 1922-); and sources cited in footnotes.

The first and second dála met chiefly in the Mansion House, Dublin: in the Round Room (the scene of the first assembly), the Oak Room, or (on some occasions after the first dáil had been obliged to suspend public meetings) the basement. Other secret meetings were held in 3 Mountjoy Square or 75 Gardiner Place, Dublin.[1] The debates on the Anglo-Irish treaty were held in the council chamber of University College at Earlsfort Terrace, Dublin. The third dáil met in the lecture theatre of Leinster House, Dublin, by arrangement with the Royal Dublin Society.[2] Leinster House became the property of the Irish Free State government on 14 August 1924, and has remained the seat of all successive dála.

After the first three dála, meetings were not adjourned in sessions, and so no distinction was made between adjournments and prorogation.

[1] J. L. McCracken, *Representative government in Ireland: a study of Dáil Éireann, 1919-48* (London, 1958), p. 24.
[2] *Dáil Éireann . . . díosbóireachtaí páirliminte (parliamentary debates)*, iv, 1562; vi, 2153.

dáil	first meeting	last meeting	dissolution
First[3]	21 Jan. 1919	10 May 1921[4]	
Second[5]	16 Aug. 1921	8 June 1922[6]	
Third	9 Sept. 1922	9 Aug. 1923[7]	
Fourth	19 Sept. 1923	20 May 1927	23 May 1927
Fifth	23 June 1927	16 Aug. 1927	25 Aug. 1927
Sixth	11 Oct. 1927	17 Jan. 1932	29 Jan. 1932
Seventh	9 Mar. 1932	22 Dec. 1932	2 Jan. 1933
Eighth	8 Feb. 1933	14 June 1937	14 June 1937
Ninth	21 July 1937	25 May 1938	27 May 1938
Tenth	30 June 1938	26 May 1943	26 June 1943

dáil	*first meeting*	*last meeting*	*dissolution*
Eleventh	1 July 1943	10 May 1944	7 June 1944
Twelfth	9 June 1944	11 Dec. 1947	12 Jan. 1948
Thirteenth	18 Feb. 1948	2 May 1951	7 May 1951
Fourteenth	13 June 1951	23 Apr. 1954	24 Apr. 1954
Fifteenth	2 June 1954	13 Dec. 1956	12 Feb. 1957
Sixteenth	20 Mar. 1957	1 Sept. 1961	15 Sept. 1961
Seventeenth	11 Oct. 1961	11 Mar. 1965	18 Mar. 1965
Eighteenth	21 Apr. 1965	21 May 1969	22 May 1969
Nineteenth	2 July 1969	14 Dec. 1972	5 Feb. 1973
Twentieth	14 Mar. 1973	25 May 1977	25 May 1977
Twenty-first	5 July 1977	21 May 1981	21 May 1981
Twenty-second	30 June 1981	26 Jan. 1982	27 Jan. 1982
Twenty-third	9 Mar. 1982	4 Nov. 1982	4 Nov. 1982
Twenty-fourth	14 Dec. 1982		

[3] The first dáil lacked official status, being a private meeting of Sinn Féin members of the United Kingdom house of commons. On 10 Sept. 1919 it was proscribed as a dangerous association (McCracken, op. cit., pp 21–7).

[4] There were twelve sessions, six in 1919 (21–2 Jan., 1–11 Apr., 9 May, 17–19 June, 19–20 Aug., and 27 Oct.), three in 1920 (29 June, 6 Aug., and 17 Sept.), three in 1921 (21–5 Jan., 11 Mar., and 10 May). Some meetings were held in public, others in secret.

[5] The second dáil at first lacked official status, being a private meeting of the Sinn Féin members of the abortive Southern Ireland house of commons plus one Sinn Féin member of the Northern Ireland house of commons, but later, under the terms of the Anglo–Irish treaty, it received effective official recognition as the parliament of Southern Ireland (McCracken, op. cit., pp 27–9, 47–8, 52–4).

[6] There were three sessions: 16 Aug.–14 Sept. 1921, 14 Dec. 1921–20 Jan. 1922, and 28 Feb.–8 June 1922.

[7] There were two sessions: the first (of the *páirlimint shealadach* or 'provisional parliament') 9 Sept.–4 Dec. 1922, the second 6 Dec. 1922–9 Aug. 1923.

V

PARLIAMENTARY ELECTIONS
FROM 1801

CONTENTS

PARLIAMENT OF THE UNITED KINGDOM: GENERAL
ELECTION IN GREAT BRITAIN, 1979

INTRODUCTION

THE following tables deal quantitatively with five major aspects of electoral history over the whole period: (1) constituencies, M.P.s, electors and population, (2) contests at general elections, (3) candidates at general elections, by parties, (4) members elected or seats won at general elections, by parties, (5) votes cast and members elected or seats won without a contest at general elections, by parties. Also included are tables of general election results for Great Britain. The numbers of seats won, rather than members returned, are given for the period 1832–1918 because during this period individuals sometimes won more than one seat. Special problems that arise in presenting the material are dealt with in introductory notes to the various sections. The principal sources used are also given in these notes. Population figures after 1921 are derived from W. E. Vaughan and A. J. Fitzpatrick (ed.), *Irish historical statistics: population 1821–1971* (Dublin, 1978; New History of Ireland Ancillary Publications II). More detailed and extended information on Irish elections is contained in *Parliamentary election results in Ireland, 1801–1921*, edited by Brian M. Walker (Dublin, 1978; New History of Ireland Ancillary Publications IV).

BRIAN M. WALKER

PARLIAMENT OF THE UNITED KINGDOM OF GREAT BRITAIN AND IRELAND, 1801-1918

1 Sources

CONSTITUENCIES, M.P.S, ELECTORS, AND POPULATION

Copy of instructions given by the chief secretary for Ireland, with reference to the cities and boroughs in Ireland sending representatives to parliament; copy of any letter or report received in answer to such instructions; reports from commissioners and plans, pp vi-xi, H.C. 1831-2 (519), xliii, 6-11.

Return of the population of the several counties in Ireland, as enumerated in 1831, p. 1, H.C. 1833 (254), xxxix, 1.

Number of electors registered under the reform act, distinguishing qualifications . . ., H.C. 1833 (177), xxvii, 289.

Amended return of electors registered in Ireland, as far as relates to Galway and Tipperary, H.C. 1833 (767), xxvii, 313.

Abstract of return of the number of registered electors in each county in Ireland, under the act 13 & 14 Vict., c. 69, distinguishing each class of electors; and similar return for each county of a city, county of a town, and borough in Ireland, returning one or more members to parliament, H.C. 1851 (383), 1, 879.

The census of Ireland for the year 1851: part VI, general report, pp 620, 644, H.C. 1856 (2134), xxxi, 765, 788.

Thom's Irish Almanac and Official Directory of the United Kingdom of Great Britain and Ireland. Dublin, 1844-1918.

Return showing for each parliamentary constituency in the United Kingdom, the number of parliamentary and local government electors on the register compiled under the Representation of the People Act, 1918, pp 20-23, H.C. 1918, xix (138), 944-7.

Peter Jupp. *British and Irish elections, 1784-1831.* Newton Abbot, 1973. (pp 152-7)

B. M. Walker, 'The Irish electorate, 1868-1915', in *I.H.S.*, xviii, no. 71 (Mar. 1973), pp 359-406.

CONTESTS, AFFILIATIONS OF CANDIDATES AND M.P.S, AND VOTES CAST

Besides the works listed below, local newspapers proved an extremely useful source for the political labels of candidates and members.

Parliamentary writs of return, 1820-65. P.R.O., Chancery papers, C219.
  Unlike the writs of return for Great Britain, the writs for Ireland contain details of the names of candidates and votes cast.

Abstract of the expenses incurred by or on behalf of each candidate at the last general election for every county, city, or borough in the United Kingdom: account sent in by each returning officer to each candidate; aggregate cost of the general election; number of electors on the register; and number who voted for each candidate, H.C. 1868-9 (424), l, 28-32.

Return of charges made to candidates at the late election by returning officers, number of members returned, and number of candidates; also the total expenses of each candidate, and number of votes polled for each. For 1874: H.C. 1874 (358), liii, 32-7; for 1880: H.C. 1880 (382-sess. 2), lvii, 36-43; for 1885: H.C. 1886 (199-sess. 1), lii, 468-83; for 1886: H.C. 1886 (199-sess. 1), lii, 553-62; for 1892: H.C. 1893-4 (423), lxx, 789-803; for 1895: H.C. 1896 (145), lxvii, 390-404; for 1900: H.C. 1901 (352), lix, 216-29; for 1906: H.C. 1906 (302), xcvi, 98-111; for 1910 (Jan.): H.C. 1910 (299), lxxiii, 769-80; for 1910 (Dec.): H.C. 1911 (272), lxii, 742-9.

Henry Stooks Smith. *The parliaments of England from 1st George I to the present time.* London, 1850; reprint with introduction by F. W. S. Craig, Chichester, 1973.

McCalmont's parliamentary poll book: British election results 1832-1918. 8th ed., with introduction by J. R. Vincent and Maurice Stenton, Brighton, 1971.

Dod's parliamentary companion. London, 1833-1918. Originally entitled *The parliamentary pocket companion.*

C. R. P. Dod. *Electoral facts, from 1832 to 1852, impartially stated, etc.* London, 1852; revised ed., with introduction by H. J. Hanham, Brighton, 1972.

Thom's Irish almanac and official directory of the United Kingdom of Great Britain and Ireland. Dublin, 1844-1918.

Debrett's illustrated house of commons and judicial bench. London, 1922 issue.

Peter Jupp. Parliamentary representation in Ireland, 1801-20. Ph.D. thesis, University of Reading, 1967.

Angus MacIntyre. *The liberator: Daniel O'Connell and the Irish party, 1830-1847.* London, 1965. (pp 299-308)

J. B. Conacher. *The Peelites and the party system, 1846-52.* Newton Abbot, 1972.

J. H. Whyte. *The independent Irish party, 1850-59.* Oxford, 1958. (pp 180-83)

David Thornley. *Isaac Butt and home rule.* London, 1964.

C. C. O'Brien. *Parnell and his party, 1880-90.* Oxford, 1957; corrected impression, 1964.

F. S. L. Lyons. *The Irish parliamentary party, 1890-1910.* London, 1951.

J. H. Whyte. The influence of the catholic clergy on elections in nineteenth-century Ireland. In *E.H.R.*, lxxxv (Apr. 1960), pp 239-59.

J. W. Boyle. The Belfast Protestant Association and the Independent Orange Order, 1901-1910. In *I.H.S.*, xiii, no. 50 (Sept. 1962), pp 117-52.

K. R. Schilling. William O'Brien and the All-for-Ireland League. M.Litt. thesis, Trinity College, Dublin, 1956.

2 Constituencies and M.P.s, 1801-1918

The figures for the number of constituencies and M.P.s apply to the period following each redistribution act. In 1832, apart from an increase in the number of borough and university M.P.s, and the alteration of some borough boundaries, no changes occurred in the number of constituencies or M.P.s. Carrickfergus, which returned one M.P., was disfranchised from 1833 to 1835. The only effect on constituencies of the reform act of 1868 was to increase the area of some of the boroughs; that of Belfast was significantly altered by the change. Sligo and Cashel, which each returned one M.P., were disfranchised in 1870. M.P.s for Dublin University were elected under a system of proportional representation after the 1918 act.

legislation	type of constituency	number of constituencies	constituencies returning		total number of M.P.s
			1 M.P.	2 M.P.s	
Act of union 1800	borough	33	31	2	35
	county	32	—	32	64
	university	1	1	—	1
	total	66	32	34	100
Representation of the People (Ireland) Act, 1832	borough	33	27	6	39
	county	32	—	32	64
	university	1	—	1	2
	total	66	27	39	105
Representation of the People (Ireland) Act, 1868	borough	33	27	6	39
	county	32	—	32	64
	university	1	—	1	2
	total	66	27	39	105
Redistribution of Seats Act, 1885	borough	15	14	1	16
	county	85	85	—	85
	university	1	—	1	2
	total	101	99	2	103
Redistribution of Seats (Ireland) Act, 1918	borough	20	19	1	21
	county	80	80	—	80
	university	3	2	1	4
	total	103	101	2	105

3 Electors and population, 1801–1918

Prior to 1832 accurate figures for the number of electors and population of constituencies are not available. The total county electorate has been estimated as about 160,000 in 1803. In 1829 this total was reduced to approximately 37,000, through the operation of the Irish parliamentary elections act of that year, which, accompanying the catholic relief act, raised the main qualification for the franchise from a forty-shilling to a £10 freehold. In the boroughs the electorate varied widely from those in which the franchise was restricted to members of the corporations to those where it included freemen and freeholders.[1]

From 1832 accurate figures for the number of electors are available, and are given below in relation to the principal franchise acts. Several points must be borne in mind when we look at these figures. First, because of the complexities of the franchise and registration laws, the electorate altered not only immediately after the franchise acts were passed but also in subsequent years; this was especially so before 1885. Secondly, there were important differences between constituencies, both borough and county, in the proportions of electors to population; these were partly the result of the operation of different franchises and the activities of registration agents, and partly the result of social and economic differences between the constituencies. Thirdly, the electorate figures contain some plural and duplicate voters, although these were not so numerous in Ireland as in England; apart from the 1830s and 1840s, when the registration system was extremely inefficient, the number under this category was, generally speaking, probably around three per cent in both counties and boroughs before 1885, and lower afterwards.

The figures for the electorate and population are those available for the year nearest to the passing of each franchise act.

legislation	constituencies	electors	population	electors as percentage of population
		1832	*1831*	
Representation	boroughs	29,471	792,151[2]	3·7
of the People	counties	60,597	6,992,385	0·9
(Ireland) Act,	university	2,073		
1832	total	92,141	7,784,536	1·2
		1851-2	*1851*	
Parliamentary	boroughs	28,301	878,430	3·2
Voters	counties	135,245	5,673,955	2·4
(Ireland) Act,	university	1,700		
1850	total	165,246	6,552,385	2·5
		1868	*1871*	
Representation	boroughs	45,625	881,588	5·3
of the People	counties	177,775	4,530,789	3·9
(Ireland) Act,	university	2,151		
1868	total	225,551	5,412,377	4·2
		1885	*1881*	
Representation	boroughs	106,314	756,430	14·1
of the People	counties	631,651	4,418,406	14·3
Act, 1884	university	4,155		
	total	742,120	5,174,836	14·3
		1918	*1911*	
Representation	boroughs	386,667	911,542	42·4
of the People	counties	1,539,607	3,478,677	44·3
Act, 1918	universities	10,399		
	total	1,936,673	4,390,219	44·1

[1] Peter Jupp, *British and Irish elections, 1784-1831* (Newton Abbot, 1973), pp 152-7.
[2] The borough population figures are based on the figures given by the boundary commissioners for the population within the proposed borough boundaries. Not all their proposals were completely accepted, but the discrepancy between the proposed and the accepted boundaries is small.

4   Contests at general elections, 1801–1918

The term 'contest' is sometimes used by historians of nineteenth-century politics to describe the situation where an election was contested until the moment when the poll was due to start. The term here refers to contests which proceeded to a poll. In the general election of 1801 there were no contests in Ireland.

1801–31 (number of constituencies: 66)

general election	contests	general election	contests
1801	—	1818	14
1802	11	1820	10
1806	12	1826	18
1807	14	1830	30
1812	18	1831	21

1832–65 (number of constituencies: 66)

general election	contests	general election	contests
1832	45	1852	44
1835	36	1857	38
1837	34	1859	26
1841	21	1865	34
1847	27		

1868–80 (number of constituencies: 66; 1870–80: 64)

general election	contests
1868	26
1874	52
1880	54

1885–1910 (number of constituencies: 101)

general election	contests	general election	contests
1885	79	1900	30
1886	33	1906	21
1892	82	1910 (Jan.)	37
1895	41	1910 (Dec.)	38

1918 (number of constituencies: 103)

general election	contests
1918	78

5 Members elected at general elections, 1801–31, by parties

For the general elections of 1801–31, it is not possible to classify candidates and M.P.s under meaningful party labels. But information supplied by Dr Peter Jupp[1] on the political divisions among M.P.s, in the form of estimates of their support for, or opposition to, governments, and also in summaries of their voting on certain important issues may be offered as follows:

Estimates of members' support for, or opposition to, governments, 1802–30

prime minister	date of estimate	for	against	independents, unknowns, or absentees
		the government		
Addington (1801–4)	July 1802	78	17	5
Pitt (1804–6)	July 1805	57	22	21
Grenville (1806–7)	1806	72	23	5
Portland (1807–9)	1808	61	39	
Liverpool (1812–27)	1813	66	34	
Liverpool (1812–27)	1819	71	28	1
Wellington (1828–30)	Sept. 1830	65	33	2

Summaries of members' votes on certain issues, 1825–31

bill	date of vote	for	against	absent (including vacant seats)
		the government		
Roman Catholic relief bill[2]	10 May 1825	54	31	15
Roman Catholic relief bill[3]	30 Mar. 1829	57	19	24
Parliamentary reform bill[4]	22 Mar. 1831	55	37	8

[1] Citing his Ph.D. thesis, 'Parliamentary representation in Ireland, 1801–20' (University of Reading, 1967), appendix A & H, and the following:
List of Irish M.P.s, 25 July 1805 (B.M., Liverpool papers, Add. MS 38359, ff 5–13).
George Canning to George Rose, 15 Aug. 1806 (B.M., George Rose papers, Add. MS 42773, f. 131).
List of Irish M.P.s during 1807–9 (B.M., Peel papers, Add. MS 40221, ff 15–42).
Jupp, op. cit., appendix H.
List of Irish M.P.s during 1818–20 (B.M., Peel papers, Add MS 40298, *passim*).
Treasury list of Irish M.P.s, 21 Sept. 1830 (B.M., Peel papers, Add. MS 40401, ff 182–95).
[2] *Hansard 2*, xiii, 558–62.   [3] Ibid., xx, 1633–8.   [4] *Hansard 3*, iii, 818.

6 Seats won at general elections, 1832–80, by parties

From 1832 information is given on the seats won at each general election by the parties, but the classification of candidates begins only in 1885; before that date it is not possible to compile consistent lists of both candidates and M.P.s according to parties, since classification of M.P.s in the period 1832–80 has sometimes to be based on their performance subsequent to elections. For the same reason, total party votes cannot be given before 1885; and in any case, the existence of so many two–member constituencies before 1885 would make such figures of little value. Some of the more difficult cases of classification in the period 1832–80 are commented on in the footnotes. Changes resulting from petitions, or from by-elections following petitions, after general elections are shown in brackets.

parties	general elections					
	1832 (Dec.)	1835 (Jan.)	1837 (July–Aug.)	1841 (July)	1847 (Aug.)	1852 (July)
conservative[1]	30	37(39)	32(34)	43(40)	31(33)	40
Peelite[2]	—	—	—	—	11	2
liberal[1]	33(35)	34	43(40)	42(47)	25(27)	15(16)
liberal (repealer)[3]	—	34(32)	30(31)	—	—	—
liberal (independent)[4]	—	—	—	—	—	48(47)
repeal	42(39)	—	—	20(18)	36(35)	—
Irish confederate	—	—	—	—	2(2)	—
total	105(104)[5]	105	105	105	105	105

parties	general elections					
	1857 (Mar.–Apr.)	1859 (May)	1865 (July)	1868 (Nov.)	1874 (Feb.)	1880 (Mar.–Apr.)
conservative[1]	44(46)	55(54)	47	39(37)	33	25
liberal[1]	48(47)	50(51)	58	66	10	15
independent opposition	13(12)[6]	—	—	—	—	—
home rule	—	—	—	—	60	36
home rule (Parnellite)[7]	—	—	—	—	—	27
total	105	105	105	105(103)[8]	103	103

[1] Throughout this period the terms conservative and liberal have been uniformly used as party labels despite the oversimplification involved.

[2] In the 1847 general election Peelites are here defined as those conservatives who had supported free trade in the previous parliament, and also those other conservatives, both newly elected and former members, who often supported Peel's friends in the new parliament. In 1852 the Peelites are defined as those conservatives who voted against the government on 16 Dec. 1852 and who regularly supported the Aberdeen coalition after it was formed, as well as others who also supported the coalition.

[3] During the 1835 and 1837 general elections the repeal party merged with the liberals. The term 'liberal (repealer)' has been used to describe liberals formerly in the repeal party, or who joined it in 1841.

[4] The Irish independent opposition party came into existence only after the 1852 general election. The term 'liberal (independent)' describes those members who in their election addresses, at their adoption meetings, at the Tenant League conference in September 1852, or at the religious equality conference in October 1852, declared themselves in favour of an independent party in parliament.

[5] See above, p. 633.

[6] This estimate of the members of the independent opposition in 1857 is based on the number of liberals who gave the conservatives their general support in 1858–9 in parliament. In the 1859 and 1865 general elections some liberals still advocated an independent parliamentary role; but they did not form a coherent group, and so no mention has been made of them in the 1859 or 1865 results.

[7] The figure for the Parnellite section of the home rule party in 1880 is based on those who voted for Parnell at the meeting in Dublin City Hall on 17 May 1880 to elect a new party chairman. It includes John Dillon, who was in the U.S.A. at the time. Parnell himself won three seats at the general election, and these are included in this figure.

[8] See above, p. 634.

7   Candidates at general elections, 1885–1918, by parties

parties	general elections				
	1885 (Nov.–Dec.)	1886 (July)	1892 (July)	1895 (July)	1900 (Sept.–Oct.)
nationalist[1]	89	97	—	—	82
anti-Parnellite nationalist	—	—	85	76	—
Parnellite nationalist	—	—	44	26	—
independent nationalist	2	—	2	2	18[2]
Sinn Féin	—	—	—	—	—
conservative/unionist[3]	67	30	49	33	26
loyalist[4]	6	—	—	—	—
independent conservative/unionist	3	—	—	—	5
liberal[5]	17	3	5	4[6]	1
liberal unionist	—	7	13	8	5[7]
independents and others	4	—	—	—	—
total	188	137	198	149	137

parties	general elections			
	1906 (Jan.)	1910 (Jan.–Feb.)	1910 (Dec.)	1918 (Dec.)
nationalist	83	84	80	55
independent nationalist	3	19[8]	25[8]	7
Sinn Féin	—	—	—	102
conservative/unionist	24	31	28	36
labour unionist	—	—	—	3
independent conservative/unionist	10[9]	2	2	4
liberal	1	7	7	—
liberal unionist[10]	3[7]	—	—	—
labour	1	1	—	5
total	125	144	142	212

[1] From 1885 the name 'nationalist' replaced 'home rule' in common usage.

[2] These independent nationalists were independent in the sense that they were not official nominees of the United Irish League. 15 of them were followers of T. M. Healy.

[3] The term 'conservative' was still widely used in 1885, but from this time onwards 'unionist' increasingly came to be used in its place.

[4] The term 'loyalist' was used in 1885 to describe candidates neither distinctly conservative nor liberal but standing on a pro-union platform.

[5] After the 1885 general election the liberals split into two, one section following Gladstone and the other forming the liberal unionist party. The section led by Gladstone, which remained the official party, has been called liberal here from 1886 onwards although contemporaries sometimes used other terms, such as 'Gladstonian liberal'.

[6] Including an independent liberal.

[7] Including an independent liberal unionist.

[8] Of these independent nationalists, 9 were followers of William O'Brien in 1910 (Jan.) and 20 in 1910 (Dec.). O'Brien formed the All-for-Ireland League in March 1910 and in the December election his followers were members of the league.

[9] Of these independent unionists, 8 were supporters of T. W. Russell.

[10] The distinction between unionist and liberal unionist in Ireland disappeared at the general elections of 1910, although the two were only formally merged in 1912.

8   Seats won at general elections, 1885-1918, by parties

Changes resulting from petitions, or from by-elections following petitions, after general elections are shown in brackets.

parties	general elections				
	1885 (Nov.-Dec.)	1886 (July)	1892 (July)	1895 (July)	1900 (Sept.-Oct.)
nationalist[1]	85	84(85)	—	—	76
anti-Parnellite nationalist	—	—	71	69(70)	—
Parnellite nationalist	—	—	9	12(11)	—
independent nationalist	—	—	—	—	5[2]
conservative/unionist	16	17(16)	19	17	17
independent conservative/unionist	2[3]	—	—	—	—
liberal	—	—	—	1	1
liberal unionist	—	2	4	4	4
total	103	103	103	103	103

parties	general elections			
	1906 (Jan.)	1910 (Jan.-Feb.)	1910 (Dec.)	1918 (Dec.)
nationalist[1]	81	70	73	6
independent nationalist	1	11[4]	10[5]	—
Sinn Féin	—	—	—	73
conservative/unionist	16	21	19	22
labour unionist	—	—	—	3
independent conservative/unionist	3[6]	—	—	1
liberal	1	1	1	—
liberal unionist	1	—	—	—
total	103	103	103	105

[1] From 1885 to 1922 T. P. O'Connor, nationalist, sat for the Scotland division of Liverpool, thus increasing the nationalist strength in the house of commons by one.

[2] The independent nationalists who held these seats were independents in the sense that they were not official nominees of the United Irish League. But except for T. M. Healy and J. L. Carew, who were expelled from the nationalist parliamentary party in December 1900, they did support the party at Westminster.

[3] Both William Johnston and E. S. W. de Cobain won these seats as independent conservatives, but supported the conservative party in Westminster. Both were accepted by their official associations for the 1886 general election.

[4] Seven seats were held by followers of William O'Brien.

[5] Seven seats were held by followers of William O'Brien, besides O'Brien himself. The other two independent nationalists, John McKean and Lawrence Ginnell, subsequently rejoined the nationalist party.

[6] Including T. W. Russell and G. R. Glendinning who subsequently became liberals.

9   Votes cast at general elections, 1885–1918, and seats won without a contest, by parties

Number of seats won without a contest are given in brackets beside the number of votes cast.

parties	general elections				
	1885 (Nov.–Dec.)	1886 (July)	1892 (July)	1895 (July)	1900 (Sept.–Oct.)
nationalist	302,315(19)	91,194(66)	297,258(9)[1]	148,393(46)[2]	63,195(57)
independent nationalist	2,889	—	2,180	3,429	24,170(1)
conservative/unionist	103,323(4)	79,977(3)	55,424(10)	36,193(14)	43,115(10)
independent conservative/unionist	7,514	—	—	—	11,690
liberal	29,943	5,710	14,472	11,960	2,869
liberal unionist	—	21,944	28,533	20,530(1)	4,354(3)
independents and others	5,482	—	—	—	—
total	451,466(23)	198,825(69)	397,867(19)	220,505(61)	149,393(71)

parties	general elections			
	1906 (Jan.)	1910 (Jan.)	1910 (Dec.)	1918 (Dec.)
nationalist	30,423(73)	78,154(55)	92,176(49)	225,557
independent nationalist	1,800(1)	45,550	36,024(4)	8,619
conservative/unionist	59,371(8)	68,982(10)	57,470(11)	293,304[3]
independent conservative/unionist	30,633	3,553	2,925	9,531
liberal	2,966	20,339	19,003	—
liberal unionist	4,872	—	—	—
independents and others	4,616	3,951	—	509,930(23)[4]
total	134,681(82)	220,529(65)	207,598(64)	1,046,941(23)[5]

[1] Including 227,007(9) for the anti-Parnellite nationalists and 70,251 for the Parnellite nationalists.
[2] Including 95,715(43) for the anti-Parnellite nationalists and 52,678(3) for the Parnellite nationalists.
[3] Including 30,304 for the labour unionists who were members of the Ulster Unionist Council.
[4] Including 497,107(23) for Sinn Féin.
[5] In the case of Dublin University the first preference votes are included.

PARLIAMENT OF THE UNITED KINGDOM OF GREAT BRITAIN AND NORTHERN IRELAND, 1921-74

10   Sources

F. W. S. Craig (ed.), *British parliamentary election results, 1918-1949.* Glasgow, 1969.
—— *British parliamentary election results, 1950-70.* Chichester, 1971.
Results and statistics for Northern Ireland constituencies in the 1974 (Feb.) general election, prepared and issued by the chief electoral officer for Northern Ireland. Typescript, Belfast, 1974; also for the 1974 (Oct.) general election, typescript, Belfast, 1974.
Irish Times, 19 Feb., 2 Mar. 1974.

11   Constituencies and M.P.s

The figures apply to the period following each redistribution act.

legislation	number of constituencies	number of constituencies returning		total number of M.P.s
		1 M.P.	2 M.P.s	
Government of Ireland Act, 1920	10[1]	7	3	13
Representation of the People Act, 1949	12	12	—	12

[1] Including the Queen's University seat, which returned 1 M.P. up to the 1949 act, and, unlike all other constituencies, had a system of proportional representation for its elections. The seat, however, was contested only in 1945 and then by only two candidates.

12   Electors and population, 1921-76

The figures for electors and population are those available for the year
nearest to the passing of each franchise act.

legislation	electors	population	electors as percentage of population
Representation of the People (Equal Franchise) Act, 1928[1]	*1929* 775,307	*1926* 1,256,561	61.7
Representation of the People Act, 1949	*1949* 865,421	*1951* 1,370,921	63.1
Representation of the People Act, 1969	*1970* 1,025,215	*1971* 1,536,065	66.7

[1] Prior to 1928 the franchise was based on the Representation of the People Act, 1918 (see above, p. 634).

13   Contests at general elections, 1922-74

1922-45 (number of constituencies: 10)

general election	contests	general election	contests
1922	2	1929	7
1923	3	1931	3
1924	7	1935	4
		1945	9

1950-74 (number of constituencies: 12)

general election	contests	general election	contests
1950	10	1964	12
1951	8	1966	12
1955	12	1970	12
1959	12	1974 (Feb.)	12
		1974 (Oct.)	12

14　Candidates at general elections, 1922–74, by parties

parties	general elections							
	1922 (Nov.)	1923 (Dec.)	1924 (Oct.)	1929 (May)	1931 (Oct.)	1935 (Nov.)	1945 (July)	1950 (Feb.)
unionist	13	13	13	11	13	13	13	12
independent unionist	—	1	1	2	—	—	1	—
nationalist[1]	2	2	—	3	3	2	3	2
independent nationalist	1	—	—	—	—	—	—	—
Northern Ireland labour	—	—	1	—	1	—	5	5
independent labour	—	1	—	—	—	—	1	—
commonwealth labour	—	—	—	—	—	—	1	—
Irish labour	—	—	—	—	—	—	—	2
liberal	—	—	—	6	—	—	—	—
Sinn Féin	—	—	8	—	—	—	—	1
republican	—	—	—	—	—	3	—	1
independents and others	—	—	—	1	—	—	2	—
total	16	17	23	23	17	18	26	23

parties	general elections							
	1951 (Oct.)	1955 (May)	1959 (Oct.)	1964 (Oct.)	1966 (Mar.)	1970 (June)	1974 (Feb.)	1974 (Oct.)
unionist	12	12	12	12	12	12	14[2]	7
unionist party of Northern Ireland	—	—	—	—	—	—	—	2
independent unionist	—	—	—	—	—	3	—	1
protestant unionist	—	—	—	—	—	2	—	—
democratic unionist	—	—	—	—	—	—	2[3]	2[4]
vanguard unionist	—	—	—	—	—	—	3[3]	3[4]
nationalist[1]	2	—	—	—	1	—	—	—
independent nationalist	1	—	—	—	—	—	—	—
national democratic	—	—	—	—	—	2	—	—
Northern Ireland labour	4	3	3	10	4	7	4	3
independent labour	—	—	1	—	—	1	—	—
Irish labour	1	1	—	—	—	—	—	—
republican labour	—	—	—	1	1	1	—	—
social democratic and labour	—	—	—	—	—	—	12	9
liberal	—	—	1	4	3	3	—	—
alliance	—	—	—	—	—	—	3	4
unity	—	—	—	—	1	5	2	1
Sinn Féin	—	12	12	—	—	—	—	—
republican	—	—	—	12	5	—	—	—
republican clubs	—	—	—	—	—	—	4	5
independents and others	—	—	—	—	—	3	4	6
total	20	28	29	39	27	39	48	43

[1] Including candidates of the new national league in 1929, nationalist abstentionists in 1935, and the anti-partition league in 1950 and 1951.

[2] These 14 claimed to be official candidates; 7 were pro-assembly unionists and 7 were endorsed by the united ulster unionist council (U.U.U.C.).

[3] Both vanguard and democratic unionist candidates were endorsed by the U.U.U.C.

[4] All were endorsed by the U.U.U.C.

15 Members elected at general elections, 1922-74, by parties

parties	general elections							
	1922 (Nov.)	1923 (Dec.)	1924 (Oct.)	1929 (May)	1931 (Oct.)	1935 (Nov.)	1945 (July)	1950 (Feb.)
unionist	11	11	13	11	11	11	9	10
independent unionist	—	—	—	—	—	—	1	—
nationalist[1]	2	2	—	2	2	2	2	2
independent labour	—	—	—	—	—	—	1	—
total	13	13	13	13	13	13	13	12

parties	general elections							
	1951 (Oct.)	1955 (May)	1959 (Oct.)	1964 (Oct.)	1966 (Mar.)	1970 (June)	1974 (Feb.)	1974 (Oct.)
unionist	9	10	12	12	11	8	7[2]	6
protestant unionist	—	—	—	—	—	1	—	—
democratic unionist	—	—	—	—	—	—	1	1
vanguard unionist	—	—	—	—	—	—	3	3
nationalist[1]	2	—	—	—	—	—	—	—
Irish labour	1	—	—	—	—	—	—	—
republican labour	—	—	—	—	1	1	—	—
social democratic and labour	—	—	—	—	—	—	1	1
unity	—	—	—	—	—	2	—	—
Sinn Féin	—	2[3]	—	—	—	—	—	—
independent	—	—	—	—	—	—	—	1
total	12	12	12	12	12	12	12	12

[1] Including members of the new national league in 1929, nationalist abstentionists in 1935, and the anti-partition league in 1950 and 1951.

[2] All the members elected were those endorsed by the U.U.U.C.

[3] T. J. Mitchell (Sinn Féin) and P. C. Clarke (Sinn Féin), both of whom were serving terms of imprisonment for treason, were disqualified and 2 unionists, George Forrest and R. G. Grosvenor, were subsequently elected.

16 Votes cast at general elections, 1922-74, and members elected unopposed, by parties

Numbers of M.P.s elected unopposed are given in brackets beside the numbers of votes cast.

parties	general elections				
	1922 (Nov.)	1923 (Dec.)	1924 (Oct.)	1929 (May)	1931 (Oct.)
unionist	107,972(10)	117,161(9)	451,278(3)	354,657(2)	149,566(9)
unofficial unionist[1]	—	15,171	517	25,057	—
Northern Ireland labour	—	—	21,122	—	9,410
independent labour[2]	—	22,255	—	—	—
nationalist[3]	99,914	87,671	—	24,177(2)	123,053
Sinn Féin/republican[4]	—	—	46,457	—	—
independents and others	—	—	—	106,162	—
total	207,886(10)	242,258(9)	519,374(3)	510,053(4)	282,029(9)

[[1] *See next page for notes to table 16.*]

16   Votes cast at general elections, 1922–74, and members elected unopposed, by parties (*continued*)

parties	general elections				
	1935 (Nov.)	1945 (July)	1950 (Feb.)	1951 (Oct.)	1955 (May)
unionist	292,840(7)	394,373(1)	352,334(2)	274,928(4)	442,647
unofficial unionist[1]	—	46,732	—	—	—
Northern Ireland labour	—	65,459	67,816	62,324	35,614
independent labour[2]	—	44,883	52,715	33,174	16,050
nationalist[3]	101,494	148,078	65,211	92,787	—
Sinn Féin/republican[4]	56,833	—	23,362	—	152,310
independents & others	—	22,891	—	—	—
total	451,167(7)	722,416(1)[5]	561,438(2)	463,213(4)	646,621

parties	general elections				
	1959 (Oct.)	1964 (Oct.)	1966 (Mar.)	1970 (June)	1974 (Feb.)	1974 (Oct.)
unionist	445,013	401,897	368,629	422,041	326,134[6]	256,065
unofficial unionist[1]	—	—	—	53,090	134,600[7]	167,149[8]
Northern Ireland labour	44,370	102,759	72,613	98,194	15,483	11,539
independent labour[2]	20,062	14,678	26,292	38,214	—	—
nationalist[3]	—	—	22,167	10,349	—	—
Sinn Féin/republican[4]	63,415	101,628	62,782	—	15,152	21,633
independents & others	3,253	17,354	43,754	157,225	225,987[9]	235,648[10]
total	576,113	638,316	596,237	779,113	717,626	702,094

[1] Including independent unionist, protestant unionist, democratic unionist, and vanguard unionist.

[2] Including independent labour, commonwealth labour, Irish labour, and republican labour.

[3] Including nationalist, independent nationalist, nationalist abstentionist, national democratic, new national league, and anti-partition league.

[4] Including republican clubs.

[5] Including votes cast for the university seat, which was elected under a system of proportional representation. However on this, the only occasion when the seat was contested, there were only 2 candidates.

[6] Including 94,301 votes for pro-assembly unionists and 232,103 for U.U.U.C. unionists.

[7] Including 75,944 votes for vanguard unionists and 58,656 for democratic unionists.

[8] Including 92,262 votes for vanguard unionists, 59,451 for democratic unionists and 20,454 for the unionist party of Northern Ireland.

[9] Including 22,660 votes for the alliance party and 160,437 for social democratic and labour.

[10] Including 35,955 votes for the alliance party and 154,193 for social democratic and labour.

PARLIAMENT AND PARLIAMENTARY ASSEMBLIES OF NORTHERN IRELAND, 1921–75

These tables cover general elections, 1921–69, to the Northern Ireland parliament, the general election of 1973 to the Northern Ireland assembly, and also the general election of 1975 to the Northern Ireland convention. For the general elections of 1921, 1925, 1973, and 1975, which were contested under systems of proportional representation, the number of votes cast by parties is for first preference votes. For elections over the period 1929–65, when Queen's University alone used a system of proportional representation, the numbers of votes given are exclusive of the university figures. The numbers of candidates and members elected do, however, include those for Queen's; footnotes give the political affiliations of these candidates and members so that an accurate comparison can be made between the tables for candidates and members and the table for votes cast.

17 Sources

Sydney Elliott (ed.), *Northern Ireland parliamentary election results, 1921–1972*. Chichester, 1973.
Report on the administration of home office services, 1970 (N.I.) [C.570], 1970, p. 53.
1973 Northern Ireland assembly election results; prepared and issued by the chief electoral office for Northern Ireland. Typescript, Belfast, 1973.
1975 Northern Ireland convention election results; prepared and issued by the chief electoral officer for Northern Ireland. Typescript, Belfast, 1975.
Local newspapers.

18   Constituencies and M.P.s

The figures apply to the period following each redistribution act.

legislation	number of constituencies	number of constituencies returning						total number of M.P.s
		I	4	5	6	7	8	
				M.P.s				
Government of Ireland Act, 1920	10	—	6	1	—	1	2	52
Method of Voting and Redistribution Act, 1929	49	48	1	—	—	—	—	52
Electoral Law (Northern Ireland) Act, 1968	52	52	—	—	—	—	—	52
Northern Ireland Constitution Act, 1973	12	—	—	1	5	5	1	78
Northern Ireland Act, 1974	12	—	—	1	5	5	1	78

19   Electors and population

The figures for electors and population are those available for the year nearest to the passing of each franchise act.

legislation	electors	population	electors as percentage of population
Representation of the People (Northern Ireland) Act, 1928[1]	*1929* 775,307	*1926* 1,256,561	62.6
Electoral Law (Northern Ireland) Act, 1968	*1969* 912,087	*1971* 1,536,065	60.0
Electoral Law (Northern Ireland) Act, 1969	*1970* 1,022,217	*1971* 1,536,065	66.5

[1] Prior to the 1928 act the franchise was based on the Representation of the People Act, 1918 (see p. 634).

20   Contests at general elections, 1921–75

1921–5 (number of constituencies: 11)

general election	contests
1921	11
1925	9

1929–69 (number of constituencies: 49)

general election	contests	general election	contests
1929	27	1953	24
1933	16	1958	22
1938	28	1962	25
1945	29	1965	29
1949	29	1969	45

1973 (number of constituencies: 12)

general election	contests
1973	12

1975 (number of constituencies: 12)

general election	contests
1975	12

21   Candidates at general elections, 1921-69,[1] by parties

parties	general elections					
	1921 (May)	1925 (Apr.)	1929 (May)	1933 (Nov.)	1938 (Feb.)	1945 (June)
unionist	40	40	43	41	43	41
independent unionist	—	4	10	8	11[2]	5
progressive unionist	—	—	—	—	11[3]	—
nationalist[4]	12	11	11	10	9	11
independent nationalist	—	—	1	1	—	—
Northern Ireland labour	—	3	5	3	7	15
independent labour	4	—	2	—	1	3
commonwealth labour	—	—	—	—	—	6
socialist republican	—	—	—	—	—	2
liberal	—	—	5	—	—	—
Sinn Féin	20	—	—	—	—	—
republican	—	6	—	4	—	—
independents and others	1	2	6	2	3	5
total	77	66	83	69	85	88

parties	general elections					
	1949 (Feb.)	1953 (Oct.)	1958 (Mar.)	1962 (May)	1965 (Nov.)	1969 (Feb.)
unionist	46	43	46	45	41	44[5]
independent unionist	3	8	5	—	—	3
protestant unionist	—	—	1	—	—	5
independent O'Neill unionist	—	—	—	—	—	15
nationalist[4]	17	8	8	9	9	9
independent nationalist	—	4	2	—	—	—
national democratic	—	—	—	—	4	7
Northern Ireland labour	9	9	8	14	17	16
independent labour	4	1	3	4	1	—
Irish labour	—	8[6]	4[7]	1	—	—
republican labour	—	1	1	1	2	5
socialist republican	1	—	—	—	—	—
liberal	—	—	1	4	4	2
people's democracy	—	—	—	—	—	8
independents and others	3	3	2	2	4	5
total	83	85	81	80	82	119

[1] Including candidates for Queen's University which were as follows: 1929, unionist 4, independent unionist 1; 1933, unionist 3, independent unionist 1, independent 1; 1938, unionist 4, independent unionist 1, independent 1; 1945, unionist 4, independent unionist 1, independent 2; 1949, unionist 4, independent 2; 1953, unionist 3, independent 2, Northern Ireland labour party 1; 1958, unionist 3, Northern Ireland labour party 1, liberal 1, independent 1; 1962, unionist 3, liberal 1, independent 1; 1965, unionist 2, liberal 1, independent 1.

[2] Including 6 candidates of the independent unionist association.

[3] Including 1 independent progressive unionist.

[4] Including candidates of the new national league in 1929 and of the anti-partition league in 1949 and 1953.

[5] Including 29 pro-O'Neill and 15 anti-O'Neill.

[6] Including 1 independent Irish labour.

[7] Including 2 independent Irish labour.

22 Members elected at general elections, 1921-69[1], by parties

parties	general elections					
	1921 (May)	1925 (Apr.)	1929 (May)	1933 (Nov.)	1938 (Feb.)	1945 (June)
unionist	40	32	37	36	39	33
independent unionist	—	4[2]	3	3	3	2
nationalist[3]	6[4]	10	11	9	8	10
Northern Ireland labour	—	3	1	2	1	2
independent labour	—	—	—	—	1	1
commonwealth labour	—	—	—	—	—	1
socialist republican	—	—	—	—	—	1
Sinn Féin	6	—	—	—	—	—
republican	—	2	—	1	—	—
independents and others	—	1	—	1	—	2
total	52	52	52	52	52	52

parties	general elections					
	1949 (Feb.)	1953 (Oct.)	1958 (Nov.)	1962 (May)	1965 (Nov.)	1969 (Feb.)
unionist	37	38	37	34	36	36[5]
independent unionist	2	1	—	—	—	—
independent O'Neill unionist	—	—	—	—	—	3
nationalist[3]	9	7	7	9	9	6
independent nationalist	—	2	1	—	—	—
national democratic	—	—	—	—	1	—
Northern Ireland labour	—	—	4	4	2	2
independent labour	1	1	1	1	—	—
Irish labour	—	1	—	1	—	—
republican labour	—	1	1	1	2	2
socialist republican	1	—	—	—	—	—
liberal	—	—	—	1	1	—
independents and others	2	1	1	1	1	3
total	52	52	52	52	52	52

[1] Including M.P.s for Queen's University. At each election 4 unionists were returned for the seat except for the following occasions: 1929, unionist 3, independent unionist 1; 1945, unionist 2, independent 2; 1949, unionist 2, independent 2; 1953, unionist 3, independent 1; 1958, unionist 3, independent 1; 1962, unionist 2, liberal 1, independent 1; 1965, unionist 3, independent 1.

[2] P. J. Woods, independent unionist, was elected for both Belfast South and Belfast West. He chose to represent the latter, and in the subsequent by-election in November 1925 for the former an official unionist, A. B. Babington, was elected. Woods has been included in these figures.

[3] Including members of the new national league in 1929 and of the anti-partition league in 1949 and 1953.

[4] Joseph Devlin, nationalist, was elected for Antrim and Belfast West. His second seat was not recontested. He has been included here twice.

[5] Including 24 pro-O'Neill and 12 anti-O'Neill.

23   Votes cast at general elections, 1921–69, and members elected unopposed,[1] by parties

Numbers of M.P.s elected unopposed are given in brackets beside the numbers of votes cast.

parties	general elections			
	1921 (May)	1925 (Apr.)	1929 (May)	1933 (Nov.)
unionist	343,377	211,662(10)	146,899(16)	72,133(27)
unofficial unionist[2]	—	34,716	41,337	35,774
Northern Ireland labour	—	18,114	23,334	14,436
independent labour[3]	3,075	—	2,442	—
nationalist[4]	60,577	91,452(1)	37,763(6)	26,480(6)
Sinn Féin republican	104,917	20,615(1)	—	20,510
independents and others	926	8,186	38,322	—
total	512,842	384,745(12)	290,097(22)	167,333(33)

parties	general elections			
	1938 (Feb.)	1945 (June)	1949 (Feb.)	1953 (Oct.)
unionist	185,854(14)	178,662(13)	234,202(14)	121,835(21)
unofficial unionist[2]	95,905	17,797(1)	2,150(2)	32,998
Northern Ireland labour	18,775(1)	66,053	26,831	31,063
independent labour[3]	5,480	47,360	7,970(2)	29,711
nationalist[4]	16,167(6)	32,546(6)	101,445(2)	39,936(4)
independents and others	7,123	12,456	623	1,207
total	329,304(21)	354,874(20)	373,221(20)	256,750(25)

parties	general elections			
	1958 (Mar.)	1962 (May)	1965 (Nov.)	1969(Feb.)
unionist	102,700(25)	143,740(20)	191,896(14)	269,501[5](6)
unofficial unionist[2]	21,241	—	—	107,043
Northern Ireland labour	37,748	76,842	66,323	45,113
independent labour[3]	29,819	20,239(1)	7,697(1)	13,155
nationalist[4]	41,181(2)	45,680(3)	41,954(6)	68,424(1)
independents and others	3,013	9,373	16,719(2)	55,851
total	235,702(27)	295,874(24)	324,589(23)	559,087(7)

[1] In 1921 and 1925 the figures are for first preference votes. From 1929 onwards the figures exclude the votes cast for the university seat because proportional representation was retained in this seat alone. Only at two elections do the figures of unopposed M.P.s include university M.P.s, namely 1925, when 4 unionists, and 1965, when 2 unionists, 1 liberal, and 1 independent, were returned without a contest.

[2] Including independent unionist, progressive unionist, protestant unionist, and independent O'Neill unionist.

[3] Including independent labour, commonwealth labour, federation of labour, Irish labour, republican labour, and socialist republican.

[4] Including nationalist, independent nationalist, new national league, anti-partition league, and national democratic.

[5] 173,805 pro-O'Neill and 95,696 anti-O'Neill.

24   Candidates, members elected, first preference votes cast, and members elected unopposed, by parties, at the general election for the Northern Ireland assembly, 28 June 1973

parties	candidates	members elected	first preference votes cast and members elected unopposed[1]
unionist (pledged)[2]	40	23	188,435
unionist	14	10	90,867
democratic unionist	17	8	78,228
vanguard unionist	25	7	75,759
West Belfast loyalist coalition	2	2	5,390
Northern Ireland labour	18	1	18,675
republican labour	1	—	1,750
social democratic and labour	28	19	159,773
nationalist	3	—	8,270
republican clubs	10	—	13,064
liberal	2	—	811
alliance	35	8	66,541
independents and others	15	—	14,678
total	210	78	722,241

[1] No members were elected unopposed.

[2] These were unionists who accepted a statement of policy drawn up by a committee of the Ulster Unionist Council pledging the party to support and work the Northern Ireland Constitution Act, 1973. They include A. L. Dickson, an unofficial unionist but a supporter of the policy.

25   Candidates, members elected, first preference votes cast and members elected unopposed, by parties, at the general election for the Northern Ireland Convention, 1 May 1975

parties	candidates	members elected	first preference votes cast and members elected unopposed[1]
unionist party of Northern Ireland[2]	18	5	50,891
unionist (official)[3]	27	19 ⎫	169,797
democratic unionist[3]	18	12 ⎬ 45	97,073
vanguard unionist[3]	17	14 ⎭	83,507
Northern Ireland labour	6	1	9,102
republican labour	—	—	—
social democratic and labour	30	17	156,049
nationalist	—	—	—
republican clubs	17	—	14,515
liberal	—	—	—
alliance	23	8	64,657
independents and others	9	2	12,570
total	165	78	658,161

[1] No members were elected unopposed.

[2] Consisting of the pro-power-sharing section of the unionist party, the U.P.N.I. came into existence formally in Sept. 1974.

[3] Members of these parties, except for Roy Bradford, official unionist, were endorsed by the United Ulster Unionist Council, which also endorsed 5 independent loyalist candidates, of whom Frank Millar alone was elected.

DÁIL ÉIREANN, 1921-73

Information on members returned to the 'first dáil' of 1918 can be found on pp 639-41 above. The 1921 general election has not been included in the tables of candidates, of members and of votes cast: it was uncontested, and 124 Sinn Féin members and 4 independents were returned. As elections to the dáil are by proportional representation, some of the material in this section—table 27 (showing the system of multi-seat constituencies) and table 32 (giving numbers of first-preference votes)—is necessarily presented on a different pattern from other sections.

26 Sources

Department of local government and public health, second report, 1925-7. Dublin: Stationery Office, 1928. (p. 52)

W. J. Flynn (ed.), *The oireachtas and Saorstat guide for 1929.* Dublin, 1929.

—— *Free State parliamentary companion for 1932.* Dublin, 1932.

—— *Irish parliamentary handbook, 1939.* Dublin, 1939.

—— *Irish parliamentary handbook, 1945.* Dublin, 1945.

Copies of the public notices of the results of the elections and of the transfer of votes in respect of: (a) general election, 1948 (b) general election, 1951 (c) bye-elections, 1944-1952 (inclusive). Dublin: Stationery Office, 1953. Continued in separate issues for each subsequent election.

Local newspapers.

27   Constituencies and T.D.s

The figures apply to the periods between each redistribution act and the next.

legislation	number of constituencies	number of constituencies returning							total number of T.D.s
		3	4	5	6	7	8	9	
					T.D.s				
Government of Ireland Act, 1920	28	3	16	4	2	1	2	—	128
Constitution of the Irish Free State, 1922, and Electoral Act, 1923	30	8	4	9	—	5	3	1	153
Electoral (Revision of Constituencies) Act, 1935	34	15	8	8	—	3	—	—	138
Electoral (Amendment) Act, 1947	40	22	9	9	—	—	—	—	147
Electoral (Amendment) Act, 1959[1]	39	21	9	9	—	—	—	—	144
Electoral (Amendment) Act, 1961	38	17	12	9	—	—	—	—	144
Electoral (Amendment) Act, 1969	42	26	14	2	—	—	—	—	144

[1] Some sections of this act were held to be repugnant to the Irish constitution and it never operated. It was replaced by the act of 1961.

28   Electors and population

legislation	electorate	population	electors as percentage of population
Constitution of the Irish Free State, 1922, and Electoral Act, 1923[1]	*1926* 1,728,943	*1926* 2,971,992	58.2
Electoral (Amendment) Act, 1973	*1973* 1,783,604	*1971* 2,978,248	59.9

[1] Prior to the 1923 act, the franchise was based on the Representation of the People Act, 1918 (see above, p. 634).

29 Contests at general elections, 1921–73

1921–2 (number of constituencies: 28)

general election	contests
1921	—
1922	20

1923–33 (number of constituencies: 30)

general election	contests
1923	29
1927 (June)	30
1927 (Sept.)	29
1932	29
1933	29

1937–44 (number of constituencies: 34)

general election	contests
1937	34
1938	32
1943	34
1944	33

1948–57 (number of constituencies: 40)

general election	contests
1948	40
1951	40
1954	40
1957	40

1961–5 (number of constituencies: 39)

general election	contests
1961	39
1965	39

1969–73 (number of constituencies: 42)

general election	contests
1969	42
1973	42

30   Candidates at general elections, 1922–73, by parties

parties	general elections								
	1922 (June)	1923 (Aug.)	1927 (June)	1927 (Sept.)	1932 (Feb.)	1933 (Jan.)	1937 (July)	1938 (June)	1943 (June)
pro-treaty	65	—	—	—	—	—	—	—	—
anti-treaty	59	—	—	—	—	—	—	—	—
Cumann na nGaedheal	—	106	96	88	100	85	—	—	—
Fine Gael	—	—	—	—	—	—	95	76	87
republican	—	85	—	—	—	—	—	—	—
Sinn Féin	—	—	15	—	—	—	—	—	—
Fianna Fáil	—	—	87	88	104	102	100	96	105
labour	18	44	44	28	33	19	23	30	70
farmers	13	65	38	20	5	—	—	—	—
Clann na Talmhan	—	—	—	—	—	—	—	—	45
national league	—	—	30	6	—	—	—	—	—
Clann Éireann	—	—	8	—	—	—	—	—	—
centre party	—	—	—	—	—	26	—	—	—
independents and others	21	75	58	34	36	13	36	11	46
total	176	375	376	264	278	245	254	213	353

parties	general elections								
	1944 (May)	1948 (Feb.)	1951 (May)	1954 (May)	1957 (Mar.)	1961 (Oct.)	1965 (Apr.)	1969 (June)	1973 (Feb.)
Fine Gael	55	82	77	89	82	96	102	125	111
Sinn Féin	—	—	—	—	19	20	—	—	10
Fianna Fáil	99	118	118	112	112	107	111	121	118
labour	30	43	37	40	30	35	43	99	55
national labour	9	14	—	—	—	—	—	—	—
Clann na Talmhan	31	24	7	10	7	6	—	—	—
Clann na Poblachta	—	93	26	20	12	5	4	—	—
national progressive democratic party	—	—	—	—	—	3	—	—	—
independents and others	27	32	31	31	26	28	20	27	40
total	251	406	296	302	288	300	280	372	334

31 Deputies elected at general elections, 1922-73, by parties

parties	general elections								
	1922 (June)	1923 (Aug.)	1927 (June)	1927 (Sept.)	1932 (Feb.)	1933 (Jan.)	1937 (July)	1938 (June)	1943 (June)
pro-treaty	58	—	—	—	—	—	—	—	—
anti-treaty	36	—	—	—	—	—	—	—	—
Cumann na nGaedheal	—	63	47	62	57	48	—	—	—
Fine Gael	—	—	—	—	—	—	48	45	32
republican	—	44	—	—	—	—	—	—	—
Sinn Féin	—	—	5	—	—	—	—	—	—
Fianna Fáil	—	—	44	57	72	77	69	77	67
labour	17	14	22	13	7	8	13	9	17
farmers	7	15	11	6	3	—`	—	—	—
Clann na Talmhan	—	—	—	—	—	—	—	—	15
national league	—	—	8	2	—	—	—	—	—
centre party	—	—	—	—	—	11	—	—	—
independents and others	10	17	16	13	14	9	8	7	7
total	128	153	153	153	153	153	138	138	138

parties	general elections								
	1944 (May)	1948 (Feb.)	1951 (May)	1954 (May)	1957 (Mar.)	1961 (Oct.)	1965 (Apr.)	1969 (June)	1973 (Feb.)
Fine Gael	30	31	40	50	40	47	47	50	54
Sinn Féin	—	—	—	—	4	—	—	—	—
Fianna Fáil	76	68	69	65	78	70	72	75	69
labour	8	14	16	19	12	16	22	18	19
national labour	4	5	—	—	—	—	—	—	—
farmers	—	—	—	—	—	—	—	—	—
Clann na Talmhan	13	7	6	5	3	2	—	—	—
Clann na Poblachta	—	10	2	3	1	1	1	—	—
national progressive democratic party	—	—	—	—	—	2	—	—	—
independents and others	7	12	14	5	9	6	2	1	2
total	138	147	147	147	147	144	144	144	144

32 First-preference votes cast at general elections, 1922–73, and deputies elected unopposed, by parties

Numbers of deputies elected unopposed are given in brackets beside the numbers of votes cast.[1]

parties	general elections		
	1922 (June)	1923 (Aug.)	1927 (June)
pro-treaty/Cumann na nGaedheal	239,195(17)	410,721	314,059(1)
anti-treaty/republican/ Fianna Fáil	135,309(17)	288,610	299,459
labour	132,565	111,933	143,859
farmers	48,718	127,810	101,425
independents and others	65,797(4)	114,594	287,187
total	621,584(38)	1,053,668(3)	1,145,989(1)

parties	general elections		
	1927 (Sept.)	1932 (Feb.)	1933 (Jan.)
Cumann na nGaedheal	453,067(1)	449,506(1)	422,295
Fianna Fáil	411,733	566,498	689,054(1)
labour	106,178	98,286	79,221
farmers	74,622	24,452	—
independents and others	125,214(3)	135,284(3)	195,788(3)
total	1,170,814(4)	1,274,026(4)	1,386,558(4)

parties	general elections		
	1937 (July)	1938 (June)	1943 (June)
Fine Gael	461,171	428,633(2)	307,490
Fianna Fáil	599,040(1)	667,996(5)	557,525(1)
labour	135,758	128,945	208,812
farmers[2]	—	—	150,938
independents and others	128,480	60,685	106,946
total	1,324,449(1)	1,286,259(7)	1,331,711(1)

parties	general elections		
	1944 (May)	1948 (Feb.)	1951 (May)
Fine Gael	249,329(1)	262,393	342,922
Fianna Fáil	595,259(3)	553,914(1)	616,212(1)
labour[3]	138,165	149,088	151,828
farmers[2]	143,034	70,063	38,872
Clann na Poblachta	—	174,823	54,210
independents and others	91,562	113,162	127,529
total	1,217,349(4)	1,323,443(1)	1,331,573(1)

parties	general elections		
	1954 (May)	1957 (Mar.)	1961 (Oct.)
Fine Gael	427,031	326,699	374,099
Fianna Fáil	578,960	592,994	512,073
labour	161,034(1)	111,747(1)	136,111(1)
farmers[2]	41,249	28,905	17,693
Clann na Poblachta	51,069	20,632	14,474
independents and others	75,859	146,042	113,954
total	1,335,202(1)	1,227,019(1)	1,168,404(1)

parties	general elections		
	1965 (Apr.)	1969 (June)	1973 (Feb.)
Fine Gael	427,081	449,749	473,781
Fianna Fáil	597,414	602,234(1)	624,528(1)
labour	192,740(1)	224,498	184,656
Clann na Poblachta	9,427	—	—
independents and others	26,460	42,472	67,572
total	1,253,122(1)	1,318,953(1)	1,350,537(1)

[1] Including the ceann comhairle, who was automatically elected. In the general elections 1927 (June)–1932, the ceann comhairle was Cumann na nGaedheal, 1933–51 Fianna Fail, 1954–65 labour, 1969–73 Fianna Fail, and labour from 1973.

[2] Including farmers and Clann na Talmhan.

[3] Including 32,732 votes for national labour in 1944 and 34,015 in 1948.

PARLIAMENT OF THE UNITED KINGDOM: GENERAL ELECTIONS IN GREAT BRITAIN, 1832-1974

From 1801 to 1921 all Ireland, and from 1921 onwards Northern Ireland, was part of the United Kingdom. Consequently the results of United Kingdom general elections in Great Britain form a necessary background to the results of general elections in Ireland to 1921 and in Northern Ireland thereafter.

33   Sources

F. W. S. Craig, *British parliamentary election results, 1832-1885*. London, 1977. (p. 622)
—— *British parliamentary election results, 1885-1918*. London, 1974. (pp 580-81)
—— *British electoral facts, 1885-1975*. London, 1976. (pp 1-30)
—— *British parliamentary election results, 1918-1949*. Glasgow, 1969.
J. B. Conacher, *The Peelites and the party system, 1846-52*. Newton Abbot, 1972.

34   Seats won at general elections in Great Britain, 1832-80, by parties[1]

parties	general elections					
	1832 (Dec.)	1835 (Jan.)	1837 (Aug.)	1841 (July)	1847 (Aug.)	1852 (July)
England						
conservative	121	204	242	281	242	248
liberal	347	264	226	187	224	216
Wales						
conservative	14	17	19	21	20	20
liberal	18	15	13	11	12	12
Scotland						
conservative	10	15	20	22	20	20
liberal	43	38	33	31	33	33
total						
conservative[2]	145	236	281	324	282	288
liberal	408	317	272	229	269	261
grand total	553	553	553	553	551	549

parties	general elections					
	1857 (Mar.-Apr.)	1859 (May)	1865 (July)	1868 (Nov.)	1874 (Feb.)	1880 (Mar.-Apr.)
England						
conservative	189	211	216	215	284	200
liberal	275	253	252	245	172	256
Wales						
conservative	17	17	14	10	14	4
liberal	15	15	18	23	19	29
Scotland						
conservative	14	13	11	7	19	7
liberal	39	40	42	53	41	53
total						
conservative	220	241	241	232	317	211
liberal[3]	329	308	312	321	232	338
grand total	549	549	553	553	549	549

[1] These figures give the number of seats won after the double and treble returns had been decided but prior to changes resulting from other types of election petitions.

[2] The figures of seats won by the conservatives include those won by liberal conservatives (Peelites), numbering 105 in 1847 and 38 in 1852 (see p. 638, n. 2, for classification).

[3] The liberal figures in 1874 and 1880 include liberal/labour.

35   Seats won at general elections in Great Britain, 1885-1918, by parties

parties	general elections			
	1885 (Nov.–Dec.)	1886 (July)	1892 (July)	1895 (July)
England				
conservative	217	282	235	296
liberal	243[1]	122	191	112
liberal unionist	—	56	31	52
labour	—	—	—	—
others[2]	1	1	4	1
Wales				
conservative	4	6	3	8
liberal	30[3]	26	31	25
liberal unionist	—	2	—	1
labour	—	—	—	—
others	—	—	—	—
Scotland				
conservative	10	12	11	19
liberal	62[4]	43	50	39
liberal unionist	—	17	11	14
labour	—	—	—	—
others	—	—	—	—
total				
conservative	231	300	249	323
liberal	335	191	272	176
liberal unionist	—	75	42	67
labour	—	—	—	—
others[2]	1	1	4	1
total	567	567	567	567

parties	general elections				
	1900 (Sept.–Oct.)	1906 (Jan.)	1910 (Jan.)	1910 (Dec.)	1918[5] (Dec.)
England					
conservative	290	109	213	211	321
liberal	122	306	188	186	108
liberal unionist	47	18	26	29	—
labour	1	26	33	34	45
others[2]	1	2	1	1	18
Wales					
conservative	6	—	2	3	4
liberal	27	33	27	26	21
liberal unionist	—	—	—	—	—
labour	1	1	5	5	9
others	—	—	—	—	2
Scotland					
conservative	21	7	8	7	32
liberal	34	58	59	58	34
liberal unionist	17	5	3	4	—
labour	—	2	2	3	7
others	—	—	—	—	1
total					
conservative	317	116	223	221	357
liberal	183	397	274	270	163
liberal unionist[6]	64	23	29	33	—
labour	2	29	40	42	61
others[2]	1	2	1	1	21
total	567	567	567	567	612

[1] Including 4 seats won by independents.

[2] Throughout this period T. P. O'Connor was returned as an Irish nationalist M.P. for Liverpool, Scotland division.

[3] Including 1 seat won by independent labour.

[4] Including 7 seats won by independents and 4 seats won by independent liberal-crofters.

[5] Seats won by M.P.s who were official candidates of the coalition at the time of the general election numbered 473, consisting of 332 conservative, 127 liberal, 4 labour, and 10 others.

[6] The liberal unionist party amalgamated with the conservative party in May 1912.

36 Members elected at general elections in Great Britain, 1922–74, by parties

parties	general elections			
	1922 (Nov.)	1923 (Dec.)	1924 (Oct.)	1929 (May)
England				
conservative	312	227	352	226
liberal	76	124	20	35
labour	95	138	109	226
others	9	3	11	5
Wales				
conservative	6	4	9	1
liberal	11	11	11	10
labour	18	19	16	25
others	1	2	—	—
Scotland				
conservative	15	16	38	22
liberal	28	23	9	14
labour	29	34	26	36
others	2	1	1	2
total				
conservative	333	247	399	249
liberal[1]	115	158	40	59
labour	142	191	151	287
others	12	6	12	7
total	602	602	602	602

parties	general elections			
	1931 (Oct.)	1935 (Nov.)	1945 (July)	1950 (Feb.)
England				
conservative	403	333	160	253
liberal	42	33	12	2
labour	40	122	331	251
others	7	4	14	—
Wales				
conservative	6	6	3	4
liberal	13	10	8	5
labour	17	19	26	27
others	—	1	1	—
Scotland				
conservative	50	37	25	31
liberal	16	11	3	2
labour	8	21	37	37
others	—	5	9	1
total				
conservative[2]	459	376	188	288
liberal[1]	71	54	23	9
labour[3]	65	162	393	315
others	7	10	25	1
total	602	602	629	613

36   Members elected at general elections in Great Britain, 1922–74, by parties (*continued*)

parties	general elections			
	1951 (Oct.)	1955 (May)	1959 (Oct.)	1964 (Oct.)
England				
conservative	271	293	315	262
liberal	2	2	3	3
labour	233	216	193	246
others	—	—	—	—
Wales				
conservative	6	6	7	6
liberal	3	3	2	2
labour	27	27	27	28
others	—	—	—	—
Scotland				
conservative	35	36	31	24
liberal	1	1	1	4
labour	35	34	38	43
others	—	—	1	—
total				
conservative[2]	312	335	353	292
liberal	6	6	6	9
labour	295	277	258	317
others	—	—	1	—
total	613	618	618	618

parties	general elections			
	1966 (Mar.)	1970 (June)	1974 (Feb.)	1974 (Oct.)
England				
conservative	219	292	268	253
liberal	6	2	9	8
labour	286	217	237	255
others	—	—	2	—
Wales				
conservative	3	7	8	8
liberal	1	1	2	2
labour	32	27	24	23
others	—	1	2	3
Scotland				
conservative	20	23	21	16
liberal	5	3	3	3
labour	46	44	40	41
others	—	1	7	11
total				
conservative[2]	242	322	297	277
liberal	12	6	14	13
labour	364	288	301	319
others	—	2	11	14
total	618	618	623	623

[1] Including 53 members of the national liberal council in 1922, 35 members of the national liberal organisation and 4 independent liberals in 1931, 33 members of the national liberal organisation in 1935, and 11 members of the national liberal organisation in 1945.

[2] Including joint members of the national liberal organisation and the conservative party: 16 in 1950, 19 in 1951, 21 in 1955, 20 in 1959, 6 in 1964, 3 in 1966.

[3] Including members of the national labour organisation, numbering 13 in 1931 and 8 in 1935. Members of the independent labour party are included among labour members until the 1935 general election, when they are included in the 'others' section, numbering 4 M.P.s in 1935 and 3 M.P.s in 1945.

APPENDIX, 1977–82

PARLIAMENT OF THE UNITED KINGDOM OF GREAT BRITAIN AND NORTHERN IRELAND, 1979

37   Sources

F. W. S. Craig (ed.), *Britain votes 2: British parliamentary election results 1974–1979.* Chichester, 1980. (pp 231–6)
—— *British electoral facts 1832–1980.* Chichester, 1981. (p. 45)

38   Candidates, members elected, and votes cast at the 1979 general election in Northern Ireland, by parties[1]

parties	candidates	members elected	votes cast
official unionist	11	5	254,978
democratic unionist	5	3	70,975
unionist party of Northern Ireland	3	—	8,021
alliance	12	—	82,892
Northern Ireland labour	3	—	4,411
social democratic and labour	9	1	126,325
republican clubs	7	—	12,093
others	14	3	113,501
total	64	12	695,887

[1] No members were elected unopposed.

NORTHERN IRELAND ASSEMBLY, 1982

39 Sources

Analysis of the 1982 Northern Ireland register of electors. Belfast, 1982.
The Northern Ireland census, 1981: preliminary report. Belfast, 1982.
Irish Times, 19 Sept., 22–5 Oct. 1982.

40 Constituencies and members

legislation	number of constituencies	number of constituencies returning						total number of members
		4	5	6	7	8	10	
				members				
Northern Ireland Assembly Election Order, 1982	12	1	3	2	3	2	1	78

41 Electors and population

electors	population	electors as percentage of population
1982	*1981*	
1,057,263	1,509,892[1]	70.02

[1] Estimated total, comprising 1,490,228 enumerated and an estimated 19,664 non-returns.

42 Candidates, members elected, and first-preference votes cast at general election, 20 October 1982, by parties

parties	candidates	members elected	first-preference votes cast
official unionist	42	26	188,277
democratic unionist	35	21	145,478
U.U.U.P.	13	—	10,927
alliance	20	10	58,887
social democratic and labour	28	14	118,891
Sinn Féin	12	5	64,191
workers' party	12	—	17,216
others	22	2[1]	28,797
total	184	78	633,664

[1] Includes one member of the U.P.U.P. and one other independent unionist.

DÁIL ÉIREANN, 1977–82

43   Sources

Census of population of Ireland, 1981. Dublin, 1982.
Dáil Éireann: election results and transfer of votes in general election (June, 1977) for twenty-first dáil . . . Dublin, [1978]. (p. 54)
Dáil Éireann: election results and transfer of votes in general election (June, 1981) for twenty-second dáil . . . Dublin, [1981]. (p. 54)
Irish Times, 19, 22 Feb., 27 Nov. 1982.

44   Constituencies and T.D.s

legislation	number of constituencies	number of constituencies returning 3 4 5 T.D.s	total number of T.D.s
Electoral (Amendment) Act, 1974	42	26 10 6	148
Electoral (Amendment) Act, 1980	41	13 13 15	166

45   Electors and population

legislation	electorate 1982	population 1981	electors as percentage of population
Electoral (Amendment) Act, 1973	2,335,153	3,443,405	67.82

46   Candidates at general elections, 1977–82, by parties

parties	general elections			
	1977	1981	1982 (Feb.)	1982 (Nov.)
Fianna Fáil	132	138	131	132
Fine Gael	116	126	113	115
labour	56	60	41	40
Sinn Féin the workers' party	16	15	15	20
others	55	64	67	59
total	375	403	367	366

47   Deputies elected at general elections, 1977-82, by parties

parties	general elections			
	1977	1981	1982 (Feb.)	1982 (Nov.)
Fianna Fáil	84	78	81	75
Fine Gael	43	65	63	70
labour	17	15	15	16
Sinn Féin the workers' party	—	1	3	2
others	4	7	4	3
total[1]	148	166	166	166

[1] Includes the ceann comhairle, who was elected unopposed. In 1977 the ceann comhairle was a labour deputy, in 1981 Fianna Fáil, in 1982 (Feb.) an independent, and in 1982 (Nov.) an independent.

48   First-preference votes cast at general elections, 1977-82, by parties

parties	general elections			
	1977	1981	1982 (Feb.)	1982 (Nov.)
Fianna Fáil	811,615	777,616	786,961	763,312
Fine Gael	488,767	626,376	621,110	662,283
labour	186,410	169,990	153,053	158,115
Sinn Féin the workers' party	27,209	29,561	38,099	54,888
others	89,026	114,668	67,130	50,120
total	1,603,027	1,718,211	1,665,353	1,688,718

PARLIAMENT OF THE UNITED KINGDOM: GENERAL ELECTION IN GREAT BRITAIN, 1979

49   Members elected at the 1979 general election in Great Britain, by parties[1]

England	
conservative	306
liberal	7
labour	203
others	—
Wales	
conservative	11
liberal	1
labour	22
others	2
Scotland	
conservative	22
liberal	3
labour	44
others	2
total	
conservative	339
liberal	11
labour	269
others	4
total	623

[1] Sources as above, p. 670.